HELP!
Windows NT 3.1

HELP!

Windows NT 3.1

Ben Ezzell

Ziff-Davis Press
Emeryville, California

Editors	Janna Clark and Jan Jue
Technical Reviewer	Robert L. Hummel
Project Coordinator	Sheila McGill
Proofreader	Cort Day
Cover Design	Carrie English
Book Design	Carrie English and Charles Cowens
Screen Graphics Editor	Cat Haglund
Word Processing	Howard Blechman, Cat Haglund, and Allison Levin
Page Layout	Tony Jonick and Anna L. Marks
Indexer	Valerie Robbins

Ziff-Davis Press books are produced on a Macintosh computer system with the following applications: FrameMaker®, Microsoft® Word, QuarkXPress®, Adobe Illustrator®, Adobe Photoshop®, Adobe Streamline™, MacLink® *Plus*, Aldus® FreeHand™, Collage Plus™.

Ziff-Davis Press
5903 Christie Avenue
Emeryville, CA 94608

ISBN 1-56276-151-X

Manufactured in the United States of America
10 9 8 7 6 5 4 3 2 1

But it was one Elephant—a new Elephant—an Elephant's Child—who was full of 'satiable curtiosity and that means that he asked ever so many questions ... and he filled all Africa with his 'satiable curtiosity.

The Elephant's Child—Rudyard Kipling

This book is respectfully dedicated to all those individuals who have offered answers and assistance, not merely to myself—although individuals in the personal category, as always, have my grateful thanks—but to any and all who suffer from "'satiable curtiosity." Perhaps this volume will offer some small repayment of your kindnesses. (After all, the best answers and greatest patience have always come from others who share the Elephant's Child's affliction.)

Contents at a Glance

Table of Contents

Introduction

HELP! Windows NT 3.1 is tailored to give you information in a format that is practical and easy to use. Its aim is to give you answers to specific questions and solutions to specific problems.

This book can help you learn about and use Windows NT in three ways:

1. As a reference, it quickly answers your "How do I...?" questions.
2. As a troubleshooter, it discusses many common problem scenarios and presents solutions to them.
3. As a learning guide, this book contains practical examples and background information so you can learn Windows NT from the ground up.

Who This Book Is For

HELP! Windows NT 3.1 is a guide to the Windows NT operating system, utility applications, and network operations. Because Windows NT is both very new and (since it's similar to Windows 3.1) very familiar, this book is designed to be a helpful reference for those who already use Windows 3.1 as well as a learning guide for all who are new to Windows NT. Whether you are a Windows expert looking to move up to the strengths and advantages of 32-bit Windows NT or a novice seeking entry into a new and convenient operating system, you'll find *HELP! Windows NT 3.1* a comprehensive guide to all phases of Windows NT operations.

How to Use This Book

You don't have to read this book from beginning to end, or in any particular order, to get help. Use the detailed Table of Contents at the front of the book or the index to find the topic you're interested in, then turn to that chapter or chapters.

Each chapter is structured so that you can quickly find the information you need about that topic. Here are the HELP! features you'll have at your fingertips:

- In each chapter you'll find step-by-step instructions for carrying out a task or using a feature.
- If you'd like to know more about the topic, read the Help Files section; here you'll find tips, advice, anecdotes, and examples.
- At the end of each chapter you'll find The Rescue Pages, a concise troubleshooting guide.
- Throughout the book you'll see notes in the margin and in the text with reminders, cautions, references to other chapters, and other information of special interest.

A Tour of the Chapters

HELP! Windows NT 3.1 covers every user-oriented feature and option found in Windows NT 3.1. Here's a quick guide to what you'll find.

The first three chapters contain basic information about Windows NT 3.1. These chapters will give you an overview of the program and help you with such tasks as using the Help features, using Program Manager to organize your programs and documents, installing applications, and setting display options.

In Chapter 4 you'll find information on customizing Windows NT with the Control Panel utilities. Chapter 5 covers file management tasks, including connecting to network drives, assigning permissions on shared directories and files, and disk maintenance. You'll learn how to manage printers and print drivers in Chapter 6, including connecting to network printers and sharing a local printer. Sharing and exchanging information is covered in Chapter 7. Here you'll find such topics as using the Clipboard and ClipBook features.

Chapters 8 through 10 cover some Windows utilities that will help you create drawings and documents and organize your work. The word processing capabilities of Notepad, Unipad, Microsoft Write, and the

Paintbrush graphics program are covered, as well as the standard and scientific calculators, the Cardfile accessory (for keeping a list of addresses, phone numbers, and even graphics), and the Clock.

Fax and modem communications are covered in Chapter 11. Here you'll learn about such topics as receiving and transmitting files by modem and printing from Windows's Terminal program. Multimedia topics are covered in Chapter 12, including a discussion of working with sound files and using CD Player and Media Player. Chapter 13 explains how to execute DOS applications under Windows NT.

Chapters 14 through 18 cover Windows's system and disk maintenance utilities, including Performance Monitor, backup utility, Disk Administrator, Event Viewer, and Registry Editor.

Scheduling and mail utilities are covered in Chapters 19 and 20. In these chapters you'll learn how to maintain an appointment calendar, schedule tasks, track meetings and projects, and handle message traffic.

Chapter 21 explains how to work with Windows NT on a network. It covers such topics as managing user accounts, using the Chat utility, and working with network settings.

Finally, two appendices are included. Appendix A offers advice and suggestions which, in the event of a serious (though unlikely) malfunction, will assist you in recovery with a minimum of disruption. (You may want to skim this appendix before a problem occurs, as a form of insurance; the potential dividends of being prepared more than outweigh your investment of reading time.) Appendix B is your guide to installing Windows NT and using the Setup utility.

CHAPTER

1

HELP! Getting Started in Windows NT

Windows NT is a graphical operating system. Unlike Windows 3.1, which operates as a shell on top of DOS and is subject to DOS's 16-bit limitations, Windows NT is a true 32-bit operating system designed to operate on both 80386/486 PCs and PCs based on 4*x*00 RISC (reduced instruction-set computing) MIPS systems. Most important, Windows NT actually uses the capabilities of either of these CPUs.

Early PCs used the 8086/8088 CPUs, but when PCs moved up to the 286 CPU, Microsoft's 16-bit DOS operating system became the standard for all PC systems. About the same time, Windows 3.0 and, more importantly, Windows 3.1 became the popular graphical environment, but Windows operated on top of the 16-bit DOS operating system and so was dependent on it. With the introduction of the 80386/80486 CPUs, both DOS and Windows 3.1 demonstrated considerable improvements in performance, but neither actually took full advantage of the newer and much more powerful CPUs.

For PCs, some of the biggest advantages offered by Windows NT—speed aside—have been the fall of the 64K (kilobyte) data-block limits, the end of 640K memory-address limits, and the end of reliance on the EMS/XMS memory standards and the slow upper-memory drivers to make use of memory beyond 1MB (megabyte).

During this same period, other parts of the computer world were relying on RISC computers that were using the UNIX operating system. Unfortunately, DOS and UNIX could

communicate only with some difficulty, and applications written for one system could be moved to the other only after extensive reprogramming.

Windows NT, however, has been written to operate on both platforms, allowing applications to execute on different types of computers (further platform expansions are expected in the near future).

This cross-platform compatibility, though, is only one part of the story. Almost from the inception of computers, communications between computers have been—at their very best—awkward. These systems have required the services of a system or network operator simply to keep the inherently cumbersome process from crashing. With Windows NT, network operations are no longer an add-on to the system, occupying memory that could be used by other applications and interfering with operations in general. Instead, under Windows NT, networking is an integral part of the operating system and, once established, is virtually transparent to users. Granted, larger networks may still require the services of a system or network manager, but he or she will be more like a network supervisor than like today's overworked troubleshooter.

For most users, however, the Windows NT operating system will not be something new. For the most part, Windows NT is—quite intentionally—the same as Windows 3.1. It works like Windows 3.1, it looks like Windows 3.1, and it responds like Windows 3.1...only better.

Still, there are differences. In part, those differences are what this book is about.

Operating in Windows NT—An Overview

▶ A Choice of Operating Systems

Windows NT on a PC system provides the FlexBoot option, permitting a choice of operating systems when the computer is powered up. With the FlexBoot option, the operating system is not loaded immediately after the computer is turned on. Instead, the following prompt appears:

```
Please select the operating system to start:
```

The prompt message is followed by a pair of choices, normally the DOS operating system and the Windows NT operating system (the latter is usually highlighted). The exact wording of the selection options can vary, as can the highlighted choice, but the up and down arrow keys can be used to change the selection. Pressing the Enter key immediately boots the highlighted selection. Below the prompts and instructions, a final message shows a countdown in seconds until the highlighted selection is booted. The default countdown is 30 seconds.

All these choices—the wording of the options, the default selection, and the delay time—can be changed either by editing the BOOT.INI file or by using the System utility from the Control Panel (see Chapter 4). The BOOT.INI file should look something like this:

```
[boot loader]
timeout=30
default=f:\nt

[operating systems]
f:\nt="Windows NT Version 3.1"
c:\="MS-DOS"
```

The drive specification used can be phrased in several different fashions. For example, on a conventional IDE hard drive, instead of a simple

```
f:\nt
```

the drive specification may be more explicitly constructed as

```
multi(0)disk(0)rdisk(0)partition(3)\nt
```

even though both are interpreted in exactly the same fashion. On a SCSI drive, this same drive specification might appear as

```
scsi(0)disk(0)rdisk(0)partition(4)\nt
```

With both forms of drive specification, the Windows NT operating system—which does not require installation on the default C drive—is identified as being located on the F partition in the \NT subdirectory. The DOS operating system—which *does* require installation on drive C—is identified as being located on drive C in the root directory.

Of course, during installation you also have the option of installing only the Windows NT operating system—in which case, only Windows NT will boot and the FlexBoot option will not appear at all.

▶ Logging On

Perhaps the biggest immediate difference between Windows 3.1 and Windows NT appears when you start the computer. Under Windows 3.1, you booted DOS and either called Windows or had a .BAT file to automatically load Windows. For Windows NT, however, DOS is out of the immediate picture. Instead, when the computer is powered up, you boot Windows NT or select WinNT from the FlexBoot display, and you are immediately greeted with a dialog box that instructs you to press Ctrl+Alt+Del.

Under DOS (or Windows 3.1), the Ctrl+Alt+Del combination resets the computer. Under Windows NT, this combination does not produce a reset, but it does prevent a Trojan horse virus from attempting to intercept your password. After pressing Ctrl+Alt+Del, the Log On dialog box appears, requesting your user name, a computer name or domain, and a password.

- The name you type in the Username box identifies the person logging on to the computer or the account being logged on to. For example, at various times, you may wish to log on under your personal account, as Adminstrator, or under some other account name.
- The From box, by default, contains the name of the local computer but can also specify a domain on the local computer, another computer on the network, and so on.
- The Password entry provides the authorization, which must, of course, match the Username entry and must be valid for the computer or domain.

After you log on, Windows NT appears and operates in essentially the same fashion as Windows 3.1—with the continuing exception, of course, of the Ctrl+Alt+Del combination.

▶ Similiarities to Windows 3.1

In most respects, Windows NT appears and acts the same as Windows 3.1. The desktop appears the same—or can be configured to appear the same—the Program Manager operates in the same fashion, the File Manager looks the same, and the same applications are included. And, overall, the similiarites are so great that it can actually be difficult to remember which version you are operating under: Windows NT or Windows 3.1.

As a matter of fact, Windows NT even has the same version number—3.1—as the previous 16-bit Windows version. However, in this book, the 32-bit Windows NT will be referred to only as Windows NT or WinNT, and the 16-bit version of Windows will be referred to as Windows 3.1. Windows version 3.0 and other earlier versions will not be mentioned.

▸ Differences from Windows 3.1

Most of the differences between Windows NT and Windows 3.1 are invisible to users (although they're quite visible to programmers) and do not affect operations aside from producing improved performance. Some differences, however, are visible in the form of new utilities, in network operations, and, not least, in the NTFS file system.

The new utilities can be categorized under two major headings: administrative utilities and general-purpose utilities. Administrative utilities (discussed in Chapter 14), which are entirely new with Windows NT, provide supervision and control—primarily for network operations. The more general utilities include a host of features, ranging from intelligent UPS (uninterruptable power supply) systems to custom cursors (in the Control Panel, discussed in Chapter 4) to network mail and schedule utilities (Chapter 15).

Network operations appear as a part of several topics; specifically, in Chapter 5's discussion of File Manager, in Chapter 16, where networks and User Manager are covered, in Chapter 19's discussion of schedule and mail facilities, as well as in Chapter 20's discussion of network operations. These operations are also covered indirectly throughout the remainder of the book.

From the programmer's standpoint, the NTFS file system—which is optional, since the DOS FAT file system can continue to be used if desired—is itself a distinct departure from DOS. From the user's standpoint, however, the NTFS file system is unlike the familiar file system in only a few respects. The NTFS file system's features are discussed in Chapter 5.

There are at least a few differences from Windows 3.1 in almost every element in the Windows NT system—certainly too many changes to

be listed in this chapter. Each difference is discussed under the appropriate topic.

One feature in Windows NT that may be of more use than any other is the on-line help system.

On-Line Help

▶ Accessing On-Line Help

Windows NT—like Windows 3.1—offers several options for accessing on-line help.

First, there's the Help icon—the yellow question mark—which summons the Help application itself. And, once the Help application is running, the File menu can be used to load any of a wide variety of Help files, which are identified by their .HLP extensions.

Second and more popular, the menu bar within virtually all applications offers a Help option that calls the Help application and loads the appropriate .HLP file.

Third, context-sensitive help is offered by many applications and not only calls the Help application and the appropriate .HLP file, but also tells Help which topic to display. In many cases, pressing F1 summons context-sensitive help. In some applications, however, the optimum method may involve highlighting text to identify a topic or clicking with the right mouse button on an icon or image.

Last, it's simple to determine which methods are relevant for any application—just ask Help.

▶ Requesting Help from Inside an Application

To request help from within an application, do one of the following:

- Choose a Help option from the application's Help menu.
- Press F1 on the keyboard.
- Select the Help button from a dialog box.

Not all applications support the F1 key. If pressing F1 does not display a Help response, use the application's Help menu.

When help is requested, a Help window appears with either text appropriate to the topic or a menu of further Help choices. In general, the F1 key and Help buttons in dialog boxes summon context-sensitive help, and the Help menu options either offer a broad choice of Help contexts (lists in which the term *Help* appears in different contexts) or offer lists of Help topics.

Selecting Help Topics

Help menus and many Help texts offer lists of Help topics. To select a Help topic:

1. Click on any bulleted topic for a list of specific Help topics.
2. Click a specific topic to view the details.

Or:

1. Use the Tab key to select a topic.
2. Press Enter to display a list of specific Help topics.
3. Use the Tab key to select the specific topic.
4. Press Enter to view the Help details.

Using Text Searches to Locate a Help Topic

When the desired Help topic is not immediately available, you can search for a topic or topics that contain a specific word or phrase. To search for a topic:

1. Call the Help utility as explained in the previous section.
2. Select the Find button from the button bar in the Help window. The Search dialog box shown in Figure 1.1 appears.
3. In the Search For edit box, enter the text desired.
   - To search for an exact match for the text entry, delimit the text by using quotes.

The Find button does not appear in most context-sensitive or application-specific Help screens.

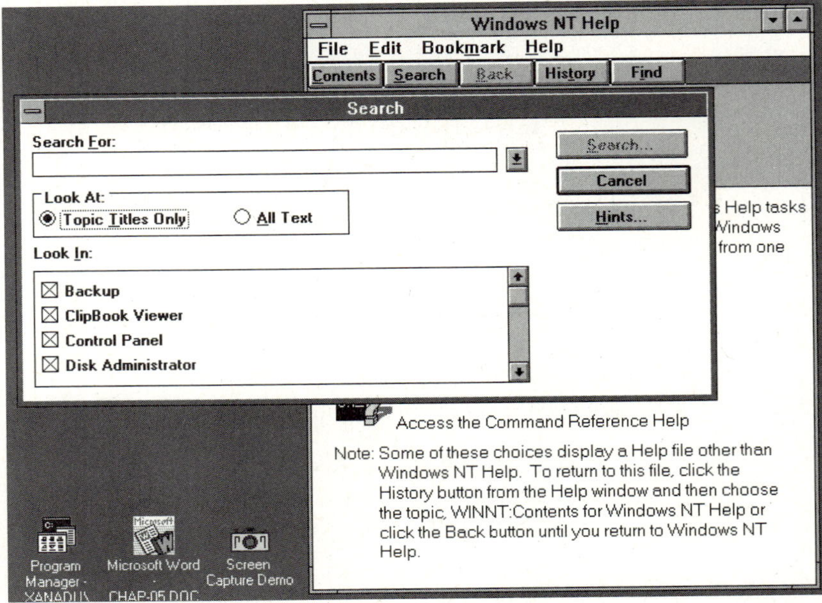

Figure 1.1
The Find dialog box

- To search for an approximate match, enter the text without quotes—the search utility will look for a match for the words in the search phrase but will not try to match the phrase and word order precisely.

In Windows NT, coded topic headings are not used, so don't clear the Topic Titles Only option.

4. The Search For edit box is also a list box (click on the down arrow at the right) and retains a list of the last ten search queries. To repeat a previous search, select an entry from this list.
5. In the Look At options, select the All Text option to search all the text within each Help topic.
6. Select which Help file to search by selecting the appropriate check box. By default, all listed Help files are searched, unless you specify a file or files.
7. Select the Search button to execute the search.
8. All topics matching the search request are listed in the results window. Select a Help topic from the list to view, and words or phrases matching the search request will be highlighted.

Use the Hints button to call up a quick reference for searches and seach conditions.

Help Files ▼ If you searched for Help information about accessing a network printer with a search request for the phrase *network print** (without quotes), Help would respond by listing all topics containing the words *network printers*, *printing over the network*, and so on. The asterisk (*) requests a search for matching words rather than a matching phrase.

▸ Setting Search Conditions

Topic searches can be made conditional in several ways by using the search operators AND, OR, NOT, and NEAR, as well as quotation marks and wild cards.

- A specific request using quotation marks, such as *"Network Printers"*, responds with topics containing the exact phrase *Network Printers*.
- A more general request, such as *Network Print**, locates topics containing both words in any order.
- A conditional request such as *Network Printers OR Network AND Printers* locates topics that contain both words but in which those words may be separated by other text.
- A conditional request such as *Network OR Printers* locates topics that contain either term but not necessarily both.
- Requesting *Network NOT Printers* locates topics that contain the word *Network* but do not contain the word *Printers*.
- The request *Network NEAR Printers* reports topics that contain both words in any order, as long as they are close to each other. The degree of proximity is set by selecting the Hints button in the Search dialog and specifying the maximum separation (in words) in the NEAR Means Within box.

- A wild card request such as *Network Print** reports topics containing the word *Network* along with *Printer*, *Printers*, or *Printing*.

▶ Opening Additional Help Files

To open another Help file:

1. Select Open from the Help File menu.
2. From the File Name list box, select the name of the Help file to open.
   - If the desired file is not in the current directory, select a different directory from the Directories box.
   - If the desired file is not on the current drive, use the Drives box to select a drive.
3. Choose the OK button.

Help Files ▼ A Help file can be opened for any application that offers help, regardless of whether you are using the application. Simply open the Help utility and then select the Help file belonging to the application desired.

▶ Keeping the Help Window Visible

To keep the Help window on top of other windows (and, therefore, visible):

- Select the Always On Top option from the Help menu in the Help Window.
- Select the Always On Top option a second time to clear this option.

Help Files ▼ A check mark appears next to the option and a shadow surrounds the Help window when the Always On Top option is selected. When the Help window is minimized (iconized), the Help icon continues to appear on top of all other windows.

The Always On Top option is useful when following Help instructions step by step or when making frequent reference to the Help files.

▸ Resizing or Repositioning the Help Window

To resize the Help window:

- Use the mouse to drag the window's corner or border until the window is the desired size.

Or:

1. Press Alt+spacebar to open the Control menu.
2. Use the Size command to change window's size.

To move the Help window:

- Use the mouse to drag the window's title bar to a new location.

Or:

1. Press Alt+spacebar to open the Control menu.
2. Use the Move command to reposition the window.

▸ Help Files

The Help window can be resized or repositioned so that both the Help window and the application window can be visible at the same time. This makes it easier to follow step-by-step procedures without continually

switching between windows. Refer also to the section "Keeping the Help Window Visible," which appears earlier in this chapter.

Scrolling through a Help Topic

To scroll through a Help topic:

- Click on the scroll-bar arrows to scroll up or down one line.
- Use the arrow keys to scroll up or down.

To scroll up or down one window at a time:

- Click above or below the thumb pad in the scroll bar.
- Use the Pg Up and Pg Dn keys.

To scroll rapidly through a Help topic:

- Use the mouse to drag the scroll-bar thumb pad.

Help Files ▼ In many cases, the information in a Help topic doesn't fit in a single window and the scroll-bar control should be used to scroll through the material.

Using the Help Contents List

To display the Help Contents:

- Select the Contents button on the Help button bar.
- Press C.

The Help Contents feature lists the available Help topics.

Selecting a Jump (Hyperlink)

To select a jump (also called a hyperlink):

1. Point to the text or graphic.
2. Click the mouse button.

Or:

1. Press Tab to move forward to select a jump.
2. Press Shift+Tab to move backward to select a jump.
3. Press Enter. If the jump selected is linked to another topic, the linked topic appears in the Help window.

To highlight all jumps in a topic:

- Press Ctrl+Tab.

Help Files ▼ In general, Help topics include text, graphics, or both that act as *jumps*, linking you to other Help topics. Jumps are customarily identified by color and, for text, by an underscore. When the cursor points to a jump, the arrow pointer changes to a pointing hand.

Selecting a Pop-Up Note

To select a pop-up note:

1. Point to the text or graphic.
2. Click the mouse button.

Or:

1. Press Tab to move forward to select a pop-up note.

2. Press Shift+Tab to move backward to select a pop-up note.
3. Press Enter. The pop-up text appears in a window over the Help text (see Figure 1.2).
4. Click the mouse to dismiss the pop-up note.

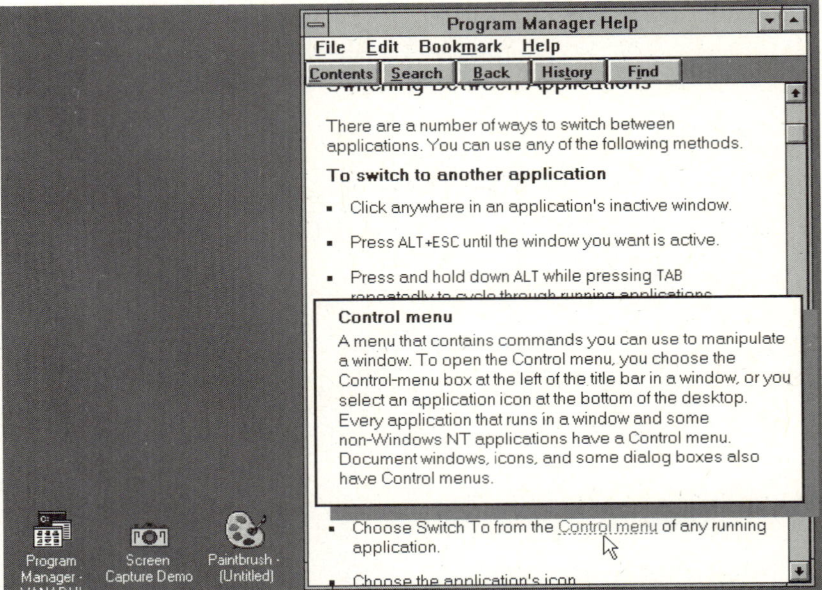

Figure 1.2
Selecting and displaying a pop-up note

To highlight all pop-ups in a topic:

- Press Ctrl+Tab.

Help Files ▼ Many Help topics include text or graphics called pop-up notes. These display additional information about the current topic. Text pop-up notes are customarily identified by color and a dotted underscore. When the cursor points to a pop-up note, the arrow pointer changes to a pointing hand.

Retracing Help Topics

To retrace Help topics:

1. Select the Back button from the Help button bar.
2. Press B.

The Help window displays the previously viewed topic, positioned within the text as it was last seen.

Help Files The Back button is used to retrace a path through the Help topics previously viewed. If there are no previous topics, the Back button is grayed (inactive). Each time the Help utility is called, a new trace record is initiated—no record is kept of previous Help inquiries.

Returning to a Previously Viewed Help Topic

To return to a previously viewed topic:

1. Select the History button from the Help button bar or press T.
2. Double-click on the topic to return to it or select a topic and press Enter.
3. If necessary, use the scroll bar to view additional topics.

To close the History window:

- Double-click on the Control-menu box (upper-left corner).
- Press Alt+F4.

Help Files ▼ The History button displays a list of up to the last 40 Help topics viewed. You may return to any topic on the list by selecting the topic from the list. A new history list is initiated each time the Help utility is called. The History window remains open until it is deliberately closed or the Help utility is exited.

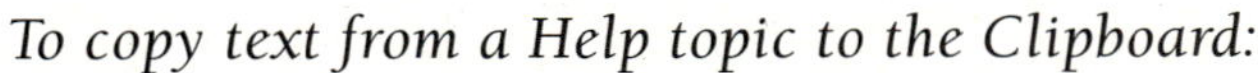

▶ Copying from Help to the Clipboard

Graphics can not be copied from a Help topic to the Clipboard.

To copy text from a Help topic to the Clipboard:

1. Select Copy from the Help Edit menu. A new window will appear with a plain-text copy of the Help text.
2. Select the Copy button to copy all text to the Clipboard, or select the text desired and then select the Copy button.

To copy an entire topic directly to the Clipboard:

- From the Help screen, press Ctrl+Ins.

▶ Annotating a Help Topic

To annotate a Help topic:

1. Select Annotate from the Help Edit menu.
2. In the Annotate dialog box, enter the text annotation.
   - Use the Backspace key for corrections.
   - Text wraps automatically, but line breaks can be entered using the Enter key.
3. Choose the Save button. A paper-clip icon appears at the left of the topic title, indicating the presence of annotated comments.

To view an annotation:

1. Click on the paper-clip icon at the left of the topic title, or press Tab to select the paper-clip icon and press Enter.
2. Select the Cancel button when finished.

To remove an annotation:

1. Click on the paper-clip icon at the left of the topic title, or press Tab to select the paper-clip icon and press Enter.
2. Select the Delete button.

To copy an annotation:

1. Click on the paper-clip icon at the left of the topic title, or press Tab to select the paper-clip icon and press Enter.
2. Select the Copy button to copy the annotation to the Clipboard.
3. Select Save.

To copy only part of the annotation text:

1. Use the mouse cursor to select the desired text, or press and hold the Shift key while using the arrow keys to select a block of text.
2. Select the Copy button to copy the annotation to the Clipboard.
3. Select Save.

To paste an annotation:

1. Copy the text desired to the Clipboard.
2. Click on the paper-clip icon at the left of the topic title, or press Tab to select the paper-clip icon and press Enter.
3. Select the Paste button or press Shift+Ins to paste the contents of the Clipboard at the beginning of the topic.
4. Select an insertion point to insert the new text, then select Paste or press Shift+Ins.
5. Select the Save button.

Help Files ▼ Annotated text can be added to Help topics for later reference. When a Help topic has been annotated, a paper-clip icon appears at the left of the topic title.

Text can be copied from an annotation and then pasted into another topic or document. Also, text from other documents can be pasted into annotations.

▶ Defining and Using Bookmarks in Help Files

To define a bookmark for a topic:

1. Select Define from the Help Bookmark menu.
2. The current topic title appears in the Bookmark Name edit box. If a different name is needed, the name can be entered directly.
3. Select the OK button. The topic name now appears in the Bookmark menu in Help.

To view a bookmark topic:

1. Select the Help Bookmark menu.
2. Select the topic desired. The first nine bookmark topic titles are preceeded by underscored numbers and can be selected by entering the appropriate number.

If more than nine bookmarks have been assigned:

1. Select the More option from the Help Bookmark menu.
2. Select the desired topic in the Go To Bookmark list box.
3. Select the OK button.

To remove a bookmark:

1. Select Define from the Help Bookmark menu.
2. Select the bookmark to remove.
3. Select the Delete button. The bookmark name is removed from the Help Bookmark menu.

Help Files ▼ Just as bookmarks can be used in books to mark specific references, bookmarks can be used to locate Help topics for rapid reference.

▸ Printing a Help Topic

Information in a pop-up window cannot be printed.

To print a Help topic:

- Select the Print Topic option from the Help File menu.

To change printers and printer options:

1. Select the Print Setup option from the Help File menu.
2. Select the printer desired.
3. Select the options desired. The available options vary, depending on the printer selected.
4. Select OK to close the printer's Setup dialog box.
5. Select OK to conclude.

Help Files ▼ Any Help topic can be printed using the default printer. If multiple printers are installed, any of them can be designated as the default printer. Also, the options for the default printer can be changed using the Printer Setup dialog.

For assistance with the Printer Setup dialog box, select the Help button or press F1 while in the dialog box.

THE RESCUE PAGES: Getting Started in Windows NT

I can't reboot. When I press Ctrl+Alt+Del, Windows NT calls up a Security dialog box.

There's nothing wrong—it's just that pressing Ctrl+Alt+Del doesn't reboot anymore. If you want to reboot, first exit from Windows NT by using the Close option from the Program Manager system menu (upper-left corner). This willl save any revisions or file changes that may be in the buffer.

Then, when the log-on prompt appears—which instructs you to press Ctrl+Alt+Del to log on—you can log on to Windows NT again under another user name. If you want to reboot at this point to return to DOS or Windows 3.1 instead, you can press the reset button on the front of the computer and select DOS from the FlexBoot options.

I can't get Help to come up.

You have a serious problem...but probably not a fatal one.

You might try calling Help from the Program Manager and then using the Search For Help On option.

If Search For Help On doesn't find anything, this probably means that you've deleted the Help file for the application or that the Help file is located in a directory where it can't be found by a search. Use the File Manager to look for the Help file and relocate it, if necessary, by placing it in the application's directory or in the \WinNT\SYSTEM32 directory.

If this is a Windows 3.1 application and you're also using Windows 3.1, you may want to duplicate the Help file, rather than move it.

If a Help file can't be found for the application at all, check the application's source disks and install the Help file. Or, if necessary, reinstall the entire application.

CHAPTER

HELP! Program Manager

The Windows NT Program Manager is a tool you can use to easily start applications and to arrange your applications and files into logical groups. Just as partitions and directories are used to organize your files on the hard drive, Program Manager uses work groups to sort applications and application files into logical collections. For the most part, these groupings are for your convenience and can be named and organized however you desire.

There are a few restrictions, however, that apply to all application, or program, groups. There are two types of application groups: personal and common. Personal program groups belong to the individual who has logged on to the computer, and these will not be displayed for or made accessible to other individuals when they log on. Common program groups, however, are displayed for and made accessible to all users who log on to the computer.

Figure 2.1 shows Program Manager with several application groups. The common program groups are shown with a small computer in the lower-right corner of the group icon. Personal program groups are identified by the human profile in the lower-right corner.

Notice also that the groups for Accessories, Administrative Tools, and Main are identified as personal program groups even though these groups are accessible to all individuals who log on to the system. This is because a personal copy of each of these groups is created for each user. Because of this, changes made to one copy of, for example, the application

group Main are not reflected in the application group that appears when another user logs on.

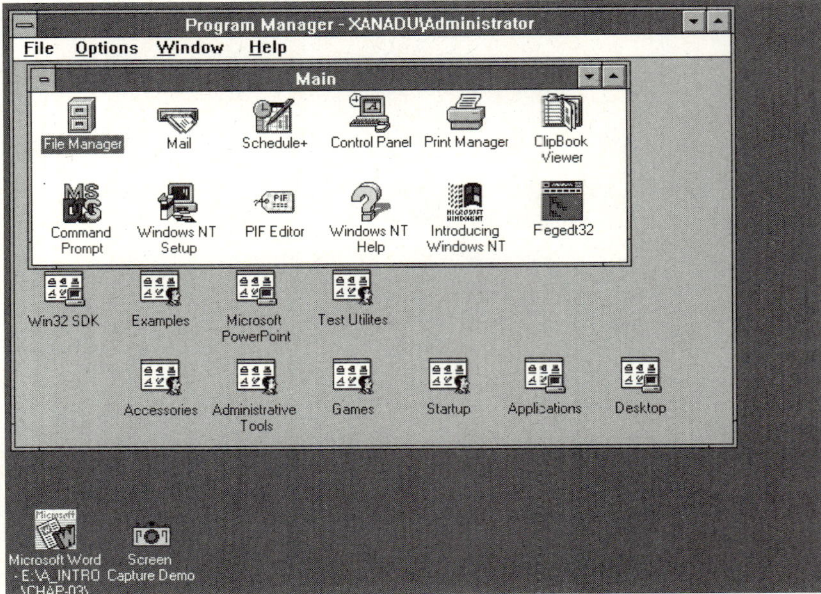

Figure 2.1
The Program Manager, application groups, and application icons

Any individuals logging on to the computer are free to create, delete, or manipulate their own personal program groups. For common program groups, however, you must be logged on as a member of the Administrators, Server Operators, or Power Users group before a new common group can be created, deleted, or otherwise changed.

Topics covered in this chapter include the following:

- Organizing applications and documents
- Starting applications and switching between applications
- Arranging windows and icons
- Saving Program Manager settings
- Quitting Windows NT

Application and Document Organization

Creating Groups

Only users logged on as members of the Administrators, Server Operators, or Power Users group are permitted to create a common program group.

To create a program group:

1. Choose New from the File menu.
2. In the New Program Object dialog box, select the Personal program group or Common program group option, and then choose the OK button.
3. In the Description box in the Program Group Properties dialog box, type a caption. This will be displayed in the title bar of the group window and will appear below the group icon in the Program Manager window.
4. Choose the OK button.

Once a new group has been created, applications can be added to the group.

Deleting Groups

To delete an application group:

1. Reduce the group to an icon by clicking on the minimize arrow at the upper-right or choosing the Minimize or Close option from the group window's system menu (in the upper-left corner of the group window).
2. Select the application group's icon—the title bar below the icon will be highlighted.
3. Choose Delete from the File menu or press the Del key.
4. In the Delete dialog box, choose the Yes button or press Enter.

HELP! *Program groups should be deleted cautiously—once deleted, a group cannot be recovered. To restore an accidentally deleted program group, you must re-create it as a new program group and install the desired applications in the new group. Deleting a group does not delete any programs or files from the disk.*

▶ Switching between Application Groups

To switch between program groups:

1. Select Windows from the Program Manager menu bar.
2. Select the desired application group from the list displayed at the bottom of the menu.
3. If you have more than nine application groups and the desired group is not listed, select More Windows from the end of the list of groups. A dialog box appears with a scrolling list box containing the names of all program groups. (The ordering appears to be more or less arbitrary.)
4. Select the desired program group from the list box.
5. Select OK or double-click on the program group name.

▶ Creating Program Items

To create a program item:

- Use the New command in File Manager.

Or:

- Create a program item by using the mouse to drag a program or document file from File Manager to a Program Manager group.

Help Files ▼ A program item icon represents an application, accessory, or document in a program group. To start an application or accessory or to open a document or file, double-click on its icon (see Figure 2.1, preceding).

▸ Adding a Program Item to a Group

To add a program to a group:

1. Open the window of the group where the program item will be placed.
2. From the File menu, choose New.
3. In the New Program Object dialog box, select the Program Item option, and then choose the OK button.
4. Fill in the Program Item Properties dialog box as necessary, and choose the OK button.

Help Files ▼ In Figure 2.2, the Desktop application group items labeled Personal, Computer, and Publishers are all identified by the same card-index icon. At the lower right, the Program Item Properties dialog box shows a typical entry, this one for the ADDRESS.CRD file.

Each of these three identical icons represents a different card file, although each uses the CARDFILE.EXE application to display the selected card file. In the case of the Winword and REGEDIT32 items, however, the program item's name simply refers to an executable application without identifying a specific data file. And in the case of the Win NT and Graph

NT icons, each calls a command-line shell but has different default-drive and directory settings. For further details, refer to "Specifying Program Item Properties," later in this chapter.

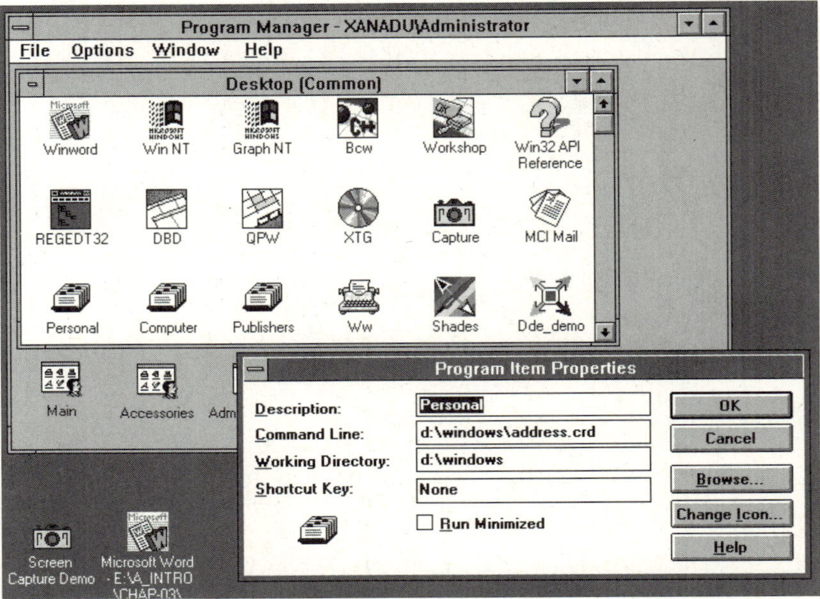

Figure 2.2
Multiple documents called as icons

▸ Deleting a Program Item from a Group

To delete a program item:

1. Select the icon for the item to be deleted.
2. Choose Delete from the File menu or press the Del key.
3. In the Delete dialog box, choose the Yes button or press Enter.

When an item is deleted from a group, the icon is removed from the group window, but the application is not deleted from the hard disk and no files or information are lost.

Moving and Copying Program Items

To move or copy a program item to another group:

1. Open the group window containing the program item you wish to move or copy.
2. Either open the destination group window or simply leave the destination group as an icon if you don't care where in the window the new icon for the item is placed.
3. Move a program item by selecting the desired application icon and using the mouse to drag it to the destination group window or the group's icon. To copy a program item, hold down the Ctrl key while dragging the program item icon.
4. Once the program's icon is inside the destination group window or on top of the destination group icon, simply release the mouse button. If the program item is being copied, of course, you should also release the Ctrl key.

Help Files

Program items can also be moved or copied using the Move or Copy commands from the File menu.

Releasing the mouse button and Ctrl key while the application icon is still inside the source group window instructs Program Manager to create a duplicate entry within the source group. (Only the Program Manager entry is duplicated; the file or application remains unchanged.)

The Move command moves the highlighted program item from its original group to another application group. This command summons the Move Program Item dialog box shown in Figure 2.3.

The item and source group are shown at the top of the dialog box, and the To Group list box displays a list of the program groups available as possible destinations. After selecting a destination group from the list (scrolling as necessary), click on the OK button to complete the move or select Cancel to terminate the operation.

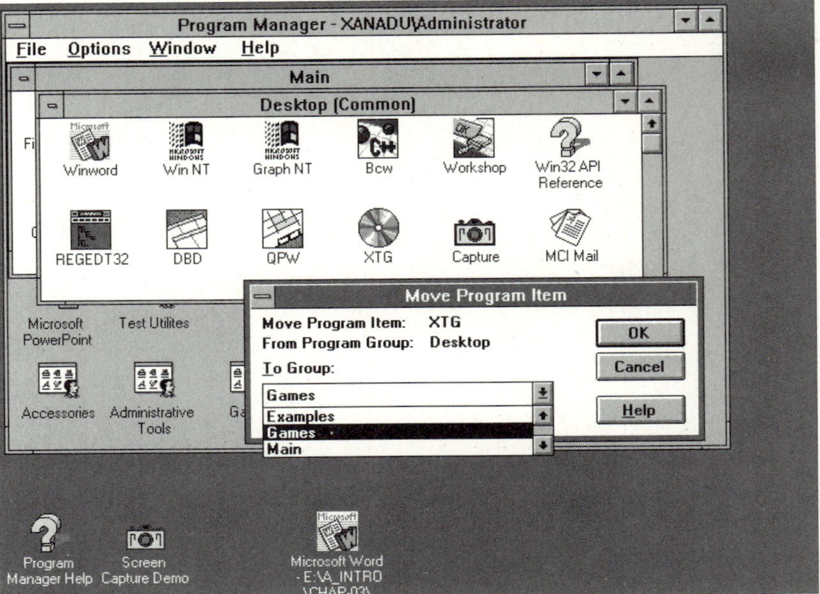

Figure 2.3
The Move Program Item dialog box

The Copy command is used to duplicate a program item in a new program group without removing it from the present program group. The steps are almost identical to those for the Move option discussed earlier; the only difference is that you hold down the Ctrl key while you drag the program item.

▸ Changing Group Properties

To change the properties of a group:

1. Select the group icon.
2. Choose Properties from the File menu or press Alt+Enter.
3. In the Program Item Properties dialog box, enter a new description.
4. Choose the OK button.

Help Files ▼ Once a personal or common group has been created, the group's one property—its description—can be changed at any time. (Remember, to change the properties of a common group or a common group's program items, you must be logged on as a member of the Administrators, Server Operators, or Power Users group.)

▶ Specifying Program Item Properties

When creating a new program item, the application's properties must be specified in the Program Item Properties dialog box. These properties include

- A description of the item (a label)
- The command-line entry used to execute the application
- A working directory where files created by the application are stored
- An optional shortcut key to call the application
- The application's icon

Help Files ▼ The Program Item Properties dialog box appears in Figure 2.2. Once a program item has been created, this dialog box can be called at any time to change any of these properties. The Description entry can be anything you wish and will become the label that appears below the icon in the Program Manager application group.

The Command Line entry specifies what text you will type from the Command Shell to call the application directly. Although Windows NT

does check its own source directory for request applications, in the example shown in Figure 2.2, the ADDRESS.CRD file is located in the Windows 3.1 directory on drive D—which Windows NT does not check—and, therefore, it is given a fully qualified (complete) drive and path specification. Even though .CRD files are not themselves executable, this extension has been associated with the CARDFILE.EXE application, which is called, automatically, to load the named card file. (Associations are assigned by File Manager.)

In other cases, the Command Line entry specifies both the executable application and the data file to be used, for example:

```
c:\winnt\cardfile.exe d:\windows\address.crd
```

In this format, the Cardfile executable application is explicitly called with a second specification naming the ADDRESS.CRD file to be loaded.

If you don't know the application or file's exact name or drive and directory path, you can use the Browse button to call the Browse dialog box, shown in Figure 2.4, to search for the desired application.

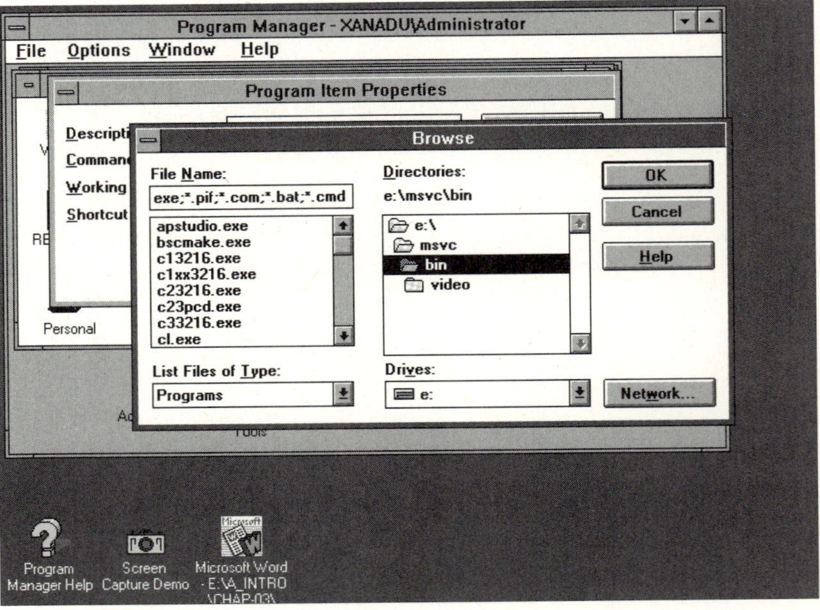

Figure 2.4
The Browse dialog box

The Working Directory entry is optional in the example shown in Figure 2.2, but in other cases it is the directory where the application's files are found or the default directory where the application's files should be written. If no directory is specified, the Windows NT directory is used by default.

The Shortcut Key entry permits you to specify a hotkey combination that can be used to call this application. The hotkey specification can be any of the following combinations:

- Ctrl+Alt+*character*
- Shift+Alt+*character*
- Ctrl+Shift+Alt+*character*

Here, *character* can be any letter, number, or special character. If you specify only the character in the Shortcut Key entry, Program Manager assumes you are selecting the Ctrl+Alt+*character* combination. Invalid characters include the Esc, Enter, Tab, spacebar, PrtSc, and Backspace keys.

The Run Minimized check box, if selected, instructs Program Manager to run the application as an icon when called.

The Change Icon button is used to select a different icon if more than one icon is available in an application or to choose an icon for applications that do not provide their own.

HELP! *If there is an error in the information provided for a program item—errors are generally in the application drive, directory, or program name or in the drive or path information specified for the application's working directory—Program Manager will report the error but will not prevent you from saving the specified configuration. An invalid configuration, however, will not function even though the application's icon—once included in a program group—will be displayed in the application group. To correct this problem, simply repeat the installation process or use the Browse feature to correctly locate the application. Alternatively, if the application has been deleted from the hard drive, delete the icon, as well.*

▶ Changing an Icon

If an application has more than one icon available or if there are no icons available, the Change Icon dialog box—illustrated in Figure 2.5—can be used to choose the icon desired or to select a source file for the icon. To change an icon:

1. Select the icon you want to replace.

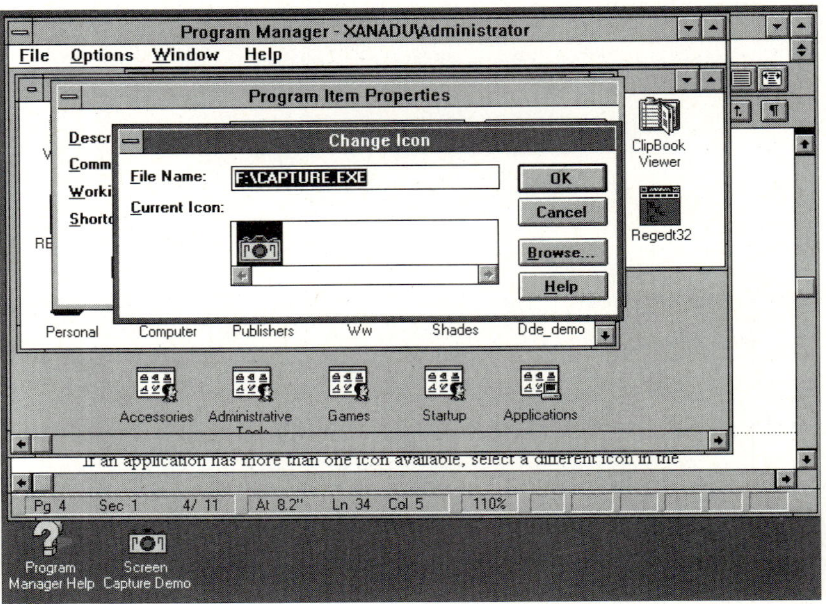

Figure 2.5
The Change Icon dialog box

2. Choose Properties from the File menu.

3. From the Program Item Properties dialog box, choose the Change Icon button. Then,

- If one or more icons are available within the application, the icons will be displayed in the Change Icon dialog box and the current icon selection will be highlighted. The scroll bar (or the left and right arrow key) can be used to scroll through the selections.

- If no icons are available within the application, Windows NT will display the icons provided by the PROGMAN.EXE program. The offered icons can be scrolled through for viewing; make a selection by clicking on the icon desired.

- Alternatively, icons can be selected from other sources, such as .ICO (icon) files, .EXE (executable) programs, or .DLL (dynamic link libraries) by selecting the Browse button to choose a source file. (Try selecting MORICONS.DLL in the WINNT\SYSTEM32 directory.) All icons available in the selected source file will be displayed in the Change Icon dialog box.

4. Choose the OK button to select an icon or choose Cancel to leave the icon unchanged.

Some applications provide more than one icon (see "Changing an Icon," preceding). When multiple icons are available, any of the supplied icons can be selected for display by Program Manager. This selection will not, however, affect the icon image displayed by the Windows NT (or Windows 3.1) desktop; only Program Manager's icon display can be selected.

Starting Applications and Switching between Applications

▶ Starting an Application from a Program Group

To start an application from a program group:

1. Open the group window containing the application's program item icon.
2. Choose the program item icon by double-clicking on it, by highlighting the item and then choosing Open from the File menu, or, if a shortcut key is assigned, by using the hotkey combination.

If the application is a document or data file that has been associated with an executable application, the executable application is called to load the document or data file.

Switching between Applications

Windows NT provides a variety of methods for switching between applications. To switch to another application:

- Click anywhere in an inactive application's window or on the application's icon.
- Press Alt+Esc to cycle through the loaded applications until the desired window is active.
- Press and hold the Alt key while pressing the Tab key repeatedly. The names of active applications cycle on the screen. When the desired application is named, release the Alt key to bring that application to the foreground.

If no applications except Program Manger are active, nothing will happen when the Alt+Tab combination is pressed.

- Press Ctrl+Esc or double-click anywhere on the desktop to open the Task List. Then select the application desired and choose the Switch To button or press Enter.
- Choose Switch To from the Control menu of any running application.

Using the Run Command to Start an Application

The Run command can be used to start applications that are used only occasionally or that haven't been added to a group. To start an application by using the Run command:

1. From the File menu, choose Run.
2. In the Command Line box, type the path and name, including the extension, of the program file.
3. Optionally, following the program name, a document or data file name can be appended (see "Specifying Program Item Properties," earlier in this chapter).
4. Select the Run Minimized check box if you want the application to be reduced to an icon when it starts.
5. Choose the OK button or press Enter.

▶ Starting Applications Automatically When You Log On to Windows NT

Windows NT establishes a Startup group for each user. Initially, this is an empty group, but any applications desired can be placed in this group and will be called when the user logs on to Windows NT. Applications can be added or copied from existing application groups or by using the New option from the Files menu.

▶ Minimizing the Program Manager Window

The Minimize On Use option on the Options menu instructs the Program Manager window to shrink itself into an icon whenever an application is started from a Program Manager application group. The Program Manager icon is placed at the lower-left corner of the desktop where it can be easily located. When selected, a check mark appears to the left of the Minimize On Use option in Program Manager's Options menu.

Window and Icon Arrangement

▶ Arranging Application Groups and Application Group Icons

Application groups and group icons can be arranged in a variety of fashions. To arrange application group windows:

- Select Cascade from the Window menu to automatically resize and arrange all open groups as overlapping windows. Each group window's title will be visible in the stacked arrangement.
- Select Tile from the Window menu to automatically resize and organize the open groups in a row or row/column arrangement. The resulting arrangement fills the Program Manager window horizontally but leaves the bottom row of group icons uncovered.

- Arrange group windows individually—in the same fashion as you would other windows—by clicking on the group window's title bar and dragging the window to the desired position.
- Resize group windows individually by placing the cursor on the window border or corner—where the cursor changes to a double-headed arrow—and then clicking and holding the left mouse button while dragging the window to the desired size.

To arrange minimized (iconized) application group:

- Use the mouse to drag the group icon to the desired position.
- Highlight any one of the group icons before selecting the Arrange Icons option from the Window menu on the menu bar. All minimized group icons will be arranged evenly, beginning at the bottom of the Program Manager window and building up in rows, as required. Open program groups will not be affected.

▸ Arranging Icons within an Application Group

Three options are provided for arranging icons with an application group. To arrange icons within a group:

- Highlight any icon within a group and then select the Arrange Icons option from the Windows menu. All the icons in the group will be evenly spaced in row/column order.
- Select individual icons and arrange them with the mouse. Press and hold the left mouse button while dragging the icon to the position desired.
- Select Auto Arrange from the Options menu on the Program Manager menu bar to automatically arrange program icons for all application groups. A check mark indicates that the option is enabled. With the Auto Arrange option in effect, all program icons in any open group window are rearranged automatically whenever the group window's size changes, or when a program icon is added or deleted.

Saving Program Manager Settings

▶ Saving Program Manager Settings Automatically

Newly created groups and program items are saved regardless of this option setting. However, the arrangement and layout of program groups is not saved automatically.

The Save Settings On Exit option on the Options menu instructs Windows NT to save the arrangement of Program Manager windows and icons when the user logs off. When the option is active, a check mark appears to the left of it in the Program Manager menu.

▶ Saving Program Manager Settings Immediately

The Save Settings Now menu option immediately saves the current arrangement of Program Manager windows and icons.

Quitting Windows NT

▶ Logging Off from Windows NT

To log off from Windows NT:

1. Choose Logoff from the File menu in Program Manager or double-click on the Control-menu box. A dialog box prompts you for confirmation that you want to log off.
2. Choose the OK button. Windows NT closes all executing applications, including Program Manager. If unsaved files remain open, you will be prompted to save work in progress.
3. When the Log On message appears, you may log on again under a different name or, if you are using FlexBoot, you may reboot the computer for DOS.

Help Files ▼ Windows NT is an operating system, unlike Windows 3.1, which executes as a shell on top of DOS. As such, Windows NT cannot exit to DOS, but it can be logged off—which causes all open applications and files to shut down. Once this is done, the user can log on again under a different name, shut down the computer, or, if the dual-boot option (FlexBoot) was selected during installation, reboot for DOS and/or Windows 3.1.

▶ Shutting Down Your Computer

To shut down Windows NT:

1. Select Shutdown from the File menu in Program Manager. A dialog box will request confirmation that you want to quit Windows NT.
2. The Restart When Shutdown Is Complete box can be checked to execute an immediate warm reboot after shutdown is completed.
3. Choose the OK button and Windows NT begins closing applications while prompting you to save any open files. After all applications and services are closed and all file buffers are flushed, you will be informed that it is safe to power down the computer.

Functionally, the Logoff command is duplicated by the Close command in Program Manager's system menu.

THE RESCUE PAGES: Program Manager

I can't find the program group I'm looking for.

There are several possible explanations why a program group might not be visible. The first step, before you panic, is to rearrange the existing program groups and program group icons so that you can see all of them. After all, the missing group might simply be hidden behind another group or group icon or might be somewhere outside Program Manager's visible window area.

If that doesn't solve the problem, call Program Manager's Window menu. A list of program groups appears on the pull-down menu. If there are more than nine program groups, the More Windows... option will call an additional dialog box, permitting selection from a list box containing the names of all available program groups. Highlight the desired program group and press Enter, or double-click on the group name to summon the program group.

To be sure that the desired program group will be visible in the future, try reducing all open program groups to icon size (click on the down arrow button for each), then highlight any program group icon and select the Arrange Icons option from Program Manager's Window menu. This will order all the program groups within Program Manager's display window.

The program group I'm looking for doesn't appear on the list at all.

Under Windows NT, you have two types of application groups: personal and common. One possibility is that the program group you are looking

for is a personal program group belonging to another user—which means that it will appear only when the other user is logged on.

You may, of course, re-create the same program group as part of your own user profile, but as a personal program group.

Or, if you have Administrator-level or equivalent access, you can create a new common program containing the same items as the personal program group (it can also have the same group title). This new group will be available to all users but does not replace the personal group that it duplicates.

An application I don't want loads every time I log on.

Certain types of applications—including fax programs, screen savers, mouse-enhancement utilities, and other background programs that, under DOS, would have been categorized as TSRs—automatically install themselves in the Startup application group. Subsequently, when you log on, Windows NT looks in the your user profile for the Startup application group and loads any applications found there.

Your solution is simple—from Program Manager, check the contents of your Startup group and remove any applications that are not wanted.

Some applications—written specifically for Windows NT—are able to install themselves for automatic start-up without appearing in the Startup program group. Refer to the RegEdit32 utility in Chapter 15 for further details.

The icon shown in Program Manager doesn't appear when the application is reduced to an icon on the desktop.

Within Program Manager, application icons can be selected from several sources: from one or more icons that belong to the application itself, from icons provided by Program Manager, or from icons provided by some other application—such as the MOREICONS.DLL library. The icons displayed by Program Manager, however, are available only within Program Manager, regardless of what source this icon image information has been read from.

In contrast, the Windows NT desktop can use only the icon information (image) that the application itself specifies. If the application is a Windows 3.1 or Windows NT program, the program itself either will

contain an icon image that it displays automatically when the program is reduced to a desktop icon or, like the Clock application, may simply generate an icon-sized display. If the application is a DOS program executing under Windows NT and using the DOS shell, the only icon that will be displayed is the default DOS icon supplied by Windows NT itself.

Although there are methods that can be used to change the icons applications display on the desktop, these are not available to the average user. Even for experienced programmers, changing an application's icons may result in errors (though these are generally annoyances rather than critical mishaps).

Nothing happens when I select an application icon.

If a program is installed in a Program Manager application group and the application itself is then deleted or moved to a different drive or directory, the Program Manager's entry is not automatically deleted or revised. The icon is there, but when the application is selected (from the application group under Program Manager), the result is…nothing.

Happily, the solution is simple.

If the application has been deleted, the obvious response is to delete the icon from the application group—or if you wish, to delete the entire group (see "Creating and Deleting Groups" or "Deleting a Program Item from a Group," earlier in this chapter).

If, on the other hand, the application or the application data files simply have been moved to a different drive or different directory (or if the directory name has been changed), all that is necessary is to update the drive and path information so that Program Manager knows where to find the program and/or the program files (refer to "Specifying Program Item Properties," earlier in this chapter).

I installed a DOS application using an icon supplied by Program Manger. Everything's fine in the Program Manager group, but when the application is reduced to an icon on the desktop, the icon changes to the MS-DOS default icon. How do I prevent this?

Quite simply, you don't. It's no problem to tell Program Manager to use an icon from its own store for a DOS application—since DOS applications

have no icons of their own—or to select alternative icons from any other Windows 3.1 or Windows NT program. These selections, however, are recognized only in Program Manager, and the applications themselves—particularly DOS applications—remain quite unaware of such alternative selections.

When a DOS application is reduced to an icon, the DOS shell manages the application, and—quite ignorant of any selections made in Program Manager—supplies the default DOS icon.

In like fashion, a Windows 3.1 or Windows NT application is ignorant of any alternative selections used by Program Manager and displays the default icon assigned by the program's author.

CHAPTER

3

HELP! Installing Applications

Regardless of whether you're running under DOS, Windows 3.1, or Windows NT, the question of how to install an application is a recurrent problem. Under DOS, installation procedures range from simply copying files onto the hard drive to using .BAT utilities to accomplish essentially the same tasks, to using interactive installation utilities, which customize the environment and, sometimes, the application itself. Under Windows—either 3.1 or NT—the parallel is generally found in a Setup program. Under Windows 3.1, that process not only decompresses and copies files as necessary but also configures or customizes the application and, frequently, creates a program group for the application and its utilities. Under Windows NT, parts of this process have changed, but other parts remain unaltered. For the most part, Windows 3.1 applications are installed in the same fashion under NT as under 3.1. DOS applications, however, may require some additional preparations under NT to optimize their execution.

Topics covered in this chapter include the following:

- Installing applications
- Executing DOS applications using .PIF files
- Setting application parameters in a .PIF file
- Memory settings

- The PIF Enhanced mode options
- Advanced options for Enhanced mode
- Setting the memory options
- Setting the display options
- Setting other options
- Windows NT options for Enhanced mode

Places where this icon appears in this chapter refer to information that does *not* apply to Windows NT but is provided for Windows 3.1 compatability.

Application Installation

▶ Installing Applications by Using File Manager

To install an application:

1. Call File Manager.
2. Place the source disk in drive A or B or, in the case of a CD-ROM, in the CD drive.
3. Log in to the source drive.
4. Double-click on the Setup program listing, or highlight the Setup program and select the Run option from the menu.
5. Follow any directions given by the Setup utility.

Beyond this point, the Setup utility will provide whatever instructions are required and guide you though the balance of the installation process—including making any modifications to the AUTOEXEC.BAT and CONFIG.SYS files.

Help Files ▼ Windows 3.1 and Windows NT applications customarily provide an installation utility titled SETUP.EXE, although a few applications have used a utility titled INSTALL.EXE. Despite the fact that its name is similar to that of a common DOS utility, INSTALL.EXE is still a Windows executable program, and it performs essentially the same task as the Setup utility.

One item to remember: If you are installing a Windows 3.1 application under Windows NT, instead of modifying your DOS AUTOEXEC.BAT and CONFIG.SYS files, you will need to direct the installation changes to the \NT\SYSTEM32 directory for AUTOEXEC.NT, and CONFIG.NT files. Undoubtedly, installation utilities will be amended in the near future to provide methods for handling both Windows 3.1 and Windows NT installation or, equally likely, provisions for dual installation. But at present, this remains a potential conflict.

The solution, although mildly inconvenient, is not terribly onerous. Normally, if changes to these two files are required, the Setup utility will offer the options of permitting you to make these changes yourself or of creating separate AUTOEXEC and/or CONFIG files rather than changing the DOS boot files. Choosing either of these options will leave your DOS files unchanged and permit you to make the required changes to the AUTOEXEC.NT and CONFIG.NT files in the \NT\SYSTEM32 directory.

Before panicking, consider this consoling thought: Most Windows applications do not expect or require any changes to either of these files, and, in general, the question of changes should not arise at all. (See also "Windows NT Options for Enhanced Mode," later in this chapter.)

▸ Installing Applications from the DOS Window

Although most Windows 3.1 and Windows NT applications expect to be installed from Windows (that is, using File Manager), some Windows

applications expect to begin at the DOS prompt, as do, of course, DOS applications. To install an application from the DOS prompt:

1. Select the MS-DOS icon from the Main program group to open a DOS window.
2. From the DOS prompt (C:), proceed exactly as you would under DOS. (Refer to any INSTALL.TXT, README.TXT, and similar files supplied in the source disk for instructions.)
3. When finished, close the DOS window to return to Windows NT.

Help Files ▼ As a general rule, DOS software packages use either an INSTALL.EXE or an INSTALL.BAT utility, although many DOS applications just provide installation instructions. Still other packages use self-extracting .ZIP files (with .EXE extensions) that expand the program and data files, creating directories and subdirectories as appropriate. (.ZIP files, named for their identifying .ZIP extension, are compressed files that contain one or more normal, usable files. When contained in a .ZIP file, a file uses much less disk space than it will after decompression. However, it cannot be used until it is extracted and decompressed to become a normal file.)

As a general rule, installation instructions should appear in the documentation, on the distribution disk label, or both. However, if the instructions are missing or have not been provided, begin by looking for likely candidates for the installation utility and simply try them. In the event that the executable program is not a DOS utility, a message should appear, stating that the application can be run only in the Windows environment.

Always be very careful of disks from unknown or unreliable sources. The Windows NT operating system includes provisions that should prevent infection by most viruses, but no one—absolutely no one—can guarantee total protection from all present and future viruses.

Executing DOS Applications by Using .PIF Files

▶ Creating a New .PIF File

To create a .PIF file:

1. Call the PIF Editor.
2. Choose New from the File menu.
3. From the Mode menu, select Enhanced as the mode the application should run in.
4. Select the options and settings appropriate to the application. For details about an option, select the option and then press F1.
5. From the File menu, choose Save As. In the File Name box, type the application's program file name adding the extension .PIF.
6. Choose the OK button.

Help Files ▼ Because all applications executing under Windows NT will run in Enhanced mode, Standard should not be selected—it is relevant only for 16-bit Windows 3.1.

When the Setup program or Program Manager is used to create a program item for a DOS application, Windows NT automatically creates a .PIF file for the application. Subsequently, when a DOS application is started, Windows NT looks for a .PIF file to provide instructions specifying how the application is to be treated. If there is no .PIF file for the application, Windows NT uses a default .PIF instruction file. If a DOS application does not have a .PIF file and does not work using the default .PIF, a new, custom .PIF file can be created for the application. (See also "Modifying the Default .PIF," later in this chapter.)

▸ Editing an Existing .PIF File

When a DOS application doesn't execute correctly, your first response should be to check the application's .PIF file. Items to check include

- The application's drive and path specification
- The application's working (default) directory specification
- Any command-line parameters expected by the application
- Reserved shortcut keys required for use by the application

To edit a PIF:

1. Call the PIF Editor.
2. Select Open from the File menu.
3. Select (or type) a file name, then click on the OK button.
4. Change any options required.
5. Select Save from the File menu.

Help Files ▼ Once an application has been installed in Program Manager, the path and default directory specified in the .PIF file can be overridden by specifications made using the Properties command from Program Manager's File menu.

▸ Modifying the Default .PIF File

To change the default .PIF file:

1. Call the PIF Editor.
2. In the Program Filename box, type the file name _DEFAULT.COM.

3. Leave the Window Title box blank.
4. Change any other settings as appropriate. For information about an option, select it and press F1.
5. From the File menu, choose Save As. Do not save changes under the original file name unless these changes are intended to apply to all DOS applications.
6. Type the file name of the application that will be using the .PIF file, replacing the application's extension with .PIF.
7. Select the OK button to save the .PIF file.

Help Files ▼ Although Windows NT does not use all the settings contained in a .PIF file (see "Setting Application Parameters in a .PIF File," following), each field must contain a valid specification because the PIF Editor verifies the contents of all fields.

When a DOS application that does not have a custom .PIF file is executed, Windows NT uses a default .PIF file named _DEFAULT.PIF. The settings in this .PIF file work with most applications, but they will not be suitable for every application.

The default .PIF can be modified, if necessary. For example, the _DEFAULT.PIF file might be changed to specify that applications should run in a window rather than execute in the full screen. However, because Windows NT will probably be using this as the default .PIF for other applications, it is always preferable to create a new .PIF—using the default .PIF as a template.

Application Parameters in a .PIF File

▶ Setting the Program File Name

The Program Filename field receives the name of the executable file including, if necessary, the drive and directory path. This program name must always include the file extension (.BAT, .COM, .EXE, or .PIF). The Program Item Properties dialog is shown in Figure 3.1.

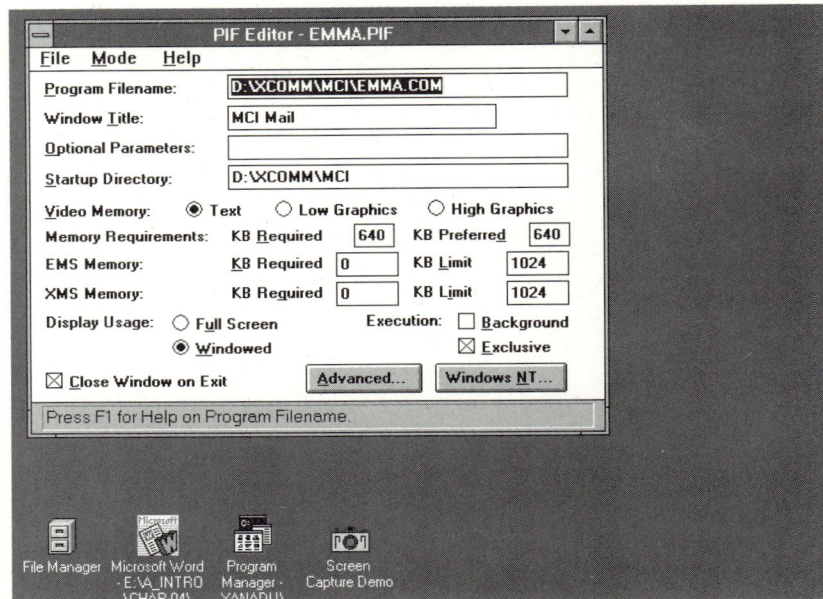

Figure 3.1
The Program Item Properties dialog box

Help Files ▼ The .PIF file name must match the program file name—that is, a .PIF file created to call XTG.EXE must be named XTG.PIF. Alternatively, if an application is started from a batch file (.BAT), the batch file name, not the application name, would be specified here. Optionally, an environmental variable can be used in the program file name.

▶ Setting the Window Title

The Window Title field supplies a descriptive name for the application. Brevity is recommended.

Help Files ▼ This descriptive name appears in the application's window title bar when the application executes and below the application's icon in Program Manager or on the desktop. If no title is specified, the application name (without the extension) is used by default.

The window title can also be specified using the Properties command in Program Manager's File menu; a title specified this way will override any title specification in the .PIF file. An environmental variable can also be used in this field.

▶ Setting Optional Parameters

The Optional Parameters field is used to specify command-line parameters for a DOS application. These are the same parameters that would be entered after an application's file name when executing the application from the DOS prompt.

Help Files ▼ Here's an example of how optional parameters work: To call XTree and log in to drive D, you would enter the characters *XTG D:* from the command-line prompt. To create a .PIF file for this same task, the D: specification would be entered in the Optional Parameters field.

If the application doesn't require any calling parameters or they are optional but not desired, simply leave this field blank. For valid parameters

and formats, refer to the application's documentation. Alternatively, if a question mark (?) is entered, Windows NT will prompt you for parameters before the application is initiated.

Optional parameters can also be entered using environmental variables.

Parameters specified in the .PIF file can be overridden when the application is called by Program Manager's or File Manager's File menu Run command. To do so, enter the parameters desired after the application name in the Run dialog box. Optional parameters can also be specified if you use the Properties command in Program Manager's File menu. In all cases, these arguments override the settings in the .PIF instruction file.

▸ Setting the Start-Up Directory

The Startup Directory field holds the drive and directory specification that the application should use as its working directory. If no start-up directory is specified, the application directory becomes the default.

Help Files ▼

Normally, the start-up directory is the location where the application's program file is found, but it can be any drive or directory desired. A start-up directory can also be specified when you use the Properties command in Program Manager's File menu; specifying the start-up directory this way will override any specification in the .PIF file. An environment variable can also be used in this field.

▸ Setting Environmental Variables

Environmental variables can be used in many of the .PIF parameter fields, but they must be identified by being enclosed in percent signs. Otherwise, they will be identified as variable references rather than as string literals.

Help Files ▼ Here's an example of how to use an environmental variable: To use a variable named MYAPPPATH, the .PIF entry would be written as %MYAPPPATH%, with MYAPPPATH defined in the AUTOEXEC.BAT file by the following set command:

```
set MYAPPPATH=d:\directory_name\directory_name
```

Memory Settings

▶ Setting Video Memory

Since the information in the Video Memory field is not used by Windows NT, these radio buttons can be left with the default setting (Text) unchanged. The PIF Editor options dialog box is shown in Figure 3.2.

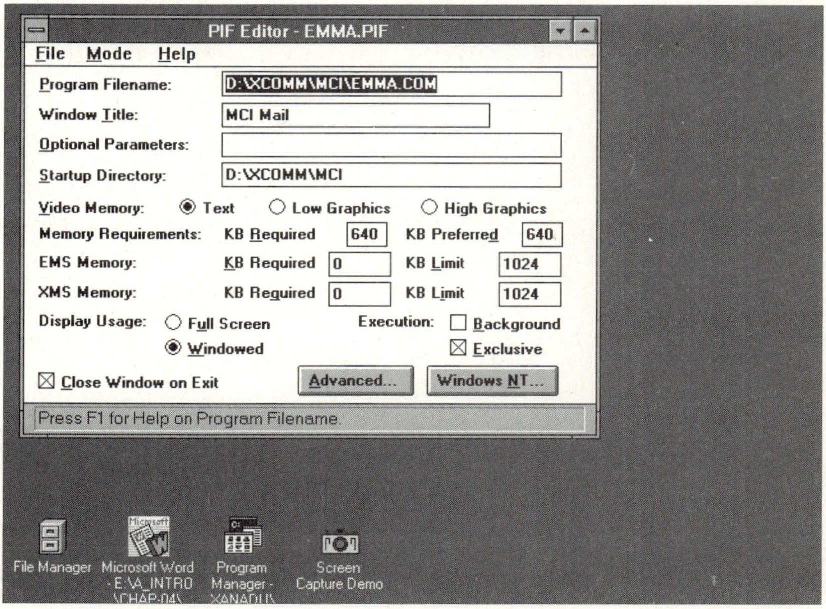

Figure 3.2
The PIF Editor options

Help Files ▼ This option specifies the video mode in which an application will start. Windows allocates system memory to display the application in accordance with the video mode you specify. Text mode uses the least amount of memory, and High (resolution) Graphics mode uses the most.

▶ Setting Base Memory Requirements

Since the information in the Memory Requirements field is not used by Windows NT, this field can be left with the default settings (128/640) unchanged. This is what the settings mean:

- KB Required indicates the minimum amount of memory (in kilobytes) that an application requires. If you are unsure, check the application's system requirements. If no minimum is stated, use the default setting. An entry of 0 indicates the application has no minimum memory requirement; –1 allocates the maximum amount of memory possible.
- KB Desired indicates the maximum amount of conventional memory that the application can use, up to 640K (kilobytes). Specifying –1 allocates the maximum amount of memory available for the application.

Help Files ▼ The Memory Requirements values are used by Windows 3.1 to allocate conventional memory for the applications.

Setting EMS Memory

The EMS Memory options are used to specify the amount of expanded memory that an application requires:

- KB Required sets the minimum amount of expanded memory (in kilobytes) that an application requires. Before setting this value, check your application's requirements, or, if the requirements are not known, leave the default setting. Use a setting of 0 for applications that do not require expanded memory.
- KB Limit sets the maximum amount of expanded memory an application may be allocated, preventing an application from demanding more expanded memory than it actually requires. The default setting is 1024K (1 megabyte). A specification of –1 allows the application to request whatever EMS memory it wishes, up to the limits of the system memory. (This will, however, slow other executing applications by restricting their memory usage.) A specification of 0 prevents the application from requesting EMS memory.

Help Files ▼ Because Windows NT runs in Enhanced mode and uses flat, 32-bit memory addressing, for applications that require expanded (EMS) or extended (XMS) memory, Windows NT simulates the presence of EMS or XMS memory.

Setting XMS Memory for Enhanced Mode

The XMS Memory options specify the amount of extended memory available to your application:

- KB Required states the minimum amount of extended memory (in kilobytes) required by an application. Check the system requirements for the application; if no requirements are stated, leave the

default settings. A specification of 0 indicates that the application does not require extended memory.

- KB Limit states the maximum amount of extended memory (in kilobytes) to be allocated for an application and prevents an application from reserving all available extended memory blocks. The default setting is 1024K, and a specification of –1 allocates as much extended memory as an application requests, up to the limit of system memory. A specification of 0 prevents an application from using extended memory.

Help Files ▼ Because few applications require extended memory, the XMS Memory options can normally be left at their default settings.

If other applications are running and Windows NT cannot provide the memory requested—whether conventional, EMS, XMS, or video—a message box will appear, suggesting that some applications may need to be closed before the current program can execute.

▶ Setting the Close Window On Exit Option

Because the information in this field is not required by Windows NT, the default (checked) for this field can be left unchanged.

The Close Window On Exit option is used by Windows 3.1. This check box should be unchecked if you want the window (or screen) to remain open when the application terminates—for example, if you are running a command or application displaying text output on the screen that is needed after the application terminates. By default, the DOS window closes when the application terminates.

Controlling How an Application Is Initially Displayed

The Display Usage options control how the application is initially displayed:

- Windowed starts the application in a window.
- Full Screen starts the application in a full screen.

Help Files ▼ Applications can be switched from full screen to a window—or vice versa—by pressing Alt+Enter. While an application is executing, display usage can be set from the Control menu by using the Settings command, which overrides the .PIF settings.

The Alt+Tab combination switches between full-screen applications and the Windows NT desktop.

On 80x86-based PCs, graphics applications execute using the full screen only. On RISC-based computers, all applications run in a window only and the Display Usage options do not apply.

Selecting Execution Background

Because the information in this field is not required by Windows NT, the default (unchecked) for this field can be left unchanged.

The background execution option is used by Windows 3.1 only where, if selected, a DOS application is permitted to run as a background application—that is, when it is not the active application.

When enabled, a DOS application is allowed to run in the background (calculating numbers, for example) while another application is being executed in the foreground. The result, however, is that other applications will run more slowly when sharing resources with background applications.

▸ Selecting Execution Exclusive

Because the information in this field is not required by Windows NT, the default (checked) for this field can be left unchanged.

The Execution Exclusive option is used only by Windows 3.1. This option gives a DOS application exclusive use of system resources while it is the active application. When set, no other applications, including those with the Background option set, can run while the current application is active.

This option can be selected for both applications running in a window and applications running full screen. However, applications running in a window do not receive all the computer's resources, because Windows NT reserves some resources for itself as well as for other executing applications.

.PIF Enhanced Mode Options

▸ Selecting Advanced Options

Choose the Advanced button to display the advanced options for Enhanced mode, as shown in Figure 3.3. Refer to details on specific options in the following sections. Grayed areas are options that are not used by Windows NT .PIF files but which have been retained for compatibility with Windows 3.1 .PIF files.

Multitasking Options

▸ Setting Background and Foreground Priority

Since the Background and Foreground Priority settings are not used by Windows NT, the default values (50/100) shown in these fields can be left unchanged.

Background and Foreground priorities are used by Windows 3.1 to determine how CPU (central processing unit) resources are allocated to applications. Priorities range from 0 to 10,000, with a default foreground priority of 100 and a default background priority of 50. The higher the priority number assigned to an application, the greater the proportion of the CPU resources allocated to the application. These settings are not used by Windows NT.

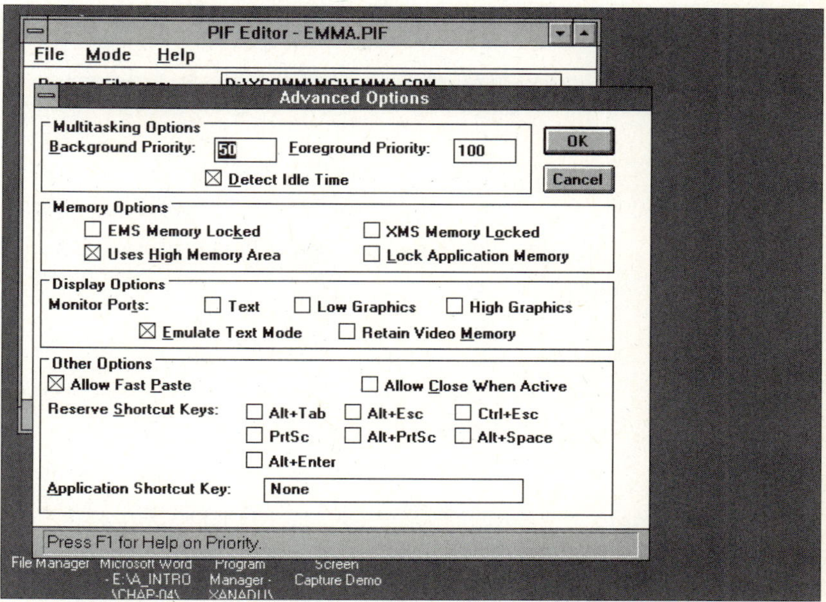

Figure 3.3
Advanced options

▶ Setting the Detect Idle Time

Since the Detect Idle Time option setting is not used by Windows NT, the default setting (enabled) for this option can be left unchanged.

The Detect Idle Time option is used by Windows 3.1 to allocate CPU resources to other applications while the current application is waiting for keyboard input. This option is not used by Windows NT.

Memory Options

▶ Setting the EMS Memory Locked Option

Since the EMS Memory Locked option is not used by Windows NT, the default setting (unchecked) for this option can be left unchanged.

The EMS Memory Locked option is used by Windows 3.1 to specify that the expanded memory allocated to the application is locked into memory and won't be swapped to the hard disk. This option is not used by Windows NT.

▶ Setting the Uses High Memory Area Option

Since the Uses High Memory Area option is not used by Windows NT, the default setting (checked) for this option can be left unchanged.

The Uses High Memory Area option is valid only in Windows 3.1. It specifies that an application has access to the high memory area (HMA) of RAM.

▶ Setting the XMS Memory Locked Option

Since the XMS Memory Locked option is not used by Windows NT, the default setting (checked) for this option can be left unchanged.

The XMS Memory Locked option is used under Windows 3.1 to lock the extended memory allocated for an application. This option is not valid under Windows NT.

▶ Setting the Lock Application Memory Option

Since the Lock Application Memory option is not used by Windows NT, the default setting (unchecked) for this option can be left unchanged.

Under Windows 3.1, when the Lock Application Memory option is selected, Windows keeps the application in memory instead of swapping parts of it to the hard disk. The application using this option speeds up but does so at the expense of other applications. Using this option also limits the number of applications that can be active. This option is not used under Windows NT.

Display Options

▸ Setting the Monitor Ports Option

Since the Monitor Ports options are not used by Windows NT, the default settings shown for these options (all unchecked) can be left unchanged.

The Monitor Ports options are used by Windows 3.1 to ensure that values used by the display adapter (hardware)—Text, Low Graphics, or High Graphics—are the same as the application expects. These options are not required by Windows NT.

▸ Setting the Emulate Text Mode Option

Since the Emulate Text Mode option is not used by Windows NT, the default setting (checked) for this option can be left unchanged.

Under Windows 3.1, many applications run with the screen display in text mode and use the standard ROM BIOS services for their output. Thus when the Emulate Text Mode option is selected, the screen update for such applications executes faster. This option is not used in Windows NT.

▸ Setting the Retain Video Memory Option

Since the Retain Video Memory option is not used by Windows NT, the default (unchecked) for this option can be left unchanged.

The Retain Video Memory option is used by Windows 3.1 and instructs Windows to set the amount of memory needed for the application's starting video mode without returning any memory to the system, even if video modes change while the application is executing. This option is not relevant in Windows NT.

Other Options

▸ Allowing Fast Paste

Since the Allow Fast Paste option is not used by Windows NT, the default setting (checked) for this option can be left unchanged.

▸ Allowing Close When Active

Since the Allow Close When Active option is not used by Windows NT, the default (checked) for this field can be left unchanged.

The Allow Close When Active check box is used by Windows 3.1 only. Selecting this option allows Windows to close an active application automatically when Windows exits. This option is ignored by Windows NT.

▸ Setting Reserve Shortcut Keys for Enhanced Mode

Shortcut keys that are defined for use with Windows NT can be reserved, instead, for use by an application when the application is active. These shortcut keys can be selected from the list displayed in Figure 3.3 by checking the boxes for the desired keys. When the application is not active, these shortcut keys function as normal under Windows NT.

▸ Setting an Application Shortcut Key

Shortcut keys, also called hotkeys, are key combinations used to load and execute an application immediately. The hotkey specification can be any of the following combinations:

- Ctrl+Alt+*character*
- Shift+Alt+*character*
- Ctrl+Shift+Alt+*character*

Here, *character* specifies any letter, number, or special character. If only the character is entered, Program Manager assumes you are selecting the Ctrl+Alt+*character* combination.

Help Files ▼ A shortcut key is entered by pressing the desired key combination. A dialog box prompts you if the selected hotkey combination is invalid. Invalid characters include the Esc, Enter, Tab, spacebar, PrtSc, and Backspace keys in any combination.

Because shortcut keys operate systemwide, only one application can use a specific key combination. Also, if the selected key combination conflicts with an access key in a Windows NT application, the access key is disabled when the NT application is active.

Shortcut keys can also be specified using Program Manager's File menu Properties command; this overrides settings assigned in a .PIF file. (See also "Setting Reserve Shortcut Keys for Enhanced Mode," earlier in this section.)

Windows NT Options for Enhanced Mode

▶ Setting the Autoexec Filename and Config Filename Options

When starting a DOS application, Windows NT uses the Autoexec Filename and Config Filename field specifications provided in the .PIF file to set path and environmental variables for the application. These batch and system files are not executed in the usual sense—as when DOS boots—but they do tell Windows NT what conditions, directory paths, and environmental variables the application would expect to find when executed under DOS. This allows Windows NT to simulate the expected environment for the application.

Figure 3.4 shows the EMMA.PIF file using the default AUTOEXEC.NT and CONFIG.NT batch and system files, which contain instructions that were copied from the DOS AUTOEXEC.BAT and CONFIG.SYS files at the time Windows NT was installed.

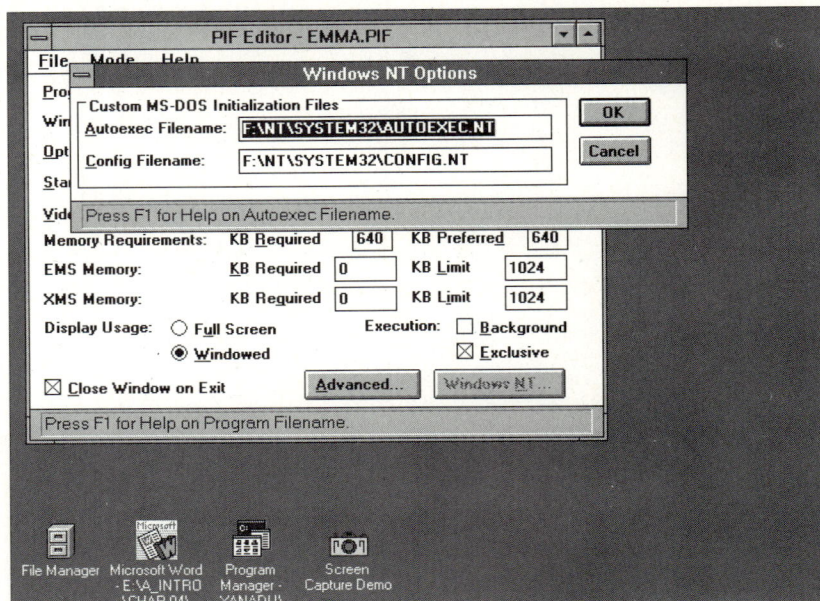

Figure 3.4
Custom DOS initialization files

The AUTOEXEC and CONFIG files can also include instructions for initiating memory-resident programs that are required or expected by the called application. The TSR utility will be loaded before the main application is called, but will be resident only in the virtual DOS shell where the main application is executed.

Help Files ▼ Customized versions of AUTOEXEC and CONFIG can be created for different applications and given new file names as appropriate. For example, if new versions were created for the EMMA application, they might be named AUTOEXEC.EMM and CONFIG.EMM, or they could be titled using some other naming convention.

One good method for ensuring that the necessary information appears in a custom start-up files is to base these on the AUTOEXEC.NT and CONFIG.NT files located in the \NT\SYSTEM32 directory.

In configuration files, the environmental variable %SystemRoot% represents the Windows NT directory and, when the file is processed, is automatically expanded.

▶ Creating Custom Start-Up Files

To create custom start-up files:

1. Using a text editor such as Notepad or Write, edit the CONFIG.NT and AUTOEXEC.NT files. These must be "plain ASCII" text files.
2. Save each file under a new name.

To include start-up files in an application's .PIF file:

1. Open the .PIF file for the application being customized.
2. Select the Windows NT button.
3. In the Autoexec Filename box, type the name of the customized AUTOEXEC file.
4. In the Config Filename box, type the name of the customized CONFIG file.
5. Select the OK button to close.

▶ Using the Mode Menu Commands

These are the Mode menu settings:

- Standard displays PIF Editor settings for Standard mode. These settings are not applicable under Windows NT.
- Enhanced displays PIF Editor settings for Enhanced mode. Only the Enhanced mode options are used to create PIFs for use with Windows NT.

THE RESCUE PAGES: Installing Applications

I installed a program in Windows 3.1 but I can't run it from Windows NT.

The same installation (setup) utility works under both 16-bit Windows 3.1 and 32-bit Windows NT—there are no special requirements and installation should proceed without a hitch. The only catch is that if you used FlexBoot for dual-boot operation to run both DOS with Windows 3.1 and Windows NT, the application was installed only in the active Windows version. So if Windows NT is active, the installation process may need to be repeated for Windows 3.1, or vice versa.

Please note that not all applications require dual installation. Many applications require nothing more than using File Manager to add the program to an application group. If, however, the install process has added a number of environmental variables—such as working and library directory paths, font specifications, palette colors, and so on—or has created its own .INI (initialization) file, you have two choices. You may either copy this information to the NT or Windows 3.1 systems or, more simply, repeat the installation after booting the alternative system.

I've installed a DOS program from Windows NT's DOS shell, but when I tried to run the program, I got path and variable errors.

The likely problem is that the installation program made changes to set path or parameter information in the CONFIG.SYS or AUTOEXEC.BAT files, and the files were not available later—or not available in the expected form. When a DOS application is executed under Windows NT, the application is executed in a DOS shell and is provided with a DOS

AUTOEXEC.BAT and CONFIG.SYS equivalent, but these are not necessarily preserved when the DOS shell is exited. Therefore, the recommended procedure for installing a DOS application for use from Windows NT is to exit from Windows NT and then boot DOS, using the FlexBoot utility. Once you are back in DOS, proceed with installation in the normal fashion, using the INSTALL.EXE or INSTALL.BAT utility if either is provided.

Once the installation process is finished, any changes made to the AUTOEXEC.BAT or CONFIG.SYS files by the install program need to be made available to the application when it executes under NT. To do this, refer to the section "Setting the Autoexec Filename and Config Filename Options," earlier in this chapter. You will also want to create a .PIF file for the application (the process is detailed in this chapter) and install the application in Program Manager—refer to Chapter 2 for details.

C H A P T E R

HELP! The Control Panel

The Windows NT Control Panel is a collection of utilities that allow you to customize many features of the Windows NT operating system, including appearances and functions. Using the Control Panel, a separate configuration can be designed for each user, allowing individuals sharing a single machine to have their own personal systems that incorporate features matching their own preferences.

Once individual preferences have been established, a user's personal configuration is loaded automatically when he or she logs on to the system. One word of caution: On a shared system, before changing the Control Panel settings, be sure that you are logged on under your own name—otherwise, you'll be changing someone else's preferences, which may not be appreciated.

The Control Panel appears by default in the Main program group but, when called, presents its own group of application icons (see Figure 4.1). Each of the icons shown represents a group of options that can be called and configured, interactively. (Please note that although the Networks and Server icons appear in the Control Pane., both are discussed in Chapter 19.)

Topics covered in this chapter include

- Customizing Windows NT
- Using the color controls

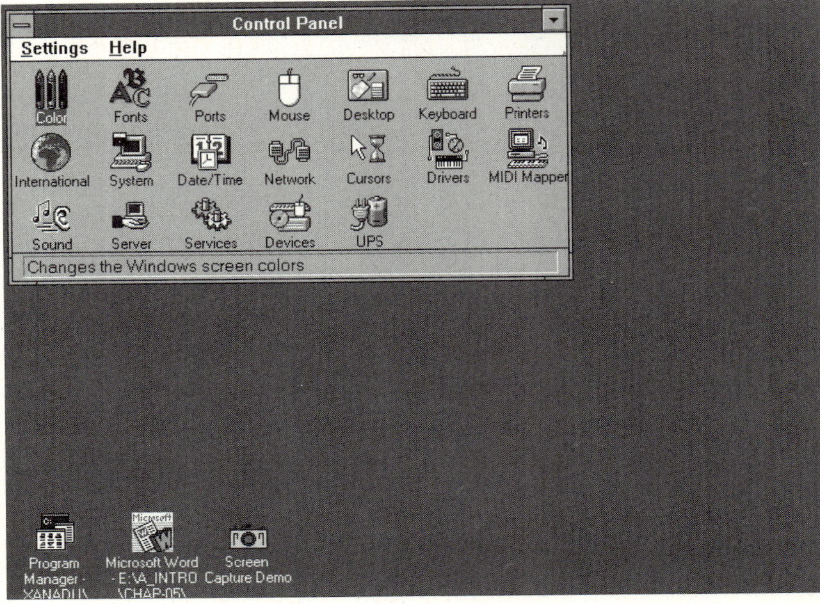

Figure 4.1
The Windows NT Control Panel

- Changing the Date/Time setting
- Configuring the Windows NT Desktop
- Setting drivers
- Selecting fonts
- Choosing International settings
- Customizing the keyboard
- Customizing the mouse
- Setting up UPS services
- Setting I/O ports
- Customizing system services
- Assigning sounds to system events
- Installing and configuring MIDI setups
- Setting system options

Windows NT Customization

▶ Using the Control Panel

Options that can be customized from the Control Panel include the following:

- Screen colors
- Desktop options governing the appearance and behavior of the screen
- System time-zone setting and the system date and time clock
- The font selection available to Windows NT applications
- I/O port settings
- Network settings
- Keyboard types
- Mouse configuration and mouse cursor selections
- International settings
- Operating system variables
- Device drivers
- MIDI (Musical Instrument Device Interface) settings
- Sound effects (sound card required)
- User resources
- Available services
- UPS (uninterruptible power supply) settings

Each of these control features is explained in the following sections.

Help Files ▼ Please be aware that some of the options shown in the Control Panel require special privileges or have restricted access. If your user profile does not have the required permissions, an access denied message will appear as a reminder.

Color Controls

▶ Selecting a Stock Color Configuration

To select any of the predefined color schemes from the pull-down list:

1. Select the Color icon in the Control Panel window.
2. In the Color Schemes list box, select the desired color scheme (the sample screen changes to reflect the selection).
3. Choose the OK button to make the selection the new default color scheme. Alternatively, select Cancel to keep the original color scheme or choose Help for assistance.

Help Files ▼ Because users have their own configurations—which are loaded when each user logs on to Windows NT—individual color schemes can be selected to suit individual tastes. For this purpose, Windows NT provides a selection of predefined color schemes that govern the appearance of all elements of an application window—including, of course, Program Manager itself.

Figure 4.2 shows the Color dialog box. At the top, the Color Schemes pull-down list offers a selection of predefined color schemes together with two buttons—Save Scheme (see "Saving a Color Scheme") and Remove Scheme (see "Removing a Color Scheme"). Immediately below, a pair of sample windows show the currently selected colors against a gray background. These two windows—an active window sample overlying an inactive sample—demonstrate all the windows elements for which colors are defined.

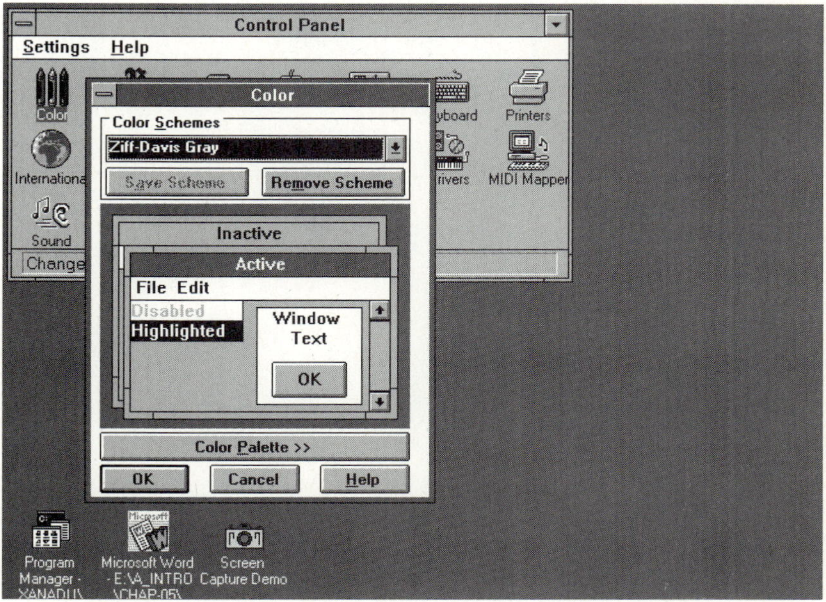

Figure 4.2
The Color dialog box

Below the sample windows is the Color Palette >> button; selecting this button calls the expanded dialog box shown in Figure 4.3. Finally, at the bottom, three buttons offer the selections OK, Cancel, and Help.

▶ Customizing a Color Configuration

To define a new color scheme:

1. Select the Color Palette >> button. The Colors dialog box is expanded—as shown in Figure 4.3—to show a pull-down list of screen

elements at the top. Below this list appears a palette of 48 basic colors and, further down, 16 custom colors, which are initially defined as white (RGB value 255, 255, 255).

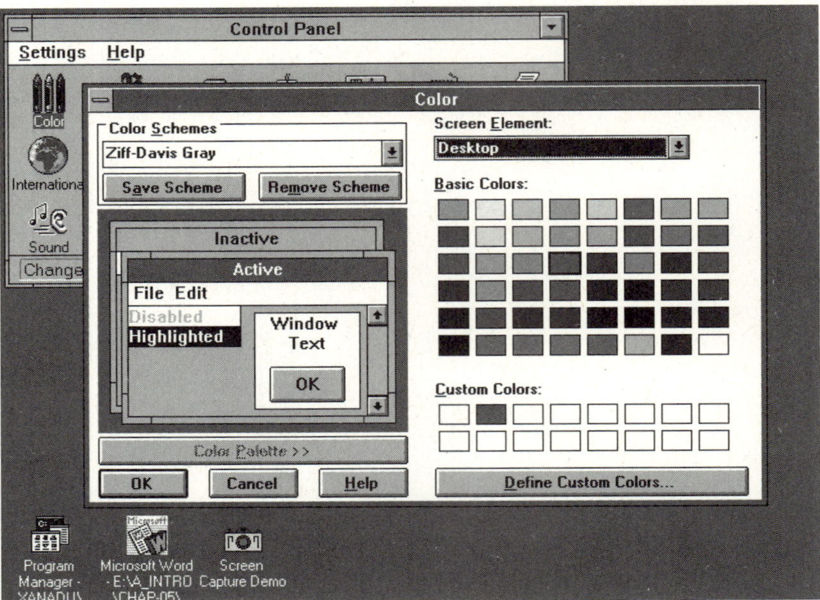

Figure 4.3
The expanded Color dialog box

2. Select the desired window element either from the Screen Element list or by clicking on the window element in the sample window (at the left).

3. Choose a new color from the Basic or Custom Colors palettes. The selected color is identified by a black outline. The screen element selection changes color to match.

4. After making all changes desired, save the color scheme under a new name or as a revision to an existing scheme. (See "Saving a Color Scheme.")

Help Files ▼ The predefined color schemes could diplomatically be described as sufficiently diverse to satisfy almost any taste (and, at the same time, to appall some tastes), but options are also provided for defining new color schemes. You do this by selecting colors from the Basic and Custom Colors palettes.

Colors are defined as RGB, or a combination of red, green, and blue values. Each color component is assigned a value in the range 0–255. Relative intensities of the three primary colors combine to produce the actual hues shown on the screen and offer a total 16,777,216 possible colors. However, while a few video cards (and monitors) can actually display the full range of 16 million plus colors, the human eye can distinguish only a small fraction of these.

Even if you are using an SVGA (Super VGA) 256-color driver, many of the basic colors shown will be dithered colors—that is, hues that are presented as a combination of pixels of other individual colors. The only solid colors available are those defined in the Windows NT default palette. Dithered colors can be used to fill areas but are not suitable for outlines, borders, or text because the results will appear as only the dominant color in the dithered combination.

▸ Saving a Color Scheme

To save a color scheme:

1. Select the Save Scheme button. In response, a dialog box appears with the name of the current color scheme highlighted.
2. To use the highlighted name, simply click the OK button.
3. To assign a new name to the scheme, type the desired name in the edit box to replace the initial entry.

Help Files ▼ Unlike file names and many other computer terms, the names used for color schemes have few—if any—restrictions and can contain spaces, punctuation, or any other printing characters. However, function, control, and alternate keys cannot be used.

▶ Removing a Color Scheme

To delete a color scheme:

1. Highlight the name of the color scheme to be removed.
2. Click on the Remove Scheme button. A dialog box appears, requesting confirmation.

Help Files ▼ The Remove Scheme button can be used to delete any of the existing color schemes, with the exception of the Windows Default color scheme, which cannot be removed.

Only one set of color schemes is maintained on each system. Thus, if a color scheme is removed—to save space, perhaps—this deletion affects all users on the system. If a color scheme selected by another user is deleted, at log on, the user's system will revert to the color scheme that followed the deleted entry on the list. If the deleted entry was the final color scheme in the list, it is replaced by the new final entry. In like fashion, when a new color scheme is defined, the new scheme becomes available to all users logging on to the computer.

Creating Custom Colors

To create a custom palette entry:

1. Click on an entry in the Custom Colors palette.
2. Select the Define Custom Colors option to summon the Custom Color Selector dialog box (see Figure 4.4).

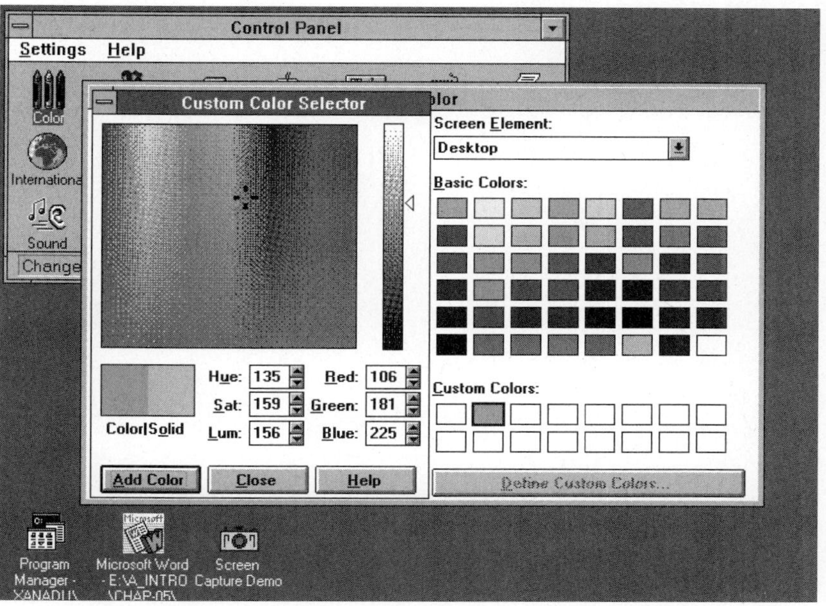

Figure 4.4
The Custom Color Selector dialog box

3. Color values may be defined in any of several fashions:
   - Values can be entered directly in the hue, saturation, and luminosity value boxes or in the red, green, and blue value box. Values must be in the range from 0–255.
   - The values in any of the color value boxes can be increased or decreased by clicking on the up or down arrows next to the box.
   - The hue and saturation values can be selected directly by clicking on the large square color box. The luminosity (intensity) is selected in the same fashion, using the tall scale box to the right.

4. To save the new color, click on the Add Color button. The color is added to the Custom Colors shown at the bottom right of the Color dialog box. Alternatively, you can click on one of the Custom Color boxes—the selected box is identified by a dotted outline—before selecting the Add Color button. The new hue will then be saved as the indicated entry.

Help Files ▼ The Custom Color Selector dialog box offers two color definition formats: red, green, and blue (RGB) values and hue, saturation, and luminosity (a system more often referred to as hue, saturation, and intensity, or HSI) values. Either system can be used; each defines the same color range.

If you use any of the three methods detailed, the color selected will appear in the Color/Solid box to the left of the HSI value boxes. The left half of the Color/Solid box shows the actual color—using dithering, if required—and the right half shows the solid supported color that is the nearest match to the requested color.

> **HELP!** *You can change the color definition to the solid color shown by double-clicking on the right (solid) side of the Color/Solid box or by pressing Alt+O.*

Date/Time Settings

▸ Setting the Date, Time, and Time Zone

The Date/Time options are used to change the system's date, time, and time zone, as well as to specify whether the computer should automatically switch to daylight saving time. To change date, time, and time zone:

1. Select the Date/Time icon from the Control Panel to call the dialog box shown in Figure 4.5.

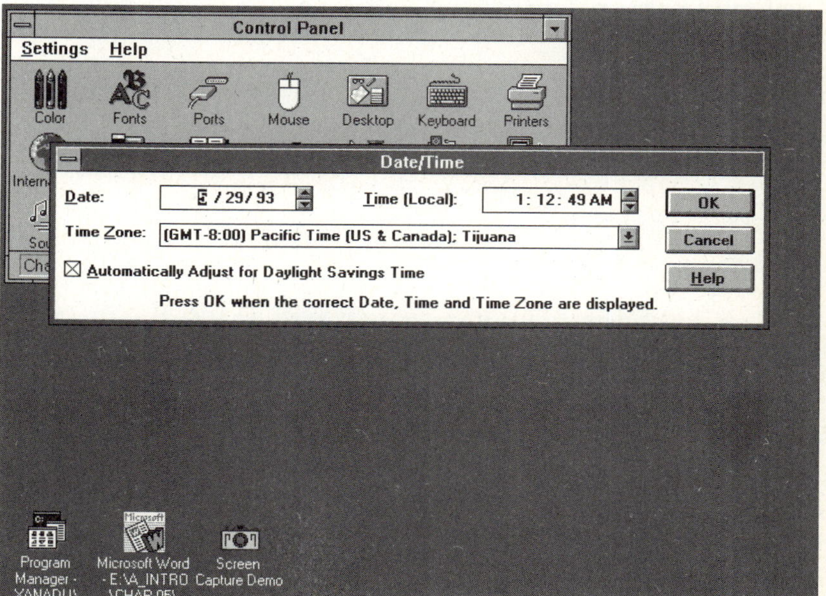

Figure 4.5
The Date/Time dialog box

2. Select the appropriate time zone from the pull-down list.
3. Select or clear the Daylight Savings Time check box, according to your personal preferences and local usage.
4. In the Date box, use the mouse cursor to select the portion of the date—the day, the month, or the year—to change, and enter the new value directly by typing or use the up or down arrows to increase or decrease the date.
5. In similar fashion, in the Time box, select the hour, minute, second or suffix (AM or PM) to change, and then type the new value or use the up or down arrows to increase or decrease the value.
6. When the Date/Time settings are correct, click on OK to set the system clock.

Help Files ▼ Before setting the date or time, you should begin by selecting the appropriate time zone. If you are associated with the military, it may be appropriate to keep the default Greenwich Mean Time (Zulu) zone setting, but most users will use the pull-down list to select a time zone appropriate to their geographical location.

If daylight saving time is used in your area, and you want the computer to automatically adjust the time accordingly, select the Daylight Savings Time check box.

The date and time settings are recognized by Windows NT applications that use the system clock, such as the Clock and Calendar programs. Other applications also use this data, such as File Manager, which recognizes these settings when providing date and time stamps for files written to disk; or Word for Windows, which can provide automatic dates for letters.

The International dialog box offers options to control how the date and time are displayed by many applications. Using these options, you can vary the order of the month, day, and year or display the time in 12- or 24-hour format. See "International Settings," later in this chapter.

The Windows NT Desktop

▶ Customizing the Desktop

The Windows NT Desktop dialog box offers a variety of options—in addition to the color options discussed earlier—that govern the appearance of the desktop (background screen). These include the following:

- Background pattern selection

- Wallpaper selection
- Screen saver and password options
- Icon and title spacing
- Sizing grid settings and options
- Text cursor (or caret) blink rate

Figure 4.6 shows the Desktop dialog box; the individual selections are discussed following.

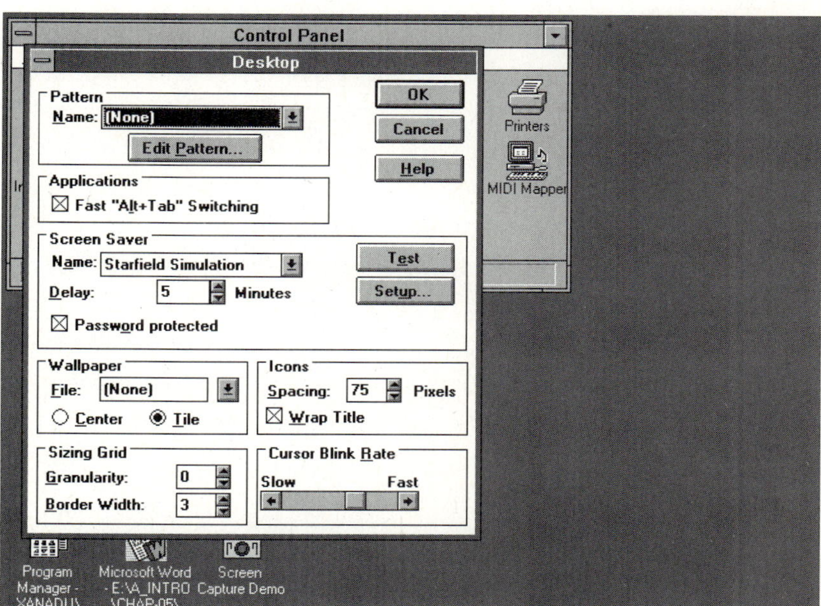

Figure 4.6
The Desktop dialog box

▶ Selecting a Background Pattern

To select a background pattern:

1. In the Pattern group, click on the arrow key at the right of the Name field to pull down the pattern list box.

2. Select the pattern desired from the displayed list or select (None) for no pattern.
3. Select OK to return to the Control Panel. The new pattern selection takes effect immediately.

Help Files ▼ Initially, Windows NT is installed with a default desktop pattern (labeled *(None)*) that produces a solid, neutral gray. The pull-down list box offers a selection of patterns, some of them rather imaginatively named, but all composed of gray and black. You may wish to use caution when selecting patterns because a background pattern may make the labels on minimized icons difficult to read.

If a wallpaper selection has been made, the area covered by the wallpaper overwrites any background pattern selection. If the bitmap does not cover the entire desktop, any selected pattern will be visible in the area surrounding the bitmap. Also, patterns may be visible as background for minimized icon titles. Any dithered colors selected as text or desktop colors, when used in a pattern, will be changed to the nearest or dominant solid color in the dither.

▶ Creating a Custom Pattern

To create a custom pattern:

1. Begin by selecting (None) as the initial pattern.
2. Call the Edit Pattern option. The dialog box shown in Figure 4.7 will show the selected pattern both as a background sample and as an 8-by-8-pixel enlargement to be edited.
3. Edit individual bits in the pattern by clicking with the mouse. The selected bits flip, changing from background to foreground and vice versa.

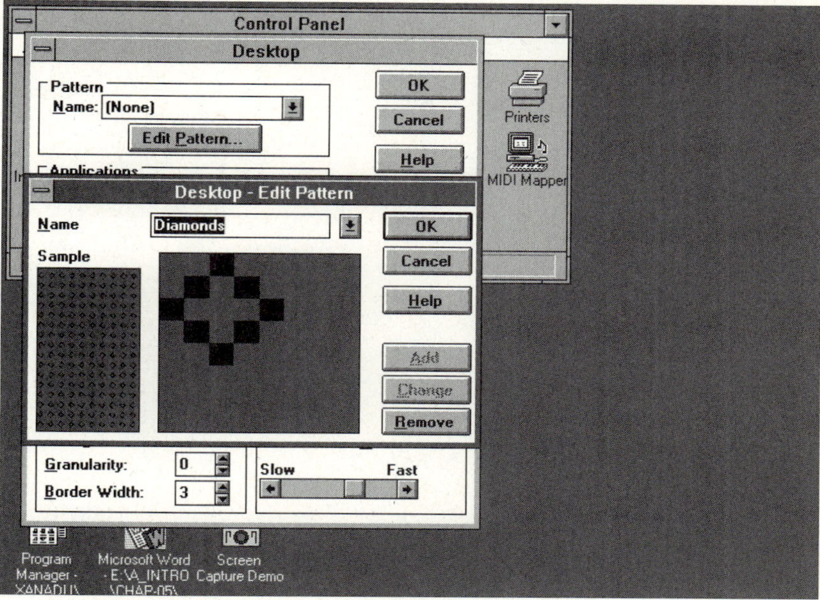

Figure 4.7
The Desktop-Edit Pattern dialog box

4. After defining a new pattern, enter a pattern name in the Name edit box.
5. Click on the Add button to save the new pattern.
6. The Remove button can be used to delete the selected pattern.

Help Files ▼ The foreground color (black by default) is the color selected in the Colors dialog box for the Windows Text screen element. The background color (gray by default) is the desktop color, again from the Colors dialog box.

Selecting Wallpaper

Wallpaper—in the form of a .BMP bitmap graphic file—is a popular choice for customizing your computer desktop. To select a bitmap for wallpaper:

1. In the Wallpaper group box, click on the arrow key at the right of the File field to pull down the bitmap list box.
2. Select the bitmap image desired from the displayed list or select (None) for no wallpaper.
3. Select either Center or Tile from the radio button options.
4. Select OK to return to the Control Panel. The new wallpaper selection appears immediately.

Help Files ▼ Several bitmap images in various sizes are distributed with Windows NT, and many more are available through bulletin boards or are distributed with various software packages. In addition, any paint program, such as Windows Paintbrush, can be used to create a bitmap image, to modify a scanned image, or to convert an image from another format to the .BMP format required for wallpaper.

Windows 3.1 bitmap images are perfectly compatible with Windows NT—your favorite images can be moved to the new system without any problems.

Bitmaps to be used as wallpaper should be stored in the WINNT directory. Although they can be stored elsewhere, to do so requires a full drive and path specification to choose the bitmap as wallpaper. This specification must be entered manually, since the directory lookup facilities provided by most programs are not included in the Desktop utility. The Wallpaper list box includes all bitmap images located in the Windows NT directory.

Two radio-button options are included in the bitmap selection: Center and Tile. Selecting Center causes the selected bitmap to be centered on the screen. Selecting Tile repeats the bitmap—horizontally and vertically, beginning at the upper left—as many times as necessary to fill the screen.

Bitmaps designed for wallpaper generally come in two forms. Full-screen bitmaps are commonly designed for a 640-by-480-pixel screens size and may come in 16- or 256-color formats. My own favorites in this format are a jungle scene by Rousseau, an electronic copy of Van Gogh's *Fields,* and an image of two iguanas engaged in an uncertain conversation. These provide a full-screen background that is certainly more entertaining to regard during idle moments than a dull gray screen would be. The second form in which you'll find bitmaps for wallpaper is in smaller designs—varying from quarter-screen sized (320-by-240) down to eighth-screen (60-by-40). These smaller bitmaps may be almost any size but are generally created as submultiples of the full screen and are designed to be tiled with patterns that repeat when matched edge to edge.

For examples, see the 256color, Leaves, Marble, and WinLogo bitmaps distributed with Windows NT. Again, a variety of tiling bitmaps are available from a variety of sources. One of my favorites is a quarter-screen image titled Circuit.BMP. Tiled, this image turns the screen into a pseudorealistic circuit board. The unidentified artist has my compliments.

Displaying bitmapped wallpaper requires more memory than displaying a solid color or patterned desktop. If an application reports insufficient memory, changing to a solid color or pattern will free some memory for use by another application. Also, if the selected bitmap is larger than the screen or if it requires more memory than is reasonably available, it will not be displayed.

▶ Setting the Sizing Grid

The sizing grid—which is invisible—is a feature used by Windows NT to set the position and alignment of application windows and icons on the desktop. To set the sizing grid elements:

1. Set the granularity either by entering a value (0 to 49) directly in the edit box or by clicking the up and down arrow buttons to increment or decrement the displayed value.

2. Set the Border Width either by entering a value directly in the edit box or by clicking the up and down arrow buttons to increase or decrease the displayed value. Recommendation: leave the default value of 3 unchanged.

3. Select OK to return to the Control Panel.

Help Files ▼ When Windows NT is installed, the sizing grid is turned off and icons and windows are not repositioned. When the sizing grid is enabled, all application windows and icons for minimized applications are aligned with the nearest grid position. Grid spacing is adjustable but is always in multiples of 8 pixels. A spacing value of 0 turns the grid off, a value of 1 sets the grid to 8-pixel intervals (both horizontal and vertical), a value of 2 sets spacing at 16 pixels, and so on. The maximum value of 49 sets the grid spacing to a rather impractical 392 pixels.

The sizing grid has no effect on windows or icons within an application—it affects only the application windows themselves and the icons on the desktop representing minimized but still active applications.

Included in the same functional group is Border Width, which controls the width of the window borders and is set at 3 by default. This value can be increased (or decreased) as desired, but there appears to be little if any reason for adjustment.

▶ Setting the Title- and Icon-Spacing Options

To set the title and icon-spacing options:

1. Enter the icon spacing directly in the edit box or use the up and down arrow buttons to increase or decrease the current value.

2. Select or clear the Wrap Title option. (Selecting it is recommended.)

3. Select the OK button to return to the Control Panel.

Help Files ▼ The sizing grid provides some control over the spacing when you move icons on the desktop, but there is a second, more important control that determines how Windows NT spaces icons on the desktop without your personal adjustments.

Whenever you reduce an application to icon size—leaving it active but minimized—Windows NT moves the icon to the bottom of the desktop (screen), where it arranges the icons in an evenly spaced row. The spacing of these icons is controlled by the Spacing control setting in the Icons control group in the Desktop dialog box.

In Figure 4.6, the spacing is 75 pixels—which is slightly more than two icons width (center to center)—positioning the icons with a bit more than the width of one icon between each pair. The spacing can be adjusted either by entering a value directly or by using the up and down arrows to increase and decrease the setting.

Before you move your icons closer together, you should know that the real problem with spacing icons is not the width of icons but the width of application titles. Many applications—their developers apparently afraid that users won't remember what the program is—have 5- to 50-word titles, and these titles require space below the icon. In fairness, of course, even applications with succinct titles may exhibit wide captions if, for example, an editor program appends a document's title to its own and then expects to display all this text below the icon.

It is quite impractical to space icons so widely that all possible captions could be displayed without overlapping. The solution is to enable (check) the Wrap Title check box, permitting long captions to be broken into two or more lines for a better fit within the available space.

Adjusting the Cursor Blink Rate

To adjust the cursor blink rate:

1. Drag the scroll bar left to slow the blink rate or right to increase the blink rate. The actual cursor blink rate is shown by a sample cursor at the right of the scroll bar.
2. Select OK to return to the Control Panel.

Help Files ▼ At the lower right of the Desktop dialog box, the Cursor Blink Rate control sets the blink rate for the text cursor used by most editor applications. A text cursor appears in the Desktop dialog box, immediately to the right of the scroll bar provided for adjustment. There are no rules for how to select a blink rate—it is purely a matter of personal preference. If you like a slow blink, set it slow. If you like it fast, speed it up. It's that simple.

Setting Options for Application Switching

To select or unselect fast Alt+Tab application switching:

1. Check or uncheck the Fast "Alt+Tab" Switching option box.
2. Select OK to return to the Control Panel.

Help Files ▼ Windows NT is designed explicitly to run multiple applications at the same time, but it's sometimes difficult to locate a specific application or to locate the application's window. The Fast Switching option—set by a check box in the Desktop dialog box—toggles between two different types of task switching.

With the Fast Switching option disabled (the check box is unchecked) pressing the Alt+Tab key combination switches between active tasks (including minimized tasks) by highlighting the title bar of each in turn. When Fast Switching is enabled (the check box is checked), instead of switching by highlighting the title bars, a dialog box appears centered on the screen with the application's icon at the far left and the application's title to the right. Holding the Alt key down and repeatedly pressing the Tab key cycles through all active applications, identifying each by its full title. Releasing the Alt key brings the selected application to the forefront, making the application the focus of activity.

Alternatively, to return to the original application, press Alt+Esc.

▶ Selecting a Screen Saver

When Windows NT is installed, by default no screen saver is selected, even though a selection of screen savers is available. To select a screen saver:

1. Under Screen Saver, select a screen saver in the Name box.
2. The Delay box sets the period of inactivity required (in minutes) before the screen saver becomes active. Use the up or down arrows to increase or decrease the delay setting.
3. Click on the Test button to immediately test the selected screen saver. To return, simply move the mouse or press any key on the keyboard.
4. Set the delay time by entering a value directly in the edit box or by using the up or down arrow buttons to increase or decrease the current value.
5. Set or clear the Password Protected option.
6. Click on the OK button to make the current selections active.

Help Files ▼ A screen saver is a utility that, when there has been no activity from the keyboard or the mouse for a set period, replaces the present screen display with a new, changing display. This feature is intended to prevent an image that's displayed for long periods of time from being burned into the monitor. If the mouse is moved or if any key is pressed, the original screen will be restored immediately.

If a third-party screen saver program is used, the desktop screen saver should be set to None. Note, however, that third-party screen savers do not provide the same password protection feature that the native Windows NT screen savers offer.

▶ Customizing a Screen Saver

To customize a screen saver:

1. From the Desktop dialog box, select the screen saver desired.
2. Choose the Setup button (if the screen saver cannot be customized, a message appears, notifying you that the screen saver has no options that you can set.) The Setup dialog box appears, with options specific to the screen saver you selected.
3. Change any settings you want.
4. Choose the OK button to return to the Desktop dialog box.
5. Choose the OK button to return to the Control Panel.

Several of the screen savers can be customized by changing the number of elements, lines, colors, shapes, or text used by the screen saver or by requiring a password before the screen saver will return. Which options are offered depends on the screen saver selected.

▶ Setting Screen Saver Passwords

The screen savers supplied by Windows NT include a password feature designed to prevent unauthorized access while you are away from your computer. When the password option is selected, instead of the screen saver vanishing whenever the mouse is moved or a key is struck, a Workstation Locked dialog box appears. The same password used to log on to the computer must be entered to cancel the screen saver.

Password protection is enabled or disabled from the Desktop dialog box by setting or clearing the Password Protect check box.

HELP! *The Windows NT screen saver WorkStation Locked dialog box directs you to press the Ctrl+Alt+Del key combination. Don't panic—under Windows NT, this action does not reset the computer and does not result in any of your applications being closed or your work being lost. Instead, pressing Ctrl+Alt+Del calls a dialog box (which is similar to the Log On dialog box) that requests a password. Entering the appropriate password returns you to normal operation.*

▶ Installing Windows 3.1 Screen Savers

Windows 3.1 screen savers can be used under Windows NT. However, not all screen savers are completely compatible with the Windows NT operating system. Experimentation is suggested before relying on a Windows 3.1 version screen saver utility.

HELP! *If a Windows 3.1 screen saver does not respond to the mouse or keyboard (if it doesn't exit when you hit move the mouse or press a key), try pressing Alt+Tab until you get to Program Manager. Or press Ctrl+Alt+Del to call the Windows NT Security dialog box, then click on the Task List button, and close the screen saver application.*

Drivers

▶ Adding New or Updated Drivers

To install a new driver

1. Select the Drivers icon in the Control Panel window. The Drivers dialog box appears (Figure 4.8).

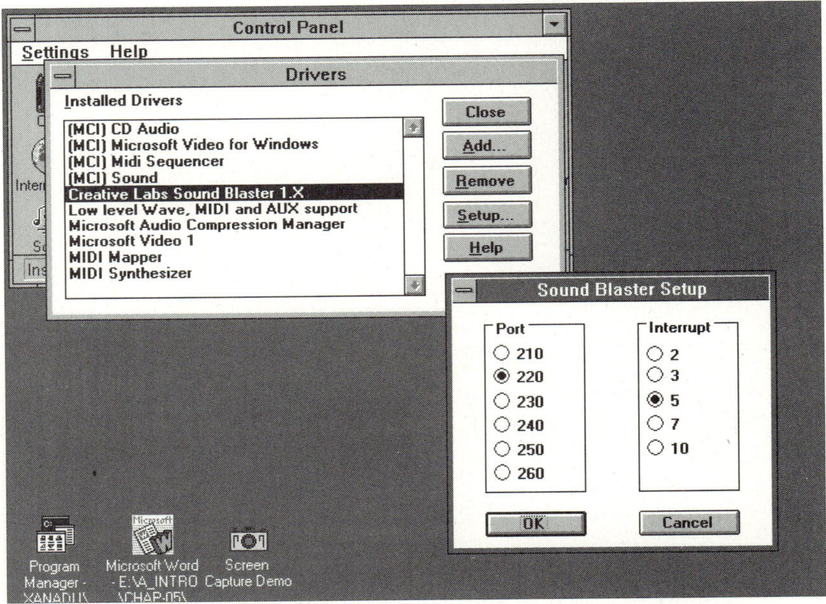

Figure 4.8
The Drivers dialog box

2. Select the Add button in the Drivers dialog box—the Add dialog box appears, listing drivers that were supplied by Windows NT.

3. From the List Of Drivers box, select the driver to be installed or, if it is not listed, select Add Unlisted Or Updated Driver. Click on the OK button to proceed.

4. Insert the driver source disk in A or, if the source is a CD or is present in another drive or directory, provide the drive and path specification in the text box. If you are not sure where to find the

driver, use the Browse button to find and select the drive and directory where the driver file is located.

Select the Restart Now button if you want your changes to take effect immediately.

HELP! *As new hardware devices such as a new video card, sound board, or printers are added to the system, the appropriate drivers to control these devices must also be installed or enabled. Until this is done, Windows NT will not recognize the new device.*

Help Files ▼ While Windows NT provides drivers for most popular devices, some devices may require manufacturer-supplied drivers, which should come with the device when purchased. If no suitable 32-bit device driver was supplied, contact the dealer or manufacturer to request such a driver.

Kernel drivers—which are any drivers that have direct access to the system hardware—can be installed only if you are logged on with Administrator privileges. Once installed, the drivers become available to all users.

Drivers already installed on the system cannot be updated with a new version until the old driver is removed from the system. If an old driver is currently installed, an error message will appear when you attempt to install the new version.

If you are installing a manufacturer-supplied driver—a driver not supplied by Windows NT—the Unlisted Or Updated Drivers dialog box appears, listing the drivers available. Select the driver desired from the list, then press the OK button.

Many drivers require specific settings before they will function correctly. When this is the case, a Setup dialog box appears. In the Driver Setup dialog box, choose the appropriate settings. The settings required by each device must not conflict with the settings used by other devices. For example, the interrupt settings used by a mouse, sound card, and network card must not conflict. If you are not certain which settings to use or if you are having difficulty, consult the manuals for each device and, where relevant, check the jumper settings on the hardware cards or devices.

In some cases, drivers are installed as groups of related drivers, and each driver in the group may require its own settings. When this occurs, multiple Setup dialog boxes may appear. Simply repeat the settings—as required—for each driver.

Select the Restart Now button if you want your changes to take effect immediately.

HELP! *Newly installed drivers do not become active immediately; they become active only when the system is booted or restarted. To have new drivers become immediately active, select the Restart Now button to exit and reenter Windows NT. Alternatively, you can simply log off in the conventional fashion and then log on again.*

▸ Removing Existing Drivers

To remove a device driver:

1. Select the Drivers icon in the Control Panel window.
2. From the Drivers dialog box, select the driver to be removed and click on the Remove button. A dialog box appears, requesting confirmation before the device is removed from the list.

Help Files ▼ If a device is no longer being used or if you need to update a device driver, the driver can be removed from the Installed Drivers list in the Drivers dialog box. Because this action does not remove the driver file from the hard drive, the same driver can be reinstalled later without requiring access to the original source disk.

The drivers that were automatically installed during the Windows NT setup are drivers that are required by the system. If a required driver is removed, the system may not function correctly in the future. Do not remove any drivers unless you are certain which driver you are removing and why!

▸ Setting Driver Options

Driver settings can be specified when the driver is installed or at any time afterward. To change a driver's configuration:

1. Select the Drivers icon in the Control Panel window.
2. From the Installed Drivers list, select the driver to configure.
3. Select the Setup button. If the driver selected requires or accepts specific settings, the Setup dialog box appears. The options offered in the Setup dialog box vary, depending on the driver being configured.
4. Refer to your device's manual for option settings.

To have your changes take effect immediately, select the Restart Now button.

HELP! *If more than one configuration is desired for a single driver, the same driver must be installed more than once. Each driver can have only one configuration at any time.*

Font Selection

▸ Adding New Fonts

The Fonts option provides a means to add new screen, plotter, or TrueType fonts to the Windows NT system, making these fonts available to your Windows NT applications. To add a new font (or fonts):

1. Select the Fonts icon in the Control Panel window. The Fonts dialog box (see Figure 4.9) appears with the currently installed fonts listed in the Installed Fonts box.
2. Select the Add button.
3. In the Add Fonts dialog box, select a font to add. If the font desired is not located in the current drive or directory, select the drive and directory where the font(s) are located. All fonts in the indicated drive and directory can be loaded at once by selecting the Select All button.

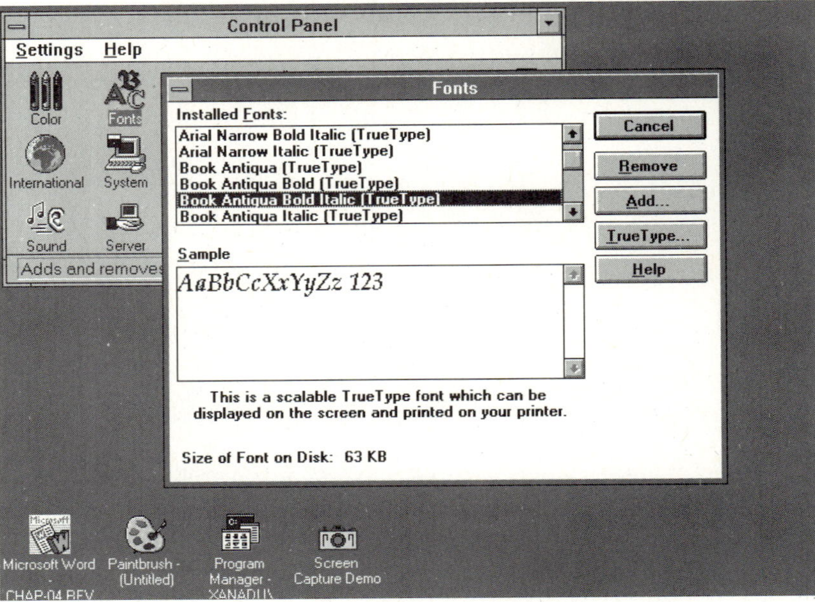

Figure 4.9
The Fonts dialog box

4. If disk space is limited, fonts can be used directly from the source directory (local or network) without copying them to the Windows NT directory. To cancel font copying, uncheck the Copy Fonts To Windows NT Directory check box.

5. Select OK, then Close to complete font installation.

Like other Windows NT resources, once fonts have been installed, further selection is made only from within an application, such as a word processor or drawing program.

▶ Removing Existing Fonts

To remove a font:

1. Select the Fonts icon in the Control Panel window.

2. Highlight (by clicking on) the font or fonts that you wish to remove.

3. Select the Remove button. A dialog box appears, requesting confirmation before the font(s) are removed from the Installed Fonts list.

4. Select the Yes button to remove a single font or, for multiple fonts, select the Yes To All button.

Help Files ▼ Because installed fonts do use memory that would otherwise be free for use by applications, you may wish to remove unneeded fonts from the Installed Fonts list. This frees memory for other uses but does not remove the font file from the hard drive (unless explicitly directed).

A few cautions:

- Do not remove the MS Sans Serif font from the Installed Fonts list. Because this font is used by most Windows NT dialog boxes, its removal may make the text in dialog boxes difficult to read.
- Removing a font from the Installed Fonts list on a particular computer makes the font unavailable to all users of the computer.
- To delete fonts from the disk as well as remove them from the Installed Fonts list, check the Delete Font File From Disk check box.
- If you are using fonts that were not installed in the Windows NT system directory—that is, fonts used from a source disk or a network drive—do not delete these fonts from the disk because they may not be recoverable.

▸ Setting TrueType Font Options

To set the TrueType font options:

1. Select the TrueType button in the Fonts dialog box.
2. In the TrueType dialog box, set or clear the Enable TrueType Fonts option.
3. Set or clear the Show Only TrueType Fonts In Applications option.
4. Select OK to return to the Fonts dialog box.

Help Files ▼ TrueType fonts are scalable fonts supported by Windows NT. A TrueType font appears the same on screen as it does in a printed document. The Enable TrueType Fonts option must be checked (this is recommended) before TrueType fonts will be available to applications. Uncheck this option only if you do not wish to use TrueType fonts at all.

The Show Only TrueType Fonts In Applications option disables all fonts that are not TrueType fonts. If the Enable TrueType Fonts option is not selected, this option will be grayed out and unavailable.

The Fonts dialog box includes a display box to show a font sample. Any font selected in the Installed Fonts list will appear in the Sample display box. Below the Sample display, a brief description of the typeface is given and, at the bottom of the dialog box, the size of the selected font file is listed.

International Settings

▶ Selecting Country and Language Options

To change the country settings:

1. Select the International icon in the Control Panel window.
2. In the Country list box, select the country and/or language settings desired.

To change the language selection:

1. Select the International icon in the Control Panel window.
2. In the Language box, select the language desired.

Help Files ▼ The Country selection sets a number of default formats for date, time, number, and currency as well as controlling the selection of paper sizes which appear in the Print Setup dialog box. These default settings can be overridden by subsequent individual settings, but by adjusting defaults to correspond to the standards popular for each country, the necessity for individual customization is greatly reduced.

Language selections affect how applications sort information. For example, some languages include accented characters, and setting the language option allows applications to correctly sort words or phrases that include accented characters.

▸ Changing the Keyboard Layout

To change the keyboard layout:

1. Select the International icon in the Control Panel window.
2. From the Keyboard list box, select the keyboard layout appropriate to your computer.

Help Files ▼ International keyboard layouts accommodate the special characters, accents, and symbols used in different languages. The International Keyboard dialog box offers a list of keyboard formats supported by Windows NT.

Selecting Units of Measurements

The measurement option is used to select either metric or English measurements. To change the units of measurement used:

1. Select the International icon in the Control Panel window.
2. In the Measurement box, select the system of measurement desired.

Changing the List Separator

The list separator box identifies the character used to separate items in a list. By default, the separator character is a comma, but any character desired can entered.

Choosing a Date Format

To change the date format:

1. Select the International icon in the Control Panel window.
2. Select the Change button in the Date Format area and the International-Date Format dialog box appears (Figure 4.10).
3. Set the options desired.

Help Files ▼ Two types of date format—short and long—are supported. A variety of formats are possible for each. Both the short and long date formats support three order formats: *MDY, DMY,* and *YMD,* each a popular format in one region of the world or another. In addition, separate separator characters can be supplied for each, leading zeros can be used or suppressed, and year formats can include or omit the century digits. The long format can, optionally, include weekdays in either full or abbreviated formats; months can be numeral, with or without leading zeros, or spelled out in full or abbreviated forms.

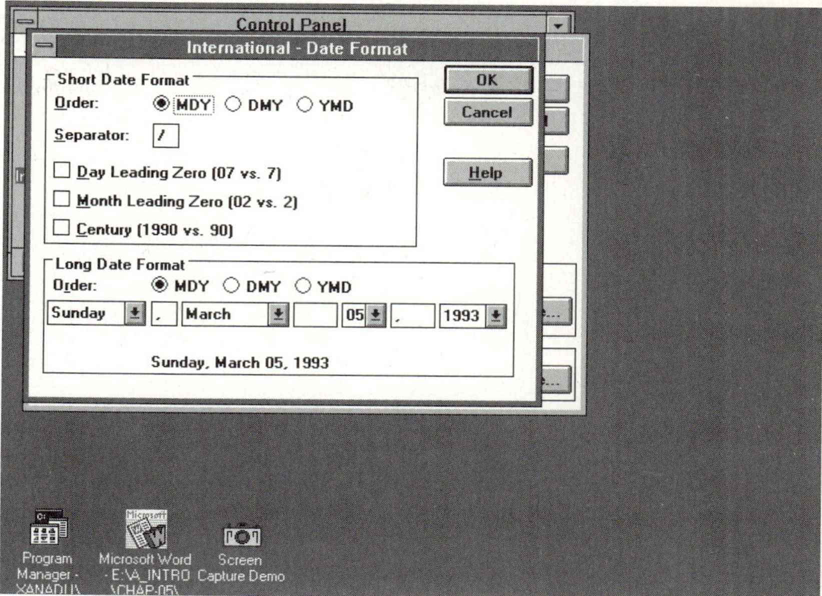

Figure 4.10
The International-Date Format dialog box

Unfortunately, only the Christian calendar is supported, and years must be entered as A.D.—a chauvinism that may be offensive to those in the world who prefer, for example, the Muslim, Buddhist, or Confucian calendars.

▸ Choosing a Time Format

To change the time format:

1. Select the International icon in the Control Panel window.
2. Select the Change button in the Time Format area. The International-Time Format dialog box appears (Figure 4.11).
3. Set the options desired.

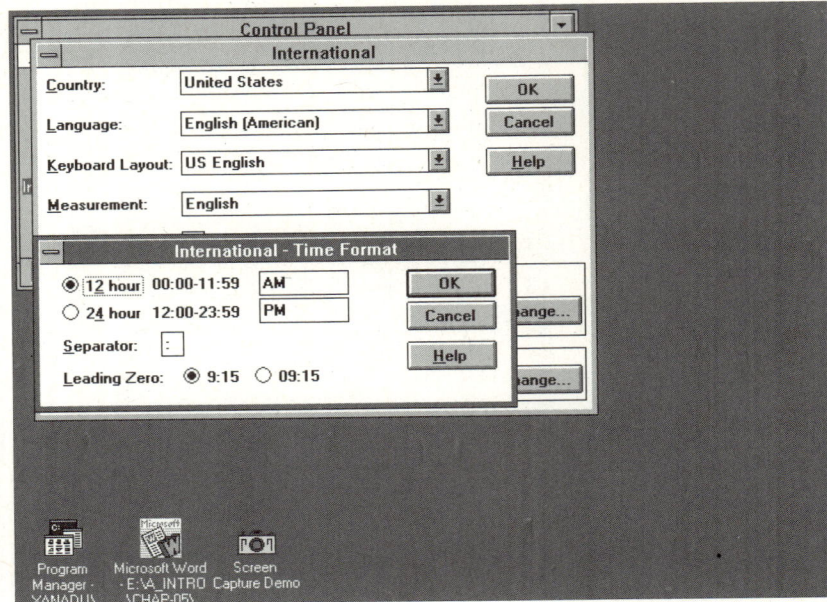

Figure 4.11
The International-Time Format dialog box

Help Files ▼ The international time formats offer fewer options than do the date formats, but the time formats do provide 12- and 24-hour formats with or without leading zeros. By default, a colon is used as the separator between hours and minutes, but any character desired can be entered in the edit box.

▶ Choosing a Currency Format

To change the currency format:

1. Select the International icon in the Control Panel window.
2. Select the Change button in the Currency Format area. The International-Currency Format dialog box appears (Figure 4.12).
3. Set the options desired.

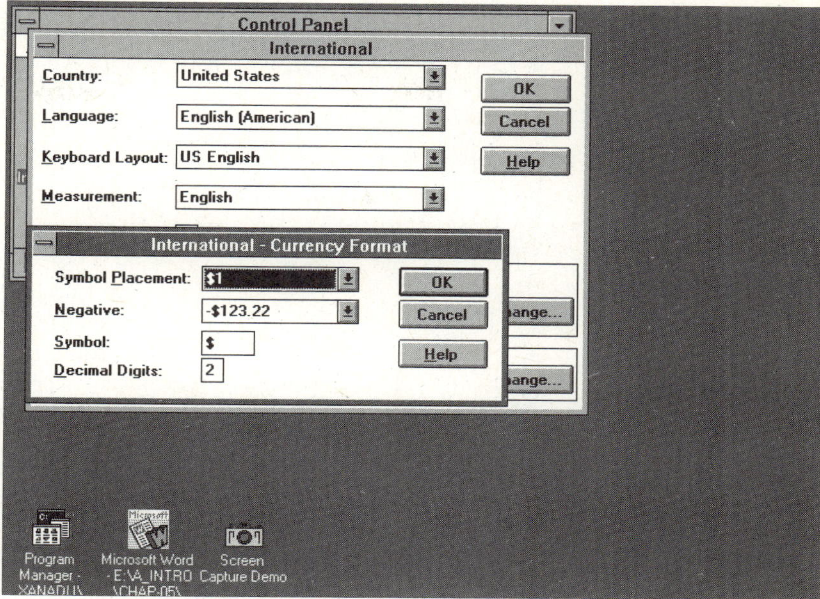

Figure 4.12
The International-Currency Format dialog box

Help Files ▼ The International-Currency Format dialog box offers a choice of leading or trailing currency symbols, a choice of how negative amounts are indicated, and an option to change the number of decimal places displayed. An edit box permits you to enter the default currency symbol desired.

▶ Choosing a Number Format

To change the number format:

1. Select the International icon in the Control Panel window.
2. Select the Change button in the Number Format area. The International-Number Format dialog box appears (Figure 4.13).
3. Set the options desired.

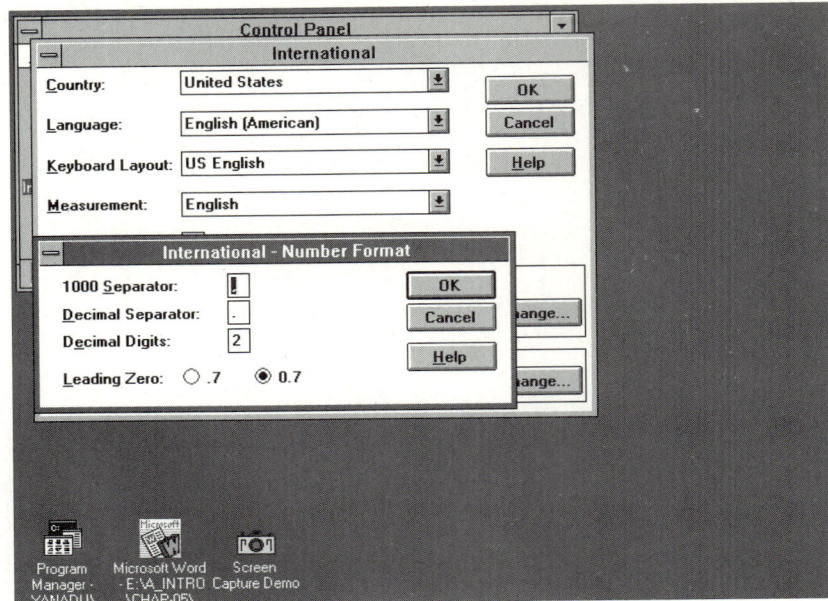

Figure 4.13
The International-Number Format dialog box

Help Files ▼ The International-Number Format dialog box lets you choose decimal and thousands separators, how many decimal places to display, and whether decimal fractions should be shown with a leading zero.

Keyboard Customization

▶ Setting the Keyboard Repeat Delay and Repeat Rate

To change the keyboard delay and repeat rate settings:

1. Select the Keyboard icon in the Control Panel window. The Keyboard dialog box appears (Figure 4.14).

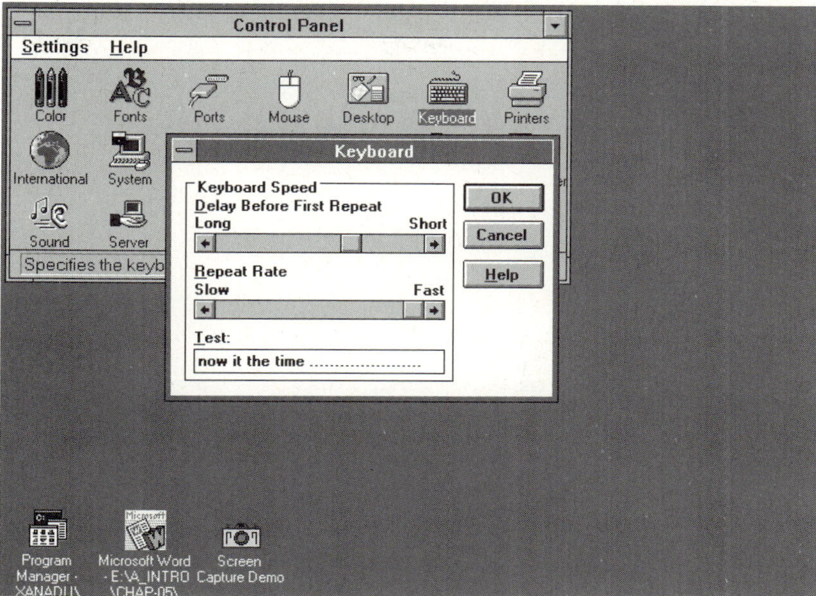

Figure 4.14
The Keyboard dialog box

2. Use the Delay scroll bar to adjust the keyboard repeat delay time.
3. Use the Repeat Rate scroll bar to adjust the keyboard repeat rate.
4. To test both settings, move to the Test box and type a brief line to test normal nonrepeat operations before holding down a single key to test the repeat delay and repeat rate. Readjust both until you find the delay and repeat rate comfortable for you.

Help Files ▼ The repeat delay setting determines how long the computer waits, after a key is held down, before the key repeat begins. The repeat rate setting determines how quickly the key repeats—that is, how many characters per second are generated.

Mouse Customization

▶ Setting Mouse Options

To customize the mouse or other pointing device:

1. From the Control Panel window, select the icon representing the pointing device. A dialog box similar to the one shown in Figure 4.15 appears.

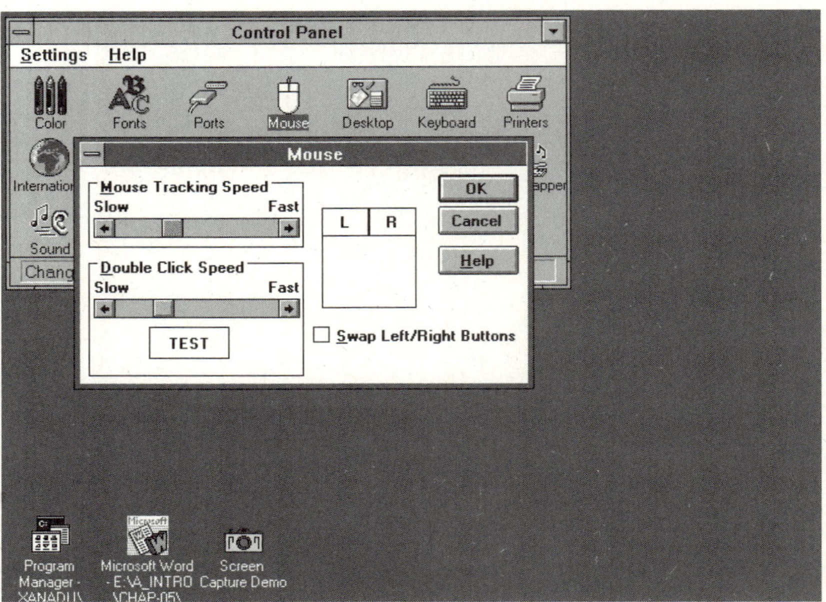

Figure 4.15
The Mouse dialog box

2. Set the options desired, then select the OK button.

Help Files ▼ Because Windows NT maintains a separate configuration profile for each user and loads each individual's profile as he or she logs on to the computer, the mouse (or other pointing device) can be individually customized for each user. Like other devices, the mouse or other pointing device (such as a trackball, light pen, and so on) must be installed—together with its driver, of course—before it can be customized. Different pointing devices install different icons in the Control Panel. For details on installing a pointing device and driver, refer to the documentation accompanying the device.

Setting the Mouse-Tracking Speed

To adjust the mouse-tracking speed:

1. Call the Mouse dialog box from the Control Panel.
2. Drag the Mouse Tracking Speed scroll-bar thumb pad left for a slower response or right for a faster response.
3. Test the new setting by moving the mouse.
4. Select OK to return to the Control Panel.

Help Files ▼ The mouse-tracking speed setting controls how rapidly the screen mouse moves in response to movement by the physical mouse. Increasing the tracking speed causes small physical movements to be echoed by large, rapid screen movements. Decreasing the tracking speed requires greater physical mouse movements to product an equivalent screen movement. The default setting—roughly midpoint in the scroll bar range—is recommended, but this can be adjusted to suit your personal preferences.

Setting and Testing the Double-Click Response Speed

To set the double-click response speed:

1. Call the Mouse dialog box from the Control Panel.
2. Drag the Double Click Speed scroll-bar thumb pad left for a slower response or right for a faster response.
3. Test the new setting by double-clicking on the Test button. A recognized double-click causes the button to change state.
4. Select OK to return to the Control Panel.

Help Files The double-click speed setting controls how rapidly the mouse button must be pressed to be recognized as a double-click. Increasing the double-click setting requires a faster double-click; decreasing the setting requires a slower double-click. The Test box below the scroll bar changes state (color) when a double-click occurs. Use this to test the speed setting and adjust the response speed to your personal tastes.

Swapping the Mouse Buttons

To swap the right and left mouse buttons:

1. Call the Mouse dialog box from the Control Panel.
2. Check or uncheck the Swap Left/Right Buttons option. The button labels on the mouse outline will change, according to the settings.
3. Press the right and left mouse buttons. The buttons on the mouse outline will change state as each button is pressed.
4. Select OK to return to the Control Panel.

Help Files ▼ Because roughly 16 percent of the population are left-handed, Windows NT has included a provision permitting the right and left mouse buttons to be swapped. This feature is selected by checking the Swap Left/Right Buttons box. The swapped button state will be reflected in the sample mouse shown in the dialog box; the right button will appear on the left and vice versa. After swapping, the right mouse button reports left button events and vice versa.

HELP! *Once the left and right mouse buttons have been swapped, the swapped state can be cleared only by clicking on the Swap Left/Right Buttons option with the right-hand button—a subtle trap inherent in the operation.*

▶ Changing the Mouse Cursor Appearance

To change a cursor:

1. Select the Cursors icon in the Control Panel window.
2. In the Cursors dialog box, select the cursor to change. The cursors are labeled with their associated actions.
3. Select Browse to call a list of .CUR cursor resource files and .ANI animated cursor files. While the initial active directory will be the \WINNT\SYSTEM32 directory, both static (.CUR) and animated (.ANI) resources can be selected from another drive or directory.
4. From the File Name list box, select a cursor file, and an example of the cursor appears in the Preview window.
5. Select OK to replace the present cursor with the selected cursor, Cancel to return without changing the selection, or choose another cursor from the File Name list box.

6. From the Cursors dialog box, select OK to make the new cursors active.
7. Any of the action cursors can be reset to the system default by highlighting the current cursor setting, then clicking the Set Default button.

Help Files ▼ The Control Panel Cursors option permits you to change the default mouse or pointer cursors, replacing these with custom cursors from .CUR cursor resources or with the animated .ANI cursors supplied by Windows NT. Figure 4.16 shows the Cursors dialog box, Figure 4.17 shows the default cursor set, and Figure 4.18 illustrates a selection of animated cursor images from Windows NT's .ANI files.

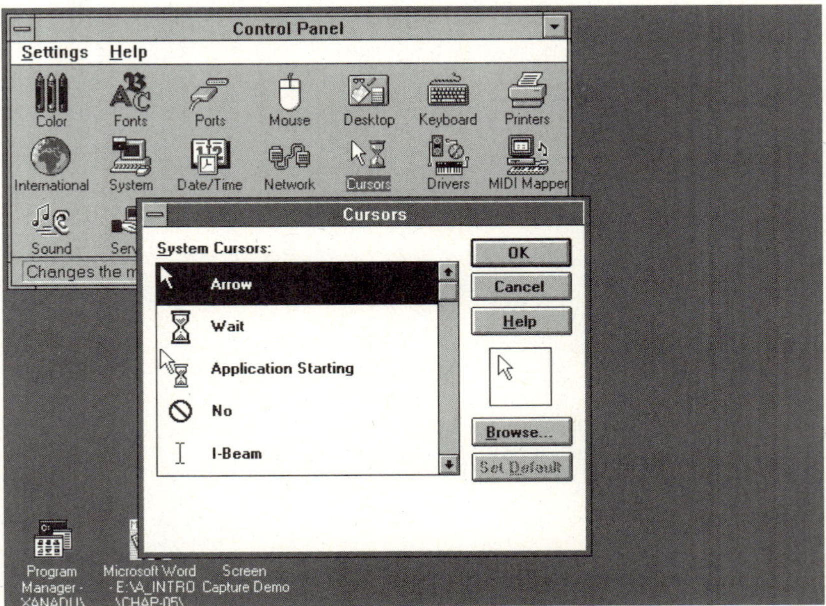

Figure 4.16
The Cursors dialog box

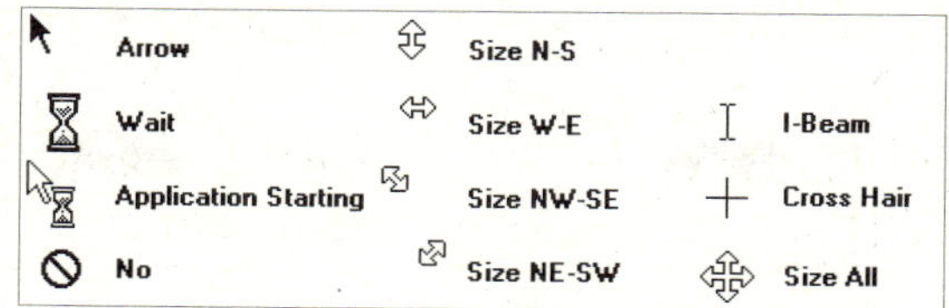

Figure 4.17
Standard cursor images

Figure 4.18
Animated cursor images

Setup for UPS (Uninterruptible Power Supply) Services

▶ Installing an Intelligent UPS

To install an intelligent UPS for a computer:

1. Double-click on the UPS icon in the Control Panel.
2. In the UPS dialog box (see Figure 4.19), check the Uninterruptible Power Supply Is Installed On check box, and select the COM port where the UPS will connect. All other options remain inactive until this check box and port have been set.

▶ Turning a UPS Off

To turn a UPS off:

1. Call the UPS dialog box from the Control Panel.
2. Clear the Uninterruptible Power Supply Is Installed On check box.

▶ Initiating UPS Services

To initiate UPS services:

1. Select the Services icon in the Control Panel window.

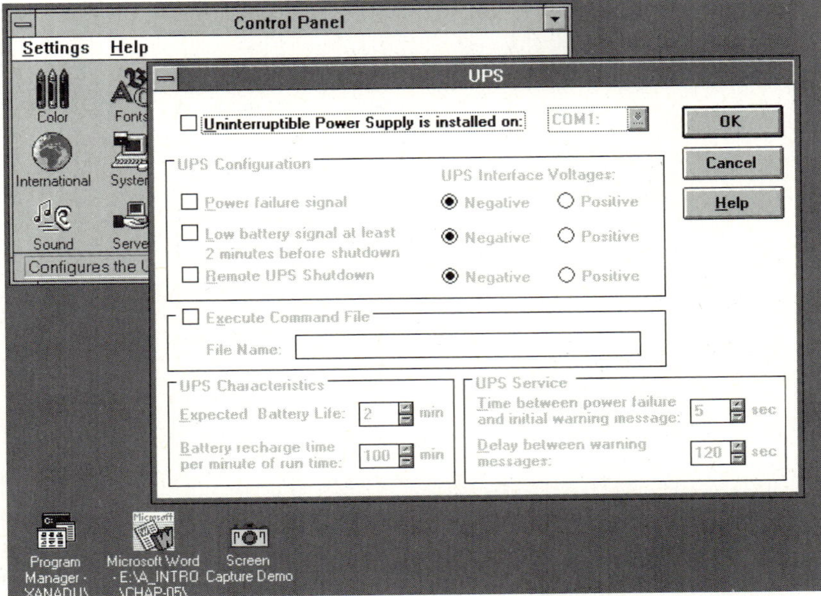

Figure 4.19
The UPS dialog box

2. Select UPS Services in the dialog box. UPS services can be started, stopped, and configured to start automatically or manually when you log on to Windows NT.

▶ Configuring the UPS

To configure the UPS:

1. Select the UPS icon in the Control Panel window.
2. From the UPS dialog box, select the desired options and settings.

Which UPS dialog box appears in response is dependent on the specific UPS hardware installed on the system. However, options that may appear include the following:

- The COM port where the battery is connected.

- The time intervals for maintaining battery power, recharging the battery, or sending warning messages after power failure.
- The Power Failure Signal check box should be checked if the UPS device can send a message reporting power supply failure (line current interruption). This setting enables a CTS (clear-to-send) cable signal on the UPS COM port connection.
- The Low Battery Signal check box should be checked if the UPS device reports when battery power is low. This setting enables a DCD (data-carrier-detect) cable signal on the UPS COM port connection.
- The Remote UPS Shutdown check box should be checked if the UPS device can accept a signal from the UPS service telling the device to shut down. This setting enables a DTR (data-terminal-ready) cable signal on the UPS COM port connection.
- The Expected Battery Life box sets the time (in minutes) that the UPS device can be expected to keep the system operating after line power fails. The range is 2 minutes (default) to 720 minutes (7 hours).
- The Battery Recharge Time box sets the time (in minutes) that the UPS battery requires for charging to support 1 minute of operation time. This value can be set for 1 to 250 minutes with a default setting of 100 minutes. Consult your UPS documentation for settings appropriate for your equipment.
- The Time Between Power Failures box specifies an interval in seconds between a power interruption and the first message sent to notify users. The range is 0 to 120 seconds, with a default of 5 seconds.
- The Delay Between Warning Messages box sets the interval (in seconds) between the initial message notifying the user of a power failure and subsequent messages advising them that power shutdown should be expected and to stop using the computer. Valid settings are 5 to 300 seconds (6 minutes) with a default setting of 120 seconds (2 minutes).

Help Files ▼ Each item checked in the UPS Configuration group requires a HIGH or LOW signal specification. These settings instruct the UPS services how to communicate with the UPS device. Refer to the documentation for the UPS device for details on signal requirements.

Your UPS documentation should offer some guidelines for determining how long the UPS device can keep your system operating. Do not, however, use the system power supply rating to determine the actual power requirements. Simply because a power supply is rated at 300 watts does not mean that the system is using 300 watts—actual usage is more likely to be half or less of the power supply's rated capacity. If all else fails, after the UPS is fully charged, simply unplug the line power cord (in noncritical circumstances) and time how long the UPS is able to support operations. Also, remember that disk access—reading from and writing to the hard drive—uses more power than does simply letting the computer run without real activity. For a default usage figure, 200 to 225 watts should cover most desktop computers with color monitors (increase this for extra-large monitors).

The default setting of 5 seconds for a minimum power interruption time is an excellent choice. Because many power interruptions are less than a second—often simply a flicker—power interruptions with a duration of less than 5 seconds will not be reported, but the user will be alerted when longer power interruptions occur. Of course, you'll probably also notice the lights going out.

I/O Port Settings

▶ Changing Serial Port Settings

The Ports option is used to configure serial (COM) port settings. To configure a COM port:

1. Select the Ports option in the Control Panel window.
2. Double-click on the desired COM port or select (highlight) the port and click on the Settings button. The Settings dialog box (Figure 4.20) allows you to specify the baud rate, data bits, parity, stop bits, and flow-control settings for the serial port selected.

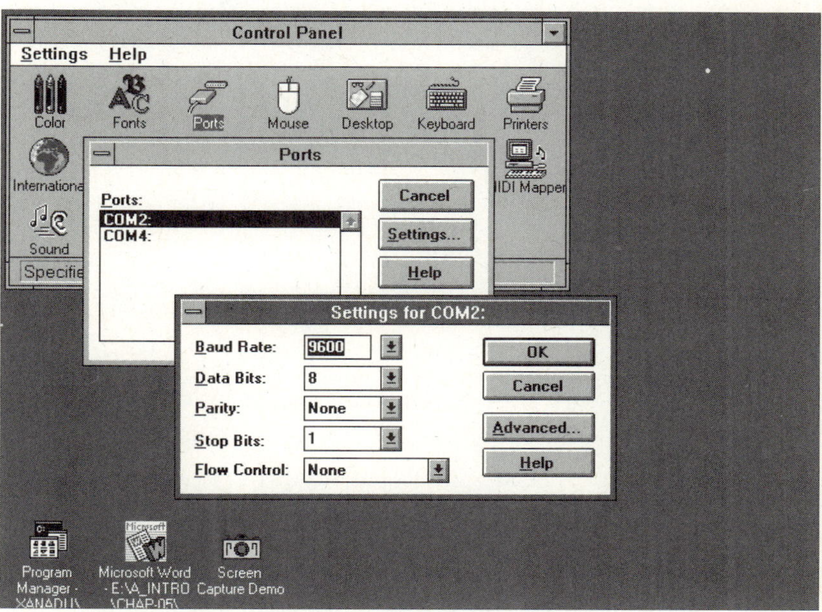

Figure 4.20
The Settings dialog box for the current port

3. Click on the scroll arrow (at the right of each option box) to display the valid settings for each.
4. Select the appropriate setting for the device connected to the COM port. For information about the correct settings, refer to the documentation supplied with the device in question.

5. When all settings are correct for the current port, select OK to return to the Ports dialog box. Click on the Close button to return to the Control Panel.

COM port setting options include the following:

- *Baud Rate* determines the rate at which information is sent to the device connected to the COM port. Valid settings are 110, 330, 660, 1200, 2400, 4800, 9600, and 19200 baud.
- *Data Bits* specifies the character size expected by the device connected to the COM port. Valid settings are 4, 5, 6, 7, or 8 bits, with most devices expecting 8 data bits per character.
- *Parity* specifies the error-checking method used by the device connected to the COM port. Valid options are Even, Odd, None, Mark, or Space with Null (or None), which is the default expected by most devices. Consult your device documentation for details on required settings.
- *Stop Bits* can be set to 1, 1.5 or 2. The default setting is 1 stop bit. (A stop bit is the time interval between transmitted characters.)
- *Flow Control* specifies how and who controls communications between the serial port and the device. Valid options are None, XOn/XOff, and Hardware. The default setting used by most devices is None.
- *Advanced* options are generally not available for most COM ports. When this option is selected, a dialog box advises *There are no user configurable Advanced I/O parameters for this COM port.*

Help Files ▼ The baud rate should always be set to the highest setting supported by the actual (physical) device (such as a modem or plotter). When connecting to a modem, use the highest baud rate setting supported by the modem itself—do not select a lower baud rate simply because it may be required by a BBS (bulletin board system) or other service called via the modem. Lower baud rates can be software-selected when required. Consult your device documentation for details on supported settings.

The default 8-bits-per-character setting should be compatible with most COM devices such as modems, plotters, and serial printers. Other settings should be used only when explicitly required by the hardware device. Consult your device documentation for details on required settings.

Stop bits are not actually transmitted bits; rather, they specify the timing interval used between transmitted characters. Consult your device documentation for details on required settings.

Most devices do not require flow control. A few devices, however, may prefer one of the control options with XOn/XOff for software control and the Hardware option for control over the communications process. Consult your device documentation for details on required settings.

HELP! *The COM settings must be configured before other services—such as the Cardfile Autodialer or a communications program—can use the attached device.*

System Service Customization

▶ Examining the Default Services

A number of default services are supplied by Windows NT. The Services dialog box (Figure 4.21) is used to start, stop, pause, or continue each of these services and to pass startup parameters to the service, if required.

The Services dialog box includes a list of services in a three-column display including the service name, current status, and startup condition. Default system services include the following:

- *Alerter Service* notifies selected users (and computers) of administrative alerts that occur on the system. This service is used by the Server and other services and requires the Messenger service.
- *Clipbook* maintains Clipboard services for local applications and clipbook services for network operation.

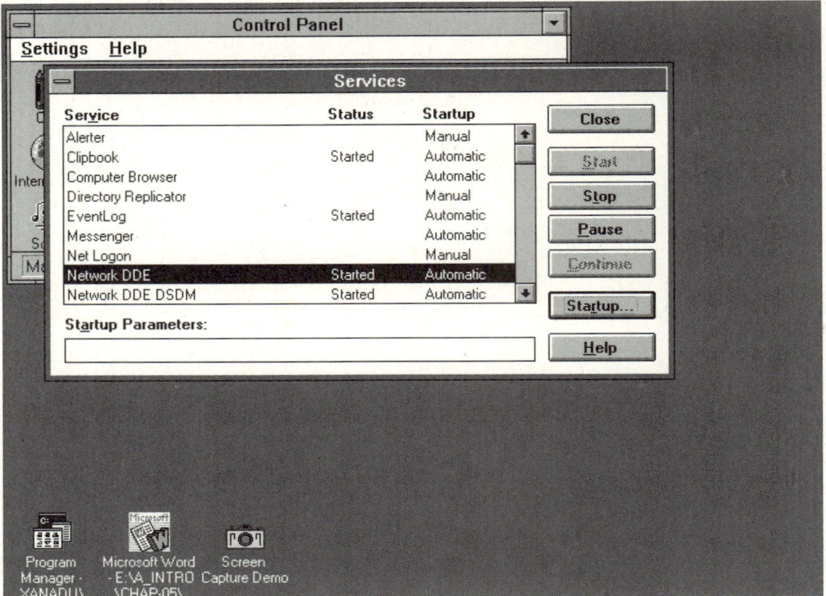

Figure 4.21
The Services dialog box

- *Computer Browser Service* maintains an up-to-date list of computers on the network, supplying this list to applications when requested to do so in the Select Computer and Select Domain dialog boxes.
- *Directory Replicator Service* replicates directories and the files in the directories between network computers.
- *Event Log Service* maintains event logs of system, security, and application events.
- *Messenger Service* sends and receives messages sent by administrators or by the Alerter service.
- *Net Logon Service* provides network logon authentication.
- *Schedule Service* is required by the AT command to schedule commands and programs to be executed at a specific time.
- *Server Service* provides remote procedure call (RPC) support as well as file, print, and named pipe sharing.

- *UPS Service* manages an intelligent UPS (uninterruptible power supply) attached to the system.
- *Workstation Service* provides network connections and network communications.

Starting and Stopping Services

To start, stop, pause, or continue a service:

1. Select the Services icon in the Control Panel window.
2. Select the service in the Services dialog box (Figure 4.21).
3. Click on the Start, Stop, Pause, or Continue button (options that are not valid for the present services will be disabled, or grayed-out).

HELP! *Stopping the Server service disconnects all remotely connected users. Always warn users before stopping this service.*

Help Files Startup parameters can also be passed to a service. Type the desired parameters in the Startup Parameters box before activating the service by clicking on the Start button. None of the default services supplied by Windows NT, however, accepts or requires any startup parameters.

Configuring Service Startup

To configure service startup:

1. Select the Services icon in the Control Panel window.
2. Select the service in the Services dialog box (Figure 4.21).
3. Click on the Startup button.

4. In the Service Startup dialog box, specify Automatic, Manual, or Disabled.

5. Select the user account where the service will log on, System Account or This Account. If This Account is selected, choose the Browse button to call the Add User dialog box. From the Add User dialog box, specify a user account, then enter the password for the account in both the Password and Confirm Password boxes.

Help Files ▼ Before a service startup can be configured, the user must be logged on under an account that has membership in the Administrators local group. The Service Configuration and Add User dialog boxes are shown in Figure 4.22.

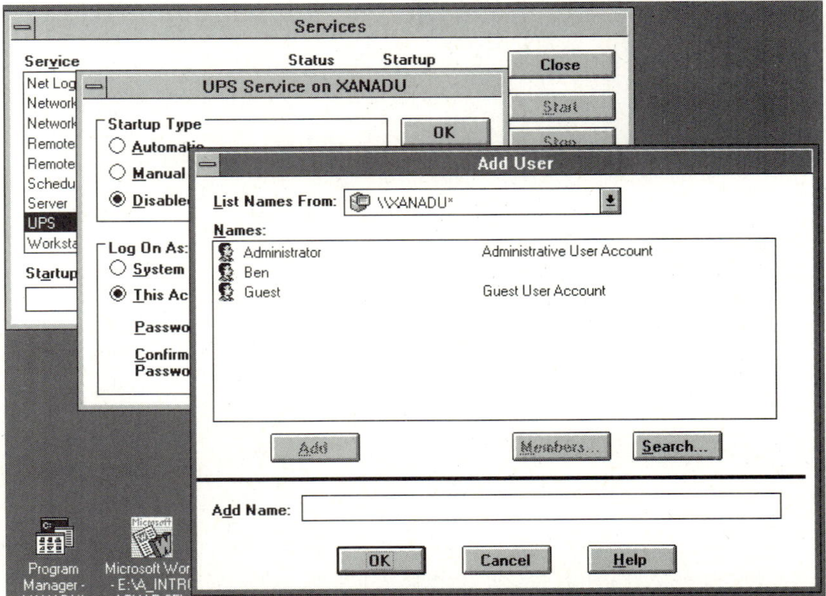

Figure 4.22
The Service Configuration and Add User dialog boxes

System Event Sounds

▸ Assigning Sounds

To assign sound waveforms to events:

1. Select the Sound icon in the Control Panel window. The Sound dialog box shown in Figure 4.23 appears.

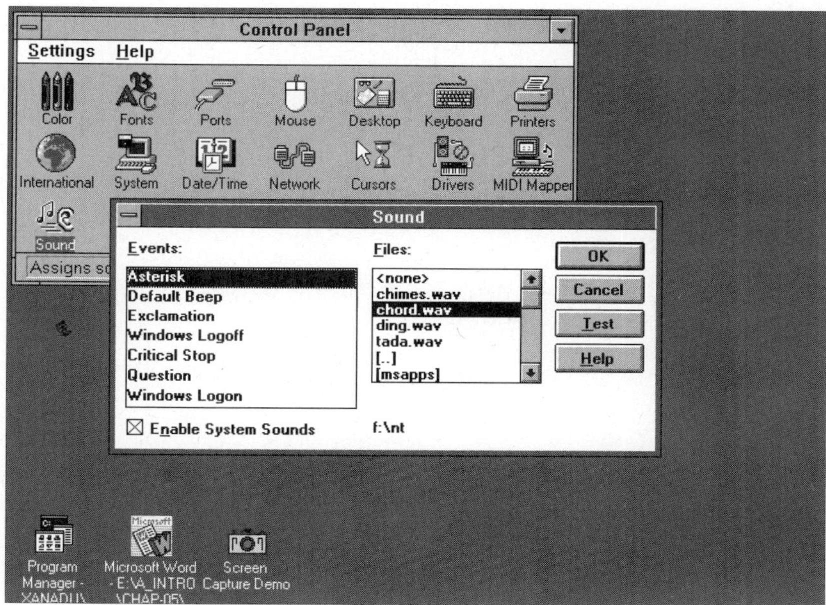

Figure 4.23
The Sound dialog box

2. From the Events list box, select the event to which a sound will be assigned.

3. From the Files list box, select the sound file desired. If the desired sound file is not located in the current directory, another drive and directory can be selected through the Files list box. Select None if no sound should be assigned.

4. Select the Test button or double-click on the event or sound file name to listen to the sound waveform.

5. The warning beep and all sounds except those assigned to Windows NT Start and Windows NT Exist can be disabled by unchecking the Enable System Sounds check box.

Help Files ▼ Different Windows NT-supplied sound (.WAV) files can be assigned to different events. For example, when Windows NT is logged on, by default, the TADA.WAV (fanfare) sound sequence is played and the CHIMES.WAV sound is used at log off. Figure 4.23 shows the Sound dialog box with the event list at the left and the standard waveform (sound files) at the right.

Sound (.WAV) files can be used—under either Windows 3.1 or Windows NT—only if a sound card is installed and configured correctly. If no sound card is installed, the Test button will be grayed-out (disabled) and the waveform sound assignments are ignored. Instead, the internal speaker will emit a warning beep when an error is encountered. Waveform sounds cannot be played through the internal speaker.

Sound waveforms can be selected before a sound card is installed but will not take effect until the card is installed.

MIDI Setups

▸ Selecting a MIDI Setup

To select a MIDI setup:

1. Select the MIDI Mapper icon in the Control Panel window. The MIDI Mapper dialog box appears (Figure 4.24).
2. Select Setup from the MIDI Mapper dialog box.
3. Open the Name list to select the desired MIDI setup.

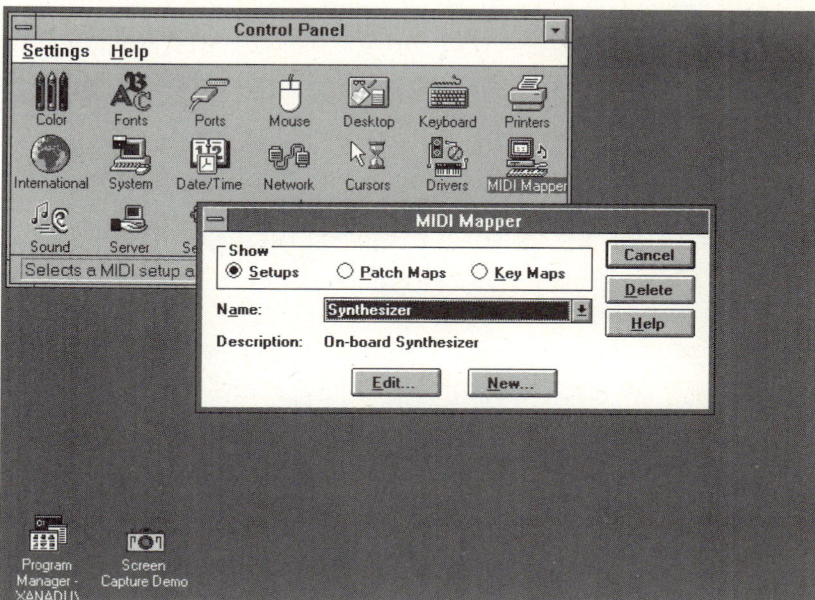

Figure 4.24
The MIDI Mapper dialog box

Help Files ▼ Applications such as Media Player require MIDI setups (and, of course, a synthesizer or synthesizer card) to play MIDI files. The MIDI setup dialog box (Figure 4.24) is used to install and configure MIDI drivers.

Before a MIDI setup can take effect, the application used to play MIDI files or to send MIDI information must use the MIDI Mapper. The application must also send patch-select messages or provide a MIDI file to include patch selections. MIDI files written for Windows NT meet these operational requirements, but this may not be true of all MIDI files and applications. Consult your MIDI application's documentation or contact your MIDI file vendor for further details.

Creating a MIDI Setup

To create a new MIDI setup, the following steps must be performed in the order shown:

1. Create a MIDI key map.
2. Create MIDI patch maps.
3. Specify channel mappings.

Help Files MIDI setups can be created for MIDI synthesizers for which Windows NT has not provided a setup. Begin by setting the synthesizer to receive MIDI messages on multiple MIDI channels. Also determine whether the synthesizer is a base-level or extended-level synthesizer and whether it is capable of playing general MIDI files. Consult your synthesizer manual to determine equipment capabilities.

A basic understanding of MIDI concepts and terminology as well as an understanding of the consequences of changes made are required before exercising the MIDI Mapper option. Those inexperienced with MIDI operations should not attempt to create a custom MIDI setup.

Editing Setups, Patch Maps, and Key Maps

To edit patch maps, key maps, or change channel mapping:

1. Select the MIDI Mapper icon in the Control Panel window.
2. Select Setups, Patch Maps, or Key Maps in the Show area of the MIDI Mapper dialog box.
3. Use the Name list to select a channel map, patch map, or key map for editing.
4. Select Edit. Figure 4.25 shows the editor with a key map file.

5. In the dialog box, make any changes you want. For details on editing MIDI files, consult your synthesizer documentation or use the Help button to summon on-line help.

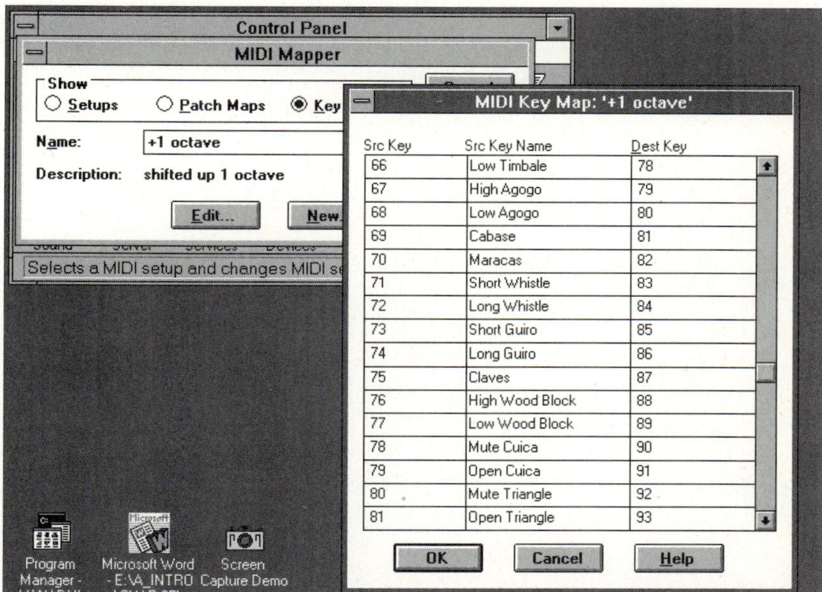

Figure 4.25
Editing a key map file

Help Files ▼ While editing is generally not required, key maps, patch maps, setups, and channel mapping can be edited for existing MIDI setups. This is normally required only if the synthesizer is not producing the expected sounds or if you need to use a Windows NT-supplied setup but require different port assignments.

Deleting Setups, Patch Maps, and Key Maps

To delete a setup, patch map, or key map:

1. Select the MIDI Mapper icon in the Control Panel window.
2. Select Setups, Patch Maps, or Key Maps in the Show area of the MIDI Mapper dialog box.
3. Use the Name list to select the name of the setup, patch map, or key map to be deleted.
4. Select the Delete button and click on Yes to confirm the deletion.

Before deleting patch maps or key maps, ensure that they are not being used by existing key maps or setup files.

Help Files ▼ While unused or unnecessary MIDI setups, patch maps, or key maps can be deleted, there are a few restrictions on that files can be deleted. Files that should not be deleted include

- The current MIDI setup (the setup initially listed in the Name box when the MIDI Mapper dialog box is called)
- A patch map used in a MIDI setup
- A key map used in a patch map

System Options

Setting System Options

To use the System tools:

Select the System icon from the Control Panel window. The System dialog box displays settings from the user profile for the user currently active on the computer. The System dialog box also provides tools to define a variety of options related to the operating system.

Changing Environmental Variables

To edit or add user environmental variables for your computer:

1. Select the System icon in the Control Panel window. The System dialog box (Figure 4.26) shows the current system environmental variables, as well as the user environmental variables for the user currently logged on to the computer.

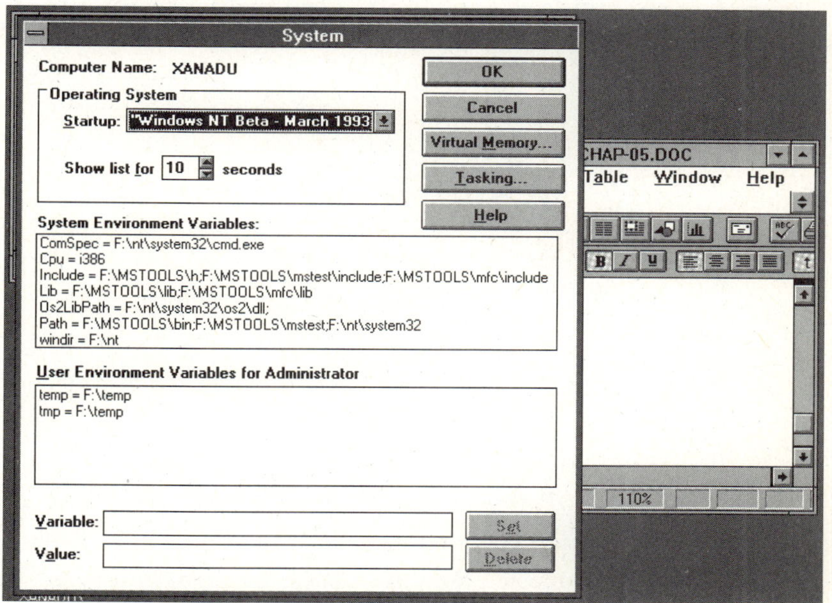

Figure 4.26
The System dialog box

2. Select the variable to edit in the User Environment Variables list box. The selected variable name appears in the Variable box, and the variable's current value appears in the Value box. Alternatively, to add a new variable, click on the Variable box and type the new variable name. The new variable is appended to the user environmental variables list and included in the current user's profile.
3. Type a new value for the variable in the Value edit box.
4. When both the Variable and Value boxes contain the desired information, click on the Set button.

5. When all changes are completed, select the OK button to save the changes in the user's profile. Or choose the Cancel button to delete all unsaved changes and restore the previous values.

To remove a user environmental variable:

1. Select the variable in the User Environment Variables box.
2. Click on the Delete button.
3. Select OK to save the new configuration or Cancel to restore the original configuration.

Help Files ▼ Environmental variables are used to locate programs and program directories, to manage memory allocations required by some applications, and, in some cases, to control an application's behavior. The environmental variables used by Windows NT are similar to environmental variables set in the DOS operating system.

Two types of environmental variables are used in Windows NT: system environmental variables, which cannot be altered by the user, and user environmental variables, which can be edited, deleted, or inserted. Changes to these variables, however, do not take effect until you log off Windows NT and log on again. Currently executing programs are not affected.

▸ Setting Virtual Memory Options

To change the size of the swap file:

1. Select the System icon in the Control Panel window.
2. Select the Virtual Memory button in the System dialog box. (If you are not logged on with Administrator privileges, the Virtual Memory button will not be available.)

3. In the Virtual Memory dialog box (Figure 4.27), use the Drive box to select the drive for the paging file.

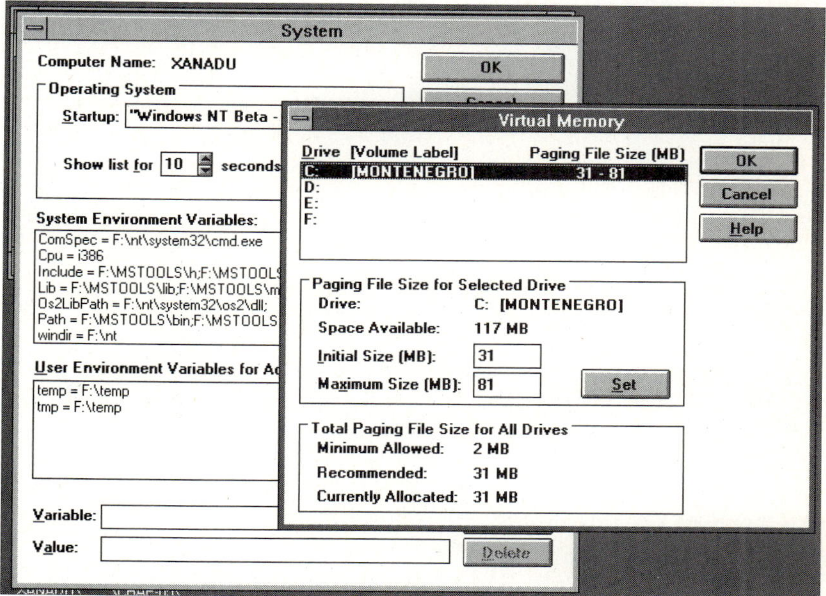

Figure 4.27
The Virtual Memory dialog box

4. In the Paging File Size boxes, set the initial and maximum sizes for the page file.

5. Select the Set button to save the paging file changes or select Cancel to leave the existing settings unchanged.

Help Files ▼ Like Windows 3.1, Windows NT uses a swap file to extend system memory. This swap file, or virtual-memory paging file, is used to write material from memory to the disk to free memory for more immediate needs, copying the swapped material back into active memory when it is required again. When Windows NT was installed, this virtual-memory paging file was created automatically.

You must be logged on as a member of the Administrators group for the computer in order to change the size of the virtual-memory paging file or create additional paging files. All paging files must reside on local hard drives—network drives cannot be used for this purpose.

As a general rule, the paging file should be left at its recommended size. However, the file size can be changed if necessary. For example, you might wish to change the file size to provide additional space while working with an application that uses unusually large amounts of data. In extreme cases, a separate hard drive, an entire drive partition, or, ideally, a flash memory drive might be devoted to the swap file.

The virtual-memory paging file is a hidden file titled PAGEFILE.SYS and is usually located in the system (boot) partition. The PAGEFILE.SYS file cannot be deleted while running Windows NT. If PAGEFILE.SYS is deleted while running under DOS, the swap file will be recreated automatically when Windows NT is booted. Unfortunately, Windows NT and Windows 3.1 are not able to share the same swap file.

If desired, swap files can be created on more than one drive (or partition), allowing the space to be used by several drives. In use, these swap files will be treated as a single swap file by Windows NT.

▶ Using FlexBoot to Boot Alternate Operating Systems

The method for adding a startup operating system (other than Windows NT) depends on the kind of processor in your computer: 80*x*86 or RISC. For an 80*x*86-based system, after installing Windows NT, edit the BOOT-.INI file to load the alternate operating system. The BOOT.INI is created automatically by Windows NT during installation. For a RISC-based system, use the ARC setup program to install the alternate operating system. Regardless of the type of processor, Windows NT's Setup utility detects the operating system present during installation and makes provisions for dual-boot operations. Not all operating systems, however, can take advantage of the alternate startup options.

To boot both DOS and Windows NT, for example, the BOOT.INI file might look like this:

```
[boot loader]
```

```
timeout=10
default=C:\
[operating systems]
scsi(0)disk(0)rdisk(0)partition(4)\nt="Windows NT 3.1"
c:\="MS-DOS"
```

The BOOT.INI contents were created during Windows NT installation and set three conditions. First, in the [boot loader] section, the time delay for booting the default operating system (timeout) was originally specified as 30 seconds but has been changed here to 10 seconds.

Second, the default boot system specification was, originally, as follows:

```
default=scsi(0)disk(0)rdisk(0)partition(4)\nt
```

The specification identifies the drive as a SCSI hard drive that is installed as disk 0, rdisk 0, partition 4—which happens to be the partition identified as drive F. This specification was written by the Windows NT installation process but can be written much more simply as

```
default=F:\nt
```

The same change would need to be made in both the [boot loader] section of the BOOT.INI file and in the [operating systems] section. In either form, however, the default boot specification would be for the Windows NT operating system.

But, if you prefer, the DOS system could be booted as the default operating system by changing the [boot loader] specification to read

```
default=C:\
```

Third, within the [operating system] section of the BOOT.INI file, two text strings identify the boot alternatives. The text strings, enclosed in quotes, can be any text desired.

```
[operating systems]
f:\="Windows NT 3.1"
c:\="MS-DOS"
```

▶ Setting the Default Operating System Using the System Utility

To set the default (startup) operating system:

1. Select the System icon in the Control Panel window.

2. Click on the scroll arrow (at the right of the Startup list box) to display a list of systems installed on the computer. Highlight the operating system desired as the default boot system.

3. In the Show List For edit box, set the number of seconds the choices should be displayed before FlexBoot automatically loads the default operating system.

Help Files ▼ If more than one operating system is installed on the computer, the System utility can be used to specify which operating system FlexBoot will use as the default operating system the next time the computer is powered up (or reset).

▶ Setting Multitasking Options

Windows NT provides three options for sharing the multitasking environment that is shared between foreground and background applications. To change the foreground and background time-sharing response:

1. Select the System option from the Control Panel window.

2. Click on the Tasking button in the System dialog box. A Tasking dialog box appears, offering three options:

   - Best Foreground Application Response Time
   - Foreground Applications More Responsive Than Background
   - Foreground and Background Applications Equally Responsive

3. Select any of these options, then click on the OK button to return to the System dialog box.

THE RESCUE PAGES: Using Control Panel Options

There isn't enough memory to run my application(s).

When memory is critical (a minimum of 8 megabytes of RAM is required for Windows NT, 12 megabytes is recommended, and 16 megabytes is strongly suggested), some memory can be saved by canceling optional features that are using some of the available RAM. Memory saving options include the following:

- Remove bitmapped wallpaper or switch to a small bitmap and use tiling.
- Remove unneeded fonts. Do not, however, remove the MS Sans Serif font, because it is used by most Windows NT dialog boxes.
- Close unneeded applications. That cute little clock or calculator or card file sitting in the corner really isn't essential, but it *is* using memory, and so is that icon animation utility that makes your icons blink, wink, and do the shimmy while you're deciding what to do next.

Of course, as a last, desperate measure, you could invest in more memory and be able to keep all your utilities open and handy.

When I have a bunch of applications open, I have trouble switching between them and bringing the right window to the top.

For convenience in switching between applications, try enabling the Fast Switching option in the Desktop dialog box. When the Fast Switching option is enabled, you have an alternative to switching windows by highlighting the title bars of each. A dialog box appears centered on the screen

with the application's icon at the far left and the application's title to the right. Holding the Alt key down and repeatedly pressing the Tab key cycles through all active applications, identifying each by its full title. Releasing the Alt key brings the selected application to the forefront, making the application the focus of activity.

Alternatively, to return to the original application, press Alt+Esc.

I can't find all my COM ports.

If you're using the Ports control, not all the installed COM ports appear on the ports list. For an example, refer back to Figure 4.20, where the Ports dialog shows COM2 and COM4 but doesn't list COM1 or COM3, despite the fact that four COM ports were installed. This may sound like an error, but there are reasons for this apparent discrepancy.

First, because the COM1 port is being used by the mouse, this port is not available for other uses and cannot be reconfigured. Therefore, it's not listed.

Second, COM3 is configured to use the same interrupt (IRQ4) as COM1, a limitation imposed by the system hardware. However, since the mouse on COM1 is effectively in continuous use, the shared interrupt cannot be spared to operate COM3. Therefore, only COM2 and COM4 (which also share a single interrupt) are listed as available ports.

My screen saver isn't working right or isn't coming up at all.

The Windows NT screen savers are pretty reliable. However, a conflict can occur when a third-party screen saver is installed and the Windows NT screen saver is not disabled. When this happens, both screen savers may be trying to operate at the same time.

The solution is simple. Either set the desktop screen saver to None or remove the third-party screen saver.

The screen saver won't let me get back to my applications without pressing Ctrl+Alt+Del, but I don't want to reset the system.

Don't panic—pressing Ctrl+Alt+Del does not reset the system. Your screen saver has the password option enabled, and, after you press Ctrl+Alt+Del, you'll be asked to enter your log on password. Simply enter the password and Windows NT restores your working screens immediately. This feature is for your protection and prevents someone else from accessing your computer when you've stepped away for a moment.

If you don't want password protection, call the Desktop dialog box from the Control Panel and turn off the password option (just below the screen saver selection).

I installed a new driver/reconfigured my system/changed environmental variables, but nothing's changed.

Newly installed drivers and other changes to the system configuration, such as environmental variables, may not take effect immediately. Drivers in particular require you to log off the system and then log back on for the new drivers to be recognized.

I plugged in a new mouse but I can't configure it.

Like other devices, the mouse or other pointing device must be installed—together with its driver, of course—before it can be customized. Since your new mouse doesn't work with the old driver, put the old mouse back while you install the new mouse drivers and select the new mouse as the default pointing device. Then turn off the computer, plug in the new mouse, and reboot the system.

For further details on installing a pointing device and driver, refer to the documentation accompanying the mouse or pointing device.

I have a UPS (uninterruptible power supply), but it doesn't have a COM port connection. Can I still use it? How do I install it in the Control Panel UPS dialog box?

The UPS dialog box in the Control Panel is only for the newer, "intelligent" UPS systems. Older, "dumb" UPS systems can still be used, just as they always have been, but they will not report power outages to the system, remind you of how long the UPS can support operations, or provide any interactive features. Unfortunately, all that the older UPS can do is to keep your computer up and running through a power outage…but that might be enough.

I have a 9600 baud modem, but I'm calling a BBS that supports only 1200 baud. Should I reconfigure my COM port for 1200 baud?

Always leave the COM port configured for the highest baud rate supported by the modem (or any other device). The modem itself can communicate with the BBS at a lower baud rate without reducing the COM port baud rate.

I have a sound card in my computer and it works fine under Windows 3.1, but under Windows NT, it only dings at me.

Installing a sound card is only half the job. You've probably forgotten either that you also need to install the sound driver for Windows NT (go to the Control Panel, Drivers option) or that you haven't enabled sounds (go to the Control Panel, Sound option).

CHAPTER

5

HELP! File Management and System Utilities

File Manager is a multipurpose utility. Not only is it used to maintain directories and files but it is also used to connect to network drives, assign permissions on shared directories and files, associate data files with applications, and even execute applications.

Topics covered in this chapter include

- The Windows NT File Manager
- Managing File Manager
- Directory and file operations
- Moving or copying directories or files
- Disk maintenance
- Network drive operations
- Working with shared directories and files
- Operating from File Manager
- Customizing File Manager

Windows NT File Manager

▶ Using File Manager

The File Manager utility is supplied by Windows NT, providing you with a means for organizing files and directories on both your hard and floppy drives. File Manager is used to do the following:

- Create and delete directories
- Copy, move, or delete files
- Access shared directories on the network
- Share directories over the network
- Secure files and directories
- Add applications or documents to program groups
- Perform other disk, directory, and file management tasks

Help Files ▼ Within File Manager, the display is divided into several sections (see Figure 5.1). The customary menu bar at the top offers a variety of options. Immediately below the menu bar, a tool bar offers icons representing various tasks. Below the tool bar, the drive bar offers a series of icons to represent the floppy drives,

hard drives (or hard-drive partitions),

and CD-ROM driver or other removable media

present on the system. Finally, in the application window itself, two child windows each display separate drive/directory listings.

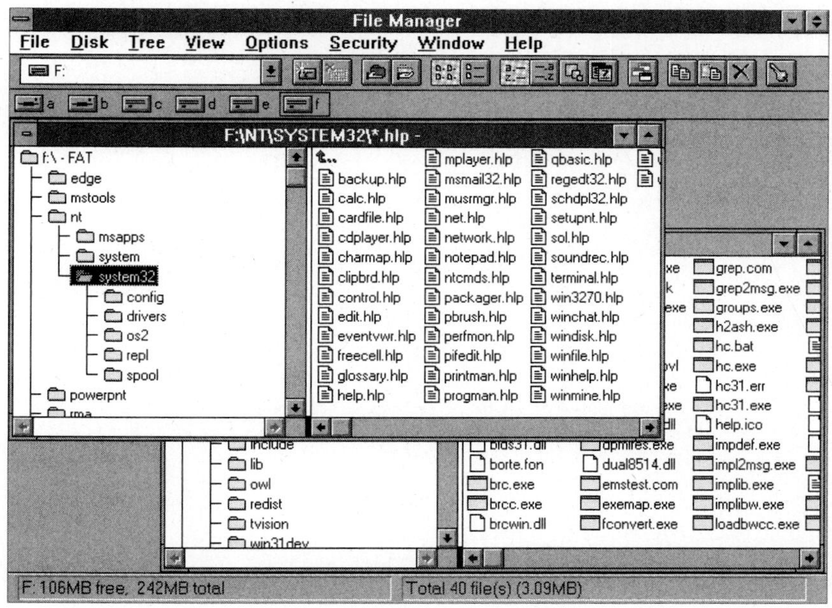

Figure 5.1
File Manager

The directory display windows show the selected drive/path and file specification in the window's title bar. The windows themselves are divided vertically to show, on the left, the directory tree and, on the right, a list of files contained in the directory (or subdirectory) highlighted in the tree.

In the directory tree, a file-folder icon

is used for each directory and subdirectory; an opened file folder

indicates the selected directory. A third file-folder icon

is used for shared directories on the network.

In the file list, three other icons identify the files as executable (.EXE, .COM, .BAT, or .PIF), recognized data files or documents (file types that are associated with an executable application), or unrecognized data-file types.

A fourth icon

is reserved for identifying system or hidden files.

Managing File Manager

▸ Entering and Exiting File Manager

To start File Manager:

- Double-click on the File Manager icon in the Main application group.

To exit from File Manager:

- Double-click on the Control-menu box (in the upper-left corner of the File Manager window).
- Pull down the Control menu and select the Close option.
- From the File menu, select Exit.

Help Files ▼ File Manager is installed, by default, in the Main program group. It can, however, be moved to another program group or duplicated in more than one program group.

When File Manager is called, it will appear in the state it was in when you last left File Manager—the same drives and directories will be open and logged, the window sizes and placement will be the same, and the same View menu settings will be in effect. If you do not wish to retain these characteristics, disable the Save Settings On Exit option.

▶ Selecting a Disk Drive

To change the drive displayed by an open directory window:

1. Select the desired directory window as the active window.
2. In the drive bar, click once on the icon for the desired disk drive.

Help Files ▼ When File Manager is called, the default display will reflect the drive(s) and directories present when File Manager was last used. In Figure 5.1, File Manager is shown with two drive windows open.

Opening Additional Drives

To open additional directory windows:

- Double-click on the icon for the desired disk drive.

Or:

1. Use the Tab key to select the drive bar.
2. Use the arrow buttons to select a drive icon.
3. Select Open from the File menu (or press Enter).

A new directory window will open, displaying the selected drive with the active directory—or root directory, if no other directory has been opened—highlighted in the directory tree.

To open an additional directory window that shows the same directory information as the active window:

- Select New Window from the Window menu.
- Click on the New Window button.

To open a directory window that displays only the contents pane for a selected directory:

- Press and hold the Shift key while double-clicking on the directory icon in an open directory window.
- Select the directory icon from the tree, then press Shift+Enter.

Help Files ▼ File Manager is not limited to displaying a single directory. Instead, multiple directory windows can be used to display directory trees and file lists for multiple disk drives or to offer multiple displays of a single drive.

Opening multiple directory windows provides a convenient method of copying or moving files between directories or between drives.

If more than one directory window is displaying the same drive/directory information, a number will appear in each window title bar, showing the order in which each window was opened.

Each new directory window inherits the display options established for the previous window. Thus, if the active window has been sized or adjusted to show only the directory tree (in the left window section), a newly opened window will also display only the directory tree.

▶ Closing Directory Windows

To close an existing directory window:

- Double-click on the Control-menu box (in the upper-left corner).

Or:

- Select the Close option from the Control menu.

If only one directory window is open, it cannot be closed.

▶ Updating Directory Windows

To update a directory window:

- Click on the drive icon for the current drive.

Or:

- Select Refresh from the Window menu.

Help Files ▼ For most operations, File Manager automatically handles updates for open directory windows. For example, when an application creates a new file, File Manager will reflect the addition immediately. There are, however,

circumstances where File Manager cannot handle updates automatically—for example, if a floppy disk has been changed or if you are using network directories. In these cases, a manual update may be required.

▶ Selecting Directory Windows

To select an open directory window,

- Click anywhere in the window.
- From the list at the bottom of the Window menu, select a directory window name.
- Press Ctrl+F6 or Ctrl+Tab to step through the directory windows.

▶ Sizing Directory Windows

Directory windows can be sized individually using the mouse. To resize a directory window:

1. Place the mouse on the window frame. The mouse cursor will change to a double arrow.
2. Press and hold the left mouse button while dragging the window frame to a new size.

Or:

- Use the minimize arrow button (in the upper-right corner) to reduce the directory window to an icon.
- Use the maximize arrow button (in the upper-right corner) to enlarge the directory window to fill the File Manager window.

▶ Repositioning Directory Windows and Icons

To reposition a directory window:

1. Position the mouse on the window title bar.

2. Press and hold the left mouse button while dragging the window frame to a new position.

Or:

- Select one of the window's menu Cascade or Tile commands to rearrange all open directory windows, making it possible to both see and select all the windows.
- The Cascade command overlaps windows diagonally, making each window's title visible.
- The Tile Horizontally command resizes the directory windows to fill the File Manager window horizontally, stacking the directory windows vertically.
- The Tile Vertically command resizes the directory windows to fill the File Manager window vertically, horizontally resizing and repositioning the windows to fit side by side.

To arrange icons for minimized directory windows:

- Use the mouse to reposition (drag) the directory window icons.

Or:

- Use the Arrange Icons command.

Help Files ▼ The Arrange Icons command arranges only minimized (iconized) directory windows. Because of this limitation, not all icons might be visible, since minimized windows may be covered by open directory windows.

Managing the Directory Window

To adjust the spacing of the window panes:

1. Point to the vertical bar separating the directory and file panes. The mouse cursor becomes a double arrow, pointing left and right.
2. Press and hold the left mouse button while dragging the bar to the desired position.

Or:

1. Select the Split option from the View menu. A vertical split bar will appear.
2. Use the arrow keys to move the split bar to the desired position, then press Enter or click the mouse button.
3. To cancel the operation, press Esc.

To display only the directory tree:

- Select the Tree Only option from the View menu.

To display only the contents of the current directory:

- Select the Directory Only option from the View menu.

To display both the tree and the contents of the current directory:

- Select the Tree and Directory option from the View menu.

Help Files ▼ Initially, a directory window displays both the directory tree for the selected drive and the contents of the current directory. The two halves of the directory window are separated by a vertical bar, which can be dragged to change the relative widths of the window panes.

Expanding the Directory Tree

To expand a single directory:

- Double-click on the icon or name of the directory to expand.

Or:

1. Select the directory.
2. Select Expand One Level from the Tree menu.

To expand an entire branch:

1. Select the icon or name of the directory.
2. Select Expand Branch from the Tree menu.

To expand all branches in a directory tree:

- Select Expand All from the Tree menu.

Help Files ▼ When a drive is logged, only the first-level directories are displayed in the directory tree, although any subdirectories belonging to the selected directory are displayed in the files list. A single click selects a directory as active, and double-clicking on the directory will expand the directory tree to show subdirectories belonging to this directory. Each subdirectory may contain additional subdirectories. A second double-click collapses an expanded directory.

Directories can be expanded as a single branch or a single level, or all the branches in the tree can be expanded at once.

▶ Collapsing Directory Branches

Just as directory can be expanded to show subdirectories, branches can also be collapsed so that the subdirectories are not included in the directory tree. To collapse a directory:

- Double-click on the icon or the directory name.

Or:

1. Select the icon or name of the directory to be collapsed.
2. Select Collapse Branch from the Tree menu.

Collapsing a directory also collapses all sub-branches belonging to that directory.

▶ Showing Expandable Directories

To identify directories that are expandable:

- Click on the Indicate Expandable Branches option in the Tree menu.

To remove identifying marking's from expandable directories:

- Click on the Indicate Expandable Branches option in the Tree menu a second time.

A check mark next to the command indicates that the feature is enabled.

Help Files ▼ Enabling the Indicate Expandable Branches command in the Tree menu is recommended. This option indicates which directories have further subdirectories by adding a plus sign (+) to each icon that represents a directory that has subdirectories. The plus sign indicates that the directory is expandable.

If the directory is already expanded, the plus sign is changed to a minus sign (–), showing that the directory is expanded but can be collapsed.

The single disadvantage of enabling the Indicate Expandable Branches option is that checking each directory for the presence of subdirectories will cause File Manager to take slightly longer to create the directory tree.

Directory and File Operations

▶ Switching Disk Drives

To change disk drives:

- Select the drive icon representing the desired drive.
- Open the Toolbar drive list box and select the desired drive.
- Press Ctrl + *drive letter.*

Or:

1. Select Select Drive from the Disk menu or double-click on the background of the drive bar to open the Select Drive dialog box (see Figure 5.2).
2. Select the drive desired.
3. Click on the OK button.

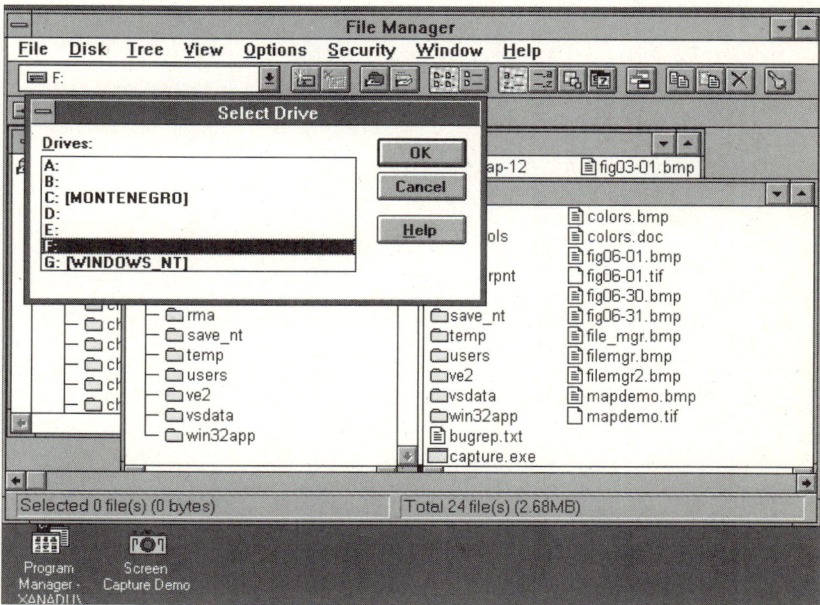

Figure 5.2
The Select Drive dialog box

Help Files ▼ Each directory window in File Manager shows the directory structure for the drive selected for the window; the drive and current file path are shown in the directory window's title bar. File Manager's drive list box also shows the drive logged by the foreground directory window, identifying the corresponding drive icon by an enclosing rectangle. As you switch between directory windows, both the drive list box and drive icon change to reflect the drive displayed by the new foreground directory window.

If a new drive is logged for a directory window—even if the drive is already displayed by another directory window—File Manager searches the selected drive to display the drive's directories, automatically focusing on the current (active) directory for that drive. Pressing Esc will stop the search, leaving a partial directory tree displayed.

▶ Changing Drive Directories

To change between directories on any drive:

- Click on the desired directory in the directory tree.
- Click on the desired subdirectory in the directory contents list.

Or:

1. Press Tab to move to the directory tree.
2. Use the arrow keys to move through the tree.
3. Select the directory desired.

Help Files ▼ In the directory tree, the current (active) directory is marked either by highlighting—if the directory window has the current focus—or by a rectangle surrounding the icon and directory name. On any drive, only one directory can be selected in a single window at a time.

From the contents list, subdirectories of the current directory can also be selected. If you double-click on one of these, however, it will become the new active directory, and the contents list will show subdirectories and files belonging to it.

Within the contents list, you can move the current directory up one level to the root of the current directory by selecting the Up icon or by pressing the Backspace key.

You can reach the root directory immediately by pressing the Home key.

Displaying File Information

To display only file and directory names:

- Select the Name option from the View menu.

Or:

- Select the Name button from the tool bar.

To display complete information for files and directories:

- Select the All File Details option from the View menu.

Or:

- Select the All File Details button from the tool bar.

To select which information to display:

1. Select Partial Details from the View menu. The Partial Details dialog box will appear.
2. In the Partial Details dialog box (see Figure 5.3), check the items to be displayed and clear items that you do not want shown.

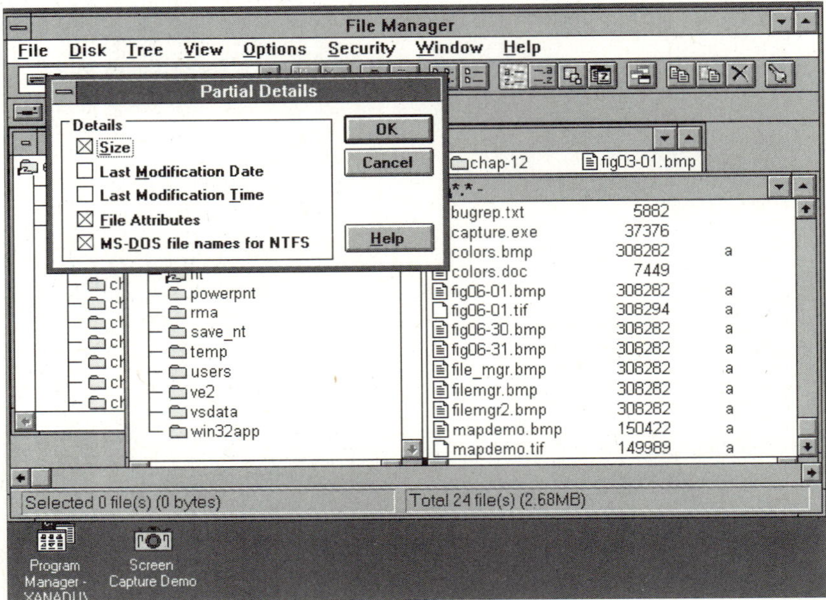

Figure 5.3
The Partial Details dialog box

Help Files ▼ Initially, File Manager displays only the directory and file names. Optionally, the contents list can also display the last modification date and time for both directories and files and, for files only, the file size and attributes. If the drive uses the NTFS (Windows NT file system) format, both a long file name and a short, DOS-format file name can be shown.

▶ Sorting Files

To sort both subdirectories and files alphabetically by name:

- Select Sort By Name from the View menu.

Or:

- Select the Sort By Name button from the tool bar.

To sort files alphabetically by type (extension):

- Select Sort By Type from the View menu.

Or:

- Select the Sort By Type button from the tool bar.

Subdirectories continue to be sorted alphabetically by name and appear first on the list.

To sort files by size:

- Select Sort By Size from the View menu.

Or:

- Select the Sort By Size button from the tool bar.

Subdirectories continue to be sorted alphabetically by name and appear first on the list.

To sort both subdirectories and files by date/time:

- Select Sort By Date from the View menu.

Or:

- Select the Sort By Date button.

Help Files ▼ By default, File Manager displays the directory contents subdirectories first, followed by file names. Both groups are sorted alphabetically. However, file names can be sorted by type (extension) or size, and directories and file names both can be sorted by name or date/time.

▸ Displaying Files Selectively

To display files selectively by type:

1. Select the By File Type option from the View menu.
2. In the By File Type dialog box (see Figure 5.4), enter a file name in the Name box to limit the display to a single file name, or use wild cards (* and ?) to list files with similar names.

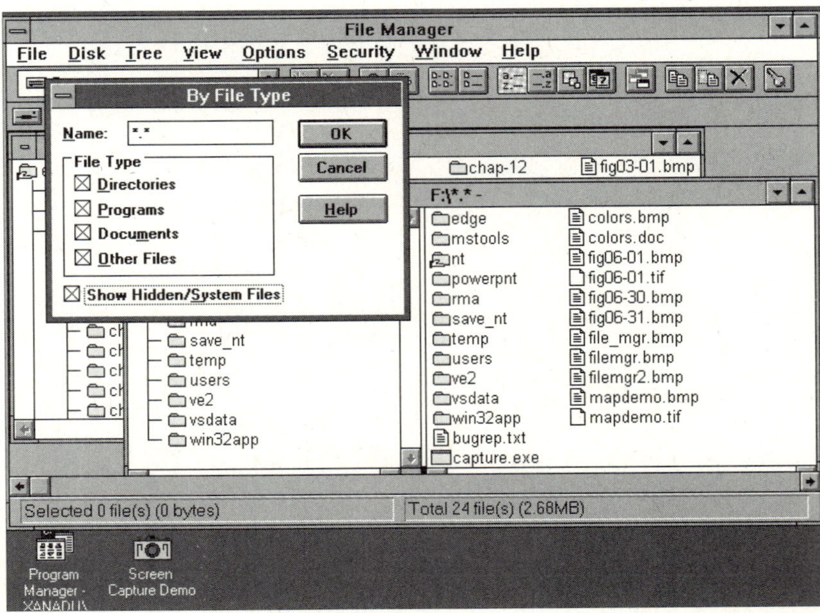

Figure 5.4
The By File Type dialog box

3. Under File Type, select the type of files to display by checking or clearing the File Type check boxes.
4. Select the Show Hidden/System Files option to display hidden and system files.

Help Files ▼ When File Manager is called, the initial contents list displays all file and directories in the current (active) directory—with the exception of hidden and system files. However, File Manager can be instructed to display only files of specific types or to include system or hidden files in the display.

> **HELP!** *Deleting or renaming system or hidden files may result in the computer failing to work correctly or failing to boot at all. Never rename or delete these files.*

A wild card can be used as a substitute for one or more characters in the file name or file extension. An asterisk (*) serves as a substitute for a group of characters, and a question mark (?) substitutes for a single character. For example, the file name specification FILE*.?X? would list all files that begin with the four characters *FILE* and whose second character in the extension is an *X*. FILELIST.TXT and FILEVIEW.EXE would match the specification. Alternatively, to display only files that have the extension .DOC, you would enter the file specification *.DOC. The default file name and extension in the Name box is *.*, which lists all files in a directory.

▸ Naming Directories and Files on NTFS Drives

Drives formatted for the NTFS (Windows NT file system) allow you to use long file and directory names, as well as the familiar FAT (DOS) format file names. NTFS uses the following naming conventions:

- NTFS file names can be up to 256 characters in length, including the extension.

- A period is used to separate the extension from the file name. The last period in the file name, which is followed by another character, is taken as the extension delimiter.
- NTFS file names preserve case, but are not case-sensitive. Thus, capitalization is retained but is not used as a distinguishing feature.
- NTFS file names can contain any uppercase or lowercase characters except the following: ? " / \ < > * | :

Short (DOS or FAT) file names are generated from the long format names according to the following rules:

- All spaces are removed.
- All periods—except for the last period, which is followed by another character—are removed. This final period is interpreted as the start of the file name's extension.
- Any characters that are not permitted in FAT (DOS) style names are converted into the underscore (_) character.
- The long file name—excluding the extension—is truncated to six characters, and a hyphen and number are appended.
- The file extension is truncated to three characters.

For example, the long file name

```
This is a long file name for. a document file"
```

would become "THISIS~1.ADO.

Help Files ▼ When a long file name is used on an NTFS drive, File Manager automatically creates a DOS-style file name that follows the eight-character-name, three-character-extension format. The short name permits Windows 3.1 or DOS-based workstations—which do not support long file names—to access the NTFS directory or file. If files using the long file name format

are copied to a FAT drive or saved using applications that do not support long file names, the long file name will be lost and only the short name will remain.

Windows NT works on both NTFS and FAT formatted drives. NTFS drives, however, are not accessible from Windows 3.1 or DOS. For floppy drives, only the FAT file system is supported, and any files copied to a 5.25- or 3.5-inch floppy will use the FAT (DOS) directory and file-name formats.

Naming Directories and Files on FAT (DOS) Drives

The FAT (DOS) file system uses the following conventions for naming directories and files:

- Names for directories or files consist of two parts: a name and an optional extension.
- The name and extension are separated by a period—for example, FILENAME.EXT.
- The directory or file name will contain one to eight characters.
- The optional directory or file extension can contain up to three characters.
- The name and extension may contain any upper or lowercase characters except the following: . " / \ [ ] : ; | = , ? * + < >
- Neither the name nor extension should contain any embedded spaces.
- The following names are reserved and cannot be used for files or directories: AUX, COM1, COM2, COM3, COM4, CON, LPT1, LPT2, LPT3, PRN, and NUL.

Help Files ▼ Windows NT works on both NTFS and FAT formatted drives, although NTFS drives are not accessible from Windows 3.1 or DOS. Windows NT permits embedded spaces—even on FAT drives—but file names that include spaces may be flagged as invalid by DOS.

▶ Using the Mouse to Select Files or Directories

To use the mouse to select a directory or file:

1. If necessary, bring the directory window to the top by using the mouse to select the window.
2. If the file or directory is not visible in the directory window, use the scroll bars in the directory or contents list to scroll to the appropriate section.
3. Click on the directory or file name to select it.

To use the mouse to select two or more items in sequence:

1. Select the directory window and scroll as necessary.
2. Click on the first directory or file name to be selected.
3. Press and hold the Shift key.
4. Click on the last directory or file name in the group to select it.

To use the mouse to select two or more items out of sequence:

1. Select the directory window and scroll as necessary.
2. Press and hold the Ctrl key.
3. Click on each directory or file name to be selected.

To use the mouse to cancel a selection:

1. Press and hold the Ctrl key.
2. Click on each directory or file name to be deselected.

To cancel all selections:

- Click on a single file or directory.

Help Files ▼ Before a directory or file can be manipulated, it must first be selected. Directories or files can be selected singly, as a group of consecutive items, or as multiple items not in sequence. In this fashion, you can select multiple files to be moved or deleted or operate on only a single file.

When a file or directory is selected, the directory or file name and the icon are highlighted if they are in the active window, or identified by a surrounding box if they are in the inactive window.

▶ Using the Keyboard to Select Files or Directories

To use the keyboard to select a directory or file:

- Press the Tab key to switch between the directory and contents lists.
- Press the up or down arrow key to move to a file above or below the current selection.
- Press the End key to move to the last directory or file in the current screen.
- Press the Home key to move to the first directory or file in the current screen.
- Press the PgUp key to move to the first directory or file in the previous screen.

- Press the PgDn key to move to the last directory or file in the next screen.
- Press any character to move to the next directory or file that begins with the selected letter or number.

To use the keyboard to select two or more items in sequence:

1. Use the arrow keys to move to the first directory or file to be selected.
2. Press and hold the Shift key.
3. Use the arrow keys to select (highlight) the remaining directories or files.

To use the keyboard to select two or more items out of sequence:

1. Use the arrow keys to move to the first directory or file to be selected.
2. Press and release the Shift+F8 keys. In response, the selection cursor will begin blinking.
3. User the arrow keys to move to the next item to select.
4. Press the spacebar to select a directory or file.
5. Press and release the Shift+F8 keys when you've finished the selection.

To use the keyboard to cancel a selection:

1. Press and release the Shift+F8 keys. In response, the selection cursor will begin blinking.
2. Use the arrow keys to move to the item to be deselected.
3. Press the spacebar to deselect the directory or file.
4. Press Shift+F8 you've finished the cancellations.

▶ Using the Select Files Command to Select Files or Directories

To use the Select Files command to select directories or files:

1. Select the Select Files option from the File menu.

Wild cards can be used in file specifications.

2. In the Select Files dialog box (see Figure 5.5), type the name of the file to be selected.

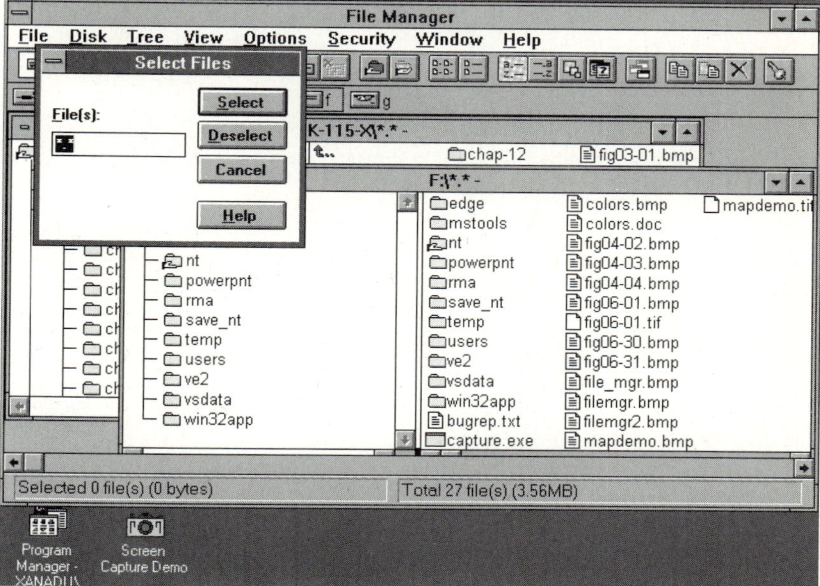

Figure 5.5
The Select Files dialog box

3. Select the Select button, or select the Deselect button to cancel a selection. The Deselect button cancels selection only for the files specified in the Files box.

4. Select the Close button when all the files desired have been selected.

▶ Creating a Directory

To create a directory:

1. In the directory tree, select the root directory where the new subdirectory will appear.

2. Select the Create Directory option from the File menu.

3. Type a new name for the directory in the Name box.

Help Files ▼ Refer to "Naming Directories and Files on NTFS Drives" or "Naming Directories and Files on FAT (DOS) Drives," earlier in this chapter, for the conventions required for naming directories.

> **HELP!** *You can create a directory anywhere—not just as a subdirectory to the current directory—by typing the full drive/path specification as well as the new directory name.*

Moving and Copying Directories or Files

▶ Using a Mouse to Move and Copy Directories or Files

To use the mouse to move or copy directories or files:

1. Ensure that both the source and destination are visible. The destination can be a drive icon, directory window, or directory window icon. If necessary, the Cascade or Tile commands from the Window menu can be used to arrange directory windows.
2. Select the directories or files to be moved or copied.
3. Drag the selected entries to the destination location. If the destination is a different drive, Windows NT assumes that you want to copy the selection. If the destination is on the same drive, Windows NT assumes that you want to move the selection.
   - To copy subdirectories or files to another location on the same drive, press and hold the Ctrl key while dragging the selections.
   - To move subdirectories or files to another drive, press and hold the Shift key while dragging the selections.

4. Release the mouse button. If the Shift or Ctrl key is being used, release these after releasing the mouse button.
5. To complete the operation of moving or copying directories or files, select Yes in the dialog box to confirm the operation.

Help Files ▼ When a directory is copied or moved, all files and subdirectories are also copied or moved. If the destination directory already contains a file or a subdirectory with the same name as a directory or file being moved or copied, a dialog box will request verification before the existing directory or file is replaced. Select Yes to replace the existing entry. If multiple directories or files are being moved or copied, select the Yes To All button to avoid further prompts.

If the destination is a drive icon, the file will be placed in the current directory of that drive.

On NTFS drives, the user must have permission to execute copy or move operations—a restriction that does not apply to FAT (DOS) drives. When directories or files are copied, ownership and auditing-information permissions are discarded and new sets of permissions are inherited from the destination directory.

HELP! *If the destination directory does not specify access permissions for files, only the owner of the file—the person copying or moving the file, not the original owner—will have access permission for the file. When either directories or files are copied or moved to a FAT drive, all permissions are discarded and are not replaced.*

▶ Using Commands to Move and Copy Directories or Files

To use commands to move or copy directories or files:

1. Select the directory(s) or file(s) to be moved or copied. Refer to the selection instructions, preceding.

   - To copy the selection(s), select Copy from the File menu or select the Copy button on the tool bar.

   - To move the selection(s), select Move from the File menu or select the Move button on the tool bar. The name of the selected directory(s) or file(s) appears in the From box in the Copy or Move dialog box (see Figure 5.6).

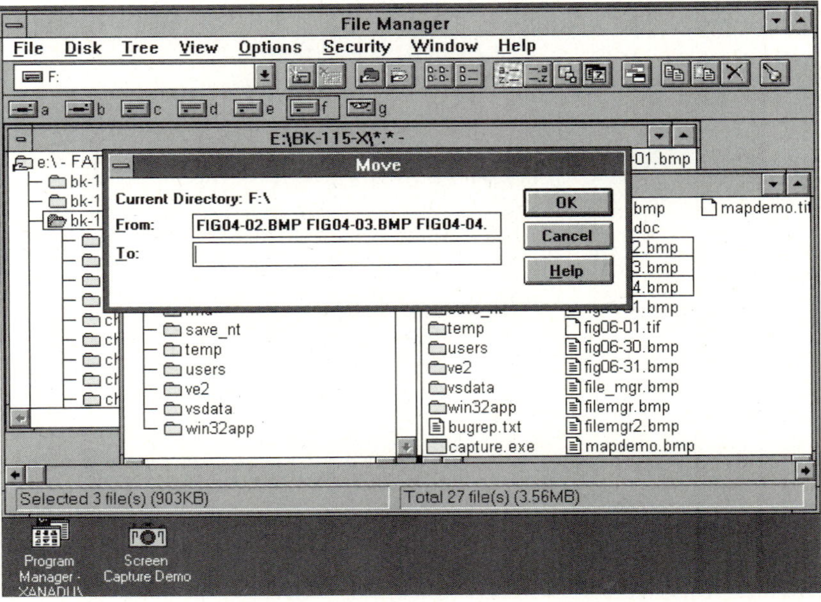

Figure 5.6
The Move dialog box

2. In the To box, specify the destination drive or directory. If a drive name is entered without a path specification, the active (current) directory on the destination drive is assumed.
3. If a new name is specified in the To box, the directory or file will be renamed when it is moved or copied.
4. Select OK.

Help Files ▼ You can use the From box to select a different file or directory by entering the name, including drive and path specifications, if appropriate.

Refer to "Using a Mouse to Move and Copy Directories or Files," preceding, for additional information.

▸ Copying a File to the Clipboard

To copy a file to the Clipboard:

1. Select the file to be copied.
2. Select Copy To Clipboard from the File menu. The file name will appear in the Destination edit box in the Copy To Clipboard dialog box.
3. Select the OK button.

Files copied to the Clipboard can be retrieved for linking to or embedding in other documents.

▸ Deleting a Directory or File

To delete a directory or file:

1. Select the directory or file to delete.

2. Select the Delete option from the File menu, select the Delete button on the tool bar or press the Del key.

3. The Delete dialog box (see Figure 5.7) will show the name of the selected directory or file in an edit box. This name can be edited, if desired.

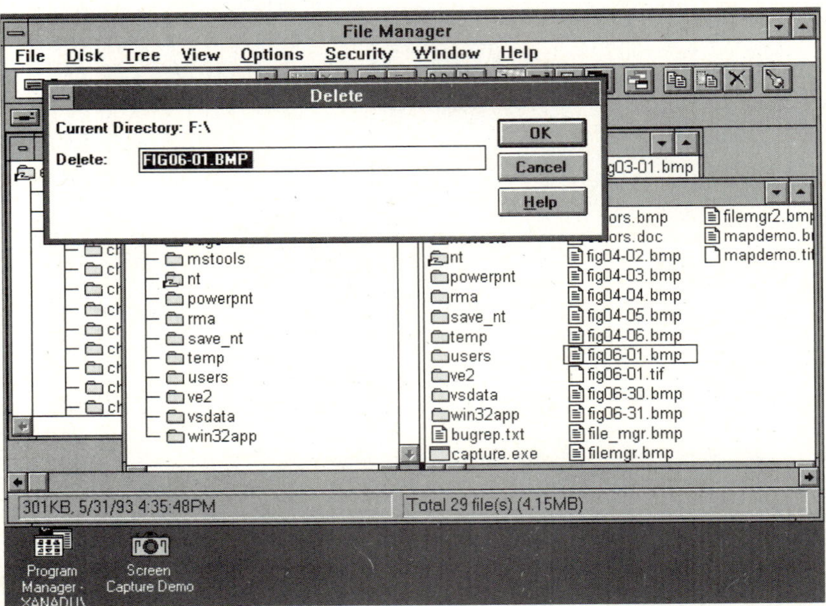

Figure 5.7
The Delete dialog box

4. Select the OK button.

5. Select Yes to confirm the deletion. To delete multiple directories or files without individual confirmation, select the Yes To All button.

6. To cancel confirmation messages, use the Confirmation command from the Options menu.

Help Files ▼ File Manager can be used to delete directories and files either singly or multiply. When a directory is deleted, all subdirectories and files contained in that directory are also deleted. On drives formatted for NTFS, permission is required before directories or files can be deleted. Once a directory or file has been deleted, the directory or file cannot be recovered.

HELP! *When entering path and file names using the NTFS long name format, if any directories or file names contain embedded spaces, be sure to enclose the entire string in quotes.*

▶ Renaming Directories or Files

To rename a directory or file:

1. Select the directory or file to rename.
2. Select Rename from the File menu. The selected directory or file name will appear in the From edit box in the Rename dialog box (see Figure 5.8).
3. To rename a group of files, edit the From entry using wild card specifications.
4. In the To box in the Rename dialog box, type a new name for the file. For multiple files, use wild card specifications.
5. Select the OK button.

Help Files ▼ To rename a directory or file, use a name that does not already exist in the destination directory. Only one file name can be specified in the From or

To edit box. However, wild cards can be used for both. For example, if you used wild cards and specified *.BAK in the From edit field and *.SAV in the To edit field, all backup files in the selected directory would be renamed as .SAV.

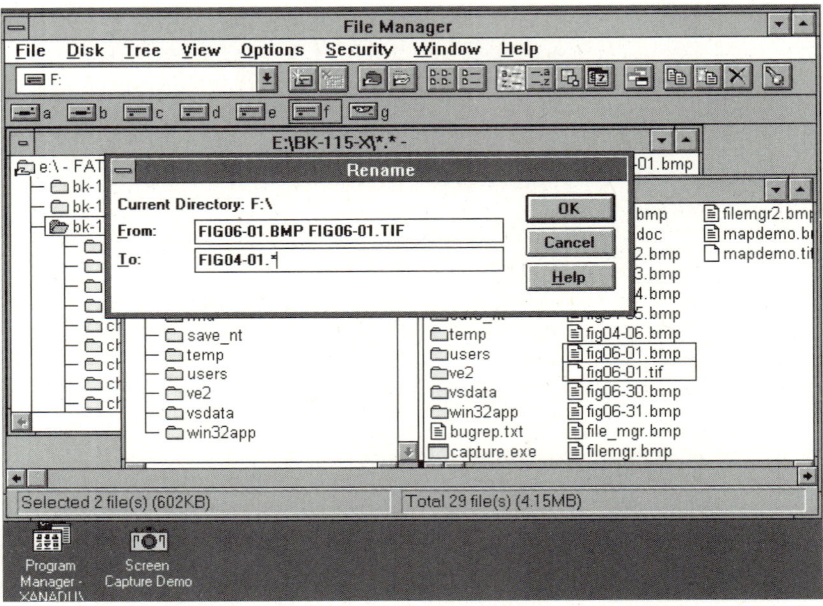

Figure 5.8
The Rename dialog box

On NTFS drives, permission is required before directories or files can be renamed.

HELP! *Use care when renaming directories or files. If a file required by the system is renamed or if its directory is renamed, the system may not function correctly or may not start at all.*

▸ Locating Directories and Files

To locate a directory or file:

1. In the File Manager display, select the start directory.

2. Select Search from the File menu. The Search dialog box (see Figure 5.9) will appear, with the selected start directory shown in the Start From edit box.

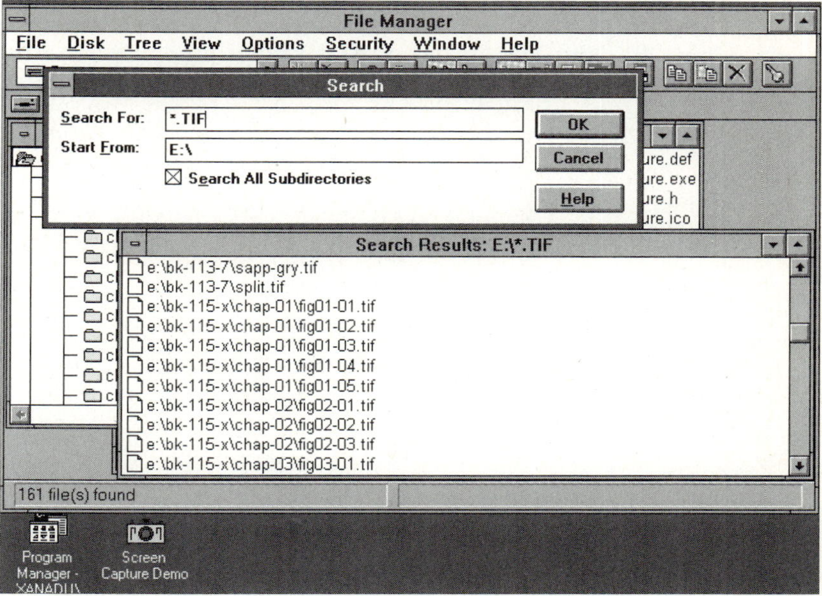

Figure 5.9
The Search dialog box

3. Enter the name of the directory or file in the Search dialog box. Wild cards may be used to search for multiple directories or files with similar names or extensions.

4. To change the start directory, enter a new path specification in the Start From edit box.

5. File Manager searches the directory specified in the Start From field, then searches all subdirectories of this directory. To exclude subdirectories from the search, clear the Search All Subdirectories option box.

6. Select the OK button to proceed. File Manager will monitor the search and display its progress in a dialog box.

7. To cancel search operations, select the Cancel button.

Help Files ▼ The Search command is used to find a file or directory. Subsequently, those directories and files can be selected from the Search Results window to be copied, deleted, moved, printed, or renamed. Details of files can be examined using the View menu options.

Other File Manager operations can continue while the search operation is executed as a background process. Use the Hide button to conceal the Search dialog box while the search is being executed. When the operation is finished, the Search Results window will appear, displaying a list of all directories and/or file names found.

If the drive being searched is modified during the search and the Search Results window is active or is made active, Windows NT will ask for permission to update the Search Results window. Select Yes to repeat the search on the modified drive.

Disk Maintenance

▸ Formatting Floppy Disks

To format a floppy disk:

1. Insert a disk in the appropriate drive.
2. Select the Format Floppy option from the Disk menu.
3. Check the Disk In box (see Figure 5.10) to ensure that the drive shown is the drive containing the floppy disk to be formatted. Correct the selection as necessary.
4. In the Capacity box, select the size of the disk to be formatted.
5. Optionally, enter a name in the Label edit box to provide a volume label for the disk.

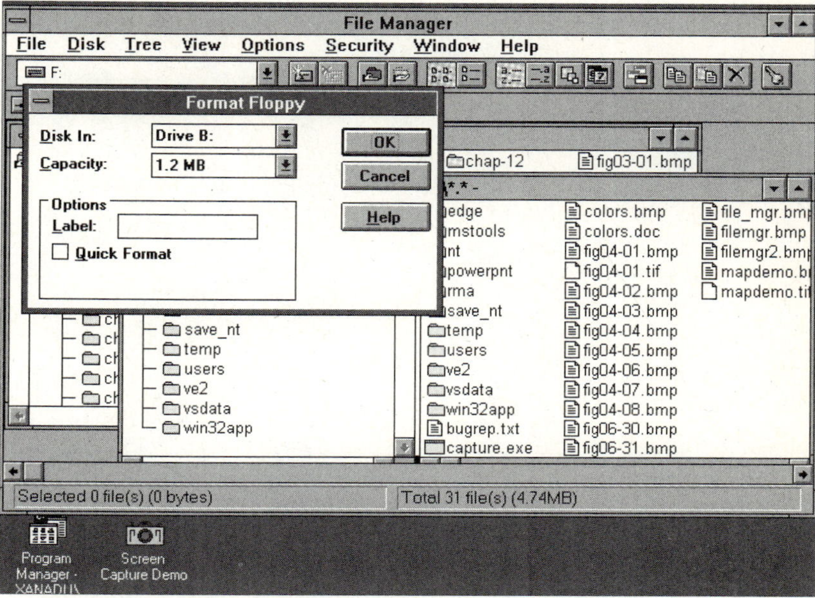

Figure 5.10
The Format Floppy dialog box

6. Select the Quick Format option if you want to rapidly reformat a disk that has been formatted previously.
7. Select OK.
8. Windows NT will request confirmation before the disk is formatted. Select Yes to proceed.
9. To hide the Format dialog box during formatting, select the Hide button.
10. To cancel formatting, select the Cancel button.

Help Files ▼ Disk formatting is carried out as a background operation. During formatting, File Manager displays its progress in a dialog box but does not prevent other operations from being carried out at the same time. When

formatting is completed, a dialog prompt will query whether another disk should be formatted.

Information on a disk that has been accidentally formatted cannot be recovered. Unlike the DOS Format utility, the Windows NT Format utility performs a disk wash, completely destroying any existing information that might be on the disk. Use care before formatting disks.

HELP! *File Manager must be running during formatting, although it can be minimized. If File Manager is terminated during disk formatting, the format option will be aborted without warning.*

All floppy disks must be formatted before files can be stored and retrieved. Floppy disks can also be formatted to remove lost files or to recover from other errors.

When formatting a floppy disk, Windows NT uses the FAT (DOS) file system, not NTFS. During formatting, all information is removed from the disk, new file allocation tables are created, and the disk medium is checked for unusable areas (bad sectors), which are then marked so that these areas will not be used later.

The Quick Format option deletes the file allocation tables and root directory but does not test the disk medium for bad sectors.

▶ Copying Floppy Disks

To copy a floppy disk:

1. Insert the source disk in the drive from which you want to copy.
2. If the system has two floppy drives of the same size, insert the destination disk in the drive to which you want to copy.
3. Select the Copy Disk option from the Disk menu.
4. If the system has two floppy drives of any size, select the letters for the source and destination drives in the Copy Disk dialog box (see Figure 5.11). If the system has only one floppy drive, this drive is assumed by default.
5. Select OK.
6. A prompt message requests confirmation before continuing. Select Yes to proceed.
7. To terminate copying, select the Cancel button.
8. To conceal the dialog box, select the Hide button.

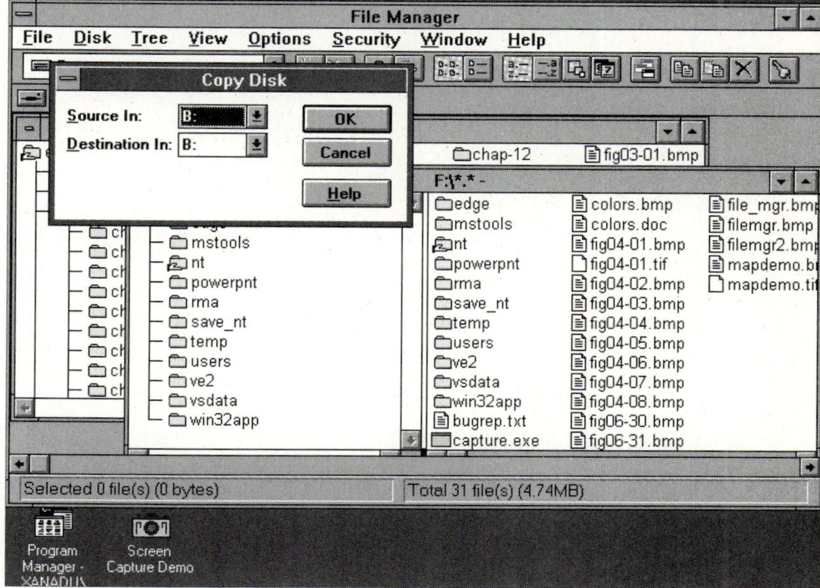

Figure 5.11
The Copy Disk dialog box

Help Files ▼

File Manager displays a progress report in a dialog box while the copy is being created. Since the copy operation is carried out as a background operation, other tasks can be carried out at the same time.

HELP! *When you use the Copy Disk command, you can only make a disk copy of a disk that has the same storage capacity as the floppy to which it is being copied. Either a single floppy drive or two floppy drives of the same size can be used. If you make copies on a single floppy drive, you will be prompted to switch source and destination disks.*

▶ Labeling Disks

To assign or change a volume label:

1. Select the drive icon for the disk to be labeled.
2. Select the Label Disk option from the Disk menu.
3. Enter the label text in the Label dialog box.
   - Labels on NTFS volumes can contain up to 32 characters.
   - Labels on FAT and HPFS volumes can contain up to 11 characters.
4. Select OK.

Network Driver Operations

▶ Connecting to a Network Drive

File Manager can be used to connect to and disconnect from network drives. Once a network drive has been connected, you can also instruct Windows NT to reconnect to the network drive each time you log on to NT.

By default, when you connect to a network drive, File Manager opens a new directory window to display the drive directory. This feature can be disabled by clearing the Open New Window On Connect option in the Options menu.

Users who are members of the Administrator, Backup Operators, or Server Operators group or who have been granted explicit permission can also connect to a network computer's root shares—for example, \\DATASERVER\C$.

To connect to a network drive:

1. Select Connect Network Drive from the Disk menu, or select the Connect Drive button from the tool bar (see Figure 5.12).

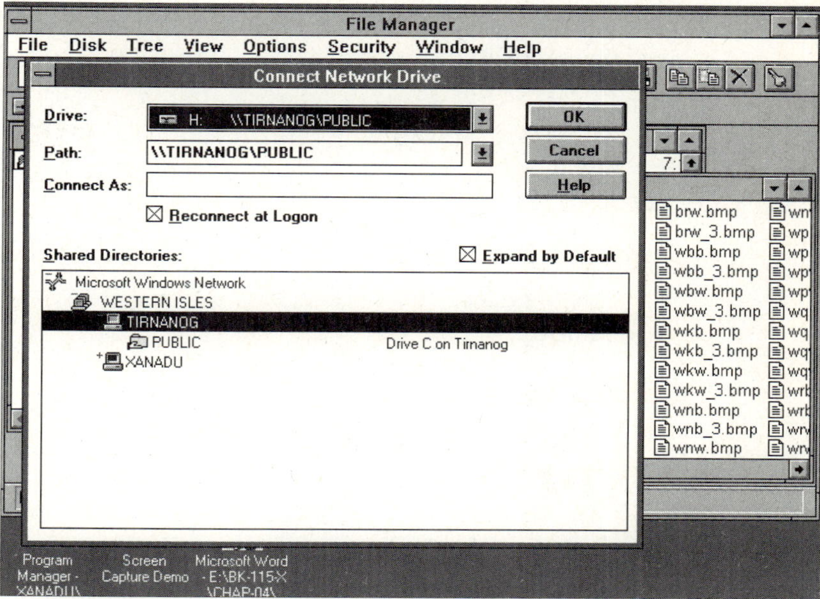

Figure 5.12
The Connect Network Drive dialog box

2. To assign the network drive to a local drive letter, File Manager displays the first free drive letter in the drive box. You can accept the displayed drive letter for this network connection or select a different drive letter.

3. In the Path box, select or type a network path consisting of a computer name and the name of a shared directory—for example, \\TIRNANOG\PUBLIC.

4. Optionally, in the Connect As box, enter a user name that is valid on the system being accessed.

5. By default, the Reconnect At Logon option is set, instructing Windows NT to reconnect to the shared directory each time the present user logs on. Change this setting if desired.

6. Select the OK button.

Help Files ▼ The Path box offers a pull-down list containing the previous ten paths/directories with which connections were established.

The Shared Directories list can be used to select a network path. In Windows networks, the Shared Directories list can be used to browse through domains, workgroups, and computers looking for shared directories. These options do not apply to all non-Windows networks.

Like directories and subdirectories on a disk drive, networks, domains, workgroups, computers, and shared directories are arranged in a tree. In the Shared Directories list, any item can be selected to expand the list. Thus, a network name can be selected to display the domains and workgroups, a domain or workgroup can be selected to display the computer names, or the computer names can be selected to show the shared directories.

Selecting the shared directory automatically fills in the Path edit field. Alternatively, you can enter a computer name in the Path field (preface the name with two backslashes, as in \\TIRNANOG), then select OK. The first shared directory on the specified computer will be displayed in the Path box and a complete list of shared directories will be displayed in the Shared Directories box.

A complete computer and directory specification can also be entered. Preface the computer name with a double backslash (\\) and the shared directory's name with a single backslash (\). See Figure 5.12 for an example.

The Connect As field is optional but does permit you to enter a different name to use for accessing the shared directory. By default, you are logged on to the shared directory under the same name used to log on to Windows NT, but you can connect using a different name. You might want to do this, for example, to gain greater access to the contents of the shared directory.

▸ Disconnecting from a Network Drive

To disconnect from a network drive:

1. Select the Disconnect Network Drive option from the Disk menu, or select the Disconnect Drive button from the tool bar.

2. Using the Disconnect Network Drive dialog box (see Figure 5.13), select one or more network drives to disconnect, then click on the OK button.

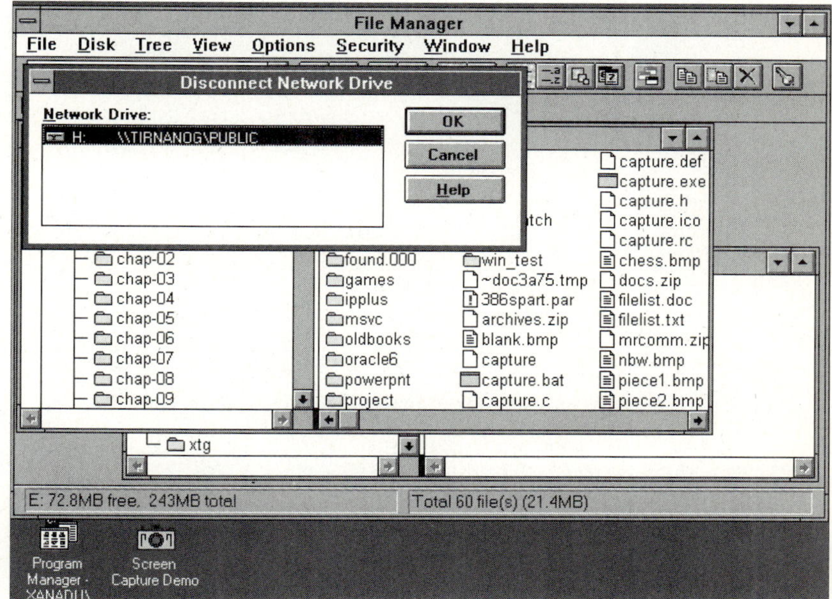

Figure 5.13
The Disconnect Network Drive dialog box

Working with Shared Directories and Files

▸ Sharing a Directory

To share a directory:

1. From the directory or contents pane in the directory window, select the directory to be shared.
2. Select the Share As option from the Disk menu or select the Share As button from the tool bar.

3. The name users need in order to connect to the shared directory is shown in the Share Name box. By default, this will be the name of the directory selected for sharing. To change the share name, enter the new name in the Share Name edit box. The share name can be up to 12 characters in length. If the directory you selected is already shared, the Share Name box shows the share names for the directory. You cannot give a shared directory a new share name; however, you can create a new share name by choosing the New Share button.
4. The Path edit box shows the local drive/path for the shared directory. To change the shared directory, enter the new path information.
5. The Comment edit box can be used to enter an optional comment directed to users who connect to the shared directory using the Connect Network Drive dialog box.
6. The User Limit box sets a limit on the number of users who can connect to the shared directory at any one time. By default, there is no limit. Change this, if necessary.
7. The Permissions button can be used to set access permissions for the shared directory.
8. Select OK.

Help Files ▼ Directories are shared to make their information available to others on the network. Before a directory can be shared, the network server service must be running. The server can be started using the Services utility from the Control Panel.

File Manager indicates that a directory is shared by displaying a shared-directory icon next to the directory name.

To share a local directory, the user must be logged on as an Administrator, Server Operator, or Power User.

Permission is required before a directory can be shared from a remote computer. If you are a member of the Administrators group or have permission, you can share a directory on a remote computer by connecting to the computer's shared root directory—for example, C$. When this is done, select the directory to share and proceed as with a local directory.

▶ Changing Share Properties

To change a shared directory's properties:

1. In either the directory or contents pane of the directory window, select the shared directory whose properties will be changed.
2. Select the Share As option from the Disk menu or select the Share As button from the tool bar.

3. If the directory has been shared more than once, in the Share Name list box, select the share name whose properties will be changed.
4. After the share name is selected, the following properties can be changed:
   - Under User Limit, set the number of users allowed to connect to the directory at any one time. Select either the Unlimited option

or the Users option and enter a limit or use the arrow buttons to raise or lower the existing entry.

- The Comment field can be edited to change the description shown to users in the Shared Directory dialog box (see Figure 5.14).

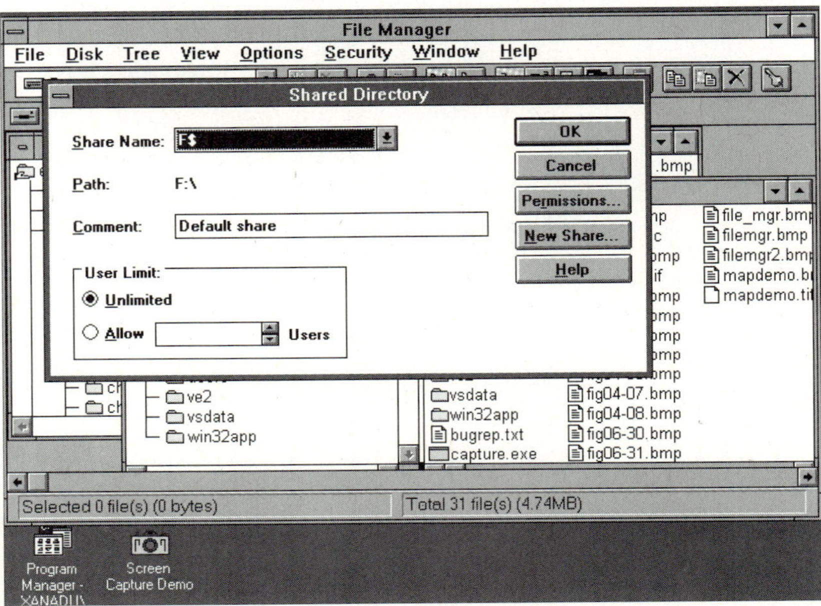

Figure 5.14
The Shared Directory dialog box

- Select the Permissions button to change the permissions for the shared directory.

5. Select OK.

Help Files ▼ To change a shared directory's properties, the user must be a member of the Administrators, Server Operators, or Power Users group. Administrators or Server Operators can also change administrative share properties.

Ending Directory Sharing

To end sharing for a directory:

1. Select the drive containing the directories by selecting the drive's directory window or drive-bar icon.
2. Select the Stop Sharing option from the Disk menu or select the Stop Sharing button from the tool bar.

3. The Stop Sharing Directory dialog box (see Figure 5.15) shows the name of the computer where the selected drive is located, and the Shared Directories On list box shows the shared directories on the drive. From the Shared Directories On list, select the directories for which you want to end sharing. If a shared directory was selected before the Stop Sharing option was selected, this directory is already selected.

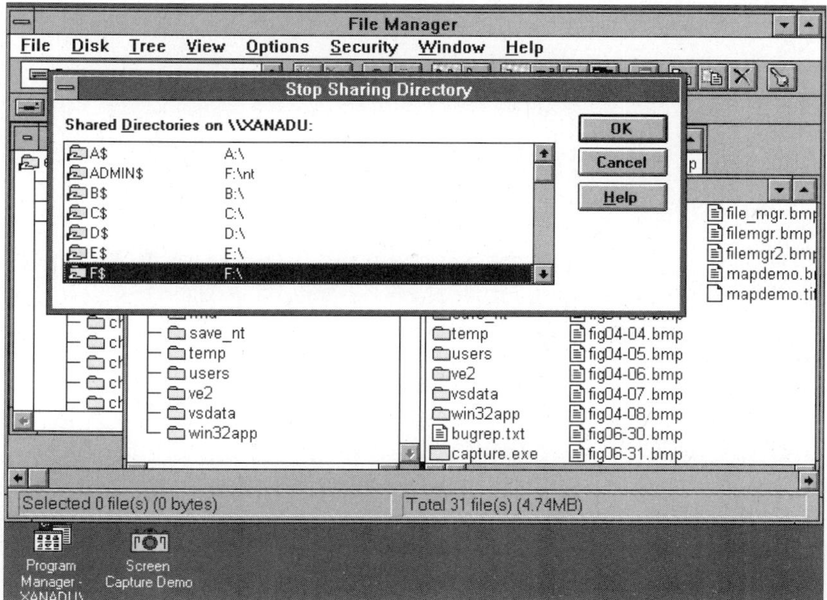

Figure 5.15
The Stop Sharing Direcory dialog box

4. Select OK to cease sharing the selected directories.

Help Files ▼

File Manager will issue a warning before sharing is stopped if any users are connected to a shared directory. If sharing is stopped while users are connected to the directory, users' data may be lost.

To end sharing for a directory, the user must be a member of the Administrators, Server Operators, or Power Users group.

▶ Viewing or Closing Shared Files

To view or to close a shared file:

1. Select the file from the contents pane of the directory window.
2. Select Properties from the File menu.
3. Select the Open By... button from the Properties dialog box (see Figure 5.16).

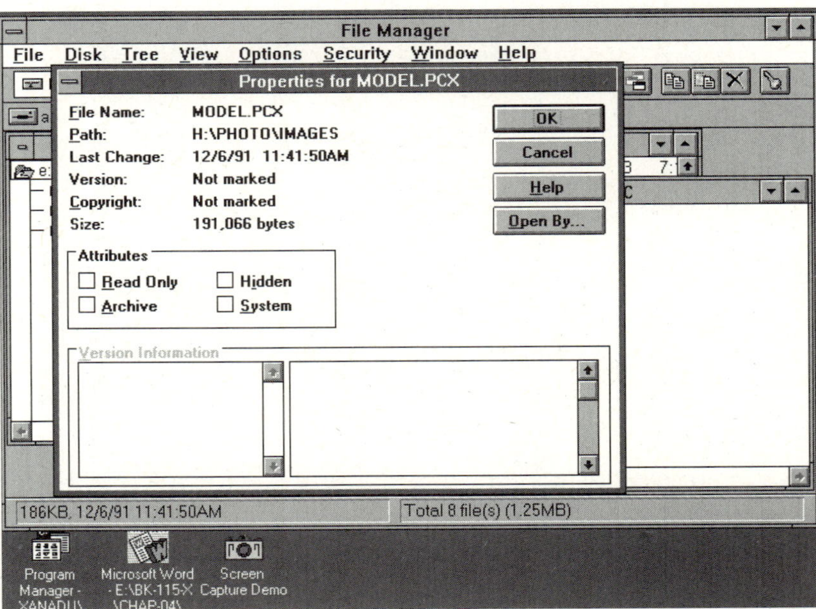

Figure 5.16
The Properties dialog box

4. To end access by one or more users, select the user name(s) and select the Close Selected button.
5. To end access by all users, select the Close All button.
6. Select OK.

Help Files ▼ Members of the Administrators, Server Operators, or Power Users group can view who is using shared files and can end access to a shared file. When access is closed to a file that is in use, changes made to the file will not be saved.

▶ Setting Directory Permissions

Permissions for a directory can be changed only by the owner of the directory or by a user who has been granted permission by the owner to do so.

To view or change directory permissions:

1. Select the directory or directories in the directory window.
2. Select Permissions from the Security menu or select the Permissions button from the tool bar.

3. By default, changes made to directory permissions affect both the directory and its files. These changes can also be applied to subdirectories and their files by selecting the Replace Permissions On Subdirectories option (see Figure 5.17).
4. Select a group or user name and select a permission type from the Type Of Access list box.
5. If you wish, customize directory and file permissions by selecting Special Directory Access or Special File Access.
6. Select OK.

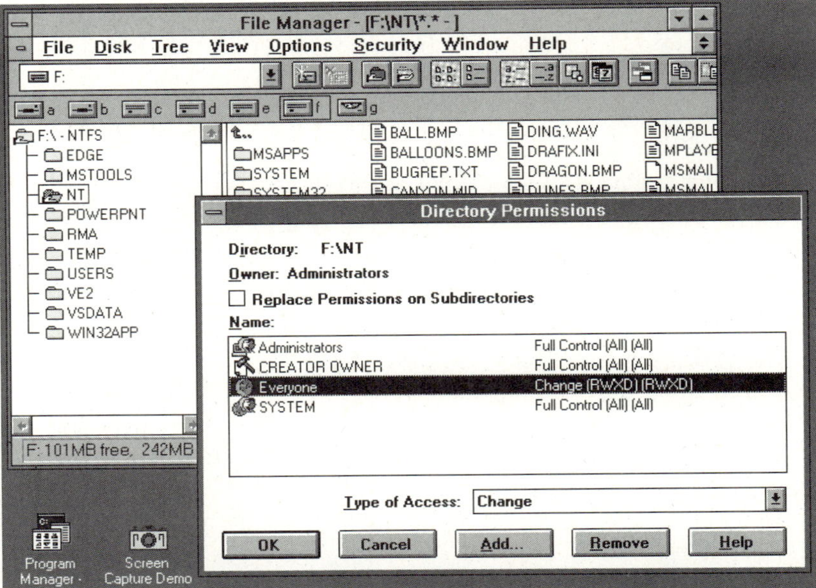

Figure 5.17
The Directory Permissions dialog box

Help Files ▼ Directory permissions can be set only on drives using NTFS. To set or change permissions on a file or directory, the user must be the owner of the file or directory, or have been granted permission by the owner to make changes.

File permissions specify what types of access are granted to a group or user. Files created in a directory inherit their permissions from the directory. When existing permissions are changed, existing subdirectories and their files do not inherit these changes unless the Replace Permissions On Subdirectories option is used. New subdirectories and files, however, inherit their access permissions from the directory.

With the exception of the No Access permission, which overrides all other permissions, permissions are cumulative. Thus, a user belonging to both a group with Read permission and a group with Change permission has Change permission.

When setting standard permissions, separate individual permissions are displayed for the directory and for the files in the directory. Thus, if Add & Read permission is assigned to a directory, the permissions displayed for the directory are RWX, signifying Read, Write, and Execute permissions for the directory, and RX for the files in the directory, signifying Read and Execute permissions.

▶ Changing Directory Permissions

To remove directory permissions:

1. Select the directory or directories in the directory window.
2. Select Permissions from the Security menu or select the Permissions button from the tool bar.

3. Select the name of a group or user in the Directory Permissions dialog box.
4. Select the Remove button.

To add a group or user to the directory permissions list:

1. Select the Add button from the Directory Permissions dialog box. The Add Users And Groups dialog box (Figure 5.18) will display a list of groups belonging to the computer or domain shown in the List Names From box.
2. Options in the Add Users And Groups dialog box can be used to display user names, identify users belonging to a group, or identify to which domain a group or user belongs.
   - Select the Show Users button to display a list of users on the selected computer or domain.
   - Select the group and select the Members button to view a group's membership.

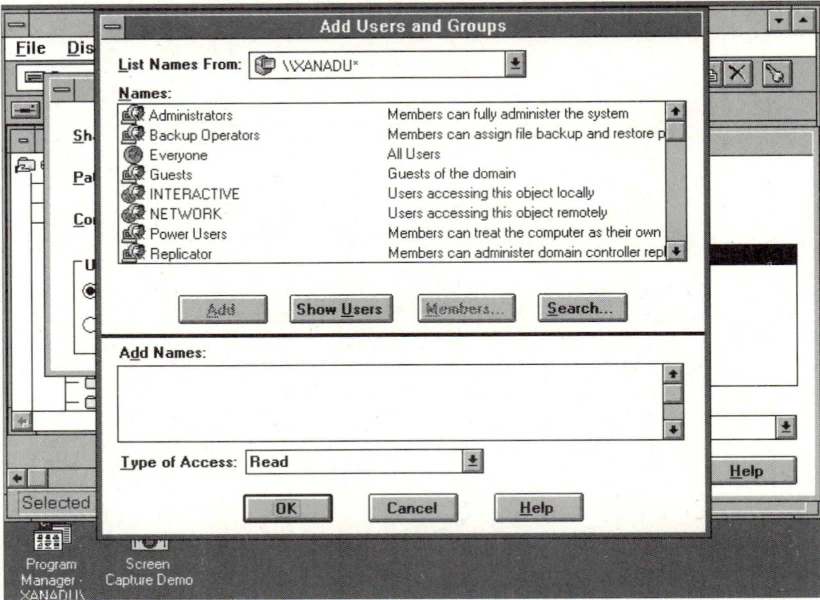

Figure 5.18
The Add Users And Groups dialog box

- Using the Windows NT Advanced Server network, global groups that are members of a local group appear in the members list. To view the names of the global group's users, select the group and select the Members button.
- To include a group in the Add Uses And Groups dialog box, select OK.
- To include only certain members of a group, select the members, then select OK.
- If the domain that contains the group or user's account is not known, select the Search button to locate the group or user's domain.
- To search domain memberships, enter the group or user name in the Find User Or Group edit box, specify the domains to search, and select the Search button.
- Select users and groups in the Search Results list box and click on the Add button to include these in the Names list in the Add Users And Groups dialog box.

3. To add groups or users to the permissions list:

   - Select group or users names in the Names list box, then select the Add button.
   - Double-click on the group or user name in the Names list box.
   - Enter the names of groups or users in the Add Names edit box, using semicolons to separate names.

4. Use the Type Of Access box to select permissions for groups or users in the Add Names list box.

5. Select OK.

Help Files ▼ Domains will be shown only if the computer is a domain member on a Windows NT Advanced Server network. The domains shown will be those that have a trust relationship with the domain containing the directory. Another domain can be selected by using the List Names From list box.

If a group or user account is not located on the computer or domain shown in the List Names From list box, the location must be specified. Enter the computer or domain name, followed by the group or user name, using a backslash to separate the names—for example, DATASERVER\TOMJONES.

▶ Setting File Permissions

To change or remove file permissions:

1. Select one or more files from the directory window contents pane.

2. Select the Permissions option from the Security menu or select the Permissions button from the tool bar.

3. Select the name of the group or user whose permissions will be changed.
4. Select a permission from the Type Of Access list box.
5. To customize the permissions for a group or user, select Special Access... from the Type Of Access list box.
6. Select OK.

To remove file permissions:

1. Select a group or user name from the File Permissions dialog box.
2. Select the Remove button.

To add a group or user to the file permissions list:

1. In the File Permissions dialog box, select the Add button.
2. The options in the Add Users And Groups dialog box can be used to display users, identify users in a group, or identify group or user domain membership. Refer to "Changing Directory Permissions," preceding, for details on access, directories, and domains.
3. To add groups or users to the permissions list:
   - Select the names of the groups or users and select the Add button.
   - Double-click on the group or user name.
   - Enter the group or user names in the Add Names list box, separating entries by semicolons.
4. Select the level of permission for the groups or users displayed in the Add Names list from the Type Of Access list box.
5. Select the OK button.

Help Files ▼ Directory permissions can be set only on drives that use NTFS. To set or change permissions on a file or directory, the user must be the owner of the file or directory or have been granted permission by the owner to make changes.

File permissions specify what types of access are granted to a group or user. Files created in a directory inherit their permissions from the directory. When existing permissions are changed, existing subdirectories and their files do not inherit these changes unless the Replace Permissions On Subdirectories option is used. New subdirectories and files, however, inherit their access permissions from the directory.

With the exception of the No Access permission, which overrides all other permissions, permissions are cumulative. Thus, a user belonging to both a group with Read permission and a group with Change permission has Change permission.

When setting standard permissions, separate individual permissions are displayed for the directory and for the files in the directory. Thus, if Add & Read permission is assigned to a directory, the permissions displayed for the directory are RWX, signifying Read, Write, and Execute permissions for the directory, and RX for the files in the directory, signifying Read and Execute Setting Special Access Permissions.

▸ Setting Special Access Permissions

To set special access permissions:

1. Select one or more directories, all files in one or more directories, or one or more individual files.
   - Select directories in the directory window from either the directory pane or the contents pane in the directory window.

- Select all files in one or more directories by selecting the files' directories either from the directory pane or from the contents pane in the directory window.
- Select one or more individual files from the contents pane in the directory window.

2. Select the Permissions option from the Security menu or select the Permissions button from the tool bar.

3. In the Permissions dialog box, select the name of the group or user to be granted special access. If no groups or users are shown, the directories or files selected have different permissions, and a group or user must be added before setting special permissions.
4. Open the Special Directory Access dialog box (see Figure 5.19) for the type of access desired. The responding Special Directory Access dialog box shows the granted access permissions based on the current standard or special permissions settings.

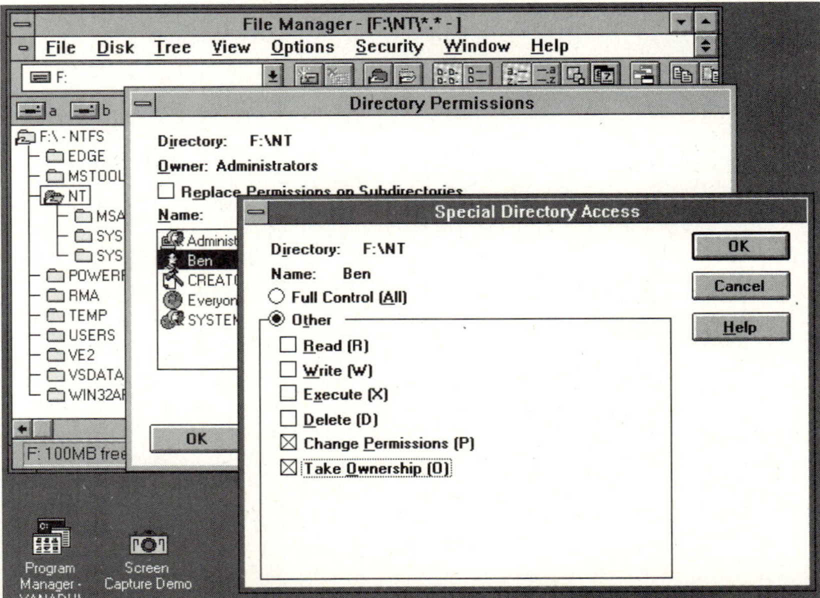

Figure 5.19
The Special Directory Access dialog box

- For directories, select the Special Directory Access option from the Type Of Access list box or double-click on the name of the group or user.
- For all files in selected directories, select Special File Access from the Type Of Access list box.
- For selected files, select Special File Access from the Type Of Access list box or double-click on the name of the group or user.

5. Select the check boxes for the special access permissions to be granted.
   - Access Not Specified can be set for all files in all selected directories. This cancels existing permissions and prevents files from inheriting permissions from their directories.
   - Full Control (All) grants full control and access.
6. Select OK.

Help Files ▼ Normally, standard directory and file permissions are sufficient to control access to directories and files. Special access permission is used to create custom permission sets on directories, files in directories, or individual files. Setting special access permission to a directory affects the directory only—it does not change the existing permissions on files in the directory.

▶ Setting Permissions via Shared Directories

To view or change permissions that were set via a shared directory:

1. Select the shared directory in either the directory or contents pane of the directory window.

2. Select the Share As option from the Disk menu or select the Share As button from the tool bar.

3. Select the Permissions button.
4. Select the name of a group or user.
5. Select a permission type from the Type Of Access list box.
6. Select the OK button.

To remove permissions set via a shared directory:

1. Select the group or user name in the Shared Directory Permissions dialog box.
2. Select the Remove button.

To add a group or user to the shared directory permissions list:

1. Select the Add button in the Access Through Share Permissions dialog box (see Figure 5.20). The Add Users And Groups dialog box will appear, displaying in the List Names From list box the groups on the computer or domain highlighted.

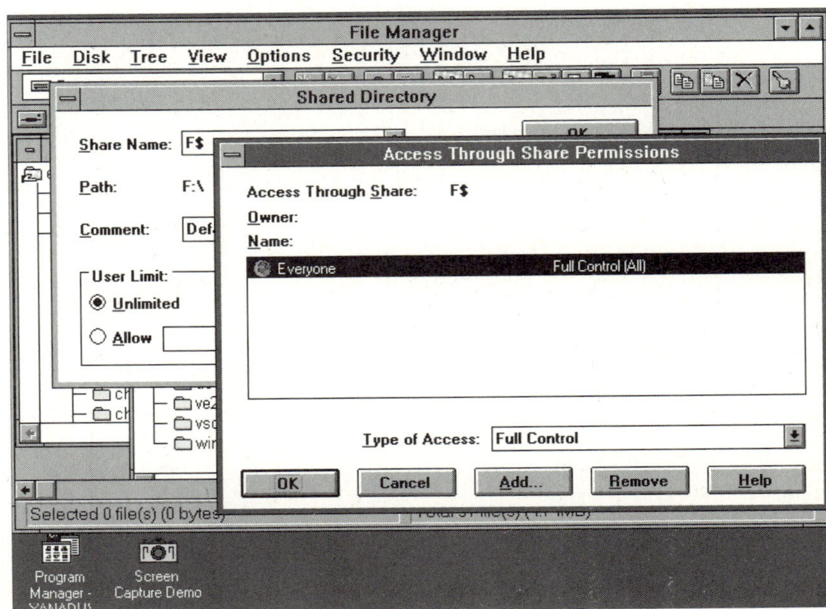

Figure 5.20
The Access Through Share Permissions dialog box

2. The Add Users And Groups dialog box offers options to identify users, users in a group, or the domain to which a group or user belongs. Refer to "Changing Directory Permissions," preceding, for details on access, directories, and domains.

3. To add users to the permissions list:

   - Select the names of groups or users to add and select the Add button.
   - Double-click on the group or user name.
   - Enter names of groups and users in the Add Names edit box, separating names by semicolons.

4. Use the Type Of Access list box to select the level of permission for the groups or users listed in the Add Names list box.

5. Select OK.

Help Files ▼ Users must be members of the Administrators, Server Operators, or Power Users group to change with shared directory permissions. Shared directory permissions can be set for directories on NTFS, FAT, or HPFS drives.

Cautions:

- Permissions set through shared directories apply only to access via the network and do not affect non-network access.
- Permissions set through shared directories govern access to all subdirectories and files in the shared directory.
- Permissions set through shared directories on NTFS volumes supplement the NTFS permissions set for the directory itself.
- Shared directory permissions specify the maximum permitted access.

Auditing Access to Directories and Files

To audit access to a directory or file:

1. Select the directory or file in the directory window.
2. Select the Auditing option from the Security menu.
3. To audit directory access, select the Replace Auditing On Existing Subdirectories check box. When this box is cleared, the auditing choices affect only the selected directory and its files.
4. Select a group or user name.
5. Select the events to be audited.
6. Select OK.

To add a group or user to the audit list:

1. Select the Add button in the Auditing dialog box. The Add Users And Groups dialog box will display in the List Names From dialog box groups on the computer or domain selected.
2. The Add Users And Groups dialog box offers options to identify users, users in a group, or the domain to which a group or user belongs. Refer to "Changing Directory Permissions," preceding, for details on access, directories, and domains.
3. To add users or groups:
   - Select the names of the groups or users to add and select the Add button.
   - Double-click on the group or user name.
   - Enter the names of the groups and users in the Add Names edit box, separating names by semicolons.
4. Select OK.

To remove a group or user from file or directory auditing:

1. Select the group or user name from the list in the Auditing dialog box.
2. Select the Remove button.

Help Files ▼ To specify auditing for directories and files, the user must be a member of the Administrators group and must set the audit policy to audit file, print, and security changes. The audit policy is set from the User Manager utility.

Auditing tracks the usage of directories and files by group or user. Provisions allow you to specify which actions to audit: successful, unsuccessful, or both. The information generated is stored in a file.

▶ Assuming Ownership of Directories and Files

To assume ownership of a directory or file:

1. Select one or more directories or files in the directory or contents pane of the directory window.
2. Select the Owner option from the Security menu.
3. Select the Take Ownership button. If multiple directories are selected, Windows NT asks if you desire to take ownership of all subdirectories and files in the selected directories.
   - Select Yes to assume ownership of the tree.
   - Select No to assume ownership only of the selected directories.

Help Files ▼ Initially, the creator of a directory or file is also the owner and grants permissions controlling how the directory or file is accessed and used. The owner of a directory or file can also grant permission to another user to assume ownership of the directory or file.

Alternatively, a member of the Administrators group can assume ownership of a directory or file but, as a security provision, cannot transfer ownership to another user, although they can change the access permissions for the directory or file.

Any user can examine the ownership of a directory or file.

Operating from File Manager

▸ Associating File Types with Applications

To create or change a file association:

1. In the directory window, select a file that has the extension to be associated.
2. Select the Associate option from the File menu. The Associate dialog box will appear.
3. The extension of the selected file will appear in the Files With Extension list box. If no file was selected, or to associate a different file extension, make a selection from the pull-down list or enter the desired extension in the edit box.
4. To complete the association, select the executable file from the Associate With list box.
5. If the appropriate executable file is not listed, use the Browse button to locate the desired executable file.
6. Select the OK button.

To remove a file association:

1. Select None in the Associate With file list.
2. Select the OK button.

Help Files ▼ A file's association with an application is established through the file's extension and the application's type. After an association is established, any file with the same extension can be selected to automatically load the executable and selected files. Once a file type has been associated with an application, File Manager will show a document-file icon next to the file name in the directory window.

Although a file extension can be associated only with a single executable application, an application can have more than one extension associated with it.

The initial application list appearing in the Associate With File Type consists only of applications distributed with Windows NT. Use the File Type Editor dialog box to create additional file types. For example, if you add Word for Windows, you can then associate .DOC files with Word.

▸ Using the File Type Editor to Create or Change File Associations

To use the File Type Editor to create or modify a file association:

1. In a directory window, select a file that has the desired extension.
2. Select Associated from the File menu.
3. Select the New Type button in the Associate dialog box (see Figure 5.21).
4. The file name extension of the selected file appears in the edit box of the Associated Extensions list. Select the Add button to add it to the list of associated extensions.
5. Enter a type description in the Description edit box.
6. Enter the executable application's name in the Command box or use the Browse button to select the application program and path.
7. Select OK to save the new association.

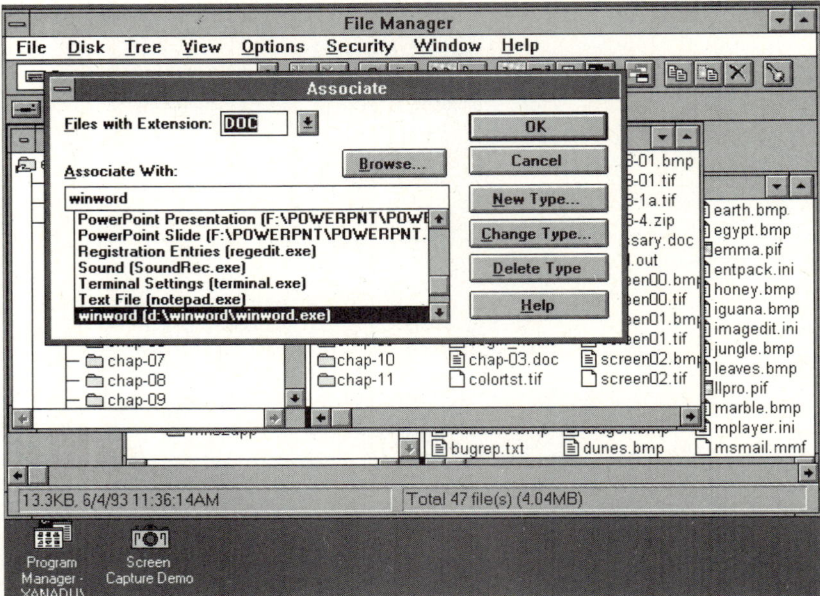

Figure 5.21
The Associate dialog box

▸ Executing an Application from File Manager

To initiate an application from File Manager:

- In the directory window, double-click on any executable file's name or on any document or data file associated with an executable application.

Or:

1. Select the file name in the directory window.
2. Select Open from the File menu or press Enter.

To start an application and open a file:

- Drag the data-file icon onto the application icon.

Or:

1. Select the application program file.
2. Select Run from the File menu.

3. In the Run dialog box, the program name appears in the Command Line edit box. If no application file was selected or if a different application is needed, a new application name can be entered together with the drive/path specification, if necessary, as well as any desired command-line arguments.

4. Select the Run Minimized option to start the application in a minimized state.

5. Select OK.

Help Files ▼ You can use File Manager to start applications by opening (double-clicking on) an application file (.BAT, .CMD, COM, .EXE, or .PIF file name extensions) or a document file associated with an application. Nonexecutable files that are associated with applications are represented by document icons in the directory windows.

▶ Printing from File Manager

File Manager can be used to print document (data) files that are associated with an application. To print a document file:

1. Select the document file from the directory window.

2. Select the Print command from the File menu.

Or:

1. Call Print Manager (from Program Manager).

2. Reduce Printer Manager to an icon.

3. Drag the document-file icon from the directory window to the Print Manager icon.

Help Files ▼ If the application does not support printing from File Manager or if the file type is not associated with an application, open the application in the conventional fashion and load the document for printing.

▶ Setting File Attributes

To change attributes for one or more files:

1. Select the files whose attributes should be changed.
2. Select the Properties option from the File menu.
3. From the Properties dialog (see Figure 5.16, preceding), set or clear the check boxes for the attribute settings.
4. Select OK.

Help Files ▼ File Manager can be used to change the attributes for a file, including attribute settings such as archive, read-only, hidden, and system. Attributes flags control access to files and the types of tasks that can be performed on files.

When multiple files are selected, any of the attribute check boxes may be grayed (disabled) if these attributes are not set consistently for all the selected files.

On NTFS drives, permission is required before file attributes can be changed.

File attributes can be viewed in the directory window by selecting the All File Details option on the View menu. Network file operations may offer additional options and attributes.

File Manager Customization

▶ Turning Confirmation Messages Off

To turn confirmation messages off:

1. Select the Confirmation option from the Options menu.
2. In the Confirmation dialog box (see Figure 5.22), clear the check boxes for whichever tasks you prefer to execute without interruption by confirmation messages.
3. Select OK to save your changes.

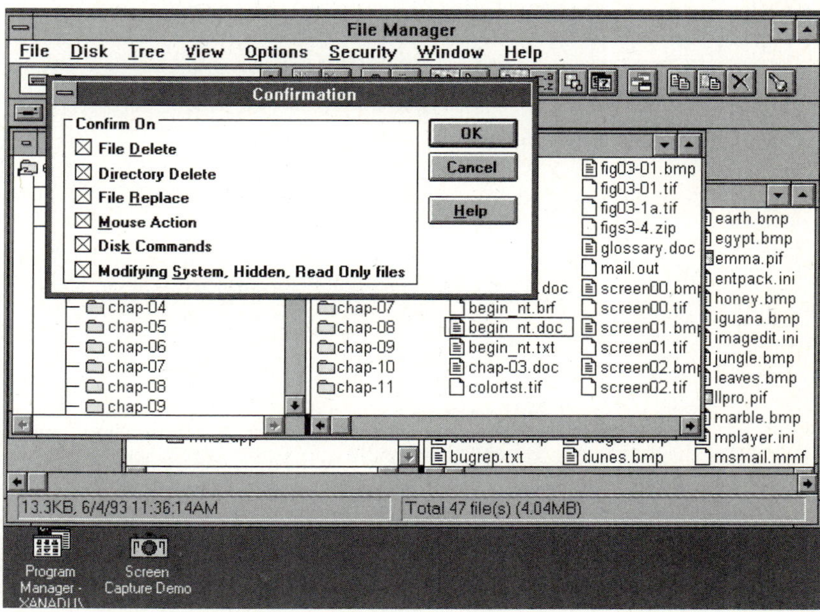

Figure 5.22
The Confirmation dialog box

Help Files ▼ Confirmation messages can be enabled or disabled for the actions of moving, copying, deleting, or replacing directories or files and for certain

mouse actions. If the confirmation messages are disabled, File Manager executes the commands immediately upon request.

HELP! *Keep the Directory Delete and File Replace confirmation options set. This will prevent you from accidentally deleting a directory with all its files and subdirectories or accidentally overwriting files.*

▶ Customizing the File Manager Tool Bar

Every command available in File Manager menus is also represented by an equivalent icon button, although not all of these are included—initially—in the tool bar. The existing tool bar buttons, however, may be rearranged or removed and new icon buttons added. To edit the tool bar buttons:

- Select the Customize Toolbar option from the Options menu or double-click anywhere on the tool bar background. In response, the Customize Toolbar dialog (see Figure 5.23) will appear.

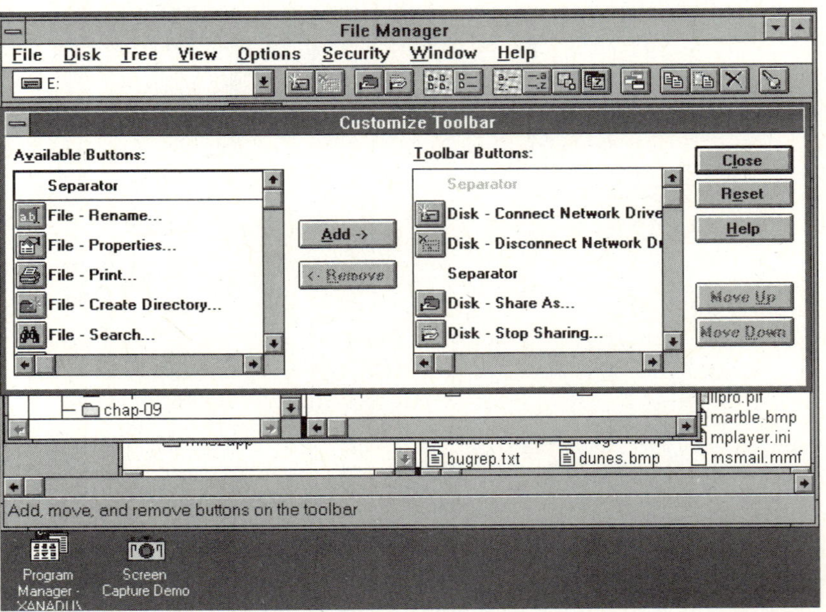

Figure 5.23
The Customize Toolbar dialog box

- To add a new command button to the tool bar, select the button desired from the Available Buttons list box (select the Separator to insert space between buttons and create groupings). The selected tool button will be highlighted while the Available Buttons list is active and will be shown by a box outline when the focus changes. Select the position in the Toolbar Buttons list where the new tool button should be inserted. Again, the selected position will be highlighted while the list is active or, after the focus changes, shown by a box outline. Finally, click on the Add button to insert the new tool control in the tool bar.
- To remove a button, from the Toolbar Buttons list, select the button or Separator to remove and click on the Remove button. Or, press and hold the Shift key while dragging the button off the tool bar.
- To change a button's position on the tool bar, from the Toolbar Buttons list, select the button or Separator to move. To move the button left, click on the Move Up button. To move the button right, click on the Move Down button. Or, simply press and hold the Shift key while dragging the tool button to a new location on the tool bar.
- To restore the default tool bar buttons, select the Reset button.

▶ Changing Fonts in File Manager

To change File Manager's font, typesize, or style:

1. Select the Font option from the Options menu. The Font dialog (see Figure 5.24) will be displayed, providing a choice of fonts, typefaces, and typesizes.
2. Select the desired font from the Font list box. The text displayed in the Sample box will appear in the selected font, style, and size.
3. Select a style option such as regular, bold, italic, or bold italic from the Font Style list.
4. Select a point size from the Size box. Point size determines the size of the characters on the screen.

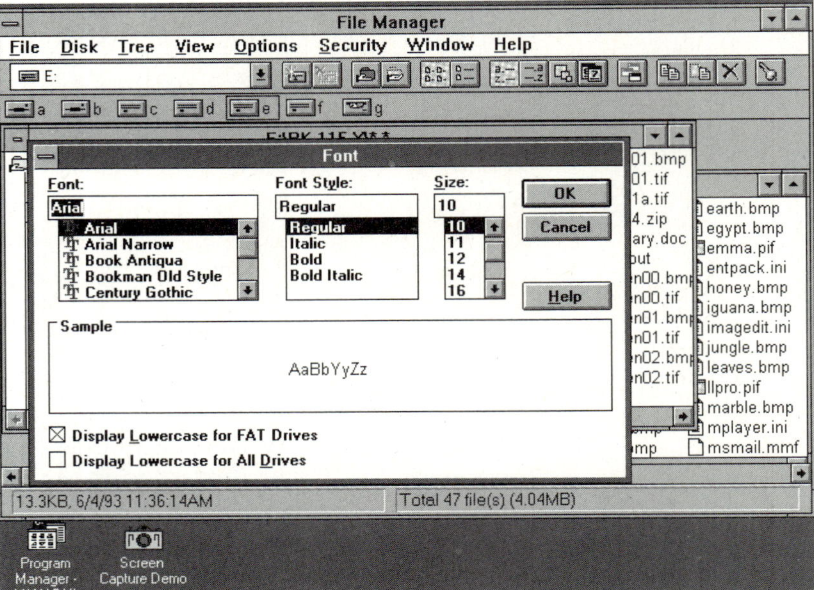

Figure 5.24
The Font dialog box

5. By default, both file and directory names are displayed in lowercase on FAT (DOS) drives and files on drives using NTFS (Windows NT file system) appear in mixed upper- and lowercase.

- Clear the Display Lowercase For FAT Drives check box to display FAT drive file names in uppercase.
- Alternatively, select the Display Lowercase For All Drives check box to display file names from all drives—both FAT and NTFS—in lowercase only.

THE RESCUE PAGES: File Manager

I've installed Windows NT and NTFS but now I can't find the drive when I boot DOS (or Windows 3.1).

Once a drive has been converted to the 32-bit NTFS file system, it simply isn't compatible with—or visible from—DOS and Windows 3.1. If you use a DOS hard-drive utility, you may find the NTFS volume identified as a non-DOS drive but, unless you go to the trouble of deleting, repartitioning, and reformatting it, the volume simply won't be visible.

Incidentally, if you are thinking of repartitioning a drive that contains an NTFS volume or two, don't do it from DOS—instead, use NT Disk Manager, which can see what it's doing and what it's working with. Besides, it's faster and simpler than the old-fashioned utilities.

How can I open two drives (or two directories) at once? Every time I click on a second drive, it replaces the first drive in the file window.

There could be two problems here. First, to select a second drive or to open a second window for the current drive, you need to double-click on the drive icon. However, if you don't hit the mouse button fast enough, the action will be interpreted as two single clicks, and the selected drive will replace the current drive. If necessary, go to the Control Panel and adjust the double-click time.

Second, if the file window (but not necessarily File Manager) is maximized, there's room only for one drive or directory to be shown. Look for a double-arrow button (a restore/minimize arrow) at the upper right, just below the maximize or restore/minimize arrow for File Manager itself. Click on this arrow to reduce the file window within the File Manager

window. Or, just go to the Window menu in File Manager and select Cascade (Shift+F4) or Tile (Shift+F5).

Refer to "Opening Additional Drives" and "Positioning Directory Windows and Icons" for further details.

I've got two file windows open: One of them shows everything, but the other shows only executable files, such as .BAT and .EXE files. Both windows show a wild card (*.*) for the file specification. What's wrong with the second file window?

Nothing, actually. The discrepancy is only in how the View/By File Type options are set for each window—it can be set differently for each. Check the By File Type dialog box and see if the second file window isn't set for executable files only. (The type category selection is independent of the file specification.)

I can see little pieces of the directory tree, but I need to see all of it. How can I make the entire tree visible without having to click on all the directories, subdirectories, subsubdirectories, ad infinitum?

Try the Expand All option from the Tree menu.

There have been security problems on our network. How can I prevent someone from copying a directory and contents to a directory where they have ownership and full permissions?

Permissions to copy directories are as important as access permissions for the files in the directories. If the files in a directory have restricted access, make the directory permissions restricted, too. There are no simple solutions when questions of security arise.

CHAPTER

HELP! Printers

As do earlier versions of Windows, Windows NT manages printers and print drivers, relieving applications of the tasks both of identifying the output device and of adapting to various codes and protocols required. Unlike other versions of Windows, however, Windows NT also has the ability to connect to network printers, to share a local printer, and to handle remote-printer administrative tasks. All these tasks, of course, are handled through Print Manager.

Topics covered in this chapter include

- Print Manager
- Printer properties
- Printer security
- Printer forms
- Document printing
- Options menu commands

Print Manager

▶ Using Print Manager

Print Manager is used to:

- Install and configure printers and printer drivers
- Control how documents are printed
- Connect to network printers
- Administer printers remotely

Help Files ▼ In Print Manager, a printer window appears for each printer installed on the local system or connected via the network. These printer windows show the current status of the printer, including current activity and pending print jobs.

Print Manager can be used to pause and restart print jobs, rearrange the order in which tasks are handled, or remove tasks from the print queue.

When several printers are available—as via a network—Print Manager can be used to locate and connect to a printer that is not busy. Through Print Manager, you can arrange network sharing for printers, set printer properties, and control access, including setting the hours during which a printer is available for use.

Print Manager also provides remote installation and access for print servers. Print servers, like individual printers, each appear in their own window. Each of these server windows shows the printers connected to that server.

Opening and Closing Print Manager

To open Print Manager:

- Select the Print Manager icon from the Main program group.

Or:

- Select the Printers icon from the Control Panel.

To close Print Manager:

- Select Exit from the Printer menu.

Help Files ▼ When Print Manager is called, by default, Print Manager's window (see Figure 6.1) appears in the same state as when it was last exited—assuming, of course, that the Save Settings On Exit option was set at that time. This preserves the sizes and positions of the various printer and server windows, as well as any window icons.

Creating a New Printer Service

To install a printer or driver, the user must be logged on as a member of the Administrators, Server Operators, Print Operators, or Power Users group.

To create a new printer service:

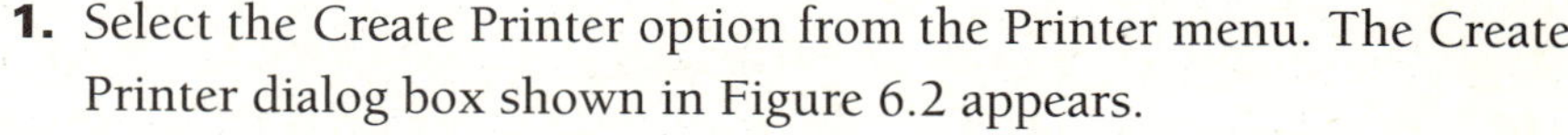

1. Select the Create Printer option from the Printer menu. The Create Printer dialog box shown in Figure 6.2 appears.
2. Enter a name for the printer in the Printer Name box. The entry may be up to 32 characters long.
3. Select the appropriate printer driver in the Driver box.

- If the printer is not listed, select a compatible printer type.
- To install an OEM (manufacturer or third-party) Windows NT-compatible driver, select Other in the Driver box, then specify the drive and path where the printer driver is located.

Print Manager - [Gutenberg - Paused]
Printer Document Options Security Window Help
Default: Gutenberg

Status	Document Name	Owner	Printed at	Pages	Size	Priority
	Microsoft Word - CHAP-06.I	Administrat	11:31 AM	17	223164 t	0
	Microsoft Word - CHAP-07.I	Administrat	11:32 AM	1	5660 b	0
	Microsoft Word - CHAP-08.I	Administrat	11:35 AM	1	4696 b	0
	Microsoft Word - PLATES.E	Administrat	11:30 AM	2	20700 b	0

Microsoft Word - CHAP-06.DOC Pages completed: 17

Program Manager - XANADU\ Screen Capture Demo

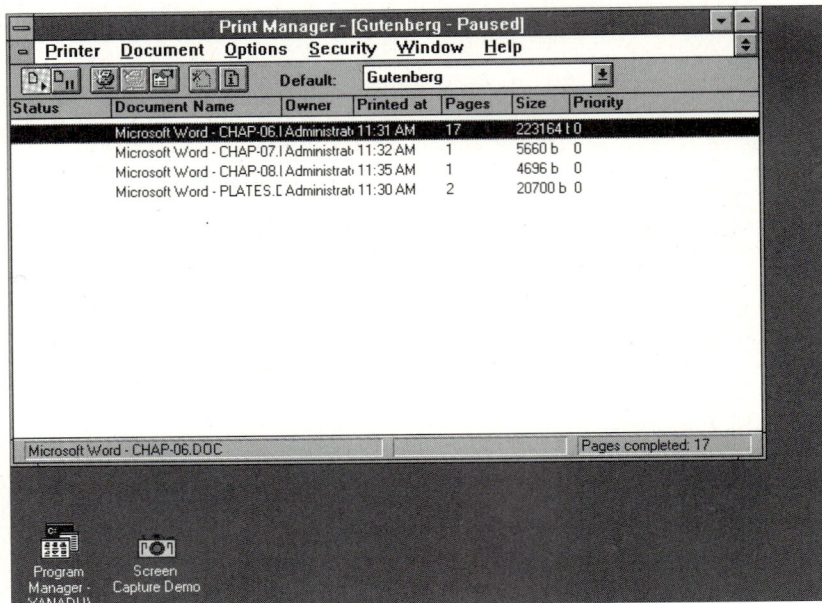

Figure 6.1
The Print Manager screen

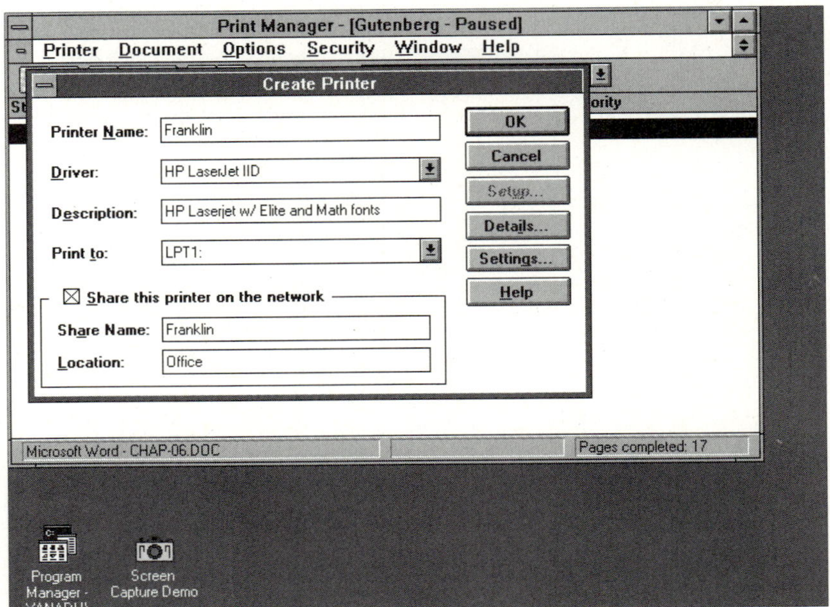

Figure 6.2
The Create Printer dialog box

4. Enter a description (optional) in the Description box. This description will assist network users who are adding the printer to their printer list.
5. In the Print To box, select the destination for printing output. (See "Selecting a Printer Destination," following.)
6. Select OK.
7. If the selected printer driver is not available on the hard drive, Windows NT will request a drive/path specification where the distribution disk can be found—showing, by default, Windows NT's original drive/path. If necessary, enter a new drive/path specification and select OK. Windows NT will prompt for additional disks, if necessary.

Help Files ▼ Print Manager's Create Printer option is used when:

- A new printer is physically installed on a computer.
- A new printer that connects directly to the network is installed.
- A printer driver is installed to print to a file.
- Multiple print drivers are defined, with differing properties, for a single physical printer.
- A printer is created for a network printer controlled by a LAN server.

When selecting a printer driver, if the specific printer does not appear in the pull-down list, the first option is to install a compatible driver. Consult your device's documentation for a list of compatible printers.

Selecting a Printer Destination

To select a printer destination for a printer that is physically installed on the local computer:

1. Select the appropriate port; for example, LPT1 in the Print To list.
2. Select OK.

To select a printer destination if the required port does not appear on the list:

1. Select Network Printer in the Print To list.
2. Select Local Port in the Print Destinations dialog box.
3. Select OK.
4. Enter the name of the port in the Port Name dialog box.
5. Select OK.

To select a printer destination for a printer driver that writes to a file:

1. Select File in the Print To list. (A prompt requesting a file name will appear when the driver is called.)
2. Select OK.

To select a printer destination for a printer controlled by a LAN Manager 2.x server:

1. Select Network Printer in the Print To list.
2. In the Print Destinations dialog box, select LAN Manager Print Share.
3. Select OK.
4. Select the print share from the Browse Network Printer dialog box or enter the name of the print share in the Path box.
5. Select OK.

To select a printer destination for a printer connected directly to the network (Hewlett-Packard):

1. Select Network Printer in the Print To list.
2. In the Print Destinations dialog box, select Hewlett-Packard Network Port.
3. Select OK. The Add A Hewlett-Packard Network Port dialog box will appear.
4. Select the network address in the Card Address box.
5. Enter a name for the port.
6. Select OK.
7. Use the Networks option in the Control Panel to install the Data Link Control protocol (required for direct HP network printers).

Installing a New Printer Driver

To install a new printer driver:

1. Select the printer's icon or window in Print Manager.
2. Select the Properties option from the Printer menu or select the Printer Properties button on the tool bar.

3. Select Other in the Driver box in the Printer Properties dialog box.
4. In the Install Driver dialog box, enter the drive/path where the printer driver is located.
5. Select OK.
6. Select OK in the Printer Properties dialog box.

Help Files ▼ When entering a network computer name, you must precede the computer name with a double backslash (\\) and the shared printer's name with a single backslash (\).

The Shared Printer list shows networks, domains, workgroups, servers, and shared printers. Double-click on any item to expand the display; for example, double-click on a domain name to display servers and shared printers on that domain.

▶ Connecting to a Network Printer

To connect to a network printer:

1. Select the Connect To Printer option from the Printer menu in Print Manager or select the Connect To Printer button from the tool bar.

2. In the Connect To Printer dialog box (see Figure 6.3), select a printer from the list or enter the names of a computer and shared printer in the Printer box.
3. Select OK. If the selected printer is shared by a Windows NT or Windows for Workgroups computer, the printer is now ready for use. If the selected printer is not on a Windows computer, Windows NT will prompt you for the installation of a driver. Select OK to call the Select Driver dialog box. Then follow these steps:

- Select the appropriate driver for the printer in the Driver box.
- Enter the drive/path where the Windows NT printer drivers are located.
- Select OK to continue. Windows NT installs the selected driver, then displays a printer window for the network printer.

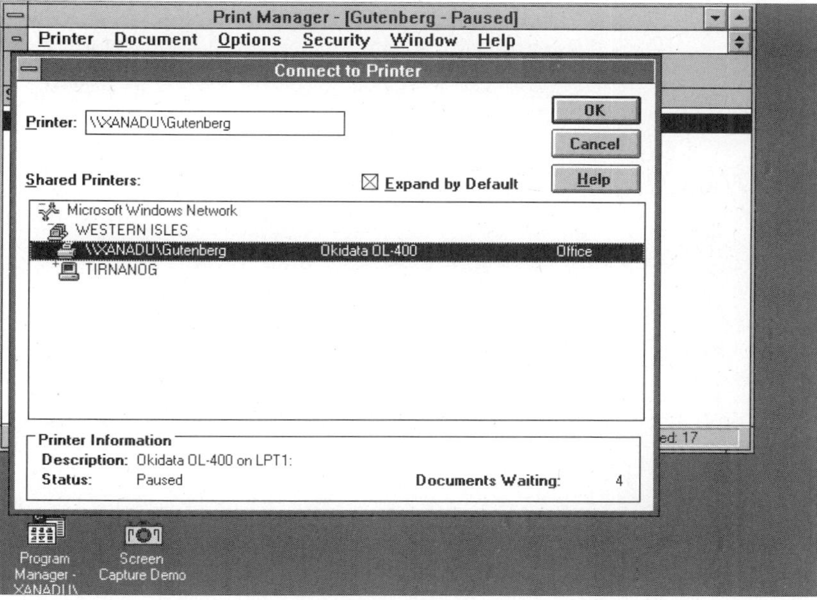

Figure 6.3
The Connect To Printer dialog box

Using a Network Printer

To use a shared network printer:

- Connect to the printer. The network printer will be added to the available printers in the Print Manager display.

Removing a Printer or Printer Driver

To remove a printer or printer driver:

1. Select the printer's window or icon.
2. Select Remove Printer from the Printer menu or select the Remove Printer button from the tool bar.

3. When prompted for confirmation, select Yes to remove the printer.

▶ Remotely Administering Network Print Servers

To prepare to remotely install, remove, or change a printer:

Printers can be administered remotely only by members of the Administrators, Server Operators, Print Operators, or Power Users group, or by those who have been granted Full Control permission for the printer.

1. Select the Server Viewer option from the Printer menu.
2. In the Select Computer dialog box (see Figure 6.4), double-click on a domain name to display the servers.

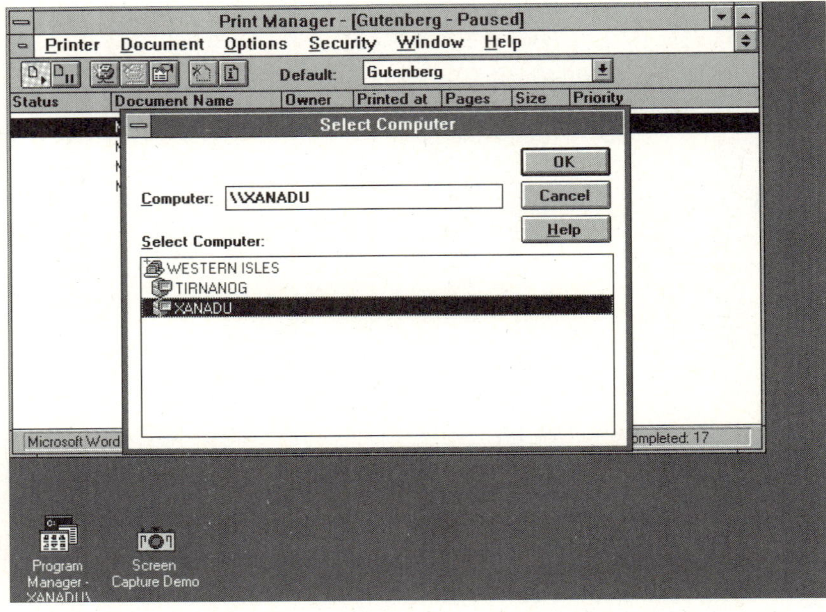

Figure 6.4
The Select Computer dialog box

3. Select the print server to administer.
4. Select OK. Print Manager displays a server window showing the printers on the selected server.

To install a new printer:

1. Select the Create Printer option from the Printer menu.
2. Proceed as for a local printer (see "Creating a New Printer Service," preceding).

To remove a printer:

1. Select the printer in the server window.
2. Select the Remove Printer option from the Printer menu.

To change a printer's properties:

1. Select the printer in the server window.
2. Select the Properties option from the Printer menu (see "Printer Properties," following).

Help Files ▼ Print Manager makes it possible to administer network print servers from a remote terminal, allowing you to install or remove printers or change the properties of existing printers.

Printer Properties

▶ Sharing a Printer

To share a printer on the network:

1. In Print Manager, select the printer's icon or window.
2. Select Properties from the Printer menu or select the Printer Properties button from the tool bar.

3. Select the Share This Printer On The Network check box in the Printer Properties dialog box (see Figure 6.2, preceding).

4. Print Manager creates a share name for the printer, conforming to DOS naming conventions, in the Share Name box.
5. Enter a description of the printer's location in the Location box.
6. Select OK.

Help Files ▼ Sharing a printer allows others on the network to connect to and use the printer. The server service must be operating before a printer can be shared. Use the Services utility from the Control Panel to initiate the server service.

Generated printer share names conform to the DOS naming conventions to permit DOS-based computers to connect to the printer. The share name can be edited, but DOS conventions should be followed for compatibility.

The printer's location description tells network users where the printer is located and, therefore, where their documents will be printed. Networks may be distributed over a wide geographical area, so these descriptions should be made as helpful as possible. After all, it can be rather annoying to realize—too late—that your hard copy is being printed in the next county.

▶ Setting Printing Options

To set or change printing options:

1. Select the printer's icon or window in Print Manager.
2. Select Properties from the Printer menu or select the Printer Properties button from the tool bar.

3. Select the Setup button in the Printer Properties dialog box to call a second Printer Properties dialog box, as shown in Figure 6.5.

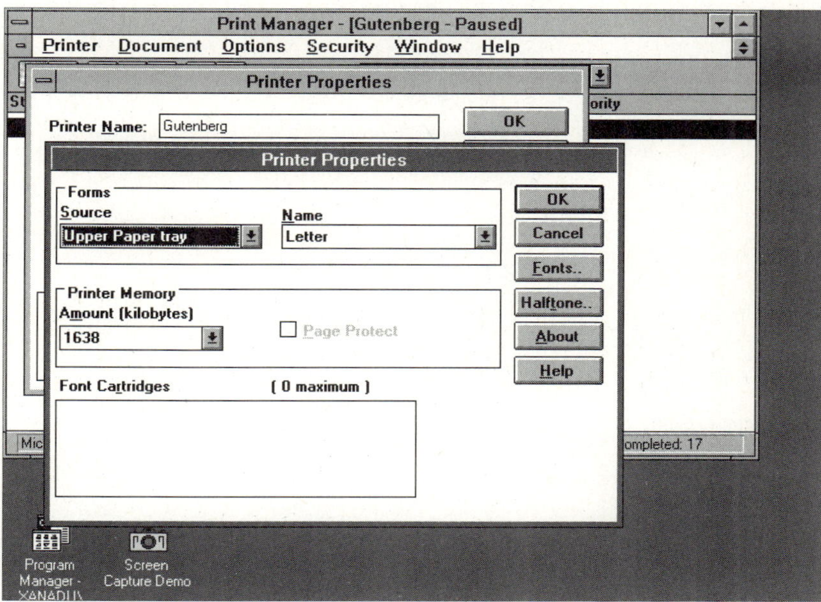

Figure 6.5
The (second) Printer Properties dialog box

4. Select the options desired.

5. Select OK.

Help Files ▼ Setup options are used to configure a printer driver so that the best use can be made of features supported by the printer. Available options and features vary, but typical setup options include

- **Font Cartridges**. Identify any font cartridges installed in the printer (this makes these fonts accessible to applications).
- **Fonts**. Set options for loading soft fonts and making font substitutions.
- **Forms**. Identify paper sizes and formats. Printers with multiple paper trays allow a different paper size to be specified for each tray.

- **Memory.** Specifies the amount of RAM available in the printer (not the computer).

▸ Limiting Printer Access Hours

To set printer access hours:

1. Select the printer's icon or window from Print Manager.
2. Select Properties from the Printer menu or select the Printer Properties button from the tool bar.

3. Select the Details button from the Printer Properties dialog box.
4. In the Printer Details dialog box (see Figure 6.6) use the Available From and To scroll buttons to set the period during which the printer will be accessible.

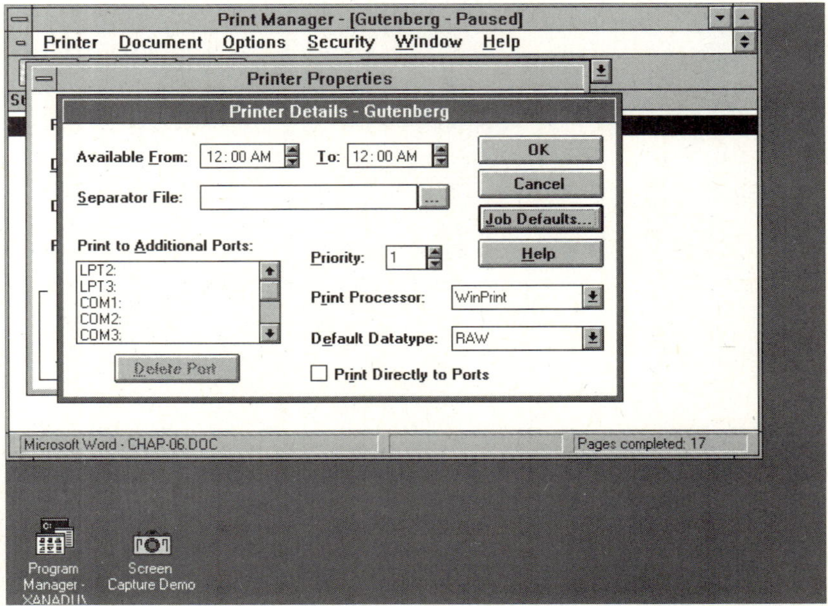

Figure 6.6
The Printer Details dialog box

For 24-hour availability:

- Make the start and stop time settings the same; for example, set both the start and stop times to 12:00 a.m. (midnight).

Help Files ▼ By default, printer access is not limited. However, you can set printer access hours to control the flow of work to a printer. For example, two printers could be created in Print Manager, both referencing a single physical printer. One printer could be given restricted access hours (say, off-hours) and used for low-priority tasks, and the other printer could be used without restrictions for immediate print tasks.

A restricted-access printer could also be shared, via the network, giving other users access to the physical printer but restricting execution of these tasks to specific hours. In this arrangement, such print tasks could be sent to the printer at any time—as long as the computer is on-line—but will be executed only during the period specified.

▶ Setting Printer Defaults

To set or change printer defaults:

1. Select the printer's icon or window from Print Manager.
2. Select Properties from the Printer menu or select the Printer Properties button from the tool bar.

3. Select the Details button in the Printer Properties dialog box.
4. Select the Job Defaults button in the Printer Details dialog box to display the Document Properties dialog box (see Figure 6.7).

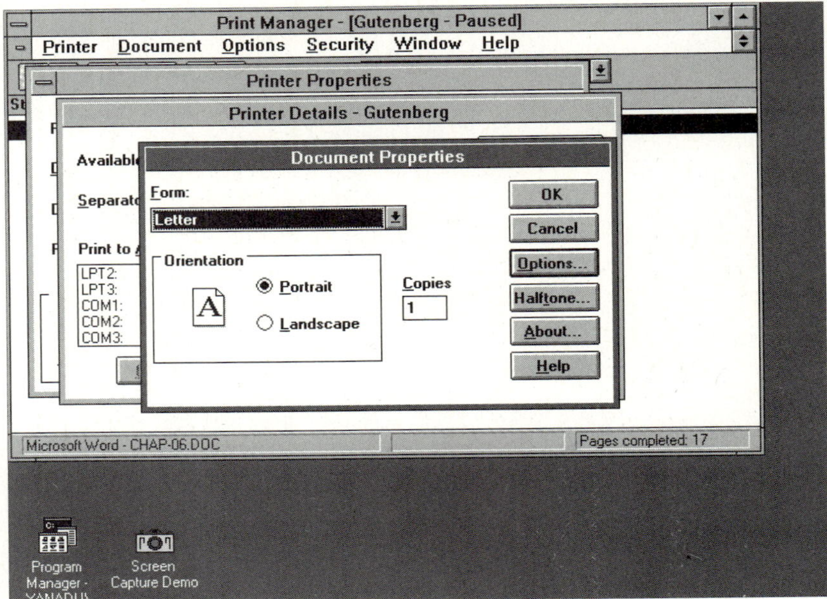

Figure 6.7
The Document Properties dialog box

5. Select the default options desired.
6. Select OK.

Help Files ▼ Printer defaults include such printer settings as the paper size, page orientation (landscape or portrait), and the number of copies printed for each page. Which options are available depend on the printer and, of course, the installed printer driver.

All printer defaults can be overridden by application settings or, for individual print tasks, changed to match the task requirements.

▸ Using Separator Files

To print a separator page:

1. Select the printer's icon or window from Print Manager.
2. Select Properties from the Printer menu or select the Printer Properties button from the tool bar.

3. Select the Details button in the Printer Properties dialog box.
4. In the Printer Details dialog box (refer back to Figure 6.6), select the Browse button (it's next to the Separator File box) and use the Select Separator Page dialog box (see Figure 6.8) to select a separator file. Alternatively, enter the name of the separator file, including the path specification, in the Separator File box.

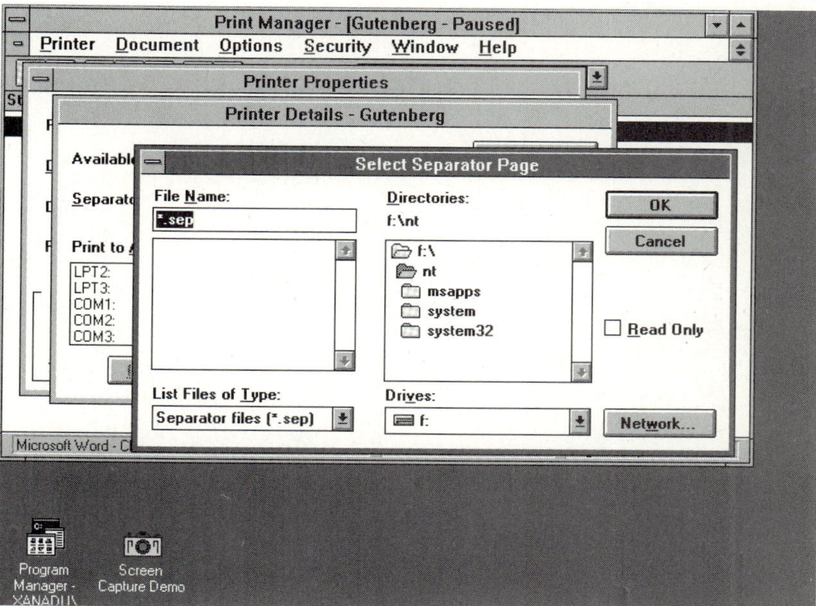

Figure 6.8
The Select Separator Page dialog box

Help Files ▼ Separator files are used for a variety of purposes, including

- To create a cover page at the beginning of a document, making it easy to locate in a stack of documents.
- To switch the printer between PostScript and PCL formats.
- To identify the owner of a printed document or to provide routing instructions for delivery.

Separator files provided by Windows NT include

- DEFAULT.SEP, which prints a page before each document (PCL compatible, not editable).
- PSLANMAN.SEP, which prints a page before each document (PostScript compatible, editable).
- PCL.SEP, which switches a printer to PCL format (editable).
- PSCRIPT.SEP, which switches printer to PostScript format (editable).

Custom separator files can also be created and used by Print Manager.

Setting Printer Task Priorities

To set or change printer task priorities:

1. Select the printer's icon or window from Print Manager.
2. Select Properties from the Printer menu or select the Printer Properties button from the tool bar.

3. Select the Details button from the Printer Properties dialog box.

4. In the Printer Details dialog box, select a priority from 1 (lowest) to 99 (highest).

Help Files ▼ Priority settings are used to control which documents sent to a printer are printed first. For example, if a physical printer is shared via a network, two virtual printers (drivers) could be installed, each with its own priority. The lower-priority printer could then be shared over the network, reserving the higher-priority printer for your own use, thus ensuring that local print jobs would be handled first.

▶ Creating a Printer Pool

To create a printer pool:

1. Select the printer's icon or window from Print Manager.
2. Select Properties from the Printer menu or select the Printer Properties button from the tool bar.

3. Select the Details button from the Printer Properties dialog box to call the Printer Details dialog box.
4. From the Print To Additional Ports box, select port names that correspond to the ports where printers are connected. If the required ports do not appear in the list, these can be added.

To add a printer port:

1. In the Printer Properties dialog box, select Network Printer in the Print To box.

2. Select Local Port from the Print Destinations dialog box.
3. Enter the name of the port to add in the Enter A Port Name box.
4. Select OK.

Help Files ▼ Pooling permits multiple printers connected to a single computer to be treated by network users as if these were, collectively, a single network printer. Each print job directed to the pooled printer is assigned by the network to one of the physical printers, sharing the work load among the units. Of course, for consistency, all printers in the pool should have the same capabilities. This is not, however, a requirement.

When a document is sent to the pool, the job is allocated to the first available printer.

▶ Bypassing the Print Spooler

To bypass the print spooler and print directly to a port:

1. Select the printer's icon or window from Print Manager.
2. Select Properties from the Printer menu or select the Printer Properties button from the tool bar.

3. Select the Details button from the Printer Properties dialog box to call the Printer Details dialog box (see Figure 6.6, preceding).
4. Select the Print Directly To Ports check box.

Help Files ▼ By default, Print Manager first sends all documents to a spool file on the hard drive, and then spools the material to the printer. This permits an application to print rapidly by outputting to the print spooler, while freeing the application to return to other tasks as the actual printing is handled in the background.

You can bypass spooling by sending output directly to the printer, but this will force the application to wait until printing is completed before carrying out any other tasks.

▶ Selecting a Print Processor or Datatype

To select a print processor or datatype:

1. Select the printer's icon or window from Print Manager.
2. Select Properties from the Printer menu or select the Printer Properties button from the tool bar.

3. Select the Details button from the Printer Properties dialog box to call the Printer Details dialog box.
4. Select the processor file name in the Print Processor box.
5. Select a datatype in the Default Datatype box.

Help Files ▼ Windows NT supports ASCII, Journal, and Raw data types, but the user probably won't need to change either the default print processor or the datatype. These options are provided principally for the benefit of specialized applications that may need to alter the printing process. Such applications may request custom printer drivers for their own use and may specify the print processor and datatypes to be used by the printer driver.

▶ Setting Printer Timeouts

To set printer timeout options:

1. Select the printer's icon or window from Print Manager.
2. Select Properties from the Printer menu or select the Printer Properties button from the tool bar.

3. Select the Settings button from the Printer Properties dialog box.
4. Set the number of seconds in the Transmission Retry box (see Figure 6.9).
5. Select OK.

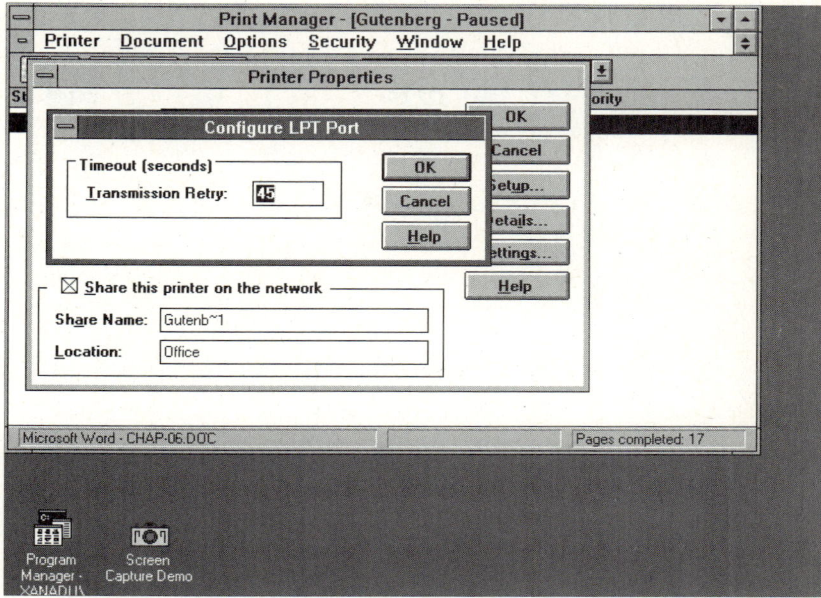

Figure 6.9
The Configure LPT Port dialog box

Help Files ▼ The Transmission Retry setting governs the amount of time that Print Manager waits for a printer to accept additional data and, therefore, the time elapsed before Print Manager notifies the user that the printer is not responding. This setting is valid only for printers connected to a parallel port—such as LPT1. Timeout settings affect not only the selected printer, but also any other local printers using the same printer driver.

Printer Security

▶ Setting and Changing Printer Permissions

To set or change printer permissions:

1. Select the printer's icon or window from Print Manager.
2. Select Permissions from the Security menu to call the Printer Permissions dialog box (see Figure 6.10).

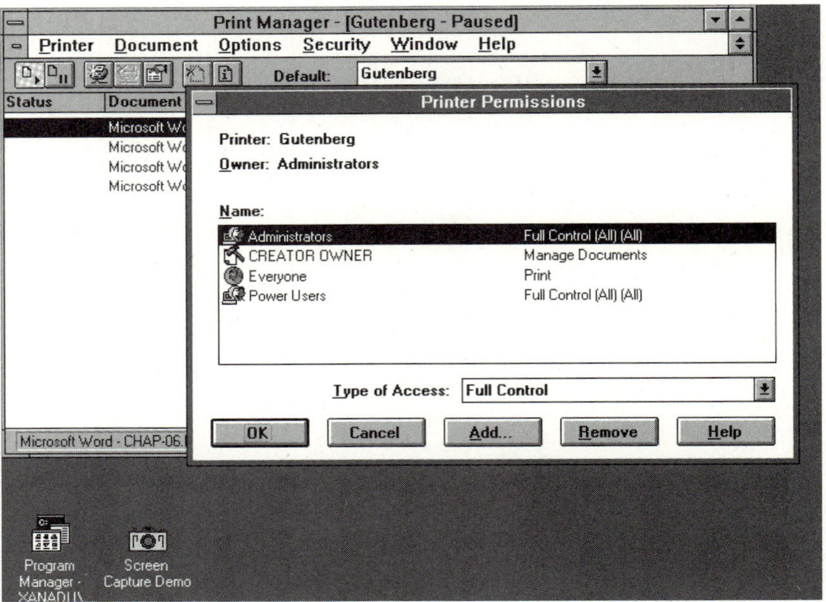

Figure 6.10
The Printer Permissions dialog box

3. Select the name of a group or user.
4. Select permissions from the Type Of Access box.
5. Select OK.

▶ Removing Printer Permissions

To remove access permissions for a printer:

1. Select the printer's icon or window from Print Manager.
2. Select Permissions from the Security menu to call the Printer Permissions dialog box.
3. Select the name of a group or user.
4. Select the Remove button.

▶ Adding Groups or Users to a Printer's Permissions List

To add a group or user to a printer's permissions list:

1. Select the printer's icon or window from Print Manager.
2. Select Permissions from the Security menu to call the Printer Permissions dialog box.
3. Select the Add button.
4. Use the List Names From box to select another domain or computer. The Add Users And Groups dialog box displays a list of the groups on the computer or domain selected.
5. Use the Add Users And Groups dialog box to identify users, identify users in a group, or identify the domain where a group or user belong.
   - Select the Show Users button for the names of users on the current computer or domain.
   - Select a group and select the Members button for the names of the group's members. Members are listed in a separate dialog box.
   - On a Windows NT Advanced Server network, global groups that are members of a local group will appear on the members list. To list a global group's members, select the group and select the Members button.

- To include a group in the Add Users And Groups dialog box, select OK.
- To include individuals, select entries from the displayed list and select OK.

6. Add groups or users to the permissions list:
   - Select groups or users and select the Add button.
   - Double-click on the name of group or user.
   - Enter the names of groups and users in the Add Names box, separating names by a semicolon.
   - If the group or user's account is not located on the computer or domain shown in the List Names In box, specify the location by giving the computer or domain name followed by the group or user name, separating the locations and names by a backslash.
7. Use the Type Of Access box to select the permission for the groups or users listed in the Add box.
8. Select OK.

To add a group or user on a Windows NT Advanced Server network:

1. Select the Search button to find the domain of a group or user.
2. In the Find Account dialog box, enter the name of the group or user in the Find User Or Group box.
3. Specify the domain(s) to search.
4. Select the Search button.
5. Select groups or users in the Search Results box.
6. Select the Add button to include the groups or users in the Add Users And Groups dialog box.

Help Files ▼ Printer permissions are used to secure access to printers. Each permission identifies the access permitted to a group or user. For example, with Print permission, documents can be printed but printer properties can not be altered.

Only the printer's owner or a user granted Full Control permission can change the permissions on a printer.

Except for the No Access permission, which overrides all other permissions, all permissions are cumulative. Thus, a user who belongs to two groups, one with Print permission and one with the more privileged Manage Documents permission, has Manage Documents permission. If permission for either group is changed to No Access, the No Access permission overrides all other permissions and the user will no longer have any access to the printer.

Print permission, by default, grants a user control over the printing of his or her own documents. The creator of a document is given the permissions granted to the Creator Owner. Permissions granted to the Creator Owner should not be changed nor should the Creator Owner be removed from the permissions list.

▶ Auditing Printer Access

To set or change printer auditing:

Before a printer can be audited, the audit policy must be set—using User Manager—to audit file, print, and security changes.

1. Select the printer window or icon for the printer to audit.
2. Select Auditing from the Security menu to display the Printer Auditing dialog box shown in Figure 6.11.
3. Select the name of the group or user to audit.
4. Mark the Success or Failure check boxes to select the events to audit.
5. Select OK.

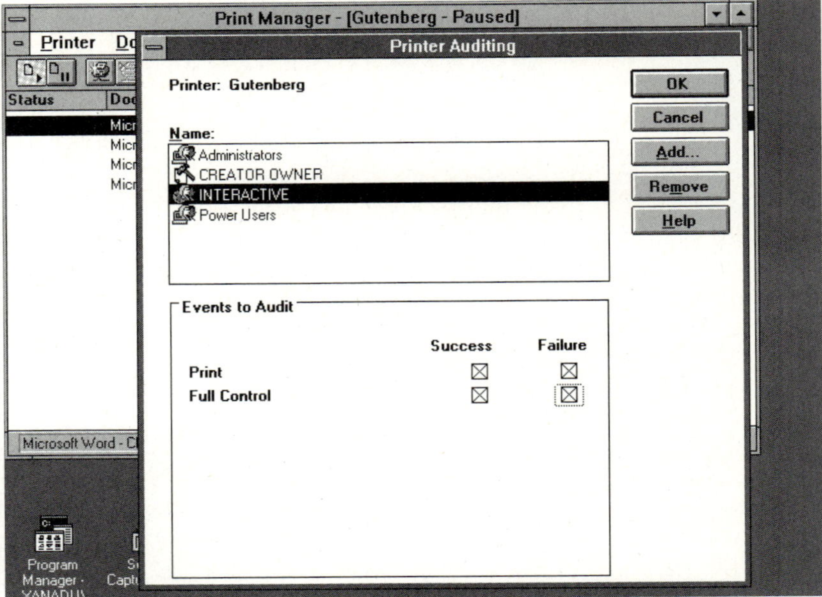

Figure 6.11
The Printer Auditing dialog box

To remove a group or user from the audit list:

1. Select the name of the group or user in the Printer Auditing dialog box.
2. Select the Remove button.

To add a group or user to the audit list:

1. Select the Add button in the Printer Auditing dialog box.
2. Use the Add Users And Groups dialog box to identify users, identify users in a group or identify the domain to which a group or user belongs. Refer to "Adding Groups or Users to a Printer's Permissions List," preceding, for instructions.
3. To add a group or users to the audit list:
   - Select groups or users and select the Add button.
   - Double-click on the names of groups or users.
   - Enter the names of groups and users in the Add Names box, separating names by a semicolon.

- If the group or user's account is not located on the computer or domain shown in the List Names In box, specify the location by giving the computer or domain name followed by the group or user name, separating the locations and names by a backslash.

4. Select OK.

Help Files ▼ Auditing is a means of tracking usage on a printer. Auditing can be specified for particular groups or users, as well as for particular activities. The Event Viewer can be used to view the audit trail.

▸ Assuming Ownership of a Printer

To assume ownership of a printer:

1. Select the printer window or icon for the printer.
2. Select Owner from the Security menu.
3. Select the Take Ownership button.

Help Files ▼ A printer's owner can change the permissions set on the printer, determining how the printer is used and by whom. To take ownership of a printer, a user must have Full Control permission or be logged on as a member of the Administrators group.

Printer Forms

▶ Creating a Printer Form

To create a printer form:

1. Select Forms from the Printer menu.
2. Use the edit fields in the Form Description box (see Figure 6.12) to describe the form:

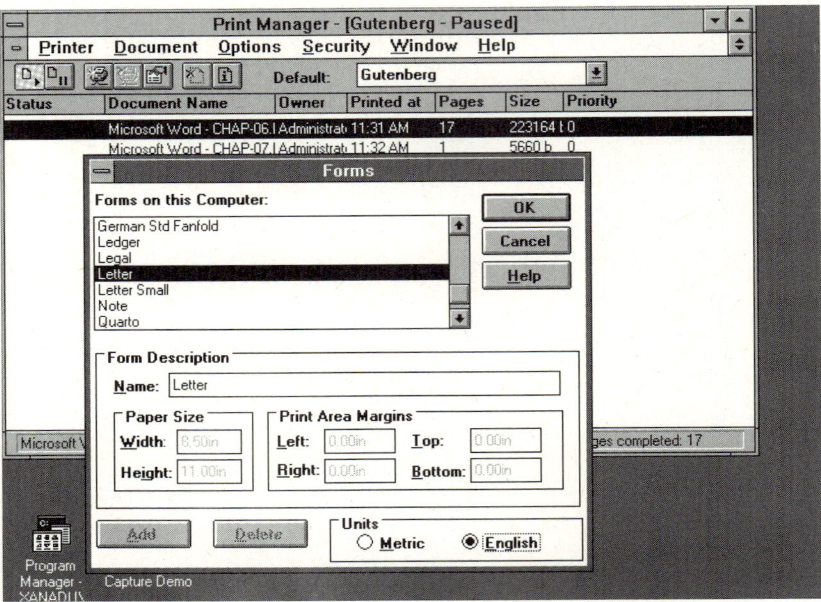

Figure 6.12
The Forms dialog box

- Enter a name for the form in the Name box.
- Specify either English or metric measurement using the option buttons in the Units box.
- Enter width and height measurements for the paper size in the Paper Size box.
- Enter measurements for the left, right, top, and bottom margins in the Print Area Margins box.

3. Select the Add button.
4. Select OK.

Help Files ▼ Predefined forms—those forms supplied by Windows NT—cannot be edited, as indicated by the grayed-out entries in the edit fields in the Forms dialog box. Only custom forms, those created by a user, can be defined or revised. Predefined forms can, however, be used as starting points for custom forms. Select the form, change its name, and then edit the form's definition.

A printer form identifies paper size and margins. Individual forms can be assigned to each of a printer's trays, as well as custom forms. For example, a form titled Logo could be designed using letter-size paper but including a top margin to allow space for preprinted letterheads. The Logo form would be assigned to a printer and paper tray reserved for letterhead stationary and used to print letters on the company stationary. Another form, titled Invoices, might be used to print half-page sheets, and so on.

Removing a Printer Form

To remove a printer form:

1. Select Forms from the Printer menu.
2. Select the form to remove from the Forms On This Computer list box.
3. Select the Delete button in the Forms dialog box.

Only custom forms can be deleted. The standard forms supplied by Windows NT cannot be removed.

Assigning a Form to a Printer

To assign a form to a printer (tray):

1. Select the printer's icon or window from Print Manager.

2. Select Properties from the Printer menu or select the Printer Properties button from the tool bar.

3. Select the Setup button from the Printer Properties dialog box.
4. Select the source tray.
5. Select the form to assign.
6. Select OK.

Document Printing

▸ Selecting a Default Printer

To select a default printer:

1. Select the Default box from the Print Manager tool bar.
2. Select a printer from the list displayed.

Help Files ▼ The default printer should be set to whatever printer is used most often because when the Print command is selected within an application, most documents are automatically sent to the default printer.

▶ Viewing Pending Documents

To view documents that are waiting to be printed or that are currently printing:

1. Select Print Manager.
2. Select the printer to view. If the printer appears as an icon within Print Manager's window, double-click on the icon to open the printer status window.

Help Files ▼ The printer window displays both waiting documents and the document currently printing. Each document is listed with its status, name, owner, time posted, size (in both pages and kilobytes), and its priority. Documents are listed in the order in which they will be printed, not in the order in which they arrived in the queue.

▶ Interrupting Printing

To interrupt (pause) printing for a document:

1. Select the document in the printer window.
2. Select Pause from the Document menu or select the Pause Document button from the tool bar.

To interrupt all printing:

1. Select the printer's window or icon.

2. If a document is currently selected in the printer window, clear the selection by pressing the right mouse button or the spacebar.

3. Select Pause from the Printer menu or select the Pause Printer button from the tool bar.

Help Files ▼ Printing can be interrupted for one document at a time or for all documents on a printer. The owner of a document can always interrupt printing for that document. To interrupt printing for other users' documents, Manage Documents or Full Control permission is required. To interrupt a printer, Full Control permission is required.

▶ Resuming Print Operations

To resume printing for an individual document:

1. Select the document in the printer window.

2. Select Resume from the Printer menu or select the Resume Document button from the tool bar.

To resume printing for all documents:

1. Select the printer's window or icon.

2. If a document is currently selected in the printer window, clear the selection by pressing the right mouse button or the spacebar.

3. Select Resume from the Printer menu or select the Resume Printer button from the tool bar.

Help Files ▼ When printing has been interrupted, printer operations can be resumed. The owner of a document can always resume printing for that document. To resume printing for other users' documents, Manage Documents or Full Control permission is required. To restart a halted printer, Full Control permission is required.

▸ Changing the Printing Order

To change the order in which documents print:

Full Control permission is required if you want to change the order in which documents are printed.

1. Select the document in the printer window
2. Drag the document to a new position in the printing order.

Or:

1. Select the document in the printer window.
2. Press Ctrl+up arrow or Ctrl+down arrow to move the selected document up or down in the printing order.

▸ Removing Pending Documents

To remove a document from the pending queue:

1. Select the document in the printer window.

2. Select Remove Document from the Document menu or select the Remove Document button on the tool bar.

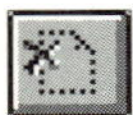

To remove all documents from the pending queue:

1. Select the printer's window or icon.
2. Select Purge Printer from the Printer menu.

Help Files ▼ Documents in the pending printing queue can be removed individually or collectively. The owner of a document can always remove a document from the printer queue. To remove other users' documents, Manage Documents or Full Control permission is required. To remove all documents from a printer's queue, Full Control permission is required.

▸ Restarting Halted Print Operations

To restart printing for a document:

Printing cannot be restarted if the Print Directly To Ports option is turned on.

1. Select the document in the printer window.
2. Select Restart from the Document menu.

Help Files ▼ Halted print operations can be restarted from Print Manager. The document will reprint in its entirety. The owner of a document can always restart printing for the document. To restart printing for other users' documents, Manage Documents or Full Control permission is required.

Setting Print Notification

To change print notification:

1. Select the document in the printer window.
2. Select Details from the Document menu or select the Document Details button from the tool bar.

3. In the Notify box in the Document Details dialog box (see Figure 6.13), enter the name of the user to be notified.

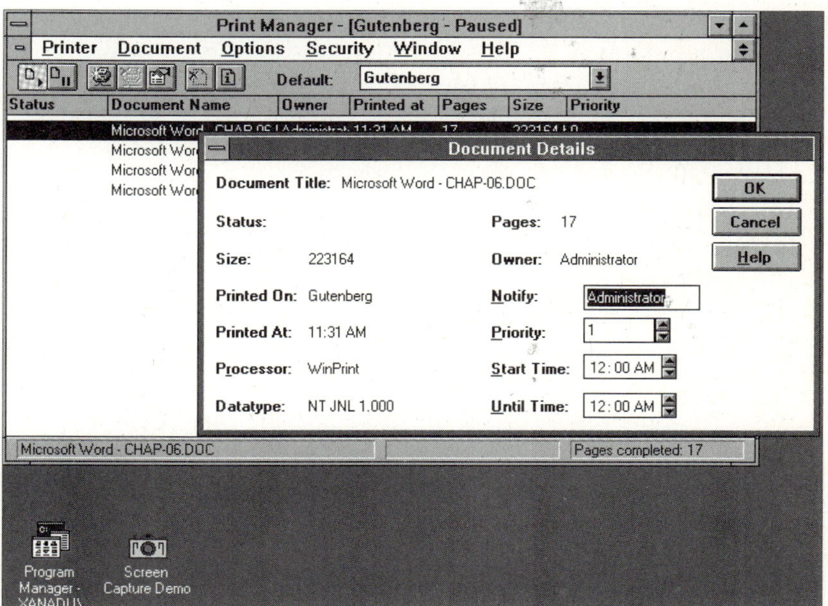

Figure 6.13
The Document Details dialog box

Help Files ▼ By default, a document's owner is notified when the document has finished printing. However, the owner can specify that another person be notified instead. To reassign notification for other users' documents, Manage Documents or Full Control permission is required.

▶ Setting Options for Individual Documents

To change the priority or printing time for an individual document:

1. Select the document in the printer window.
2. Select Details from the Document menu or select the Document Details button from the tool bar.

3. Use the scroll button to change the Priority settings. Valid priorities range from 1 (lowest) to 99 (highest). (Refer to Figure 6.13, preceding.)
4. Use the scroll buttons to change the Start Time and Until Time settings to set the time during which the document will be printed.

Help Files ▼ By default, no time restrictions are placed on individual documents and a default priority of 1 is assigned. The owner of a document can always assign time restrictions and priorities for a document. To assign time

restrictions or priorities for other users' documents, Manage Documents or Full Control permission is required.

Options Menu Commands

▶ Saving Print Manager Settings

The Options menu's Save Settings On Exit option saves the appearance and arrangement of the Print Manager window when Print Manager is exited. When this option is enabled, a check mark appears to the left of the command.

THE RESCUE PAGES: Using Print Manager

I need to install a printer but I can't find it listed in the printer drivers.

If you can't find your printer model listed, there are two solutions:

First, you can ask the manufacturer for a compatible driver or check any disks supplied with the printer for Windows NT-compatible drivers. Refer to "Creating a New Printer Service," preceding, for instructions on installing OEM drivers.

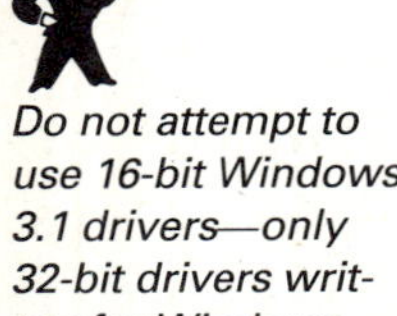

Do not attempt to use 16-bit Windows 3.1 drivers—only 32-bit drivers written for Windows NT provide compatible operations.

Second, refer to your printer's documentation for compatible printer types or look in the supported printer list for a similar model from the same manufacturer. In general, handling and features do not vary extensively from one model to another and even printers from different manufacturers often use essentially the same drivers.

My printer is shared—via the network—and it seems like it's always tied up with other people's print jobs. How can I get my documents printed?

There are three good solutions to this problem: limiting who has access to the shared printer, limiting the hours of access to the shared printer, and creating separate drivers.

Of these three, the separate drivers solution is probably the best. By establishing two drivers, one personal and one shared, the shared driver can be assigned a lower priority (refer to "Setting Printer Task Priorities") than the personal driver. In this fashion, local, personal print tasks will receive priority over network print tasks. Of course, this doesn't mean that a job currently printing will be interrupted so that you can run off a quick letter, but it does mean that your task will be first in line when the current job finishes.

Limiting hours of access is a second solution (see "Limiting Printer Access Hours"). If network access is limited, for example, to periods when the printer is not being used locally, network users can continue to upload documents at any time for printing during the time specified for access.

Finally, as a last-ditch solution, printer access could be limited to fewer users (refer to "Setting and Changing Printer Permissions"). Diplomacy, of course, suggests that you should discuss the problem with other users before simply rescinding everyone's access.

Of course, you could also try to solve the problem by using various combinations of these three suggestions. You might begin by using one driver to give yourself local priority, assigning a second driver with a lower priority to users who still need immediate access, assigning a third driver for routine jobs that can be printed during off-hours, and so on.

How can I print on letterhead without printing over the logo? I keep forgetting to insert enough blank lines at the beginning of the text.

The simple solution is to create a form to fit the letterhead and then to assign the form definition to the printer (or printer tray) used with the letterhead. By assigning a top margin that allows enough room for the logo, you can restrict printing automatically to the blank part of the page. Refer to "Creating a Printer Form" for details.

CHAPTER

HELP! The Clipboard, the ClipBook, and Information Exchanges

One essential element in a multitasking environment is the ability to share or exchange informations—and, sometimes, tasks—among quite different applications. In Windows 3.1, data exchange is provided by the Clipboard utility. In Windows NT, however, the Clipboard has been supplemented by the *ClipBook* and *ClipBook Viewer* applications—both of which are integral to topics discussed in this chapter.

The ClipBook itself—the actual mechanism providing the transfer facilities—is an invisible feature of Windows NT. Because it can't be seen, it is the ClipBook Viewer utility that is referred to commonly as the ClipBook. It is briefly introduced here.

The ClipBook Viewer window contains two smaller windows: the Local ClipBook and the Clipboard (see Figure 7.1). The Local ClipBook window opens when you first start ClipBook Viewer, and the Clipboard window appears as an icon. The Clipboard temporarily stores information you are transferring between documents, and the ClipBook permanently stores information you want to save and share with others.

The Clipboard window shows the current contents of the Clipboard. When you cut or copy information from an application, it is placed onto the Clipboard and remains there until you clear the Clipboard or cut or copy another piece of information. You can paste the information into any document as often as you like.

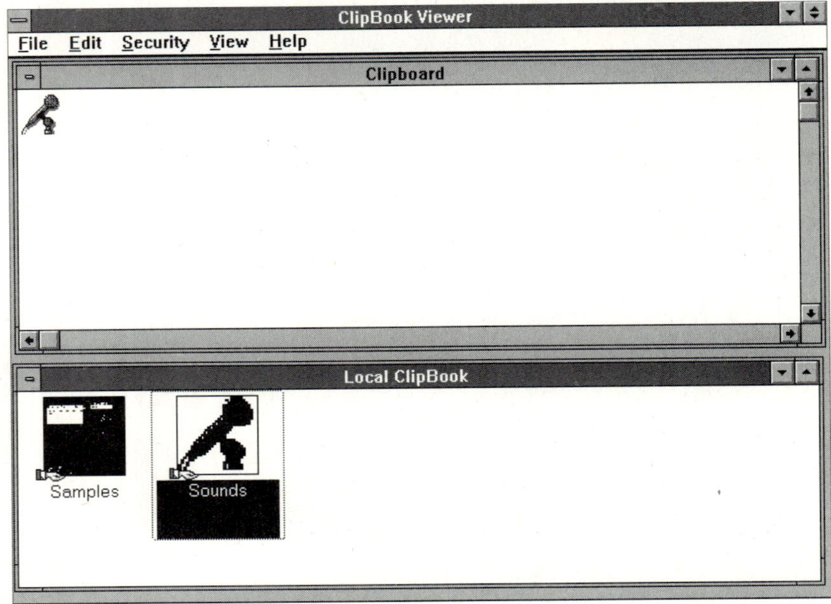

Figure 7.1
The ClipBook Viewer, Clipboard, and Local ClipBook screens

You can permanently save the current contents of the Clipboard by copying it onto your Local ClipBook. You can save several pieces of information (called pages) on it and then copy the information back onto the Clipboard when you want to paste it into a document.

After information is saved as a page, you can share it. Each computer has its own ClipBook. You can connect to a ClipBook on another computer, and others can connect to the ClipBook on your computer to use the information in shared pages.

The term document is used in Windows to refer to any type of work file—including text files, spreadsheets, database files, images, and so on.

Along with copying or transferring information, other mechanisms provide means to embed or link objects from a source application to one or more documents managed by other applications.

Finally, in addition to provisions allowing applications to copy and retrieve information from the ClipBook, Windows NT also provides mechanisms that allow cutting and pasting of information to and from applications executing in the DOS windows (see "Capturing and Transferring Information").

Topics discussed in this chapter include:

- The Clipboard and the ClipBook Viewer

- Network sharing for ClipBook pages
- Managing ClipBook access
- Linking and embedding objects
- Capturing and transferring information

The Clipboard and the ClipBook Viewer

▸ Displaying ClipBook Pages

There are three views in which you can view Local ClipBook pages:

- Table Of Contents displays page titles alphabetically.
- Thumbnail displays a miniature snapshot of each page.
- Full Page displays complete page contents.

Figure 7.1 (preceding) shows the Local ClipBook with two pages displayed in Thumbnail view.

▸ Viewing a ClipBook Page in Different Formats

To select a Full Page view:

1. Select the ClipBook window.
2. Select the page to view.
3. Click on the Full Page button on the tool bar or select Full Page from the View menu.

To select a different format:

1. Select the page.
2. Select the format name from the View menu.

To return to the original format:

- Select Default Format from the View menu.

Help Files ▼ Information saved as a ClipBook page is saved in multiple formats. Before the information format can be changed, the page must be selected in Full Page view. The type of display driver used determines whether the page contents from another computer's ClipBook can be viewed in bitmap format.

▸ Viewing the Contents of the Clipboard in Different Formats

To view the contents of the Clipboard:

- Select the Clipboard icon from the ClipBook Viewer window.

To view the Clipboard contents in a different format:

- Select a format name from the View menu.

To return to the initial format:

- Select Default Format from the View menu.

Help Files ▼ Information on the Clipboard is stored in multiple formats to facilitate information transfers among applications using different formats.

Text on the Clipboard can be stored in a variety of formats, including:

- Owner Display, which employs the character fonts used when the document was originally created, listing the source application (for example, Word Formatted Text)
- Rich Text format
- Text character set, which is used by most Windows NT applications
- OEM Text, which is used by DOS applications
- Unicode Text, which supports international alphabets

The View menu lists all supported formats, although not all formats can be displayed on screen. Formats that cannot be displayed are grayed out and cannot be selected. The active format appears with a check mark at the left.

Clearing the Clipboard Contents

To clear the Clipboard contents:

1. Select the Clipboard icon or window.
2. Click on the Delete button on the tool bar or select Delete from the Edit menu.

Help Files ▼ The Clipboard stores information in multiple formats, so clearing the Clipboard may free memory required by other applications.

Copying a ClipBook Page to the Clipboard

To copy a ClipBook page to the Clipboard:

1. Select the page to transfer from the Local ClipBook.

2. Select the Copy button from the tool bar or select Copy from the Edit menu.

Help Files ▼ A ClipBook page must be copied back to the Clipboard before it can be inserted into a document. If, however, no new information has been copied to the Clipboard (i.e., the Clipboard and ClipBook contents are the same), the information is already available and does not need to be copied.

▸ Saving Clipboard Contents to a File

To save the contents of the Clipboard to a file:

1. Select the Clipboard icon or window.
2. Select Save As from the File menu.
3. Enter a file name in the Save As dialog box (the default extension used for Clipboard files is .CLP).
4. Select OK.

To open a Clipboard file:

Clipboard files cannot be shared with network users. For shared material, use pages in the Local ClipBook.

1. Select the Clipboard icon or window.
2. Select Open from the File menu.
3. Select the desired .CLP file from the File Name box.
4. Select OK.

▸ Saving the Clipboard to the Local ClipBook

To save the Clipboard contents to the Local ClipBook:

1. Select the Local ClipBook window.

2. Select the Paste button from the tool bar or select Paste from the Edit menu.
3. In the Page Name box, enter a name for the page on which the information is saved.
4. Select the Share Item Now check box to make the page available to others.
5. Select OK to open the Share ClipBook Page dialog box.
6. Select the share conditions for the page.
7. Select OK.

Help Files ▼ The Clipboard contents can be saved either to a page on the Local ClipBook—which can be viewed, retrieved, and shared—or to the local Clipboard, which is not shared.

Network Sharing for ClipBook Pages

▶ Connecting to a Remote ClipBook

To connect to a ClipBook on a remote computer:

1. Select the Connect button from the tool bar or select Connect from the File menu.
2. In the Select Computer dialog box, enter the name of the computer with the desired ClipBook or select the name from the Computers list.
3. Select OK. A window opens to display the contents of the remote ClipBook.

Help Files ▼ A network connection must be established to the remote computer and that computer's ClipBook before the information in the shared pages can be accessed.

▶ Sharing ClipBook Pages

To share a page from the Local ClipBook:

1. Select the ClipBook window with the page to share.
2. Select the page to share.
3. Select the Share button from the tool bar or select Share from the File menu.
4. Select sharing options by selecting the check boxes for:
   - Start Application On Connect
   - Run Minimized
5. Optionally, select the Permissions button to set sharing permission.
6. Select OK.

Help Files ▼ Information that has been saved as a page on the Local ClipBook can be shared with other network users. Depending on the type of password protection, these users can view or change the shared information.

Shared pages are identified by the Shared icon appearing next to each page.

▶ Ending the Sharing of ClipBook Pages

To stop sharing pages from the Local ClipBook:

1. Select a shared page.
2. Select the Stop Sharing button from the tool bar or select Stop Sharing from the File menu.

▶ Disconnecting from a Remote ClipBook

To disconnect from a ClipBook on a remote computer:

1. Select the ClipBook window.
2. Select the Disconnect button on the tool bar or select Disconnect from the File menu.

ClipBook Access

▶ Establishing ClipBook Page Permissions

To add groups or users to the ClipBook permissions list:

1. Select the Add button in the ClipBook Permissions dialog box.
2. Use the options in the Add Users And Groups dialog box to display users, identify users in a group, or identify the domain to which a group or user belongs.
3. Select groups or users and select the Add button, double-click on the name of the group or user, or enter the names in the Add Names box, separating each by a semicolon.
4. Select the permission in the Type Of Access box for the groups or users shown in the Add Names box.
5. Select OK.

To change permissions for a ClipBook page:

1. Select a ClipBook page from the contents pane of the ClipBook window.
2. Select Permissions from the Security menu.
3. Select the groups or users for whom you want to change permissions.
4. Select the new permission from the Type Of Access box.
5. Select OK.

Permissions can be set or cleared only for ClipBook pages that are shared.

To remove permissions for a ClipBook page:

1. Select a ClipBook page from the contents pane of the ClipBook window.
2. Select Permissions from the Security menu.
3. Select the groups or users for whom you want to remove permissions.
4. Select the Remove button.

Help Files ▼ By setting permissions for a ClipBook page, you specify the type of access permitted to a group or user. Except for No Access permission, which overrides all other permissions, permissions are cumulative. Thus, if a user belongs to one group with Read permission and another with Change permission, the user will have Change permission.

Permissions can be changed only by the owner of the ClipBook page or by a user to whom permission to do so has been granted by the owner.

The Add Users And Groups dialog box is used to display the groups on the computer in the domain selected in the List Names From list box. Another domain or computer can be selected from the List Names From list box.

Domains appear only if the computer is a member of a domain belonging to a Windows NT Advanced Server network. Any domains listed will have a trust relationship with the domain containing the ClipBook page.

The Show Users button is used to display the names of users on a selected computer or domain. To view the members of a group, select the group and select the Members button. Users belonging to the group will be listed in a Members dialog box. On a Windows NT Advanced Server network, the list will include global groups that are members of a local group. To view global group users, select the group and select the Members button.

To include a group in the Add Users And Groups dialog box, select the Add button. To include only specified users from a group, select the users and select the Add button.

Before a domain group or domain user can be added, the domain containing the group or user's account must be known. On a Windows NT Advanced Server network, select the Search button to identify the domain for a group or user.

Enter the name of the group or user in the Find User Or Group box in the Find Account dialog box. Specify the domains to search and select the Search button.

To include groups or users in the Add User And Groups dialog box, select the group or user in the Search Results list box and select the Add button.

▶ Auditing ClipBook Pages

To audit a ClipBook page:

1. Select the ClipBook page in the ClipBook window.
2. Select Auditing from the Security menu.
3. Select a group or user.
4. Select the events to audit.
5. Select OK.

To add groups or users to the audit list:

1. Select the Add button in the Auditing dialog box.
2. Use the options in the Add Users And Groups dialog box to display users, identify users in a group, or identify the domain to which a group or user belongs.
3. Select groups or users and select the Add button, double-click on the name of the group or user, or enter the names of groups and users in the Add Names box, separating each by a semicolon.
4. Select OK.

ClipBook pages can be audited only by a member of the Administrators group.

To cancel ClipBook-page auditing for a group or user:

1. Select the name of the group or user from the list in the Auditing dialog box.
2. Select the Remove button.

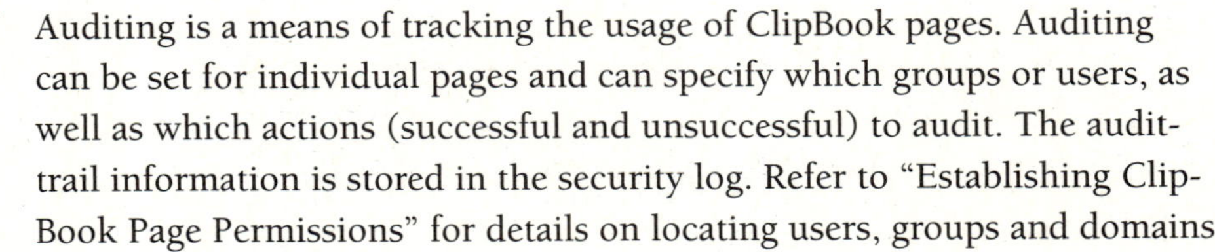

Help Files ▼ Auditing is a means of tracking the usage of ClipBook pages. Auditing can be set for individual pages and can specify which groups or users, as well as which actions (successful and unsuccessful) to audit. The audit-trail information is stored in the security log. Refer to "Establishing ClipBook Page Permissions" for details on locating users, groups and domains.

Audit policy for file and object access must be set in User Manager before ClipBook pages can be audited.

▸ Assuming Ownership of a ClipBook Page

To assume ownership of a ClipBook page:

1. Select the ClipBook page from the ClipBook Viewer window.
2. Select Owner from the Security menu.
3. Select the Take Ownership button.

Help Files ▼ The creator of a ClipBook page becomes the owner by default and, by granting permissions, controls who and how the ClipBook page is accessed. The owner of a ClipBook page can grant permission to another user to assume ownership.

Alternatively, a member of the Administrators group can assume ownership; however, in the interests of ensuring security, he or she is not allowed to transfer ownership to another user. Also, if No Access permission is set on a ClipBook page, access can be gained only by an administrator who takes ownership and changes the permissions.

Linking and Embedding Objects

▶ Embedding Objects on the Clipboard

To embed an object on the Clipboard:

1. Open the source document.
2. Select the object.
3. Select Copy from the source's Edit menu to copy the object to the Clipboard.
4. Open the destination document.
5. Select Paste from the destination's Edit menu.

Help Files ▼

To embed an object, the application creating the object must support embedding. Refer to the application for details and menu commands. (Of course, the application receiving the object must also recognize embedded objects.)

When an object or document is embedded in an application, a copy of an object created by one application is placed in another. For example, a Paintbrush image could be embedded in a Write document. Further, the image could be edited in the Write document by calling the application that created the object—in this case, the Paintbrush program.

Embedded objects are temporarily stored on the Clipboard while being transferred from the source to the destination.

Source and destination may be on a single computer or, with a network, can be on different computers. In the latter case, a connection must be made to the ClipBook on the remote computer, and the object must be saved as a page on the ClipBook and marked as shared.

▶ Embedding an Object from a Remote Computer

To embed an object from a remote computer:

1. Select the Connect button from the tool bar or select Connect from the File menu.
2. In the Select Computer dialog box, enter the name of the computer to connect to or select the name from the Computers list.
3. Select OK. The ClipBook window will show the shared pages available from the remote computer's ClipBook.
4. Select the page to be embedded.
5. Select Copy from the Edit menu. A copy of the object is placed in the Clipboard.
6. Open the document where the object will be embedded.
7. Select Paste from the Edit menu.

Help Files ▼

When an object is embedded in an application, a copy of an object created by one application is placed in another. For example, a Paintbrush image could be embedded in a Write document. Further, the image could be edited in the Write document by calling the application that created the object—in this case, the Paintbrush program.

To embed an object, the application creating the object must support embedding. Refer to the application for details and menu commands.

Embedded objects are temporarily stored on the Clipboard while being transferred from the source to the destination.

Source and destination may be on a single computer or, with a network, can be on different computers. In the latter case, a connection must be made to the ClipBook on the remote computer, and the object must be saved as a page on the ClipBook and must be marked as shared.

An embedded object can be edited only when the application used to create the object is installed on the local computer. Objects embedded from a remote computer cannot be edited.

▶ Linking an Object from a Remote Computer

To create a link to an object from a remote computer:

To link an object, the application creating the object must support linking. Refer to the application for details and menu commands.

1. Select the Connect button from the tool bar or select Connect from the File menu.
2. In the Select Computer dialog box, enter the name of the computer to connect to or select the name from the Computers list.
3. Select OK. The ClipBook window will show the shared pages available from the remote computer's ClipBook.
4. Select the page to be linked.
5. Select Copy from the Edit menu. A copy of the object is placed in the Clipboard.
6. Open the document where the object will be linked.

7. Select Paste Special from the Edit menu.
8. Select the format desired.
9. Select the Paste Link button.

Help Files ▼ A linked object cannot be edited if the source application is on a remote computer only. Changes made to the source object can, however, be received over the link.

Capturing and Transferring Information

▶ Copying Information from a DOS Application

To copy selected information to the Clipboard:

1. Execute the application in a DOS window (not a full screen).
2. Select the window's Control menu (click the Control-menu box in the upper-left corner or press Alt+spacebar).
3. Select Edit from the Control menu.
4. Select Mark from the Edit menu.
5. Select the information to copy from the application's display.
6. Select the application's Control menu.
7. Select Edit from the Control menu.
8. Select Copy from the Edit menu.

To copy an image of the active window to the Clipboard:

- Press Alt+PrtSc.

To copy an image of the entire screen to the Clipboard:

- Press PrtSc.

Help Files ▼ With a DOS application executing in a window in text mode, all or part of the text information can be copied to the Clipboard, or an image of the window or the desktop can be copied to the Clipboard. If the application is executed full screen or executed in graphics mode, only an image of the entire screen can be captured.

▶ Pasting Information to a DOS Application

To paste text information to a full-screen DOS application:

1. Copy the information to the Clipboard.
2. Switch to the destination application.
3. Place the insertion point where the information should appear.
4. Press Alt+spacebar to open the window's Control menu.
5. Select Edit from the Control menu.
6. Select Paste from the Edit menu.

To paste text information to a windowed DOS application:

1. Copy the information to the Clipboard.
2. Switch to the destination application.
3. Place the insertion point where the information should appear.
4. Select the window's Control menu (click on the Control-menu box in the upper-left corner or press Alt+spacebar).
5. Select Edit from the Control menu.
6. Select Paste from the Edit menu.

Help Files ▼ If an application is executing full screen and requires the Alt+spacebar combination for its own use, the Ctrl+Esc key combination can be used to call the Task List without exiting the DOS application. The DOS application will be reduced to an icon and placed at the bottom of the screen. Click on the DOS application's icon to open the Control menu.

▶ Transferring Information between Windows NT (or Windows 3.1) Applications

To transfer information via the Clipboard:

1. Go to the source application.
2. Select the information to copy or move.
3. Select Copy or Cut from the Edit menu.
4. Switch to the destination application if it is different from the source.
5. Position the insertion point where the information should appear.
6. Select Paste from the Edit menu to insert the information.

To copy an image of the active window to the Clipboard:

- Press Alt+PrtSc.

To copy an image of the entire screen to the Clipboard:

- Press PrtSc.

Help Files ▼ The Cut, Copy, and Paste commands provided in the Edit menus of most applications are used to copy or move information within an application, between application windows, or between applications. The Clipboard is used to temporarily store information that is being transferred from one application to another. Once information has been copied to the Clipboard, it can be saved, viewed in other formats, or deleted.

THE RESCUE PAGES: The Clipboard, the ClipBook, and Information Exchanges

I used the Copy command to save a lot of material but now I can't find the data.

Let's hope that you simply aren't looking in the right place. After selecting the ClipBook, open the Clipboard window—this is where your material was copied to from the application.

The Clipboard is a vulnerable repository. Normally, it holds only one block of data of any type; the previously saved block is discarded when a new block is saved. If the Clipboard window doesn't reveal your material, you can be pretty sure that your data has suffered this fate.

If you want to save material securely, you can copy the Clipboard contents out to a Clipboard file (the default extension is .CLP) or, better yet, copy the material from the Clipboard to a page in the Local ClipBook (see "Saving the Clipboard to the Local ClipBook").

I've saved material in the Local ClipBook but another user needs to access it. Do I have to write it to a shared file or what?

Instead of creating a file for sharing, the simple solution is to share the page (or pages) in the Local ClipBook. In this fashion, your colleague can access the ClipBook page over the network, either to read the material or to write changes back. Remember, however, that a connection to the ClipBook on the remote computer must be established before the information in the shared pages can be accessed.

I want to share some ClipBook pages containing personal information, but I don't want everyone to have access to them.

If these are personal matters, there may, of course, be advantages to not having anything in writing. And, any way you look at it, the electronic media is a pretty impersonal medium. Still, sharing *can* be limited to specific users, access can be limited to viewing only, or a password can be required for access. You can also use any combination of these.

However, unless you're the Administrator, remember there is no absolute security. It's is like the old Russian proverb that cautions "Three can keep a secret only if two are dead."

I can't capture a DOS graphics image by using the Clipboard.

The best solution is to capture the image the same way you'd do it under DOS—by using a TSR capture utility such as HiJack or Grab.

First, open the DOS window and load your captured TSR, then load your graphics application (in the same DOS window). When you're ready, call the capture utility in the usual fashion and save the image to a file.

Afterward, if desired, the image file can still be loaded into the Clipboard, transferred to a page in the Local ClipBook, or shared over the network.

If your TSR doesn't work (there are no guarantees), you can also try using the Alt+PrtSc key combination to capture an image of the DOS window or simply press PrtSc to capture an image of the entire screen.

Last, if all else fails, try a different TSR capture utility…or go back to DOS.

The ClipBook page I want is locked!

Well, you have two options. First, you can ask the owner for permission. Second, if you're the Administrator, you can assume ownership of the object. This will automatically give you access. Otherwise, you're pretty much out of luck—which, after all, is the whole point of security.

My Thumbnail view is blank.

Basically, this means that there's nothing in that page of the ClipBook. Either nothing has been pasted to the ClipBook or the thing that's been saved simply doesn't show—such as blank lines of text.

CHAPTER

8

HELP! Calculator, Cardfile, and Clock Accessories

In one sense, Windows NT is simply a collection of utilities that provide an environment and features supporting the operation of other applications. A few of these supplementary utilities, however, go a step or two beyond filling a supporting role and are useful programs in their own right. These include the Calculator, Cardfile, and Clock accessories.

Under DOS, a variety of TSR (terminate and stay resident) utilities have served similar functions—usually with varying degrees of success and compatibility. Under Windows NT, however, the problems inherent in TSRs are no longer a consideration, making utility applications useful features instead of annoyances and stumbling blocks.

Topics in this chapter include

- Using the standard and scientific calculators
- The Cardfile accessory
- The Clock utility

The Calculator Accessory

Windows NT supplies a pair of calculators that work like the screen equivalents of standard and scientific pocket calculators. The Calculator is installed by default in the Accessories program group.

▶ Switching Calculator Types

To switch calculators:

- Select Standard or Scientific from the View menu.

▶ Operating the Calculator

To enter calculations:

1. Enter a number by using the mouse or the keypad.
2. Select an operation (select an operator key).
3. Enter the next number.
4. Use the Back button or Backspace key to delete individual digits.
5. Select the CE button or press the Del key to clear an entire entry.
6. Enter any additional operations and values.
7. Select the equal button (=), press Enter, or press the equal (=) key. The results of the calculation are displayed in the Calculator window.
8. To clear the entire calculation, select the C button or press the Esc key.

Help Files ▼

To use the number pad, the Number Lock must be active (the Num Lock light should be on).

The calculator can be operated by using the mouse to click on the Calculator buttons (see Figure 8.1) or, for numerical values, by using the number pad on the keyboard.

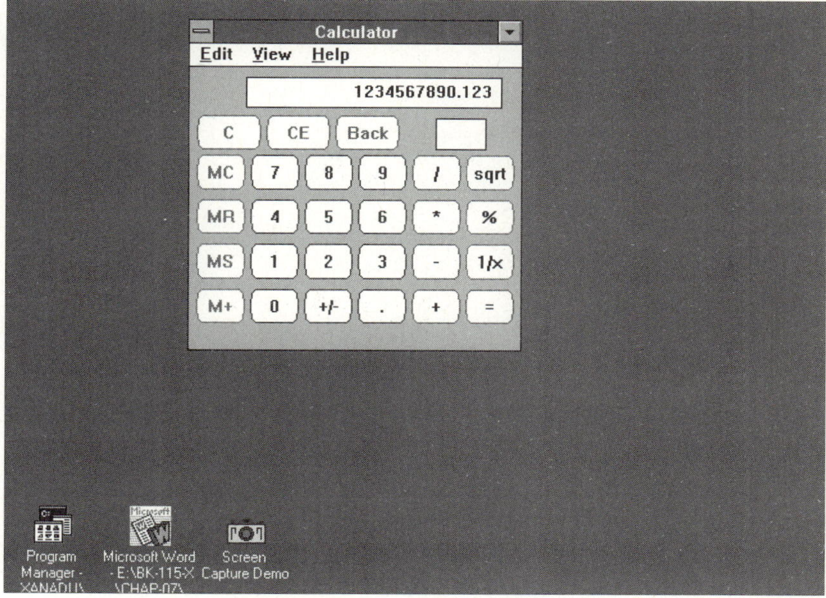

Figure 8.1
The standard calculator

▸ Using Standard Calculator Functions

To use the standard calculator functions, select the buttons shown in Table 8.1, or press the equivalent keys.

Table 8.1
Standard Calculator Functions

Button	Key	Function
+	+	Adds two numbers.
-	-	Subtracts two numbers.
*	*	Multiplies two numbers.

Table 8.1
Standard Calculator Functions (Continued)

Button	Key	Function
/	/	Divides two numbers.
+/-	F9	Inverts the sign of the displayed entry.
.	. *or* ,	Inserts a decimal point in the displayed entry.*
sqrt	@	Executes a square root calculation.
%	%	Calculates a percentage.
=	= *or* Enter	Completes an operation—select again to repeat the last operation.
1/x	r	Calculates the reciprocal of the value displayed.
Back	Backspace	Deletes the rightmost digit from the displayed value.
C	Esc	Clears and resets the present calculations.
CE	Del	Clears the current entry.
MS	Ctrl+M	Stores the displayed value in memory.
M+	Ctrl+P	Adds the displayed value to a value in memory (if any).
MC	Ctrl+L	Clears memory.
MR	Ctrl+R	Recalls a value from memory without clearing memory.

* A period is the default decimal separator, but you can select the comma for the decimal separator setting in the Control Panel.

Help Files ▼ When a value is stored in memory, the letter *M* appears in a box below the display area. Storing a second value replaces the current value. Storing a zero or adding a value to memory that leaves a zero result is the equivalent of clearing memory and removes the *M* prompt.

▸ Using the Scientific Calculator

To use the scientific calculator:

1. Select the scientific calculator from the View menu (see Figure 8.2).

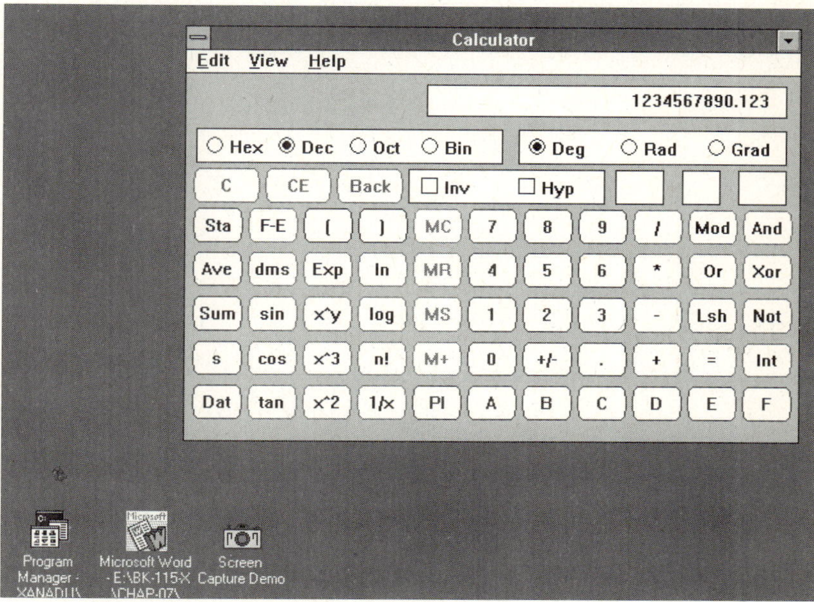

Figure 8.2
The scientific calculator

2. Enter values as described for the standard calculator.
3. Select operations by clicking on the appropriate buttons or pressing the keyboard equivalents shown in Table 8.2.

Table 8.2
Scientific Calculator Buttons

Button	Key	Function
(	(	Opens a new level of parentheses up to a maximum of 25 levels. The current level appears below the display.*
)	)	Closes the current level of parentheses.*
And	&	Executes a bitwise AND operation.
Int	;	Displays the integer portion of a decimal value.
Inv+Int		Displays the fractional portion of a decimal value.

Table 8.2
Scientific Calculator Buttons (Continued)

Button	Key	Function
Lsh	<	Executes a left-shift operation on the value currently displayed. Selection should be followed by the number of positions (binary) to shift the value. Press the equal (=) key to conclude.
Inv+Lsh		Performs a right-shift operation (see left-shift operation, above).
Mod	%	Performs a modulo operation (remainder) for *x/y*.
Not	~	Performs a bitwise inversion.
Or	|	Executes a bitwise OR operation.
Xor	^	Executes a bitwise eXclusive OR operation.

* Parentheses must be closed manually. Pressing Enter does not automatically close open parentheses.

▶ Using Advanced Functions

To use the advanced functions of the scientific calculator, click on the buttons or press the keyboard equivalents shown in Table 8.3.

Table 8.3
Advanced Scientific Calculator Functions

Button	Key	Function
cos	o	Calculates the cosine of the displayed number.
cos+Inv		Calculates the arc cosine of the displayed value.
cos+Hyp		Calculates the hyperbolic cosine of the displayed value.
cos+Inv+Hyp		Calculates the arc hyperbolic cosine of the displayed value.
Deg	F2	Selects trigonometric input in degrees. Used in decimal mode only.
dms	m	Converts the displayed value (assumes decimal degree format) to degree-minute-second format.
dms+Inv		Converts the displayed value (assumes degree-minute-second format) to decimal degrees.
Exp	x	Permits entry in scientific notation with an exponent limit of +307. Used only in decimal format.
F-E	v	Turns scientific notation on and off. Used only in decimal format.*

Table 8.3
Advanced Scientific Calculator Functions (Continued)

Button	Key	Function
Grad	F4	Selects gradient mode for trigonometric input. Used in decimal format only.
Hyp	h	Selects hyperbolic functions for the sin, cos, and tan functions.
Inv	i	Selects inverse functions for the sin, cos, tan, PI, x^y, x^2, x^3, ln, log, Ave, and Sum functions.
ln	n	Calculates the natural (base *e*) logarithm of displayed value.
ln+Inv		Calculates *e* to the xth power, *x* = displayed value.
log	l	Calculates the base-10 logarithm of displayed value.
log+Inv		Calculates 10 to the xth power, *x* = displayed value.
n!	!	Calculates the factorial result of the displayed value (integers only).
PI	p	Enters the value of pi (3.14159265359...).
PI+Inv		Enters the value of 2 * pi (6.28318530718...).
Rad	F3	Selects trigonometric input in radians. Used in decimal mode only.
sin	s	Calculates the sine of the displayed value.
sin+Inv		Calculates the arc sine of the displayed value.
sin+Hyp		Calculates the hyperbolic sine of the displayed value.
sin+Inv+Hyp		Calculates the arc hyperbolic sine of the displayed value.
tan	t	Calculates the tangent of the displayed value.
tan+Inv		Calculates the arc tangent of the displayed value.
tan+Hyp		Calculates the hyperbolic tangent of the displayed value.
tan+Inv+Hyp		Calculates the arc hyperbolic tangent of the displayed value.
x^2	@	Calculates the square of the displayed value.
x^2+Inv		Calculates the square root of the displayed value.
x^3	#	Calculates the cube of the displayed value.

Table 8.3
Advanced Scientific Calculator Functions (Continued)

Button	Key	Function
x^3+Inv		Calculates the cube root of the displayed value.
x^y	y	Calculates *x* raised to the yth power, *x* = displayed value and *y* is entered after the operation is selected.
x^y+Inv		Calculates the yth root of *x*, *x* = displayed value and *y* is entered after the operation is selected.

* Exponential display is always used for values greater than 10^{15}.

Help Files ▼ The Inv and Hyp check boxes can be selected to change the primary function of other operators. Inv can be used with the sin, cos, tan, PI, x^y, x^2, x^3, ln, log, Ave, and Sum functions. Hyp can be used with the sin, cos, and tan functions. To use the Inv and/or Hyp options, select the option check boxes before selecting the operator. Both the Inv and Hyp options are canceled automatically after the operator is selected.

▶ Converting Values between Number Base Systems

To convert a value to a different number base:

1. Enter the value.
2. Select the number base desired. Options are
   - Bin (binary—base 2)
   - Oct (octal—base 8)
   - Dec (decimal—base 10)
   - Hex (hexadecimal—base 16)
3. Select a different unit of measurement to modify the value display. Options in binary, octal, or hexadecimal are

- DWord—double word, four bytes or 32 bits, maximum value displayed is FFFFFFFFh (4,294,967,295 decimal)
- Word—two bytes or 16 bits, maximum value displayed is FFFFh (65,535 decimal)
- Byte—8 bits, maximum value displayed is FFh (255 decimal)

Help Files ▼ Only integer values can be converted from base 10 to other number bases. Decimal fractions will be truncated to their integer portions. Values exceeding the maximum that can be displayed for a format (including exponential values) cannot be converted.

Negative decimal values are converted to their hexadecimal, octal, or binary equivalents in one's-complement format. Remember, however, that the ranges for negative values are reduced by one bit with the high (most significant) bit reserved for the sign.

Conversion options and keyboard equivalents are listed in Table 8.4.

Table 8.4
Numerical Format Conversion Options

Button	Key	Function
Dword	F2	Displays values in full 32-bit format (8 characters in hexadecimal, 16 in octal, or 32 in binary).*
Word	F3	Displays the low word of the value in 16-bit format (4 characters in hexadecimal, 8 in octal, or 16 in binary).*
Byte	F4	Displays the low byte of the value in 8-bit format (2 characters in hexadecimal, 4 in octal, or 8 in binary).*
Hex	F5	Represents values in hexadecimal format.
Dec	F6	Represents values in decimal format. Dword, Word, and Byte options do not apply. Decimal format is used by default.
Oct	F7	Represents values in octal format.
Bin	F8	Represents values in binary format.

* The Dword, Word, and Byte formats are not used in decimal mode.

HELP! *Values greater than 255 displayed in Byte format and those greater than 65,335 displayed in Word format are truncated only for display purposes. The actual value is not affected.*

▶ Executing Statistical Calculations

To perform statistical calculations:

1. Select the Sta button to call the Statistics Box shown in Figure 8.3.

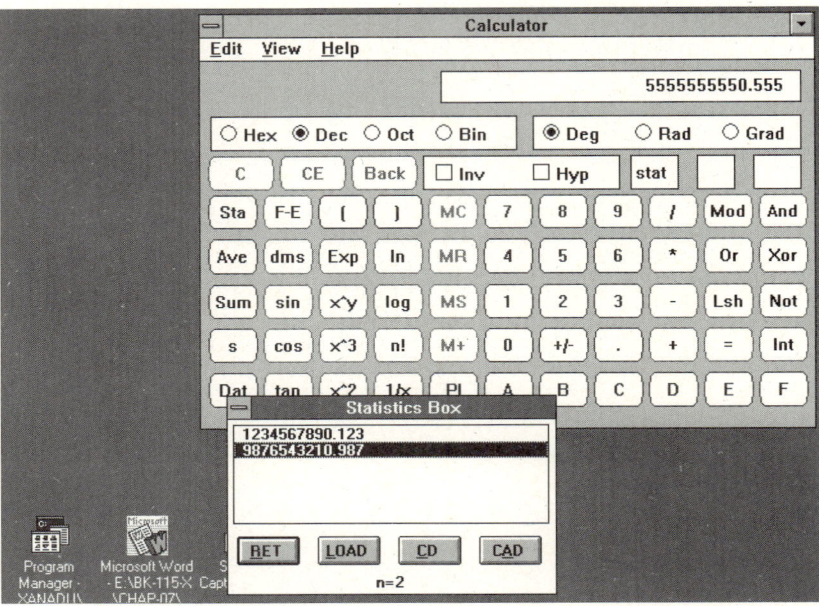

Figure 8.3
The Statistics Box with the scientific calculator

2. Position the Statistics Box in such a way that both the Statistics Box and Calculator are accessible.

3. Begin calculations by entering the first value:

   - Use the mouse to operate the calculator keys.
   - Press Alt+R (for the RET button) to make the Calculator window active, permitting use of the keyboard keypad.

4. To enter the value shown on the calculator into the Statistics Box, select the Dat button.

The number of entries is limited only by the computer's memory. The list box can be scrolled if necessary.

5. Enter additional values for calculation, selecting the Dat button after each to transfer the entries to the Statistics Box.
6. Select the statistical operation desired. The results are displayed in the Calculator window. Options are
   - Ave—average
   - Sum—total
   - s—standard deviation
7. Select Dat to include the statistical result in the Statistics Box.
8. Options for manipulating entries in the Statistics Box are
   - RET switches from the Statistics Box to the calculator without loosing statistics entries. (Use the calculator's Sta button to return to the Statistics Box.)
   - LOAD copies a selected entry from the Statistics Box to the Calculator window.
   - CD deletes a selected entry from the Statistics Box.
   - CAD (Clear All Data) deletes all entries from the Statistics Box.
9. To close the Statistics Box, select Close from the Control menu.

Help Files ▼ Statistical calculation options are shown in Table 8.5.

Table 8.5
Statistical Operator Options

Button	Key	Function
Ave	Ctrl+A	Calculates the mean of the values displayed.
Ave+Inv		Calculates the mean of the squares of the values displayed.
Dat	INS	Copies a value from the calculator to the Statistics Box.

Table 8.5
Statistical Operator Options (Continued)

Button	Key	Function
s	Ctrl+D	Calculates standard deviation for a population of *n*-1 items.
s+Inv		Calculates standard deviation for a population of *n* items.
Sta	Ctrl+S	Opens the Statistics Box.
Sum	Ctrl+T	Calculates the sum of values in the Statistics Box.
Sum+Inv		Calculates the sum of the squares of the values in the Statistics Box.

▶ Operating between the Calculator and the Clipboard

To copy a value from the Calculator to the Clipboard:

- Select Copy from the Calculator's Edit menu.

To paste a character sequence from the Clipboard to the Calculator:

1. For the scientific calculator, select a number system.
2. Select Paste from the Calculator's Edit menu.

Help Files ▼ The Windows NT Calculator can perform calculations for other applications by passing data and results via the Clipboard.

The Calculator interprets characters received from the Clipboard as if these were being entered on the keyboard. Some two-character sequences—those initiated by a colon (:)—are interpreted as key sequences or function keys, as shown in Table 8.6.

Table 8.6
Interpreted Character Sequences

Character	Function
:c	Clears memory. Equivalent to Ctrl+L or the MC button.
:e	In decimal mode, indicates an entry using scientific notation. Can, optionally, be followed by a plus (+) or minus (–) sign indicating the sign of the exponent.*
:m	Copies to memory. Equivalent to Ctrl+M or the MS button.
:p	Adds to memory. Equivalent to Ctrl+P or the M+ button.
:q	Clears the current calculation. Equivalent to the Esc key and the C button.
:r	Recalls from memory. Equivalent to Ctrl+R or the MR button.
\	Copies a value from the calculator to the Statistics Box. Equivalent to the Dat button or Ins key. Statistics Box must be active before use.

* The *e* may also specify the number *E* in hexadecimal mode.

The Cardfile Accessory

▶ Creating Card Entries

To add a new card to a card file:

1. Select Add from the Card menu.
2. Enter text for the index line.
3. Select OK.
4. Enter additional text in the information area of the card.

Help Files ▼ New cards are inserted in alphabetical order; the card file scrolls to display the new card immediately. All cards are maintained in alphabetical order by index line entry.

Switching between Card and List Views

To switch the view:

- Select Card from the Cardfile View menu to view the file as overlapping cards (see the upper-left portion of Figure 8.4).

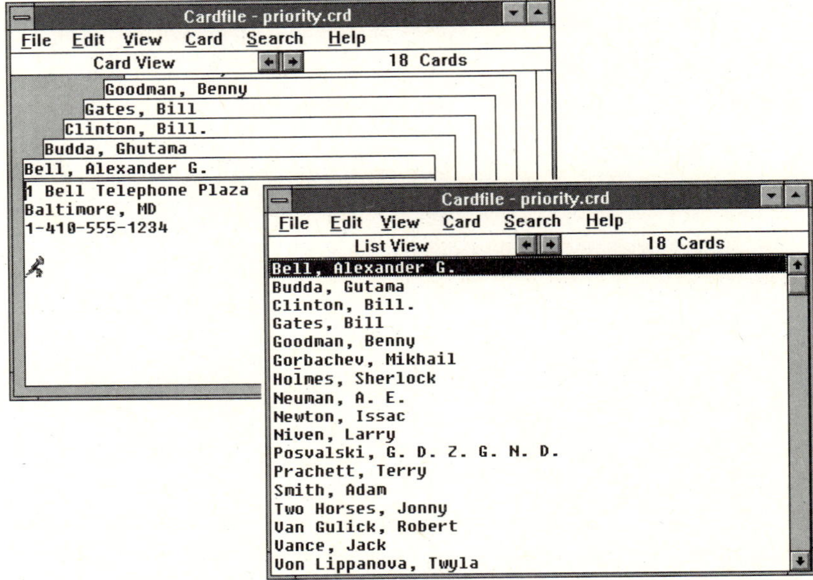

Figure 8.4
The Cardfile in Card and List views

Or:

- Select List from the Cardfile View menu to view the file as an index list (see the lower-right portion of Figure 8.4).

Deleting Cards

To delete a card from a card file:

1. Select the card to delete.
2. Select Delete from the Card menu. A dialog box will request confirmation.
3. Select OK.

Help Files ▼ Individual cards can be deleted only one at a time. To delete an entire file of cards, use File Manager to delete the corresponding .CRD file.

▶ Duplicating a Card

To duplicate a card in a card file:

1. Select the card to duplicate.
2. Select Duplicate from the Cardfile menu.

Help Files ▼ Existing cards can be duplicated within a card deck and edited and revised as desired. No restrictions are placed on duplicate index entries.

▶ Locating Cards

To move through the cards in a file:

- In Card view, click on any card visible to bring that card to the front.
- Select the left or right arrow buttons from the status bar to move forward or backward one item in either Card or List view.

Or, using the keyboard:

- Select the PgDn key to scroll forward one card in Card view or to move forward one page (of index lines) in List view.
- Select the PgUp key to scroll backward one card in Card view or move backward one page (of index lines) in List view.

- Select Ctrl+Home to display the first card in the file.
- Enter Ctrl+Shift+*character* to display the first card that has an index line beginning with the selected letter or number.
- Select the up or down arrow key to scroll one card forward or backward in List view.

▸ Selecting Cards

To select a card in Card view:

1. Scroll or search as necessary to locate the desired card.
2. Click on the card's index line to bring it to the front.

To select a card by using the Go To command:

1. Select Go To from the Search menu.
2. Enter text from the card's index line.
3. Select OK. The first matching card will be brought to the front.

HELP! *Case is ignored on all searches. Go To searches the card's entire index line, but does not search the contents of cards. Use the Find command to search the contents of the index cards.*

To select a card in List view:

1. Scroll or search as necessary to locate the desired index entry.
2. Select the card's index line.
3. Select Card from the View menu to view the card's contents.

▸ Dialing from the Cardfile

To use Cardfile entries to dial telephone numbers:

1. Select the card that contains the number to call.
2. Select Autodial from the Card menu. Cardfile displays the first number found on the card (see Figure 8.5).

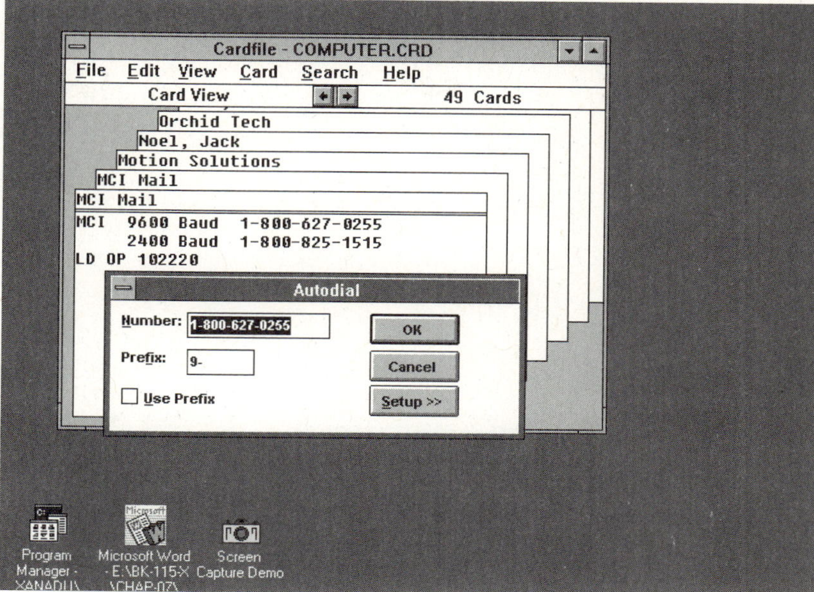

Figure 8.5
The Autodial dialog box

3. Change the number shown by
   - Editing the number in the Autodial dialog box
   - Highlighting a number on the card before selecting the Autodial option
4. If required (for example, by a phone switchboard), use the prefix displayed in the Prefix box by selecting the Use Prefix check box.
5. Select the Setup button to change modem settings. Select the appropriate settings from the Autodial Setup dialog box (see Figure 8.6).
6. Select OK to dial.

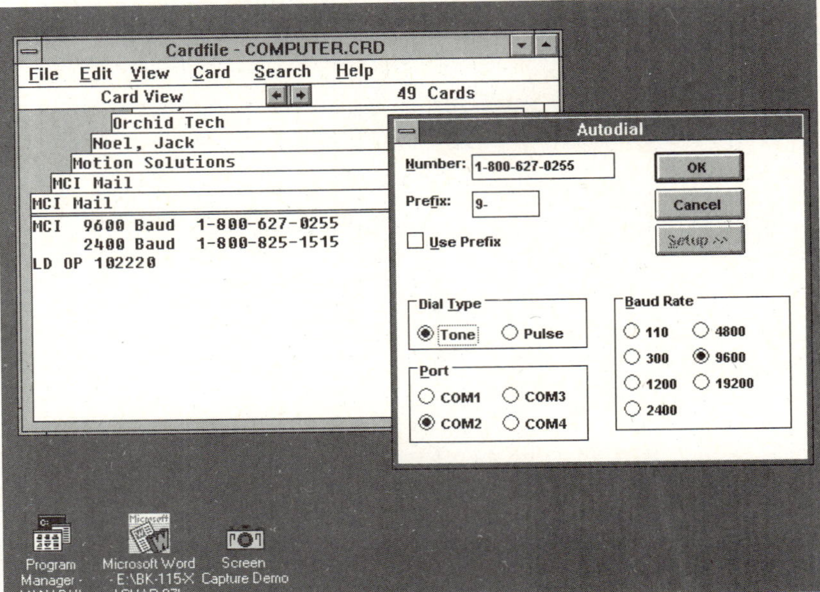

Figure 8.6
The Autodial Setup dialog box

Help Files ▼ Before Cardfile can be used to dial the phone, there are two requirements that must be met.

- A Hayes or Hayes command set-compatible modem is required. (Most modems follow this standard.)
- The first number appearing on the card (but not on the card index) should be a valid phone number.
  - Phone number entries cannot contain any spaces. Parentheses and dashes are permitted.
  - Phone number entries should appear exactly as they will be dialed, including prefixes required for long distance, area codes, and so on.

For example, an entry to dial 800 Information could be written as 1-800-555-1212. Or, if you prefer an abbreviated format, 18005551212 is also acceptable.

The prefix field is ideal for specifying a switchboard prefix, such as 9 to request an outside line or #73 to cancel call waiting. However, if the Use Prefix option is selected, the prefix is used for *all* calls. Prefixes that apply only to specific entries—such as the long-distance prefix 1—should be included in the phone number entry on individual cards.

▸ Editing a Card's Index

To edit a card's index:

1. Select the card to edit.
2. Select Index from the Edit menu or double-click on the index line.
3. Edit or revise the text as desired. Up to 40 characters can be entered.
4. Select OK when completed.
5. Select Save from the File menu.

▸ Editing a Card's Contents

To edit the text contents of a card:

1. Select the card to edit.
2. Click anywhere in the contents section of the card.
3. Revise the text display as desired.
4. Select Save from the File menu when changes are complete.

▸ Searching Cards for Contents

To search for text on a card:

1. Select Find from the Search menu.
2. Enter the text to search for in the Find What box.
3. Select the Match Case option to match capitalization.
4. Select the Find Next button.
5. To repeat a search, select the Find Next button again or press F3.

Restoring an Index Card

To restore an index card:

- Select the Restore option from the Edit menu.

Help Files ▼ All changes made to a card can be undone if the card remains at the front of the file and the file has not been saved to disk.

Using the Clipboard to Copy Text to and from the Cardfile

To move or copy text from one card to another:

1. Select the text to be moved or copied.
2. Select Copy or Cut from the Edit menu to copy or move text.
3. Select the card to insert the text.
4. Use the mouse cursor to select an insertion point or select a block of text to replace.
5. Select Paste from the Edit menu. The text will appear on the destination card.

Help Files ▼ The Clipboard can be used to copy text between cards within a card file, between cards in different card files, or between the card file and other applications.

Including Images on Index Cards

There are three methods for including images in cards: copying, embedding, and linking. Which method(s) can be used depends on the source application. See Figure 8.7 for an example.

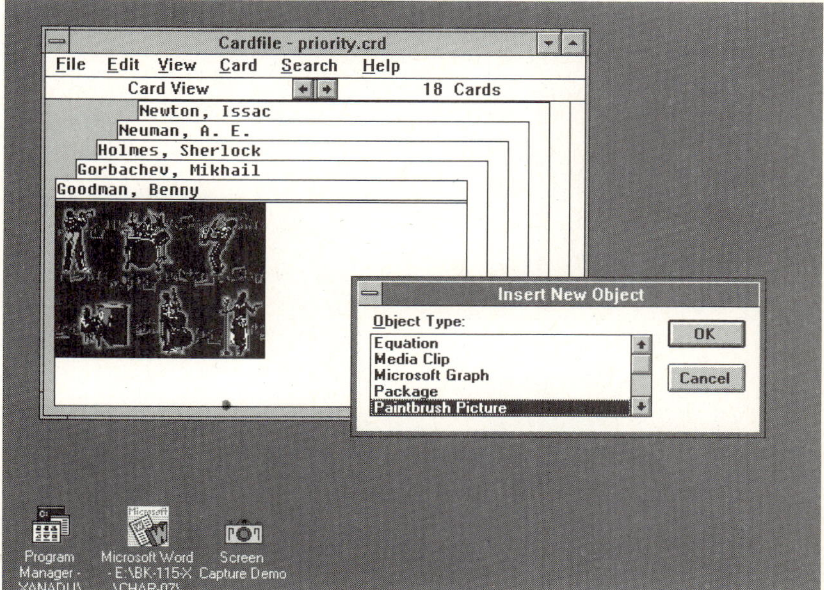

Figure 8.7
Pasting an image to a card

Pasting an Image to a Card

To paste (copy) an image to a card:

1. Copy the image to the Clipboard.
2. Switch to the Cardfile, loading a card index or adding a card, if necessary.
3. Select the card where the image will be placed.
4. Select Picture mode from the Edit menu.
5. Select the Paste operation from the Edit menu to transfer the image to the card.
6. Position the image by dragging or using the arrow keys.
7. Select Text mode from the Edit menu.

Help Files ▼ Copying an image to a card file is done in the same fashion as other Clipboard paste operations. Once an image has been copied to a card, it can be revised only by replacing it with another image—that is, by deleting the existing image to replace it with a new image. Use the Paste command from the Edit menu to insert an image from the Clipboard.

The Paste command is used either to copy or to embed an image. If the image was created by a server application, the image will be embedded. Otherwise, the image will be copied.

▶ Copying and Cutting Images to and from Cards

Each card can contain only one image.

To copy or move images between cards:

1. Select the card containing the image.
2. Select Picture mode from the Edit menu.
3. Select the Copy or Cut command from the Edit menu.
4. Select a destination card.
5. Select Paste from the Edit menu.
6. Position the image by dragging or using the arrow keys.
7. Select Text from the Edit menu to conclude.

Help Files ▼ The Cut and Copy commands copy an image to the Clipboard. From there, it can be pasted to another card or application. If the original image was created by a server application, the image will be embedded. Otherwise, the image will simply be copied.

Embedding Images

The text, if any, on a card may be covered by an image; however, the text is not erased. Thus, a card file of images might also contain phone numbers (for use by the Autodialer), even though the text entries might not be visible.

To embed an image:

1. Create or open an image by using Paintbrush or another application with similar capabilities.
2. Select the image by using the Pick or Scissors tool.
3. Select Copy from the Edit menu. A copy of the drawing is placed in the Clipboard.
4. Select the Save option from the File menu to save any changes.
5. Switch to Cardfile, opening a card file in which to embed the image, if necessary. Select the destination card.
6. Select Picture mode from the Edit menu.
7. Select Paste from the Edit menu.
8. Position the image by dragging or using the arrow keys.
9. Select Text from the Edit menu to return to text mode.

Help Files ▼ Embedding is similar to copying, but it allows the image to retain a connection to the original source so that the image can be edited from within Cardfile. Use the Paste command from the Edit menu to embed an image from the Clipboard.

Editing an Embedded Image

To edit an embedded image:

1. Select Picture mode from the Edit menu.
2. Double-click on the linked drawing or, from the Edit menu, select Edit Paintbrush Picture Object. (The type named in the command will change to reflect the object type selected.) The application originally used to create the image will be started.
3. Edit the drawing as desired.
4. Select Update from the Paintbrush File menu.
5. From the Paintbrush File menu, choose Exit & Return To *name of document*.

   HELP! *The Undo command from the Edit menu can be used to undo these changes.*

Linking an Image

To link an image:

1. Create or open an image by using Paintbrush or another application with similar capabilities.
2. Select the image by using the Pick or Scissors tool.
3. Select Copy from the Edit menu. A copy of the drawing is placed in the Clipboard.
4. Select the Save option from the File menu to save any changes.
5. Switch to Cardfile, opening a file in which to embed the image, if necessary. Select the destination card.
6. Select Picture mode from the Edit menu.
7. Select Paste Link from the Edit menu.
8. Position the image by dragging or using the arrow keys. Any text on the card may be covered by the image.
9. Select Text from the Edit menu to return to text mode.

Help Files ▼ Linking creates a dynamic connection between two files such that changes to one are automatically reflected in the other. To link an image from the Clipboard, use the Paste Link command from the Edit menu.

To see how this works, use the Paintbrush utility to create or edit a drawing, and then link the drawing to a Cardfile card. The linked image on the card will immediately reflect subsequent changes made to the original image in Paintbrush.

When an image is linked, only a representation of the image is displayed; the original (actual) image continues to be stored in its original file. After the link is established, the image can be edited either from the Cardfile card or from the Paintbrush program. Any changes will be reflected in both, as well as anywhere else where a link has been established to the image.

▶ Editing a Linked Image

To edit a linked image:

1. Select Picture from the Edit menu.
2. Double-click on the linked-drawing or, from the Edit menu, select Edit Paintbrush Picture Object. (The type named in the command will change to reflect the object type selected.)
3. The Paintbrush application appears with the image ready for editing.
4. After editing, select Save from the File menu. The representation in Cardfile of the linked image is automatically updated to reflect any changes.
5. From the File menu, choose Exit & Return To *name of document*.

Help Files ▼ Linked images are edited in the same fashion as embedded images. However, any changes made are reflected in all linked instances. If the Update option is set to Manual, linked instances are not updated until an update is explicitly requested.

Selecting Manual update prevents the embedded image from being repainted until changes are complete, thus speeding operations when more than one copy of an image is visible.

▶ Updating Linked Images

To change the update options for linked images:

1. Select the Cardfile card with the linked image.
2. Select Link from the Edit menu.
3. Select Automatic or Manual.
4. Select OK.

To manually update linked images:

1. Select Link from the Edit menu.
2. Select the Update Now button.
3. Select OK.

Help Files ▼ Linked images can be updated automatically (the default) or manually. If the Update option is set to Manual, linked instances are not updated until an update is explicitly requested.

Embedding a Sound File in a Cardfile Card

To embed a sound file in a Cardfile card:

1. Select a card file and card in which to embed a sound file. The sound file will be inserted at the upper-left corner of the card.
2. Select Picture from the Edit menu.
3. Select Insert Object from the Edit menu. A dialog box appears, listing all applications on the computer that support object linking and embedding.
4. Select Sound or Sound Recorder and OK to open the Sound Recorder.
5. Select the Insert File command from the Sound Recorder Edit menu.
6. In the Insert File dialog box, select the sound file to be embedded and select OK, or record a new sound file.
7. Select Update from the Sound Recorder File menu to embed the selected sound file in the Cardfile card (or other document). The sound file is represented by an icon, as shown in Figure 8.4, preceding.
8. Select Exit from the Sound Recorder File menu to return to the Cardfile card.

Editing an Embedded Sound File

Sound files can be edited only by using the Sound Recorder.

To edit an embedded sound file:

1. Select the embedded sound file to edit.
2. Select Sound Object from the Edit menu in Cardfile.
3. Select Edit from the resulting menu to open the Sound Recorder with the sound file displayed.
4. Edit the sound file as needed.
5. Select Update from the Sound Recorder File menu to update the embedded sound file in the Cardfile card.
6. Select Exit from the Sound Recorder File menu to return to the Cardfile.

Linking a Sound File to a Cardfile Card

To link a sound file to a Cardfile card:

1. Open the Sound Recorder.
2. Create and save a sound file or open the sound file to be linked.
3. Select Copy from the Edit menu.
4. Select a card file and card to link to a sound file. The sound file will be inserted at the upper-left corner of the card.
5. Select Picture from the Edit menu.
6. Select Paste Link from the Edit menu. (See Figure 8.4, preceding, where the sound file has been moved lower on the card.)

Editing a Linked Sound File

To edit a linked sound file:

1. Select the card with the linked sound file to edit.
2. Select Sound Object from the Cardfile Edit menu.
3. Select Edit from the resulting menu to open the Sound Recorder with the selected sound file displayed.
4. Edit the sound file as required.
5. Select Save from the Sound Recorder File menu to update the linked sound file.
6. Select Exit from the Sound Recorder File menu to return to the Cardfile.

Opening and Saving Card Files

To open a card file:

1. Select Open from the File menu. The Open dialog box appears with the file specification *.CRD.
2. Change the extension if the desired card file uses a different file extension.

3. Change drive and directories as required to locate the desired card file.
4. Locate the desired card file.
5. If desired, select the Read-Only check box to specify that the card file cannot be changed.
6. Double-click on the file name or select OK.

To save an existing card file:

- Select Save from the File menu.

To save a new file or save changes under a new name:

1. Select Save As from the File menu.
2. Using the Save As dialog box, select the drive and directory where the file should be saved.
3. Enter a file name in the File Name box. If no extension is specified, the default extension .CRD is added.
4. Select OK.

▸ Merging Existing Index Files

To merge two card files:

1. Open the first file to be merged.
2. Select Merge from the File menu.
3. From the Files box, select the second file to be merged. Or, type the name of the file in the File Name box.
4. Select OK. The files are merged and sorted.
5. Save the merged file.
   - Select the Save option from the File menu to save the merged file under the name of the first file selected.
   - Select the Save As option to save the merged file under a different file name.

Help Files ▼ The Merge option permits you to consolidate two sets of index cards, merging all cards of the two files in correct alphabetical order.

▶ Printing Cards

To print a single card from a card file:

1. Select the file.
2. Select the card to print.
3. Select Print from the File menu.

To print an entire card file:

1. Select the file.
2. Select Print All from the File menu.

▶ Changing Printers or Printer Options

To change printers from Cardfile:

1. Select the Print Setup option from the File menu.
2. Select the Default Printer or the Specific Printer options in the Printer box. If the Specific Printer option is selected, select the printer desired from the list of available printers.
3. Select orientation and paper specifications as appropriate.
4. Select the Options button for options specific to the selected printer driver.
5. Select OK.

▶ Including Headers and Footers

To include headers or footers while printing cards:

1. Select Page Setup from the File menu.
2. Enter the header or footer text and/or codes.
3. Select OK.

Help Files ▼ You can use codes to include automatic features in headers and footers. Codes are shown in Table 8.7.

Table 8.7
Printer Header and Footer Codes

Code	Printed Results
&d	Prints the current date.
&t	Prints the current time.
&p	Prints the page numbers.
&f	Prints the name of the file.
&l	Left-aligns all text following the code.
&c	Centers all text following the code.
&r	Right-aligns all text following the code.

The Clock Utility

A check mark appears at the left of each selected option on the Clock menu.

▶ Selecting a Clock Format

To select a clock format:

1. Select Settings.
2. Select either digital or analog display (see Figure 8.8).

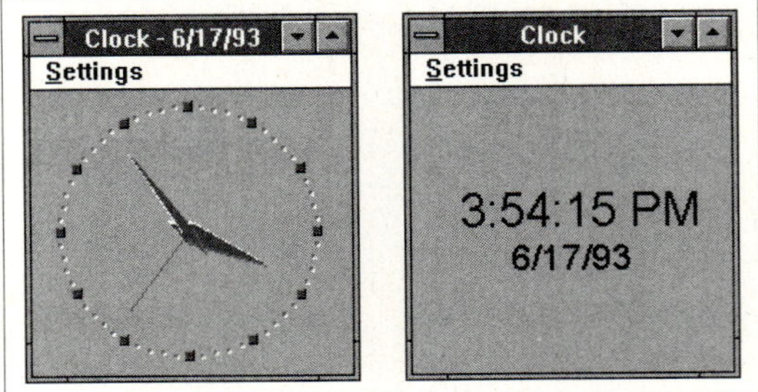

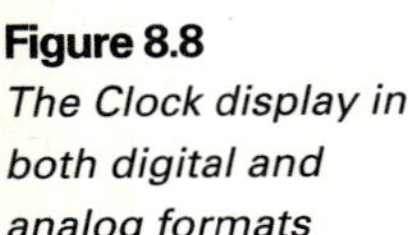

Figure 8.8
The Clock display in both digital and analog formats

3. Select Seconds to include a sweep second hand in the analog display or to include seconds in the digital display.
4. Select Date to include the date in the title bar.
5. Select GMT to switch to the Greenwich Mean Time (Zulu) zone setting.

▶ Keeping the Clock on Top

To keep the clock on top of other applications:

1. Select the Control menu (in the upper-left corner of the Clock window).
2. Select the Always On Top option.

Help Files ▼ In analog format, the date is displayed only if the Clock window is large enough to support the date as well as the title. In digital format, the date appears below the time display.

When the Always on Top option is selected, the Clock window will always appear on top of other windows—even when reduced to an icon.

THE RESCUE PAGES: Using Accessories

The Calculator doesn't seem to respond to the keyboard.

First, make sure that the Calculator has the focus—that is, that the Calculator is the active application. If the Calculator is inactive, the title bar will be grayed. Use the mouse to click on the title bar or press Alt+Tab to step though open applications until the Calculator is made active.

Second, check to be sure that Num Lock is on (the Num Lock light on the keyboard should be lit). When Num Lock is off, the keypad keys are interpreted as arrow (cursor) keys and are not recognized by the Calculator.

Third, if you have a keyboard with a built-in calculator, make sure that the calculator on the keyboard is off. When the keyboard calculator is on, the keypad is entirely disabled.

The Cardfile Autodial feature keeps trying to dial the street address.

The Cardfile Autodialer is sophisticated but not intelligent. When Autodial is requested, the current card is checked for the first sequence of numbers that resembles a telephone number. If a street address appears before the telephone number, Autodialer may select it. Or it may miss a prefix or an area code and notice only the local number.

If you're going to use the Autodial feature, use a format that Cardfile can easily recognize. Make the telephone number the first line on the card, and include the prefix and area code if necessary. Use hyphens if desired but do not use any spaces in the telephone number.

If you have more than one number, use the mouse to highlight the phone number desired before selecting Autodial.

The Cardfile tries to dial the phone but nothing happens.

First, go to the Control Panel and select Ports. From the Ports utility, check to make sure that all port assignments are correct and that the ports are correctly configured.

Second, from the Autodial dialog box, select Setup. Check the port assignment, baud rate, and dial type.

Last, make sure the modem and phone line are connected.

I've linked images to several cards in the Cardfile. Now, paging through the cards takes forever.

Instead of linking or embedding images to or in cards in the Cardfile, try simply copying the image. Linking or embedding sends requests for updates to the source, slowing things down. A simple image copy does not.

I can't see the card I want.

You can use the Search/Go To or Search/Find options to find the card. Or, perhaps more conveniently, you can click repeatedly on the top card (the back of the stack) until the desired card appears in the display stack, then click on the card. Of course, you can also click on the forward and backward arrows above the card stack.

I entered 6 (3+2) = in the Calculator—exactly as it appears in my textbook—but I get a wrong result.

Well, the formula may look fine on paper, but when you enter it this way, the Calculator interprets the information inside the parentheses as if it were a numbered entered from the keyboard. This is why you get the unwanted result 65. To calculate the formula correctly, the Calculator requires a more explicit instruction, such as 6 * (3+2) =, which will give you a correct result of 30.

If you'd like to play around with this, try another example: enter 6 (9+8) =. Did you expect a result of 617? Are you wondering where the 77 came from? The 6 was moved to the tens column and the parenthetical total—17—was added in the ones column.

Or try this: enter 6 (9*9). The result is 621 (which is 69 multipled by 9). Now, aren't computers fun?

When I try to edit an embedded object, nothing happens.

There are a couple of possibilities. The first (and most probable) is that the object is not embedded—it might simply have been copied and pasted. The second possibility is that you could be out of memory and not have space to run the source application.

CHAPTER

HELP! Word Processors

Windows NT supplies two (or, depending on your viewpoint, three) native word processors: the Windows NT Notepad and Unipad editors, and the Microsoft Write word processor.

The Windows NT Notepad is a simple text editor useful for handling small text files—such as .BAT batch files—that require an unformatted text output. The Unipad editor is essentially the same as Notepad, except that it handles the international Unicode character set.

In contrast, Windows NT Write is a word processor that can be used to create and print formatted documents, including images. While less sophisticated than, for example, Microsoft Word, Microsoft Write still provides a surprising degree of flexibility and enough features to handle many word processing tasks.

Topics covered in this chapter include

- The Notepad and Unipad editors
- Editing in Notepad
- Managing Microsoft Write document files
- Printing from Microsoft Write
- Editing text documents

- Formatting text
- Formatting paragraphs
- Operating in a Write document
- Working with images
- Working with Sound Recorder files

The Notepad and Unipad Editors

▶ Differences between Notepad and Unipad

The Notepad and Unipad editors use the same menu structures and execute the same tasks in essentially the same fashion. The difference is that the Unipad editor is written for the international character set—16-bit characters instead of 8-bit ASCII/ANSI.

Consult the on-line help documentation for changes that were not available at the time of publication.

▶ Opening Notepad Files

To open a Notepad file:

1. Select Open from the File menu. The Open dialog box (see Figure 9.1) appears in response.
2. If required, select a drive in the Drivers list box.
3. Select the directory in the Directories list box.
4. Select a file extension or file specification from the File Type list box. The default specification is *.TXT.
5. Select a file in the Files list box.
6. Double-click on the file name, or choose the OK button.

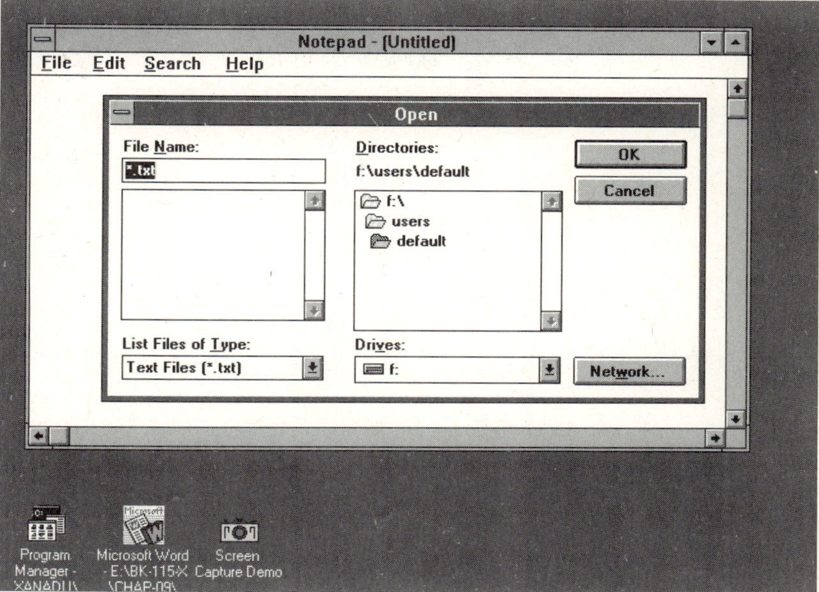

Figure 9.1
The Open dialog box

▶ Saving Notepad Files

To save an existing file:

- Select Save from the File menu. The work file will be saved under its existing name, and you will remain in Notepad.

To save a new file or save an existing file under a new name:

1. Select Save As from the File menu. The Save As dialog box (see Figure 9.2) appears in response.
2. Select a destination drive in the Drives list box.
3. Select a directory in the Directories list box.
4. Enter a name for the file in the File Name edit box.
5. Optionally, specify a file extension either in the File Name edit box or in the Save File As Type box. If no extension is specified, the default extension .TXT is used, as shown.
6. Select OK.

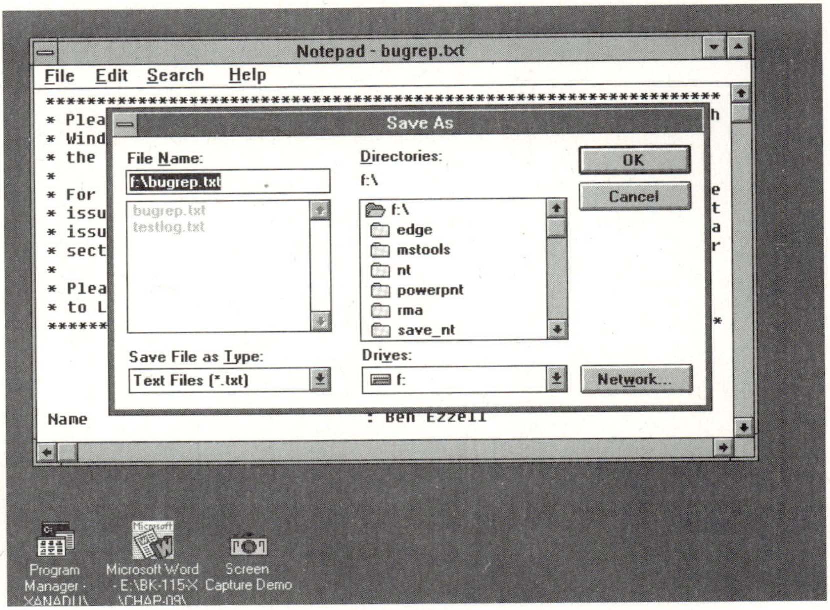

Figure 9.2
The Save As dialog box

▸ Printing Notepad Documents

To print Notepad documents:

Notepad always prints to the default printer.

- Select Print from the File menu.
- Select the Cancel button to terminate printing.
- Select the Print Setup command from the File menu to choose a different printer as the default printer. (See "Changing Printers and Printer Options," following.)

▸ Adjusting Page Margins

To set page margins before printing a Notepad document:

The measurement units used (English or metric) are set via the International option in the Control Panel.

1. Select the Page Setup option from the File menu. The Page Setup dialog box (see Figure 9.3) appears.
2. Enter the margin settings desired in the Margins area.
3. Select OK.

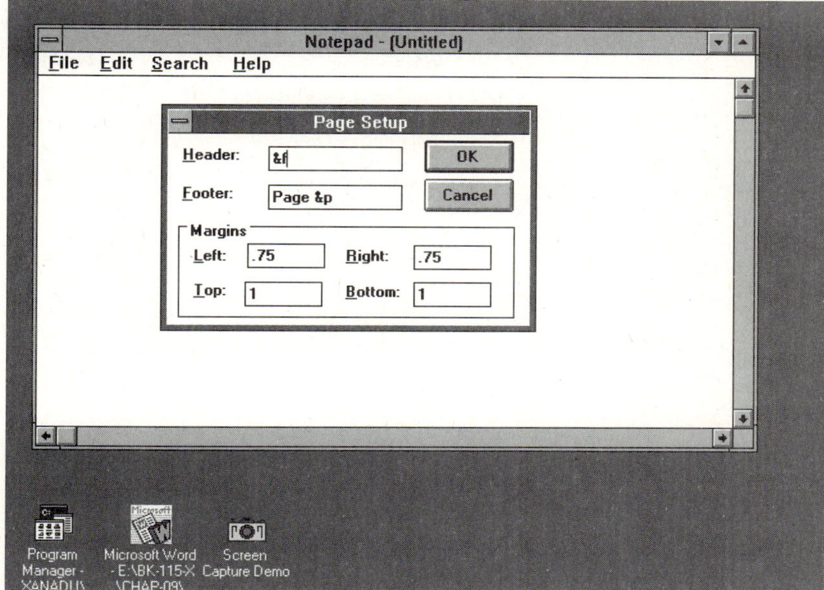

Figure 9.3
The Page Setup dialog box

Help Files ▼ By default, Notepad uses the standard margin settings shown in the Page Setup dialog box. To change the print margins, adjust the settings before selecting the Print command.

▶ Printing Headers and Footers for Notepad Documents

To include a header or footer when printing a Notepad document:

More than one code can be included in a header or footer line.

1. Select Page Setup from the File menu (see Figure 9.3, preceding).
2. Enter the header or footer text in the Header or Footer edit box of the Page Setup dialog box. Optional codes are shown in Table 9.1.
3. Select OK.

Table 9.1
Header and Footer Codes

Code	Prints
&p	Page numbers
&f	Name of file
&d	Current date
&t	Current time
&l	Left-aligns following text
&c	Centers following text (default setting)
&r	Right-aligns following text

Help Files ▼ Printed Notepad documents can include header and footer text displaying text, date and time information, file names, and page numbers using left, center, and right alignments.

▶ Changing Printers and Printer Options

To change printers or printer options:

1. Select Print Setup from the File menu. The Print Setup dialog box (see Figure 9.4) appears.
2. Select the Default Printer or Specific Printer options from the Printer box.
3. If Specific Printer is selected, select the printer desired from the list displayed.
4. Select orientation and paper specifications as desired.
5. Select the Options button to display options specific to the selected printer driver.
6. Select OK. The new printer or options become the default settings.

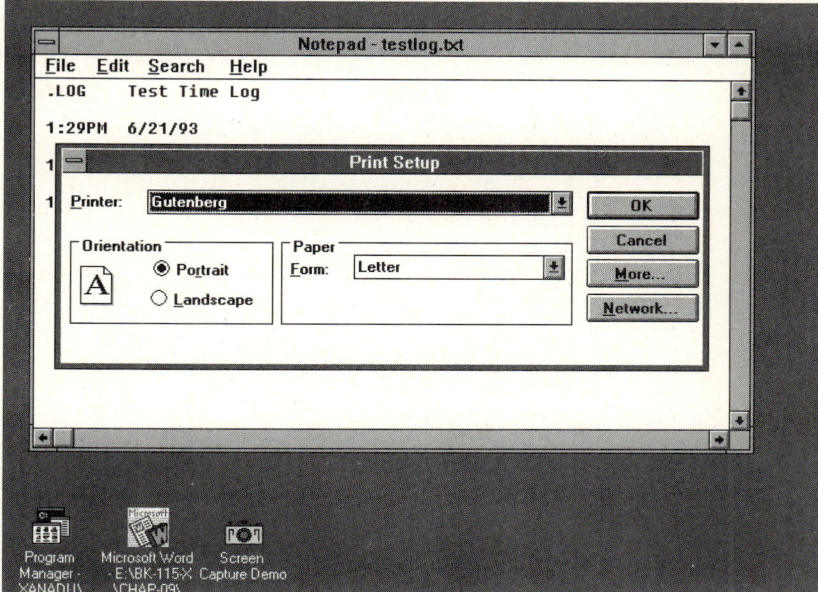

Figure 9.4
The Print Setup dialog box

Help Files ▼ The Notepad utility prints only to the default printer selection. To change printers or printer options, select the Printer Setup option from the File menu and select a new default printer or new default options.

Editing in Notepad

▶ Formatting Text

To enable or disable the Word Wrap option:

- Select Word Wrap from the Edit menu. A check mark appears when Word Wrap is enabled.

To format text:

- Press Enter to end a line.
- Select the beginning or end of a line and press Enter to insert a blank line.
- Enter Tab at the beginning of a line to indent the line. Press Tab anywhere else to insert a tab within a line.

Help Files ▼ When the Word Wrap option is selected, Notepad formats text lines to wrap text on screen so a new line begins when text reaches the right window margin. No line breaks, however, are entered in the actual text file.

When Word Wrap is not selected, the Enter key must be used to begin a new line of text or to break existing lines.

Word Wrap remains in effect until the Word Wrap option is selected again.

▶ Positioning within a Notepad Document

To position the cursor within a Notepad document:

- Select Home to move to the beginning of a line.
- Select End to move to the end of a line.
- Select Ctrl+Home to move to the beginning of the document.
- Select Ctrl+End to move to the end of the document.
- Use the arrow keys to move the text cursor by line and character position.
- Use the scroll bars to scroll through a document.
- Click the mouse to position the cursor anywhere within the document window.

▶ Selecting a Block within a Notepad Document

To select a block of text:

1. Position the mouse cursor at the beginning of the block.
2. Press and hold the mouse button.
3. Move to the end of the block, highlighting it.

▶ Deleting Text

To delete text by single characters:

- Press Backspace to delete the character immediately to the left of the cursor.

Or:

- Press the Del key to delete the character immediately to the right of the cursor.

To delete multiple characters:

1. Select the block of text to delete.
2. Press the Backspace or Del key, or select Delete from the Edit menu.

Help Files ▼ To save deleted text to the Clipboard, use the Cut option from the Edit menu. Remember, however, that the Clipboard will hold only one block of text and that the existing contents are overwritten when a new block is copied.

To delete text without overwriting material on the clipboard, use the Backspace or Del key, or the Delete command from the Edit menu.

Cut and Paste Operations

The Copy, Cut, and Paste commands are used to transfer information to and from the Clipboard as well as within a document.

To copy or move text within a document:

1. Select (highlight) the text to copy or move.
2. Select Copy or Cut from the Edit menu.
3. Move the cursor to the location where the text should be inserted or select (highlight) a block of text to be replaced by the copied text.
4. Select Paste from the Edit menu.

Selecting All Text within a Document

To select all text within a Notepad document:

- Select the Select All option from the Edit menu. The entire document will be highlighted.

Or:

- Click the mouse anywhere within the text window to cancel the selection.

Help Files The Select All option can be used to copy an entire document to the Clipboard. From the Clipboard (see Chapter 7), the document contents can be merged with another document file or can be inserted in a document under another application.

Searching Documents

The matching text may be concealed if the Find dialog box overlaps the Notepad window.

To locate specific text—either specific characters or words—within a document:

1. Place the cursor at the point where the search should begin.
2. Select Find from the Search menu.
3. Enter the characters or words to locate in the Find What edit box in the Find dialog box (see Figure 9.5).

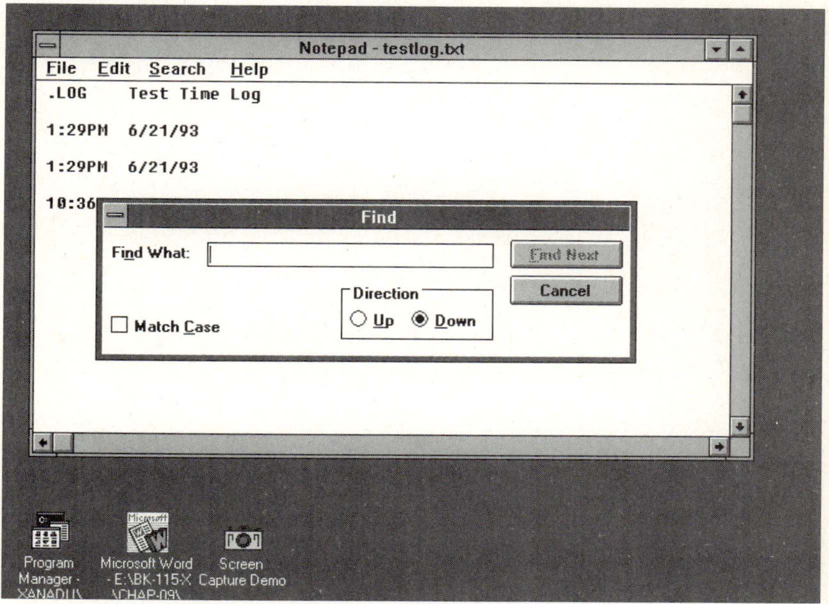

Figure 9.5
The Find dialog box

4. Select Match Case to match capitalization precisely.
5. Select Up or Down (the default) to set the search direction.
6. Select Find Next to initiate the search. The first matching text entry will be highlighted.
7. If no match is found, a message reports the lack of success. Select OK.
8. Select the Find Next button to locate the next match.

Help Files ▼ A search can be initiated from any location within a Notepad document. By default, the search begins at the start point and works toward the end of the file.

Once a search target has been specified, a repeat search can be initiated—without calling the Find dialog box—by selecting Find Next from the Search menu or by pressing the F3 key.

▶ Inserting Date and Time Information in Documents

To add the date or time to a Notepad document:

1. Move the cursor to the point where the time and date should appear or select a block of text to be replaced by the time and date.
2. Select Time/Date from the Edit menu. The current time and date are inserted using the format specified in the International settings in the Control Panel.

▶ Creating a Time Log

To create a time-log document:

1. Enter .LOG at the left margin of the first line within a Notepad document.
2. Enter any comments or text desired in the document.
3. Select Save from the File menu.

Help Files ▼ A time-log document, designated by the .LOG flag, can be used to keep track of time spent on various projects or tasks. Each time the log document is opened, Notepad enters the current system time and date at the end of the document. Comments can be added as desired. Following is a sample time-log document.

```
.LOG    Time Log Test File

1:29PM 6/21/93
working on XYZ account

6:29PM 6/21/93
finished XYZ -- supper time
```

Managing Microsoft Write Document Files

▶ Opening a Microsoft Write Document

To open a Microsoft Write document:

1. Select Open from the File menu. The Open dialog box shown in Figure 9.1, preceding, appears in response.
2. If required, select a drive in the Drivers list box.
3. Select the directory in the Directories list box.
4. Select a file extension or file specification in the File Type list box. The default specification is *.WRI.
5. Select a file from the Files list box.
6. Double-click on the file name, or choose the OK button.

To open a non-Microsoft Write document:

1. Select Open from the File menu (see Figure 9.1, preceding).

2. If required, select a drive in the Drivers list box.
3. Select the directory in the Directories list box.
4. Select a file extension or file specification in the File Type list box.
5. Select a file in the Files list box.
6. Double-click on the file name, or choose the OK button. The Conversion dialog box (see Figure 9.6) appears, offering a choice of format conversions.

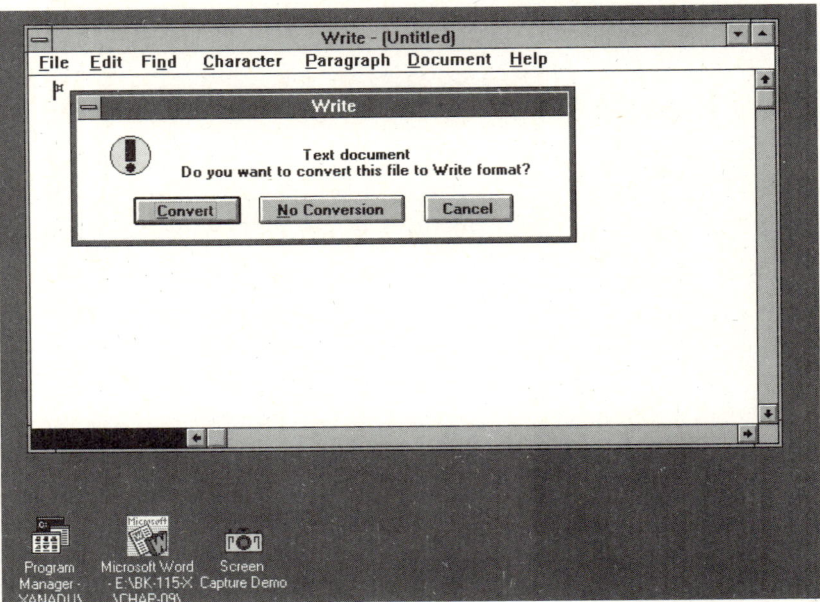

Figure 9.6
Conversion options

7. Select the appropriate format conversion option:
   - Select the No Conversion button to open documents created by Windows applications or Write documents saved in text-only format.
   - Select the Convert button for Microsoft Word documents or for non-Windows text-only documents.

To convert a Microsoft Word document to the Microsoft Write format:

- Select the Convert button from the Conversion dialog box.

To edit a Windows NT data file without converting it to Write format:

- Select the No Conversion button from the Conversion dialog box.

To convert a non-Windows NT text file to Write format:

- Select the Convert button from the Conversion dialog box.

Help Files ▼ Microsoft Write can be used with both Windows and non-Windows-based text files. Because most Windows NT text files are in the same format as Write files, no conversion is necessary. However, documents that were not created using the Windows NT character format must be converted to Microsoft Write format before editing.

▶ Saving Documents

To save a document from Write:

- Select Save from the File menu.

To save an untitled document or to save a titled document under a new name:

1. Select Save As from the File menu.
2. Enter a file name.
3. Select OK.

To save a document in a non-Write format:

1. Select Save As from the File menu. The Save As dialog box is shown in Figure 9.7.

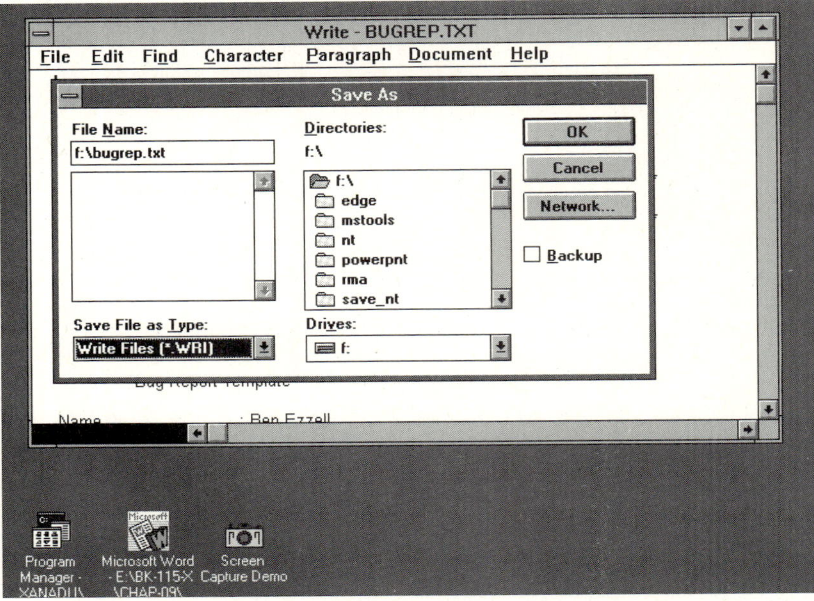

Figure 9.7
The Save As dialog box

2. Enter a file name.
3. Select a format from the Save File As Type list.
4. Select OK to save the file.

To save automatic backup copies of a document:

1. Select Save As from the File menu.
2. Select the Backup check box.
3. Select the backup format desired from the Save File As Type list.
4. Select OK.

Help Files ▼ When a Write document is saved in text or Microsoft Word format, all formatting and graphics information is lost.

Windows 3.1 does not require any special compatibility provisions.

If any embedded or linked objects are included in a Write file, the Windows 3.0 Write Format option appears. Selecting Windows 3.0 compatibility deletes any embedded or linked objects; all static objects remain unchanged.

Use the Backup option to have Write automatically create a backup copy when saving a file.

Printing from Microsoft Write

▶ Printing Documents

To print a document from Microsoft Write:

1. Select Print from the File menu.
2. Select the print options desired from the Print dialog box shown in Figure 9.8.

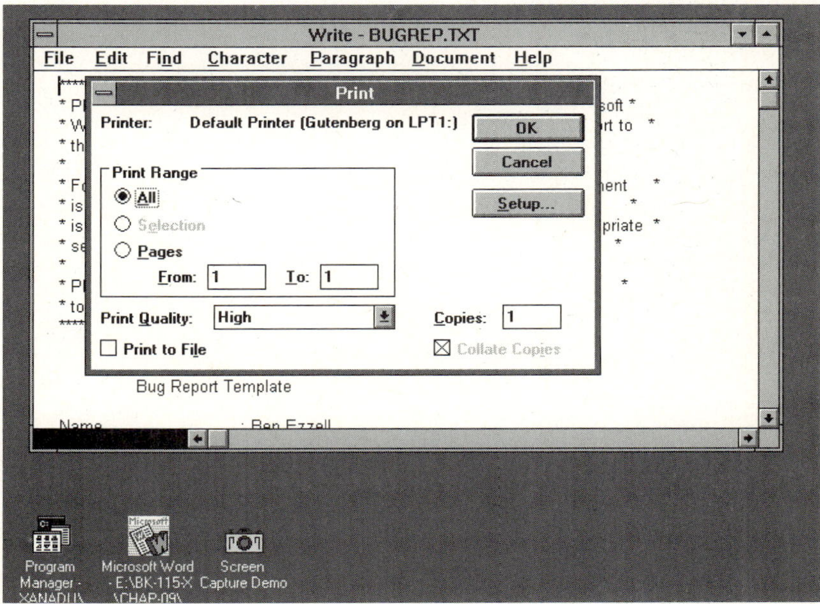

Figure 9.8
The Print dialog box

- Copies—enter the number of copies to print.
- All—prints all pages in the document.
- Selection—prints only the selected (highlighted) text.
- Pages: From/To—prints only the pages specified.
- Print Quality—depending on the printer, this option offers a choice of output qualities; for example, High, Medium, Low, and Draft.
- Print To File—prompts for a file name and saves output to a file containing printer format commands.
- Collate Copies—used for multiple copies. Each copy printed entire and in order.

3. Select OK to print.

Help Files ▼ The Print Quality options offered depend on the output device. In many cases—such as with most laser-quality printers—the various qualities offered may be indistinguishable. In other cases (with lower resolution printers), draft quality may print an unformatted copy with images rendered as empty boxes.

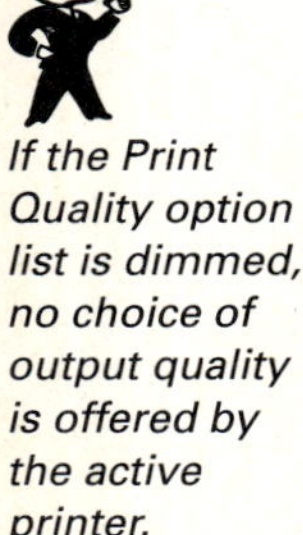

If the Print Quality option list is dimmed, no choice of output quality is offered by the active printer.

▶ Changing Printers/Printer Options

To change printers or printer options:

1. Select Print Setup from the File menu.
2. Select the Default Printer or Specific Printer options in the Printer box.
3. If the Specific Printer option is selected, select the printer desired from the list displayed.
4. Select orientation and paper specifications as desired.

5. Select the Options button to display options specific to the selected printer driver.
6. Select OK. The new printer or options become the default settings.

Help Files ▼ Microsoft Write prints only to the default printer selection. To change printers or printer options, select the Printer Setup option from the File menu and select a new default printer or new default options.

Editing Text Documents

▶ Selecting Text Using the Selection Area

To select

- A single line, from the selection area (left margin), point to the line desired and click the mouse button once.
- Several lines, from the selection area, point to a line, then click and hold the mouse button while dragging the pointer up or down.
- An entire paragraph, from the selection area, point to a paragraph and double-click.
- Several paragraphs, from the selection area, point to a paragraph and double-click. Then drag the pointer up or down while holding the mouse button down.
- A range of text, from the selection area, point to a starting line or paragraph and click with the mouse. Then press and hold the Shift key while clicking on the last line or paragraph. Everything between the two points is selected (highlighted).
- The entire document, press the Ctrl key, then click the mouse anywhere in the selection area.

To cancel a selection:

- Click anywhere within the document area.

Help Files ▼ The document selection area extends vertically along the left margin of the document. When the mouse is in the selection area, the mouse cursor changes to a slanted arrow. In the document area, the mouse cursor appears as an I-beam.

▶ Copying, Cutting, and Pasting Text

To copy text using the mouse:

1. Select a block of text to copy or move.
2. Move the mouse cursor to the location where the text should appear.
3. Press and hold the Alt key, then click the mouse.

To move text using the mouse:

1. Select the text you want to move.
2. Move the mouse cursor to the location where the text should appear.
3. Press and hold the Shift+Alt combination, then click the mouse.

To copy or move text using the keyboard:

The Copy, Cut, and Paste commands are used to transfer text to and from the Clipboard and within a document.

1. Select a block of text to copy or move.
2. Select Copy or Cut from the Edit menu.
3. Move the text cursor to the location where the text should appear or select a block of text to replace.
4. Select Paste from the Edit menu.

▶ Locating Text

To locate text in a document:

1. Position the cursor at the location to start the search.
2. Select the Find option from the Find menu. The Find dialog box shown in Figure 9.9 appears.

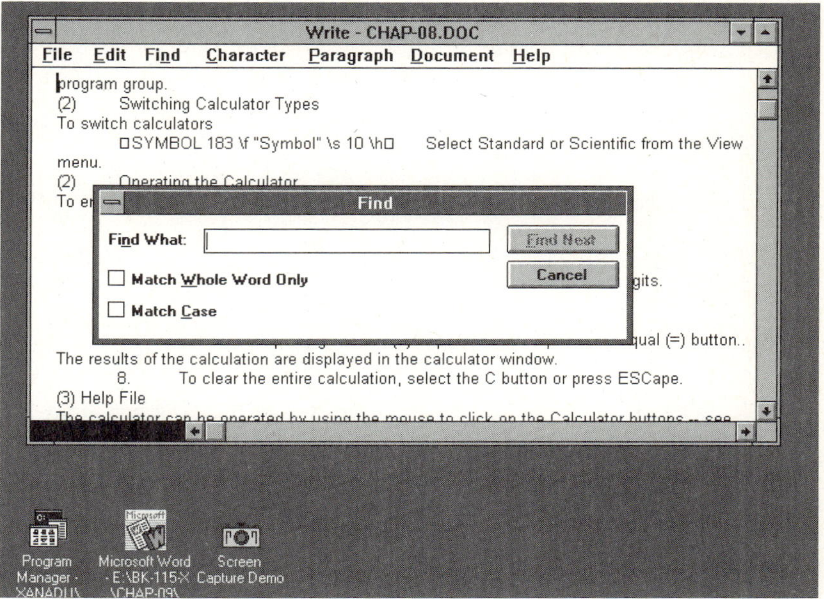

Figure 9.9
The Find dialog box

3. Enter the search text in the Find What edit box.
4. Select the Match Whole Word Only check box to match entire words only.
5. Select the Match Case check box to match capitalization precisely.
6. Select the Find Next button to initiate a search.
7. Press Alt+F6 or click in the text to switch back to the document.
8. Select the Find Next button to locate the next occurrence of the search text.
9. Select Cancel to close the Find dialog box.

To repeat a search without using the Find dialog box:

1. Select Cancel to close the Find dialog box.
2. Select Repeat Last Find from the Find menu or press F3 to locate the next occurrence of the search text.

To search for text including spaces, tabs, paragraph marks, or manual page breaks, use the following special characters in the Find What edit box:

- ^w identifies a space character.
- ^t identifies a tab character.
- ^p identifies a paragraph break.
- ^d identifies a page break inserted by using Ctrl+Enter.
- ? provides a wild card matching any character or string of characters.

Help Files ▼ The Find commands can be used to search for a single character, a word, or a string in a Write document.

The wild card ? can be used to identify any single character. For example, entering a search specification *thin?* will locate both *thing* and *things*, as well as *thinner*, *thinnest*, *think* and *thins*. It will even identify *thin* when it occurs at the end of a line, by matching the wild card with the following carriage return character.

A search specification of *t?in* would identify the previous matches but would also find matches such as *string* and not *in*cluded.

The search match is identified by highlighting.

Replacing Text

To find and replace text in a document:

1. Position the cursor at the location at which you want to start the search or select (highlight) a block of text to limit the search-and-replace operation to a portion of the document.
2. Select the Replace option from the Find menu to call the Replace dialog box shown in Figure 9.10.

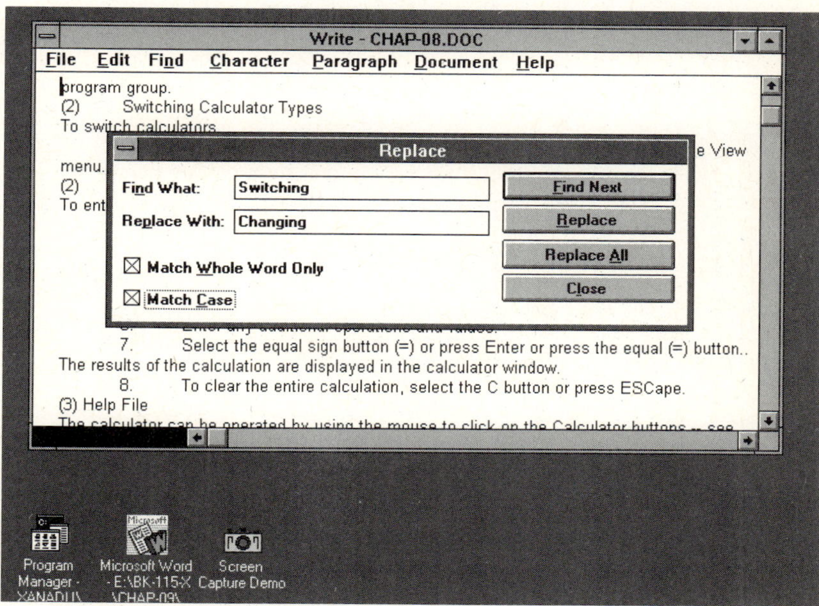

Figure 9.10
The Replace dialog box

3. Enter the search text in the Find What edit box.
4. Enter the replacement text in the Replace With edit box.
5. Select the Match Whole Word Only check box to match entire words only.
6. Select the Match Case check box to match capitalization precisely.
7. Select the desired replacement option.

- Find Next finds the next occurrence of the search text but does not replace it.
- Replace finds the next occurrence of the search text and changes it to the replacement text.
- Replace All locates and changes all occurrences of the search text.
- Replace Selection locates and changes all occurrences of the search text in the selected portion of the document only.

8. Select Close to close the Replace dialog box.

Formatting Text

▸ Changing Character Styles

Multiple character styles can be applied to a block of text.

To apply a character style to text:

1. Move the text cursor to the location where text will be entered or select (highlight) a block of text to which to apply the style change.
2. Select the desired style from the Character menu. The style(s) selected—Bold, Italic, Underline, Superscript, or Subscript—are identified by check marks.
   - If a location was selected, new text entered will appear in the style selected.
   - If a block of text was selected, the block will appear in the style selected.
3. If necessary, select the Undo option from the Edit menu to cancel the change.

To cancel a character style:

1. Select the text block for which to cancel a style.
2. Select the style to be canceled from the Character menu.

The Regular style cannot be canceled.

To cancel all character styles:

1. Select the text block for which to cancel styles.
2. Select Regular from the Character menu.

To change styles for an entire document:

1. Select the entire document (see "Selecting Text Using the Selection Area," preceding.)
2. Select Fonts from the Character menu to open the Font dialog box shown in Figure 9.11.

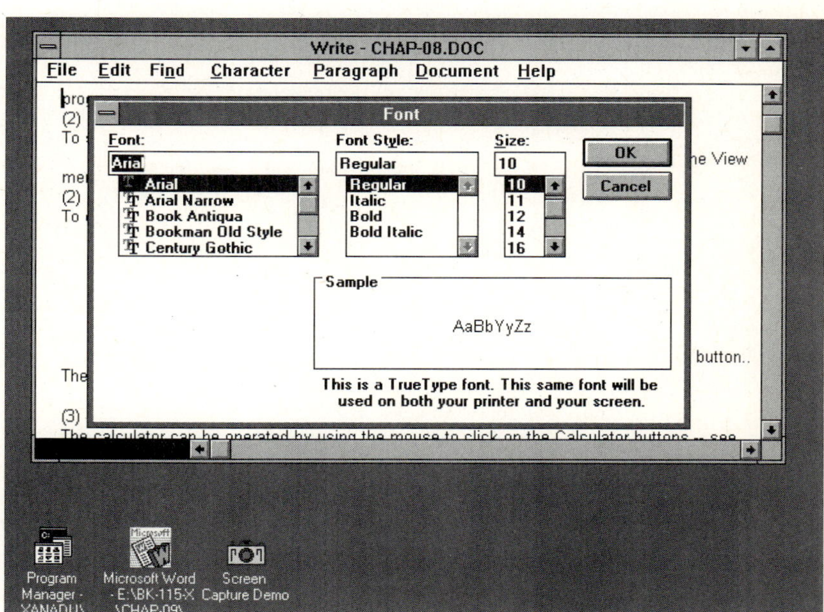

Figure 9.11
The Font dialog box

3. Select the style from the Font Style list box or enter the style name, or select Regular to remove all current style settings.
4. Select OK.

▸ Changing Fonts and Font Sizes

To change fonts or font sizes using the Fonts command:

1. Move the text cursor to the location where text will be entered or select (highlight) a block of text to which to apply the style change.
2. Select Fonts from the Character menu.
3. Select a font from the Font list box or enter a font name.
4. Select a style from the Font Style list box.
5. Select a font size from the Size list box.
6. Select OK.

To change the font size using the font-size commands:

1. Move the text cursor to the location where text will be entered or select (highlight) a block of text to which to apply the font change.
2. Select the Reduce Font or Enlarge Font options from the Character menu.

Help Files ▼ Fonts (or typefaces) determine the appearance of all text, numerals, and other characters. They can be selected from a variety of type styles supplied with Windows NT as TrueType fonts or from third-party sources. Each font is available in a range of point sizes.

The Fonts option from the Character menu provides the opportunity to change typefaces, type styles (normal, bold, italic, and so on), and point sizes. Existing fonts will be replaced by global changes in typefaces, but local style selections—such as bold and italic—remain unchanged. Font and style changes made to selected portions of a document will not affect the document as a whole.

Creating Subscripts and Superscripts

To create a subscript or superscript:

1. Move the text cursor to the location where the subscript or superscript will be entered or select (highlight) a block of text to be subscripted or superscripted.
2. Select Subscript or Superscript from the Character menu.

Help Files ▼ Superscripts appear offset below other text, and superscripts are offset above. Both forms are scaled to a smaller type size.

Supplying Conditional Hyphenation

To insert an optional (conditional) hyphen:

- Press Ctrl+Shift+hyphen (-) at the desired hyphenation point.

Help Files ▼ Conditional hyphens offer Microsoft Write an opportunity to break a line within a word; for example, to eliminate the gap left at the end of a line when a long word doesn't fit. A conditional hyphen does not appear except when it occurs at the end of a line.

Formatting Paragraphs

▶ Displaying the Ruler

To display the Ruler:

- Select Ruler On from the Document menu. The Ruler is shown in Figure 9.12.

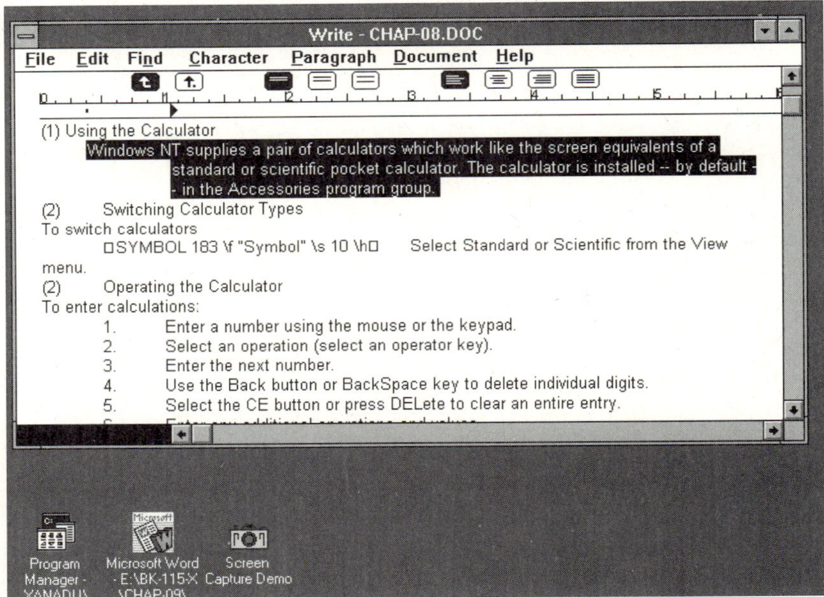

Figure 9.12
The Ruler and icons

To turn the Ruler off:

- Select Ruler Off from the Document menu.

To change units of measurement:

- Select the Page Layout command from the Document menu.

Help Files ▼ The Ruler appears at the top of the Write window and is used to format paragraphs, set tab spacings, and adjust the appearance of a document.

▶ Using the Ruler to Format Paragraphs

To format paragraphs with the Ruler:

To change paragraph formats, you must have a mouse.

1. Select Ruler On from the Document menu.
2. Place the text cursor in the paragraph to be formatted or select multiple paragraphs to be formatted (see "Selecting Text Using the Selection Area," preceding).
3. Select the appropriate format options.
   - Select the paragraph alignment icon from the four alignment icons at the right side of the Ruler.

   - Select the line-spacing icon from the three line-spacing icons at the middle of the Ruler.

4. Adjust indentation by dragging one or both of the indent markers to the desired locations. (Until adjustment is made, the two markers are superimposed on the Ruler, toward the left.)
   - The left indent marker—identified as a triangle—controls the position of the left margin of the paragraph.

- The first-line indent marker—identified as a dot—controls the indentation of the first line of the paragraph.

▶ Changing Paragraph Indentations

To change paragraph indentations:

1. Place the text cursor in the paragraph to be changed or select multiple paragraphs for changing (see "Selecting Text Using the Selection Area," preceding).
2. Select Indents from the Paragraph menu to call the Indents dialog box shown in Figure 9.13.

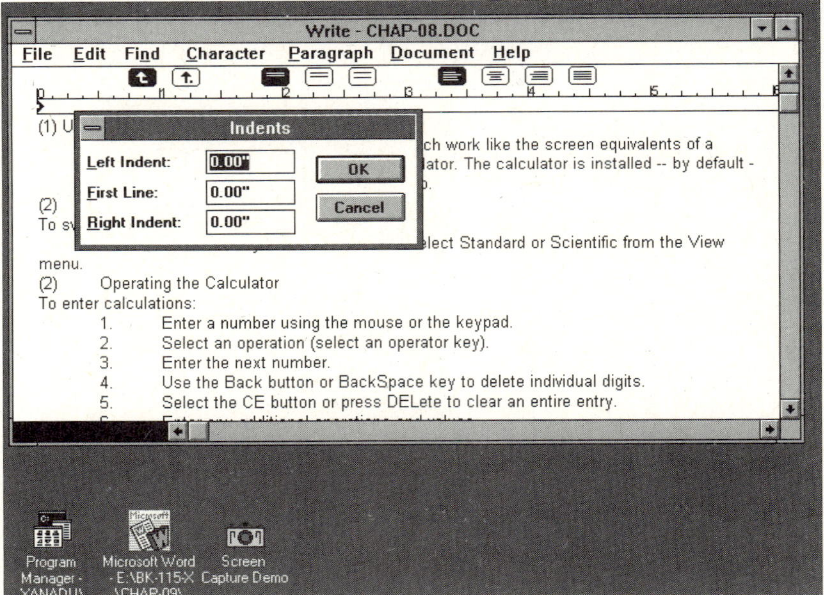

Figure 9.13
The Indents dialog box

3. Enter new measurements for any indentations to be changed.
   - The Left Indent field specifies the distance a paragraph is indented from the left margin.
   - The Right Indent field specifies the distance a paragraph is indented from the right margin.

- The First Line field specifies the indentation (or, with a negative argument, the outdent) of the first line, relative to the body of the paragraph.

4. Select OK.

Help Files ▼ Entire paragraphs can be indented from the right or left margins. Measurements are made in inches or centimeters, depending on the Measurements selection in the Page Layout dialog box.

Indenting can also be applied to pictures or other embedded information contained in a Write document.

▶ Setting Hanging Indents

To create a hanging indent:

1. Place the text cursor in the paragraph to be changed or select multiple paragraphs for changing (see "Selecting Text Using the Selection Area," preceding).
2. Select Indents from the Paragraph menu.
3. Enter a positive value in the Left Indent field.
4. Enter a negative value in the First Line field. The absolute value of the number entered (8 is the absolute value of –8, for example) cannot be greater than the positive number used for the Left Indent.
5. Select OK.

Help Files ▼ In a hanging indent format, the first line of a paragraph extends further to the left than does the body of the paragraph.

▶ Changing Paragraph Alignment

To change paragraph alignment

1. Place the text cursor in the paragraph to be changed or select multiple paragraphs for changing (see "Selecting Text Using the Selection Area," preceding).
2. Select Normal, Left, Centered, Right, or Justified from the Paragraph menu or the Ruler icons.
   - *Normal* aligns the paragraph at the left margin, and makes it single spaced.
   - *Left* aligns the paragraph at the left margin with a ragged right margin.
   - *Centered* centers each line with ragged left and right margins.
   - *Right* aligns the paragraph at the right margin with a ragged left margin.
   - *Justified* spaces characters and words on each line to produce smooth margins on both left and right.

▶ Selecting Paragraph Line Spacing

To change paragraph line spacing:

1. Place the text cursor in the paragraph to be changed or select multiple paragraphs for changing (see "Selecting Text Using the Selection Area," preceding).

2. Select Single Space, 1½ Space, or Double Space from the Paragraph menu or the Ruler icons.

▸ Using the Ruler to Change Tabs

To use the Ruler to set tab positions:

1. Select Ruler On from the Document menu.
2. Select (click on) one of the two tab icons above the Ruler.
   - The plain tab icon is used for normal tabs.

   - The tab icon with the period is used for decimal tabs.

3. Click on the Ruler at the point the tab should be set.
4. Alternatively, an existing tab marker can be dragged to a new position.

To remove a tab:

- Drag the tab marker away from the Ruler.

▸ Using the Tabs Command to Change Tabs

To use the Tabs command to set a tab stop:

1. Select Tabs from the Document menu.
2. Select a position box.
3. Enter the distance from the left margin for the tab stop.
4. For a decimal tab, select the Decimal check box.
5. Select OK.

To delete a tab stop:

1. Select Tabs from the Document menu. The Tabs dialog box shown in Figure 9.14 appears.

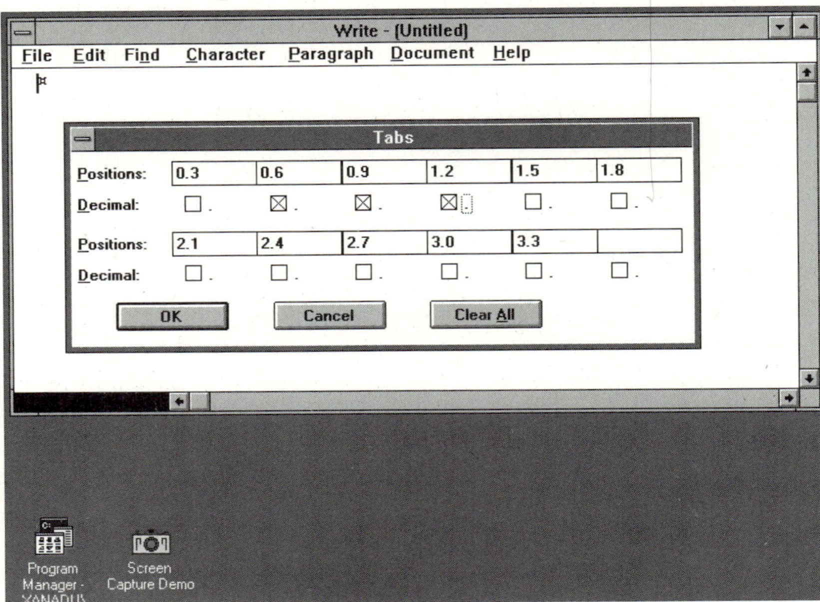

Figure 9.14
The Tabs dialog box

2. Select the position box for the tab to be deleted.
3. Select the Del or Backspace key.

To delete all tabs:

1. Select Tabs from the Document menu.
2. Select the Clear All button.

Help Files ▼ All tab settings replace preset tabs. The default tabs are spaced at ½-inch intervals.

Operating in a Write Document

▶ Positioning within a Write Document

To move around within a document, in addition to the mouse and scroll bar(s), the cursor control keys can also be used in several combinations, as shown in Table 9.2.

Table 9.2
Movement Keys

Press	Move To
Ctrl+right arrow	Next word
Ctrl+left arrow	Previous word
5+right arrow	Next sentence
5+left arrow	Previous sentence
5+down arrow	Next paragraph
5+up arrow	Previous paragraph
Home	Beginning of a line
End	End of a line
Ctrl+PgDn	Bottom of window
Ctrl+PgUp	Top of window
PgDn	One screen down
PgUp	One screen up
5+PgDn	One page down
5+PgUp	One page up
Ctrl+Home	Beginning of a document
Ctrl+Home	End of a document

The 5 key mentioned here is the center key on the keypad. The 5 at the top of the keyboard cannot be substituted.

Help Files ▼ With the exception of key combinations that move to the beginning of a line or of the document or to the end of the document, the text cursor can be moved continuously by holding down any of the key combinations listed.

The 5+PgDn and 5+PgUp key combinations can be used to move to the next page or previous page only after the document has been printed (which imposes paging) or after the Repaginate command has been used to assign pages.

▸ Inserting and Removing Paragraph Marks

To insert a paragraph mark:

1. Press Enter at the end of a paragraph.
2. To add a blank line between paragraphs, press Enter again.

To remove a paragraph mark:

1. Position the text cursor at the beginning of the paragraph following the paragraph mark to be removed.
2. Press Backspace.
3. If a blank line appears after the paragraph, press Backspace a second time.

Help Files ▼ Paragraph marks—hard carriage returns—are not visible in a document but are used to mark the end of a paragraph or to create a blank line.

Locating and Moving to Specific Pages

To assign pages to a document:

- Select the Repaginate command from the File menu.

Or:

- Print the document (this process assigns pages before printing).

To move to a specific page:

1. Select Go To Page from the Find menu.
2. Enter the page number desired.
3. Select OK.

Help Files ▼ Before the Go To Page command can be used, page breaks must be assigned by printing or repaginating the document. Until this is done, Microsoft Write treats the document as a single page, irrespective of length.

Setting Margins, Page Lengths, and Numbering

To change margins, page lengths, or page numbers:

1. Select Page Layout from the Document menu. The Page Layout dialog box (see Figure 9.15) appears.
2. Enter a starting page number in the Start Page Numbers At edit box.
3. Enter right, left, top, and bottom margins in the Margins edit boxes.
4. Select the units of measurement desired by selecting the Inch or Cm (centimeters) option.
5. Select OK.

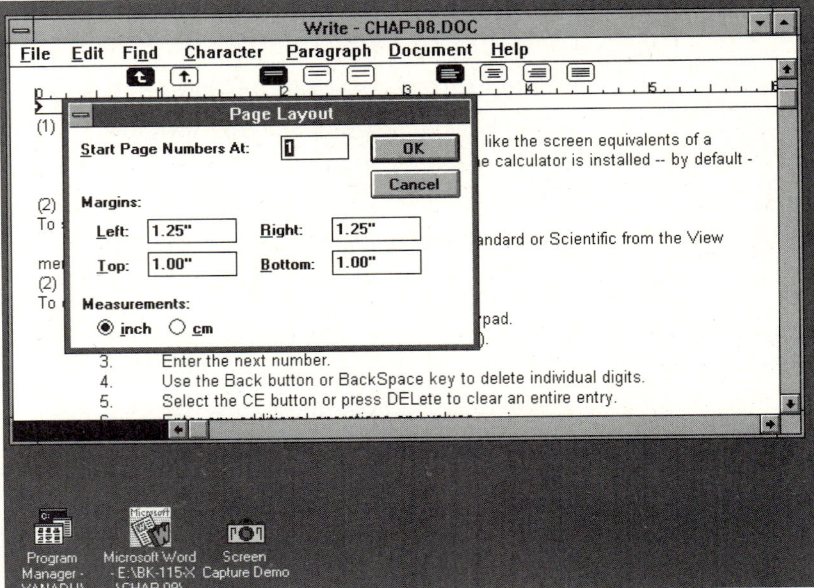

Figure 9.15
The Page Layout dialog box

Help Files ▼ The measurement option selected here is also applied to other measurements, including headers, footers, and indents.

These changes affect the default values used by Write for margin width, page numbers, and units of measurement. The preset values are

- Measurements expressed in inches
- Top and bottom margins of 1 inch
- Right and left margins of 1.25 inches
- Page numbers beginning at 1

▶ Repaginating Documents

To repaginate a document:

1. Select Repaginate from the File menu.
2. Select the Confirm Page Breaks option to approve each page break position during pagination.
3. Select OK to repaginate the document.
4. If Confirm Page Breaks is selected
   - Use the up arrow button to move an automatic page break up from the proposed location.
   - Use the down arrow button to move an automatic page break down again.
   - Use the Confirm button to proceed to the next page-break location.
5. Select the Keep or Remove button for manually inserted page breaks.

To insert manual page breaks:

1. Position the text cursor at the location where the page break is required.
2. Press Ctrl+Enter.

Help Files ▼ A Write document can be repaginated at any time. Automatic page breaks are designated by arrows in the left margin and manual page breaks are designated by dotted lines extending across the page.

Confirming Automatic and Manual Page Breaks

To confirm page breaks:

1. Select Repaginate Document from the Edit menu.
2. Select the Confirm option from the Repaginate Document dialog box.

Help Files ▼ With the Confirm option, Write pauses at each page break during repagination, allowing the page break to be moved up or to be restored. When a manual page break is encountered, the page break must be confirmed or removed.

Including Headers, Footers, and Page Numbers

To add a header or footer to a document:

1. Select Header or Footer from the Document menu. Both a Header or Footer document window and a Page Header or Page Footer dialog box appear in response (see Figure 9.16).
2. Select the Clear button to delete previously entered header or footer text.
3. Enter text for the header or footer. Include text formatting as desired.
4. Select the Page Header or Page Footer dialog box or press Alt+F6.
5. To change the spacing between the header or footer and the page edge, enter the spacing in the Distance From Top or Distance From Bottom edit box.

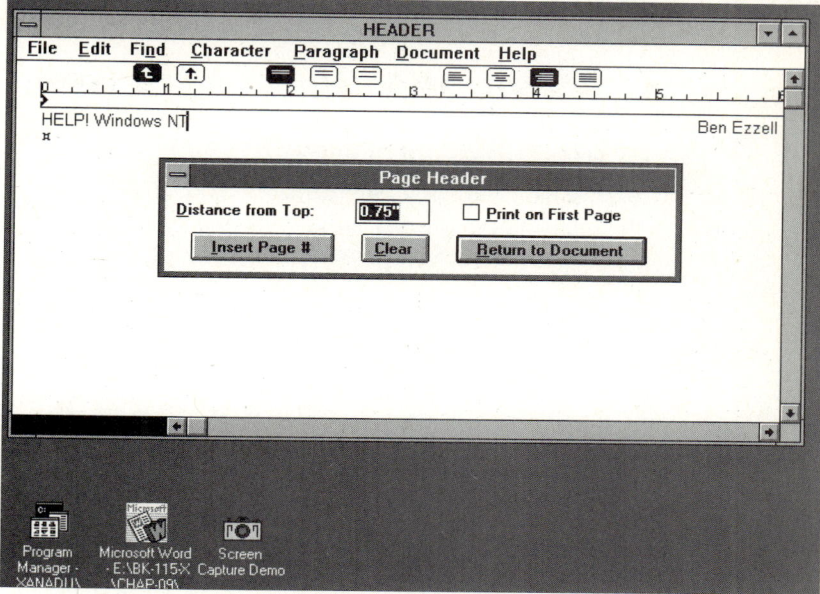

Figure 9.16
The Header document window and Page Header dialog box

6. Select the Print On First Page option for the header or footer to appear on the first page of the printed document. Otherwise, the header or footer will begin on the second page.
7. To include page numbers in the printed document, select the Insert Page # button.
8. The page-number positioning can be changed by selecting Centered, Left, or Right from the Paragraph menu.
9. Select Return To Document when finished or press the Esc key.

Help Files ▼ Headers and footers do not appear on the screen but do appear when the document is printed. Header and footer measurements will be in inches or centimeters, according to the Measurements setting in the Page Layout dialog box.

Working with Images

▸ Copying, Cutting, and Pasting Images

To paste an image into a Write document:

1. Use the Pick or Scissors tool in Paintbrush to select the image.
2. Select Copy from the Edit menu.
3. Save the image.
4. Exit Paintbrush.
5. Open Microsoft Write.
6. Open the document in which to insert the image.
7. Move the text cursor to the position at which to insert the image.
8. Select Paste from the Edit menu.

To copy or cut an image from a Write document:

1. Select by clicking on the image or use the up or down arrow keys to move the text cursor to the image.
2. Select Copy or Cut from the Edit menu.

Help Files ▼ Pasted images can be copied, embedded, or linked in Write documents, depending on whether the application supplying the image is a server application and supports the format. Refer to the application's documentation for details. Refer to Chapter 7 for further details on copying, embedding, and linking processes.

Moving Images

To move a picture horizontally:

1. Select the image by clicking on it, or use the up or down arrow key to move the text cursor to the image.
2. Select the Move Picture option from the Edit menu.
3. Without pressing a mouse key, move the mouse right or left, or use the right or left arrow keys.
4. Press Esc to restore an image to its original position.
5. Click the mouse or press Enter when the image is located as desired.
6. To restore an image to its original position, immediately select Undo from the Edit menu.

HELP! *Images in a document can be moved only left or right. Use the Cut and Paste commands to change the position vertically.*

To move an image using formatting commands:

1. Select the image by clicking on it, or use the up or down arrow key to move the text cursor to the image.
2. Select Left, Centered, or Right from the Paragraph menu.

Changing Image Sizes

To change the size of an image:

1. Select the image by clicking on it, or use the up or down arrow key to move the text cursor to the image.
2. Select the Size Picture option from the Edit menu. A dotted outline will surround the image.
3. Move the mouse cursor to the midpoint on the left, right, or bottom edge of the outline or on either of the lower corners, or use the arrow keys to position the cursor.
4. Drag the cursor or use the arrow keys to enlarge or reduce the image.

5. To return the image to its original size, press Esc.
6. When the image is the size desired, click the mouse button or press Enter.
7. To restore an image to its original size, immediately select Undo from the Edit menu.

Help Files ▼ When the Size Picture option is selected, sizing information is displayed as *x* and *y* location values in the lower-left corner of the window. Keeping the *x* and *y* values as integers rather than fractions will help to prevent distortion.

Working with Sound Recorder Files

▶ Linking and Embedding Sound Recorder Files

Sound Recorder files can be embedded or linked in Write documents. Refer to Chapter 7 for further details on copying, embedding, and linking processes.

THE RESCUE PAGES: Word Processors

I saved my Notepad file but now I can't find it.

This probably means that you saved your file to the wrong drive or directory. You can use File Manager to search for your missing text in two ways.

In File Manager, select By File Type from the View menu and enter the document name. Then start checking directories.

Or, simply select Search from the File menu, then enter the name of your document file and let File Manager do the searching. For best results, of course, start the search in the root directory for each drive and be sure to select the Search Subdirectories check box. Of course, this search looks only for a file name and doesn't search the contents of the file, so you can't do a keyword search. However, there are other, third-party utilities such as XTREE that can execute keyword or phrase searches.

When I print from Notepad, the margins come out wrong!

Check what units—English or metric—are set. This selection is made through the International option from the Control Panel.

Page numbers show up when I print my Notepad document, but I can't see any page numbers in the screen document.

When I'm typing, everything scrolls off to the left where I can't see it. How do I get line breaks, like I would with other word processors?

Probably, the solution is simply to turn on the Word Wrap option from the Edit menu. If Word Wrap isn't enabled, you need to enter line breaks manually, using the Enter key. When Word Wrap is enabled, you need to

use the Enter key only when you want a paragraph break—the bulk of your text is automatically broken to accommodate the width of the Notepad window.

When I change the size of Notepad's window, the text formatting changes, too. Now my columns don't line up correctly.

Turn the Word Wrap option off (see the preceding discussion). With Word Wrap off, a line will break only when you hit the Enter key. Of course, you may need to go back and insert line breaks in your existing material, but this shouldn't be any real problem.

My Notepad window doesn't show exactly what I get when I print.

Unfortunately, it would be asking too much of Notepad to show an accurate representation of the layout of your document. If you want this, you need to be using a real word processor/editor program—preferably one with WYSIWYG features (the acronym for What You See Is What You Get, pronounced *wizzywig*.) You might try using the Write program instead.

I imported my WordPerfect file into Write using the Convert option but everything's garbage!

If you really want to import from WordPerfect, begin by using WordPerfect to save the document as a text (ASCII) file, and then import it in this form. The conversion features are not that elaborate or sophisticated and, at best, you will lose a lot of special formatting. Also, depending on the original source, you may find blocks of indecipherable characters at the beginning and/or end of the document after importing. All you can do is delete these portions. An incidental note: Word for Windows files are particularly difficult to import.

I can't make a word break where I want it to in Write.

Assuming that you want a break in the middle of a word, simply insert a hyphen and press Enter to break the line.

Alternatively, you can insert a conditional hyphen in a word by using Ctrl+Shift+hyphen (-) at the desired hyphenation point. The conditional

hyphen *allows* a line break at this point but doesn't insist that it must break. The conditional hyphen appears in print or on the screen only when it is at the end of the line.

I can't figure out what page I'm on in my Write document.

Select Repaginate from the File menu. Until a file has been printed or repaginated, Write treats the document as a single page, regardless of its length.

CHAPTER

10

HELP! The Windows NT Paintbrush Program

The Windows NT Paintbrush program is used to create or edit images and other drawings. Paintbrush works both with color and with black and white images; handles bitmaps, Paintbrush, and Microsoft Paint file formats; supports custom color palettes; and prints hardcopy images.

Topics covered in this chapter include

- Creating simple drawings
- Working with Paint and Eraser tools
- Working with Line, Curve, and Geometric tools
- Working with Cutouts and Cutout tools
- Working with text
- Working with custom colors
- Managing the drawing space
- Managing Paintbrush files
- Importing images
- Printing images

Creating Simple Drawings

▶ Selecting a Drawing Mode

To select a drawing mode:

1. Select the Image Attributes option from the Options menu. The Image Attributes dialog box (see Figure 10.1) appears in response.

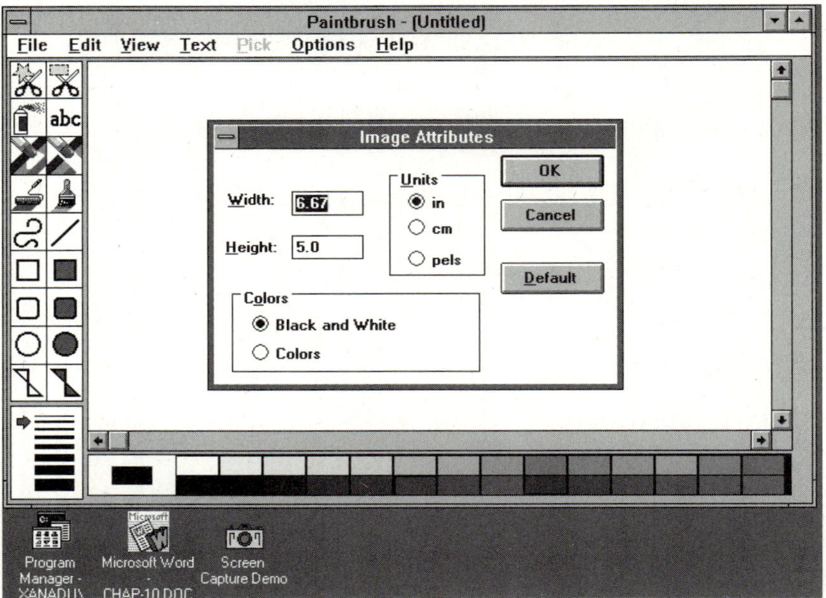

Figure 10.1
The Image Attributes dialog box

2. Select the Black And White or Colors drawing mode option.
3. Select Units to change measurement units.
4. Optionally, select a new image size. Default is 640×480 pixels (pels).
5. Select the Default button to restore default settings.
6. Select OK.

Help Files ▼ The default settings are for inches and an image size of 6.67 inches wide by 5.0 inches high—which, at 96 pixels per inch, becomes 640×480 pixels. The Colors/Black And White option is not reset by the Default button.

Changes in size or color mode can be made only when starting a new image. Existing images cannot be resized or changed from color to black and white.

Selecting Colors

To set the foreground color:

- Select a color from the Palette (see Figure 10.2) by clicking on the color with the left mouse button.
- Use the Tab and arrow keys to select a color, then press Ins.

Figure 10.2
The Paintbrush Palette

To set the background color:

- Select a color from the Palette by clicking on the color with the right mouse button.
- Use the Tab and arrow keys to select a color, then press Del.

To set colors for a new drawing:

1. Select background and foreground colors.
2. Select New from the File menu.

Help Files ▼ Initially, Paintbrush's foreground color is black and the background is white. At the left of the Palette (color) bar, the foreground color appears as the center rectangle surrounded by the background color.

▶ Selecting a Drawing Width

To select a drawing width:

- Click on a sample line in the Linesize box.

Or:

- Use the Tab and arrow keys to select a line width (shown by the arrow at the left), then press Ins.

Help Files ▼ The drawing width controls the width of lines, as well as the thickness of object borders and the size of some tools. Sample line widths are shown in the Linesize box (lower-left corner); the top line is 1 pixel wide. The default width is a 2-pixel line.

Selecting a Drawing Tool

To select a drawing tool:

- Select a tool from the Toolbox at the left by clicking on the desired tool.

Or:

- Use the Tab and arrow keys to select a tool, then press Ins.

Using a Drawing Tool

To work with a tool:

1. Select a tool from the Toolbox.
2. Position the cursor at the start location.
3. Press the left mouse button and drag the tool to draw or, using the keyboard, press and hold the Ins key while using the arrow keys to drag the tool.
4. Release the mouse button or Ins key to stop drawing.

Help Files ▼ When drawing an object, such as a box or circle, a flexible outline expands and shrinks to follow the tool's movements. The object is drawn when the mouse button or Ins key is released.

Undoing Changes

To use the Undo command:

- Select Undo from the Edit menu.

Or:

- Press Ctrl+Z.

Everything that was drawn using the current tool is undone—including color changes—restoring the previous image.

To undo a portion of a drawing:

1. Press the Backspace key. The cursor becomes a square containing an X. The size of the square is determined by the selected drawing width.
2. Press and hold the mouse button (or Ins key) while dragging the cursor over the area to undo.
3. Release the mouse button (or Ins key) when finished. The previous tool is restored.

Help Files ▼ The Undo command and the Backspace key act to undo items that were drawn with the currently selected drawing tool. Images drawn prior to selecting the current tool cannot be undone.

To avoid undoing a completed section, reselect the tool from the Toolbox. This will paste down the finished work, preventing it from being undone.

▸ Substituting Keyboard Commands for Mouse Actions

Keyboard commands can be substituted for mouse actions either in the absence of a mouse or when a finer degree of control is desired. Keyboard substitutions are shown in Table 10.1.

Table 10.1
Keyboard Substitutes for Mouse Actions

Use	Instead Of
Ins	Clicking or pressing the left mouse button
Del	Clicking or pressing the right mouse button
F9+Ins	Double-clicking the left mouse button
F9+Del	Double-clicking the right mouse button
Ins+arrow keys	Dragging the cursor

Paint and Eraser Tools

▸ Using the Airbrush

To use the Airbrush:

1. Select the foreground color and drawing width.
2. Select the Airbrush tool and move to the drawing area.
3. Press the left mouse button to begin spraying.
4. Move the Airbrush over the area to paint. The speed of movement controls the density of the paint applied.
5. Release the mouse button to stop spraying.

Help Files ▼ The Airbrush produces a spray of dots in the foreground color. For a light spray, move the Airbrush quickly or tap the mouse button repeatedly for an intermittent spray. For a heavier spray, move the Airbrush slowly while holding the mouse button down.

▸ Using the Eraser

To use the Eraser:

1. Select a drawing width.
2. Select the Eraser tool.
3. Move to the position in the drawing area where you wish to start erasing.
4. Hold the left mouse button down while dragging the Eraser. Hold the Shift button down to make the Eraser move in a straight horizontal or vertical line.
5. Release the mouse button to stop erasing.

Help Files ▼ The Eraser changes the area covered to the background color. The same effect can be achieved by selecting the background color as the active drawing color and then using the Brush.

▸ Using the Color Eraser

To erase a single color:

1. Make the color you want to erase the foreground color.
2. Make the replacement color the background color.
3. Select a drawing width.
4. Select the Color Eraser tool.
5. Move to the position in the drawing area where you wish to start erasing.
6. Hold the left mouse button down while dragging the Color Eraser. Hold the Shift button down to make the Color Eraser move in a straight horizontal or vertical line.
7. Release the mouse button to stop erasing.

To completely replace one color with a second color:

1. Make the color you want to replace the foreground color.
2. Make the replacement color the background color.
3. Double-click on the Color Eraser tool. The foreground color will be completely replaced by the background color.

Help Files ▼ The Color Eraser replaces one color with a second color. You can replace all instances or just selected instances of a color. The complete color replacement affects only the area of the image that is visible within the Paintbrush window. Regions outside the visible screen are not affected.

▶ Using the Paint Roller

To use the Paint Roller:

1. Select a foreground color.
2. Select the Paint Roller tool.
3. Move the Paint Roller to the area to fill.
4. Click on the left mouse button.

Help Files ▼ The Paint Roller fills a closed area with the foreground color. The fill action stops when Paintbrush encounters a color other than the one that occupied the point where the fill began. This means that any break in the area outline, however small, will allow the fill to leak into the surrounding regions.

▶ Using the Brush

To paint using the Brush:

1. Select a foreground color and drawing width.
2. Select the Brush tool.
3. Move the Brush to the drawing area.
4. Press the left mouse button and drag the Brush to draw freehand shapes.

5. To draw a horizontal or vertical line, hold the Shift key down while dragging the Brush in the desired direction.
6. Release the mouse button to stop drawing.

To change the Brush shape:

1. Double-click on the Brush tool or select Brush Shapes from the Options menu.
2. Select the brush shape desired.
3. Select OK.

Line, Curve, and Geometric Tools

▶ Drawing a Straight Line

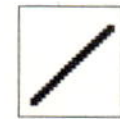

To draw a straight line:

1. Select a foreground color and drawing width.
2. Select the Line tool.
3. Move the cursor to the drawing area.
4. Press the left mouse button to anchor the start point for the line.
5. Hold the mouse button down while dragging the cursor. An elastic line stretches from the anchor point to the cursor position.
6. To draw a horizontal, vertical, or 45-degree diagonal line, hold the Shift key down while dragging the cursor in the desired direction.
7. Release the mouse button to terminate the line or click the right mouse button to undo the line.

▸ Drawing a Curve

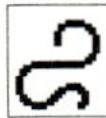

To draw a curve:

1. Select a foreground color and drawing width.
2. Select the Curve tool.
3. Move the cross hair cursor to the drawing area.
4. Press the left mouse button to set the start point for the curve.
5. Hold the left mouse button down while dragging the cursor to the end point of the curve. Release the mouse button to anchor the end point. A straight but flexible line connects the two points.
6. Press the left mouse button again and drag the cursor to shape the curve.
7. Release the mouse button. To undo the curve and start shaping again, click the right mouse button.
8. To end the curve with the current shape, click again on the end point of the curve.
9. To add a second curve to the line, position the cross hair cursor off the line, press the mouse button, and drag the cursor to finish shaping the curve.
10. Release the mouse button. The curve assumes its final shape, color, and thickness.

▸ Drawing a Box or Rounded Box

To draw a square-cornered or rounded box:

1. Select a foreground color and drawing width. The drawing width determines the thickness of the box outline.

2. Select the Box or the Rounded Box tool.
3. Move the cross hair cursor to the drawing area.
4. Press the left mouse button to anchor one corner of the box.
5. Hold the mouse button while dragging the cursor to shape the box. A rectangular elastic outline connects the anchor point and the cursor. Press and hold the Shift key while dragging the mouse to if you want to create a square box.
6. Release the mouse button to anchor the box or click the right mouse button to undo the box.

▶ Drawing a Filled Box or Filled Rounded Box

To draw a filled square-cornered or rounded box:

1. Select a foreground color for the box fill color.
2. Select a background color for the box outline color.
3. Select a drawing width to determine the thickness of the box outline.
4. Select the Filled Box or the Filled Rounded Box tool.
5. Move the cross hair cursor to the drawing area.
6. Press the left mouse button to anchor one corner of the box.
7. Hold the mouse button while dragging the cursor to shape the box. A rectangular elastic outline connects the anchor point and the cursor. Press and hold the Shift key while dragging the mouse if you want to create a square box.
8. Release the mouse button to anchor the box or click the right mouse button to undo the box.

Drawing a Circle or Ellipse

To draw a circle or ellipse:

1. Select a foreground color and drawing width. The drawing width determines the thickness of the circle or ellipse outline.
2. Select the Circle tool.
3. Move the cross hair cursor to the drawing area.
4. Press the left mouse button to anchor the corner of an invisible box surrounding the circle or ellipse.
5. Hold the mouse button while dragging the cursor to shape the ellipse. The cursor acts as the diagonally opposite corner of an invisible box surrounding the ellipse. Press and hold the Shift key while dragging the mouse if you want to create a circle.
6. Release the mouse button to anchor the ellipse or circle, or click the right mouse button to undo the shape.

Drawing a Filled Circle or Ellipse

To draw a filled circle or ellipse:

1. Select a foreground color for the fill color.
2. Select a background color for the outline color.
3. Select a drawing width to determine the thickness of the outline.
4. Select the Filled Circle tool.
5. Move the cross hair cursor to the drawing area.
6. Press the left mouse button to anchor the corner of an invisible box surrounding the circle or ellipse.

7. Hold the mouse button while dragging the cursor to shape the ellipse. The cursor acts as the diagonally opposite corner of an invisible box surrounding the ellipse. Press and hold the Shift key while dragging the mouse if you want to create a circle.
8. Release the mouse button to anchor the ellipse or circle, or click the right mouse button to undo the shape.

▶ Drawing a Polygon

To draw a polygon:

1. Select a foreground color and drawing width. The drawing width determines the thickness of the outline.
2. Select the Polygon tool.
3. Move the cross hair cursor to the drawing area.
4. Press the left mouse button to anchor the first vertex of the polygon.
5. Hold the mouse button while dragging the cursor to create the first side of the polygon. An elastic line connects the anchor point and the cursor.
6. To draw a horizontal, vertical, or 45-degree diagonal line, hold the Shift key down while dragging the cursor in the desired direction.
7. Release the mouse button at the point where the line segment should end. The end of the first line segment becomes the anchor point for the next segment.
8. Press the left mouse button and drag the cursor to add the next side to the polygon, or move to the next corner of the polygon and press the mouse button. Adjust the position as necessary before releasing the button.
9. Continue adding sides to the polygon. Click the right mouse button at any time to start the polygon again.

10. Double-click to close the polygon and complete the drawing.

▸ Drawing a Filled Polygon

To draw a filled polygon:

1. Select a foreground color for the fill color.
2. Select a background color for the outline color.
3. Select a drawing width to determine the thickness of the outline.
4. Select the Filled Polygon tool.
5. Move the cross hair cursor to the drawing area.
6. Press the left mouse button to anchor the first vertex of the polygon.
7. Hold the mouse button while dragging the cursor to create the first side of the polygon. An elastic line connects the anchor point and the cursor.
8. To draw a horizontal, vertical, or 45-degree diagonal line, hold the Shift key down while dragging the cursor in the desired direction.
9. Release the mouse button at the point where the line segment should end. The end of the first line segment becomes the anchor point for the next segment.
10. Press the left mouse button and drag the cursor to add the next side to the polygon, or move to the next corner of the polygon and press the mouse button. Adjust the position as necessary before releasing the button.
11. Continue adding sides to the polygon. Click the right mouse button at any time to start the polygon over.
12. Double-click to close the polygon and complete the drawing.

Cutouts and Cutout Tools

▸ Using the Pick Tool to Select an Area

To use the Pick tool to select an area:

1. Select the Pick tool.
2. Move the cursor to the drawing area.
3. Press the left mouse button to anchor one corner of an elastic box.
4. Hold the mouse button while dragging the elastic box to enclose the area desired.
5. Release the mouse button when finished. If you want to cancel the cutout selection, click anywhere on the screen.

Help Files ▼ The Pick tool is used to define a rectangular cutout. If the area desired is larger than the display window, select the Zoom Out option from the View menu.

▸ Using the Scissors Tool to Select an Area

To use the Scissors tool to select an area:

1. Select the Scissors tool.
2. Move to the drawing area.
3. Press the left mouse button to begin defining an area.

4. While holding the mouse button, drag the cursor to draw a line around the area for the cutout.

5. After the area is enclosed, release the mouse button. If you want to cancel the cutout selection, click anywhere on the screen.

Help Files ▼ The Scissors tool is used to define a free-form cutout that needs to closely follow an object's contours. If the area desired is larger than the display window, select the Zoom Out option from the View menu.

▶ Copying, Cutting, and Pasting Cutouts

To copy or move a cutout within an image:

1. Use the Pick or Scissors tool to select a cutout.
2. Position the cursor inside the cutout.
3. To move the cutout, press and hold the Ctrl key.
4. Press and hold the mouse button while dragging the cutout or its copy to the new location.
   - Use the left mouse button to paste the image transparently. The background color should not be changed during this operation.
   - Use the right mouse button to paste the image opaquely.
5. Release the Ctrl key, if necessary.
6. Release the mouse button when the cutout or its copy is positioned.
7. To paste the cutout in position, click anywhere outside the cutout or select a tool.

To paste a cutout into another image:

1. Use the Pick or Scissors tool to select a cutout.

2. Select Copy from the Edit menu or press Ctrl+C to copy the cutout, or select Cut from the Edit menu or press Ctrl+X to move the cutout.
3. Open the destination Paintbrush image file.
4. Select Paste from the Edit menu or press Ctrl+V to paste the cutout. The pasted cutout appears at the upper left of the image window.
5. Position the cursor inside the cutout.
6. Hold the mouse button while dragging the cutout to the desired location.
   - Use the left mouse button to paste the image transparently. The background color for the cutout and the current background color must be the same.
   - Use the right mouse button to paste the image opaquely.
7. Click outside the cutout to paste it, or select any tool.

Help Files ▼ When using the Zoom Out mode for pasting cutouts larger than the working window, a few restrictions apply:

- The image does not appear inside a cutout frame.
- The cutout can be pasted only opaquely (use either button).
- If the cutout is as large as the drawing, click outside the drawing to paste the cutout into position.

The Copy, Cut, and Paste commands from the Edit menu are used to transfer cutouts to and from the Clipboard. Refer to Chapter 7 for details on Clipboard operations.

Copying, Embedding, and Linking Cutouts

How Paintbrush images or cutouts are inserted into another application's file determines how changes can be made. Images can be copied, embedded, or linked, although the latter two methods can be used only if the destination application supports these processes.

- Copying an object places a duplicate of the object in the destination application. After copying, changes can be made only by deleting the copy and replacing it.
- Embedding an object permits the object to be edited in the destination file, using the source application's facilities.
- Linking creates a dynamic link between two documents (files) such that changes to the source file automatically update the information contained in the destination file.

An object can be copied, embedded, or linked by using the Copy command from the Edit menu. The commands used to insert or paste the object from the Clipboard to the destination application determine whether the object is copied, embedded, or linked.

For further details on linking and embedding operations, refer to "Linking and Embedding" in Chapter 7.

Limiting Clipboard Formats

To limit the formats used when copying to the Clipboard:

1. Select the Omit Picture Format option from the Options menu.
2. Select the image.
3. Copy the image to the Clipboard.

Help Files ▼ A drawing copied to the Clipboard is copied in several formats, ensuring that other applications will be able to display the image. Since some applications cannot read all the formats used, the Omit Picture Format option is provided. Refer to the destination application's documentation to determine whether this provision is required.

▶ Saving a Cutout as a File

To save a cutout to a disk file:

1. Define the cutout by using the Pick or Scissors tool.
2. Select Copy To from the Edit menu. The Copy To dialog box (see Figure 10.3) appears in response.

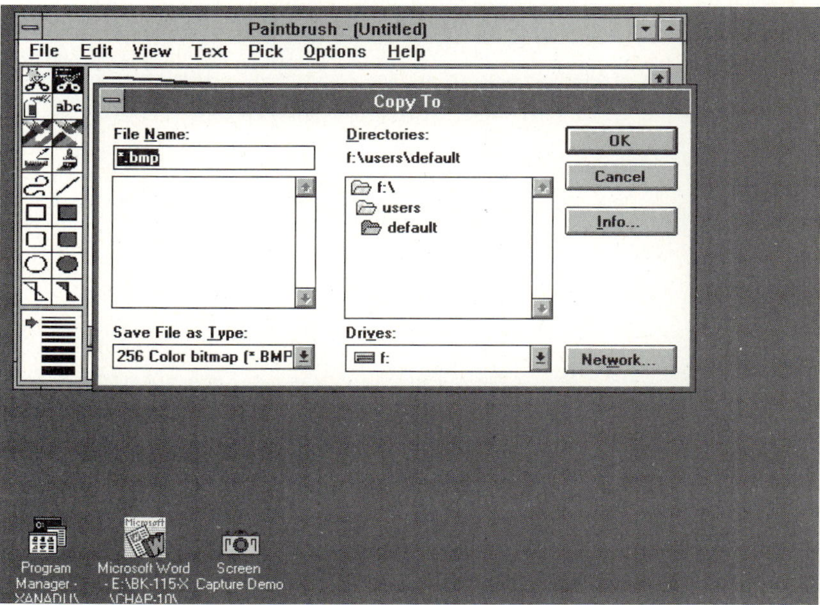

Figure 10.3
The Copy To dialog box

3. Enter a name for the file in the File Name edit box.
4. Select the image format to use from the Save File As Type list box.
5. Select the Info button for details on the cutout's height, width, color resolution, and color planes.
6. Select OK.

Help Files ▼ Cutouts can be saved as .PCX (Paintbrush) or .BMP (Windows bitmap) images. The latter format is used by default.

▶ Retrieving a Cutout

To retrieve an image from a file:

1. Select the Paste From option from the Edit menu.
2. Select a file type from the List Files Of Type list box.
3. Select the file name from the list box or enter a file name in the edit field.
4. Select the Info button for details on the cutout's height, width, color resolution, and color planes.
5. Select OK to load the image. The cutout image will be positioned in the upper-left corner of the drawing area.
6. Position the cursor inside the cutout.
7. Press the mouse button and drag the cutout to the desired location.
8. To paste the cutout into the image, release the mouse button, then click outside the cutout or select any tool.

Help Files ▼ A saved image can be retrieved from a file and copied to the drawing area. If a color image is pasted to a black and white drawing, the colors are translated to black and white patterns.

▶ Inverting Colors in an Image

To invert image colors:

1. Define a cutout using the Pick or Scissors tool, or define the entire image as a cutout.
2. Select the Inverse option from the Pick menu.
3. Paste the inverted colors into the image by clicking outside the cutout or by selecting any tool.

Help Files ▼ Colors can be inverted, either in a cutout or for the entire image, by selecting the entire image as a cutout. In black and white drawings, black pixels are swapped for white and white pixels for black. In color images, each color becomes its complement; for example, red changes to a muddy blue-gray and green becomes a bad purple.

▶ Sweeping a Cutout

To create a succession of cutout copies across the drawing area:

1. Use the Pick or Scissors tool to select a cutout.
2. Position the cursor inside the cutout.
3. Press and hold the Shift key.

4. Hold the mouse button while dragging the cutout to the desired location.
   - Use the left mouse button to sweep the cutout transparently.
   - Use the right mouse button to sweep the cutout opaquely.
5. Release the Shift key and the mouse button when finished.
6. To paste the cutout, click outside the cutout or select any tool.

Help Files ▼ How fast you drag the cutout determines how the copies are spaced.

▸ Shrinking or Enlarging a Cutout

To shrink or enlarge a cutout:

1. Use the Pick or Scissors tool to select a cutout.
2. Select the Shrink+Grow option from the Pick menu.
3. Select Clear from the Pick menu if you want to erase the original cutout area after the size change.
4. Position the cursor to anchor a corner of the cutout.
5. Press the left mouse button and drag the elastic outline to define the new size for the cutout.
6. To retain the original proportions of the cutout, press and hold the Shift key while dragging the outline.
7. Release the mouse button. If the Clear option is selected, the original cutout is repainted with the background color before the cutout shrinks or grows to fit the outline.
8. Select any tool or select Shrink+Grow from the Pick menu again to exit the current Shrink+Grow operation.

▶ Tilting a Cutout

To tilt a cutout:

1. Use the Pick or Scissors tool to select a cutout.
2. Select Tilt from the Pick menu.
3. Select Clear from the Pick menu if you want to erase the original cutout area after the cutout is tilted.
4. Position the cursor to anchor the upper-left corner of the cutout.
5. Press and hold the left mouse button.
6. Move the mouse right or left. The outline base will shift with the mouse movement.
7. Release the mouse button when the desired angle is achieved. The tilted cutout will appear.
8. The cutout can be positioned and tilted repeatedly if desired.

▶ Flipping a Cutout

To flip a cutout:

No provisions exist for image rotation.

1. Use the Pick or Scissors tool to select a cutout.
2. Select Flip Horizontal or Flip Vertical from the Pick menu.
3. Paste the cutout by clicking outside the cutout or by selecting any tool.

Text

▶ Entering Text in an Image

To enter text in an image:

1. Select the foreground color.

2. Select the Text tool.

abc

3. Position the cursor in the drawing area.

4. Type the text entry.

Help Files ▼ Entry of typed text halts when the text reaches the right margin of the drawing area. Press Enter to begin a new line of text or click to reposition the entry point. The Shift+arrow key combination may be used to scroll the image.

▶ Editing Text

The Paintbrush application is not a text editor or word processor and provides only very simple editing capabilities. Simple text errors can be deleted using the Backspace key.

The Backspace key cannot be used if:

- The text cursor has been repositioned.
- The image has been scrolled.
- The window has been resized.
- Another tool has been selected.
- The user has switched to another application.

When any of these actions occur, Paintbrush pastes the text into the image. Further changes can be made only by erasing or overpainting the existing text and entering new text.

▶ Setting Fonts and Font Sizes

To select a font or font size:

1. Select the Fonts option from the Text menu. The Font dialog box (see Figure 10.4) appears in response.

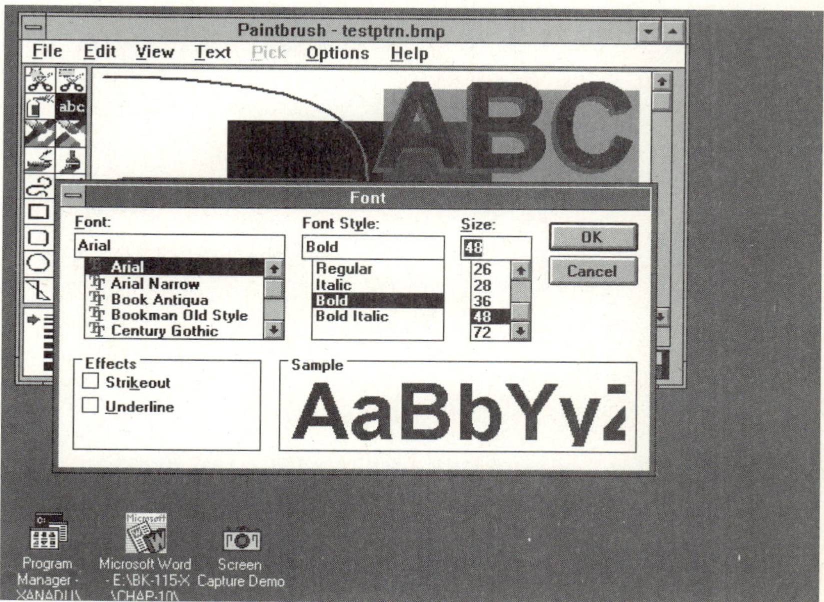

Figure 10.4
The Font dialog box

2. Select a font from the Font list box.
3. Select a size from the Size list box.
4. Optionally, font styles can also be selected.
5. Select OK.

Help Files ▼ Available fonts and font sizes depend, in part, on the display adapter and what fonts have been installed on the computer. Figure 10.4 shows

a selection of TrueType fonts that are supplied with Windows NT. If additional fonts from third-party sources have been installed, these will also appear in the Font list box.

Font, size, and style selections affect text yet to be typed, as well as any text that is not yet pasted down in the drawing area.

▸ Selecting Text Styles from the Text Menu

To select a specific text style:

- Select the style name from the Text menu. A check mark appears by the selected style.

To cancel an individual text style:

- Select the style name again from the Text menu. The check mark will be cleared.

To cancel all current style selections:

- Select Regular from the Text menu. All marked styles are cleared.

Help Files ▼ Style selections include bold, italic, and underline formats, as well as outline and shadow text. Text shadow appears in the selected background color.

Style selections affect text yet to be typed, as well as any text that is not yet pasted down in the drawing area. Styles can also be selected in the Font dialog box. The outline and shadow options, however, appear only in the Paintbrush Font menu as special effects applied to a typeface.

Custom Colors

▸ Defining Custom Colors

To define a custom color:

1. Select as the foreground color a Palette entry to be modified.
2. Select Edit Colors from the Options menu or double-click on the Palette entry. In response, the Edit Colors dialog box (see Figure 10.5) appears.

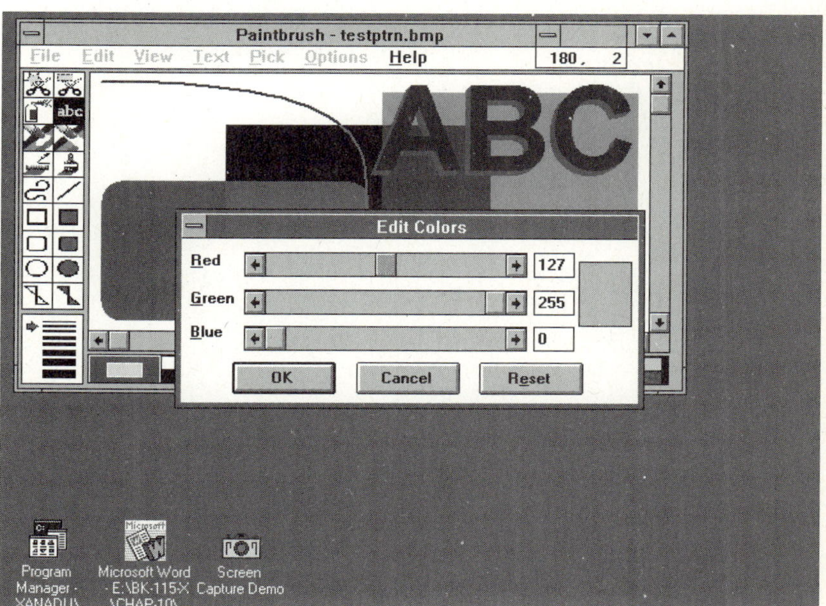

Figure 10.5
The Edit Colors dialog box

3. Drag the scrollbars to adjust the proportions and intensities of the red, green, and blue that are combined to create the color entry. Or, enter Red, Green, and Blue values directly in the edit boxes. The valid range for each is 0 to 255.
4. Finish by doing one of the following:
   - Select OK to accept the defined color, replacing the current Palette entry.

- Select Cancel to keep the previous color.
- Select Reset to restore the original Palette entry.

Help Files ▼ All computer (screen) colors are created by varying the intensities and proportions of the three primary colors: red, green, and blue. Black is created by setting all three intensities to 0, white by setting all three to 255, and all other colors by varying the proportions of the three.

Defining a new Palette color does not affect the existing drawing or the colors presently in the drawing, aside from providing additional color options.

▶ Saving and Retrieving a Custom Palette

To save a custom color Palette:

1. Select Save Colors from the Options menu.
2. Enter a file name for the Palette file in the edit box—the default extension for a Palette file is .PAL.
3. Select OK.

To retrieve a custom color Palette:

1. Select Get Colors from the Options menu.
2. Select a file from the File Names list or enter a file name in the edit box.
3. Select OK.

Drawing Space

▶ Establishing Default Settings for a New Drawing

To establish default settings for a new drawing:

1. Select the Image Attributes option from the Options menu. (The Image Attributes dialog box appears in Figure 10.1.)
2. Select or enter the options and settings desired.
   - *Width* sets the drawing's width.
   - *Height* sets the drawing's height.
   - *Units* selects the units of measurement used for width and height as inches, centimeters, or pixels.
   - Colors can be selected as color or black and white.
   - The Default button resets the drawing area to the image (pixel) size used by the video display. No other settings are affected.
3. Select OK. A message dialog box asks if a new drawing should be created using the new settings.
4. Select Yes to create a new image.

Help Files ▼ The dimension settings for an image must be set before the image is drawn. Once drawing has begun, the only practical method of changing the image size is to save the present work, create a new image in the desired size, and then import the saved image.

Settings specified for new drawings will continue to be used until a new set of image attributes are assigned.

To begin a new image quickly, double-click on the Eraser tool.

Enlarging the Work (Drawing) Area

To remove the Toolbox and Linesize box:

- Select Tools And Linesize from the View menu.

To remove the Palette:

- Select Palette from the View menu.

To redisplay the Toolbox and Linesize box:

- Select Tools And Linesize from the View menu a second time.

To redisplay the Palette:

- Select Palette from the View menu a second time.

Help Files The drawing (working) area can be enlarged by removing the Toolbox, Linesize box, and Palette. Removing these areas does not prevent you from working with the currently selected tool, line width, and foreground and background color selections.

Viewing an Image in a Full Screen

To display an image using the full screen:

- Select View Picture from the View menu.
- Press Ctrl+P.
- Double-click on the Pick tool in the Toolbox.

To return to the working view:

- Click either mouse button.
- Press any key.

Help Files ▼ If the image is too large to fit the screen, only part of the image will be visible. The image cannot be edited in a full-screen view.

▶ Displaying an Image Larger than the Screen

To display an entire image that is larger than the drawing area:

- Select Zoom Out from the View menu.
- Press Ctrl+D.

To cancel Zoom Out:

- Select Zoom In from the View menu.
- Press Esc.

Help Files ▼ The Zoom Out option shrinks an image to fit the drawing area. The Pick and Scissors tools and the Edit menu can still be used to copy, cut, and paste cutouts, but the drawing tools cannot be used in Zoom Out.

▶ Using the Zoom In Option

To edit magnified images:

1. Select Zoom In from the View menu or press Ctrl+N. The cursor changes to a rectangle.
2. Position the rectangle over the area to be magnified.

3. Click. The enclosed portion of the image is magnified to fill the drawing window; a small box at the upper left shows the same area without magnification. In the magnified image, individual pixels appear outlined in black.

4. To edit individual pixels:

   - Use the left mouse button for the foreground color.
   - Use the right mouse button for the background color.
   - Press and drag the mouse to change multiple pixels.

5. To change groups of pixels within the magnified area, use the Paint Roller tool.

6. Select Undo from the Edit menu or press Ctrl+Z to return to normal resolution and to cancel any changes.

7. Select Zoom Out from the View menu to save changes and return to normal resolution.

Help Files ▼ The Zoom In option is useful for locating and patching leaks that occur when using the Paint Roller.

▸ Using the Cursor Position Window

To display the cursor position's xy *coordinates:*

- Select Cursor Position from the View menu. The Cursor Position window appears in the upper-right corner of the Paintbrush frame but can be relocated anywhere outside of the drawing area, including outside the Paintbrush window.

To remove the Cursor Position window:

- Select Cursor Position from the View menu a second time.

Help Files ▼ The Cursor Position window shows the *xy* coordinates of the cursor, provided that the cursor is within the drawing window. These coordinates can be used to align text or space lines when creating charts or tables.

If the cursor moves outside the drawing area, the coordinates displayed show the cursor's last position before it left the drawing window.

▸ Using the Keyboard to Navigate

To use the keyboard to navigate through Paintbrush, use the key combinations in Table 10.2 to substitute for mouse actions.

Table 10.2
Navigating Paintbrush Using Keyboard Commands

Select	To Move
Tab	Counterclockwise among Toolbox, Linesize box, Palette, and drawing areas
Shift+Tab	Clockwise among Toolbox, Linesize box, Palette, and drawing areas
Arrow keys	Within drawing area
Home	To top of drawing area
End	To bottom of drawing area
PgUp	Up one screen
PgDn	Down one screen
Shift+PgUp	Left one screen
Shift+PgDn	Right one screen
Shift+Home	To left edge of drawing area
Shift+End	To right edge of drawing area

Table 10.2
Navigating Paintbrush Using Keyboard Commands (Continued)

Select	To Move
Shift+up arrow	Up one line (~10 pixels)
Shift+down arrow	Down one line (~10 pixels)
Shift+left arrow	To left one space (~10 pixels)
Shift+right arrow	To right one space (~10 pixels)

Paintbrush Files

Opening and Saving Paintbrush Files

To open a Paintbrush file:

1. Select Open from the File menu. The Open dialog box (see Figure 10.6) appears.

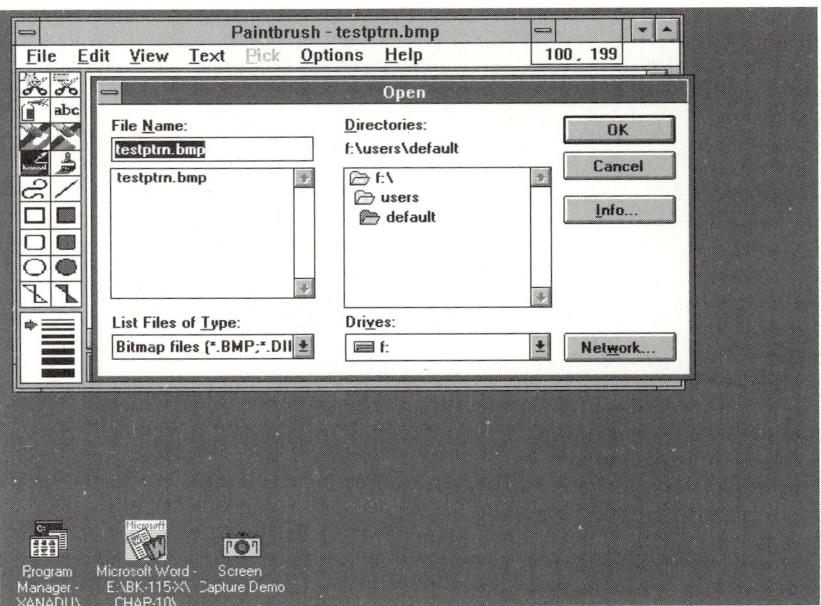

Figure 10.6
The Open dialog box

2. Select the drive from the Drives list box.

3. Select the directory from the Directories list box.

4. Select the file type from the List Files Of Type list box. Options are *.BMP, *.DIB, *.MSP, *.PCX, or *.* (all) file formats.

5. Select a file from the Files list box.

6. Double-click on the file name or select the OK button to load the image file.

To save an existing Paintbrush file:

- Select Save from the File menu.

To save a new file or save an existing file under a new name:

1. Select Save As from the File menu. (The Save As dialog box is identical to the Open dialog box in Figure 10.6, except for its title.)

2. Select the drive from the Drives list box.

3. Select the directory from the Directories list box.

4. Select the file type from the List Files Of Type list box. Options are .PCX or .BMP file formats.

5. Enter a file name in the File Name edit box. If no extension is specified, the extension from the List Files Of Type selection will be used.

6. Select OK.

Importing Images

▶ Working with Microsoft Paint Files

To convert a Microsoft Paint file to a Paintbrush file:

Microsoft Paint files can be converted to Paintbrush file formats, but not vice versa.

1. Select Open from the File menu (see Figure 10.6, preceding).

2. Select the drive from the Drives list box.

3. Select the directory from the Directories list box.

4. Select the .MSP file type from the List Files Of Type list box. Other options are *.BMP, *.DIB, *.PCX, or *.* (all) file formats.

5. Select a file from the Files list box.
6. Double-click on the file name or select the OK button to load the image file. A dialog box asks if the image file should be converted to a Paintbrush file.
7. Select OK to confirm the conversion.
8. Edit the image as required.
9. Select Save from the File menu. The image is saved under the same file name but using the .BMP extension.

Printing Images

▶ Printing an Image

To print the current drawing:

1. Select Print from the File menu. The Print dialog box (see Figure 10.7) appears in response.

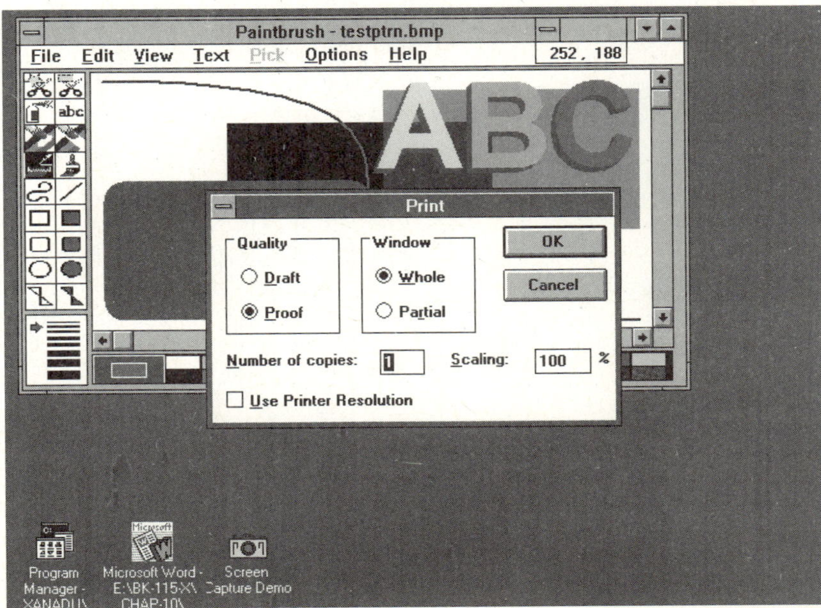

Figure 10.7
The Print dialog box

2. Select the appropriate options.
    - *Draft* uses the fastest printer speed available, which usually results in lower resolution.
    - *Proof* produces the clearest image possible using any advanced features supported by the printer.
    - *Whole* prints the entire drawing, including parts not showing in the drawing area.
    - *Partial* prints only a selected portion of an image.
    - *Number Of Copies* specifies the number of copies to print.
    - *Scaling* sizes the image proportionally. A setting of 100% produces no scaling.
    - *Use Printer Resolution* uses printer dot resolutions instead of screen dimensions.
3. Select OK.

Help Files ▼ Many printers—particularly laser-type printers—support only one setting for printing, in which case Draft and Proof produce the same results.

By default, Paintbrush prints an image the same size as it appears on screen (or approximately the same). However because a 640×480 image on screen is imaged at 96 pixels per inch, the same image on a 300dpi printer requires 2000×1500 dots—which requires enlargement.

If the Use Printer Resolution option is selected, the same image will be printed at 640 dots by 480 dots—reducing the printed image from 6.67 inches wide to 2.13 inches wide. In some cases, using the printer resolution may reduce or prevent stretch distortion. In general, however, this option is better suited to lower-resolution devices, such as dot-matrix printers.

▸ Printing a Portion of an Image

To print only a part of a drawing:

1. Select Print from the File menu.
2. Select the Partial option.
3. Select OK. The image is reduced to fit in the drawing window.
4. Press the mouse button to anchor one corner of an elastic box.
5. Hold the mouse button down while dragging the elastic box to enclose the area to be printed.
6. Release the mouse button. The enclosed area is printed.

▸ Printing Images with Headers and Footers

To add a header or footer to the printed image:

1. Select Page Setup from the File menu. The Page Setup dialog box (see Figure 10.8) appears.

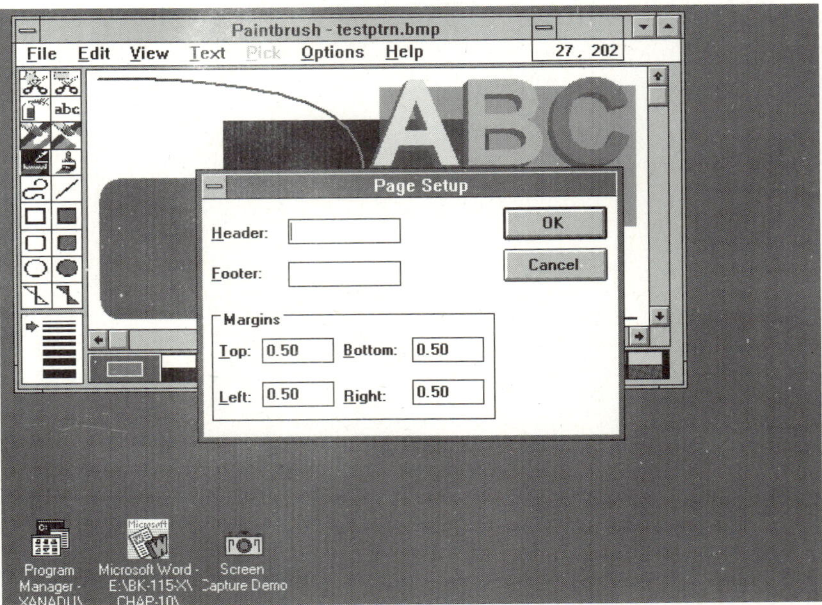

Figure 10.8
The Page Setup dialog box

2. Enter header or footer text and/or codes.
3. Select OK.

Help Files ▼ The Header and Footer boxes scroll as text is entered. Codes (see Table 10.3) can be used to include date/time information, file names, page numbers, or to align text entries.

Table 10.3
Header/Footer Codes

Code	Result
&d	Prints current date
&t	Prints current time
&p	Prints page numbers
&f	Prints file name
&l	Left-aligns text following code
&c	Centers text following code
&r	Right-aligns text following code

Header and footer text and codes are not preserved with saved files. New header and footer information must be entered each time a file is loaded.

Headers are printed in the top margin and footers in the bottom margin, regardless of margin settings.

▶ Setting Page Margins for Printing

To set the margins used for printing:

1. Select Page Setup from the File menu. The Page Setup dialog box (see Figure 10.8) appears.

2. Enter measurements for the page margin settings in the Margins edit boxes.

3. Select OK.

Help Files ▼ The margin settings in the Page Setup dialog box control how Paintbrush positions an image on the page. If the margin settings are too low to permit you to print an image, a warning message will be displayed and the upper-left corner of the image will be positioned according to the Top and Left margin settings.

▸ Changing Printers and Printer Options

To change printers or set printer options:

1. Select Print Setup from the File menu. (See Figure 10.9).

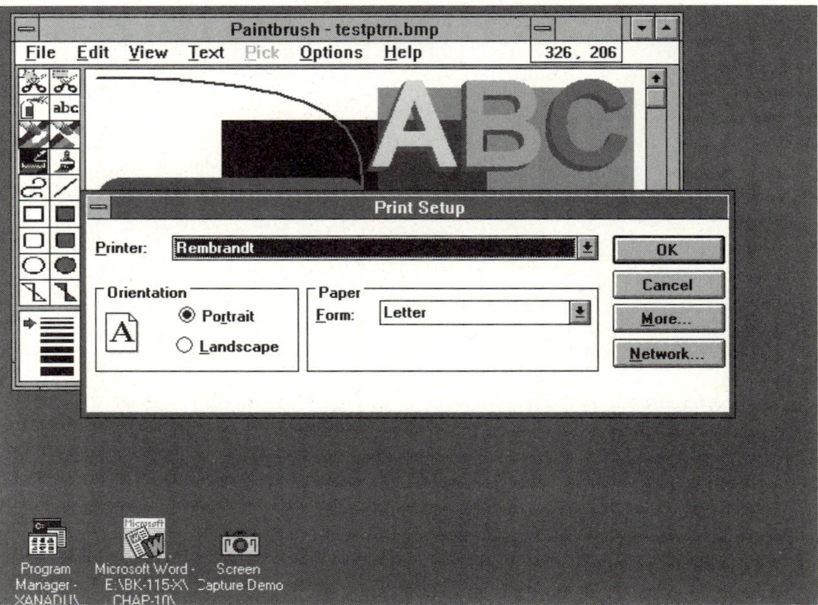

Figure 10.9
The Print Setup dialog box

2. Select the Default Printer or Specific Printer option in the Printer box.
3. If the Specific Printer option is selected, select a printer from the Printer list.
4. Set the Orientation and Paper specifications as desired.
5. To display options specific to a selected printer driver, select the More… button.
6. Select OK to save changes.

Help Files ▼ Paintbrush directs all documents to the default printer. To select a different printer, the preferred printer must be selected as the default.

THE RESCUE PAGES: Using the Windows NT Paintbrush Program

I want to draw a color image, but the Palette offers only black and white (or vice versa).

Select the Image Attributes option from the Options menu and select the Color mode from the dialog box. Image size can also be set at this point. Two cautions: Existing images cannot be resized or be changed from one mode to the other. Any changes in the Image Attributes can be applied only to a new image.

You may, however, save a black and white image and then paste the image into a color format or vice versa. Of course, color images copied to a black and white format are changed to black and white in the process.

Help! I messed up my drawing!

Okay, mistakes happen...but, before you do anything else, select Undo from the Edit menu or press Ctrl+Z. Everything you've drawn using the current tool selection is undone and the previous image is restored.

Alternatively, you can undo a portion of a drawing by pressing the Backspace key. The cursor is replaced by a square with an X inside. Press the mouse button and drag the cursor across the area to undo. Release the mouse button when finished.

I chose the wrong color. I need to replace all of it with another color.

Use the Color Eraser to replace one color with another. Select the original color as the foreground color and the replacement color as background.

Then, either drag the Color Eraser across the image or double-click on the Color Eraser tool to replace all instances of a particular color in the entire image.

I tried to use the Paint Roller to fill an area, but it keeps leaking.

Even a 1-pixel break in an outline allows sufficient room for a leak. Unfortunately, leaks are hard to locate because the fill action occurs too rapidly to follow.

One approach is to localize the leak by subdividing the area to fill. First, select a thin line width, then draw a line in the fill color to roughly bisect the area to be filled. Next, use the Paint Roller on one half of the area. If the fill leaks, select Undo and try the other side. If both sides leak, keep subdividing.

When the leaking area has been located, use the Zoom In option to examine the border area in greater detail, plugging leaks as required. Then use Zoom Out and complete the fill.

I've tried to paste an image from the Clipboard into another application, but I get a message saying that the format isn't recognized.

When an image is copied to the Clipboard, it is copied in multiple formats; for example, bitmap, native, enhanced metafile, picture, and ownerlink formats. The problem may be that the application you are using simply doesn't recognize the multiple formats supplied by the Clipboard.

The solution is to select the Omit Picture Format option from the Options menu in the Paintbrush program before copying the image to the Clipboard. This reduces the format options to bitmap, native, and ownerlink, with bitmap as the default. At least one of these formats should be acceptable to any Windows/Windows NT application.

Incidentally, just in case you've exited from Paintbrush before finding out that the image isn't acceptable, but you didn't save the image to a file, you can save the Clipboard image as a file or load it back into Paintbrush directly.

I need to include a block of text in an image, but Paintbrush's text capabilities are too cumbersome.

Even though text can be copied from another text editor to the Clipboard and viewed on the Clipboard with fonts and formatting intact, when this same text is transferred from the Clipboard to Paintbrush, all formatting, fonts, and so forth are lost. Tabs appear as print characters, and only line breaks are preserved. Further, once the text has been pasted from the Clipboard, it becomes a part of the image and cannot be edited.

Text copied from the Clipboard will, however, be inserted using the currently selected typeface and font size.

If you frequently need to combine text and images, you need a more sophisticated graphics application. You might wish to consider something such as Power Point, CorelDraw, or Publisher's Paintshop.

I can't seem to draw several items the same size (or space them equally).

There is no spacing grid supplied, but the Cursor Position window can behave like one. For example, to draw a series of vertical lines 25 pixels apart from one another, open the Cursor Position window from the View menu. Then, with the Line tool, draw the first line from 10,10 to 10,200 (use the Shift key to draw a vertical line). Position the cursor at 35,10 to draw the next line. Start the next at 60,10, and so on.

I load a picture and it looks great—almost photographic. Then, later, when I come back to Paintbrush, the colors are all wrong.

Unfortunately, it's easier to explain what's happening here than it is to suggest a cure, even though the problem is not serious. Some other application has changed the active, displayed Palette, affecting your picture. However, because the picture has not actually been changed, it still retains its original Palette colors…even if they aren't visible at the moment.

When you click on the Paintbrush program, Paintbrush should, in theory, check to ensure that its Palette is actually the active Palette. However, Paintbrush does not always restore the Palette and some intervention may be required on your part to nudge it into action. First, try reducing the Paintbrush window to an icon, then restoring it to force

Paintbrush to do a complete repaint. If this doesn't work, save your image file—under a new name, if necessary—and then reload it. This is the one move that definitely will reset the active Palette.

CHAPTER

11

HELP! Fax and Modem Utilities

Windows NT Terminal is an application that you can use to connect your computer to other computers and exchange information.

Topics covered in this chapter include

- Remote communications with a modem
- Configuring and customizing the Terminal program
- Connecting to another computer
- Receiving and transmitting text files
- Binary file transfers
- Working with text in the Terminal window
- Printing from Terminal
- Ending a communications session

Remote Communications with a Modem

▸ Requirements for Establishing a Modem Connection

Several initial provisions are necessary before communications can be opened with a remote computer, including

- Using the Communications dialog box to define communications options
- Using the Modem Commands dialog box to define modem commands and other default settings
- Using the Terminal Emulation dialog box to select a terminal emulation type

Once defined, these basic communications settings can be saved in a settings file with different configurations saved for different remote connection requirements. Refer to "Saving a Settings File" and "Loading Terminal Settings on Startup," following.

Finally, a phone number must be entered in the Phone Number dialog box to establish the telephone link.

HELP! *Remember, the COM port settings must be established from the Control Panel before the Terminal utility will function correctly.*

▸ Creating or Opening a Terminal Settings File

To create a new settings file:

- Select New from the File menu to begin with the default settings.
- Open an existing settings file to use as a basis for the new settings.

To open an existing settings file:

1. Select Open from the File menu. The Open dialog box (see Figure 11.1) appears.
2. Select the drive and directory as necessary.
3. Select a .TRM file from the File Name list box.

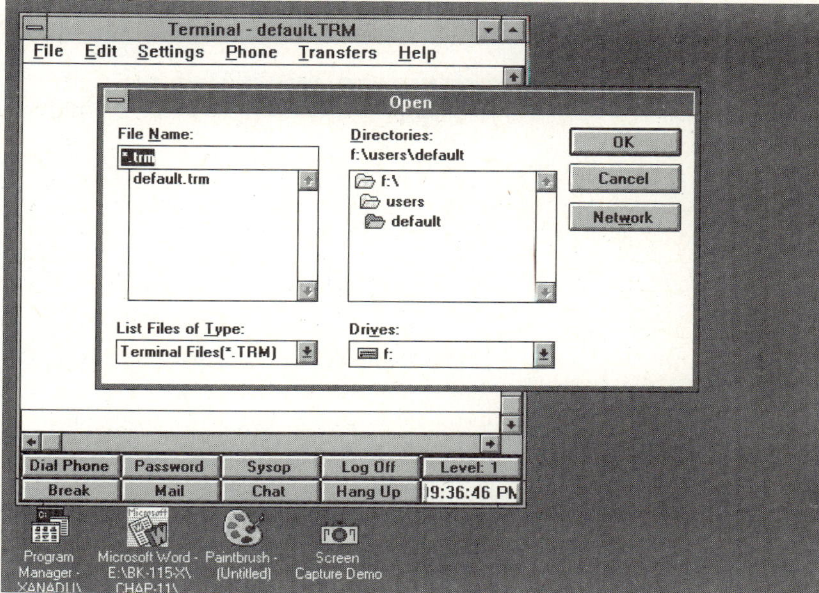

Figure 11.1
The Open dialog box

4. Select OK to load the .TRM file.

▸ Defining Communications Settings

To define communications settings:

1. Select Communications from the Settings menu. The Communications dialog box (see Figure 11.2) appears.
2. Select the options appropriate for both the local system and the remote computer.
3. Select OK.

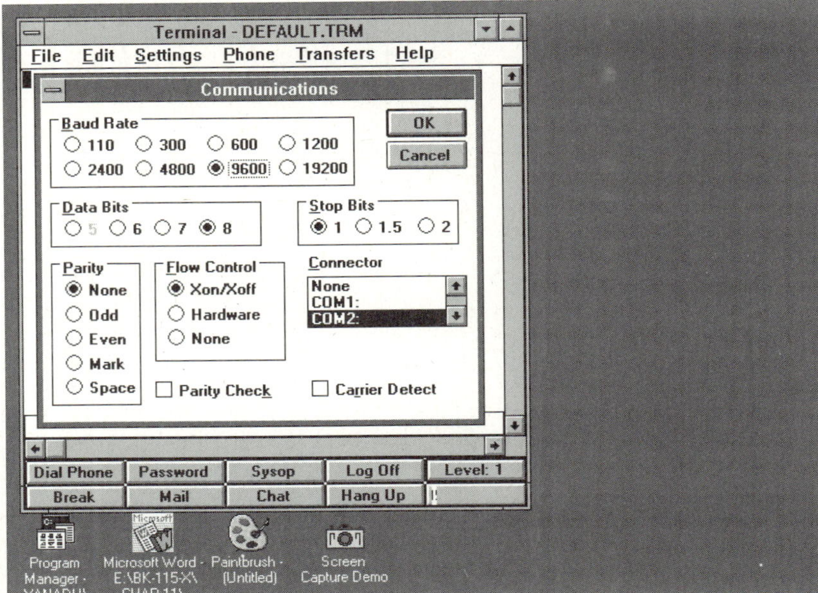

Figure 11.2
The Communications dialog box

Help Files ▼ Conventionally, communications protocols are stated in a shorthand format as, for example, 2400 N 8 1 or 9600 N 8 1. The first term is the highest baud rate supported by the host's modem—in these examples, 2400 baud or 9600 baud. The last three terms in each are the communications protocols. The two most common protocols (they are used by almost everyone) are N 8 1 (no parity, 8 bits, 1 stop bit, used by most BBSs) and E 7 1 (even parity, 7 bits, 1 stop bit, used by CompuServe).

Protocols and settings are described further here:

- *Baud Rate* sets the transfer rate used by the modem to communicate with the remote system. This must be a rate supported by the remote computer service as well as by the local modem (hardware). Most modems support multiple baud rates; select the highest baud rate compatible with both the local modem and the remote system.

- *Data Bits* sets the number of bits in each data packet transferred between the local and remote computers. Most host computers require 7 or 8 data bits; a few, however, may require 5 or 6 data bits.
- *Parity* selects the parity type used to check communications accuracy. If 8 data bits are used, set Parity to none.
- *Parity Check* shows any characters that were not received correctly, replacing the error with a question mark. Of course, the Parity Check option can't be selected unless Parity has been selected.
- *Carrier Detect* tells Terminal to use the carrier-detect signal to determine if the modem is on-line. If Carrier Detect is not selected, Terminal watches for the modem response string—a string returned by smart modems using the Hayes protocols—to determine if the modem is on-line. If Carrier Detect is selected but the modem appears to be having difficulty connecting to the remote computer, try clearing the Carrier Detect option and relying on string protocols.
- *Connector* selects the communications port where the modem is connected. If None is selected, Terminal checks COM1 first, then COM2, and so on. On most computers, only two communication ports are installed, as COM1 and COM2. One of these is used for the mouse and the other is used by the modem. However, up to eight communications ports may be installed on some systems.
- *Stop Bits* sets the interval between selected characters. One stop bit is the common interval, but some systems may require longer lapses.
- *Flow Control* selects a hand-shaking method to permit the remote computer to tell Terminal to stop sending data when the remote buffer is too full to receive additional data. Select Hardware, Xon/Xoff, or None. The Hardware flow control option is normally used only with a dummy modem, when two computers are cabled together directly. None is selected if no overflow control is used; if the flow control method is not known (the most common circumstance), select Xon/Xoff.

Windows NT also needs to know the base port address and interrupt request line (IRQ) settings for the communications port. These, however, were detected during the Windows NT installation. (Refer to Chapter 4).

Setting Modem Command Strings

To define modem command strings:

1. Select the Modem Commands option from the Settings menu. The Modem Commands dialog box (see Figure 11.3) appears.

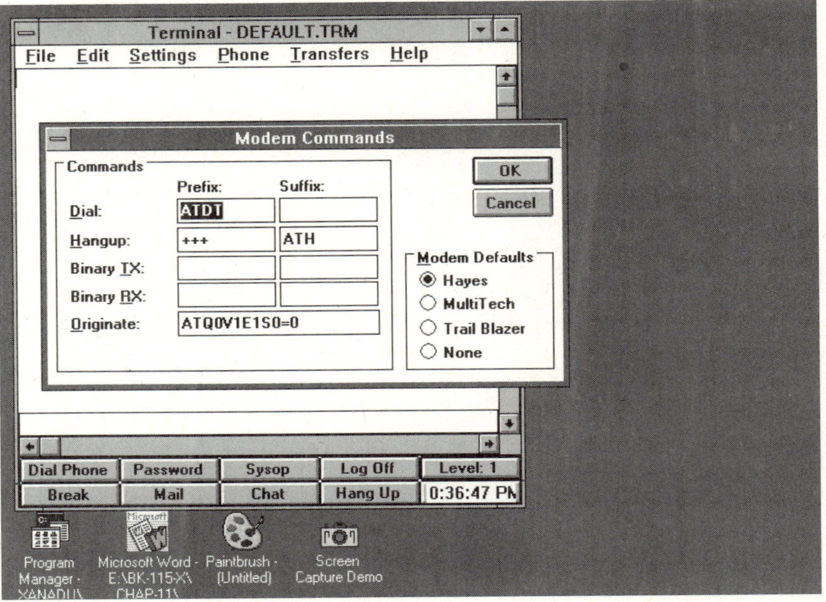

Figure 11.3
The Modem Commands dialog box

2. Select a modem type from the Modem Defaults buttons.
3. Modify any of the default commands, if necessary, to fit.
4. Select OK.

Help Files ▼ If the modem in use is not listed, select either a compatible modem type, or select None and define command strings appropriately.

The Hayes command set is the current de facto standard, and most modems sold today are Hayes-compatible, but some modems may require changes to the command strings for optimum operation. Refer to your modem manual for details on compatibility and on command strings.

▸ Selecting a Terminal Emulation Type

To select a terminal emulation type:

1. Select Terminal Emulation from the Settings menu. The Terminal Emulation dialog box (see Figure 11.4) appears.

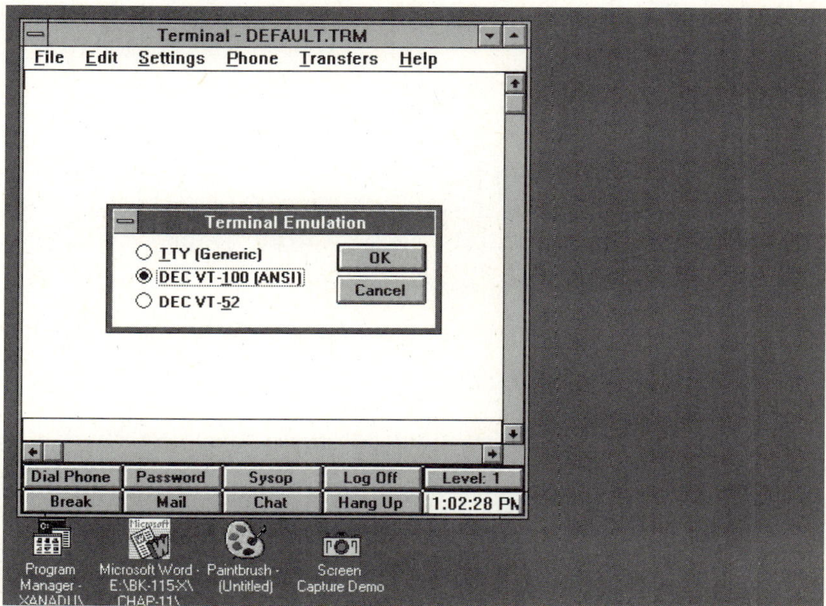

Figure 11.4
The Terminal Emulation dialog box

2. Select a terminal type.

3. Select OK.

Help Files ▼ The Terminal program is able to emulate several terminal types that can be expected by the remote computer. The DEC VT-100 (ANSI) terminal mode is compatible with most remote systems. In cases of difficulty, however, the TTY terminal type (TeleTYpe) can be selected as a lowest common denominator. It uses format codes only for carriage returns, backspaces, and tab characters.

If you use DEC VT-100 (ANSI) emulation, the Scroll Lock (keyboard) option must be turned on to enable the VT-100 function keys. If Scroll Lock is off, the function and arrow keys operate normally with Windows NT functions.

Configuring and Customizing the Terminal Program

▶ Setting Terminal's Emulation Mode

To set a terminal emulation mode:

1. Select Terminal Preferences from the Settings menu. The Terminal Preferences dialog box (see Figure 11.5) appears.

2. Select the appropriate Terminal Modes check boxes.

   - *Line Wrap* automatically wraps characters that exceed the specified column width.

   - *Local Echo* displays keystrokes as they are typed rather than waiting for the echo sent from the remote terminal. If double characters appear, leave the Local Echo option off.

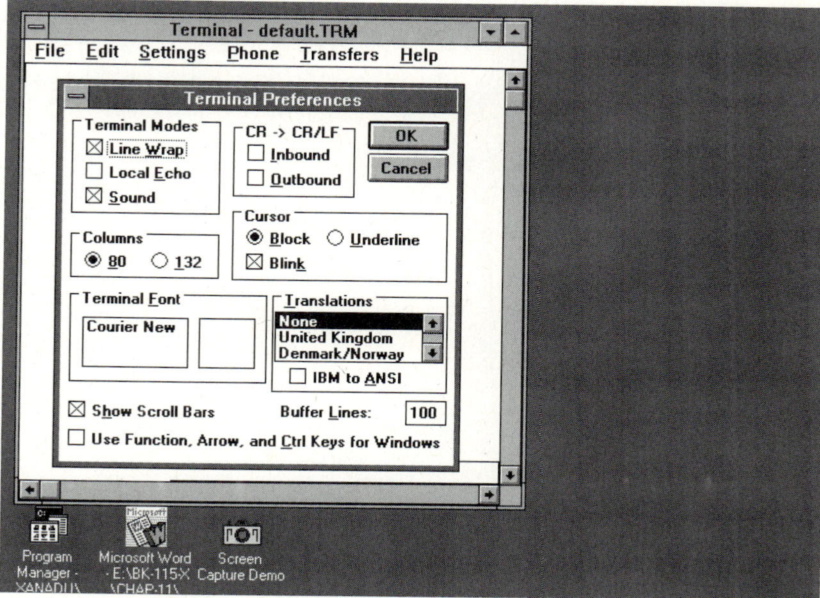

Figure 11.5
The Terminal Preferences dialog box

- *Sound* enables the system speaker to respond when a bell instruction is received from the remote computer.

3. Select OK.

Help Files ▼ Enabling the Line Wrap option is a good default setting. If it is not required, it has no effect; however, if, for example, the remote host sends text in a 132-column format but the local display is only 80 columns, the Line Wrap option will wrap the lines to fit the display width. Alternatively, the horizontal scroll bar can be used to view lines extending beyond the display width.

Full-duplex remote systems echo all keystrokes received, returning characters typed for local display. Half-duplex systems do not echo and,

therefore, you must select the Local Echo option in order to see what you are typing.

Setting the Screen Column Width

To set the display column width:

1. Select Terminal Preferences from the Settings menu (see Figure 11.5).
2. Select a column width of 80 or 132.
3. Select OK.

Help Files ▼ The 132-column setting instructs the Terminal application to reserve a text display suitable for 132 columns, regardless of what the physical display can handle and what the remote terminal is actually sending. Use the scroll bars to view a 132-column display on an 80-column screen.

Selecting a Display Font

To select a display font:

1. Select Terminal Preferences from the Settings menu (see Figure 11.5).
2. Select a font and font size.
3. Select OK.

Help Files ▼ All characters typed or received appear in the Terminal window in the selected font and type size. Multiple fonts, formatting, and WYSIWYG typesetting are not supported by Terminal (nor by most other communications protocols/software packages).

Setting Language Preferences

To change language selection:

1. Select Terminal Preferences from the Settings menu (see Figure 11.5).
2. Select a country or language setting from the Translation list box.
3. Enable (check) the IBM To ANSI check box if the language selected uses extended or accented characters.
4. Select OK.

Help Files Selecting a language or country name specifies which ISO (International Standards Organization) character set will be used. Of course, the remote host computer must also recognize the selected character set.

Displaying Scroll Bars

To display scroll bars for the Terminal window:

1. Select Terminal Preferences from the Settings menu (see Figure 11.5).
2. Select Show Scroll Bars.
3. Select OK.

Help Files ▼ The scroll bars allow you to see any information that is not presently visible in the Terminal window. For example, even if an 80-column display is selected, only part of the text received may be visible, because the actual window can be any size. Using the scroll bars, the window contents can be scrolled for viewing.

▶ Selecting a Buffer Size

To set the buffer size (the number of lines of text that can be saved in the buffer):

1. Select Terminal Preferences from the Settings menu (see Figure 11.5).
2. Enter a number in the Buffer Lines box. (The minimum range for either width is 25. The maximum is 399 in 80-column mode or 244 in 132-column mode. Default is 100.)
3. Select OK.

Help Files ▼ The Terminal program reserves a minimum buffer size of 25 lines (2K) with a maximum size of 399 or 244 lines (32K). If the setting requested exceeds the maximum, the buffer is set to the maximum permitted. If fewer than 25 lines are requested, a minimum of 25 lines are reserved.

Setting Usage for the Arrow Keys, Ctrl Key, and Functions Keys

To specify how the arrow, Ctrl, and function keys are used:

1. Select Terminal Preferences from the Settings menu (see Figure 11.5).
2. Enable (check) the Use Function, Arrow, And Ctrl Keys For Windows NT check box to make these keys available for Windows NT functions. Disable (clear) the check box to send these keys to the remote terminal.
3. Select OK.

Help Files ▼ The arrow keys, Ctrl key, and function keys either can be used by Windows NT—for example, press F1 for Help or Ctrl+Esc to display the Task List—or can simply be passed through to the remote terminal if, for example, the remote computer requires a Ctrl+C key combination. Alternatively, see "Assigning Function Key Tasks for Terminal," following.

To use the arrow, Ctrl, and function keys locally, enable this option; to send these keys to the remote terminal, clear this check box.

Setting Handling for Carriage Returns and Line Feeds (CR to CR/LF)

To add line feed characters to carriage returns in incoming files:

1. Select Terminal Preferences from the Settings menu (see Figure 11.5).
2. Select the Inbound check box to add line feed characters to carriage returns.
3. Select OK.

To add line feed characters to carriage returns in outgoing files:

1. Select Terminal Preferences from the Settings menu (see Figure 11.5).
2. Select the Outbound check box to add line feed characters to carriage returns.
3. Select OK.

Help Files ▼ By itself, the carriage return character is intended simply to move the print head or the cursor back to the left margin; a line feed character moves the paper in a printer up one line or moves the cursor on screen down one line. Thus, to correctly display text, both printer and text display expect each line of text to end with a carriage return character followed by a line feed character—a CR/LF pair.

Many editors and word processors, however, use carriage returns only at the end of paragraphs (hard line breaks) and do not use line feed characters at all. Therefore, when a text file is sent, the sending computer may need to insert carriage returns to provide formatting line breaks but may or may not include line feed characters, leaving it to the receiving computer to supply these.

In short, there are no hard-and-fast standards for how text files are transferred. Therefore, if the remote computer appends line feeds to carriage returns when sending a text file, clear the Inbound check box. Likewise, if the remote computer appends line feeds to carriage returns when receiving a text file, clear the Outbound check box. (See also "Receiving and Transmitting Text Files," following.)

▶ Assigning Function-Key Tasks for Terminal

To assign tasks to function keys for the Terminal application:

1. Select Function Keys from the Settings menu. See the Function Keys dialog box in Figure 11.6.

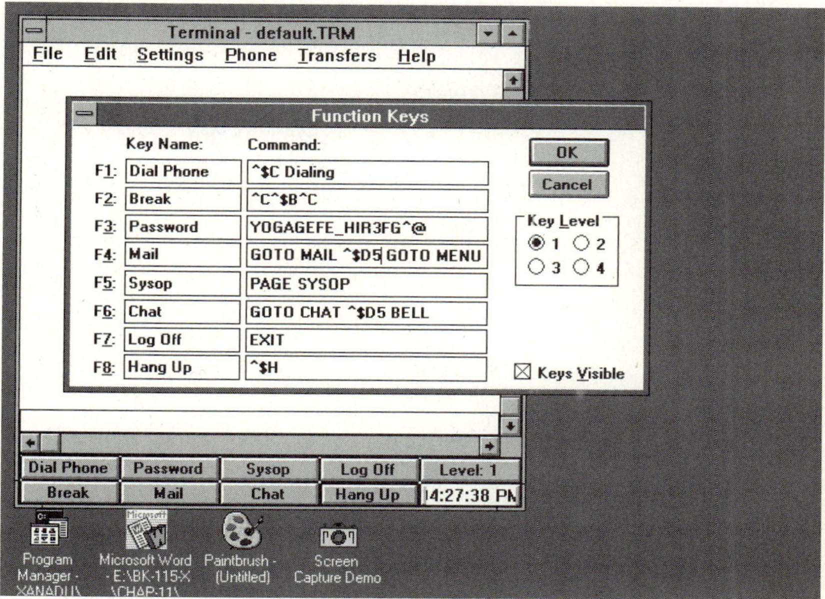

Figure 11.6
The Function Keys dialog box

2. From the Key Level buttons, select a level for the group of function keys.
3. In the Key Name edit box, enter an optional name for each function key.
4. In the Command edit box, enter text, control codes, or any combination of the two. Entries may be up to 41 characters in length. Control codes are listed in Table 11.1.

Table 11.1
Terminal Control Codes

Control Code	Operation
^A ... ^Z	Transmits Ctrl+A ... Ctrl+Z to remote host computer.
^$D*nn*	Delays *nn* seconds before continuing.
^$B	Transmits 117-millisecond break code.

Table 11.1
Terminal Control Codes (Continued)

Control Code	Operation
^$C	Selects Dial command from Phone menu.
^$H	Selects Hangup command from Phone menu.
^$L1 ... ^$L4	Changes to another key level in which keys are defined.
^^	Transmits caret (^) character to remote computer.
^@	Transmits NULL character to remote computer.
^[*n*	Transmits one or more escape-code sequences to remote computer with *n* representing one or more codes.

5. Select a new level, then repeat steps 2 through 4 to assign additional function keys.
6. Select OK.

Help Files ▼ Four levels of function-key assignments are permitted, allowing as many as four tasks to be assigned to each function key. Change levels to access a different group of functions (tasks).

▶ Using Function Keys

To display a function key:

1. Select the Function Keys option from the Settings menu. See the Function Keys dialog box in Figure 11.6.
2. Select the level of function key to display from the Key Level buttons.
3. Select the Keys Visible option to display the function keys at the base of the Terminal window.
4. Select OK.

To use a function key:

- Select the function key from the keypad at the base of the Terminal window.
- Press Ctrl+Alt+function key.

To change function-key level (if more than one level is defined):

- Click on the Level button (lower right).
- Select the level desired from the Function Keys dialog box.

Help Files ▼ The Level button operates only if definitions have been entered for function keys on more than one level.

▶ Concealing or Displaying the Function Keys

To display the function keys:

- Select Show Function Keys from the Settings menu.

To conceal the function keys:

- Select Hide Function Keys from the Settings menu.

▶ Saving a Settings File

To save Terminal settings to a file:

- Select Save from the File menu.

Help Files ▼ If the Terminal settings have not been saved previously, a dialog box appears (it is similar to that shown in Figure 11.1) wherein the drive, directory, and file name can be specified. If no file extension is specified, the default extension .TRM will be appended.

▶ Loading Terminal Settings on Start-Up

To load saved settings when Terminal starts:

1. Select the Terminal icon from Program Manager.
2. Select Properties from the File menu in Program Manager. The Program Item Properties dialog box is shown in Figure 11.7.

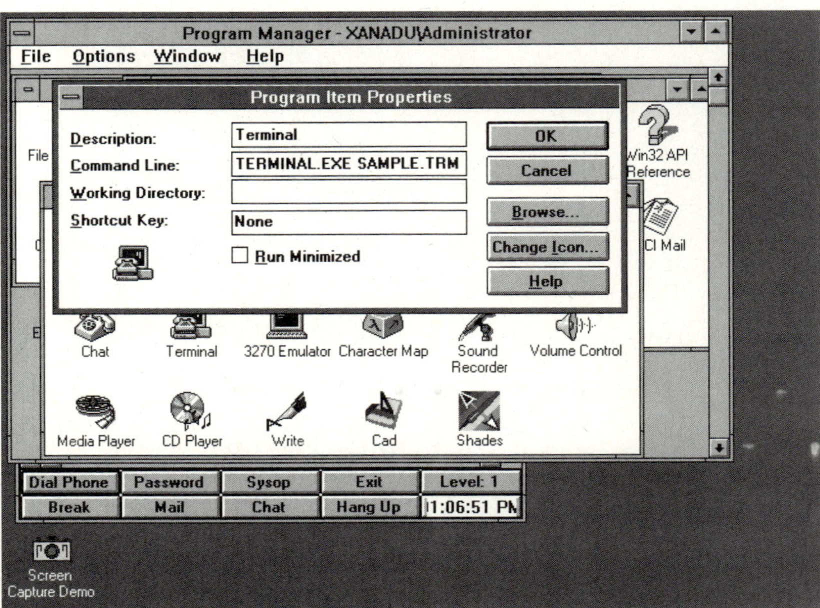

Figure 11.7
The Program Item Properties dialog box

3. Add the name of a settings file—Sample.TRM in the example shown—in the Command Line edit box.

4. Select OK to save the revisions.

Help Files ▼ Instead of adding the .TRM file to the Command Line specification, TERMINAL.EXE can be replaced with the name of a start-up settings file—for example, SAMPLE.TRM. However, in this format, the .TRM extension is required, since this extension is associated with the Terminal program. Alternatively, a different extension could also be associated with the Terminal program. Refer to Chapter 2 for details on associating file extensions with executable programs.

Connecting to Another Computer

▶ Dialing a Phone Number

To have Terminal dial the telephone:

1. Select Phone Number from the Settings menu. The Phone Number dialog box is shown in Figure 11.8.

2. Enter a phone number in the Dial box.

3. Select any additional options required.

   - *Time-Out If Not Connected In* determines how long (in seconds) Terminal waits for a connect signal from the remote host. The minimum wait is 30 seconds.

   - *Redial After Timing Out* instructs Terminal to keep trying the phone number until a connection is established.

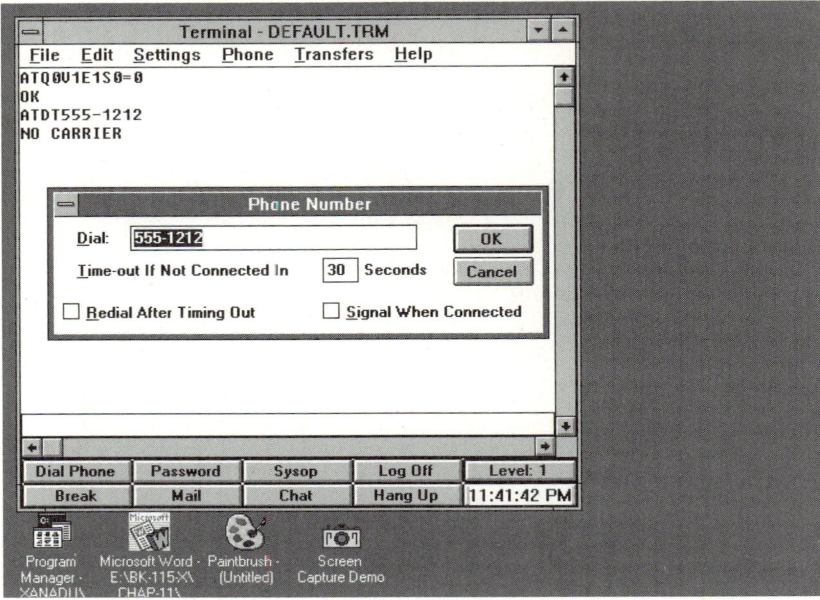

Figure 11.8
The Phone Number dialog box

- *Signal When Connected* instructs Terminal to ring the system bell when a successful connection is established.

4. Select OK to place the call, or select Phone/Dial.

Help Files ▼ Phone number entries can include parentheses and dashes, although these are not required. A comma in a dial command produces a brief delay before proceeding. Multiple commas can be used for longer delays.

To save a phone number for a future occasion, save the Terminal settings in a file using the file name to identify the BBS or service being called. When the settings file is loaded, the saved phone number can be dialed by selecting Phone/Dial from the Main menu.

Dialing a Preset Number

To connect to a remote computer:

1. Load the appropriate settings file or use the Settings/Phone Number commands to enter the phone number and any additional options.
2. Select Dial from the Phone menu.
3. Select Cancel to terminate.

Timing an On-Line Session

To time an on-line session:

1. Select Timer Mode from the Settings menu.
2. Select Timer Mode a second time to reset the timer.
3. Click on the timer display to switch between system time and the elapsed time without resetting the timer.

Help Files ▼ When the Terminal function keypad is displayed (at the bottom of the Terminal window), a box at the bottom-right corner will display either the system time or the elapsed time.

Receiving and Transmitting Text Files

Preparing for File Transfers

To both receive and transmit text files:

1. Use the Text Transfers option from the Settings menu to select flow control settings (refer to "Setting Text Transfer Protocols," following).

2. Select either the Receive Text File or Send Text File option from the Transfers menu (refer to "Receiving a Text File" or "Sending a Text File," following).
3. For an incoming text file, select the drive and directory where the incoming file will be stored, and determine whether a new file should be created, whether the incoming data should be appended to an existing file or an existing file should be replaced, and how format instructions that might be in the file will be handled.
4. To transmit a text file, use the Send Text File dialog box to select a source drive, directory, and file name and select handling for line feed characters.
5. Select the OK button to transmit or receive the text file.

▶ Setting Text Transfer Protocols

To set text transfer (send/receive) protocols:

1. Select Text Transfers from the Settings menu.
2. Select one of the following flow control types:
   - Standard Flow Control
   - Character At A Time
   - Line At A Time
3. For text files created using a word processor, select the Word Wrap Outgoing Text At Column option to produce hard line breaks and set a column width. For text files created using a text editor (such as Notepad or Unipad), hard carriage returns are already present.
4. Select OK.

Help Files ▼ Both the sending and receiving computers must be using the same protocols and transfer methods before reliable communications and data transfers can be possible.

▶ Using Standard Flow Control

To select standard flow control:

1. Select Text Transfers from the Settings menu. The Text Transfers dialog box (see Figure 11.9) appears.

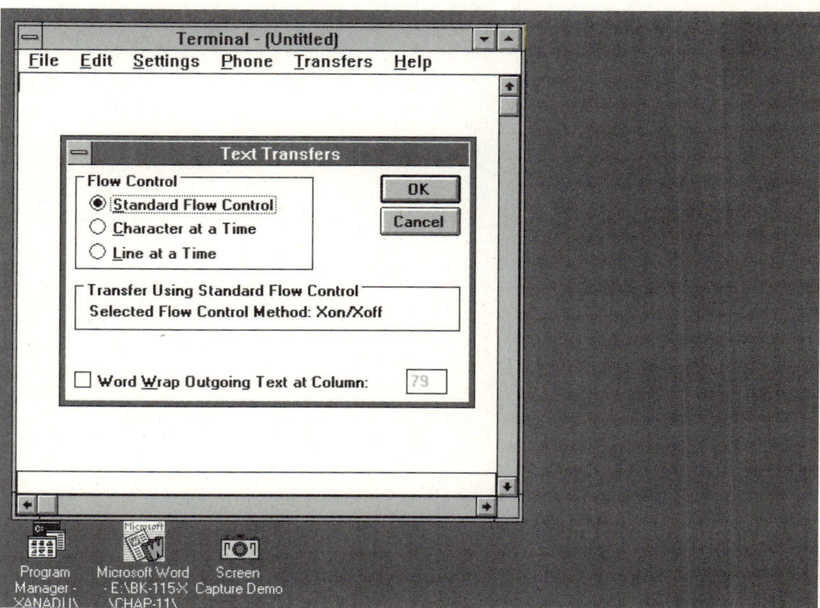

Figure 11.9
The Text Transfers dialog box with the Standard Flow Control option selected

2. Select Standard Flow Control from the Flow Control radio button group.
3. Select OK.

Help Files ▼ Selecting the Standard Flow Control option allows Terminal to transmit characters until the receiving terminal buffer reports that it is full. At that point, Terminal will pause until the receiving buffer can accept additional data.

The standard flow control method—Xon/Xoff—was selected via the Communications option on the Settings menu. Refer to "Defining Communications Settings," preceding.

▶ Using Character At A Time Flow Control

To select Character At A Time flow control:

1. Select Text Transfers from the Settings menu.
2. Select Character At A Time from the Flow Control radio button group, as shown in Figure 11.10.

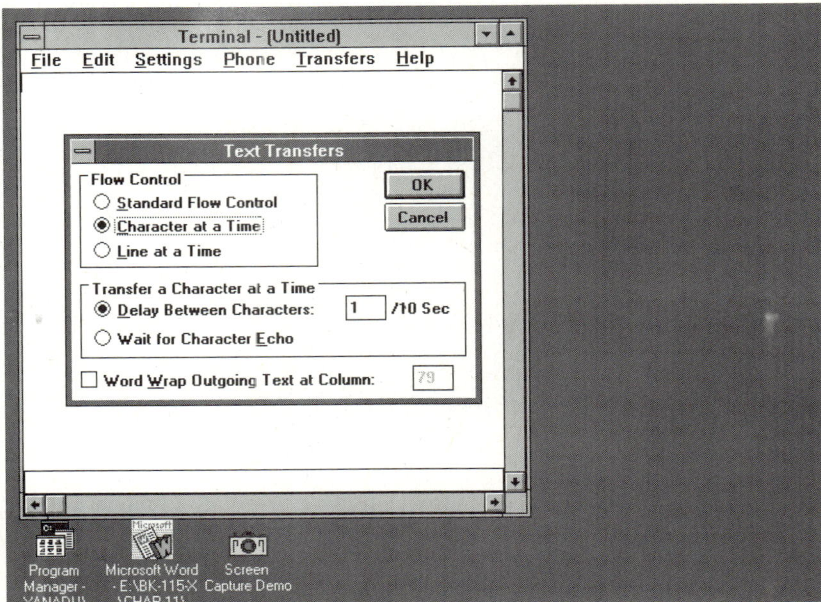

Figure 11.10
The Text Transfers dialog box with the Character At A Time flow control option selected

3. Select either the Delay Between Characters or the Wait For Character Echo option. If the Delay Between Characters option is selected, set how long Terminal should delay between characters in tenths of a second.

4. Select OK.

Help Files ▼ The Delay Between Characters setting is used to slow transmission enough to prevent errors. When this method of character-at-a-time transmission is used, there is no verification of the data transmission and no feedback from the remote system.

The Wait For Character Echo setting is used to send a single character at a time and then to wait for that character to be returned before sending the next 8-bit character. This is a very slow transmission method.

▶ Using Line At A Time Flow Control

To select Line At A Time text data transfer:

1. Select Text Transfers from the Settings menu.

2. Select Line At A Time from the Flow Control radio button group, as shown in Figure 11.11.

3. Select either the Delay Between Lines or the Wait For Prompt String option.

   - If the Delay Between Lines option is selected, set how long Terminal should delay between lines in tenths of a second.

   - If the Wait For Prompt String option is selected, enter the return prompt or character.

4. Select OK.

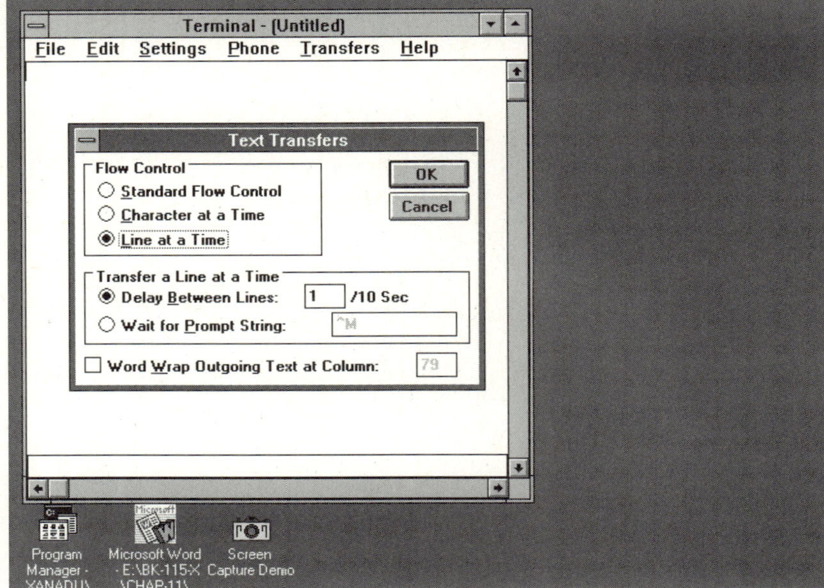

Figure 11.11 *The Text Transfers dialog box with the Line At A Time flow control option selected*

Help Files ▼ The Delay Between Lines setting is used to slow transmission enough to prevent errors. When this method of transmission is used, there is no verification of the data transmission and no feedback from the remote system.

The Wait For Prompt String setting instructs Terminal to send a line of text and then to wait until the remote computer replies with a prompt message or end-of-line code before sending the next line. The end-of-line code shown in the edit box—^M (or Ctrl+M)—is the carriage return character. The Wait For Prompt String method is faster than the Wait For Character option and does not suffer from dependency on accurate character echoes.

▶ Setting Word Wrap for Text File Transfers

To set word wrap for outgoing text transfers:

1. Select Text Transfers from the Settings menu.
2. Select the Word Wrap Outgoing Text At Column check box.
3. Enter the column number in the edit box.
4. Select OK.

Help Files ▼

Always set the width one or two characters narrower than the column width to allow space in the buffer for the carriage return character (^M) ending each line.

Text files created by formatting word processors—often referred to as WYSIWYG editors—commonly place a carriage return character only at the end of a paragraph, depending on active formatting to produce the line breaks and word wraps required to format the text on screen. At the same time, plain-text text editors such as Notepad and Unipad insert hard line breaks (^M characters) for every line.

This latter format is what is expected by most modem communications programs, and the Word Wrap option is used to format long lines to fit in an 80- or 132-column screen. Any column break desired can be set, but a column width of 78 or 79 is commonly used for an 80-column screen and a width of 130 or 131 for a 132-column screen.

▶ Transmitting a Text File

To transmit a text file:

1. Select Send Text File from the Transfers menu. The Send Text File dialog box is shown in Figure 11.12.
2. Select the drive and directory where the source file is located.
3. Select the file in the File Name list box or enter the file name in the File Name edit field.

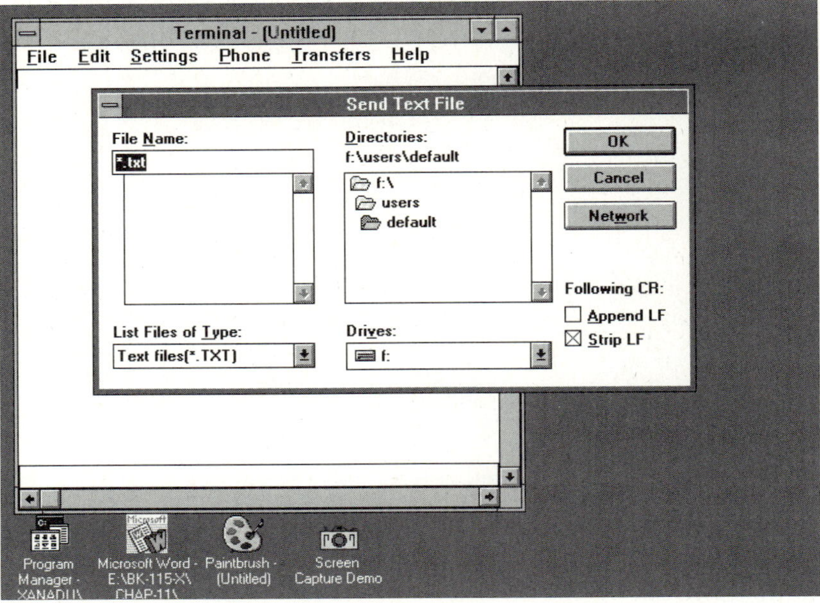

Figure 11.12
The Send Text File dialog box

4. Select the end-of-line handling in the Following CR section.
   - Set the Append LF check box to add a line feed character to the end of each line sent.
   - Set the Strip LF check box to remove existing line feed characters from the end of each line.
5. Select OK to begin file transmission.

Help Files ▼ If the remote computer already adds line feed characters, any existing line feed characters should be stripped before the file is transmitted. However, if the remote computer does not append line feed character where needed, these should be added before the file is transmitted.

Receiving a Text File

To receive a text file:

1. Select Receive Text File from the Transfers menu. The Receive Text File dialog box is shown in Figure 11.13.

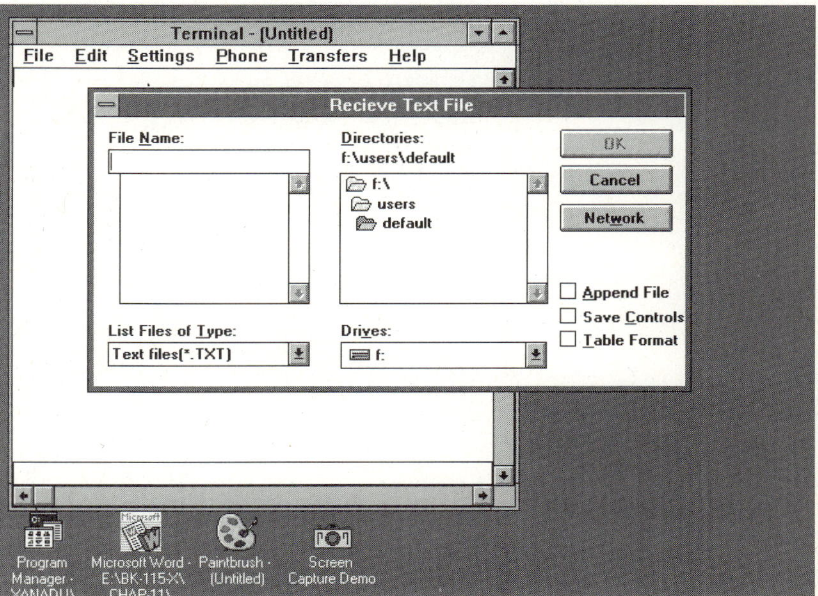

Figure 11.13
The Receive Text File dialog box

2. Select the drive and directory where the incoming file will be saved.
3. Provide a name for the incoming file.
   - To create a new file to save the incoming text, enter a new file name in the File Name edit box.
   - To append the incoming text to an existing file or to overwrite an existing file, select the file name from the File Name list box.
4. If an existing file name was selected, check the Append File option to add the incoming text to the existing file, or clear the check box to overwrite the existing file. Windows NT will request confirmation before overwriting a file.
5. Select OK to receive the text file transmission.

To receive incoming text in tabular format:

- Select the Table Format check box.

To save control codes:

- Select the Save Controls check box.

Help Files ▼ If the Table Format check box is selected, two or more consecutive spaces in the incoming text are replaced by a tab character—the standard separator for table format data.

Even when a file is saved in text format, not all word processors or spreadsheets remove all their formatting codes. Enabling the Save Controls option prevents these codes from being stripped out of incoming files.

▶ Pausing, Resuming, and Stopping Text Transfers

To pause, resume, or stop a transfer:

- Select Pause, Resume, or Stop from the Transfers menu.
- Click on the Pause, Resume, or Stop button from the button bar. These buttons appear automatically when a file transfer is initiated.

Help Files ▼ Text file transfers can be paused, resumed, or stopped. Binary file transfers, however, can be stopped but cannot be paused or resumed.

Binary File Transfers

▶ Preparing for a Binary File Transfer

To establish protocols for a binary file transfer:

1. Select Binary Transfers from the Settings menu.
2. Select either the XModem/CRC or Kermit protocol.
3. Select OK.

Help Files ▼ While a wide variety of protocols are in use under various names—including YModem, ZModem, CompuServe B, TeLink SeaLink, and others—only two protocols are supported by the Terminal program. These two protocols, however, are widely supported; one, if not both, should be available on most systems.

The XModem/CRC protocol transfers data in bytes (8-bit packets), requiring the Parity option to be set to None. Error checking is accomplished using cyclic redundancy checks (CRC), and binary transfers using XModem are both efficient and convenient.

The Kermit protocol (which is not related to frogs) uses 7- or 8-bit packets with Parity set to Even, Odd, or None. For 8-bit data packets (recommended), Parity should be set to None.

The Parity option is set using the Communications command from the Settings menu.

▶ Sending Binary Files

To send a binary data file or to send a text file as a binary format:

1. Select Send Binary File from the Transfers menu. The Send Binary File dialog box (see Figure 11.14) appears.

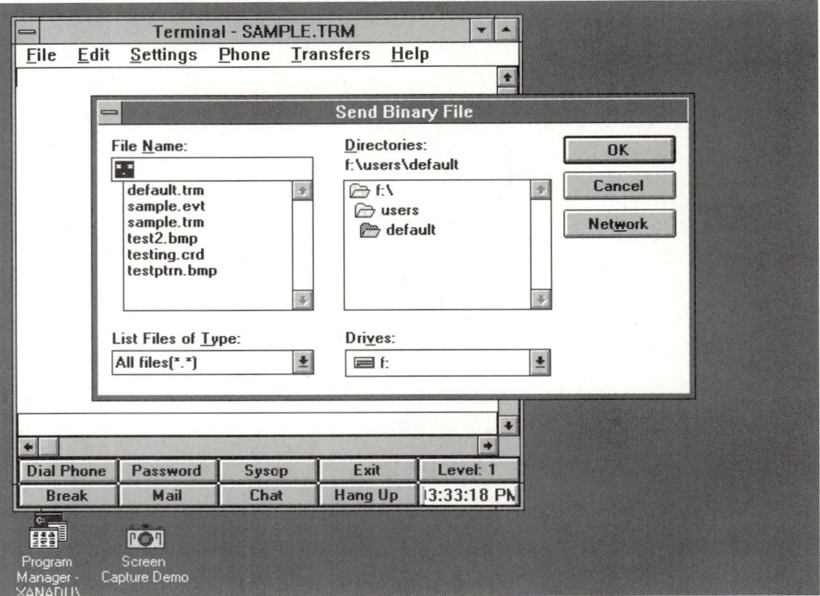

Figure 11.14
The Send Binary File dialog box

2. Select the drive, directory and file type from the Send Binary File dialog box.
3. Select a file from the File Name list or enter the name of the file to send.
4. Select OK to transmit the file.

Help Files ▼ Binary files are transmitted using the protocol selected via the Binary Transfers option in the Settings menu.

▶ Receiving Binary Files

To receive a binary file:

A binary file transfer cannot be paused or resumed, only stopped.

1. Select Receive Binary File from the Transfers menu. The Receive Binary File dialog box (see Figure 11.15) appears.

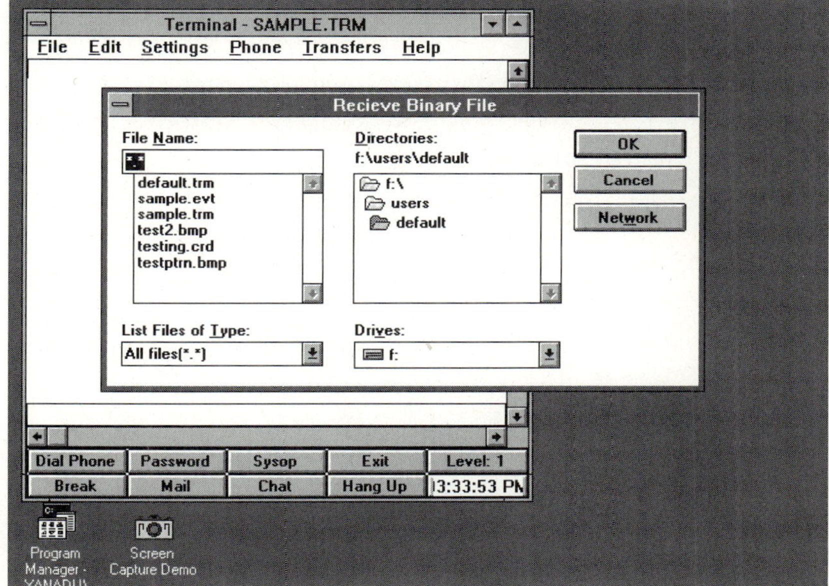

Figure 11.15
The Receive Binary File dialog box

2. Select the drive and directory where the file will be stored from the Receive Binary File dialog box.
3. Enter the file name in the File Name edit field or select a file name from the list.
4. Select OK to receive the file.
5. If the file name matches an existing file, select OK to confirm that you want to overwrite the file.
6. To interrupt the transfer, select the Stop button or the Stop option from the Transfers menu.

Help Files ▼ Binary files are transmitted using the protocol selected via the Binary Transfers option in the Settings menu.

Binary file transfers are executed by data block, with the size of the block varying according to the protocol and transfer method. Various provisions are used to ensure the validity of each data block. However, noise on the line or other communications errors can prevent a successful file transfer, requiring the remote computer to send the data block again. The XModem/CRC protocol will retry a maximum of 20 times, and the Kermit protocol a maximum of five times, before aborting the file transfer.

Transmission errors aside, if the binary transfer is not working, check whether the same transfer protocol has been selected at both ends. Use the Binary Transfers option in the Transfers menu to change protocols.

Text in the Terminal Window

▸ Viewing a Text File

To view a text file in the Terminal window:

1. Select View Text File from the Transfers menu.
2. Use the Drive and Directory lists to select the drive and path for the file desired.
3. Select the file to view from the File Name list or enter a file name.
4. Select the Append LF check box to add line feed characters for viewing.
5. Select the Strip LF check box to remove existing line feeds.
6. Select OK to view the file. The file contents are scrolled in the Terminal window.
7. Use the Pause, Resume, or Stop button to control scrolling.

Help Files ▼ Text files can be viewed in the Terminal window before being sent to or after being received from a remote computer. Viewing a file before receipt, however, remains a matter for psychics, not computers.

▸ Copying Text to and from the Clipboard

To copy text to the Clipboard:

1. Select (highlight) the text to copy.
2. Select Copy from the Edit menu.

To copy text from the Clipboard:

1. Position the cursor at the point where the text should be inserted.
2. Select Paste from the Edit menu (see the help files for "Transmitting the Clipboard Contents").

▸ Transmitting the Clipboard Contents

To send the contents of the Clipboard to a remote system:

- Select Paste from the Edit menu.

Help Files ▼ When text is pasted from the Clipboard to the Terminal window, a copy of the text is also sent to the remote system, exactly as if the text had been typed on the local terminal. The Clipboard contents are not altered.

▸ Transmitting Selected Text

To send selected text from the Terminal window:

1. Select (highlight) the text to send.
2. Select Send from the Edit menu.

Help Files ▼ Selecting the Send command is the equivalent of selecting the Copy and Paste commands. Selecting Send first copies the highlighted text to the Clipboard and then transmits it to the remote computer.

▸ Selecting All Text

To select all text in the Terminal scroll buffer:

- Select the Select All option from the Edit menu.

Help Files ▼ Using the Select All option is the equivalent of using the mouse (or keyboard) to highlight all the text in the Terminal window and scroll buffer. Once selected, the text can be copied to the Clipboard or transmitted to the remote computer.

▸ Clearing the Scroll Buffer

To clear both the scroll buffer and the Terminal window:

- Select Clear Buffer from the Edit menu.

Help Files ▼ All text entered in Terminal or echoed from a remote computer is copied to a scroll buffer (see "Selecting a Buffer Size," preceding) and can be viewed using the scroll bars. When the buffer is filled, the oldest material is discarded to make room for newer text. The Clear Buffer command empties the scroll buffer and, consequently, the Terminal window.

Printing from Terminal

▶ Printing Incoming Text

To print incoming text:

- Select Printer Echo from the Settings menu. All incoming text is passed directly to the printer.

To stop printing or to eject a page:

- Select Printer Echo again. A form feed command is sent to the printer.

▶ Changing the Printer and Printer Options

To change printers or set printer options:

1. Select Print Setup from the File menu.
2. Select either the Default Printer or the Specific Printer option in the Printer box.
3. If the Specific Printer option is selected, select the printer to use from the list.
4. Set the printer's orientation and paper specifications as required.

5. Select the Options button to display options specific to the selected printer driver.

6. Select OK.

Help Files ▼ Terminal echoes only to the default printer. If the echoed output should be sent to a different printer, use Printer Setup to select the desired printer as the default printer.

▶ Printing Selected Text

To print text from the Terminal scroll buffer:

1. Select (highlight) the text to print. To print the entire scroll buffer, select the Select All option from the Edit menu.

2. Select Copy from the Edit menu to copy selected text to the Clipboard.

3. Start a Windows or Windows NT word processor or text editor, such as Write, Notepad, or Unipad.

4. Paste the Clipboard contents to the word processor or text editor.

5. Print the selection from the word processor or text editor.

Help Files ▼ Because printing operations may cause conflicts with the timing required for remote communications, the optimum procedure would be to wait until the communications session is finished before printing. In the interim, text copy can be pasted to an editor for safekeeping or can be written to a disk file.

Ending a Communications Session

▶ Disconnecting from a Remote Computer

To disconnect from a remote computer:

1. Enter the exit command for the remote computer.
2. Select Hangup from the Phone menu.

Help Files ▼ As a general rule, remote host computers prefer that users issue a disconnect command before breaking the phone connection. The specific commands vary from system to system, depending on the host software, but generally take the form of a command such as "exit" or "bye," or offer a menu option for disconnecting. To determine the proper disconnect protocols, consult the service documentation or request on-line help from the host. (The commands "Help" or "?" usually bring a response.)

If you simply hang up without disconnecting from the remote host, the host may remain on-line (continue to hold the phone connection) and may, if you are connected to a fee service, continue charging your account until the remote host realizes that the connection has been broken. In any case, it is certainly better manners to disconnect properly than to simply hang up.

▶ Quitting Terminal

To exit the Terminal program:

- Select Exit from the File menu.

If changes have been made to Terminal's settings but have not been saved, a prompt will offer a choice of exit options:

- Select Save to save the current settings.

- Select Abandon to forget changes.
- Select Cancel to remain in Terminal.

Selecting Fax and Modem Utilities

▶ Fax and Modem Hardware Requirements

Hardware requirements for a modem or fax/modem under Windows NT are the same as under DOS or Windows 3.1. If the modem or fax/modem (external or internal card) is compatible with the computer, no compatibility problems with Windows NT should arise.

▶ Fax Software Requirements

DOS-based fax software, which is designed to operate on a TSR (terminate and stay resident) basis, cannot be expected to function particularly well under Windows NT (nor under DOS, for that matter). Windows 3.1 fax software should function under Windows NT in essentially the same fashion as in its original environment. If, however, a Windows NT version of the fax software is available, this should be used.

In any case, for receiving faxes, a stand-alone fax machine continues to hold advantages over both external fax/modem units and internal fax cards.

▶ Modem Communication Software Requirements

Most modem communications software—whether DOS, Windows 3.1 or Windows NT—should run without problems. Unlike fax software, modem software does not expect to remain resident and, unless very unusual operations are involved, should operate in essentially the same fashion under Windows NT as under DOS or Windows 3.1.

The Rescue Pages: Remote Computer Communications

My modem doesn't dial the phone.

First, check the protocol setup under the Communication option in the Settings menu and make sure that the correct communications (COM) port has been selected. If you aren't sure which COM port the modem is connected to, select None, and the Terminal program will query the COM ports for a response.

Second, check the Modem Commands option in the Settings menu to be sure that the correct instruction strings are being sent to the modem.

Third, for external modems, check the cables, power supply, and power-on switch.

Last, check the phone line and make sure the modem is connected to the phone system.

My modem dials the phone but doesn't make a connection.

The probable cause—wrong numbers and problems on the remote computer aside—is that incorrect settings have been specified for the remote computer. Check the protocol setups under the Communications option in the Settings menu.

I need to send a text file but I don't understand this business about protocols, carriage returns, and all that stuff.

If you listen carefully, you just might hear the distant but sympathetic voice of the author assuring you that you are in very good company

indeed...because text file transfers, particularly when the computer on the other end is an unknown factor, require some real finagling.

Fortunately, there's an easy alternative because a binary file transfer—which works just fine for text files, too—does have well-defined and standardized protocols that don't require hours of research to use. Refer to "Binary File Transfers," preceding.

My modem (or fax) works fine under DOS, but not under Windows NT.

Communications ports that are available under DOS may not be available under Windows NT—not because of any deficiency in Windows NT but because the mouse may be using a COM port and interrupt, preventing another COM port from being used. For example, both COM1 and COM3 normally share a single interrupt, as do COM2 and COM4. If your mouse is attached to COM1 and your modem to COM3, a conflict occurs under Windows NT. Unlike under DOS, where the mouse can be temporarily displaced while the modem is used, the mouse is continually using the shared interrupt under Windows NT, rendering the paired COM port unavailable.

The solution—assuming the mouse is on COM1—would be to move the modem to COM2 or COM4 and simply forget about COM3. Otherwise, unless you abandon the mouse, COM3 will not be available.

If, however, you absolutely need more COM ports, you might try using a bus mouse (a mouse with its own internal card) with or without a multi-IO card (a specialty card providing eight or 16 COM ports). Of course, there may be problems here as well since the multi-IO cards require driver software...which also must be 32-bit Windows NT compatible.

The final solution is a bit more expensive. There are motherboards (the main board in the computer) that support as many as eight communications ports. Consult your dealer or computer supplier for further information.

When I try to print, my remote communications link breaks down (goes haywire, and so on).

Because printer timing requirements may interfere with modem operations, the best solution is to wait until the communications session is finished and then print. In the interim, text can be copied to an editor such as Notepad for safekeeping or can be saved to a file.

The clock at the bottom of the Terminal display shows the wrong time, but when I check the system clock, the time's right.

Sounds like you're looking at the timer, not the clock display. The display can be toggled between elapsed and current time.

CHAPTER

12

HELP! Multimedia

Windows NT provides a number of multimedia extensions, including Sound Recorder, CD Player, and Media Player. Sound Recorder can be used to play, record, and edit sound (.WAV) files. CD Player is used to play audio compact disks using a CD-ROM drive attached to the computer. Media Player plays waveforms and MIDI (Musical Instrument Device Interface) sound and video sequences, as well as controlling any MCI (Media Control Interface) multimedia devices such as audio compact disks or video disks.

Topics covered in this chapter include

- Working with sound files
- Using CD Player
- Using Media Player

Sound Recorder and Sound Files

▶ Installing Sound Recorder

To install Sound Recorder:

1. Install a sound board, such as Sound Blaster.
2. Use the Driver option from the Control Panel to install a driver that matches the hardware.

▶ Setting up Sound Recorder for Recording

To set up Sound Recorder for recording:

- Connect a microphone to the sound card or use an audio cable to hook up to another sound source.

Help Files ▼ Refer to the sound card documentation for details on using microphones and other audio sources.

Keep these limitations in mind:

- Not all sound cards provide recording support.
- Direct recording from external audio sources requires careful adjustment of sound levels. (Low signal levels are suggested.)

The terms waveform file and sound file are used interchangeably. Both refer to data files that can be played back as audio recordings.

▶ Playing a Sound File

To play a sound file:

1. Select Open from the File menu. The Open dialog box (see Figure 12.1) appears.
2. Select a .WAV waveform file.

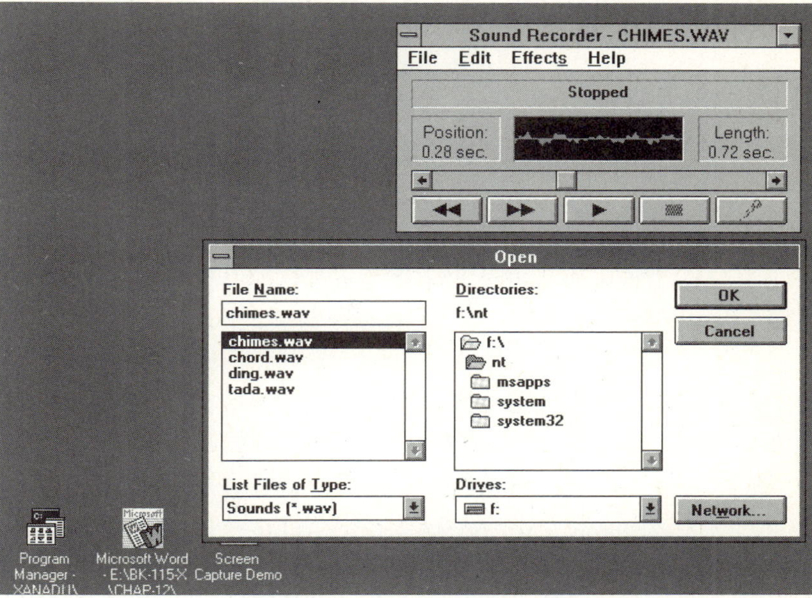

Figure 12.1
The Open dialog box

3. Select OK to load the waveform file.
4. Select the Play button. The status bar displays the prompt *Playing*.
5. Select the Stop button to stop playing. The status bar message changes to *Stopped*.
6. Select Play again to resume.

Help Files ▼ When the Play button is selected, Sound Recorder plays the waveform file either from the beginning or from the point where it was stopped or set. While a sound file is playing, the wave box displays the sound waveform.

To play only a part of a file and return to the starting point, hold the Shift key while selecting the Play button.

▸ Positioning within a Sound File

To move to a point within a sound file:

- Play the sound file and click on Stop when the desired point is reached.
- Adjust the scroll bar by dragging the thumb pad, clicking on the scroll arrows, or clicking on the scroll bar. The scroll arrows move in intervals of one-tenth of a second; the scroll bar, in 1-second intervals.
- Tab to reach the scroll bar, then use the left and right arrow keys to adjust the scroll bar position. The arrow keys move in intervals of one-tenth of a second.

To move to the end of a sound file:

- Select the Forward button.
- Press the End key.

To move to the beginning of a sound file:

- Select the Rewind button.
- Press the Home key.

Help Files ▼ The Shift key can be held down for finer control. This allows you to move by one sound sample per press of an arrow key or click on the arrow buttons, or by ten sound samples per click on the scroll bar.

Hold the Shift key down while selecting Play to play the waveform and then return to the start point.

▶ Recording a New Sound File

To record a new sound file:

1. Select New from the File menu.
2. Select the Record button to begin recording from the microphone or audio cable.
3. Select the Stop button.
4. Select Save As from the File menu.

Help Files ▼ Sound Recorder will record continuously for a maximum of 60 seconds. The maximum length of a sound file, however, is determined by the available memory. A longer file can be created by selecting Record a second time or by adding several sound files together.

▶ Saving and Restoring Sound Files

To save an existing sound file:

- Select Save from the File menu.

To save a new sound file or an existing sound file under a new name:

1. Select Save As from the File menu. The Save As dialog box (see Figure 12.2) appears.
2. Select the drive from the Drives list box.
3. Select the directory from the Directories list box.
4. Enter a file name in the File Name edit field. If no file name extension is specified, the default extension .WAV will be added.
5. Select OK to save the waveform file.

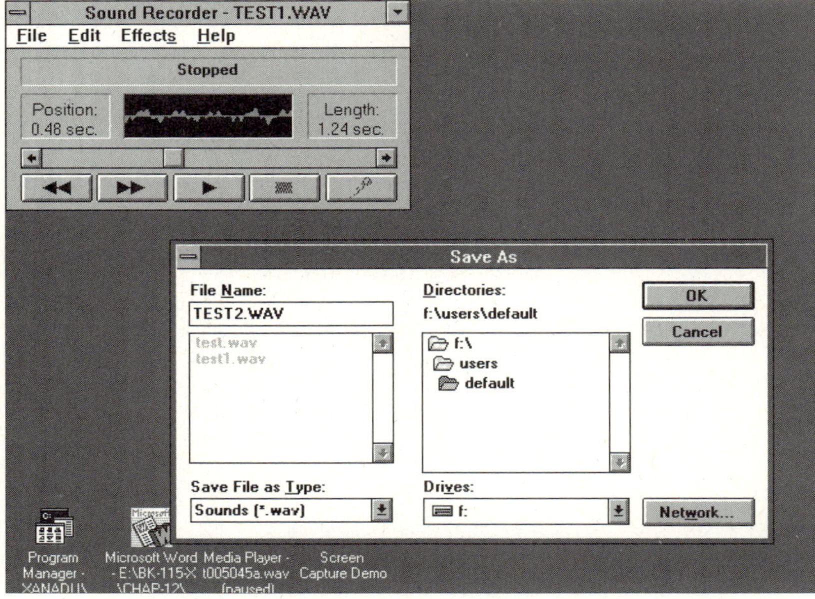

Figure 12.2
The Save As dialog box

To restore a sound file to its last saved state:

1. Select Revert from the File menu.
2. Select Yes to confirm restoration.

After a sound file is saved, changes cannot be undone.

▶ Changing the Sound Volume

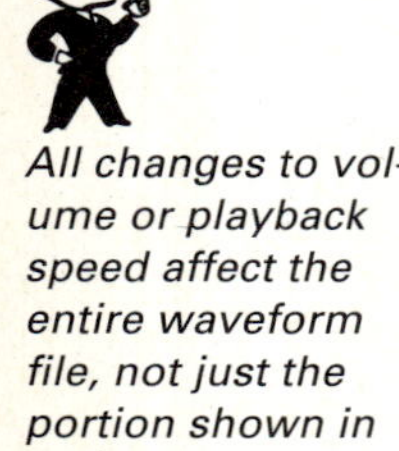

All changes to volume or playback speed affect the entire waveform file, not just the portion shown in the window.

To decrease the volume of a waveform:

- Select Decrease Volume from the Effects menu.

To increase the volume of a waveform:

- Select Increase Volume from the Effects menu.

To restore the original volume:

- Immediately select the opposite volume change from the Effects menu.

HELP! *Increasing the volume of a waveform to the maximum may flatten the waveform. Decreasing the volume afterward will not restore the original waveform.*

Help Files ▼ Sound volume can be increased or decreased by 25 percent.

▶ Changing the Waveform Speed

To decrease the waveform speed:

- Select Decrease Speed from the Effects menu.

To increase the waveform speed:

- Select Increase Speed from the Effects menu.

To restore the previous waveform speed:

- Immediately select the opposite speed change from the Effects menu.

Help Files ▼ The waveform speed can be decreased by 50 percent or increased by 100 percent. This does, of course, shorten the duration by half or double the duration.

Speeding up a waveform and then slowing it down can introduce some distortion. However, slowing the waveform and then speeding it up again does *not* produce distortion.

Reversing a Sound

Playing a waveform in reverse does not produce the same effect as generating sounds in reversed order. Because attack and decay times are also reversed, the reversed playback sounds quite different from the original. In particular, voice recordings have a much different effect when reversed.

To reverse a waveform:

- Select Reverse from the Effects menu.

To restore the waveform:

- Select the Reverse command a second time.

Adding Echo to a Sound

To add echo to a sound:

1. Select Add Echo from the Effects menu.
2. Repeat to add more echoes.

To undo an added echo:

- Select the Revert command from the File menu.

Recording into an Existing Sound File

For fine scrolling, hold the Shift key down while scrolling.

To record into an existing sound file:

1. Select Open from the File menu. The Open dialog box (see Figure 12.1) appears.
2. Select a sound file from the file list or enter a file name.
3. Select OK to load the sound file.
4. Use the Play and Stop buttons or the scroll bar to locate the point in the sound file where you want to insert the new recording.
5. Select the Record button to begin recording.
6. Select the Stop button when finished.
7. Select Save from the File menu to save the modified sound file.

Help Files ▼ The ability to record depends on whether the hardware playing the sound file supports recording. Record capabilities vary and are not provided by all sound cards.

When a new recording is added to an existing file, the new recording overwrites the existing sound. If recording begins at the end of the existing file, the recording is appended, increasing the length of the file.

The maximum play length of a file is determined by the available memory. However, Sound Recorder will not record beyond 60 seconds. To create a longer sound file, the recording must be done in increments of 60 or fewer seconds, appending each increment at the end of the sound file.

▶ Inserting Another Sound File

For fine scrolling, hold the Shift key down while scrolling.

To insert a sound file into an existing file:

1. Open the first sound file.
2. Use the Play and Stop buttons or the scroll bar to locate the point in the sound file where insertion should begin.
3. Select Insert File from the Edit menu. The Insert File dialog box (which is identical to the Open dialog box shown in Figure 12.1) appears.
4. Select the file to insert or enter the file name.
5. Select OK.

To undo a sound file insertion:

- Select Revert from the File menu.

Help Files ▼ The contents of one sound file can be inserted into another. The resulting sound file will play the first part of the original, then the inserted file, then the remainer of the original file. The maximum file length is determined by the amount of memory available.

▶ Merging (Mixing) Sound Files

For fine scrolling, hold the Shift key down while scrolling.

To merge or mix two sound files:

1. Open the first sound file.
2. Use the Play and Stop buttons or the scroll bar to locate the point in the sound file where mixing should begin.
3. Select Mix With File from the Edit menu. The Mix With File dialog box (which is identical to the Open dialog box shown in Figure 12.1) appears.
4. Select the file to mix or enter the file name.
5. Select OK.

To undo a sound file merge:

- Select Revert from the File menu.

Help Files ▼ The contents of two sound files can be blended (mixed) together to play simultaneously. The maximum file length is determined by the amount of memory available.

▶ Deleting a Portion of a Sound File

For fine scrolling, hold the Shift key down while scrolling.

To delete a portion before the current position:

1. Use the Play and Stop buttons or the scroll bar to locate the point in the sound file where you want to stop deleting.
2. Select Delete Before Current Position from the Edit menu.
3. Select Yes to confirm deletion.

To delete a portion after the current position:

1. Use the Play and Stop buttons or the scroll bar to locate the point in the sound file where you want to start deleting.
2. Select Delete After Current Position from the Edit menu.
3. Select Yes to confirm deletion.

To undo a deletion:

- Select Revert from the File menu.

Help Files ▼ A sound file can be deleted before or after a selected play position. Until the revisions are saved to a file, all changes can be undone using the Revert command from the File menu.

▶ Embedding a Sound File

To embed a sound file in an application file:

1. Open Sound Recorder.
2. Create a new sound file, or open the sound file to embed.
3. Select Copy from the Edit menu to place a copy of the sound file in the Clipboard.

4. To keep any modifications, save the sound file.
5. Open the application where the sound file will be embedded.
6. Position the cursor at the location where the sound file should appear.
7. Select Paste from the destination application's Edit menu. A Sound Recorder icon representing the embedded sound file appears.
8. Save the destination application.

Help Files ▼ Sound files can be embedded from within Sound Recorder—as described—or from within the document where the sound file will appear. To work from within the destination, refer to the destination application's documentation for instructions.

In some applications, such as Cardfile, the Sound Recorder icon appears initially in the upper-left corner of the document. The Sound Recorder icon can be repositioned using the conventional editing processes for the document.

▶ Playing an Embedded Sound File

To play an embedded sound file:

- Double-click on the Sound Recorder icon.

Or:

1. Select the Sound Recorder icon.
2. Select the Sound Object option from the application's Edit menu.
3. Select Play from the cascading menu.

▶ Editing Embedded Sound Files

To edit an embedded sound file:

1. Select the embedded sound file to edit.
2. Select Sound Object from the Edit menu in the destination document.
3. Select Edit from the cascading menu. Sound Recorder is opened and the selected sound file is displayed.
4. Edit the sound file as desired.
5. Select Update from the File menu in Sound Recorder.
6. Select Exit from the File menu in Sound Recorder.

▶ Linking Sound Files

To link a sound file to an application file:

1. Open Sound Recorder.
2. Create a new sound file, or open the sound file to link.
3. If the sound file is new or modified, save the sound file.
4. Select Copy from the Edit menu to place a copy of the sound file in the Clipboard.
5. Open the application and document where the sound file will be linked.
6. Position the cursor at the location where the sound file should appear.
7. Select Paste Link from the destination application's Edit menu. A Sound Recorder icon representing the linked sound file appears.
8. Save the destination application.

Help Files ▼ A sound file must be saved to disk as a file before it can be linked to another document.

In some applications, such as Cardfile, the Sound Recorder icon appears initially in the upper-left corner of the document. The Sound Recorder icon can be repositioned using the conventional editing processes for the document.

▶ Playing a Linked Sound File

To play a linked sound file:

- Double-click on the Sound Recorder icon.

Or:

1. Select the Sound Recorder icon.
2. Select the Sound Object option from the application's Edit menu.
3. Select Play from the cascading menu.

▶ Editing a Linked Sound File

To edit a linked sound file:

1. Select the linked sound file to edit.
2. Select Sound Object from the Edit menu in the destination document.
3. Select Edit from the cascading menu. Sound Recorder is opened with the selected sound file displayed.
4. Edit the sound file as desired.

5. Select Save from the File menu in Sound Recorder to update the linked sound file. The changes are reflected in the linked document.
6. Select Exit from the File menu in Sound Recorder.

Help Files ▼ Changes made in a linked sound file are reflected in all documents containing links to the sound file. Updates are immediate, irrespective of whether a manual or automatic update was selected for the link.

CD Player

▶ Starting CD Player

To start CD Player from Program Manager:

- Select the CD Player icon.

Help Files ▼ If no CD-ROM drive or drivers are detected, CD Player displays an error message and does not start.

▶ Quitting CD Player

To exit from CD Player:

- Select Close from the Control menu.
- Select Exit from the Disc menu.
- Double-click on the Control-menu box.

Playing an Audio CD

To play an audio CD:

- Select the Play button from the CD Player window.

To pause play:

- Select the Pause button in the CD Player window.

To resume playing:

- Select the Pause button a second time.
- Select the Play button.

To stop playing an audio CD:

- Select the Stop button from the CD Player window.

To eject the CD disk:

- Select the Eject button in the CD Player window.

Not all CD Players support remote Eject instructions. If your CD Player does not support this instruction, use the physical eject button on the front of the CD unit.

Help Files ▼

If a playlist has been created, CD Player plays the selected tracks in the listed order. If no playlist has been created, CD Player begins with the first track and plays the tracks in order. CD Player continues to play whether expanded or minimized.

▶ Identifying the CD

To set the CD title:

1. Select Edit Playlist from the Disc menu or select the Edit Playlist button from the tool bar.

The CD Player: Disc Settings dialog box (see Figure 12.3) appears.

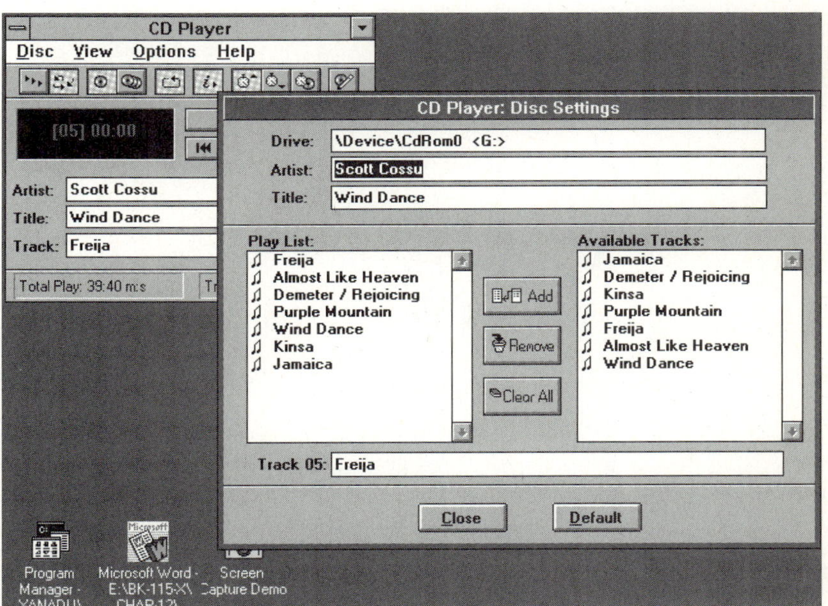

Figure 12.3
The CD Player: Disc Settings dialog box

2. Enter the CD Title in the Title edit box.
3. Enter the artist's name in the Artist edit box.
4. Replace the default track names (*Track 1*, and so on) with the CD track titles.
5. Select Close.
6. Select Yes to save the changes and additions.

To store the track titles for a CD:

1. Select Edit Playlist from the Disc menu or select the Edit Playlist button from the tool bar.

   The CD Player: Disc Settings dialog box (see Figure 12.3) appears.
2. Select a track from the Available Tracks list box.
3. Enter the track name in the Track box.
4. Repeat steps 2 and 3 to enter additional track titles.
5. Select Close.
6. Select Yes to save the changes and additions.

▶ Creating a Playlist

To create a custom playlist:

1. Select Edit Playlist from the Disc menu or select the Edit Playlist button from the tool bar.

   (The CD Player: Disc Settings dialog box is shown in Figure 12.3.)
2. To clear the current playlist, choose the Clear All button.
3. Select a track to add to the Play List from the Available Tracks list box.
4. Select the Add button. The select track is appended to the bottom of the list.
5. Repeat steps 3 and 4 as desired.
6. Select Close when finished.
7. Select Yes to save changes.

A playlist consists of a list of CD tracks to be played. Each track (selection) is played in the order listed. Tracks can appear in any order desired and any individual tracks can be listed as many times as desired.

To remove tracks from the playlist:

1. Select a track from the Play List in the Disc Settings dialog box.
2. Select the Remove button.
3. Select Close when finished.
4. Select Yes to save changes.

Changing Tracks on the Current Disc

To change CD tracks:

- Select the Skip Forward or Skip Back button from the CD Player window.

Or:

1. Click on the drop-down button at the right of the Track list box. All tracks on the CD are listed in their current play order.
2. Select the track desired, using the scroll bar as necessary.
3. Select the Play button.

Changing to a Disc in Another Drive

To change to another drive in a multi-CD system or another disk in a carousel system:

1. Click on the drop-down button at the right of the Artist list box. All available disks are listed.
2. Select the drive or disk desired, using the scroll bar as necessary.

Selecting Carousel or Multidisc Play

To play multiple discs:

- Select Multidisc Play from the Options menu or select the Multidisc button from the tool bar.

Help Files The multidisc option is available only if more than one CD-ROM drive is available or if a multidisc (carousel) CD-ROM drive is available. With a multidisc system, selecting Single Disc Play plays a single CD once, then stops.

Selecting Play Order for the CD-ROM

To play CD tracks in selected order:

- Select the Selected Order option from the Options menu or select the Selected Order button from the tool bar.

To play CD tracks in random order:

- Select Random Order from the Options menu or select the Random Order button from the tool bar.

Help Files ▼ The Selected Order option plays a CD disk in the order specified in the Play List or, if no playlist has been created, in numerical order. With a multidisc CD-ROM, tracks are played from each CD in random order.

▶ Setting Continuous Play

To select continuous play:

- Select Continuous from the Options menu or select the Continuous button from the tool bar.

Help Files ▼ The Continuous option can be combined with Selected or Random play order.

▶ Viewing the Current Track Time

To view the current track time:

- Select the Current Track Time button from the tool bar.

Or:

- Click on the Time Display window.

Help Files ▼ The Current Track Time shows how long the present CD track has been playing.

▶ Viewing the Remaining Track Time

To view the remaining track time:

- Select the Remaining Track Time button from the tool bar.

Or:

- Click on the Time Display window.

Help Files ▼ The Remaining Track Time button shows the time remaining on the current track.

▶ Viewing the Remaining Playlist Time

To view remaining playlist time:

- Select the Remaining Play List Time button from the tool bar.

Or:

- Click on the Time Display window.

Help Files ▼ The Remaining Play List Time shows the play time remaining for the current disk.

Media Player

▶ Selecting a Media Device

To select a simple media device:

- Select the media device from the Device menu.

Compound media device names are followed by an ellipsis (...); simple media devices lack the ellipsis.

To select a compound device:

1. Select the media device from the Device menu. The Open dialog box appears.
2. Select the name of the file to play from the file list or enter the file name.
3. Select OK.

Help Files ▼ Media Player supports both simple and compound devices. The Device menu reflects the system configuration, listing all devices and software drivers that are installed and configured on the systems.

If a simple device is selected, Media Player is immediately ready to play whatever may be loaded in the hardware device. If a compound device is selected, in addition to the device name, the name of a specific media file—such as a synthesizer to play audio waveforms—is also required.

When a compound device is first selected, the File Open dialog box is displayed to allow you to select the device file. Subsequently, the Open command is used to select drivers and the Device menu is used to select devices.

▶ Opening a Device File

To open a device file:

1. Select Open from the File menu. The Open dialog box (see Figure 12.4) appears.

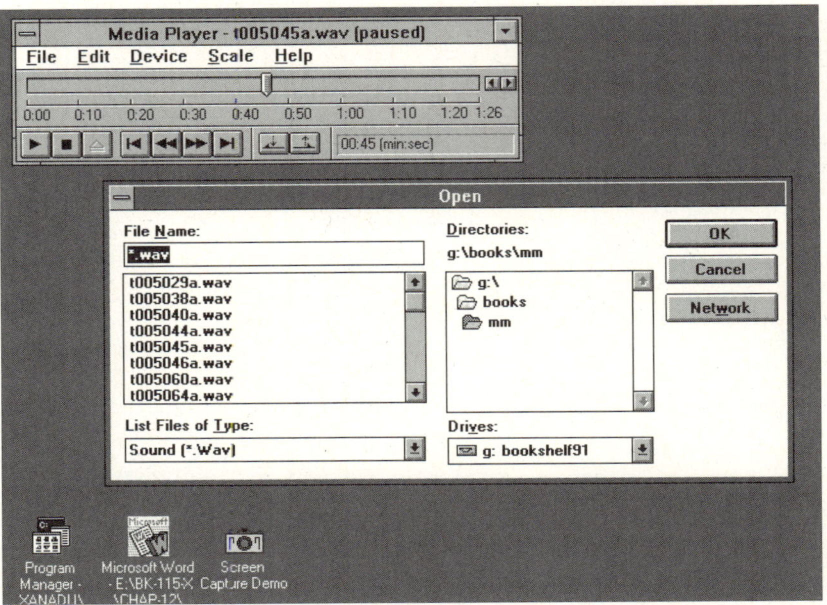

Figure 12.4
The Media Player Open dialog box

2. Select the drive and directory, if necessary.
3. Select the name of the file from the files list or enter the file name.
4. To change the device type, select a device type from the List Files Of Type list box.
5. Select OK.

Help Files ▼ If a compound device is already selected, Media Player can open and play any file appropriate to the device, such as MIDI files for a MIDI Sequencer or waveform files for a sound card. The device type can be changed from the Open dialog box or from the Device menu. Media Player automatically allocates resources according to the device selection and the file type.

▶ Closing a Media Device

To close a media device:

- Select Close from the File menu.

Help Files ▼ Closing Media Player releases control of any devices that may be in use. The effects of closing on simple and compound media devices, however, differ markedly. If Media Player was used to access a simple device (for example, to play a CD audio disk), closing Media Player simply releases control of the device but does not terminate the playback. In contrast, however, closing Media Player terminates any playback sequences for a compound media device.

▶ Quitting Media Player

To exit from Media Player:

- Select Exit from the File menu.

To exit from a media clip object:

- Either select another item or select another area from the application containing the media clip.

Help Files ▼ On exit, simple devices (such as CD Audio) will continue to play; for compound devices, play is terminated.

▶ Changing Trackbar Scales

To change trackbar scales:

When you change scales, you also erase any markers set in the sequence.

- Select Time from the Scale menu to show time intervals.
- Select Frames from the Scale menu to show frames in a video sequence.
- Select Tracks from the Scale menu to show tracks (as for an audio CD).

▶ Controlling Media Player's Appearance

To switch between the normal and abbreviated formats:

- Double-click on the Media Player title bar.
- Press Ctrl+W.

To resize the abbreviated display window:

- Select the Maximize button (upper-right corner) to double the display window size.
- Drag the display window frame to increase the window size.
- Select the Restore button (upper-right corner) to restore the display window to the default image size.

Help Files ▼ Media Player offers an abbrieviated control format. For audio devices, the abbreviated controls consist of the trackbar, Play/Pause, and Stop buttons. For video and animation devices using a video window, the playback window appears above the abbreviated controls.

▸ Setting Video-Viewing Characteristics

To set video-viewing characteristics:

1. Select Configure from the Device menu.
2. Select the viewing mode and other video sequence options from the Video Playback options dialog box.
3. Select OK.

Help Files ▼ The Configure option appears only after an .AVI file containing a video sequence has been selected. Media Player uses the Video for Windows NT device for video sequences captured and edited in the Video for Windows NT format. (The Video for Windows NT device is an MCI device with its own configuration options.)

▸ Setting Media Player Options

To select playback options for Media Player:

1. Select Options from the Edit menu. The Options dialog box (see Figure 12.5) appears.

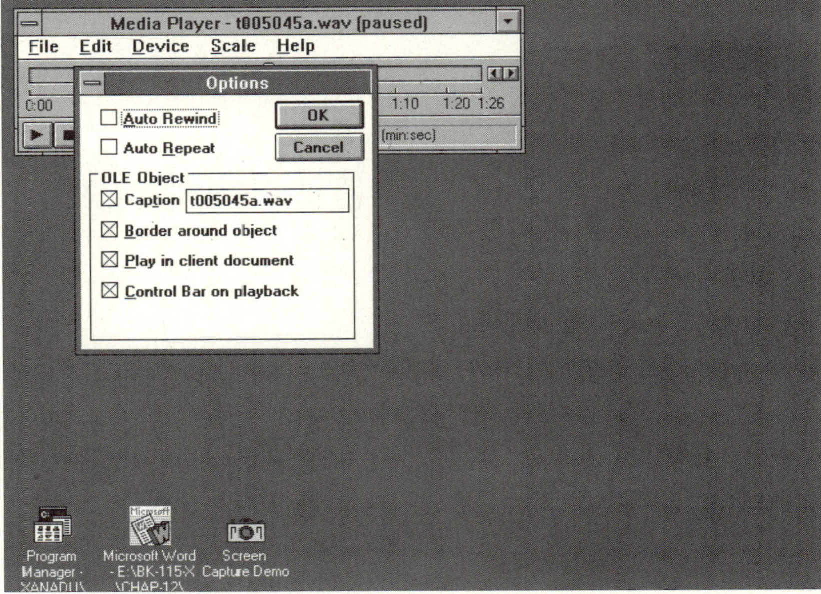

Figure 12.5
The Media Player Options dialog box

2. Select presentation and playback options.
3. Select OK.

Help Files ▼ The Options dialog box offers playback and display options that are applied to media clips being copied to other applications. The Auto Rewind and Auto Repeat options, however, are also valid when Media Player is used as a stand-alone application.

▶ Playing and Pausing a Media Sequence

To play a media sequence or restart a paused sequence:

- Select the Play button. The title bar adds the word (*Playing*) to the device title.

To play or restart a media sequence embedded in an application document:

- Double-click on the media clip icon.

To play a marked selection in a media sequence:

- With Media Player operating alone, press the Alt key while selecting the Play button.
- For an embedded media clip, select Play.

To pause playback:

- Select the Pause button. The title bar adds the word (*Paused*) to the device title.

Stopping a Media Sequence

To stop play:

- Select the Stop button. The title bar adds the word (*Stopped*) to the device title.

To stop an embedded or full-screen media clip:

- Press either the Esc or Alt key or the Ctrl+S combination.

To stop a media clip object in the Media Player window:

- Click the right mouse button, double-click on the system menu, or press Alt+F4.

To eject a compact disc or other media element:

- Select the Eject button.

The Eject button is provided only for devices supporting a software eject function.

Changing the Playback Position

To change the playback position:

- Drag the trackbar slider to the desired position.

- Select the scroll arrows at the right end of the trackbar.
- Use the PgUp, PgDn, Home, or End key, or left or right arrow key.
- Select from the Page Right, Page Left, Next Mark, and Previous Mark buttons.

Help Files ▼ The playback position permits selecting portions of a video or audio sequence without requiring you to play the entire media sequence.

▶ Selecting a Portion of a Media Sequence

To use Media Player controls to mark a selection:

1. Drag the slider to the start of the selection.
2. Select the Mark In button.
3. Drag the slider to the end of the selection.
4. Choose the Mark Out button.

Or:

1. Drag the slider to the start of the selection.
2. Hold the Shift key down.
3. Drag the slider to the end of the selection.

To use the Selection command to mark a selection:

1. Select the Selection option from the Edit menu or double-click on the scale's ruler. The Set Selection-Time Mode dialog box (see Figure 12.6) appears.
2. Select From and enter the beginning time, frame, or track/time for the selection.

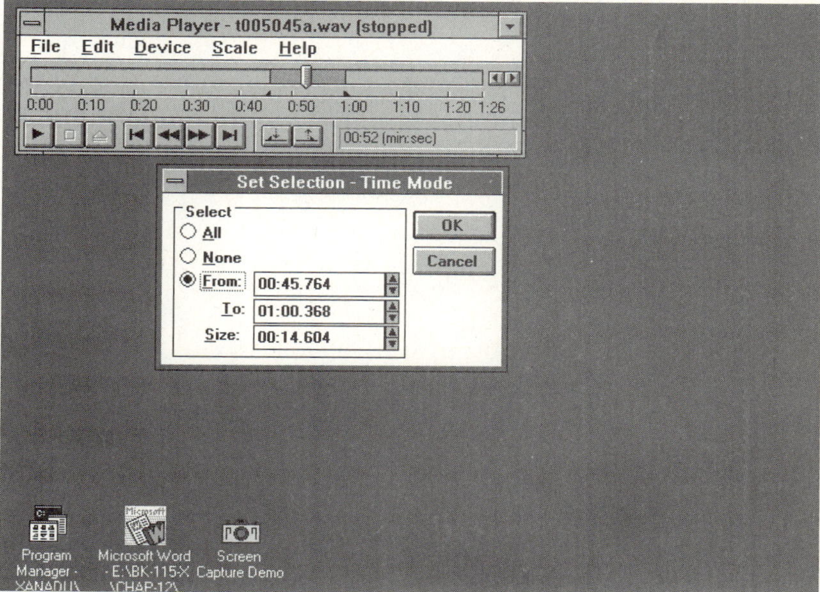

Figure 12.6
The Set Selection-Time Mode dialog box

3. Set the length of the selection using either the To or Size edit box.
   - Use the To edit box to enter the end time, frame, or track/time.
   - Use the Size box to enter the length as an elapsed time, number of frames, or as tracks/time duration.
4. Select OK.

Help Files ▼ The selection is shown as a shadowed section on the trackbar. After a selection is made, changing the trackbar scale will clear the selection.

▸ Playing a Selection

To play a selected sequence:

1. Position the slider at the first of the marked sequence.
   - Drag the slider to the first of the sequence.
   - Use the start or end button to move the slider.
2. Select the Play button.

▸ Embedding a Media Sequence in an Application Document

To embed a media clip in an application document:

1. Start Media Player.
2. Select Open from the File menu.
3. Select the file or device to play.
4. For a video clip or animation, move the slider to a representative frame. The selected frame will be used as a place marker for the media clip object.
5. Select Copy Object from the Edit menu in Media Player.
6. Open the application and document where the media clip will be inserted.
7. Select the Paste or Paste Special command from the application's Edit menu to embed the media clip.

Help Files ▼ In addition to using Media Player alone to play sound and video files, you can embed media clips in other application's documents—for example, in a spreadsheet file. When the marker for the embedded object is selected, the sound or video clip is played back.

If the Paste or Paste Special command doesn't insert the media clip correctly, refer to the destination application's documentation for information on using OLE objects.

▶ Editing an Embedded Media Clip

To edit an embedded media clip:

1. Open the document where the media clip is embedded.
2. Select the embedded clip.
3. Select Media Clip Object from the Edit menu. The Media Clip menu appears next to the command.
4. Select Edit from the Media Clip menu. Media Player opens with the file or device identified by the embedded clip.
5. Edit the media clip as desired.
6. Select Update from the File menu in Media Player. The embedded media clip is updated in the destination application.
7. Select Edit from the File menu in Media Player to return to the original application and document.

▶ Adjusting MIDI Volume and Balance

To adjust MIDI playback volume on Media Player:

- Drag the Master or Synthesizer volume bar (see Figure 12.7).

To adjust the MIDI balance on the Media Player:

- Drag the Master or Synthesizer balance bar.

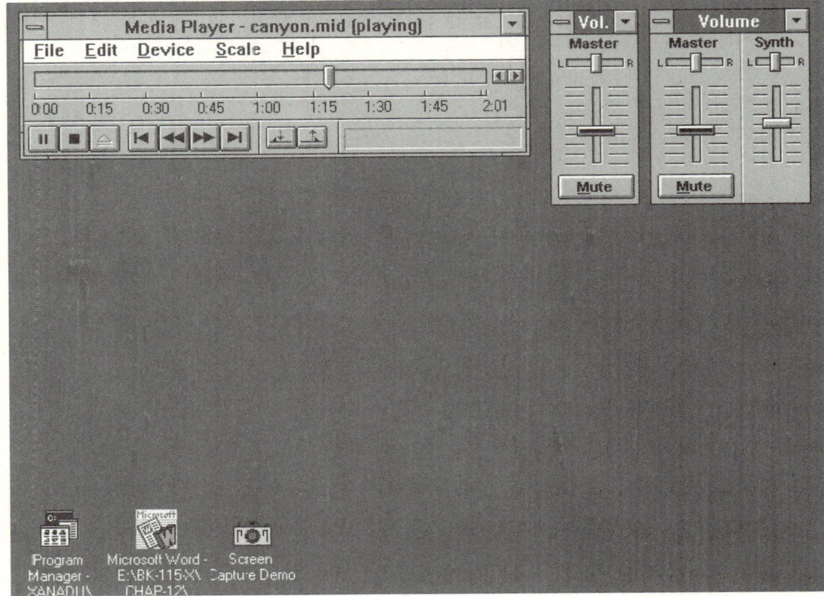

Figure 12.7
Two views of the Volume Control utility

Help Files ▼ The Volume Control works only when Media Player is playing back a MIDI sound file. The Volume Control does not work with CD audio disks controlled from Media Player, with sound files (.WAV files) played on Media Player, or with CD Player or Sound Recorder.

▶ Setting Volume Control Options

To show both the Master and Synthesizer volume controls:

1. Do one of the following:
   - Select Expanded View from the Control menu (upper-left corner).
   - Press Alt+E.

2. Repeat the selection to cancel.

To keep the Volume Control on top of other windows:

1. Select the Always On Top option from the Control menu (upper-left corner).
2. Repeat the selection to cancel.

Help Files ▼ The Always On Top and Expanded View options appear with check marks when selected.

RESCUE PAGES: Multimedia

I've tried using both CD Player and Media Player with my favorite audio CD in the computer's CD drive, but nothing happens. I know the sound card works because I've used the Sound utility from the Control Panel to test it.

Probably nothing's wrong…except for an understandable misunderstanding. While the CD drive can be controlled from the computer, using either CD Player or Media Player to play audio CDs, the sound is not played back through the sound card or the sound card's speakers. Instead, if your CD drive is external, you should find a stereo headset jack—probably a miniature one—on the front and a pair of RCA jacks (the same kind found on the back of your TV, stereo, and VCR) on the back of the unit. The computer's CD player can be cabled into your stereo for playback or you can attach a pair of speakers, but the player has to be controlled from your computer.

If your CD drive is internal, the miniature stereo jack should still be on the front; however, on the back, instead of a pair of RCA jacks, look for a three-pin connector labeled "Audio Out" or "Stereo Out." Unfortunately, a plug and adapter to fit this connector may be hard to find (but not too difficult to make). However, a stereo adapter to plug into the front jack should be available at your local electronics supply or stereo store…or you can simply plug in a set of miniature stereo speakers or a head set.

Also, in case you're wondering, no, you can't play the Windows NT distribution disk over the stereo and you can't play the Microsoft Bookshelf back through your TV—at least, not for a while yet.

I listed my audio CDs on my computer, but now I can't figure out how to get rid of them. CD Player doesn't seem to offer any erase options.

CD Player offers no erase options for obsolete or unwanted CD listings. However, these listings can be found in the file titled CDPLAYER.INI, which is located in your Windows NT root directory. This is a plain text file and can be edited using the Notepad, Write, or Unipad utility or any plain text editor.

One suggestion: Before making changes, make a backup copy of the .INI file—just in case.

The Eject button on CD Player doesn't eject the disk from the CD drive. Instead, I get an error report.

If the CD Player Eject button used to work and doesn't now, it might mean that something is wrong. However, the Eject button is not compatible with all CD players. As long as the Eject button on CD Player—the CD drive itself—works, don't worry about the one on the screen.

I experimented with making changes to a sound file (.WAV). But when I undid the changes, the result didn't sound like the original.

The first thing to do—*before* experimenting with a sound file—is to make a duplicate copy of the sound file under another name...because not every change can be undone (at least, not perfectly). For example, compressing the sound file (making it run faster) results in a loss of some information that cannot be recreated by expanding (slowing) the sound. Of course, if you really want to edit sound files or create long sound files, you should probably be looking at some more sophisticated utility, such as a MIDI setup with voice capabilities.

A 60-second sound file just isn't long enough.

If you really need more than 60 seconds of sound, you can combine sound files in several ways, including appending sound files, recording at the end of a sound file, or merging sound files.

If you need quite a long sound file, however, you probably should look at MIDI rather than .WAV sound files. Sound files (.WAV) require considerable memory and disk space, ranging in size from 10 to 15K per second, and MIDI files (.MID) are considerably smaller, on the order of 300 bytes per second of play time. Thus, a 2-minute MIDI sequence might use 40K, where the equivalent .WAV file could require anywhere from 1.5 to 2MB of file space...as well as the same amount of RAM for playback.

CD Player (or Media Player) says that there's no disc in the CD drive, even though I have a disk in the drive.

There may be a disk in the CD cartridge...but is it an audio CD? CD discs come in a variety of formats, and a data disk isn't the same as an audio disk isn't the same as a game disk. The Windows NT distribution disk, for example, is a data disk that can be read by File Manager but not by CD Player or Media Player. At the same time, a game disk, such as the Sherlock Holmes series, may be readable by File Manager or Media Player, but neither application knows how to handle the audio/visual file format.

CHAPTER

13

HELP! DOS Applications under Windows NT

While Windows NT is itself an operating system, replacing the DOS (MS-DOS, DR-DOS, or other version) operating system, you still need to be able both to execute DOS applications and to exercise command-line instructions—many of which parallel existing DOS instructions, a few of which are new to Windows NT.

For those reasons, Windows NT supplies the Command Prompt (or DOS shell) utility which, functionally, acts like the familiar DOS screen, provides a workspace for DOS applications, and offers a command-line input format for direct entry of instructions.

Still, for all its familiarity, there are differences as well in the Windows NT DOS shell or DOS windows.

Under DOS, there was only one operating environment and only one prompt. DOS occupied the entire machine, exercised total control, and did precisely as it wished...or was instructed to do. And, under Windows 3.1, the MS-DOS shell operated quite similarly, including preempting virtually all of the system's resources during its operation.

Under Windows NT, however, not only can there be more than one DOS shell at any time, but each copy of DOS also operates as a "virtual machine"—acting as if each were a separate computer, isolated and entirely separate from the others. Physically, of course, all of these virtual machines share a single system—one display monitor, one keyboard, one CPU, and so on. Each of these virtual machines does, however, have its own memory space

where none of the others can intrude and where, within its slice of time and resources, it is independent of all others.

For practical purposes, the mechanics of how are unimportant. Instead, what is relevant is, first, that you can have more than one of these virtual machines active, and second, that Windows NT offers some provisions—discussed shortly—to share information between applications operating in these virtual machines and other Windows NT applications—a feature that was not available under Windows 3.1. Third, while not directly relevant to executing DOS applications, Windows NT also offers several provisions for customizing the DOS windows.

There are also other aspects relevant to DOS applications—such as using PIF instructions files and providing icons to install DOS applications in the Program Manager—which were discussed in Chapter 3 and are not repeated here.

Topics covered in this chapter include

- Operating in the DOS shell
- Using the Command Prompt reference

Operating in the DOS Shell

▶ Executing a DOS Application

To execute a DOS application under Windows NT:

The term DOS shell *is used here to refer to the virtual DOS machine executing in a Command Prompt window under Windows NT.*

1. Call the MS-DOS shell (Command Prompt) from the Main application window. Figure 13.1 shows the DOS shell as a window. (The DOS shell may also be used full screen.)
2. From the Command Prompt, change drives and/or directories as required.
3. Type an application name or instruction and press Enter.

To leave the DOS window:

- Click on an application outside of the DOS window.

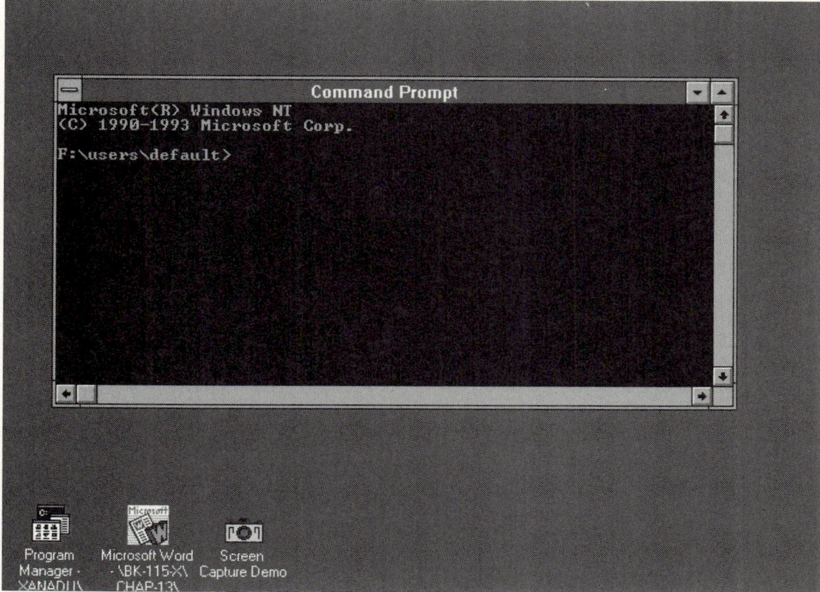

Figure 13.1
The DOS shell

- Or reduce the DOS window to an icon.
- Or use the Switch To option from the system menu or press Ctrl+Esc to call the Task List window and select a different task.

To terminate the DOS window:

- Select Close from the system menu.
- Or use the Terminate button from the Settings dialog box.
- Or use the Switch To option from the system menu or press Ctrl+Esc to call the Task List window and select End Task.

To leave the full-screen DOS shell:

- Press Ctrl+Esc to call the Task List window and select a different task.

To terminate the full-screen DOS shell:

- Press Ctrl+Esc to call the Task List window and select End Task.

Help Files ▼ When the DOS shell or Command Prompt is called from Program Manager's Main application group, the shell may be full screen or a window (see "Customizing the DOS Shell," later in this chapter). As either a window or full screen, the shell can be treated exactly as if you were under DOS, with a few exceptions in the form of commands or utilities that are provided by DOS but not supported under Windows NT.

▸ Using the System Menu from the DOS Shell

The DOS shell's system menu is available only if the shell is run as a window or has been minimized. If the DOS shell is maximized as full screen, the menu is not available.

To use the system menu:

- Click on the menu box at the upper-left corner of the window frame. The system menu is shown in Figure 13.2.

Help Files ▼ In addition to the stock Restore, Move, Size, Minimize, Maximize, and Close options, the DOS shell's system menu also offers a number of options allowing you to copy and paste from the DOS application window and to change window settings, fonts and display options, and screen colors. While these options are detailed shortly, remember that the DOS Command Prompt must be a window, not a full screen, before these features can be used.

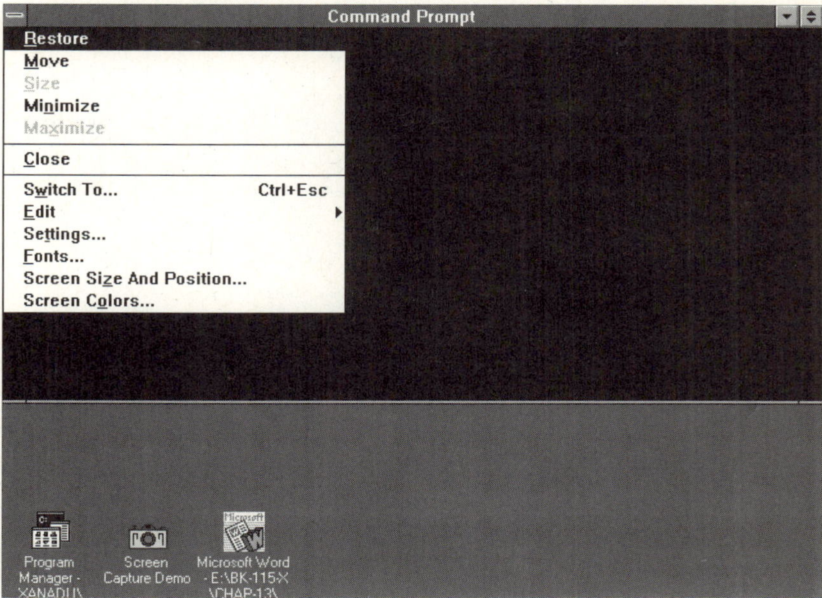

Figure 13.2
The system menu in the DOS shell

▶ Cutting and Pasting from a DOS Window

To copy text from a DOS application:

1. If the Quick Edit option (see "Changing DOS Command Prompt Settings" below) is not enabled, select Mark from the Edit menu in the Command Prompt system menu. If the Quick Edit option is enabled, this step can be ignored.

2. Using the Windows mouse cursor, click the mouse to select a start point.

3. Press and hold the left mouse button while dragging the mouse to define the area to copy. The selected area will be highlighted, as shown in Figure 13.3.

4. Press Enter or select Copy from the system menu Edit submenu. The selected text is copied to the Clipboard.

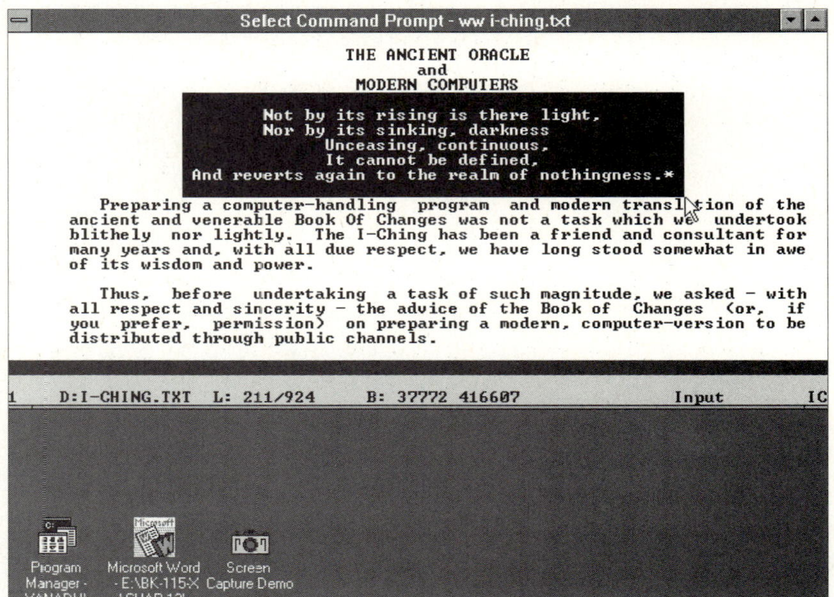

Figure 13.3
Copying text from a DOS application

To paste text to a DOS application:

1. Select a paste insert position by using the Windows NT mouse cursor to click on the location desired.

   - Or, because not all applications will recognize the Windows NT mouser, select an insertion point by positioning the application cursor.

2. Select Paste from the system menu Edit submenu. The Clipboard text is copied to the application as if it were typed from the keyboard.

▸ Changing DOS Command Prompt Settings

Figure 13.4 shows the Command Prompt dialog box.

To set display options:

- Select Window for a window display complete with system menu, title bar, resizable window frame, and Windows NT mouse cursor.

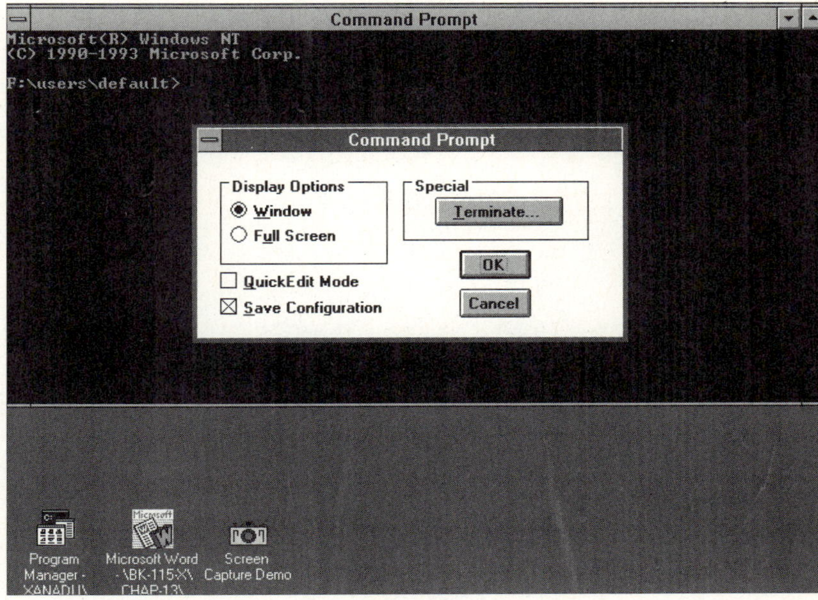

Figure 13.4
The Command Prompt dialog box

- Select Full Screen display to have the Command Prompt window fill the entire screen, enabling the application mouse—if any.

To enable fast copy operations:

- Select the QuickEdit Mode check box.

To save Command Prompt configuration changes:

- Select the Save Configuration check box.

To end a hung application:

- Select the Terminate option. A dialog box appears warning that any unsaved information in any open application will be lost. Use Cancel to return to the DOS window or OK to close the window and any application executing in the window.

The Terminate button in the Command Prompt dialog box is a last-ditch exit for a hung-up application.

Selecting Display Fonts for the DOS Window

To change font sizes for the DOS window:

1. Select Fonts from the Command Prompt system menu.
2. Select a font size from the Font list box. Figure 13.5 shows the Font Selection dialog box with a series of fixed-width font sizes.

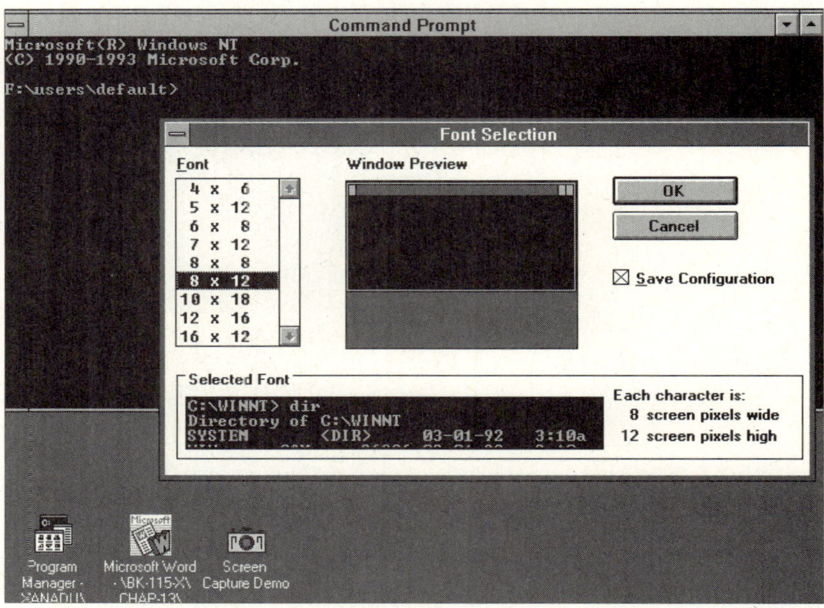

Figure 13.5
The Font Selection dialog box

3. Select OK to save the font selection or Cancel to exit without changes. The last selection saved will also be the default font selection for the next DOS window opened.

To make only local font size changes:

- Clear the Save Configuration check box before saving the selection. Only the current DOS window will be affected, and the selection will not affect later DOS windows.

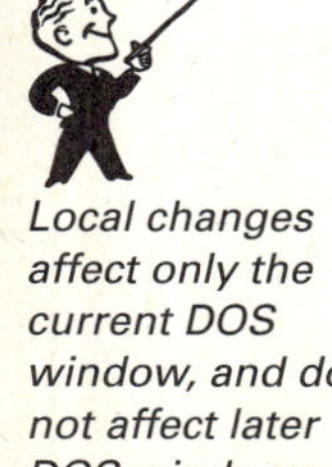

Local changes affect only the current DOS window, and do not affect later DOS windows.

To select different font sizes for different DOS windows:

- Select a font size from the Font Selection dialog box in each DOS window. DOS windows already opened will not be affected.

Figure 13.6 shows three DOS windows, each with a different font setting. Beginning at the top, the font size is 16 x 12, then 12 x 16 and, at the bottom, the default 8 x 12.

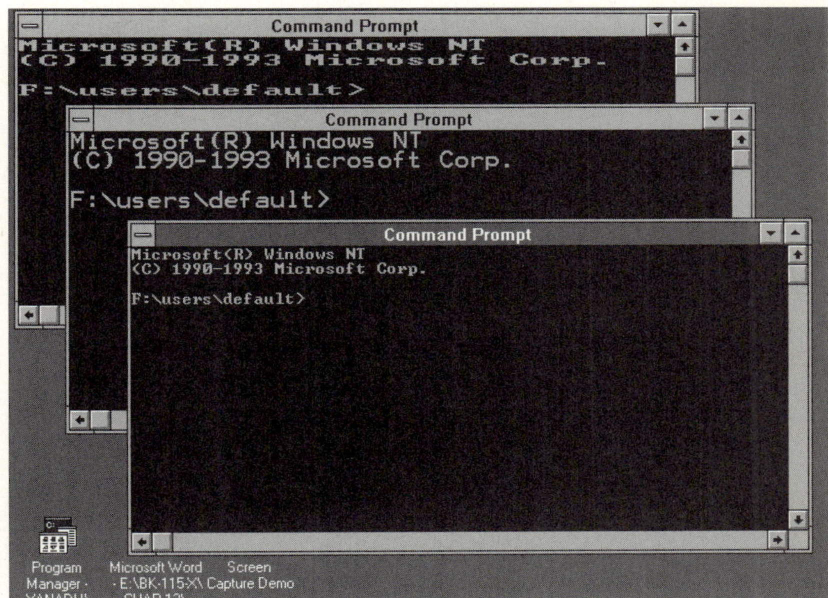

Figure 13.6
DOS windows with different font settings

Help Files ▼ TrueType (graphics) fonts are not available in the DOS window—only fixed-width system fonts. Changes in font size, however, also affect the display size of the DOS window. Because the display size is always a set number of characters in width and height, selecting a wider or taller font immediately changes the size of the display window to reflect the change.

Both the current size and position are shown in the Window Preview box, while a font sample is shown in the Selected Font box at the bottom.

Setting the DOS Screen Buffer Size

To set the buffer size for the DOS (Command Prompt) shell:

1. Select the Screen Size and Position option from the system menu. The Screen Size And Position dialog box is shown in Figure 13.7.

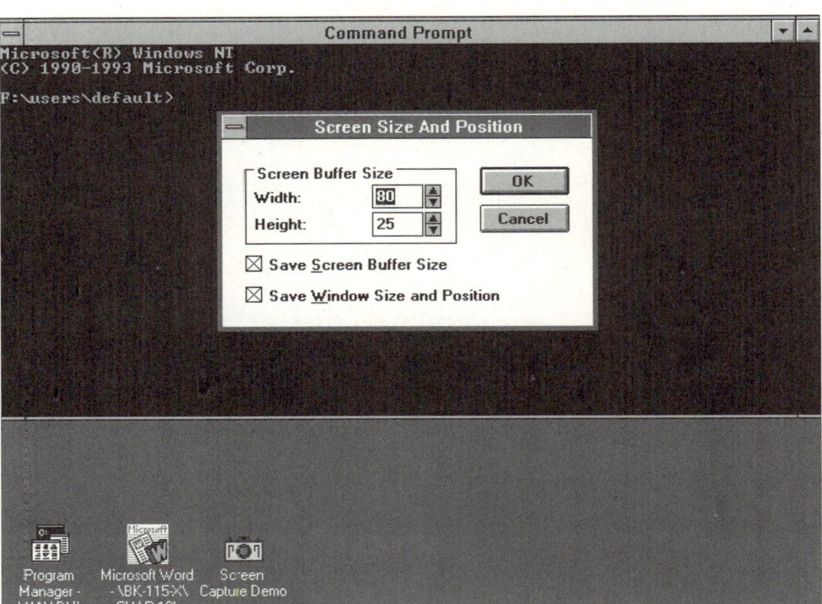

Figure 13.7
The Screen Size And Position dialog box

2. In the Screen Buffer Size box, enter width and height values in the edit boxes, or use the scroll arrows to change the present settings.
3. Select OK.

To use changes without setting defaults:

- Clear the Save Screen Buffer Size and Save Window Size and Position check boxes before selecting the OK button.

Help Files ▼ Increasing the Screen Buffer Size does not change the display window size, but will add horizontal or vertical scroll bars when the defined window size is larger than the displayed window. If the designated buffer size becomes smaller than the display size, the display size is shrunk to match.

Both the Save Screen Buffer Size and Save Window Size and Position check boxes will be set each time the Screen Size And Position dialog box is called. These check boxes can be cleared during any individual action but will be set again the next time the dialog box is called. Also, because the default window size and position setting is saved, as multiple copies of the DOS window are opened, each appears the same size at the same position.

The MODE command (see "Command Prompt Reference," following) can also be used to set the default screen buffer width and height.

▶ Selecting Color Settings for the DOS Window

To select foreground and background color settings:

1. Select the Screen Colors option from the system menu. The Screen Colors dialog box shown in Figure 13.8 appears.
2. Select the Screen Text, Screen Background, Popup Text, or Popup Background button.
3. Select the desired color from the color bar. Color selections are displayed in the two sample windows at the bottom.
4. Select OK.

Local changes affect only the current DOS window, and do not affect later DOS windows.

To make changes locally only:

- Clear the Save Configuration check box. Color selections will affect the current DOS window only, but will not be saved as defaults.

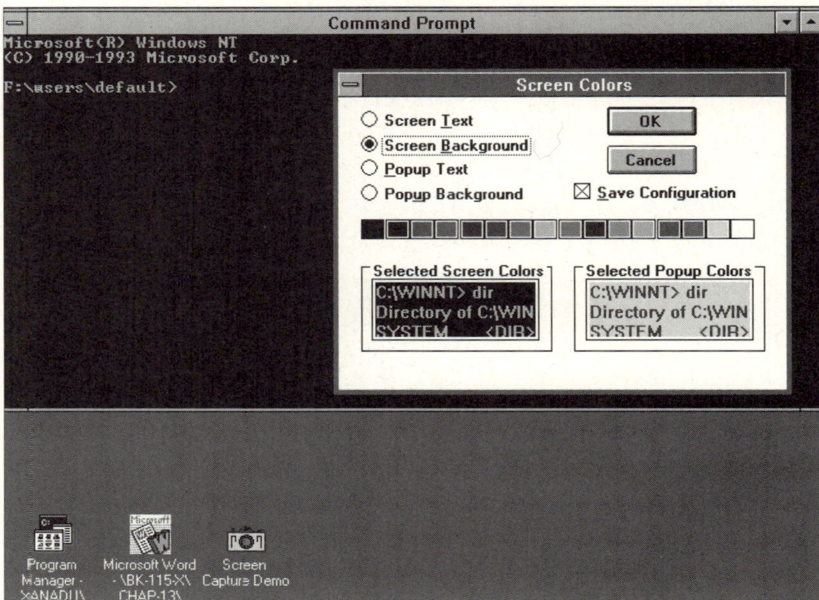

Figure 13.8
The Screen Colors dialog box

Help Files ▼ The Selected Screen Colors settings control the default appearance of the DOS window, but may still be overridden by DOS applications. The Popup color settings—while not recognized by many DOS applications—are used by some DOS (system) utilities such as Doskey.

Command Prompt Reference

▶ Using the DOS Shell and Command Prompt Reference

The DOS shell or Command Prompt window provides a virtual DOS machine—a simulation of the DOS environment where DOS applications can execute and where many DOS utility commands are either simulated or supported by 32-bit Windows NT versions. The DOS environment is

independent of any DOS version that may be installed and does not depend on DOS being installed.

For those using MS-DOS version 6.0 or 6.1 or DR-DOS 6.0, the Windows NT DOS simulation is the equivalent of DOS version 5.0 and does not explicitly support commands provided by any later versions.

Also, Windows NT does not support all DOS version 5.0 commands—only a selected subset of these that are relevant or compatible with Windows NT. In the following Command Prompt Reference list, DOS version 5.0 commands that are not compatible with or emulated by Windows NT are listed simply as *Not Supported by Windows NT.*

Next, commands that function essentially the same in both Windows NT and DOS are identified as *DOS/NT.*

And last, commands that are new to Windows NT but which do not exist under DOS are identified simply as *NT Only.*

▶ ACLCONV (NT Only)

The ACLCONV command converts OS/2 Lanman Server access control lists for Windows NT use.

Usage:

```
ACLCONV /DATA:datafile /LOG:logfile
ACLCONV /LOG:logfile /LIST
```

Parameters for the ACLCONV command are

/DATA:*datafile*	Specifies an OS/2 Lanman BACKACC data file.
/LOG:*logfile*	Specifies an ACLCONV log file.
/LIST	Lists the contents of a specified log file.

▶ APPEND (DOS/NT)

The APPEND command allows programs to open data files in specified directories as if they were in the current directory. The command is not commonly required under Windows NT.

Usage:

```
APPEND [drive:]path [...]
```

▶ ASSIGN (Not Supported by Windows NT)

The ASSIGN command was used in DOS to redirect requests for disk operations on one drive to a different drive.

▶ AT (NT Only)

The AT command requires the Schedule service to be operating and is used to schedule commands and programs to run on a computer at a specified time and date.

Usage:

```
AT[\\computername] [ [id] [/DELETE] | /DELETE [/YES]]
AT[\\computername] time[/EVERY:date[,...] |/NEXT:date[,...]]"command"
```

Parameters for the AT command are

computername	Identifies a remote computer on the net. If omitted, commands are scheduled on the local computer.
id	An optional identification number assigned to a scheduled command.
/DELETE	Cancels a scheduled command. If *id* is omitted, all scheduled commands on the specified computer are canceled.
/YES	Used with an instruction to cancel all jobs when no further confirmation is desired.
time	Specifies the time when the command or batch file is to execute.
/EVERY:*date*[,...]	May be one or more weekdays or days of the month. The command or batch file is executed on each specified day(s) of the week or month. If omitted, the current day of the month is assumed.
/NEXT:*date*[,...]	May be one or more weekdays or days of the month. The command or batch file is executed on the next occurrence of the day (for example, Thursday) or date (for example, the 13th). If omitted, the current day of the month is assumed.
"*command*"	Identifies the Windows NT command or batch program to be executed.

If the system time is changed on a remote computer (*computername*), the AT scheduler for the remote computer should be synchronized by typing:

```
AT \\computername
```

ATTRIB (DOS/NT)

The ATTRIB command displays or changes file attributes.

Usage:

```
ATTRIB [+R|-R][+A|-A][+S|-S][+H|-H][[drive:][path]filename][/S]
```

Parameters for the ATTRIB command are

+	Sets an attribute.
–	Clears an attribute.
R	Read-only file attribute.
A	Archive file attribute.
S	System file attribute.
H	Hidden file attribute.
/S	Processes files in all directories in the specified path.

BACKUP (DOS/NT)

The BACKUP command backs up one or more files from one disk to another.

Usage:

```
BACKUP source destination-drive: [/s] [/m] [/a]
       [/f[:size]] [/d:date [/t:time]]
       [/l[:[drive:][path]logfile]]
```

The BACKUP command can be used to back up files either to a hard drive (partition) or to floppy disks or from one floppy disk to another, irrespective of size and format.

Parameters and flags used with the BACKUP utility include

source:	Specifies the location of files to back up (*source* may consist of a drive letter and colon, a directory name, a file name, or any combination of these.)

destination-drive:	Specifies the drive containing the destination disk where the backup files will be written. Backup files are stored under the names BACKUP.*nnn* and CONTROL.*nnn*, where *nnn* begins with 001 on the first backup disk, incrementing for each subsequent disk.
/s	Subdirectory flag—backs up the contents of all subdirectories of the specified path.
/m	Modified flag—backs up only files that have changed since the last backup, turning off the archive attribute of the original files.
/a	Add flag—adds backup files to existing backup disks without deleting the existing file(s). The /a switch is ignored if the existing backup files were created from MS-DOS version 3.2 or earlier.
/f[:*size*]	Format flag—formats the destination disk(s) to the size specified. The Format utility must be in a directory specified by the current path. If no size is specified, the default drive size is used. Unformatted disks are formatted regardless of the /f switch. Value sizes are as follows:

Size Argument	**Disk Type**
160 / 160k / 160kb	160K, single-sided, double-density, 5.25-inch disk
180 / 180k / 180kb	180K, single-sided, double-density, 5.25-inch disk
320 / 320k / 320kb	320K, double-sided, double-density, 5.25-inch disk
360 / 360k / 360kb	360K, double-sided, double-density, 5.25-inch disk
720 / 720k / 720kb	720K, double-sided, double-density, 3.5-inch disk
1200 / 1200k / 1200kb / 1.2 / 1.2m / 1.2mb	1.2MB, double-sided, quadruple-density, 5.25-inch disk
1440 / 1440k / 1440kb / 1.44 / 1.44m / 1.44mb	1.44MB, double-sided, quadruple-density, 3.5-inch disk

Size Argument	Disk Type
2880 / 2880k / 2880kb / 2.88 / 2.88m / 2.88mb	2.88MB, double-sided, 3.5-inch disk

/d:*date*	Backs up only files modified on or after the date specified. The date format used is determined by the country settings in effect.
/t:*time*	Backs up only files modified on or after the date and time specified. The time format is determined by the country settings in effect.
/l[:[*drive*:][*path*]*logfile*]	Creates a log file, entering a record of the backup operation to the file. If no location is specified for the log file, the log file is placed in the root directory of the source drive. If no file name is specified, the default name BACKUP.LOG is used. A removable media drive (floppy drive) should not be used for the log file destination.

Refer also to the RESTORE command.

▶ BREAK (DOS/NT)

The BREAK command is used to set or clear extended Ctrl+C checking and is provided for compatibility with DOS systems, but has no effect under Windows NT's DOS shell.

▶ CALL (DOS/NT)

The CALL command calls one batch program from another.

Usage:

```
CALL [drive:][path]filename [batch-parameters]
```

The *batch-parameters* provide any command-line information required by the called batch program.

CD *See CHDIR*

CHCP (DOS/NT)

The CHCP command displays or sets the active code page number.

Usage:

```
CHCP [nnn]
```

The argument *nnn* is a numerical value identifying a specific code page number. Called without an argument, CHCP displays the active (current) code page number.

CHDIR / CD (DOS/NT)

The CHDIR/CD command displays the name of or changes the default directory on the specified or default drive.

Usage:

```
CHDIR [drive:][path]
CHDIR[..]
CD [drive:][path]
CD[..]
```

The argument .. changes to the parent of the default directory. If a drive argument but no path is supplied, the active (default) directory for the specified drive is displayed. If no arguments at all are specified, the active (current) drive and directory are displayed.

CHKDSK (DOS/NT)

The CHKDSK utility checks a disk and reports disk status, space available, the number of files on the drive (including subdirectory contents), and disk space used.

Usage:

```
CHKDSK [drive:][[path]filename][/F][/V][/R]
```

Parameters for the CHKDSK function are

drive:	Identifies the drive to check. If no drive is specified, the active drive is tested.
path	Identifies the directory path to check. If no path is specified, the active directory and any subdirectories are tested.
filename	Identifies a specific file or files to check for fragmentation. Wild cards may be used in the *filename* to identify a group of files.
/F (Fix)	Flag required before any identified errors will be corrected. If the /F argument is not supplied, errors will be reported but will not be corrected.
/V (Verbose)	Displays the full path and name of each file on the disk.
/R (Repair)	Locates and marks bad sectors, recovering readable information when possible—requires /F.

The CHKDSK utility is executed automatically for all hard-drive partitions when Windows NT boots, but may be called at any time with or without the /F flag.

Example:

```
F:\users\default>chkdsk
The type of the file system is FAT.
Volume Serial Number is 1859-12E4

255565824 bytes total disk space.
 14331904 bytes in 3 hidden files.
   946176 bytes in 231 directories.
170827776 bytes in 3130 user files.
 69459968 bytes available on disk.

     4096 bytes in each allocation unit.
    62394 total allocation units on disk.
    16958 allocation units available on disk.
```

CLS (DOS/NT)

The CLS command clears (erases) the screen or the DOS window.

Usage:

```
CLS
```

CMD (NT Only)

The CMD command calls a new instance of the Windows NT command interpreter. Under MS-DOS, the COMMAND instruction provides an equivalent function.

Usage:

```
CMD [[/C | /K] string]
```

Parameters for CMD are

/C	Carries out a command specified by the string argument, and then terminates.
/K	Carries out a command specified by the string argument but remains active.
string	Specifies a command to be executed.

Multiple commands can be enclosed in quotes and separated by the command separator '&&'.

Use the EXIT command to terminate the new command interpreter and return control to the previous command interpreter. Use the EXIT command to terminate the new command interpreter and return control to the previous command interpreter. If this is the first command interpreter, the task is terminated and the DOS shell is closed, returning to the Windows NT desktop.

COMMAND (Not Supported by Windows NT)

COMMAND starts a new instance of the MS-DOS command interpreter. Under Windows NT, the CMD command provides the equivalent function.

COMP (DOS/NT)

The COMP utility compares the contents of two files or two sets of files.

Usage:

```
COMP [data1] [data2][/D | /A][/L][/N=nnn][/C]
```

Parameters and flags for COMP are

data1	Identifies the first file or group of files to compare by drive, path, and file name. Wild cards may be used in the file-name specification to identify a group of files.
data2	Identifies the second file or group of files to compare by drive, path, and file name. Wild cards may be used in the file-name specification to identify a group of files.
/D	Differences are displayed in decimal format (default).
/A	Differences are displayed in ASCII characters.
/L	Displays line numbers where differences are found.
/N=*nnn*	Compares only the first *nnn* lines in each file.
/C	Disregards case of ASCII characters when comparing files.

CONVERT (NT Only)

The CONVERT utility changes FAT or HPFS volumes to NTFS. The current (active) drive cannot be converted.

Usage:

```
CONVERT drive: /FS:NTFS
```

Arguments used are

drive:	Identifies the drive to convert to NTFS.
/FS:NTFS	Converts the volume to NTFS format.

COPY (DOS/NT)

The COPY command copies one or more files to another location.

Usage:

```
COPY [/A | /B] source [/A | /B] [+ source [/A | /B] [+ ...]]
        [destination [/A | /B]] [/V]
```

Parameters and flags for COPY are

source	Specifies the file or files to be copied.
destination	Specifies the directory and/or file name(s) for the copied file(s).
/A	Identifies an ASCII text file.
/B	Identifies a binary file.
/V	Verifies that new files can be read correctly.

Files can be appended by specifying a single destination file with multiple sources either using a wild-card specification or by using the format: *file1* + *file2* + *file3*.

CTTY (Not Supported by Windows NT)

The CTTY command was used under DOS to change the terminal device used to control your system.

DATE (DOS/NT)

The DATE command displays or sets the date on the system clock.

Usage:

```
DATE [date]
```

Entering DATE without parameters displays the current date together with a prompt for the entry of a new date. Press Enter to retain the current date setting.

▶ DEBUG (DOS/NT)

The DEBUG command runs the Debug program, which is used by application developers to test and edit executable programs. The Debug utility should not be employed by inexperienced users.

▶ DEL (DOS/NT)

The DEL command is used to delete a file or files.

Usage:

```
DEL [/P][/F][/S][/Q][/A:attributes] [drive:][path]filename
```

Accepted parameters and flags are

[*drive*:] [*path*]*filename*	Identifies the file or, using wild cards, files to delete.
/P	Prompt—requests confirmation before deleting each file.
/F	Forces delete for read-only files.
/S	Deletes all matching files from all subdirectories.
/Q	Quiet mode—no prompt on global wild card (*.*).
/A	Selects files to delete based on file *attributes* (see ATTRIB command, above).

Refer also to the ERASE command.

▶ DIR (DOS/NT)

The DIR command displays a list of files and subdirectories in a directory.

Usage:

```
DIR [drive:][path][filename] [/P][/W][/D][/A[[:]attributes]]
    [/O[[:]sortorder]][/T[[:]timefield]][/S][/B][/L][/N][/X]
```

Parameters and flags for DIR are:

[*drive*:] [*path*]*filename*	Identifies the file or, using wild cards, files to list.

/A	Selects files to delete based on file *attributes*. For example: /A–R identifies files that are not flagged as Read Only. (See ATTRIB command, above.)
/P	Pauses when screen (window) is filled.
/W	Uses wide-list (multicolumn) format.
/D	Uses wide-list format, sorting files by column.
/O	Lists files in sorted order according to ordering instructions, as follows:

N	Sort by name (alphabetic).
S	Sort by size (smallest first).
E	Sort by extension (alphabetic).
D	Sort by date and time (earliest first).
G	Group directories first.
–	Use as prefix to reverse sort order.

If no sort order is specified, files are listed in order of occurrence in the directory.

/T	Specifies which time field is displayed or is used for sorting files (NTFS systems only).

C	Uses date/time stamp when file was created.
A	Uses date/time stamp when file was last accessed.
W	Uses date/time stamp when file was last written.

The FAT file system supports only last-write access time stamps.

/S	Displays files in specified directory and all subdirectories.
/B	Uses bare file list format (no heading information, summary, or time/date/size).

/L	Displays file names in lowercase.
/N (NTFS only)	Uses new, long file-name format with file names on the far right.
/X (NTFS only)	Displays FAT-compatible short (generated) file names with the short name inserted before the long name. If no short name is generated, blanks are displayed.

Directory switches may also be preset using the DIRCMD variable (use the System utility from the Control Panel for system variable settings), but can be overridden individually by prefixing any switch with a hyphen (-) as, for example, /-W.

▶ DISKCOMP (DOS/NT)

The DISKCOMP utility compares the contents of two floppy disks.

Usage:

```
DISKCOMP [drive1: [drive2:]]
```

If only one drive is specified, comparison is made between two disks alternating in the same drive.

▶ DISKCOPY (DOS/NT)

The DISKCOPY utility makes an exact copy of a floppy disk.

Usage:

```
DISKCOPY drive1: drive2: [/V]
```

Parameters and flags for DISKCOPY are

drive1:	Source drive to copy from.
drive2:	Destination drive to copy to.
/V	Verifies that the destination disk can be read.

Both floppy disks must be the same size end capacity. The same drive can be specified as both source and destination, but if two separate drives are used, they must both be 5.25-inch or 3.5-inch sizes.

▶ DOSKEY (DOS/NT)

The DOSKEY utility edits command lines, recalls MS-DOS or Windows NT commands, and creates macros.

```
DOSKEY [/REINSTALL] [/LISTSIZE=size]
       [/MACROS[:ALL | :exename]]
       [/HISTORY] [/INSERT | /OVERSTRIKE] [/EXENAME=exename]
       [/MACROFILE=filename]
       [macroname=[text]]
```

Accepted parameters and flags are

/REINSTALL	Installs a new copy of Doskey.
/LISTSIZE=*size*	Sets command history buffer size.
/MACROS	Displays all Doskey macros.
/MACROS:ALL	Displays all Doskey macros for all executable files that have Doskey macros.
/MACROS:*exename*	Displays all Doskey macros for a specific executable files.
/HISTORY	Displays all commands stored in memory.
/INSERT	New text typed is inserted in old text.
/OVERSTRIKE	New text typed overwrites old text.
/EXENAME=*exename*	Identifies an executable program.
/MACROFILE=*filename*	Identifies a macro file to install.
macroname	Specifies a name for a macro to create.
text	Specifies commands to record.

DOSKEY commands include

Up or down arrow key	Recalls commands.
Escape	Clears the command line.
F7	Displays command history.
ALT+F7	Clears command history.
F8	Searches command history.
F9	Selects a command by number.
ALT+F10	Clears macro definitions.

DOSKEY macro codes include

$T	Command separator, allows multiple commands in a macro.
$1..$9	Batch parameters, equivalent to %1..%9 in batch programs.
$*	The symbol is replaced in the macro by the entire command-line entry following the macro name.

▶ DOSSHELL (Not Supported by Windows NT)

The DOSSHELL command starts MS-DOS Shell from DOS 5.0.

Usage:

```
DOSSHELL
```

While the MS-DOS shell is not supported by Windows NT, it can still be called from the DOS window if desired.

▶ ECHO (DOS/NT)

The ECHO command displays messages or turns command echoing on or off.

Usage:

```
ECHO [ON | OFF]
ECHO [message]
```

Type ECHO without parameters to display the current echo setting.

▶ EDIT (DOS/NT)

The EDIT command starts MS-DOS Editor, which creates and changes ASCII files. The Notepad or Unipad editors provide equivalent functions, although the MS-DOS Editor can be called from the MS-DOS shell under Windows NT.

Usage:

```
EDIT [filename]
```

▶ EDLIN (Not Supported by Windows NT)

The EDLIN command starts Edlin, a line-oriented text editor. Under Windows NT, the Notepad or Unipad editors provide equivalent functions.

▶ EMM386 (Not Supported by Windows NT)

The EMM386 command turns on or off EMM386 expanded memory support. Under Windows NT, expanded memory is handled by simulation. Refer to the PIF Editor instructions for equivalent settings.

▶ ENDLOCAL (NT Only)

The ENDLOCAL command ends localization of environment changes in a batch file.

Usage:

```
ENDLOCAL
```

After the ENDLOCAL command is executed, further environment changes are not local to the batch file, and previous settings are not restored on termination of the batch file. Refer also to the SETLOCAL command. The default condition is global.

▶ ERASE (DOS/NT)

The ERASE command is used to delete a file or files.

Usage:

```
ERASE [/P] [drive:][path]filename
```

Parameters and flags for ERASE are

[*drive*:][*path*]*filename*	Identifies the file or, using wild cards, files to delete.
/P	Prompt—requests confirmation before deleting each file.

Refer also to the DEL command.

▶ EXE2BIN (Not Supported by Windows NT)

The EXE2BIN command converts .EXE (executable) files to binary format—available under Windows NT but not relevant to Windows executable files.

▶ EXIT (DOS/NT)

The EXIT command quits the CMD.EXE (command interpreter) program under Windows NT or the COMMAND.COM program under DOS, or exits to the next lower shell.

Usage:

```
EXIT
```

▶ EXPAND (Not Supported by Windows NT)

The EXPAND command was used to expand files on the MS-DOS 5.0 distribution disks and is not required by Windows NT.

▶ FASTOPEN (Not Supported by Windows NT)

The FASTOPEN command is used under DOS to decrease the amount of time needed to open frequently used files and directories.

▶ FC (DOS/NT)

The FC (file compare) utility compares two files or sets of files, displaying the differences between them.

Usage:

```
FC [/A][/C][/L][/LBn][/N][/T][/W][/nnnn][drive1:][path1]filename1
                                         [drive2:][path2]filename2
FC /B [drive1:][path1]filename1 [drive2:][path2]filename2
```

Flags and arguments for EXPAND include

/A Displays on the first and last lines for each set of differences found.

/B	Compares files as binary format—no other switches are valid in binary mode.
/C	Ignores upper- and lowercase differences.
/L	Compares files as ASCII text.
/LB*n*	Ends comparison after *n* consecutive mismatched lines are found.
/N	Displays the line numbers on an ASCII comparison.
/T	Does not expand tabs to spaces.
/W	Compresses white space (tabs and spaces) for comparison.
/*nnnn*	Requires *nnnn* consecutive matching lines following a mismatch.

FDISK (Not Supported by Windows NT)

The FDISK command configures a hard disk for use with MS-DOS. Attempts to execute FDISK under Windows NT will produce an error prompt and should be terminated without execution. See the Disk Manager and the Format command for Windows NT.

FIND (DOS/NT)

The FIND command searches for a text string in a file or files.

Usage:

```
FIND [/V][/C][/N][/I] "string" [[drive:][path]filename[ ...]]
```

Arguments and flags for FIND include

"*string*"	Specifies the text string to search for.
[*drive:*][*path*]*filename*	Specifies a file or files to search.
/V	Displays only lines that do not contain the specified string.
/C	Displays only the line count for lines containing the search string.
/N	Displays both line numbers and matching lines.
/I	Ignores upper-/ lowercase while matching strings.

If no path name is specified, FIND searches the text typed at the prompt or piped from another command. Refer also to FINDSTR

FINDSTR (NT Only)

The FINDSTR command searches for strings in files.

Usage:

```
FINDSTR [/B][/E][/L][/R][/S][/I][/X][/V][/N][/M][/O]
        [/F:file] [/C:string] [/G:file] [strings]
        [[drive:][path]filename[ ...]]
```

Arguments and flags for FINSTR include

strings	Specify the text strings to search for. Strings should be enclosed in quotes and separated by spaces.
[*drive*] [*path*]*filename*	Specifies a file or files to search.
/C:*string*	Uses specified string as a literal search string—see notes, following.
/F:*file*	Reads a list of files to search from the specified file.
/G:*file*	Retrieves search strings from the specified file.
/B	Matches a search string only at the beginning of a line.
/E	Matches a search string only at the end of a line.
/L	Uses search strings literally.
/R	Uses search strings as regular expressions.
/S	Searches for matching files in the current directory and all subdirectories.
/I	Ignores upper- and lowercase while matching strings.
/X	Prints lines containing string match.
/V	Prints only lines which do not contain a string match.

/N	Prints a line number before each line containing a string match.
/M	Prints only the names of files containing a string match.
/O	Prints the character offset where the match begins at the first of each matching line.

The /C flag identifies the search string as a string literal. Using the /C flag, for example, the search string "hello world" will search only for a literal match for both words. Without the /C flag, matches will be found for both "hello" and "world," with space in the string treated as a delimiter separating multiple strings.

The /S flag searches for matching files in the current directory and all subdirectories. However, subdirectory searches are executed in two modes, depending on how the file name(s) specification is entered. If the file name is placed in quotes—as, for example, FINDSTR /S "hello world" "*.doc"—all files in the current directory and all subdirectories matching the wild-card file specification are searched. Alternatively, if the file specification is not in quotes, the only files searched in the subdirectories will be files with the same file names as those matched in the current directory.

FINDSTR is also capable of finding string matches using wild cards or other conditions by searching for patterns rather than exact string matches. To specify pattern searches instead of literal (string) searches, metacharacters are used in the search string specification. Metacharacters recognized by FINDSTR are listed in Table 13.1.

Table 3.1
Metacharacters for Search Patterns

Metacharacter	Type	Explanation
. (Period)	Wild card	Matches any character.
\x	Escape	Literal use of metacharacter *x*. Thus, use \. to include a period in a search string or \\ to include a single \ character.
*	Repeat	Matches zero or more occurrences of the previous character or class.
^	Line position	Match must occur at the beginning of a line.
$	Line position	Match must occur at the end of a line.

Table 3.1 (Continued) *Metacharacters for Search Patterns (Continued)*

Metacharacter	Type	Explanation
\<*word*	Word position	Match must occur at the beginning of a word.
\>*word*	Word position	Match must occur at the end of a word.
[*class*]	Character class	Matches any one character in set, that is, any character in a specified set such as [*abcxyz*].
[^*class*]	Inverse class	Matches any one character not in set, that is, any character not in a specified set such as [^*abcxyz*].
[*x-y*]	Range	Matches any one character within the specified range, that is, the range [*a-f*] encompasses the characters *a* through *f*.

Metacharacters are used in various combinations as well as singly. For example, the wild card (.) and repeat (*) characters can be combined as .* to match any string of characters that are a part of a long string—as, for example, *b*.*ing, which not only matches words like "*b*eginn*ing*" and "*b*elong*ing*," but also matches phrases such as "*b*efore display*ing*" and "*b*y the search str*ing*".

▸ FOR (DOS/NT)

The FOR command executes a specific command for each file in a set of files.

Usage:

```
FOR %variable IN (set) DO command [command-parameters]
```

Parameters and arguments used in the preceding example are

%variable	Identifies a variable parameter. (To use FOR in batch file, use %%variable instead of %variable).
(set)	Can be a file or set of files; wild-card arguments can be used.
command	Specifies the command to carry out for each file.
command-parameters	Optional parameters or switches required by the specified command.

FORMAT (DOS/NT)

The FORMAT command formats a disk for use with MS-DOS and/or Windows NT.

Usage:

```
FORMAT drive: [/FS:file-system] [/V:label] [/Q] [/A:size]
FORMAT drive: [/V:label] [/Q] [/F:size]
FORMAT drive: [/V:label] [/Q] [/T:tracks /N:sectors]
FORMAT drive: [/V:label] [/Q] [/1] [/4]
FORMAT drive: [/Q] [/1] [/4] [/8]
```

Parameters and flags used with the FORMAT command are

/FS:*file-system*	Selects the file system type as FAT, HPFS, or NTFS.
/V:*label*	Provides an optional volume label.
/Q	Uses quick format.
/A:*size*	Sets the allocation unit size as 512, 1024, 2048, or 4096 bytes.
/F:*size*	For floppy disks only, set format capacity as 160, 180, 320, 360, or 720K or 1.2, 1.44, 2.88, or 20.8MB.
/T:*tracks*	Specifies the number of tracks per disk (per side).
/N:*sectors*	Sets the number of *sectors* per track.
/1	Formats a floppy disk as a single-sided disk.
/4	Formats a 5.25-inch 360K floppy disk in a high-density drive.
/8	Formats a 5.25-inch floppy disk using eight sectors per track.

GOTO (DOS/NT)

The GOTO command is used during execution of a batch instruction file (.BAT) to direct execution to a labeled line in the batch program.

Usage:

```
GOTO label
```

A batch file label is a text string, beginning with a colon, that is used to label a position within the .BAT file. The label must appear on a line by itself. Execution proceeds with the next instruction line in the batch file.

▶ GRAFTABL (DOS/NT)

The GRAFTABL command enables MS-DOS or Windows NT to display an extended character set in CGA graphics mode.

Usage:

```
GRAFTABL [xxx]
GRAFTABL /STATUS
```

Parameters and flags for GRAFTABL are

xxx	Numerical value specifying a code page number.
/STATUS	Shows the current code page selected for use with GRAFTABL.

▶ GRAPHICS (Not Supported by Windows NT)

Loads a program that can print graphics—not used in Windows NT.

▶ HELP (DOS/NT)

Provides Help information for MS-DOS or Windows NT commands.

Usage:

```
HELP [command]
```

The *command* parameter identifies the command or topic for which help is requested. The Windows NT Command Reference Help utility can also be used to search for command topics.

▶ IF (DOS/NT)

The IF command performs conditional processing or branching in batch programs.

Usage:

```
IF [NOT] ERRORLEVEL nnn command
IF [NOT] string1==string2 command
IF [NOT] EXIST filename command
```

Modifiers, conditionals, and arguments permitted include

NOT	Negates the IF condition, executing the command only when the condition evaluates as false.
ERRORLEVEL *nnn*	Evaluates as true if the last program or command executed returned an exit code equal to or greater than *nnn*.
command	Specifies a command or instruction to execute if the condition evaluates as true.
*string*1==*string*2	Evaluates as true if the two text strings match. (Double equal signs are required.)
EXIST *filename*	Evaluates as true if *filename* exists.

▶ JOIN (Not Supported by Windows NT)

The JOIN command is used by DOS to join a disk drive to a directory on another drive. The equivalent function under Windows NT is supplied by Disk Manager (in the Administrative Tools program group).

▶ KEYB (DOS/NT)

The KEYB command configures a keyboard for a specific language.

Usage:

```
KEYB [xx[,[yyy][,[drive:][path]filename]]] [/E] [/ID:nnn]
```

Arguments used with the KEYB command are

xx	A two-letter keyboard code to identify the country.
yyy	Numerical value specifying a console code page.

[*drive*:][*path*]*filename*	This parameter is provided for compatibility with DOS, but is ignored under Windows NT.
/E	This parameter is provided for compatibility with DOS, but is ignored under Windows NT.
/ID:*nnn*	This parameter is provided for compatibility with DOS, but is ignored under Windows NT.

▶ LABEL (DOS/NT)

The LABEL command creates, changes, or deletes the volume label of a disk or logical partition.

Usage:

```
LABEL [drive:][label]
```

The *label* argument is a string—up to 13 characters in length—used as the disk label. If no label is specified, the drive is unlabeled. If no drive is specified, the current (active) drive is assumed. An error occurs if the drive label duplicates a file name in the root directory or a subdirectory name in the root directory.

▶ LH *See LOADHIGH*

▶ LOADFIX (Not Supported by Windows NT)

The LOADFIX command loads a program above the first 64K of memory and runs the program.

▶ LOADHIGH/LH (Not Supported by Windows NT)

The LOADHIGH command loads a program into the upper memory area.

▶ MD *See MKDIR*

MEM (Not Supported by Windows NT)

The MEM command displays the amount of used and free memory in your system. Under the Windows NT DOS shell, the MEM command reports memory available to DOS applications.

MIRROR (Not Supported by Windows NT)

The MIRROR command records information about one or more disks. Not valid under Windows NT even though this command may be recognized.

MKDIR/MD (DOS/NT)

The MKDIR command creates a subdirectory.

Usage:

```
MKDIR [drive:][dir]path
MD [drive:][dir]path
```

If no drive is specified, the current (active) drive is assumed. If no directory is specified, the new directory is created as a subdirectory of the current directory.

MODE (DOS/NT)

The MODE command configures a system device, performing such tasks as displaying system status, changing system settings, or reconfiguring ports or devices. The MODE command performs a variety of tasks, each requiring a different syntax and parameters. A list of tasks performed by the MODE command follows.

Serial port:

```
MODE COMm[:] [BAUD=b] [PARITY=p] [DATA=d] [STOP=s]
             [to=on|off] [xon=on|off] [odsr=on|off]
             [octs=on|off] [dtr=on|off|hs]
             [rts=on|off|hs|tg] [idsr=on|off]
```

The MODE command can be used to configure a serial communications port (COM1, COM2, COM3, and so on). The parameters used for configuring a serial port are

COM*m*	*m* identifies the number of the asynchronous communications (COM) port.
BAUD=*b*	Sets the transmission rate (baud rate) in bits per second. Valid settings are specified by abbreviation as:

11	110 baud
15	150 baud
30	300 baud
60	600 baud
12	1200 baud
24	2400 baud
48	4800 baud
96	9600 baud
19	19,200 baud

PARITY=*p*	Sets how the parity bit is used to check for transmission errors. *p* can be one of the following: *n* (none), *e* (even)(default), *o* (odd), *m* (mark), or *s* (space). Mark and space are not supported by all remotes.
DATA=*d*	Sets the number of data bits in a character. Entries for *d* are valid in the range 5 through 8 with a default value of 7. Values 5 and 6 are not supported by all computers.
STOP=*s*	Sets the number of stop bits with valid arguments: 1, 1.5, and 2. The default stop value at 110 baud is 2, otherwise the default is 1. Not all computers support a stop-bit spacing of 1.5, which is valid only for DATA=5 and which should be selected automatically by UART.
to=on|off	Sets infinite time-out processing—the default is off.
xon=on|off	Sets the xon/xoff protocol for data flow on or off.

odsr=on|off	Sets the output handshaking using the Data Set Ready (DSR) on or off.
octs=on|off	Sets the output handshaking using the Clear To Send (CTS) on or off.
dtr=on|off	Sets the Data Terminal Ready (DTR) handshaking on or off.
rts=on|off|hs|tg	Sets the Request To Send (RTS) handshaking to on, off, handshake, or toggle.
idsr=on|off	Sets the Data Set Ready (DSR) sensitivity to on or off.

Device status:

```
MODE [device] [/STATUS]
```

The MODE command is used to display the status of one or all of the devices installed on the system. The parameters used are

none	Without parameters, MODE displays the status of all devices installed on the system.
device	Names the device to display the status for, as MODE LPT1.
/STATUS	Requests the status of any redirected parallel printers. Without this flag switch, all other installed devices are reported. The flag can be abbreviated as /STA.

Redirect printing:

```
MODE LPTn[:]=COMm[:]
```

The MODE command can be used to redirect printer output from a parallel port to a serial device where LPT*n* and COM*m* identify the parallel and serial ports, respectively.

Configure printer:

```
MODE LPTn[:] [cols=c] [lines=l]
MODE LPTn[:] [c][,[l]]
```

The MODE command can be used to configure an IBM-compatible or Epson-compatible printer connected to a parallel printer port (PRN, LPT1, LPT2, or LPT3). Parameters used are

LPT*n*	Identifies the parallel port where the printer is installed: *n* = 1, 2, or 3.
cols=*c*	Sets the characters width (columns) to 80 (default) or 132 characters per line. The *cols=* can be omitted, specifying only the width parameter.
lines=*l*	Sets the vertical line spacing (lines per inch) to 6 (default) or 8. The *lines=* can be omitted, specifying only the number of lines, but if so must be preceded by a comma.

Select code page/Code page status:

```
MODE CON[:] CP SELECT=yyy
MODE CON[:] CP [/STATUS]
```

The MODE command can be used to set device code pages or to report code page status. The parameters used are

CON	Specifies the device for which the code page is selected (CON is the only valid device name).
CP SELECT	Selects a code page to be used with the specified device. *Codepage* and *select* can be abbreviated as *cp* and *sel*, respectively.
yyy	Identifies the number of the code page to select. Refer to the Command Reference (on-line) for a list of code page numbers.
/STATUS	Displays the numbers of the code pages, if any, that are selected for the specified device. Can be abbreviated as /STA or omitted entirely.

Display mode:

```
MODE CON[:] [COLS=c] [LINES=n]
```

The MODE command is used to change the width and depth (size) of the command prompt screen buffer (DOS window), producing the same effect as using the mouse to resize the DOS window. Parameters used are

CON[:]	Identifies the command prompt window (console).

COLS=*c*	Sets the command prompt screen buffer column width (in characters).
LINES=*n*	Sets the command prompt screen buffer depth (number of lines).

Typematic rate:

```
MODE CON[:] [RATE=r DELAY=d]
```

The MODE command can be used to set the keyboard *typematic rate*—the rate at which Windows NT repeats a character when a key is held down. The typematic rate consists of two elements: the delay (before repeat) and the repeat rate. If either the repeat rate or delay is changed, both must be set. The parameters used are

CON[:]	Identifies the console keyboard.
RATE=*r*	*r* sets the repeat rate with valid arguments in the range 1 through 32 equivalent (approximately) to 2 to 30 characters per second with default settings of 20 for AT-compatible keyboards and 21 for PS/2 compatible keyboards.
DELAY=*d*	*d* sets the delay time, after a key is pressed, before auto-repeat begins. Valid values are 1, 2, 3 or 4—respectively, 0.25, 0.50, 0.75, or 1.0 seconds—with a default of 2.

▶ MORE (DOS/NT)

The MORE command is used to display screen output one screen at a time.

Usage:

```
command-name | MORE [/E [/C] [/P] [/S] [/Tn] [+n]]
MORE [/E [/C] [/P] [/S] [/Tn] [+n]] < [drive:][path]filename
MORE /E [/C] [/P] [/S] [/Tn] [+n] [files]
```

The MORE command is used in several formats with parameters and flags as follow:

[*drive:*] [*path*]*filename*	Specifies a file to display one screen at a time.
command-name	Specifies a command whose output will be displayed by screens.
/E	Enables extended features—see extended feature commands, following.

/C	Clears screen before displaying page.
/P	Expands Form Feed characters.
/S	Squeezes multiple blank lines into a single line.
/T*n*	Expands tabs to *n* spaces (default 8).

The preceding switches can be specified on the command line or can be present in the MORE environment variable.

+*n*	Begins displaying the first file at line *n*.
files	List of files to be displayed. Files in the list are separated by blanks.

If extended features are enabled, the following commands can be entered at the -- More -- prompt:

P *n*	Display next *n* lines.
S *n*	Skip next *n* lines.
F	Display next file.
Q	Quit.
=	Show line number.
?	Show help line.
<space>	Display next page.
<ret>	Display next line.

▶ MOVE (NT Only)

The MOVE command moves one or more files from one directory to another directory on the same or another drive.

Usage:

```
MOVE [source] [destination]
```

The MOVE parameters are

source	Specifies the path and name(s) of the file(s) to move.
destination	Specifies the path and (optionally) name to move file(s) to.

NLSFUNC (Not Supported by Windows NT)

Loads country-specific information.

PATH (DOS/NT)

Displays or sets a search path for executable files.

Usage:

```
PATH [[drive:]path[;...][;%PATH%]
PATH ;
```

Including %PATH% in a new path specification appends the old path specification to the new.

PATH	(Without parameters) displays the current path specification.
PATH ;	Clears all search-path settings. CMD.EXE searches only the current directory.

PAUSE (DOS/NT)

Suspends processing of a batch program, displaying the message:

```
Press any key to continue . . .
```

POPD (NT Only)

The POPD command restores the previous directory saved by PUSHD instruction.

Usage:

```
POPD
```

PRINT (DOS/NT)

The PRINT command prints a text file.

Usage:

```
PRINT [/D:device] [[drive:][path]filename[…]]
```

Arguments used with PRINT include

/D:*device* *device* specifies a print device other than the default PRN.

PROMPT (DOS/NT)

The PROMPT command changes the CMD.EXE (DOS shell) Command Prompt under Windows NT or the DOS Command Prompt under MS-DOS.

Usage:

```
PROMPT [text]
```

The *text* string specifies a new command prompt composed of both normal characters and any of the following special codes:

Code	Prints
$A	& (ampersand)
$B	| (Pipe)
$C	((left parenthesis)
$D	Current date
$E	Escape code (ASCII code 27)
$F	) (right parenthesis)
$G	> (greater-than sign)
$H	Backspace (erases previous character)
$L	< (less-than sign)
$N	Current drive
$P	Current drive and path
$Q	= (equal sign)
$S	(space)
$T	Current time
$V	Windows NT version number
$_	Carriage return and line feed
$$	$ (dollar sign)

One popular Command Prompt, "$P $G", produces "F:\users\default > ", showing the current drive and path followed by a space and then the

angle bracket prompt. Other popular prompts show the time or, occasionally, pipe another utility to the Command Prompt.

PUSHD (NT Only)

The PUSHD command saves the current directory setting for later restoration by the POPD command, and then changes to the directory specified.

Usage:

```
PUSHD [path | ..]
```

The *path* parameter specifies the directory to change to. If no argument is supplied, the current directory setting is not saved. Use the .. argument to move to the parent of the current directory while saving the current directory.

The PUSHD and POPD commands can be used repeatedly to make several directory changes and then step back through the originals in reverse order.

QBASIC (Not Supported by Windows NT)

The command QBASIC starts the MS-DOS QBasic programming environment. While QBASIC will execute in the DOS window, it is not designed for Windows NT programming.

RD *See RMDIR*

RECOVER (DOS/NT)

The RECOVER utility recovers readable information from a bad or defective disk.

Usage:

```
RECOVER [drive:][path]filename
```

The RECOVER command reads a file sector by sector and recovers data from the good sectors. Data in bad sectors is lost. The RECOVER parameters are

[*drive:*] [*path*] *filename*	These parameters specify the location and name of the file to recover.

To check the hard drive or floppy for bad sectors, refer to the CHKDSK command.

▶ REM (DOS/NT)

The REM or remark command is used to record comments (remarks) in batch files or in the CONFIG.SYS file.

Usage:

```
REM [comment]
```

All text following the REM statement on the same line is ignored when a batch file is executed.

▶ RENAME/REN (DOS/NT)

The RENAME command renames a file or—using wild cards—a group of files.

Usage:

```
RENAME [drive:][path]filename1 filename2
REN [drive:][path]filename1 filename2
```

While the RENAME command renames a file or files, it cannot be used to change the drive or path where the files are located. Instead, use the MOVE command.

▶ REPLACE (DOS/NT)

The REPLACE command is used to copy and replace files.

Usage:

```
REPLACE [drive1:][path1]filename [drive2:][path2]
        [/A][/P][/R][/W]
REPLACE [drive1:][path1]filename [drive2:][path2]
        [/P][/R][/S][/W][/U]
```

Arguments and flags used with the REPLACE command are

[*drive1*:][*path1*]*filename*	Specifies the source file or files.
[*drive2*:][*path2*]	Specifies the directory where files are to be replaced.
/A	Adds only new files to destination directory—cannot be used with the /S or /U switches.
/P	Prompts for confirmation before replacing a file or adding a source file.
/R	Replaces read-only files as well as unprotected files.
/S	Replaces files in all subdirectories of the destination directory—cannot be used with the /A switch.
/W	Waits for a source disk to be inserted before beginning.
/U	Only replaces (updates) files older than source files—cannot be used with the /A switch.

▸ RESTORE (DOS/NT)

The RESTORE command is used to restore files backed up using the DOS BACKUP command.

Usage:

```
RESTORE drive1: drive2:[path[filename]] [/S] [/P]
        [/B:date] [/A:date] [/E:time]
        [/L:time] [/M] [/N] [/D]
```

The RESTORE parameters and flags include

drive1:	Identifies the drive where the backup files are located.
drive2:[*path*[*filename*]]	Identifies the file(s) to restore.
/S	Restores files in all subdirectories in the path.
/P	Prompts before restoring read-only files or any files that have changed since the last backup (that is, files with the archive attribute bit set).
/B	Before flag—restores only files last changed on or before the specified date.
/A	After flag—restores only files changed on or after the specified date.
/E	Earlier flag—restores only files last changed at or earlier than the specified time.
/L	Later flag—restores only files changed at or later than the specified time.
/M	Modified flag—restores only files changed since the last backup.
/N	Not present flag—restores only files that no longer exist on the destination disk.
/D	Displays all files on the backup disk(s) that match the specifications.

▸ RMDIR/RD (DOS/NT)

The RMDIR command removes a directory optionally with any files or subdirectories belonging to that directory.

Usage:

```
RMDIR [/S] [drive:][path]directory
RD [/S] [drive:][path]directory
```

Parameters with the RMDIR command include

drive:	Identifies the drive where the directory is located. If not specified, the current (active) drive is assumed.
path	Identifies the path (parent directory) where the directory is located. If not specified, the current (active) directory is assumed.
directory	Identifies the directory to be removed. The directory must be empty. If not, the /S switch can be used.
/S	Removes all directories and files in the specified directory together with the directory itself—used to remove a directory tree.

▸ SET (DOS/NT)

The SET command is used to display, set, or remove environment variables.

Usage:

```
SET [variable=[string]]
```

Parameters used with the SET command include

variable	Specifies the environment variable name.
string	Specifies a string to assign to the variable name.

Enter SET without parameters to display the current environment variables.

▸ SETLOCAL (NT Only)

The SETLOCAL command begins localization of environment changes in a batch file.

Usage:

```
SETLOCAL
```

Environment changes made following the SETLOCAL command are local to the batch file. The previous settings are restored once the batch file terminates.

▶ SETVER (Not Supported by Windows NT)

The SETVER command sets the version number that MS-DOS reports to a program.

▶ SHARE (Not Supported by Windows NT)

The SHARE command installs file-sharing and -locking capabilities on the hard drive.

▶ SHIFT (DOS/NT)

The SHIFT command shifts the position of replaceable parameters used in a batch file.

Usage:

```
SHIFT
```

The SHIFT command shifts the values of the variable parameters %0 through %9 by copying each parameter into the previous variable. Thus the value in %1 is moved (shifted) into %0, %2 to %1, and so on. This permits creating a batch file that performs an operation or series of operations on more than ten command-line parameters. (Initially, the %0 parameter is the program name.)

Alternatively, the SHIFT command can be used to create a batch file that can accept more than ten parameters by shifting the additional parameters, one at a time, into the tenth variable (%9).

However, for whatever reason, each time the SHIFT command is used, the first (%0) parameter in the variable list is lost and cannot be recovered.

▶ SORT (DOS/NT)

The SORT command is used to sort an input stream, writing the sorted results to the screen, a file, or another device.

Usage:

```
SORT [/R] [/+n] < [drive1:][path1]infile
```

```
                  [ > [drive2:][path2]outfile ]
command SORT [/R] [/+n]
                  [ > [drive2:][path2]outfile ]
```

Parameters and flags used with the SORT command are

[drive1:][path1]infile	Identifies a file to be sorted.
[drive2:][path2]outfile	Identifies a file where the sort results will be written.
command	Specifies a command whose output will be sorted.
/R	Reverses the sort order; sorting from Z to A and 9 to 0.
/+*n*	Sorts the file according to characters in column *n*.

START (NT Only)

The START command starts a separate window to run a specified program or command.

Usage:

```
START ["title"] [/dpath] [/i] [size] [priority]
                [/b] [filename] [parameters]
```

Parameters used with the START command include

none	Called without parameters, START opens a second Command Prompt window with the path name of CMD.EXE in the title bar.
"*title*"	Specifies a title to display in the window title bar.
/*dpath*	Identifies *path* as the start-up directory.
/i	Passes the present CMD.EXE start-up environment to the new window.
size	Use /min to minimize or /max to maximize the new window on start-up.
priority	Use /low to start the application in the idle priority class, /normal for normal priority, /high for high priority or /realtime for real-time priority.

/b	A new window is not created. Unless the application enables Ctrl+C handling, Ctrl+C is ignored, and Ctrl+Break must be used to interrupt the application.
filename	Specifies a DOS or NT command or program to start.
parameters	Specifies command-line parameters to pass to the command or program.

SUBST (DOS/NT)

The SUBST command associates a path with a drive letter to create a virtual drive.

Usage:

```
SUBST [drive1: [drive2:]path]
SUBST drive1: /d
```

The path specified is assigned to a drive letter as a virtual drive allowing the drive letter to be used as if it represented a physical drive. Parameters used with the SUBST command are

none	Called without any parameters, SUBST displays the names of all current virtual drive assignments.
path	Identifies the path to assign to a virtual drive. The path must already exist.
drive1:	Identifies the virtual drive assigned the path.
drive2:	Identifies the physical drive containing the path specification if it is not the current drive.
/d	Deletes a virtual drive.

SYS (Not Supported by Windows NT)

The SYS command is used under DOS to copy the MS-DOS system files and command interpreter to a floppy disk or from a floppy disk to a hard drive or between hard drives. This command is not supported under Windows NT, and the Windows NT system will not fit on a standard 1.2MB or 1.44MB floppy disk.

▶ TIME (DOS/NT)

The TIME command displays or sets the system time.

Usage:

```
TIME [hours:[minutes[:seconds[.hundredths]]][A|P]]
```

The TIME command is used to display the system time or to set the computer's internal clock. The time information is used to provide a time stamp whenever a file is changed or created. Parameters used in calling the TIME command include

none	Used without parameters, TIME displays the computer's clock time and prompts for the new time. Press Enter to leave the time unchanged, or type the new time and press Enter to set the clock
hours	Sets the hours as 0 through 23.
minutes	Sets the minutes as 0 through 59.
seconds	Sets the seconds as 0 through 59.
hundredths	Sets hundredths of a second as 0 through 99.
A|P	Specifies AM or PM for the 12-hour time format. If a valid 12-hour time is entered but A/P is not specified, AM is assumed.

Refer to the DATE command to change the current date.

▶ TITLE (NT Only)

The TITLE command sets the window title for the Command Prompt window.

Usage:

```
TITLE [string]
```

The argument *string* provides the title for the Command Prompt window.

▶ TREE (DOS/NT)

The TREE command graphically displays the directory structure of a drive or path.

Usage:

```
TREE [drive:][path] [/F] [/A]
```

drive:	Identifies the drive for the directory tree to be displayed. If not specified, the current drive is assumed.
path	Identifies a path directory where the tree should begin. If not specified, the current directory is assumed.
/F	Displays the names of the files in each directory.
/A	Uses ASCII rather than extended characters.

HELP! *Using the Tree command on a substitute drive—a drive created using the SUBST command—may produce an error message.*

▶ TYPE (DOS/NT)

The TYPE command displays the contents of a text file.

Usage:

```
TYPE [drive:][path]filename
```

The calling parameter *[drive:] [path] filename* identifies the location and name of the file to view.

If TYPE is used to view a non-text file, a document file containing formatting instructions, or a binary file of any kind (such as an executable .EXE or an image file), the results are likely to be a screen full of strange characters not readily understandable. The TYPE command is not intended for use with binary files.

▶ UNDELETE (Not Supported by Windows NT)

The UNDELETE command is used under DOS to recover files which have been deleted.

▸ UNFORMAT (Not Supported by Windows NT)

Under DOS, the UNFORMAT command restores a disk erased by the FORMAT command or restructured by the RECOVER command.

▸ VER (DOS/NT)

The VER command displays the MS-DOS subsystem version from the MS-DOS shell under Windows NT, or the DOS version under MS-DOS.

Usage:

```
VER
```

▸ VERIFY (DOS/NT)

The VERIFY command turns verification on or off, verifying that files written to a disk can be read without error.

Usage:

```
VERIFY [ON | OFF]
```

Type VERIFY without a parameter to display the current VERIFY setting. (Default is ON).

▸ VOL (DOS/NT)

The VOL command displays a disk volume label and serial number.

Usage:

```
VOL [drive:]
```

The drive parameter can be used to identify the disk drive. If no drive is specified, the current (active) drive is assumed.

HELP! *The VOL command does not work on a substituted drive—that is, on a drive created using the SUBST command.*

▸ XCOPY (DOS/NT)

The XCOPY command copies files and directory trees.

Usage:

```
XCOPY source [destination] [/A | /M] [/D[:date]]
                           [/P] [/S [/E]] [/V] [/W]
                           [/C] [/I] [/Q] [/F] [/L]
                           [/H] [/R] [/T] [/U] [/K]
```

Parameters and flags used with the XCOPY command include

source	Identifies the file or files to copy (wild cards can be used in the specification).
destination	Identifies the destination and/or name(s) of new files.
/A	Copies files with the archive attribute set; doesn't change the attribute.
/M	Copies files with the archive attribute set; turns off the archive attribute.
/D:date	Copies files changed on or after the specified date. If no date is given, copies only files whose source date and time are newer than the destination date and time.
/P	Displays a confirmation prompt before creating each destination file.
/S	Copies all directories and subdirectories that are not empty. Use /S with /E to copy empty directories.
/E	Copies all directories and subdirectories, including empty ones. May be used only with /T or /S.
/V	Verifies that each new file can be read without error.
/W	Prompts for a keypress before copying, allowing the user to swap disks.
/C	Continues copying even if errors occur.
/I	If destination does not exist and you are copying more than one file, assumes that the destination must be a directory to create.
/Q	File names are not displayed during copying.
/F	Displays full source and destination file names during copying.
/L	Displays files which would be copied but does not copy them.
/H	Copies system and hidden files.

/R	Forces overwrite for read-only files.
/T	Copies directory structure only. Does not copy empty directories or subdirectories. Use with /E to copy empty directories.
/U	Updates any files already present in destination by overwriting existing files of the same name.
/K	Copies attributes exactly. If not specified, XCOPY resets (clears) read-only attributes on new files.

THE RESCUE PAGES: The DOS Shell/ Command Prompt

My DOS application doesn't run under Windows NT. Instead I get violation error messages.

Not all DOS applications will execute under Windows NT, and some that do execute may or may not function entirely as they would under DOS or may fail to perform some functions that executed correctly under DOS—all of which is, for the present, good reason for using the FlexBoot utility and retaining the ability to boot DOS and/or Windows 3.1 as well as Windows NT.

Some applications fail because they attempt to use system (hardware) resources in a fashion that is simply not permitted under Windows NT and that is not compatible with any shared environment. In other words, some applications simply operate in a manner incompatible with a multitasking environment and can only be operated in a system where they have complete control of all system resources—that is, under DOS.

The best solution—in such cases—is to look for a Windows 3.1 / Windows NT analog of the offending application.

My DOS application's hung and I can't exit from it or from the DOS window.

Calm down, don't panic…and, above all, don't reboot.

First, if the problem occurs because the DOS window is full screen, try pressing Alt+Esc—this should reduce the full-screen DOS window to an icon, which can be dealt with more conveniently.

Second, if the problem has occurred with the DOS shell as a window but you still can't get out of the window, the chances are that you initiated

a copy or paste operation which wasn't compatible with the application—try pressing Esc to cancel the shell operation. Then you should be able to move outside of the DOS shell window—using the mouse cursor, for example—and do something else.

Another alternative is the Alt+Tab combination, which allows you to step through all of the active applications—including Program Manager.

I copied a block of text from a DOS editor and then pasted it into another application, but it has odd characters and isn't aligned right.

Yes, this can happen. In a way, the amazing thing is that you can cut and paste from a windowed DOS application at all—if the operation doesn't always work perfectly, maybe that shouldn't be such a big surprise.

Anyway, you may encounter a few problems—such as tabs and other embedded control characters that may or may not be compatible when moving a block of text from one application to another.

Also, you may lose alignment because of the way the paste operation works. Windows NT can't simply paste into an application's memory buffer. Instead, to paste text into a non-Windows application, Windows NT inserts the text characters—including carriage returns and line feeds—into the keyboard buffer for the application. The result is that the text appears as if it were being typed in.

Of course, this is also a reason why alignment can be lost. The characters are not being placed on the screen or positioned in a text memory buffer, they're simply being fed in through the keyboard, and create their own line breaks and alignment…or lack thereof.

Alignment can be preserved—to some degree and in some cases—by copying text beginning at the left margin and pasting text in from the left margin. This will help…but isn't a guarantee.

I resized the DOS window's screen buffer after an application was already running—now the text display is being formatted incorrectly.

A minimum 80-by-25 window size is a good idea for any DOS application—first, try resetting the screen buffer size, then hit the Minimize and

Maximize buttons to resize the window. This should reset the display. The real cure, of course, is simply to keep the screen buffer sized appropriately for the application.

I used the Convert utility to convert my D drive to NTFS but now—after rebooting—I can't find it from DOS. What happened?

Sorry, but you'll have to reboot and go back to Windows NT. NTFS volumes are only accessible from Windows NT and aren't even visible from DOS or Windows 3.1. Further (sorry again) there is no convenient utility to convert the drive back to FAT.

Restoring the converted NTFS drive is going to require a bit of work:

1. From Windows NT, back up all of the files from the NTFS drive (either to tape or to floppy disks).
2. Reboot DOS and use the FDisk utility to reformat the drive or partition. Or reboot Windows NT and use the Format utility to reformat the drive as a FAT drive. If the NTFS drive was your Windows NT boot drive, you may need to reinstall Windows NT as well.
3. Restore the files from tape or disks.

Of course, if you're only using Windows NT—or if you don't need to access that drive from DOS or Windows 3.1—an NTFS drive has its own advantages.

Some of my DOS macros and .BAT files don't work in the Windows NT DOS shell. How come?

Are you getting a "command not recognized" message? Check the syntax and commands used against those supported by Windows NT. First, Windows NT emulates MS-DOS version 5.0—but does not actually run any version of DOS—only its own emulation version and even then only selected commands and utilities.

CHAPTER

14

HELP! The Performance Monitor

The Performance Monitor is a utility designed principally for administrators (but usable by anyone) for monitoring system usage to determine performance and system capacity.

The Performance Monitor graphically displays usage for objects such as the CPU, memory, cache, treads, and processes both on the local computer and for other computers on the network. Each system object has an associated set of counters to provide information on device usage, queue lengths, and delays as well as throughput and internal congestion.

Further, in addition to reporting and charting current activity, the Performance Monitor can also maintain a file log of events for later review, viewing recorded events in the same fashion as current activities.

The Performance Monitor lets you:

- View simultaneous event data from multiple computers.
- Create log files for specific object data from individual computers on the network.
- Set system alerts to detect and list events in the Alert Log, including options for issuing notification to a specific user or as a network alert.

- Set one-shot or repeat triggers to execute a utility program when a specified counter falls above or below a user-defined threshold.
- Display and dynamically adjust graphics charts of current activity.
- Update charts and data at user-defined intervals.
- View both current activity and logged activities.
- Create reports from current and/or logged activities.
- Export data from charts, logs, alert records, and reports to spreadsheets, database applications, or word processors for further manipulation, report generation, and printing.
- Append and concatenate portions of existing logs to create long-term archives.
- Save individual records, charts, alert logs, report settings, or workspace conditions for later reuse.

All users may access the Performance Monitor without requiring special access permission, although the DiskPerm command—which controls disk monitoring—does require Administrators group access.

The Performance Monitor consists of four main windows—Chart, Alert, Log, and Report—each sharing a menu bar, status bar, and tool bar, but presenting different information in different formats.

Topics covered in this chapter include

- Setup for the Performance Monitor
- Monitoring performance
- Managing the Chart view
- Managing the Log view
- Managing alerts
- Creating reports
- Working with recorded log files

Setup for the Performance Monitor

▶ Activating the Disk Counters

To activate the physical and logical disk counters:

1. If you are not already logged on as a member of the Administrators group, exit Windows NT and log on again as an Administrator.
2. Call the Command Prompt (DOS shell).
3. From the Command Prompt, enter **DISKPERF -Y** to enable the disk performance counters. A response prompt reports the previous status—enabled or disabled—of the disk performance counters. Use the /? instruction for Help.
4. Log off and restart the computer to activate the disk performance counters.

The DiskPerf command is called as:

```
DISKPERF [-Y | -N][\\computername]
```

The arguments used with the DiskPerf command are

-Y	Instructs the system to start the disk performance counters when the system is rebooted.
-N	Instructs the system not to start the disk performance counters when the system is rebooted.
computername	Specifies the computer name to set or view disk performance counters.

If no arguments are specified, DiskPerf reports the current status settings.

▶ Saving Settings

To save the Performance Monitor settings from any view:

1. Select the Save *..view..* Settings command from the File menu (the "view" in the Save option name reflects the current view as selected by the View menu). If no file name has been assigned yet, the Save As dialog box appears.

2. Enter a file name in the File Name box.
3. Select OK—the assigned file name will appear in the Performance Monitor's status bar (bottom at left).

To change the settings file name:

1. Select the Save *..view..* Settings As command from the File menu (again, the Save option name reflects the current view). The Save As dialog box appears.
2. Enter a file name in the File Name edit box or select a name from the displayed list of existing file names.
3. Select OK—the new file name will appear in the Performance Monitor's status bar (bottom left).

To save related settings from all four view windows:

1. Select the Save Workspace command from the File menu. The Save Workspace As dialog box appears. Caption and default extensions aside, the Save Workspace As dialog box is the same as the Save As dialog box preceding.
2. Enter a name in the File Name edit box or select a name from the listed file names.
3. Select OK.

Help Files ▼ Individual charts, alert settings, logs, report settings, or the entire workspace can be saved to a file before exiting the Performance Monitor, retaining view settings or a combination of settings for future use.

Exiting the Performance Monitor

To exit from the Performance Monitor:

- Select Exit from the File menu.

Or:

- Select Close from the Control menu (upper-left corner).

Help Files ▼ Before exiting the Performance Monitor, be certain to save chart, alert, log, or report settings or the entire workspace to a settings file—unless, of course, you are certain the current settings will not be wanted later.

Selecting the Screen to View

To select the screen to view:

- From the View menu, select from the Chart, Alert, Log, or Report views.

Help Files ▼ The four view windows share the Menu and Title option, the Toolbar option, and the Status Bar option. Each of these can be enabled or disabled to change the screen space available for display. The Always On Top option—also shared with all four views—ensures that the Performance Monitor remains visible even if it has been reduced to an icon or when another application is active.

▶ Organizing the Performance Monitor's Screen

To organize the Performance Monitor's screen:

- Select the options to hide or show from the Options menu. Display elements that can be hidden include

Menu and Title	The menu and title bar at the top of the window
Toolbar	The tool icons immediately below the menu bar
Status Bar	The status bar at the bottom of the Performance Monitor

To access the menu bar after it has been hidden:

- Double-click anywhere in the display area that does not show text information. The menu bar will appear at the top of the window.

To restore the original display:

- Double-click anywhere in the display area that does not show text information. The original display arrangement will reappear.

To keep the Performance Monitor visible:

- Select the Always On Top option (off by default) from the Options menu—when the option is enabled, the Performance Monitor remains on top of all other applications.

To move the Performance Monitor when the title bar is hidden:

1. Click anywhere in the display area that does not show text information.
2. Hold the mouse button down while dragging the window to a new position.

To turn Chart highlighting on and off:

Monochrome monitors will show shaded lines.

- Press Ctrl+H—the selected counter (bottom window) is highlighted in the graph window (upper window) by changing the trace from a colored line to a heavier white line.
- Press Ctrl+H a second time to restore the original display.

Monitoring Performance

▶ Working with Information on Current Activity

To work with current activity information (in any view):

1. Select a new settings file or open an existing view file from the File menu. The default file extensions match the view window type as follows:
   - Chart settings files use the extension .PMC.
   - Alert settings files use the extension .PMA.
   - Log settings files use the extension .PML.
   - Report settings files use the extension .PMR.
   - Workspace settings files use the extension .PMW and contain settings for all four windows.
2. Select the Add To option from the Edit menu or the Add To button from the tool bar to add computers, objects, counters, or instances to the monitor.

   The Add To Chart dialog—see Figure 14.1—appears.

To select several objects or counters, select the first item from the Add To Chart dialog box to add to the chart, and then:

1. Press and hold the Shift key while selecting the last contiguous item.
   - Or drag the mouse to the last contiguous item.
   - Or press and hold the Ctrl key while selecting non-contiguous items.
2. Select the Add To or Edit commands to change how selections are represented.

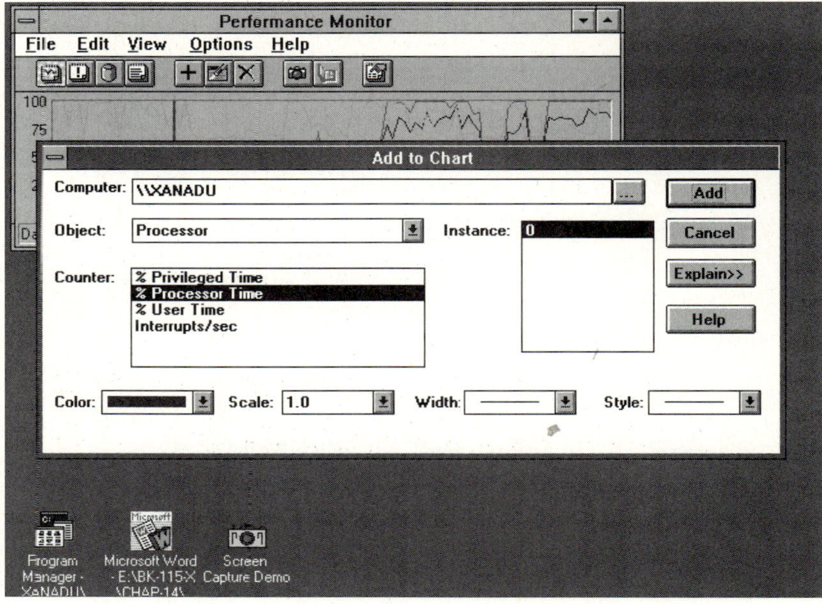

Figure 14.1
The Add To Chart dialog box

3. Use the Options menu to select options customizing each view, including setting the time interval and update method, displaying items, selecting graphics formats, turning logging on or off, setting bookmarks, and establishing notification methods.
4. Save any changes—using the File menu—in a new settings file or as an update to the current settings file.
5. If related information is contained in more than one window, save settings for the entire workspace.

▶ Selecting Local or Remote Computers

To select a local or remote computer:

1. Select the Add To *..view..* option from the Edit menu.
2. Enter the computer's name in the Computer edit box.
   - Or select the Browse button (right end of the edit box) to display the Select Computer dialog box shown in Figure 14.2.

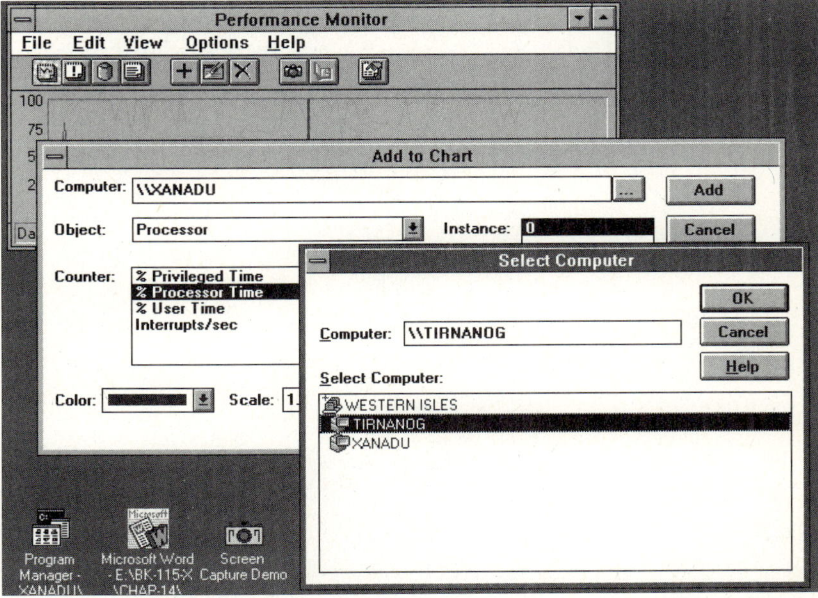

Figure 14.2
The Select Computer dialog box

3. The Select Computer dialog box lists the names of domains and work groups that can be accessed. (A brief delay may occur while the Performance Monitor searches for member computers.)
4. Double-click on a domain or work group name to display the names of servers and work groups.
5. Select the server or work group to monitor.
6. Select OK to add the server or work group to the Performance Monitor.

Help Files ▼ When a server or work group is added to the Performance Monitor, the Add button will be disabled while the named computer is searched for. Once the computer is found, the Add button is reenabled, and the display shows the default settings for the selected computer. If the specified

computer is not found, a report appears stating the problem, and the Performance Monitor returns to the default selections.

Clearing the Display

To clear the values displayed on the screen:

- Select Clear Display from the Edit menu.

Help Files ▼ The Clear Display command is used in all four views to clear the data from the display screen.

Deleting Selections

To delete a selection:

1. Select the legend, log, or report item to delete.
2. Select the Delete command from the Edit menu.
   - Or select the Delete button from the tool bar.

Help Files ▼ The same instructions are used in all four views to delete display elements.

▶ Updating the Display

To update the screen display (any view):

- Select Update Now from the Options menu.

Or:

- Select the Update Now button from the tool bar.

To change update methods within a view:

1. Select the view from the View menu.
2. Select the *..view..* option from the Options menu. The appropriate Options dialog box for each view will appear. Figure 14.3 shows the Chart Options dialog box.

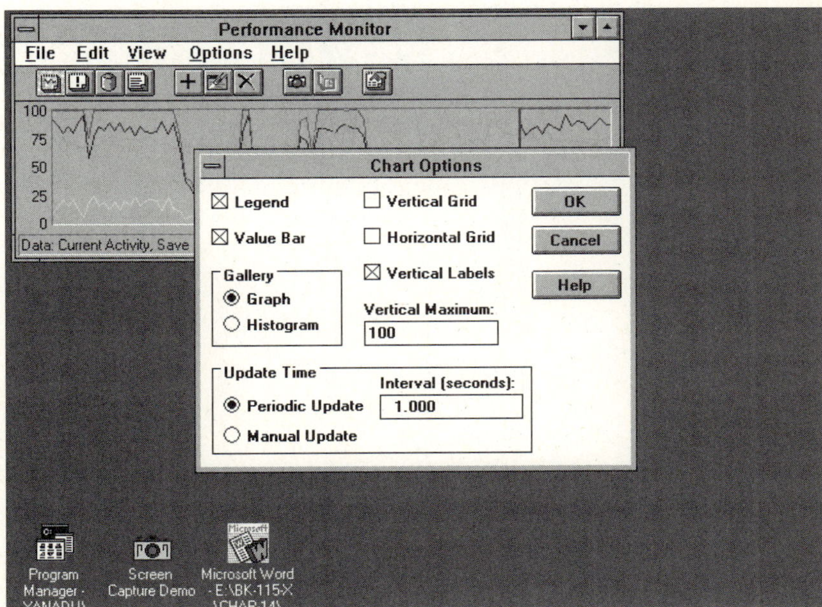

Figure 14.3
The Chart Options dialog box

3. Select Periodic Update or Manual Update from the Options dialog box (refer also to "Selecting Chart Options").
4. If Periodic Update is selected, enter a value in the Interval edit box to set the time, in seconds, between updates.
5. Select OK.

Help Files ▼ Each of the four views has its own Options dialog box and Update Time interval, or can be set to manual updates. Likewise, each view has both an Update Now command and button for manual updates. When automatic updating is active, the Update Now command or button may still be used to request a snapshot of the current status.

▶ Printing the Window Display

To print a snapshot of the current display window:

1. Press Alt+PrtSc to copy a view of the active window to the Clipboard. (Pressing PrtSc alone will copy the entire desktop.)
2. Load the Paintbrush program from the Accessories group.
3. Select Paste to copy the captured image from the Clipboard to the Paintbrush program.
4. Select Save As to save the bitmap image for future reference.
5. Select Print to produce a hard copy of the bitmap image.

Help Files ▼ The PrtSc key captures the entire desktop, while Alt+PrtSc captures only the active window. In either case, the captured image is copied to the Clipboard, where it can be pasted into a paint application for retouching, saving as a file, or printing.

▶ Exporting Data

To export data to a spreadsheet or database:

1. Select Export from the File menu. The Export As dialog box shown in Figure 14.4 appears.

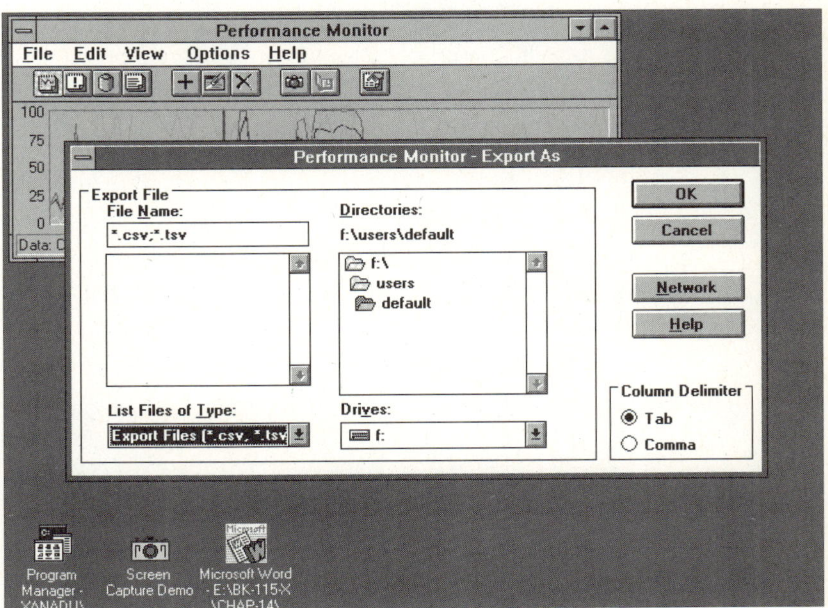

Figure 14.4
The Export As dialog box

2. Select either Tab characters (*.TSV files) or commas (*.CSV files) to delimit (separate) column data in the file, depending on the format required by the intended recipient of the data.
3. Enter or select a path and file name—using the appropriate extension to match the selected column delimiter—for the exported file.
4. If the file should be written to a remote computer, use the Network button to display and select a destination from the Network Connections box.
5. Select OK to write the file.
6. Load a spreadsheet or database program.
7. Import the Performance Monitor file into the spreadsheet or database application.

Help Files ▼ Using the Export option, the Performance Monitor data can be saved to a spreadsheet or database program for analysis, manipulation, or printing.

▸ Working with Log File Data

To work with data from log files (any view):

1. Select Data From from the Options menu to select an existing data log.
2. Select Time Window from the Edit menu, if necessary, to change the start and stop times.
3. Select the Add To command or Add To button to select one or more computers to monitor or to select objects, counters, or instances.

- Or select the Open command from the File menu to open an existing settings or workspace file.

4. Select either the Add To or Edit command, as appropriate, to change how selections are represented.
5. Save selections in a new settings file or as an update to the current settings file.
6. Use the Options menu to change options for hiding and displaying items, changing graphics formats, starting and stopping relogging, setting log intervals, or adding bookmarks.
7. Change windows or views and repeat the process for a different perspective on the same data or to examine another aspect of the data.
8. If related information is shown in two or more windows, save settings for the entire workspace.

Managing the Chart View

▶ Viewing the Chart Window

To view the Chart window:

- Select Chart from the View menu.

Or:

- Select the Chart button from the tool bar.

Help Files ▼ When you switch the Performance Monitor from another view, the Chart window will be blank unless a chart has previously been created or opened during the current session.

▶ Highlighting a Chart Selection

To highlight a chart selection:

1. Select the chart element to highlight from the legends window.
2. Press Ctrl+H to turn highlighting on.

To change the highlighted selection:

- Select a different chart element from the Legends window.

To end highlighting:

- Press Ctrl+H.

Help Files ▼ Chart highlighting makes it easier to watch a chart element by changing a selected counter's screen trace to white. If the selected line width is narrow, the line is thickened. Also, if a line style is used, the line becomes solid.

▸ Opening Existing Chart Settings

To open an existing chart settings file:

1. Select Open from the File menu. The File Open dialog box shown in Figure 14.5 appears.

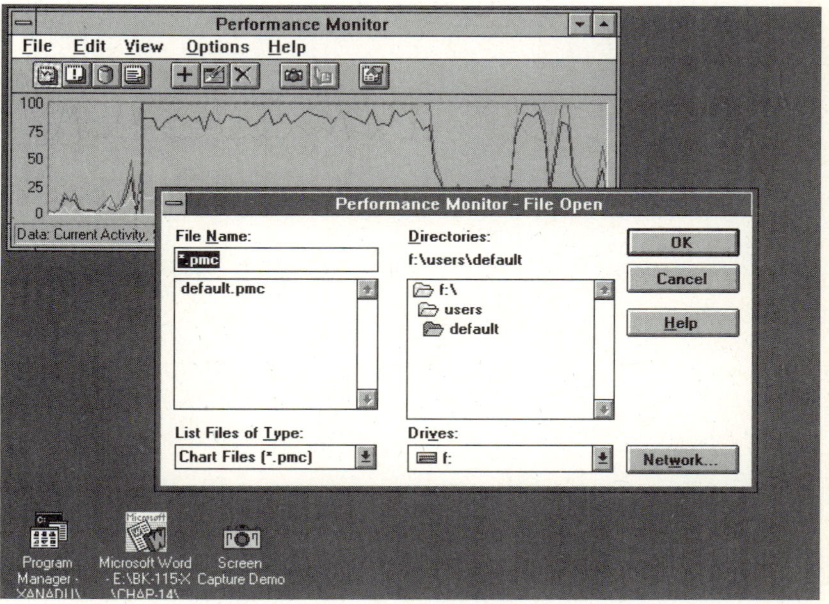

Figure 14.5
The File Open dialog box

2. Enter a path and file name for the .PMC file containing the desired Chart settings.

   ■ Or select a path and file from the File Open dialog box.

3. If the desired .PMC file is located on another computer, select the Network button to call the Network Connections dialog box.
4. Select OK to load the Chart settings.

To create a new, blank chart:

■ Select New Chart from the File menu.

Help Files ▼ Customized charts are used to monitor the performance of selected counters and instances for such purposes as:

- Identifying slow or inefficient operations or applications.
- Monitoring systems for intermittent performance bottlenecks.
- Determining capacity requirements.

Click the Explain button from the Add To Chart dialog box to display the Counter Definition box with a brief explanation of the selected counter.

▶ Adding Chart Selections

To add objects, counters, and instances to a chart:

1. Select Add To Chart from the Edit menu.

   - Or select the Add To Chart button from the tool bar.

   The Add To Chart dialog box shown in Figure 14.6 appears.

2. Select an object to monitor from the pull-down Object list box. The list shows all of the resources available on the computer. The Counter and Instance boxes provide a list of items available for the selected object on the selected computer.

3. Select one or more counters from the Counter list box. Click on the Explain button for a brief definition of the selected counter. (See the bottom of Figure 14.6.)

4. Select one or more instances—as appropriate—from the Instance list box.

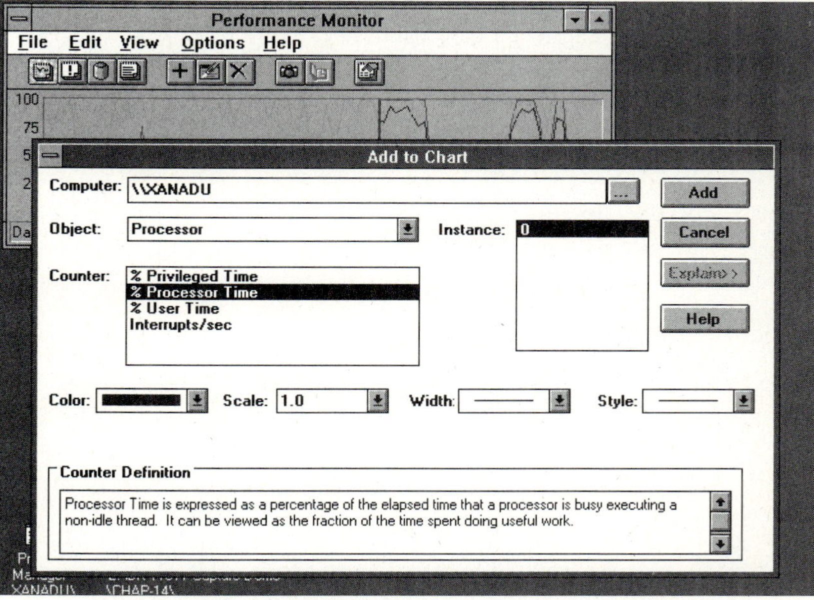

Figure 14.6
The Add To Chart dialog box

5. Select color, scale, line width, and line style (or accept the defaults assigned).
6. Select the Add button to add the object to the chart display.
7. Repeat steps 2 through 6 to add additional objects or computers.
8. Select Close when selections are complete.

Help Files ▼ Each successive object added to the chart is assigned the next available color and the default scale, line width, and style. Each of these display characteristics can be changed as desired (see "Changing Chart Styles" below). A list of the selections and their chart styles appears in the legend window at the bottom of the Performance Monitor (see "Organizing the Performance Monitor's Screen").

Changing the scale factor affects all currently selected counters and is used as a multiplication factor times the counter value for display purposes. The value bar (at the left of the window), however, does not change scales to match the scale factor.

▶ Changing Chart Styles

To change the line style and colors used on the chart:

1. Select the counter to change from the legend window.
2. Double-click the selected counter.
   - Or select Edit Chart Line from the Edit menu.
   - Or select the Edit Chart Line button from the tool bar.

3. Change any of the following options:

Colors	Select according to personal preferences.
Scale	Set scale multiplier for chart display.
Width	Select line width (thick lines can not be styled).
Style	Select line style.

4. Select OK. Changes are selected in the chart and legend information windows.

▶ Selecting Chart Options

To change chart options:

1. Select Chart from the Options menu or select the Options button from the tool bar.

   The Chart Options dialog box appears as shown in Figure 14.7.

2. Select display options from the Chart Options dialog box.

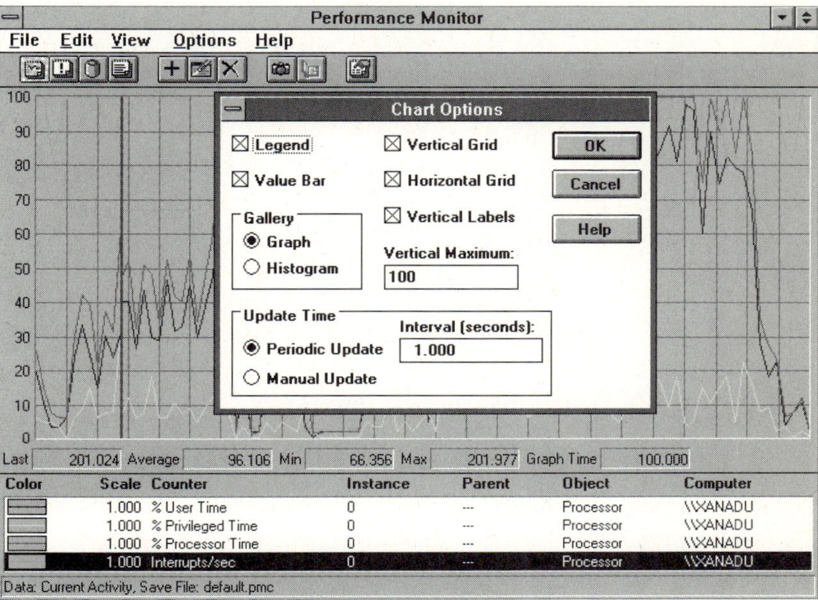

Figure 14.7
The Chart Options dialog box

3. Enter a maximum value for the vertical axis in the Vertical Maximum edit box.
4. Select Periodic Update or Manual Update in the Update Time box.
5. If Periodic Update is selected, enter a value—in seconds—in the Interval edit box. The Graph Time displayed in the value bar below the chart shows the duration, in seconds, for a complete horizontal trace.
6. Select a Graph or Histogram display in the Gallery box.
7. Select OK.

Managing the Log View

▶ Viewing the Log Window

To view the Log window:

- Select Log from the View menu.

Or:

- Select the Log button from the tool bar.

Help Files ▼ When switching to the Performance Monitor from another view, the Log window will be blank unless a log has previously been created or opened during the current session.

▸ Opening Existing Log Settings

To open an existing log settings file:

1. Select Open from the File menu. The File Open dialog box—see Figure 14.5, preceding—appears.
2. Enter a path and file name for the .PML file containing the desired Log settings.
   - Or select a path and file from the File Open dialog box.
3. If the desired .PML file is located on another computer, select the Network button to call the Network Connections dialog box.
4. Select OK to load the Log settings.

To create a new, blank log:

- Select New Log Settings from the File menu.

Help Files ▼ Logs are used to monitor the performance of selected objects and computers for later viewing. Log files can maintain data on the performances of counters and object instances, collect data from multiple systems, collect data for long-term planning, and analyze trends over longer periods.

▶ Adding to a Log

To add objects to a log:

1. Select Add To Log from the Edit menu, or select the Add To Log button from the tool bar.

   The Add To Log dialog box shown in Figure 14.8 appears.

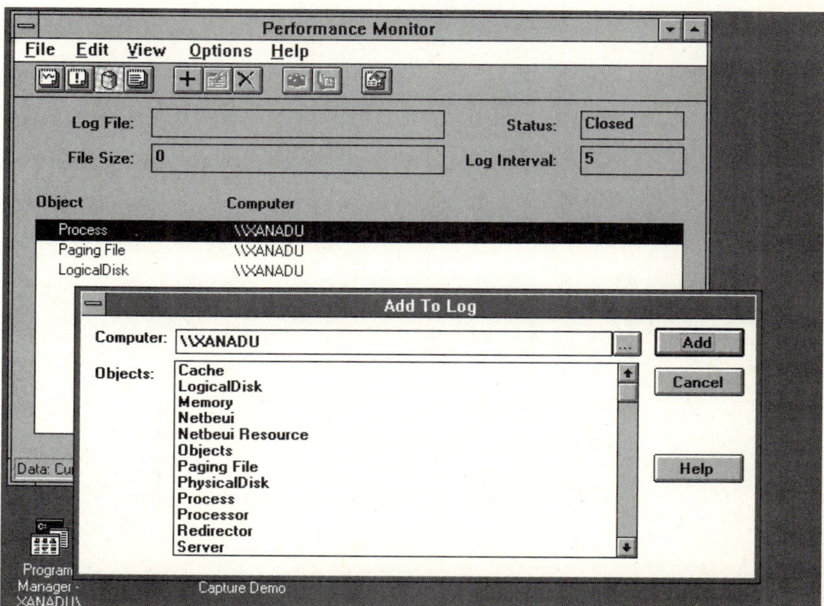

Figure 14.8
The Add To Log objects list

2. Select the computer by entering the computer name or using the Browse button (...) (located at right end of the Computer entry box) to select a computer from a list of those available.
3. Select an object or set of objects from the Objects list box to monitor. The list shows all of the resources available on the computer. The Counter and Instance boxes provide a list of items available for the selected object on the selected computer.
4. Select the Add button to add the object to the Log list.
5. Repeat steps 2 through 4 for any additional computer which needs to be monitored.
6. Select Cancel when finished. Log selections appear in the Objects list in the Log view.

Help Files ▼ Different logs can be created to accumulate information about the behavior of selected objects on different computers, with the logged information saved for later study. Log profiles can also be saved as .PML files for later reuse—select Save Log Settings As from the File menu.

▸ Changing Log Options

To change log options:

1. Select Log from the Options menu, or select the Options button on the tool bar.

The Log Options dialog box shown in Figure 14.9 appears.

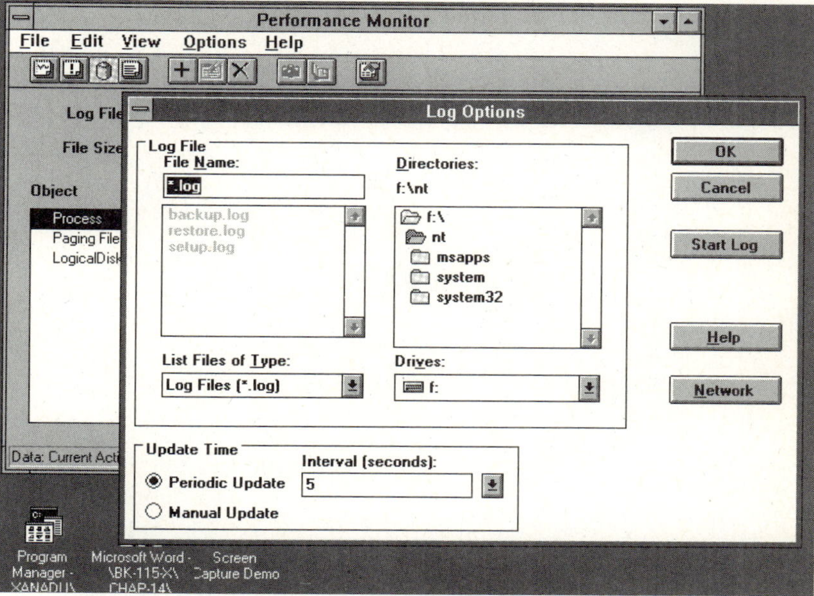

Figure 14.9
The Log Options dialog box

2. Enter a name for the log file or select a log file from the File list box. If an existing file is used, the new data will be appended to the existing data. To replace old data, either choose a new file name, or delete the old file and then create a new file with the same name.
3. Select Periodic Update or Manual Update from the Update Time box.
4. If Periodic Update is selected, set the interval, in seconds, between log updates.
5. Select the Start Log button to begin logging immediately, or select OK to defer logging without losing settings and selections.

To start logging:

1. Select Log from the Options menu. The Log Options dialog box appears.
2. If the Start Log button is not enabled, a log file name and log profile must be created.

3. Select the Start Log button to initiate logging. (The Start Log button changes to Stop Log.)

To stop logging:

- Select the Stop Log button. (The Stop Log button changes to Start Log.)

Help Files ▼ After logging is initiated, a log symbol appears on the right of the status bar together with a changing total for the file size.

The log symbol appears in all four of the Performance Monitor views.

▶ Adding Bookmarks

To add a bookmark to a log file:

1. Select Bookmark from the Options menu or select the Bookmark button from the tool bar.

2. Enter a comment in the Bookmark Comment box.
3. Select the Add button.

Help Files ▼ Bookmarks are used to add comments at various intervals during logging. Bookmarks serve to identify circumstances or highlight major points and provide a reference or reminder of what was happening at each point during the log's creation.

Managing Alerts

▶ Viewing the Alert Window

To view the Alert window:

- Select Alert from the View menu.

Or:

- Select the Alert button from the tool bar.

When you switch the Performance Monitor from another view, the Alert window will be blank unless an alert log has previously been created or opened during the current session.

To open an existing alert log settings file:

1. Select Open from the File menu. A File Open dialog box similar to the one shown in Figure 14.5, preceding, appears.
2. Enter a path and file name for the .PMA file containing the desired Alert settings.
   - Or select a path and file from the File Open dialog box.
3. If the desired .PMA file is located on another computer, select the Network button to call the Network Connections dialog box.
4. Select OK to load the Alert settings.

To create a new, blank alert log file:

- Select New Alert Settings from the File menu.

Help Files ▼ Alert settings allow the user to work on other jobs while the Performance Monitor tracks events and conditions, issuing notification when and as defined in the alert log.

The alert log permits monitoring several counters simultaneously. When a counter exceeds a set value, the date/time for the event are recorded in the Alert window up to a total of 1,000 event records; after which the oldest event records are discarded to make space for new events. An event can also generate a network alert or execute a utility or program.

▶ Adding Alerts

To add alert watches to an alert log:

1. Select Add To Alert from the Edit menu or select the Add To Alert button from the tool bar.

   The Add To Alert dialog box, shown in Figure 14.10, appears with the default settings and the local workstation or server listed in the Computer box.

2. Select the computer by entering the computer name or using the Browse button (located at the right end of the Computer entry box) to select a computer from a list of those available.

3. Select an object from the pull-down Object list box. The Instance and Counter list boxes change to reflect items available for the selected object.

4. In the Counter box, select one or more counters. For a brief definition of the selected counter, select the Explain button.

5. If appropriate, select one or more instances from the Instance box.

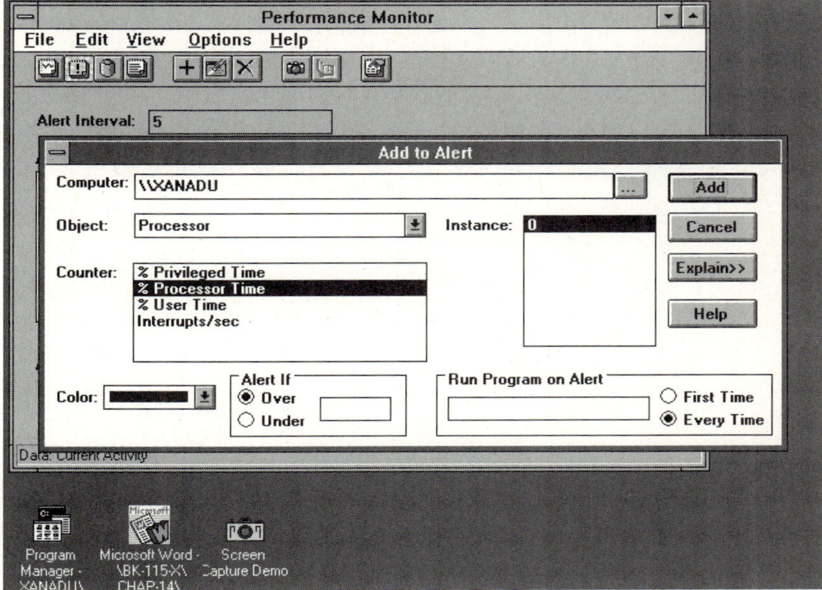

Figure 14.10
The Add To Alert dialog box

6. Select a specific color from the pull-down list, or accept the next available color by default.
7. Select either Over or Under in the Alert If box, and set an appropriate value for the counter.
8. If desired, select a program or macro to execute when the alert is triggered.
9. Select the Add button.
10. Repeat steps 2 through 9 to monitor additional objects or computers.
11. Select Cancel when finished.

To execute a program or a macro when an alert is triggered:

1. Select either First Time or Every Time from the Run Program On Alert box.
2. Enter the complete path and file name for the program or macro. The Alert Log entry is passed as a command-line parameter.

To switch to the Alert view automatically when an alert occurs:

1. Select Alert from the Options menu.
2. Select the Switch To Alert View check box in the Alert Options dialog box (see "Changing Alert Options," following).

Help Files ▼ Alert requests are displayed in the Alert Legend box at the bottom of the Performance Monitor window, while alert events are listed in the Alert Log window.

Anytime an alert occurs while the Performance Monitor is not in the Alert view, the alert icon appears in the status bar showing the number of alerts occurring since the Alert view was last displayed.

Save alert log selections using the Save Alert Settings As option from the File menu. Alert logs can be created to provide warnings for varying problems and circumstances and then saved for reuse at later times.

▶ Changing Alert Conditions and Selections

To modify alert conditions and options:

1. Double-click a selected counter in the Alert Legend list.
   - Or select Edit Alert Entry from the Edit menu.
   - Or select the Edit Alert Entry button from the tool bar.

   A dialog box similar to Figure 14.10 appears, showing only the information relevant to the counter selected from the Alert Legend list.
2. Three of the alert options can be revised as:
   - Color selection

- The Alert If warning criterion
- The Run Program On Alert options

3. Select OK for the alert revisions to take effect.

▶ Changing Alert Options

To change alert options:

1. Select Alert from the Options menu or select the Options button from the tool bar.

   The Alert Options dialog box shown in Figure 14.11 appears.

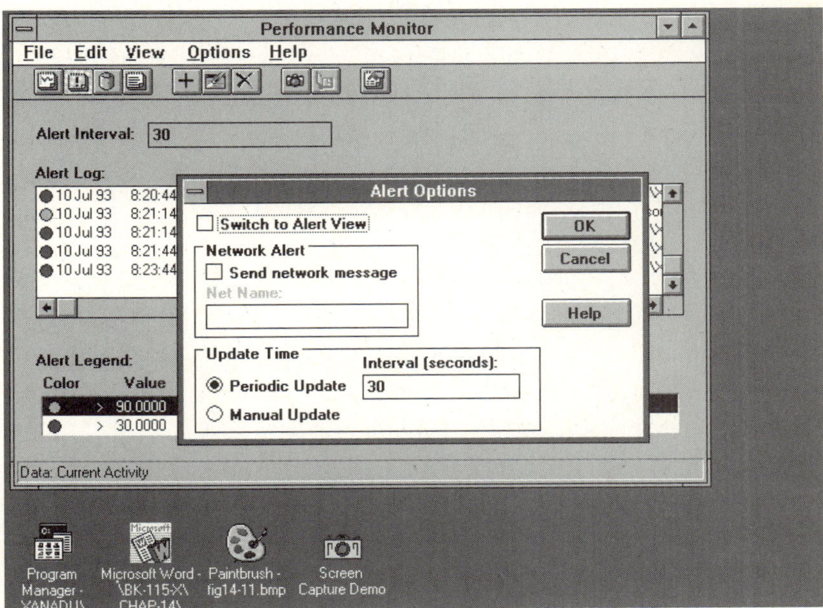

Figure 14.11
The Alert Options dialog box

2. Select the Switch To Alert View check box to automatically switch to the Alert view in Performance Monitor when an alert is triggered.

3. Select the Send Network Message check box and enter the computer name—without backslashes (\\)—for the recipient's computer or for another predefined name on the recipient's computer in the Net Name box.

4. Select either Periodic Update or Manual Update from the Update Time box.

5. If Periodic Update is selected, enter a value in the Interval box setting the time, in seconds, between updates of the alert log.

6. Select OK to save the changed settings.

Help Files ▼ To use predefined network names for network notification messages, the Messager service must already be active and the net name defined on the recipient's computer.

Creating Reports

▶ Viewing the Report Window

To view the Report window:

- Select Report from the View menu.

Or:

- Select the Report button from the tool bar.

Help Files ▼ When you switch to the Performance Monitor from another view, the Report window will be blank unless a report file has previously been created or opened during the current session.

▶ Opening Existing Report Settings

To open an existing report settings file:

1. Select Open from the File menu. The File Open dialog box—see Figure 14.5, preceding—appears.
2. Enter a path and file name for the .PMR file containing the desired Report settings.
   - Or select a path and file from the File Open dialog.
3. If the desired .PMR file is located on another computer, select the Network button to call the Network Connections dialog box.
4. Select OK to load the Report settings. A sample report is shown in Figure 14.12.

To create a new, blank report file:

- Select New Report Settings from the File menu.

Help Files ▼ The Report view offers a simple report format for displaying information on counter and instance values for selected objects in a simple column format. Report intervals can be adjusted, snapshots printed, and data exported.

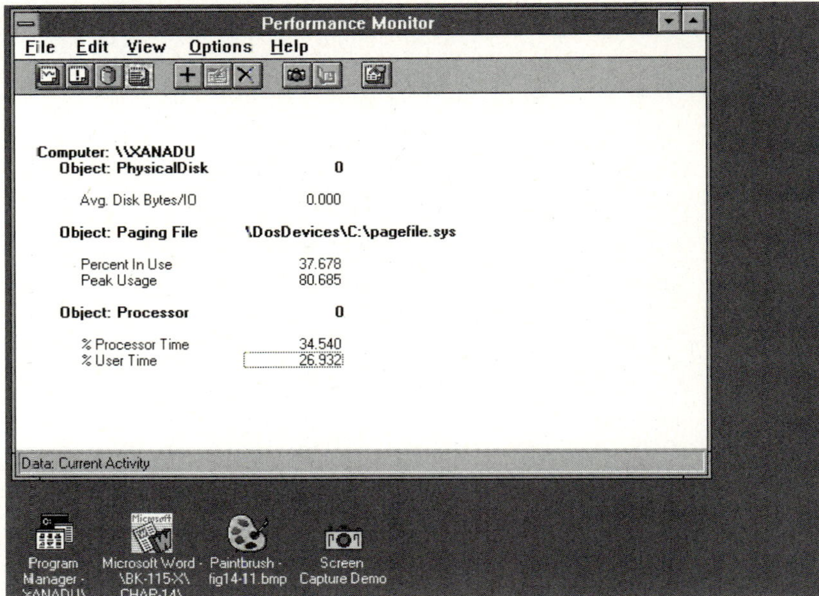

Figure 14.12
Viewing a report

▶ Adding to a Report

To add selections to a report:

1. Select Add To Report from the Edit menu or select the Add To Report button from the tool bar.

   The Add To Report dialog box shown in Figure 14.13 appears.

2. Select the computer by entering the computer name or using the Browse button (located at the right end of the Computer entry box) to select a computer from a list of those available.
3. Select an object from the pull-down Object list box. The Instance and Counter list boxes change to reflect items available for the selected object.
4. In the Counter box, select one or more counters. For a brief definition of the selected counter, select the Explain button.
5. If appropriate, select one or more instances from the Instance box.

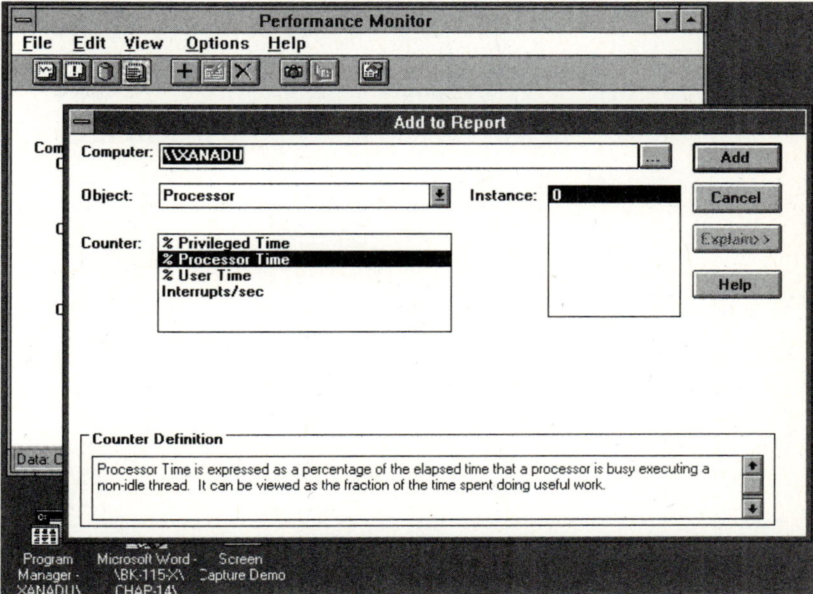

Figure 14.13
The Add To Report dialog box

6. Select the Add button.
7. Repeat steps 2 through 6 to monitor additional objects or computers.
8. Select Cancel when finished.

Help Files ▼ Reports can be created paralleling the information gathered for a Chart or Log view or simply to provide a different view of the information. For example, a report might be generated for all of the counters relating to the hard drive and the swap file, providing a convenient view of their performance under different loads. As with other views, the report settings can be saved as a file for later reuse. Refer also to "Creating Reports from Log Files," below.

▶ Changing the Report Interval Options

To change the report interval time option:

1. Select Report from the Options menu or select the Options button from the tool bar.

2. Select Periodic Update or Manual Update from the Update Time box.
3. If Periodic Update is selected, enter a value in the Interval box setting the time, in seconds, between updates of the report.
4. Select OK.

Working with Recorded Log Files

▶ Selecting a Log File

To select an existing log file:

1. Select Data From from the Options menu.
2. Select Log File from the Data Values Displayed From box.
3. Enter the log file name in the Log File edit box or click the Browse button (located at the right end of the Log File edit box) to display the Open Input Log File dialog box.
4. If the desired log file is located on another computer, select the Network button to call the Network Connections dialog box.
5. Select the OK button. This action also activates the Time Window command in the Edit menu.

Help Files ▼ Saved log files offer a wealth of information both for troubleshooting and for planning system usage and requirements. Where current activity charting, alerts, and reports are well suited for rapid feedback, log files permit examining information over a longer baseline from a more flexible choice of perspectives.

Information from a log file can be examined at leisure in a much more thorough fashion than trying to make sense of events as they are happening. Changing the start and stop times offers the convenience of moving through the log to examine different intervals (use the Time Window command from the Edit menu).

▸ Changing the Time Window

To change the Time Window:

- Select Time Window from the Edit menu. The Input Log File Timeframe dialog box shown in Figure 14.14 will appear.

To change the start and stop points for the display:

- Drag the corresponding ends of the time interval slide bar.

To use bookmarks as start and stop points:

1. Select a bookmark from the list.
2. Select the Set As Start or Set As Stop button.

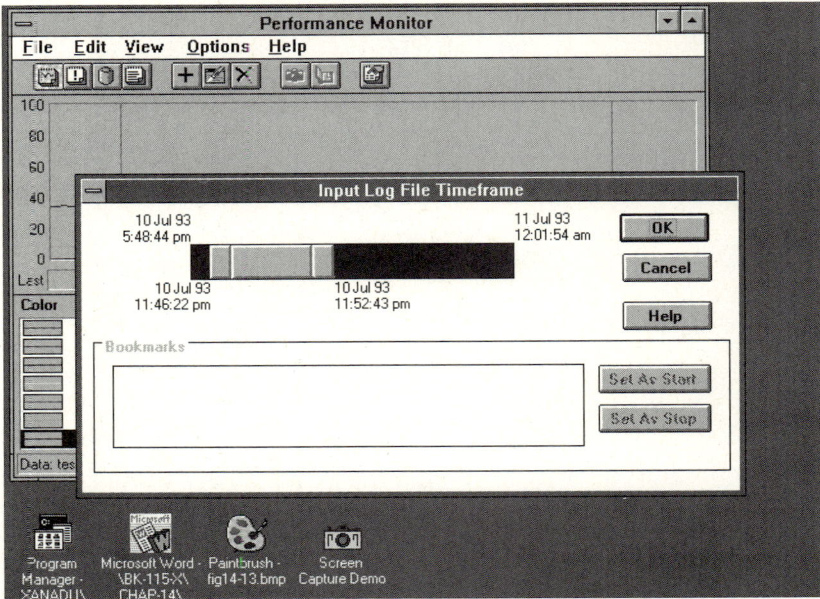

Figure 14.14
The Input Log File Timeframe dialog box

Help Files ▼

Dragging either end of the slide bar also moves two gray, vertical lines on the chart, showing the range covered by the interval selection. When selection is complete, the chart will be redrawn to show only the selected interval.

▶ Charting Input Log Files

To chart an input log file:

1. Select the Chart view window.
2. Select Data From from the Options menu.
3. Select a log file name from the local computer or from the network.

4. From the Edit menu, select
   - The Add To Chart option to select counters from specific computers to chart.
   - The Edit Chart Line option to change selection settings.
   - The Delete From Chart option to remove any unwanted counters.
   - The Time Window option to select the time interval for display.
5. Select Chart from the Options menu to hide or display individual items, change the vertical maximum or switch between graph and histogram formats.
6. From the File menu, select
   - The Save Chart Settings As option to update changes to the current chart settings file or to save these as a new file.
   - The Export Chart option to export data to a spreadsheet or database program.

Help Files ▼ The Chart view can be used to create a graphic view of a log file showing how factors change over time. Time intervals can be adjusted, different counters selected for charting, charts can be edited, snapshots printed, and data exported to a spreadsheet or database program for further processing.

▸ Setting Alerts on Input Log Files

To set alerts in an input log file:

1. Select Data From from the Options menu in the Alert view.
2. Select a log file name from the local computer or from the network.

3. From the Edit menu, select
   - Add To Alert to select computers and counters to relog with alerts.
   - Edit Alert Entry to revise selection settings.
   - Delete Alert to remove any counters not wanted.
   - Time Window to revise start and stop points.
4. Select Alert from the Options menu to set the update-time interval.
5. From the File menu, select
   - Save Alert Settings As to update the current alert settings file or to create a new alert settings file.
   - Export Alert to export data to a spreadsheet or database program.

Help Files ▼ Alerts can be set in log files to determine where values exceed or fall below specified alert values. The Add To Alert dialog box will list counters for all objects originally selected for logging.

▶ Relogging Input Log Files

To relog an input log file:

1. Select Data From from the Options menu in the Log view.
2. Select a log file name from the local computer or from the network.
3. From the Edit menu, select
   - Add To Log to select computer and objects to relog.
   - Delete From Log to remove any unwanted objects.
   - Time Window to revise start and stop points.

4. Select Log from the Options menu to change the log file name, the logging interval, or to start or stop relogging.
5. From the File menu, select
   - Save Log Settings As to update the current log settings file or to create a new log settings file.
   - Export Log to export the log settings to a spreadsheet or database program.

Help Files ▼ A file name must be selected and objects chosen for logging before the Relog button will be enabled. When relogging, large log files can be condensed by relogging with a longer time interval for all or selected objects in the original log file, or by changing the start and stop times and relogging only the data within the interval. If an existing log file is selected for output, the data will be appended to the file.

▶ Creating Reports from Log Files

To create a report from an input log file:

1. Select Data From from the Options menu in the Report view.
2. Select a log file name from the local computer or from the network.
3. From the Edit menu, select
   - Add To Report to select computers and counters to display in the report.
   - Delete From Report to remove unwanted counters.
   - Time Window to change the start and stop points.

4. From the File menu, select

   - Save Report Settings As to update the current report settings file or to create a new report settings file.
   - Export Report to export the data to a spreadsheet or database program.

Help Files ▼ Reports can be created from existing log files in the same fashion as with current activity values. However, when reports are created from log data, the values reported show counter values for the selected time interval rather than current values.

THE RESCUE PAGES: Using the Performance Monitor

I can't monitor disk usage. I've loaded a half-dozen disk activities in the Performance Monitor, but all I get is a flat-line trace like my disk was dead.

Well, be glad this isn't the Emergency Room. Anyway, your disk isn't dead, it's just that you haven't hooked up the EKG yet—or the computer equivalent thereof. The solution begins by calling the Command Prompt (DOS shell) and entering the command **DISKPERF -Y**. Then the bad news—you need to log off and restart, because the disk performance counters have to be activated on start-up.

Of course, you might go back to the Performance Monitor and save your profile before exiting—this, at least, will save you a little bit of trouble when you restart.

I hid the menu to save space. How do I get back to it?

Double-click anywhere in the graph on report or chart, and so on, to switch the view. The menu should come back into view. Double-click again to restore the previous view.

The graph moves too fast—I'm having trouble figuring out what's going on.

A couple of solutions here.

First, reduce the sample rate to produce a slower graph. Of course, you'll probably need to adjust the scale factor to compensate—for example, if you change the sample rate from 1 to 10 seconds, you may need to

change the scale multiplier from 1 to 0.1 to compensate. Remember, each trace has its own scale factor assignment, while the sample rate is global.

A second solution is to write the data to a file. Then you can call-in the log at leisure and select the time period to view and look at it as long as you wish...and from several angles as well. For long-term processes, this is probably the best choice, since you can show a longer or shorter scale period. Of course, you may run out of disk space....

One trace seems to be consistently off-scale—at least it always seems to be at the top of the grid, and I can't tell if there are any variations.

Definitely sounds like a case for changing the display scale. Begin by double-clicking on the trace in the Legend window (at the bottom) to bring up the Edit Chart Line dialog box. The default scale is 1.0, but no, you cannot enter the value of your choice such as 0.3. You can, however, pick off a value from the pull-down scale list. Since the line seems to be off-scale, try using a scale factor of 0.1. The scale factor runs from 0.000001 to 100000.0, but only adjusts by magnitude factors.

CHAPTER

15

HELP! The Backup Utility

The Backup utility is used to operate a tape backup to save and restore files to and from NTFS, FAT, and HPFS file system hard drives. Unlike DOS tape backup utilities, however, the Windows NT Backup utility is multitasking and does not tie up the entire computer system during backup operations. Supported capabilities include

- Selecting files for backup or restoration by volume, directory, or individual file
- Viewing detailed file information including size and modification date
- Ensuring correct backup and restoration by a verification pass
- Performing normal, copy, incremental, differential, and daily copy backups
- Copying multiple backup sets to a tape
- Appending new backup sets or replacing older backup sets with newer ones
- Spanning multiple tapes with backup sets or files
- Creating batch files to automate repeated backups
- Reviewing backup sets, individual files, and directories to select files for restoration
- Controlling restoration destination drive and directories

- Controlling overwrites on restoration
- Saving backup log information as a disk file
- Viewing tape operations in the Event Viewer

Principal topics covered in this chapter include

- Configuring the Backup utility
- Backing up disk files to tape
- Restoring tape files to disk
- Tape maintenance

Configuring the Backup Utility

▶ Selecting Tape Drives

To switch between tape backup devices:

1. Select Hardware Setup from the Operations menu.
2. Select a tape backup device from the Hardware Setup dialog box.
3. Select OK.

Help Files ▼ If more than one tape backup device is available, the Hardware Setup command can be used to select the desired active device. Windows NT supports both high-capacity SCSI tape drives for 4mm DAT, 8mm and $^1/_4$-inch drives as well as the less expensive but popular minicartridge drives. More than one tape drive may be mounted on a system, but only one tape drive can be selected as active.

When Windows NT boots, the system automatically checks for and initializes the tape hardware. However, the physical tape drive must be

turned on before starting Windows NT for the drivers to be loaded properly. For internal tape drives, of course, this presents no problems, but for external tape drives, power must be supplied before or at the same time the computer is powered up.

Concealing or Displaying the Status Bar and Tool Bar

To conceal or display the status bar:

- Select the Status Bar option from the View menu (see Figure 15.1).

To conceal or display the tool bar:

- Select the Toolbar option from the View menu (see Figure 15.1).

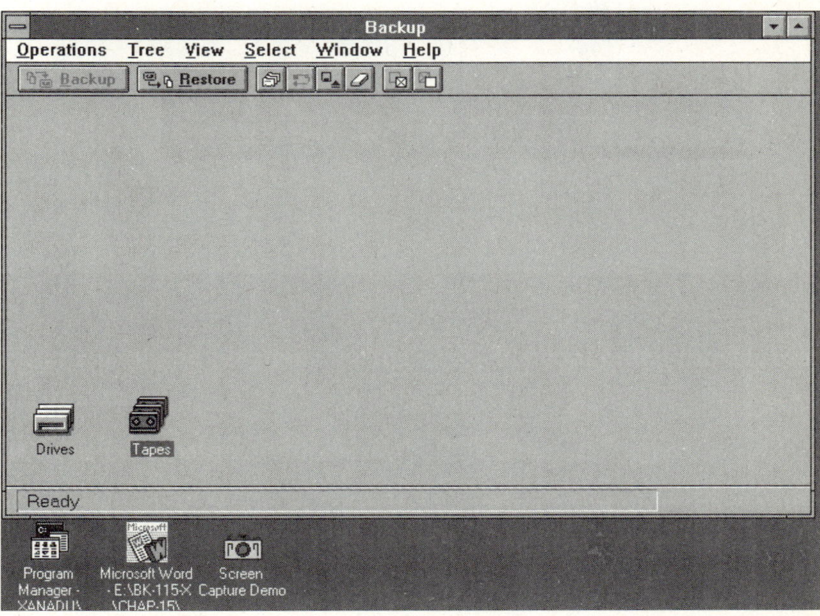

Figure 15.1
The Backup utility with both the status bar and tool bar

Help Files ▼ A check mark appears next to either option when selected; the status bar or tool bar is displayed or hidden according to the selection.

The Tree, View, and Window menus in the Backup utility offer commands similar to File Manager for selecting and displaying drives, directories and files. The tool bar at the top of the window offers easy access to commonly used commands, while the status bar at the bottom of the window offers command descriptions and program status information.

▸ Changing Fonts

To change the font used by Backup to display file and directory lists:

1. Select Font from the View menu. The Font dialog box shown in Figure 15.2 appears.

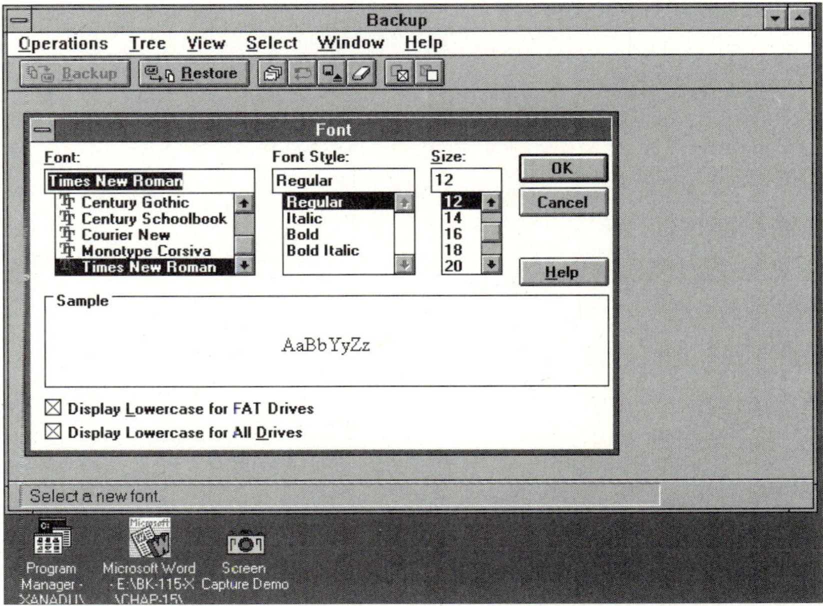

Figure 15.2
The Font dialog box

2. Select the font, style, and size desired. The text in the Sample box reflects the selection.
3. Clear the Lowercase check boxes to display only uppercase characters.
4. Select OK to save the font selection. The text in all directory windows is displayed using the new font.

Backing Up Disk Files to Tape

▶ Opening and Updating the Drives Window

To reopen and update the Drives window:

1. Double-click on the Drives icon in the main Backup window or select the Drives window from the Window menu.

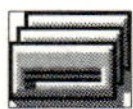

2. Select Refresh from the Window menu to update the information in the Drives window.

Help Files ▼ The Drives window is normally open when the Backup utility is started. The Drives window can, however, be minimized and reopened when required. Also, the backup operator can leave the Backup program, start File Manager to connect to another network drive and then return to Backup. However, Backup will require the Drives window to be updated before the additional network drive(s) can be recognized.

Backing Up All the Files

To back up all the files on a disk:

1. Select the disk drive to back up from the Drives window.
2. Select the Check command from the Select menu.
   - Or click the Check button on the tool bar.

   - Or select the check box for the drive in the Drives window.
3. Select the Backup command from the Operations menu.
   - Or select the Backup button from the tool bar.

Help Files ▼ All files on a disk can be selected by selecting the drive in the Drives window. However, when a disk drive is selected, Backup will not access any files or directories that the user does not have security access to read. This includes files hidden in a directory without read permissions (the directory will be displayed with an exclamation mark on the file icon). When files are backed up, all file attributes, including permissions, are preserved.

Selectively Backing Up Files

To back up files selectively:

1. Double-click the drive icon or letter in the Drives window to open the Disk File Selection window shown in Figure 15.3.

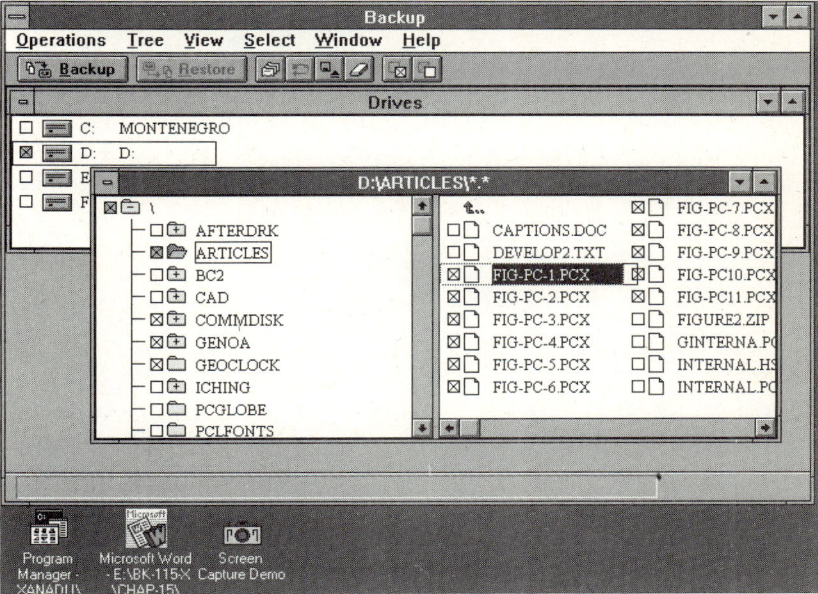

Figure 15.3
The Disk File Selection window

2. To select a block of files, begin by selecting (highlighting) the first file name, and then:
   - Press and hold the Shift key while selecting the last contiguous file name.
   - Drag the mouse to the last contiguous file name.
   - Press and hold the Ctrl key while selecting individual file names.
3. Select the Check command from the Select menu or the tool bar's Check button to mark the selected files' check boxes.

4. To undo file selections, select the UnCheck command from the Select menu or select the tool bar's UnCheck button.

All selections will be cleared.

5. Select the Backup command from the Operations menu or the Backup button on the tool bar.

Backup

Help Files ▼ For selective backups, the Disk and Tape File Selection windows use the same organization as File Manager, including the same view options for tree structures and directory and file lists. To select only a few files, the fastest choice is to select the check boxes for each file name. When only a few files are selected, the corresponding drive and directory check boxes are shown with a gray background.

▶ Setting Tape Options

To set the tape volume options:

1. After selecting the disk drives or files for backup, select the Backup command from the Operations menu to open the Backup Information dialog box shown in Figure 15.4. The upper section of the dialog box provides information about the tape currently in the tape drive.
2. Select the backup operation type from the Operation box:
   - Select Append to append the new backup set after the last backup set on the tape.
   - Select Replace to overwrite any existing backup information on the tape, that is, erasing the tape.
3. Enter a name for the tape in the Tape Name box. The maximum name length is 32 characters.
4. Select the Verify After Backup check box to use a second pass to verify an accurate backup.

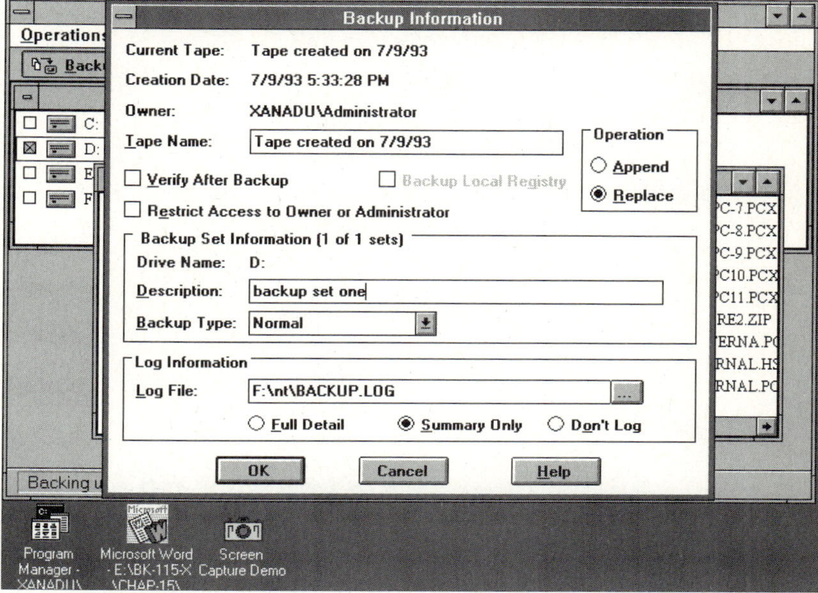

Figure 15.4
The Backup Information dialog box

5. Select the Backup Local Registry check box to add a copy of the Windows NT registry files to the backup set.

6. To limit tape access, select the Restrict Access To Owner Or Administrator check box.

▶ Setting the Backup Set Options

To set the Backup set options:

1. Enter a description for the backup set in the Backup Set Information edit box.

2. Open the Backup Type list box to select the backup operation type.

Help Files ▼ The lower section of the Backup Information dialog box—see Figure 15.4—shows how many backup sets have been made. If more than one disk drive has been selected or files have been selected from more than one drive, each drive will be backed up as a separate set. Use the scroll bar to move between sets, entering separate descriptions from each, and optionally, selecting different backup types for each drive.

▶ Setting the Backup Log Options

To set the Backup log options:

1. Select the logging option desired or select Don't Log.
2. Enter the name in the Log File box for a text file where completed tape operations will be recorded. Alternately, use the Browse button (at the end of the Log File edit box) to select a log file name.
3. Select OK to display the Backup Status dialog box and begin the backup process.

Help Files ▼ The Backup Log option creates a log file containing either a summary or full details of all backup operations.

▶ Checking the Backup Status

To view the Backup Status dialog box and control backup operations:

1. Select the OK button from the Backup Information dialog box. The backup operation begins as the Backup Status dialog box appears.
2. Select the Abort button to interrupt a backup before completion, and then select Yes from the Backup Abort message to confirm. If the current file being backed up is less than 1Mb, backup for the file will be completed. If the current file is larger than 1MB, a query message will ask whether to stop immediately and show the present file as corrupted, or to finish backup for the current file.

Help Files ▼ The Backup Status dialog box shows an active status area—the names of the drive, directory, and file(s) being backed up. The Summary section shows a log of the major operations including the completion status of the operations. If a backup operation reaches the end of a tape before completion, the Insert New Tape dialog box appears prompting for the insertion of a new tape.

If the status area shows any corrupt files, a list is kept in a file titled CORRUPT.LST. Before attempting to restore a tape, check the CORRUPT.LST file and then delete it. Otherwise a message will appear warning about the existence of corrupt files whenever restoration is attempted from this tape or any other.

▶ Backups from Batch Files

A command-line batch file can be created to automatically back up one or more drives on a regular basis: The batch command parameters offer essentially the same functionality provided by the Backup utility's graphics interface.

The command format used is

```
NTBACKUP [operation pathnames [options]]
```

The *operation* parameter would, of course, be simply BACKUP. The *pathnames* parameter takes the form

```
d:[\directory_path\...]
```

The *options* parameters include Mode, Verify, Restrict_Access, Description, Backup_Local_Registry, Backup_Type, and Log_Options. Individually, these can be entered as shorthand, thus:

Mode	/A[ppend] (default is overwrite)
Verify	/V[erify]
Restrict_Access	/R[estrict]
Description	/D[escription] "*text_description*"
Backup_Local_Registry	/B
Backup_Type	/T[ype] *typename*. Valid types are Normal, Copy, Incremental, Differential, and Daily_Copy.
Log_Options	/L[ogfile] "*log_filename*"
log exceptions only	/E[xceptions] "*exceptions_filename*"

Restoring Tape Files to Disk

▶ Opening the Tapes Window

To open the Tapes window:

- Double-click the Tapes icon in the main Backup window.

Or:

- Select the Tapes window from the Window menu.

The Tapes window shown in Figure 15.5 appears.

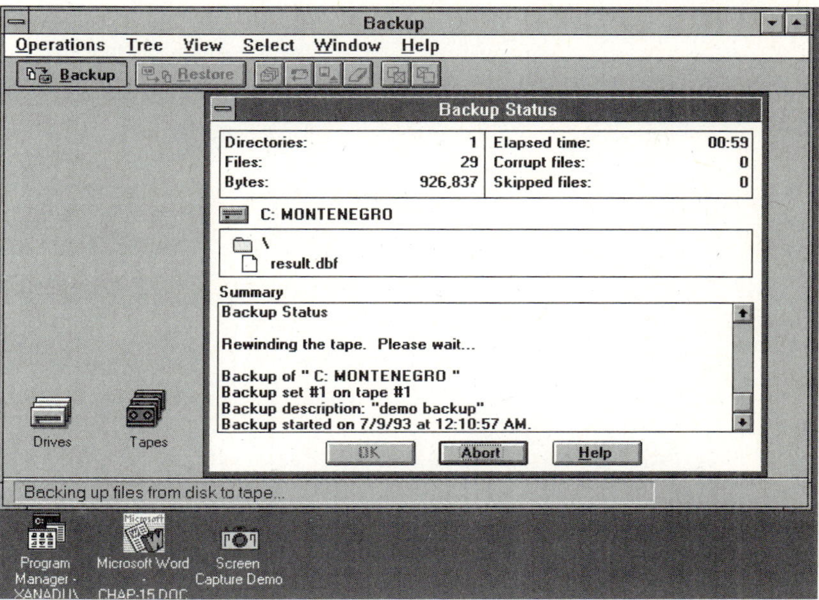

Figure 15.5
The Tapes window

The tape name appears in the left pane of the Tapes window while the right panel shows

- Drive ID
- Backup set number
- Tape number/number in set
- Backup type
- Date and time of backup
- Backup description

Help Files ▼ Normally, when Backup is called, the Tapes window is closed. Once opened, the Tapes window shows the backup sets. Selections include

restoring the current tape, restoring one or more backup sets, or restoring individual files. Catalog information is maintained on the tape corresponding to a backup set. Family sets—sets of two or more related tapes—have the catalog information on the last tape in the set.

Loading Catalogs

To load catalogs for tapes and backup sets:

1. Select the tape or backup set from the Tapes window.
2. Double-click on the tape's icon.
   - Or highlight the tape's icon and select Catalog from the Operations menu.
   - Or highlight the tape's icon and select the Catalog button from the tool bar.

3. The Backup Status dialog box appears—see Figure 15.6—offering the option of aborting the cataloging process.
4. When the catalog process is completed, a list of backup sets appears in the right half of the Tapes window. If the tape contains multiple backup sets, question marks appear on the set icons showing that the individual catalogs have not been loaded.
5. Double-click on a backup set's icon to load the set's catalog of directories and files.
   - Or highlight the backup set and select Catalog from the Operations menu.
   - Or highlight the backup set and select the Catalog button from the tool bar.

6. If the backup set spans more than one tape, a prompt appears—see Figure 15.7—requesting a new tape.

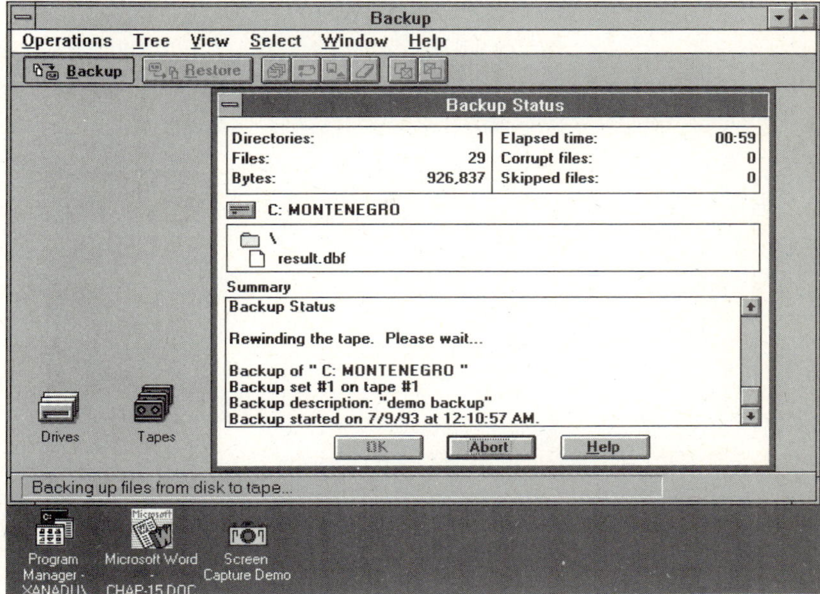

Figure 15.6
The Backup Status dialog box

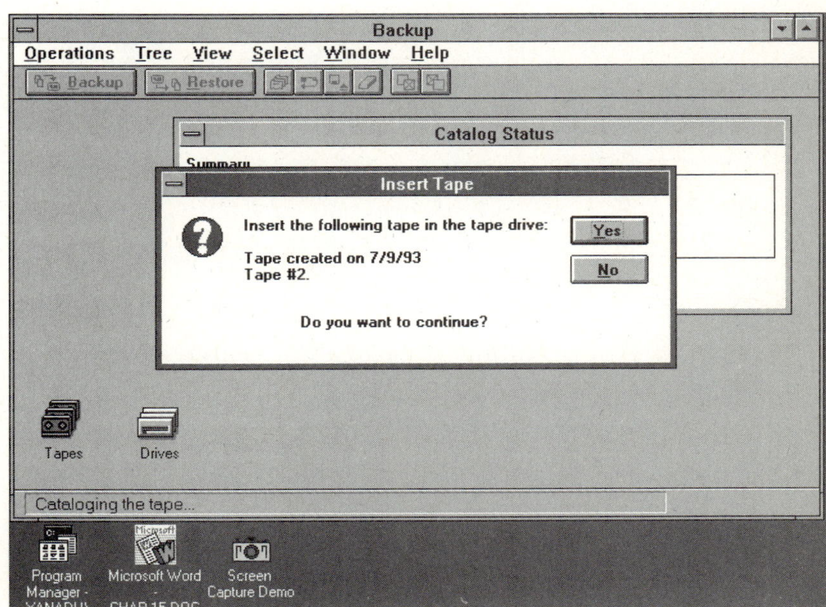

Figure 15.7
The Insert Tape prompt

7. After the tape is searched, a complete directory and file list for the backup set appears in the Tape File Selection window, while the set icon in the Tapes window shows a plus sign indicating that it has been cataloged. Corrupt files (files containing an error) and their directories are marked by an icon with a red "X."

Help Files ▼ When a new tape is inserted in the drive, only the first backup set is shown in the Tapes window's right panel. To redisplay the entire tape, load the tape's catalog to show a list of backup sets. To view files in each backup set, load the individual catalogs for each backup set.

▸ Restoring Tapes or Backup Sets

To restore a tape or individual backup sets:

1. Load the tape's catalog of backup sets.
2. Select the check box for the desired tape in the Tapes window.
   - Or select the tape and select the Check button from the tool bar.

3. To restore one or more backup sets, select the check box for each backup set from the right panel of the Tapes window.

When a tape has multiple backup sets but only certain sets are selected, the corresponding tape check box shows a gray interior.

To select multiple backup sets:

1. Select the first backup set.
2. Press and hold the Shift key while selecting the last contiguous backup set.
   - Or drag the mouse to the last contiguous backup set.
   - Or press and hold the Ctrl key while selecting (clicking) non-contiguous backup sets.

3. To select backup sets, click on the backup set's check box.
    - Or highlight the backup set and select the Check command from the Select menu.
    - Or highlight the backup set and select the Check button from the tool bar.

To undo individual selections:

- Click a second time on any selected check box.

To undo all selections:

- Select the UnCheck command from the Select menu.

Or:

- Select the UnCheck button from the Select menu.

To restore backup set(s):

- Select the Restore command from the Operations menu.
- Select the Restore button from the tool bar.

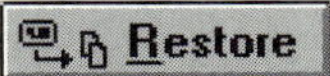

Help Files ▼ Procedures for selecting files to restore are similar to selecting files for backup. However, when a tape is loaded, initially only the first backup set on the tape is displayed and the tape's catalog must be loaded to display all backup sets. If Restore is selected without first loading the tape catalog, only the first backup set on the tape will be restored.

▶ Restoring Individual Files

To restore individual files from a backup set:

1. Load the desired backup set catalog from the Tapes window. The catalog of directories and files appears in a Tape File Selection window as shown in Figure 15.8.

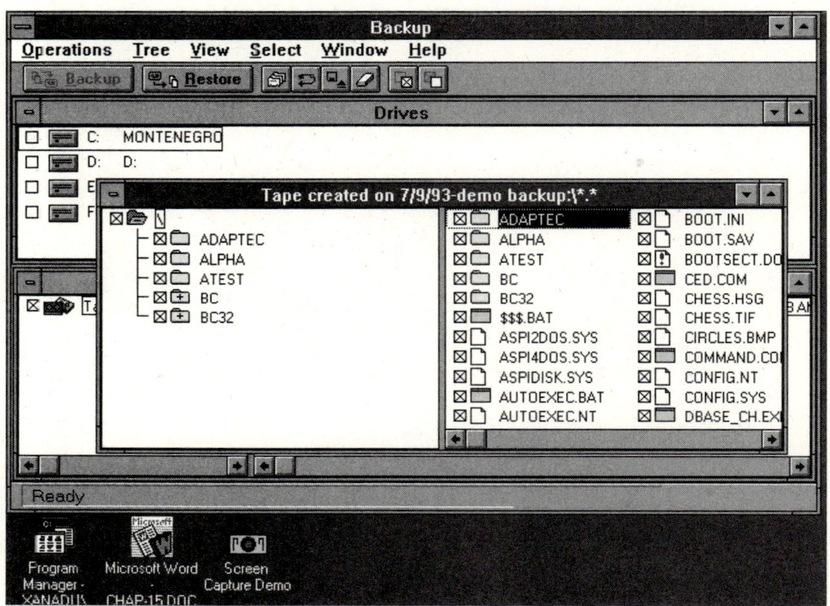

Figure 15.8
The Tape File Selection window

2. Select individual files to be restored.
3. Select the Restore command from the Operations menu.
   - Or select the Restore button from the tool bar.

To select files:

- Click on the check box by each file name.
- Or highlight the file name and select the Check command from the Select menu.

- Or highlight the file name and select the Check button from the tool bar.

To select individual files for restoration:

- Click on the check boxes by individual file names.

Or:

- Press and hold the Ctrl key while selecting individual file names using the Check command or Check button.

To select a group of contiguous files:

- Select the first file name, then press and hold the Shift key while:
  - Selecting the last contiguous file name.
  - Or dragging the mouse to the last contiguous file name.

To uncheck individual selections:

When individual files are selected, the corresponding drive and directory check boxes are also shown checked but with a gray background.

- Click a second time on individual selections.
- Or highlight the item and select the UnCheck command from the Select menu.
- Or highlight the item and select the UnCheck button from the tool bar.

To uncheck all selections:

- Select the files or group of files to uncheck and
  - Select the UnCheck button from the tool bar.

  - Or select the UnCheck command from the Select menu.

Help Files ▼ Procedures for selecting files to restore are similar to selecting files for backup. However, when a tape is loaded, initially only the first backup set on the tape is displayed, and the tape's catalog must be loaded to display all backup sets. If Restore is selected without first loading the tape catalog, only the first backup set on the tape will be restored.

▶ Building Partial Tape and Backup Set Catalogs

To build a catalog from a tape lacking a complete on-tape catalog:

1. Insert the tape in the tape drive.
2. Load the available on-tape catalog information. The Backup Status dialog box offers the option of aborting the catalog process.

Help Files ▼ If a backup operation has spanned more than one tape, on restoration you will be prompted to insert the last tape in the set to load the catalog information and a list of all backup sets and their locations. If the last tape in the family set is missing or damaged, a partial tape catalog must be created by inserting the available tapes and loading the catalog of backup sets from each. To locate specific directories or files from a backup spanning several tapes, it may also be necessary to load each backup set's catalog of directories and files.

Files can also be restored from tapes that were not created using the Windows NT Backup program as long as the tape was created using the Microsoft/Maynard Tape Format (MTF). The tape may not, however, have the full on-tape catalog (OTC) information that is required by the Windows NT Backup program, or the tape device may not support creating an on-tape catalog.

If no catalog information is available, the entire tape is searched—first, for backup sets, and then a second time, slowly, to determine the contents for each backup set.

▶ Selecting Restore Options

The Restore Information dialog box—see Figure 15.9—appears when the Restore button or Restore command is selected.

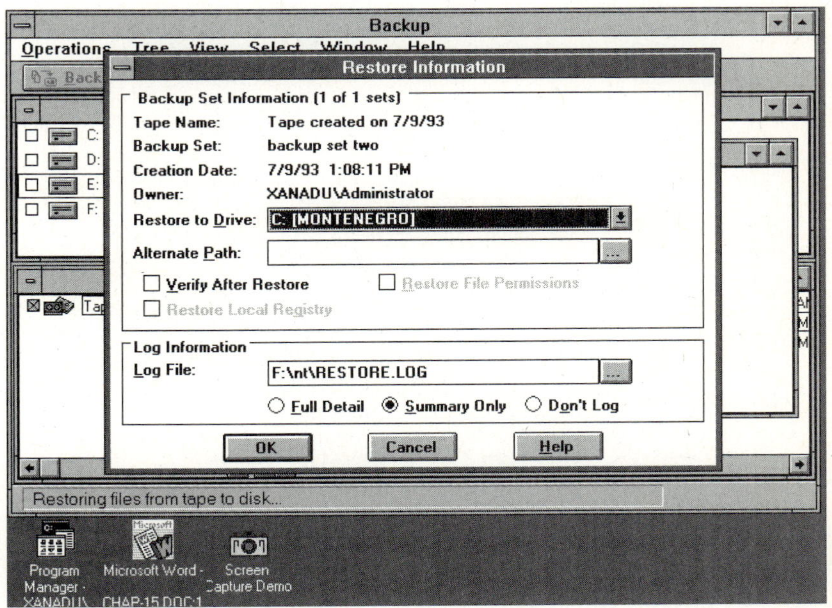

Figure 15.9
The Restore Information dialog box

To set restore options:

1. Select a drive destination for restored files from the Restore to Drive list box.
2. An alternate directory path can be specified by:
   - Entering a directory path in the Alternate Path edit box.

- Or clicking the Browse button (right) and selecting a directory path from the Browse Directory dialog box.

3. Select the Verify After Restore check box to verify the contents of restored disk files against the tape copies.
4. Select the Restore Local Registry check box to restore Registry files. A log off/log on is required before the restored information takes effect. (Not used with FAT drives.)
5. Select the Restore File Permissions check box to restore permissions information along with the restored files. By default, restored files inherit permissions from the directory where they're restored. (Not used on FAT drives.)

▸ Selecting Log Options

To set the log options:

1. Select the desired log type—Full Detail or Summary Only—or select Don't Log.
2. Enter a drive, directory, and log file name in the Log File edit box, or use the Browse button to select a log file directory and name.
3. Select OK. The Restore Status dialog box appears and the restore process begins.

▸ Restoring from Tape

To begin restoring files:

- Select OK from the Restore Information dialog box. The Restore Status dialog box—see Figure 15.10—appears and the restore operation begins.

To abort restoration:

1. Select the Abort button from the Restore Status dialog box.
2. Select Yes from the Restore Abort prompt.

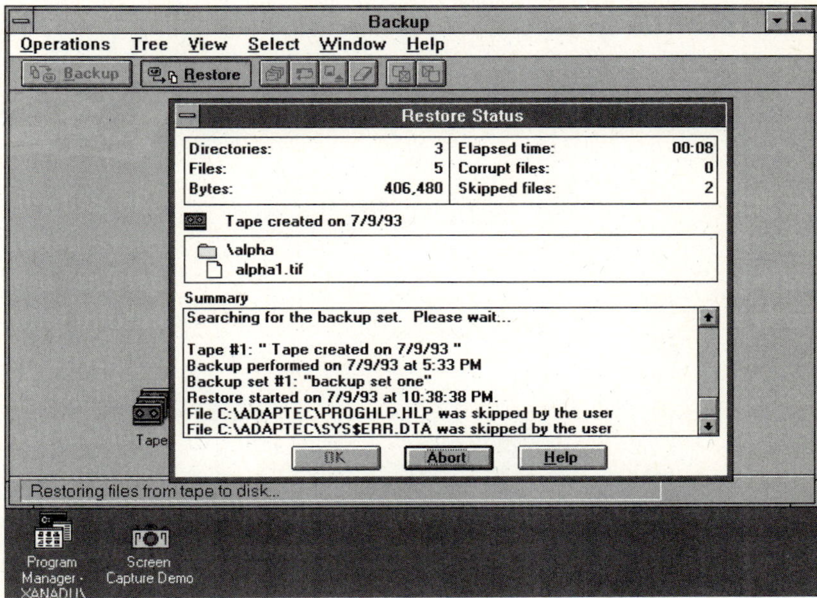

Figure 15.10
The Restore Status dialog box

Help Files ▼ The Restore Status dialog box consists of an active status area reporting the names of the drive, directory, and files being restored and a Summary section showing an operations log.

If the end of the tape is reached before the restoration is completed, the Insert New Tape dialog box will prompt for the next tape in the series.

If restoration is aborted, the current file restoration will be completed if less than 1MB remains. Otherwise, a message requests permission to finish restoring the current file.

Tape Maintenance

Erasing Tapes

To erase a tape:

1. Select the Erase Tape option from the Operations menu.
   - Or select the Erase Tape button from the tool bar.

2. Select either Quick Erase or Secure Erase from the Erase Tape dialog box.
3. A cautionary message reminds you that all information on the tape will be destroyed, adding the name of the tape and the date created. Select Continue to proceed.

Help Files The Erase Tape command erases the entire tape. The Quick Erase option rewrites the tape header, while the Secure Erase option rewrites the entire tape (slow, but better security).

Retensioning Tapes

To retension a tape:

- Select Retension Tape from the Operations menu.
- Select the Retension button from the tool bar.

Help Files ▼ Retensioning a tape executes a fast forward to the end of the tape, and then rewinds the entire tape in a single, continuous operation, thus ensuring that the entire tape is evenly wound and will run smoothly during record or playback.

To minimize tape slippage, manufacturers recommend retensioning $^1/_4$-inch tapes every 20 uses. Since 4mm and 8mm tapes do not require retensioning, this option is not offered for 4mm and 8mm drives.

▶ Rewinding Tapes

To rewind a tape:

- Select the Eject Tape option from the Operations menu.

Or:

- Select the Rewind/Eject button from the tool bar.

Help Files ▼ While the Eject option isn't supported by all tape drives, it is a good idea to rewind tapes before removing them from the drive.

THE RESCUE PAGES: Using the Backup Utility

I have a high-capacity tape backup drive on my computer, but Windows NT doesn't seem to have a driver that recognizes it.

Unfortunately, there are no certain or easy solutions to this problem. You can contact the tape drive manufacturers for OEM drivers for Windows NT, or you can see if any of the provided drivers—which are not well identified—will work with your tape. If neither of these offers a solution, however, your only real solution will be to use the FlexBoot utility and operate your tape backup using OEM-supplied software from DOS.

A caution, however, is also in order: If you are using the NTFS file system on any drives, these drives will not be visible from DOS and cannot be backed up using the DOS tape utility.

I had a backup tape containing several incremental backups, but when I restored the tape, the only files restored were from an early backup.

Before restoring any tape, your first step should be to load the tape catalog to show all backup sets on the tape. When a tape is initially inserted in the drive, only the first backup set is shown. If the tape is restored without logging the catalog, this is the only set that will be restored.

I'm doing a backup, but the current tape is full and I don't have any blanks. What now? Can I quit without losing what did get saved?

In a word, yes…you can. If you respond to the Insert Tape prompt with a No, the backup will be interrupted at the current point. When you restore from this tape, however, you may get a warning about a corrupt file (a file incompletely backed up) or about a missing file catalog (which would have been written to the last volume in the backup), and you may need to generate a new catalog (see "Building Partial Tape and Backup Set Catalogs").

However, the files that have been written to the tape should be secure.

I have backup tapes that were formatted by my old tape software. Will these work with Windows NT's Backup utility?

If Windows NT recognizes the tape drive, it shouldn't have any trouble with the tape format. However, if there's any question, you can always reformat the tape.

I have backup tapes that were written by tape software operating from DOS. Can I restore these under Windows NT?

That's a good question, but the answers aren't so simple. The best bet is to try logging the tape using Backup. If Backup can recognize the tape directory—or if Backup can create a tape directory—then you should be safe restoring files from these tapes.

On the other hand, if Backup identifies the tape as "Foreign Tape," then the odds are pretty bad. If you really need to restore files from this tape, your best bet is to go back to DOS, restore the files, and then back them up again using Backup.

For example, a tape created using Colorado Memory System's (CMS's) software can not be read by Windows NT's Backup utility (and vice versa) even though both are using exactly the same hardware (tape drive). For CMS's Tape utility, the Windows NT backup tape is simply reported as corrupted or invalid. Likewise, under Windows NT, the Backup utility reports Tape's cartridge as a "Foreign Tape."

Can I run my old tape backup software under Windows NT?

Sorry, but probably not! You should certainly feel free to experiment, but the odds are not good. For example, Colorado Memory System's CBW (CMS Backup for Windows) in theory should execute under Windows NT, but actually comes up with a fault error and cannot be executed. A separate attempt to execute a DOS-based tape software package for a 700MB tape drive simply reports that no tape hardware can be found at all. Both packages, of course, execute flawlessly from, respectively, Windows 3.1 and DOS, but neither was able to execute under Windows NT.

CHAPTER

16

HELP! Disk Administrator

The Disk Administrator utility provides the tools necessary for managing disk resources, replacing DOS-based disk management tools such as FDISK, and providing new functions not previously supplied. Capabilities offered by Disk Administrator include tools to:

- Create and delete partitions on a hard disk and create or delete logical drives within an extended partition
- Read disk status information including partition size and unformatted free space available for creating additional partitions
- Read status information for Windows NT volumes including drive-letter assignments, volume labels, file system types, and sizes
- Reassign drive letters
- Create and delete volume sets
- Extend volumes and volume sets
- Create and delete stripe sets with or without parity

Topics covered in this chapter include

- Starting and quitting Disk Administrator
- Organizing the Disk Manager screen
- Partitioning disks
- Working with volumes and volume sets
- Working with stripe sets

Starting and Quitting Disk Administrator

▶ Starting Disk Administrator

To start Disk Administrator:

- Double-click the Disk Administrator icon in the Administrative Tools group.

Disk Administrator can only be opened by members of the Administrators group.

Or:

- Enter **WINDISK** or **START WINDISK** from the Command Prompt.

The Disk Administrator screen is shown in Figure 16.1.

▶ Quitting Disk Administrator

To quit Disk Administrator:

- Select Exit from the Partition menu.

Or:

- Select Close from the Control menu.

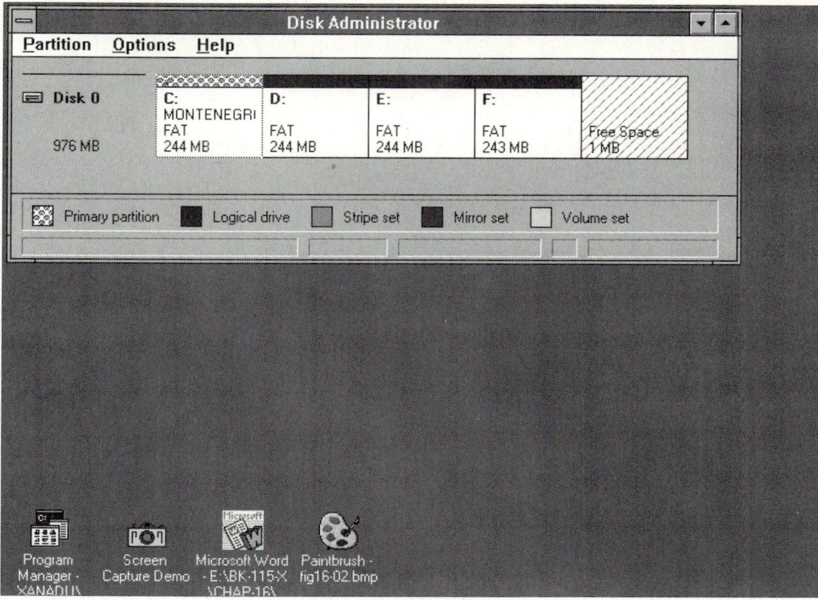

Figure 16.1
The Disk Administrator screen

Help Files ▼ Disk Administrator displays a scrollable graphic representation of the physical disk drives connected to the local computer together with their partitions. The status bar at the base of the window offers basic information about partitions, while a color-coded legend at the top of the status bar identifies partition color codes and patterns. All Disk Administrator commands are provided with context-sensitive help.

On exit, if any significant changes have been made to the disk partitions or drive letter assignments, Disk Administrator will display a reminder that emphasizes any irreversible changes such as deleting a partition and requests confirmation before saving the changes. The actual updates and changes to the disk drives are made only on exit and following confirmation. Select No to exit without changes or select Cancel to remain in Disk Administrator without changes.

On exit with confirmed changes, Disk Administrator begins executing the requested modifications. When the disk drives have been successfully updated, it displays a message that the completed changes will require a system reboot. Click the OK button and a complete system shutdown will be initiated, closing all open applications. When shutdown is completed, the system will be rebooted.

Any new volumes will be accessible following reboot and may then be formatted and labeled.

Organizing the Disk Manager Screen

▶ Displaying or Concealing the Status Bar and Legend

To display or conceal the status bar and legend:

- Select the Status Bar or Legend options from the Options menu. A check mark appears next to each when enabled.

Help Files ▼ Both the status bar and legend are displayed by default, but one or both may be hidden to provide additional display space for data on multiple disk drives.

▶ Selecting Colors and Patterns to Identify Disk Volumes

To change colors and patterns for the disk volumes:

1. Select Color And Patterns from the Options menu. The Colors And Patterns dialog box is shown in Figure 16.2.

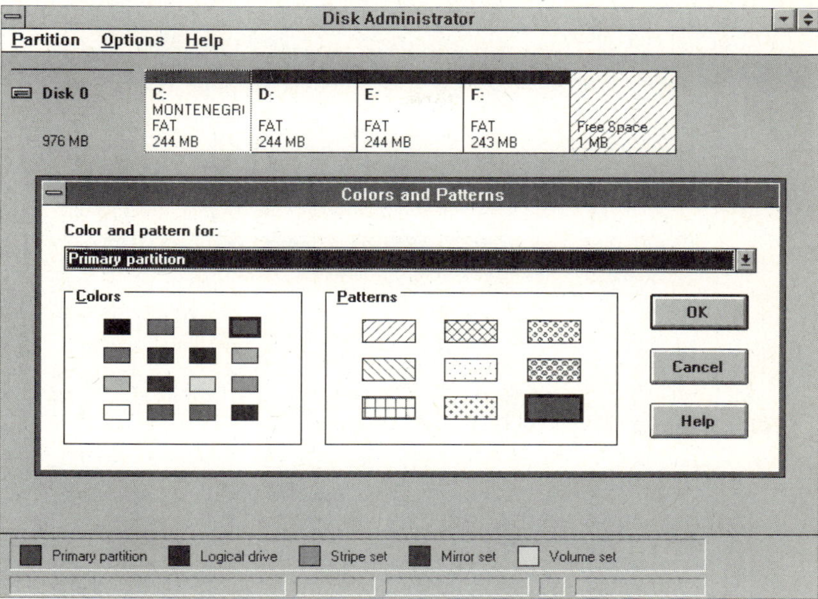

Figure 16.2
The Colors And Patterns dialog box

2. Select the volume type to change from the pull-down list box.
3. Select a new color and pattern from the Colors And Patterns boxes—selected colors and patterns are identified by heavy black outlines.
4. Select OK.

Help Files ▼ Initially, the default pattern for all partitions is solid. Both colors and patterns can be modified for the five partition types shown in the legend bar. The Free Space section shown with a striped background in Figure 16.2 is not modifiable.

▸ Changing How Regions Are Displayed

To change how regions are displayed:

1. Select Region Display from the Options menu. The Region Display Options dialog box shown in Figure 16.3 appears.

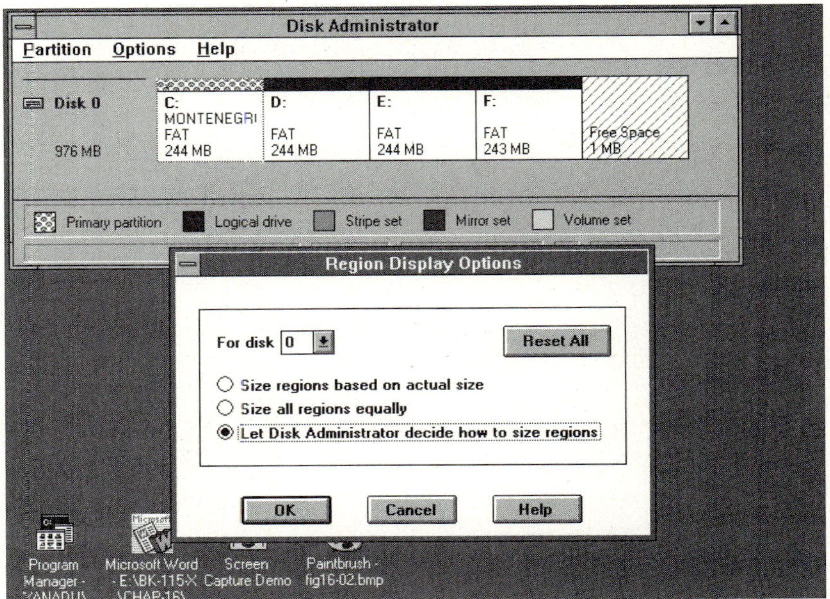

Figure 16.3
The Region Display Options dialog box

2. If you have more than one physical disk, use the For Disk pull-down list to select the number of the disk to change.
3. Select a display option for the regions.
4. Repeat steps 2 and 3 for each disk.
5. Select the Reset All button to allow the Disk Administrator to decide how to display all the disks.
6. Select OK.

Help Files ▼ Because different physical drives may have a wide variety of capacities and a wide variety of partition sizes, each physical drive may be displayed proportionally according to size, or with all partitions equally sized. Or you may allow Disk Administrator to decide which format to use.

For multiple hard-disk drives, the total lengths of the bars representing each disk are proportional to the sizes of the disks. The smallest single disk, however, will never be less than one-fourth the size of the largest.

Partitioning Disks

▶ Creating Primary Partitions

To create a primary partition:

1. Select the disk where the partition will be created.
2. Select an area of free space from the Disk bar by clicking on the area.
3. Select Create from the Partition menu. The Create Primary Partition dialog box—Figure 16.4—displays the minimum and maximum sizes permitted for a primary partition.
4. Enter the size desired in the Create Primary Partition dialog box.
5. Select OK.

▶ Creating an Extended Partition

Only one extended partition can be created on each disk drive.

To create an extended partition:

1. Select the disk where the partition will be created.
2. Select an area of free space.

Disk Administrator
Partition Options Help
Disk 0 976 MB
C: MONTENEGRI FAT 244 MB | D: FAT 244 MB | E: FAT 244 MB | F: FAT 243 MB | Free Space 1 MB
Primary partition | Logical drive | Stripe set | Mirror set | Volume set
Free space | 1 MB

Create Primary Partition
Minimum size for the partition is 1 MB
Maximum size for the partition is 1 MB
Create partition of size 1 MB
OK | Cancel | Help

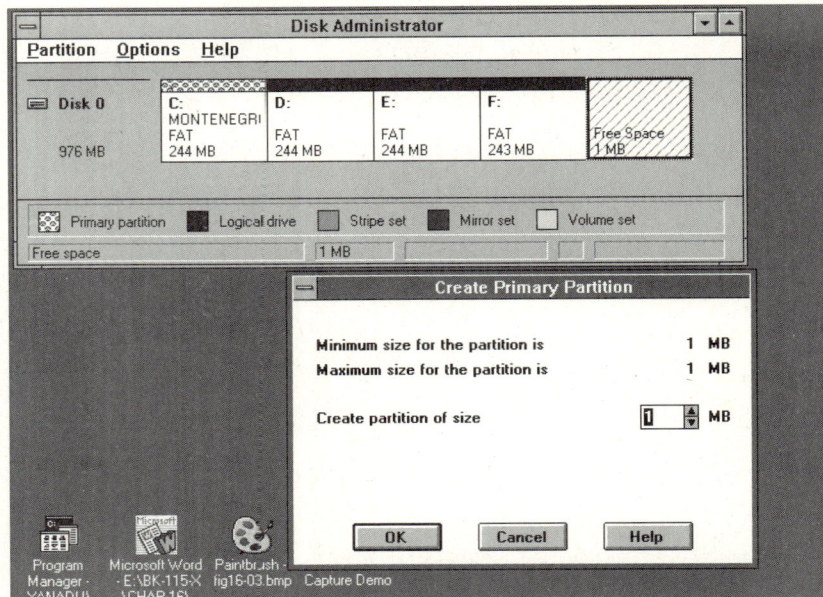

Figure 16.4
The Create Primary Partition dialog box

3. Select Create Extend from the Partition menu. The Create Extended Partition dialog box—similar to Figure 16.4—displays the minimum and maximum sizes permitted for an extended partition.
4. Enter the size desired in the Create Extended Partition dialog box.
5. Select OK.

Help Files ▼ An extended partition can be used to create multiple logical disk drives or to create volume sets or other fault-tolerant volume types.

Creating Logical Drives in an Extended Partition

To create a logical drive in an extended partition:

1. Select a drive with an extended partition.
2. Select an area of free space.
3. Select Create from the Partition menu. The Create Logical Drive dialog box—similar to Figure 16.4, preceding—shows the minimum and maximum sizes permitted for a logical drive.
4. Enter the size desired in the Create Logical Drive dialog box.
5. Repeat steps 2 through 4 to create additional logical drives.
6. Select OK.

Formatting Partitions

To format a partition:

1. If Disk Manager has been used to create partitions, exit from Disk Manager (so the new partitions can actually be created) and allow the system to reboot.
2. Select the Command Prompt (DOS Window).
3. Enter **FORMAT /?** at the Command Prompt to list the Format command syntax and switches, or refer to Chapter 13 for details.

Help Files ▼ Before directories can be created or files written to a new partition, the partition must be formatted using the FAT, HPFS, or NTFS file systems. Be careful not to reformat a partition that already contains files and directories—the information lost will not be recoverable.

Labeling Partitions

To label a new volume or to change or delete a volume label:

1. Select the Command Prompt (DOS Window).
2. Enter **LABEL** [***drive***:][***label***] <CR>. Refer to Chapter 13 for details on using the Label command.
3. If no volume label is specified, the system reports the current label (if any) and volume serial number before prompting for a new label.
4. Press Enter without supplying a new label to delete the current label and leave the volume unlabeled.

Marking an Active Partition on an 80*x*86 Computer

To mark a partition active on an 80x86 computer:

The system partition can never be part of a stripe set or volume set.

1. Select the primary partition containing the start-up (system) files for the operating system to activate.
2. Select Mark Active from the Partition menu. A message appears advising that the partition has been marked active (an asterisk appears in the partition's color bar) and that the operating system located on that partition will be started when the computer is next powered up.
3. Select OK from the message box.

Help Files ▼ The partition containing the start-up files is commonly referred to as the system partition, while the partition containing the operating system files is referred to as the boot partition. Under DOS, the system and boot partitions have conventionally been one and the same, but this is not always the case.

On 80x86 computers, the system partition must be a primary partition marked as active for start-up purposes and must be located on a local disk accessible when the computer is powered up. Only one partition can be active at a time.

However, two or more primary partitions may exist on a single drive or on multiple drives, and different operating systems may be made bootable by changing the active system partition and then restarting the computer.

Marking an Active Partition on a RISC-based Computer

Partitions on RISC computers are not marked active. Instead, RISC computer drives are configured by a hardware configuration program supplied by the manufacturer. System partitions on RISC computers must be formatted using the FAT file system.

The system partition can never be part of a stripe set or volume set.

Assigning Static Drive Letters

To assign a static drive letter:

1. Select the partition or logical drive to assign.
2. Select Drive Letter from the Partition menu. The Assign Drive Letter dialog box shown in Figure 16.5 appears.
3. Select the appropriate option button from the Assign Drive Letter dialog box.
4. To assign a static drive letter, accept the next letter available.Or, select a static drive letter from the pull-down list.
5. Select OK.
6. Repeat steps 1 through 5 for additional partitions or logical drives.

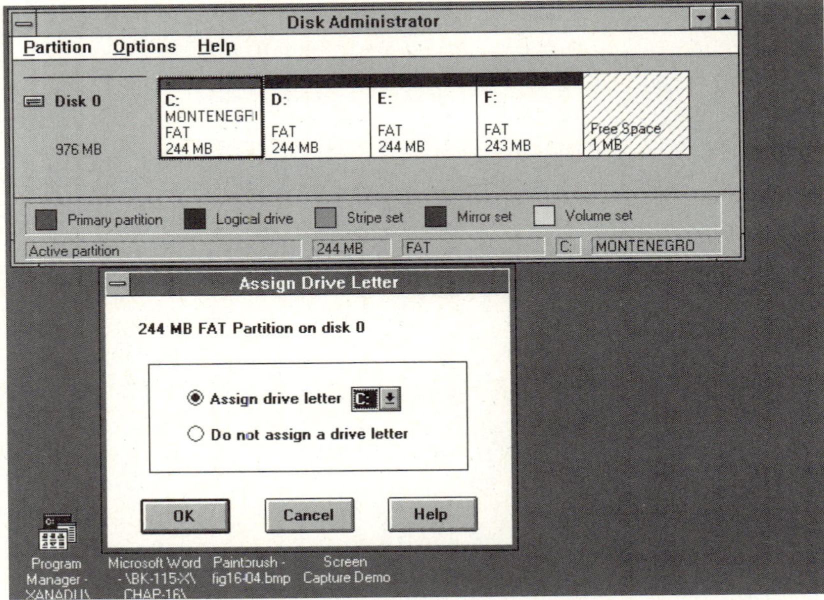

Figure 16.5
The Assign Drive Letter dialog box

Help Files ▼

Static drive letters assigned by Windows NT do not affect the drive letters assigned when the computer is booted under DOS or Windows 3.1.

Windows NT will permit creating more than 24 volumes, but only 24 letters are available for accessing these volumes. (Drive letters A and B continue to be reserved for floppy disk drives.)

Unlike DOS, however, Windows NT allows the static assignment of drive letters, permitting a drive letter to be permanently assigned to a specific hard drive and partition or volume. Thus, when a new hard drive is added to the existing system, the statistically assigned drive letters remain unaffected.

Until static drive letters are assigned by Disk Administrator, or if no drive letter is assigned to a partition, drive letters are assigned in the same fashion as DOS. First, the primary partition on each hard drive is assigned sequentially beginning with "C." Second, available drive letters are assigned sequentially to each logical partition on each hard drive.

Third, available drive letters are assigned sequentially to the secondary partitions on each. Typically the active system partition is drive C.

Use caution when assigning drive-letters. Remember that many DOS and Windows programs create references to specific drive letters which are—at best—difficult to locate and reassign.

Deleting Partitions, Volumes, or Logical Drives

To delete a partition, volume, or logical drive:

1. Select the partition, volume, or logical drive.
2. Select Delete from the Partition menu.
   - If the partition or logical drive is the active partition or contains the Windows NT system files, a message appears warning that this partition or drive cannot be deleted.
   - If the partition is part of a set, the partition cannot be deleted without deleting the entire set.
   - If the partition is an extended partition, all logical drives or other volumes must be deleted before the extended partition can be deleted.
3. A cautionary prompt warns that all data in the partition, volume, or logical drive will be lost and requests confirmation. Select Yes to continue.
4. The partition, volume, or logical drive is deleted and the space is shown as free. No changes are actually made, however, until Disk Administrator is exited and confirmation is given to save the changes.

Be careful using the Delete command on a RISC computer, where it is possible to delete the system partition containing the files needed to load Windows NT.

Help Files Before deleting any partitions, volumes, or logical drives under Windows NT, any information that may be needed later—both files and directories—should be backed up to tape or to another disk drive.

▶ Saving the Disk Configuration

Any changes made to the disk configuration during the current session are not saved.

To save disk configuration data:

1. Select Configuration from the Partition menu.
2. Select Save from the Configuration menu. A message appears detailing what information will be saved and suggesting the Emergency Repair Disk as an appropriate destination.
3. Select OK to continue.
4. Insert a blank, formatted floppy disk, a floppy disk with a previous version of the configuration data, or the Emergency Repair Disk in drive A.
5. Select OK.

Help Files ▼ During Windows NT setup, the Emergency Repair Disk created contains a copy of the disk configuration data in effect at that time. Disk Administrator can save this data to the Emergency Repair Disk or to a separate floppy disk. The saved information includes assigned drive letters, volume sets, stripe sets, parity stripe sets, and mirror sets.

▶ Restoring a Saved Disk Configuration

To restore previously saved disk configuration data:

Any changes made to the disk configuration during the current session will be lost.

1. Select Configuration from the Partition menu.
2. Select Restore from the Configuration menu. A message appears warning that the saved information will overwrite the current disk configuration data.
3. Select Yes to continue.
4. Insert the floppy disk containing the saved configuration information.
5. Select OK.

Help Files ▼ During Windows NT setup, the Emergency Repair Disk created contains a copy of the disk configuration data in effect at that time. Since then this data may have been updated to the Emergency Repair Disk or to a separate floppy disk and can be restored if Disk Administrator overwrites the current data and settings. The saved information includes assigned drive letters, volume sets, stripe sets, parity stripe sets, and mirror sets.

▶ Searching for Configuration Data

To search for disk configuration data:

Any changes made to the disk configuration during the current session will be lost.

1. Select Configuration from the Partition menu.
2. Select Search from the Configuration menu. A message appears warning that this operation will overwrite the current disk configuration data with data from a different installation of Windows NT.
3. Select OK to continue. Disk Administrator scans the local hard drive(s) for other Windows NT installations, displaying a list of the installations found—if any.
4. Select an installation from those listed.
5. Select OK.

Help Files ▼ Disk configuration information can be searched for among other installed versions of Windows NT and a specific version selected as a replacement. The alternate version, however, should be updated whenever changes are made to the disk configuration. Make changes under one version, quit

Disk Administrator, restart the computer and Disk Administrator, and then save the new configuration and quit Disk Administrator.

Deleting Mirror Sets

To convert the unmirrored partition to free space:

1. Select the unmirrored partition to be freed.
2. Select Delete from the Partition menu. A message advises that all data will be lost and requests confirmation.
3. Select Yes to confirm.

Help Files Establishing and breaking mirror sets without deleting the information in both volumes is part of the fault-tolerance functionality provided with Windows NT Advanced Server. Windows NT, however, will not recognize such volumes unless the configuration data is first saved from Windows NT Advanced Server to a floppy disk and restored under Windows NT. The two volumes will then appear in the disk bar with color bars identifying them as primary partitions or logical drives but without drive letters assigned. They may be assigned drive letters as is, or may be deleted to regain and reassign the disk space.

Working with Volumes and Volume Sets

Creating a Volume Set

To create a volume set:

1. Select two or more free areas by selecting the first free area and then pressing Ctrl and clicking the additional areas. Selection may be made from a single physical drive or from as many as 32 drives.

2. Select Create Volume Set from the Partition menu. The Create Volume Set dialog box displays the minimum and maximum sizes for the volume set.
3. Enter the size of the volume set to create.
4. Select OK.

Help Files ▼ Volume sets are a mechanism used to combine scattered free areas from a single drive or from multiple drives to create a single large volume that is treated as a single partition. Remember, however, that other operating systems such as DOS that lack volume-set functionality will not recognize volume sets created by Windows NT. Thus, any volume sets created on a dual-boot computer will be invisible to DOS.

If a volume set is created using less than the total space available from the selected areas, Disk Administrator divides the total size by the number of disks, using roughly the same space—insofar as it's practical—from each of the selected disks. A single drive letter is assigned to the volume set.

▶ Deleting a Volume Set

To delete a volume set:

1. Select the volume set to delete.
2. Select Delete from the Partition menu. A message advises that all data will be lost and requests confirmation.
3. Select Yes to confirm.

Help Files ▼ Deleting a volume set deletes all information contained in the volume set. Save any information, directories, and files that will be needed later by backing up to a tape or copying to another partition, volume, or logical drive before deleting the volume.

▶ Extending Volumes and Volume Sets

To extend a volume or volume set:

1. Select an existing volume (which is not part of a stripe set or mirror set), or a volume set and one or more areas of free space.
2. Select Extend Volume Set from the Partition menu. The Create Extended Volume Set dialog box displays the minimum and maximum sizes for the volume set.
3. Enter the total size of the volume set to create.
4. Select OK.

Help Files ▼ Existing NTFS volumes and volume sets can be extended by adding free space. Disk Administrator—on exit—reboots the system and formats the added area without affecting any existing files in the original volume or volume set.

Working with Stripe Sets

▶ Creating a Stripe Set

To create a stripe set:

1. Select two or more free areas from two or more hard drives. Only one area can be selected from any hard drive. Up to 32 areas and hard drives may be used.
   - Select the first area of free space from the first drive.
   - Press Ctrl and click on additional areas from each of the other hard drives.
2. Select Create Stripe Set from the Partition menu. The Create Stripe Set dialog box displays the minimum and maximum sizes for the stripe set.
3. Enter the size of the stripe set to create.
4. Select OK.

Help Files ▼ Stripe sets are similar to volume sets, but are created under a different series of restrictions. Each member partition of the stripe set must be on a different disk, but may use up to 32 physical disks. Each partition will be approximately the same size, with Disk Administrator dividing the total size by the number of disks. If the size cannot be divided equally, the size will be rounded up or down to the closest divisible value. The stripe set will be assigned a single drive letter and is treated as a single volume.

Remember, operating systems such as DOS that lack stripe-set functionality will not recognize stripe sets created by Windows NT. Thus, any volume sets created on a dual-boot computer will be invisible to DOS.

Deleting a Stripe Set

To delete a stripe set:

1. Select the stripe set to delete.
2. Select Delete from the Partition menu. A message advises that all data will be lost and requests confirmation.
3. Select Yes to confirm.

Help Files Deleting a stripe set deletes all information contained in the stripe set. Save any information, directories, and files that will be needed later by backing up to a tape or copying to another partition, volume, or logical drive before deleting the stripe set.

THE RESCUE PAGES: Disk Administrator

If I can't use the Assign command to swap the A and B drives, what about using Disk Administrator to assign new drive letters?

Nice idea, but one problem—Disk Administrator doesn't do floppies.

Okay, frivolity aside, the A and B drive letters are reserved and, effectively, inviolate. And, as for those annoying programs that insist on being installed from the A drive but only come on floppies fitting the B drive, the only real solution is to boot DOS where you can use the ASSIGN command. Besides, it has to be a DOS program, doesn't it?

I assigned static drive letters to all the drives on the system, but when I boot DOS, the assignments don't show up.

The static drive letter assignments only apply under Windows NT. Under DOS, the drive letters are assigned following the standard rules. If it's really necessary, you could use the DOS ASSIGN command to reassign drives to match the Windows NT assignments.

Help! I accidentally deleted a drive (partition, and so on) with critical files on it.

Okay, don't panic. Nothing is actually deleted until you exit Disk Administrator and, when you exit, you'll be asked to confirm your changes. Say *No!*

However, if you already exited and saved the changes…there's still hope. The Emergency Repair Disk contains a copy of the drive setups and assignments that can be restored. The trick is that deleting the drive or partition doesn't erase the drive, it just tells the system that the drive or partition is unassigned, empty, and unformatted…which means that

nothing can be found on it. Thus, restoring the original disk configuration makes the drive visible again without overwriting the file system as formatting would. Refer to "Restoring a Saved Disk Configuration" for details.

CHAPTER

17

HELP! Event Viewer

Event Viewer is used to view event logs such as the System, Security, and Application logs; to archive event logs; and to maintain event logs.

Critical events—such as printer errors, a server malfunctions, or problems writing a file—are reported immediately by on-screen error message dialog boxes. Other problems, which are less drastic and which do not require immediate attention, are written to an event log file without interrupting the user's activites. Error event logging is initiated automatically when Windows NT starts.

In addition to error events, logging can also be requested for security events, tracking changes to the security system, and identifying breaches in system security. Security event tracking is set by the Policies/Audit dialog box in User Manager but is reported in Event Viewer. Finally, the application log details errors found and reported by System applications.

Topics covered in this chapter include

- Event Viewer
- Using and managing event logs
- Working with event log archives

Event Viewer

▶ Using Event Viewer

To turn general event logging on or off:

- Select the Services utility in the Control Panel.

To turn security event logging on or off:

- Select the Audit option from the Policies menu in User Manager.

To turn file and directory access auditing on or off:

- Select the Auditing option from the Security menu in File Manager.

Help Files ▼ Event logging begins automatically when Windows NT is started, but can be turned on and off from the Services utility in the Control Panel. Auditing for security events is controlled from the Audit option in the Policies menu from User Manager. Auditing for file and directory access is controlled from the Auditing option on the Security menu in File Manager. The Event Viewer screen is shown in Figure 17.1.

Information in Event Viewer is arranged in seven columns, with an icon in the left column identifying the event type as Error, Warning, Information, Success Audit, or Failure Audit. The event columns are as follows:

- *Date* and *Time* show, of course, the date and time the event occurred.
- *Source* identifies the software that logged the event and may be an application name, a system component, or an application such as a driver name. For example: *Print* identifies Print Manager, while *QIC117* identifies the tape driver.
- *Category* identifies the event classification as defined by the source. For example: Security event categories are logon and logoff, file and object access, user rights, user, and group management. *None* simply means that no specific event category has been assigned.

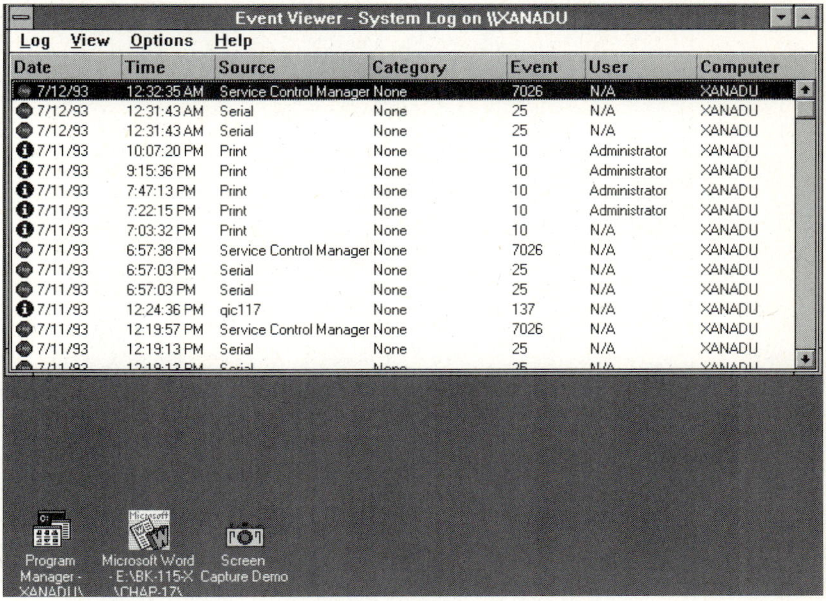

Event Viewer - System Log on \\XANADU

Log View Options Help

Date	Time	Source	Category	Event	User	Computer
7/12/93	12:32:35 AM	Service Control Manager	None	7026	N/A	XANADU
7/12/93	12:31:43 AM	Serial	None	25	N/A	XANADU
7/12/93	12:31:43 AM	Serial	None	25	N/A	XANADU
7/11/93	10:07:20 PM	Print	None	10	Administrator	XANADU
7/11/93	9:15:36 PM	Print	None	10	Administrator	XANADU
7/11/93	7:47:13 PM	Print	None	10	Administrator	XANADU
7/11/93	7:22:15 PM	Print	None	10	Administrator	XANADU
7/11/93	7:03:32 PM	Print	None	10	N/A	XANADU
7/11/93	6:57:38 PM	Service Control Manager	None	7026	N/A	XANADU
7/11/93	6:57:03 PM	Serial	None	25	N/A	XANADU
7/11/93	6:57:03 PM	Serial	None	25	N/A	XANADU
7/11/93	12:24:36 PM	qic117	None	137	N/A	XANADU
7/11/93	12:19:57 PM	Service Control Manager	None	7026	N/A	XANADU
7/11/93	12:19:13 PM	Serial	None	25	N/A	XANADU

Program Manager - XANADU\ Microsoft Word - E:\BK-115-X\CHAP-17\ Screen Capture Demo

Figure 17.1
The Event Viewer screen

- *Event* provides a specific event number identifying the event. The Event ID can be used by product support representatives to track whatever event occurred in the system.
- *User* identifies a user name or *N/A* (not applicable) for system events.
- *Computer* identifies the specific computer—by computer name—where the event occurred.

▶ Viewing Event Logs

To select another log for viewing:

- Select System, Security, or Application from the Log menu.

To select another computer for viewing:

- Select the Select Computer option from the Log menu.

Help Files ▼ Event Viewer can select three different event logs recording system, security, or application events and can select any of these event logs from any computer on the net. Events from logs maintained by separate computers can be combined for comparison purposes.

▶ Customizing Log Views

To sort events chronologically:

- Select Oldest First or Newest First (default) from the View menu. See "Sorting Events," following.

To view only events with specific characteristics:

- Select Filter Events from the View menu. See "Selecting and Filtering Events," following.

To identify events based on specific characteristics or event descriptions:

- Select Find from the View menu. See "Searching for Events," following.

To view descriptions and details of logged events:

- Select Detail from the View menu.

Or:

- Double-click on the event listing. Refer to "Viewing Event Details," following.

▶ Refreshing Event Viewer

To update the events shown in Event Viewer:

- Select the Refresh command from the View menu.

Help Files ▼ When an event log is opened, Event Viewer displays all current information contained in the log, but the displayed contents are not updated, even though new events may be added to the event log. Selecting a different log for viewing does, of course, update the newly displayed list.

The Refresh command is not available when viewing archived event logs.

▶ Selecting the Computer for Viewing

The Select Computer option is available only to users logged on as members of the Administrators group.

To select a computer for viewing:

1. Select the Select Computer option from the Log menu. The Select Computer dialog box shown in Figure 17.2 appears.
2. Select a computer name from the list.
   - Or type the computer name in the Edit box.

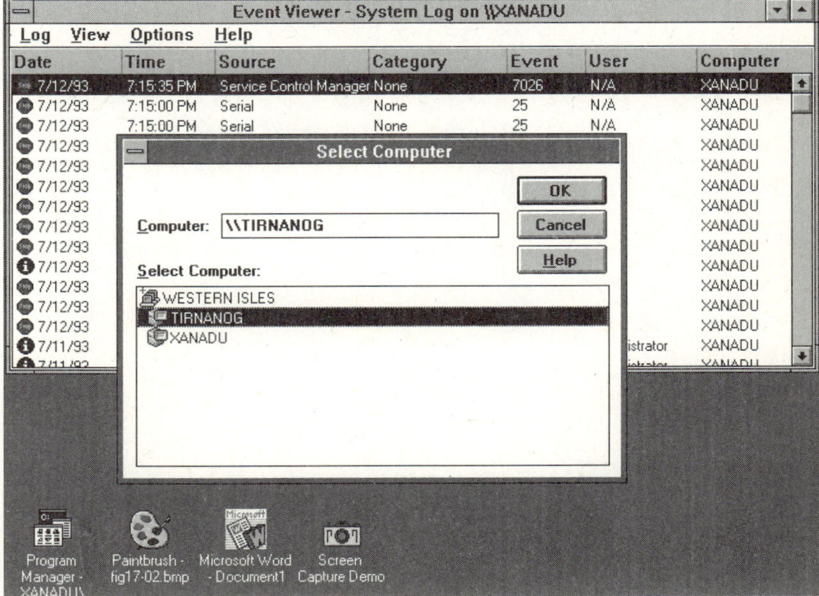

Figure 17.2
The Select Computer dialog box

Using and Managing Event Logs

▶ Sorting Events

To specify sort order:

- Select either Newest First or Oldest First from the View menu. The currently selected order is identified by a check mark.

Help Files ▼ Events displayed appear in the order of date and time of occurrence. The default list order places the newest events first. When an event log is archived in a text or comma-delimited format file, the current sort order determines the order in which event records are written. The display sort order does not, however, affect the ordering of records in a log file format. If the Save Settings On Exit command—from the Options menu—is selected (checked), the selected sort order will be the default when Event Viewer is next loaded.

▶ Selecting and Filtering Events

To filter events:

1. Select Filter Events from the View menu. The Filter dialog box shown in Figure 17.3 appears.
2. Select characteristics to qualify an event for display—see "Setting Filter Conditions," following.
3. Select the Clear button to restore the default criteria.
4. Select OK to view the filtered events.

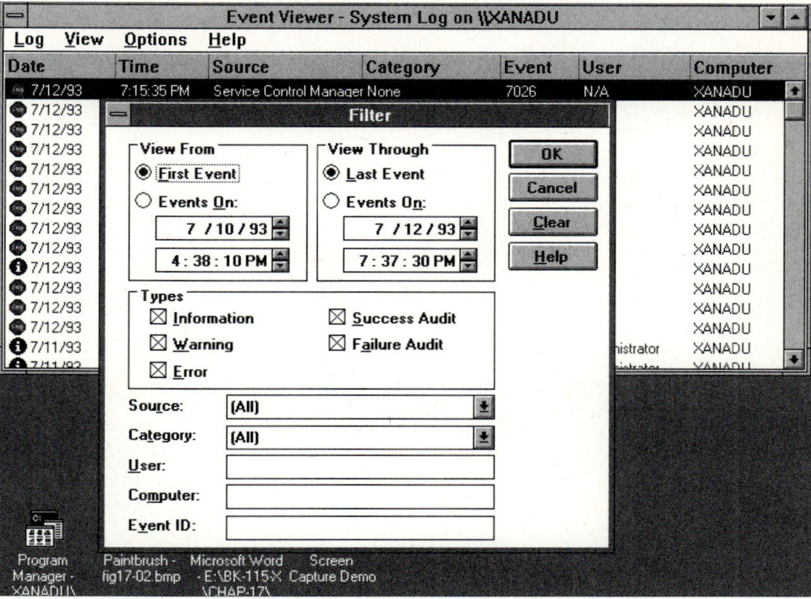

Figure 17.3
The Filter dialog box

To turn event filtering off:

- Select the All Events option from the View menu.

Help Files ▼ When Event Viewer is loaded, no filtering is applied and all events in a selected log are displayed. When a log is saved as an archive, no filtering is applied and the unfiltered log is saved.

▶ Setting Filter Conditions

To set filter conditions:

1. In the View From box:
   - Select First Event (default) to view events from the earliest entry.

- Select Events On and enter a date and time to begin event listings.

2. In the View Through box:
   - Select Last Event (default) to view events through the final entry.
   - Select Events On and enter a date and time to end event listings.
3. Check the event types to display in the Types box.
4. Use the pull-down Source list to select a source to display.
   - Or enter a source name in the edit field.
5. Use the pull-down Category list to select a category to display.
   - Or enter a category name in the edit field.
6. Enter a user's name in the User field to display only events resulting from a specified user's actions.
7. Enter a computer name in the Computer field to display only events from a specific computer.
8. Enter a value in Event ID to limit the display to specific events.

▶ Searching for Events

To search an event log for events of a specific nature:

1. Select Find from the View menu. The Find dialog box shown in Figure 17.4 appears.
2. Select one or more event types from the Types box.
3. Set additional specifications using the Source, Category, Event ID, Computer, and User fields—see "Setting Filter Conditions," preceding.
4. Enter text in the Description box to match any portion of an event record description.
5. Select Up or Down as the search direction.
6. Select Clear to restore the default search criteria.
7. Select Find Next to begin the search.

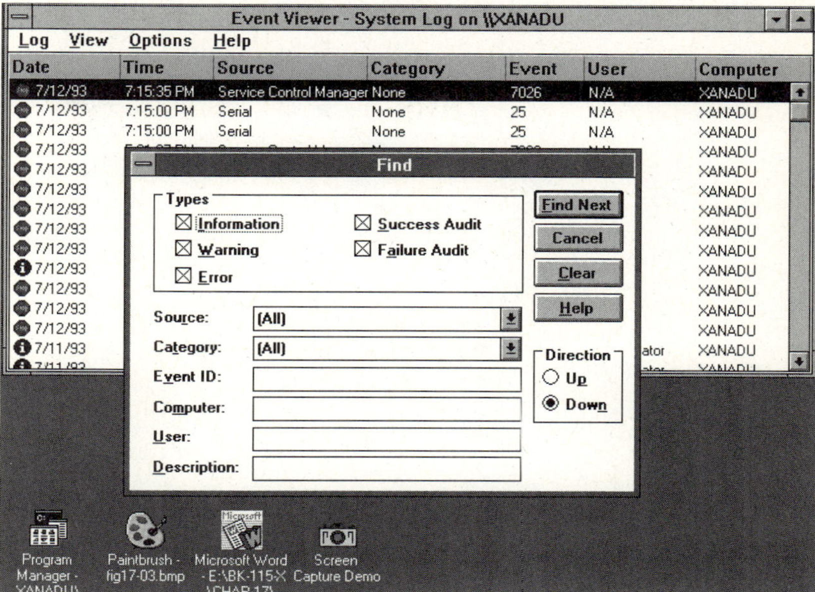

Figure 17.4
The Find dialog box

Help Files ▼ Event Viewer can search for events to match a specified type, source, category, user, or event ID. Further, the Description field can be used to search for a matching text entry in the event record description. Once search criteria have been defined, pressing the F3 key will search for the next matching event without displaying the Find dialog box.

▶ Viewing Event Details

To view additional details about an event:

1. Double-click on the event or select Detail from the View menu after selecting an event. The Event Detail dialog box is shown in Figure 17.5.
2. Select Next or Previous to view other events in sort-order sequence.
3. Select OK to return to Event Viewer.

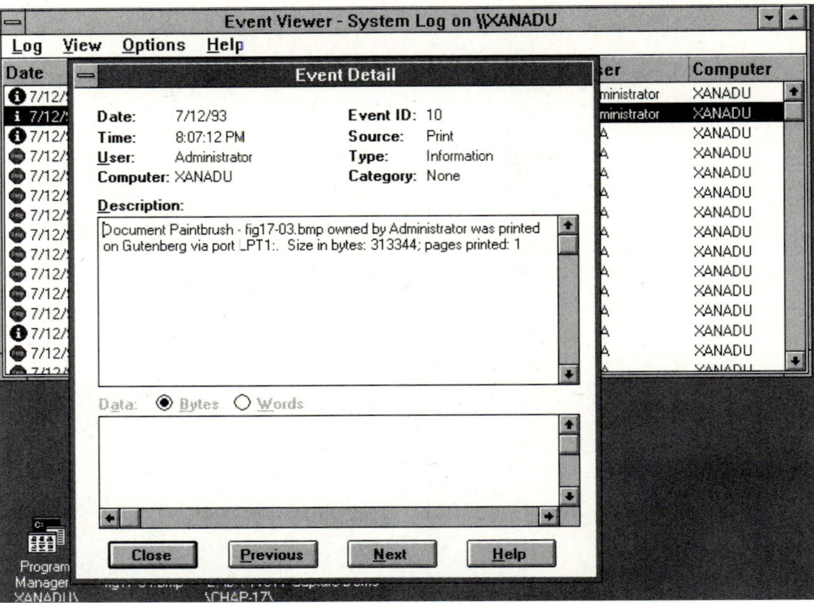

Figure 17.5
The Event Detail dialog box

Help Files ▼ While the listing in Event Viewer is tersely brief, additional information is available in the form of a text description provided by the application generating the event message—although not all sources or events generate a detailed description.

The Description box displays a text report amplifying the event occurrence, while the Data box displays binary data in hexadecimal format for use by support technicians or experienced programmers.

Event descriptions are saved in all archived event logs. Binary event data, however, is saved only in log file format archives, but is discarded when text or comma-delimited text archives are created.

Setting Event Logging Options

To set options for event logging:

1. Select Log Settings from the Log menu. The Event Log Settings dialog box is shown in Figure 17.6.

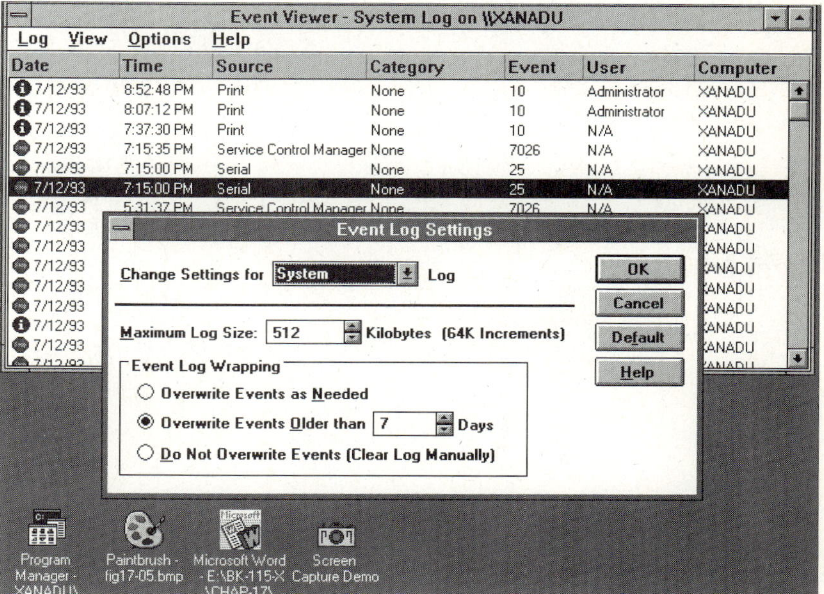

Figure 17.6
The Event Log Settings dialog box

2. Select the log type from the Change Settings For box.
3. Set a maximum log size—in kilobytes—in the Maximum Log Size edit box.
4. Select an Event Log Wrapping option to define how events are retained or erased:
   - Overwrite Events As Needed—When the log is filled, the oldest events are discarded to make space for the new.
   - Overwrite Events Older Than [*n*] Days—Logged events are retained a minimum of *n* days before they can be overwritten. *n* may have any value from 1 to 365, but defaults to 7 days.

- Do Not Overwrite Events—Logged events can only be cleared manually, ensuring that no events are overwritten or discarded. For security purposes, the Halt System When Full option may be selected from the Auditing Policies dialog box from User Manager.

5. Select the Default button to restore default settings.
6. Select OK.

Help Files ▼ A maximum log size can be defined for each type of log, but the size must be some multiple of 64K. If no overwrites are permitted and the system is halted when the log is full, the log size cannot be increased to resume operations. Instead, the event log must be saved and cleared manually before resizing.

▶ Clearing Event Logs

To clear an event log:

1. Select the event log to clear.
2. Select Clear All Events from the Log menu. A message appears, asking if the currently logged events should be archived.
3. Select Yes to call the Save As dialog box and archive the log contents.
4. Select No to proceed without archiving the log contents.

Working with Event Log Archives

▸ Archiving an Event Log

To archive an event log:

1. Select Save As from the Log menu. The Save As dialog box appears.
2. Select a file format from the Save File As Type list box.
3. Enter a file name in the File Name edit box or select a file name from the list.
4. Select OK to proceed.

Help Files ▼ Event logs can be archived in log file format (.EVT) for later use in Event Viewer or in text or comma-delimited text formats (.TXT) for export to a database, spreadsheet, or other application.

▸ Viewing a Log Archived in Log File Format

To display an archived log in Event Viewer:

1. Select Open from the Log menu. The Open dialog box appears.
2. Select the .EVT archive log file to view.
3. Select OK to load the file.
4. From the Open File Type dialog box, select the original log type—System, Security, or Application.
5. Select OK to return to Event Viewer.

Help Files ▼ If the log type is not specified correctly, the Description field in the Event Detail dialog box will not be reported correctly. Archived files can be viewed only if the file was saved in log file format. Also, the Refresh and Clear All Events commands are not valid for archived logs.

THE RESCUE PAGES: Event Viewer

The same error events keep showing up in the system log every time someone logs on. The problem is that there doesn't seem to be a problem—everything seems to be working—except for the error events...and there are a bunch of them.

Well, yes, this happens. And there are no simple solutions—aside from ignoring the error events. What usually happens is that some very simple event—such as an incorrectly identified serial port—produces a cascade of error events.

To troubleshoot the problem, begin by looking at the earliest event in the sequence. All of the events in the sequence are—probably—time-stamped within a maximum interval of a minute or two. If the initial error event can be corrected, the rest will probably disappear.

How you troubleshoot the error event is not quite so simple, but check the description for amplifying clues. If the error originates in an application, check with the application's programmers. If the error originates in Windows NT, check the error code documentation. And, of course, look for something stupidly simple before wasting time looking for something complex.

I can't select another computer to view the event logs. Do I need a password or something?

No passwords are required, but you must be logged on as a member of the Administrators group before you can access remote event logs.

I loaded an archived event log, but the Description under Event Detail doesn't make any sense. Is the event log archive trashed?

Probably not. It's more likely that the wrong log type was selected when the archive was loaded. Reload the archive and specify the correct log type. Of course, if you're not sure about the log type, there are only three possibilities, and in one of these, the Description field should begin to make sense.

The reason for the problem is simple. The event log does not store the complete description, only the portions of the description that are specific to this event report. The bulk of the description is called from the Source application and combined with the stored reference. Thus, as an example, a Print event reports the following description. The portions actually contained in the event log are in italics, the rest is obtained from Print Manager when the message is displayed.

Document *Paintbrush - fig17-03.bmp* owned by *Administrator* was printed on *Gutenberg* via port *LPT1:*. Size in bytes: *313344*; pages printed: *1*

If this same information was inserted into a different message template—because the wrong log type had been selected—the data might not fit the format or might accidentally fit but simply not make any sense.

CHAPTER

18

HELP! The Registry Editor Utility

The RegEdt32 (Registry Editor) utility is used to inspect and to modify the Registry database. Modifications, however, should be made only with extreme care. Errors or injudicious modifications may seriously damage your system. Administrators should not permit system users casual access to Registry Editor.

Windows NT uses the Registry database to replace the information that previously was contained in the AUTOEXEC.BAT and CONFIG.SYS files as well as the WIN.INI and other configuration files. The AUTOEXEC.BAT and CONFIG.SYS files continue to exist to provide compatibility with DOS and Windows 3.1 applications. Many of the latter will continue to create and depend on .INI files for application data, but the majority of the important system information is now located in the Registry database and accessible using the Registry Editor utility.

For an example: The Registry subkey HKEY_LOCAL_MACHINE\SYSTEM identifies device drivers to be loaded when Windows NT boots, while subkeys under HKEY_CURRENT_USER contain per-user data, which previously would have been stored in the WIN.INI file.

Topics discussed in this chapter include

- Elements of the Registry Editor interface
- Managing Registry information

Caution: Erroneous Registry modifications can seriously damage your system!

- Adding and deleting information in Registry Editor
- Editing Registry data
- Editing Registry entry values
- Maintaining Registry data security
- Changing the appearance of Registry Editor
- Printers and printer options

Elements of the Registry Editor Interface

The Windows NT Registry Editor (see Figure 18.1) appears with four windows representing four predefined keys:

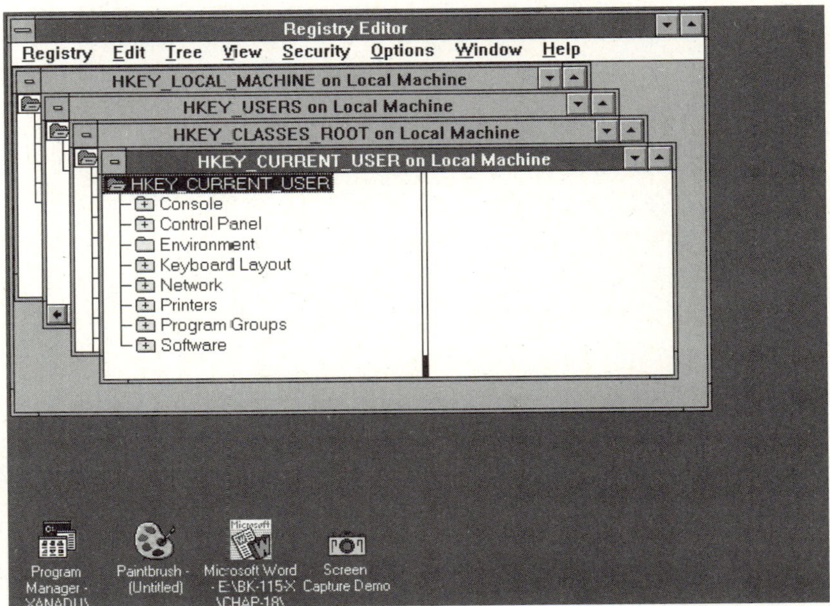

Figure 18.1
The Registry Editor screen

- HKEY_CURRENT_USER is a subkey of HKEY_USERS and contains configuration information for the current user, including the user's program groups, screen colors, and control panel settings.

- HKEY_CLASSES_ROOT is a subkey of HKEY_LOCAL_MACHINE\SOFTWARE and contains information used to open the right application when a file is opened from File Manager (file association) and for Object Linking and Embedding (OLE).
- HKEY_USERS contains user profiles for all users on the local computer.
- HKEY_LOCAL_MACHINE contains configuration information particular to the computer (for any user).

Registry Editor can be used to assign value entries to new keys or to alter values assigned to keys.

In each window, the left pane shows a tree view similar to the directory trees used in File Manager. Branches in the tree offer folders representing keys in Registry Editor. The right pane shows the values contained in a key and can be edited by double-clicking on any entry to invoke an edit dialog box.

Value entries in Registry Editor appear as strings composed of three elements:

- Value name
- Value entry type (class)
- Actual assigned value

Five categories of value type are identified as:

- REG_BINARY—a binary entry
- REG_DWORD—a double-word entry
- REG_SZ—a data string
- REG_MULTI_SZ—a multiple string
- REG_EXPAND_SZ—an expandable string

An editor dialog box for each value class is invoked by double-clicking on the value entry or by selecting the appropriate option from the Edit menu.

Managing Registry Information

▶ Opening Registry Editor

To open Registry Editor:

- Select REGEDT32 from Program Manager or File Manager.

Or:

- Enter "START REGEDT32" in the Command Prompt window.

Help Files ▼ The local Registry is loaded by default when REGEDT32 is started.

▶ Opening the Local Registry

To open the Local Registry:

- Select Open Local Registry from the Registry menu. The four Local Registry windows appear, each bearing the name of a predefined key.

▶ Accessing Registry Editor in a Remote Computer

To access a remote Registry Editor:

1. Refer to "Accessing a Remote Computer Drive," below.
2. After a computer is selected, two remote Registry keys—HKEY_USERS and HKEY_LOCAL_MACHINE—appear in the local Registry Editor.

▶ Updating Registry Information

To update all information in all Registry windows:

- Select the Refresh All option.

To update only the information in the active Registry window:

- Select the Refresh Active option.

To automatically update changes made in Registry Editor:

- Select the Auto Refresh option.

▶ Closing Registry Windows

To close a local or remote Registry window:

1. Select the window to close.
2. Select Close Registry from the Registry menu.

▶ Saving a Subtree to a Text File

To save a Registry subtree as a text file:

1. Select the subkey to save.
2. Select the Save Subtree As option from the Registry menu. The Save As directory dialog box appears.
3. Select the desired drive from the Drivers list box.
4. Select the desired directory from the Directories list box.
5. Select a file name from the File Name list box or enter a name for the file.
6. Select or enter a file extension in the Save File As Type list box.
7. Select OK.

To save a Registry subtree text file to a network drive that is not currently accessible:

1. Select the subkey to save.
2. Select the Save Subtree As option from the Registry menu. The Save As directory dialog box appears.
3. Refer to "Accessing a Remote Computer Drive," below.

Help Files ▼ Registry Editor saves selected subtrees—including all descendent keys and value entries—as a text file written to a drive/path, server, workstation, or shared directory. The text file can be used as a convenient record of system settings, but cannot be used to regenerate the Registry data directly.

Adding and Deleting Information in Registry Editor

▸ Adding Keys to Registry Editor

To add a key to Registry Editor:

1. Select the key or subkey under which the new key should appear. This must be a key or subkey owned by the user or one for which the owner has granted permission to the user.
2. Select the Add Key option in the Edit menu or press the Ins key. The Add Key dialog box shown in Figure 18.2 appears.
3. Enter a key name in the Key Name box.
4. Optionally, enter a Class to assign to the key in the Class box.
5. Select OK. The new key appears in the Registry Editor window.

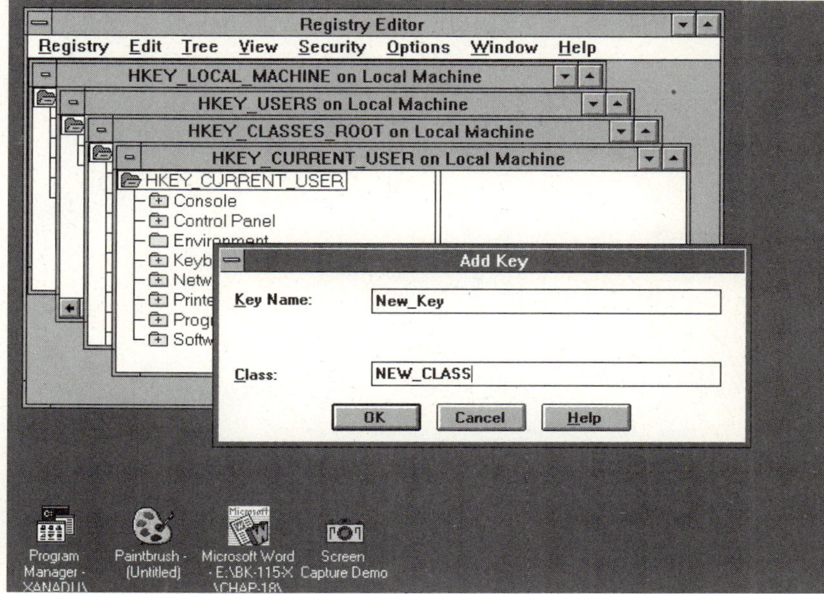

Figure 18.2
The Add Key dialog box

Help Files ▼ Registry Editor includes the capacity to add a new Registry key (subkey) to store new data in the Registry.

▶ Assigning a Registry Key Value

To add a value entry to a Registry key:

1. Select the Registry key.
2. Select Add Value from the Edit menu. The Add Value dialog box shown in Figure 18.3 appears.
3. Enter a name in the Value Name edit box.
4. Select the data type from the pull-down Data list box.

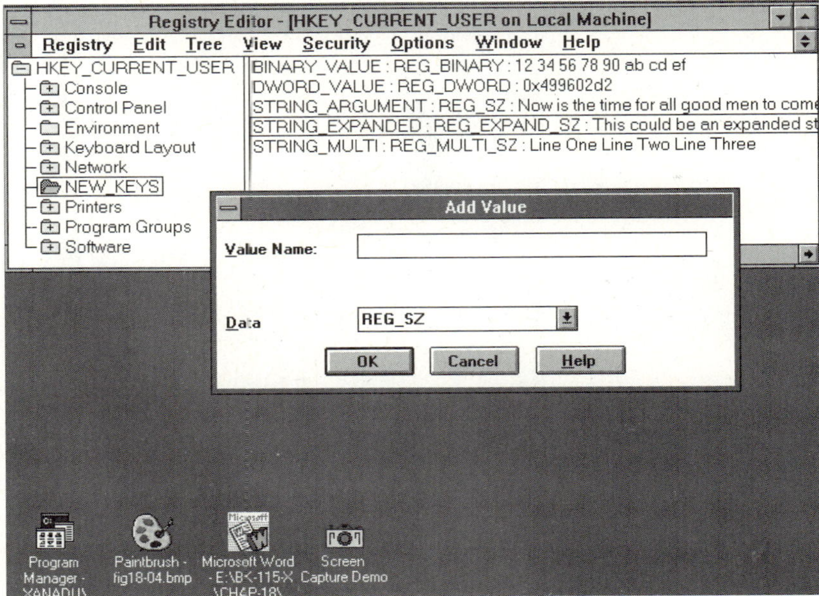

Figure 18.3
The Add Value dialog box

5. Select OK. Registry Editor calls an entry editor appropriate for the selected data type.
6. Enter the value or data for the key. The new key value and value entry appear in the right (data) pane.

▶ Saving a Registry Key

To save a Registry key:

1. Select the predefined key to save.
2. Select the Save Key option from the Registry menu. The Save Key dialog box appears in response.
3. Select the desired drive from the Drivers list box.
4. Select the desired directory from the Directories list box.
5. Select a file name from the File Name list box or enter a name for the file.

6. Select or enter a file extension in the Save File As Type list box.
7. Select OK. The selected key—together with its subkeys and values—is saved as a file of type hive and can be recalled when the Load Hive option is used.

To save a Registry key to a network drive that is not currently accessible:

1. Select the predefined key to save.
2. Select the Save Key option from the Registry menu. The Save Key dialog box appears in response.
3. Refer to "Accessing a Remote Computer Drive," below.

Help Files ▼ Registry Editor provides a number of options for system maintenance—such as the Load Hive and Unload Hive options, which permit a portion of the system to be temporarily copied to another workstation for maintenance. However, before a hive can be loaded, it must be saved to a floppy or hard drive by using the Save Key option.

▶ Loading and Unloading Registry Hives

To load a hive into Registry Editor:

1. Select Load Hive from the Registry menu. The Open dialog box appears.
2. Select the Drive and Directory where the hive is located.
3. Select the file containing the hive definition.
4. Select OK. The selected hives now appear in the predefined HKEY_USERS and HKEY_LOCAL_MACHINE keys.

To load a hive file from a network drive that is not currently accessible:

- Refer to "Accessing a Remote Computer Drive," below.

To unload a hive from Registry Editor:

- Select the Unload Hive option from the Registry menu. The hive previously loaded is removed from Registry Editor.

Help Files ▼ The Load Hive and Unload Hive options are used to display and perform maintenance on another workstation's Registry. These options affect only the predefined HKEY_USERS and HKEY_LOCAL_MACHINE keys.

▸ Restoring a Registry Key

To make a hive file a permanent part of the system configuration:

1. Select the predefined key in which to restore the hive.
2. Select the Restore option from the Registry menu. The Restore Key dialog box appears.
3. Select the source drive from the Drives list.
4. Select the source directory from the Directories list.
5. Select the file name from the File Name list.
6. Select OK. The selected hive is restored to the system.

To load a hive file from a network drive that is not currently accessible:

- Refer to "Accessing a Remote Computer Drive," below.

To provisionally restore a key to the system configuration:

1. Select the Restore Volatile option from the Registry menu.

2. Execute steps 3 through 6, preceding. The selected hive becomes a provisional addition to the system configuration and will be removed when the system is shut down.

Help Files ▼ Registry Editor offers two options for restoring hive functions as a part of the system configuration: the Restore option, which makes permanent changes, and the Restore Volatile option, whose changes are lost when the computer is shut down.

▶ Deleting Registry Keys or Registry Key Value Entries

To delete a Registry key or a Registry key value entry:

1. Select the key or value entry to delete.
2. Select Delete from the Edit menu or press the Del key.
3. If Confirm On Delete is active (Options menu), a warning dialog box requests confirmation.
4. Select OK to delete or Cancel to return.

Help Files ▼ Both keys and key values can be deleted from the Registry. However, predefined keys such as HKEY_CURRENT_USER cannot be deleted or changed.

Confirming a Deletion

To enable the Confirm Delete option:

- Select Confirm On Delete from the Options menu.

Help Files The Confirm On Delete option can be selected to protect Registry data. When selected, a request for confirmation is made anytime a Registry key or value entry is deleted.

Accessing a Remote Computer Drive

To access a remote computer drive:

1. Select the Networks button from the Open, Restore Key, or Save As dialog boxes. The Connect Network Drive dialog box appears.
2. Select a drive from the Drive list box where the network connection will be assigned.
3. If the local computer is already connected to the server needed, select the server in the Shared Directories option box, and then select OK.
   - Otherwise, select a drive from the Drive list box where the network connection will be assigned.
4. Enter a server command path in the Path box.
   - Or select the server, workstation, or shared directory from the Shared Directories box, and the path will appear automatically in the Path box.
5. Enter your user name in the Connect As option.
6. Select the Reconnect At Logon option to reestablish this network connection at the next log on.

7. Select the Expand By Default option to have the Shared Directories dialog box display all of the computers and shared directories automatically at log on.

8. Select OK.

9. If the Open dialog box is used, select any appropriate options.

10. Select OK.

Editing Registry Data

▶ Searching for Keys in Registry Editor

To search for a key in Registry Editor:

1. Select Find Key from the View menu. The Find dialog box shown in Figure 18.4 appears.

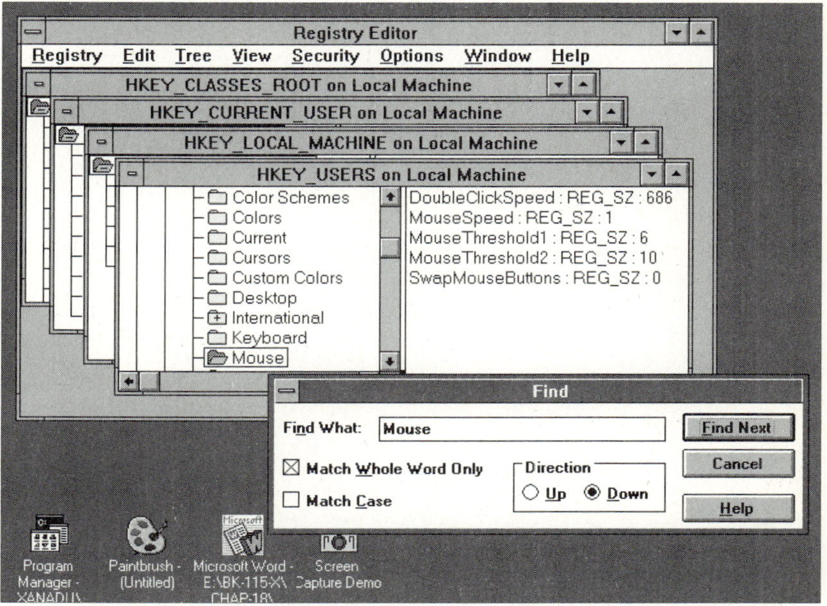

Figure 18.4
The Find dialog box

2. Enter the name of the key to find in the Find What edit box.
3. Select the Match Whole Word Only check box to locate only occurrences that are not part of a longer word or term.
4. Select Match Case to require an exact match for upper- and lowercase letters.
5. Select a search direction from the Direction box.
   - Up searches from the current position or selection to the beginning of Registry Editor.
   - Down searches from the current position or selection to the end of Registry Editor.
6. Select the Find Next button to locate the next occurrence of the specified text.
7. Select Cancel.

Help Files ▼ Registry Editor's Find option searches for keys in the Registry on the basis of a supplied key name. The Find Next option repeats the search.

Editing Registry Entry Values

▶ Invoking String Editor

To invoke String Editor:

1. Select the value entry to edit.
2. Double-click on the REG_SZ or REG_EXPAND_SZ value entry.
   - Or select the String option from the Edit menu. The String Editor dialog box shown in Figure 18.5 appears.

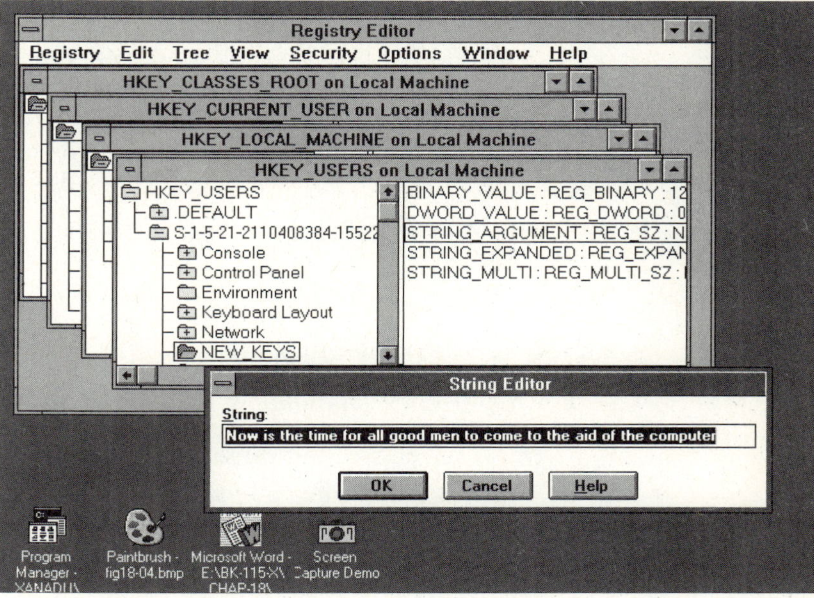

Figure 18.5
The String Editor dialog box

3. Edit the string data.
4. Select OK to return to Registry Editor. The selected value entry now reflects the changes made.

Help Files ▼ A REG_SZ string is a simple text string, usually a phrase, caption, or other readable instruction. A REG_EXPAND_SZ or expandable string may also consist of readable text, but contains one or more variable references that will be replaced by system constants when called by an application. For example, the value entry for File Manager/Add-Ons might appear as:

```
Mail File Manager Extension : REG_EXPAND_SZ :
                              %SystemRoot%\system32\SendFl32.DLL
```

The term %SystemRoot% is defined elsewhere but identifies the drive and system directory. Thus, the Mail File Manager Extension is expanded in use with %SystemRoot% and is replaced by the actual location of the drive and directory containing the Windows NT system files.

▶ Invoking Multi-String Editor

To invoke Multi-String Editor:

1. Select the value entry to edit.
2. Double-click on the REG_MULTI_SZ value entry.
   - Or select the Multi-String option from the Edit menu. The Multi-String Editor dialog box shown in Figure 18.6 appears.

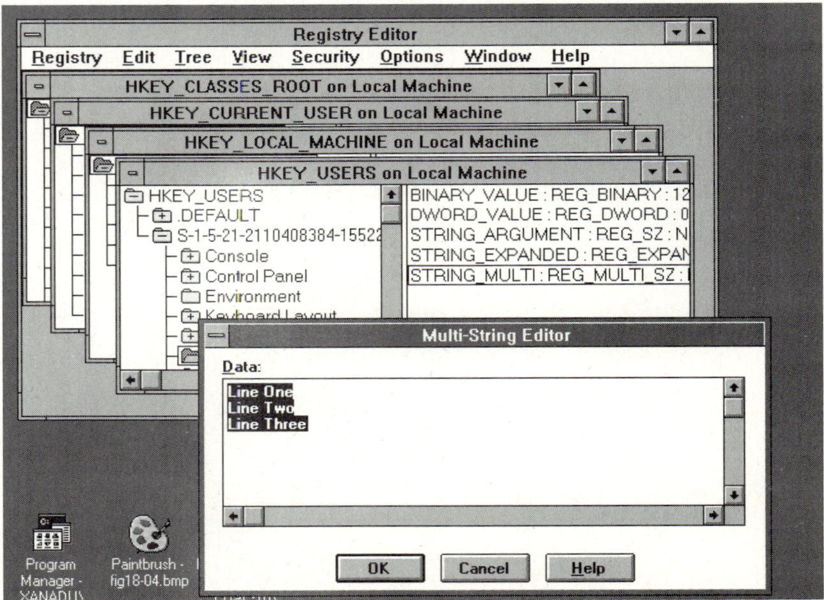

Figure 18.6
The Multi-String Editor dialog box

3. Edit the string data.
4. Select OK to return to Registry Editor. The selected value entry now reflects the changes made.

Help Files ▼ Multi-String Editor permits editing a key value that has multiple lines of text broken by carriage return characters.

▸ Invoking Binary Editor

To invoke Binary Editor:

1. Select the value entry to edit.
2. Double-click on the REG_BINARY value entry.
   - Or select the Binary option from the Edit menu. The Binary Editor dialog box shown in Figure 18.7 appears.

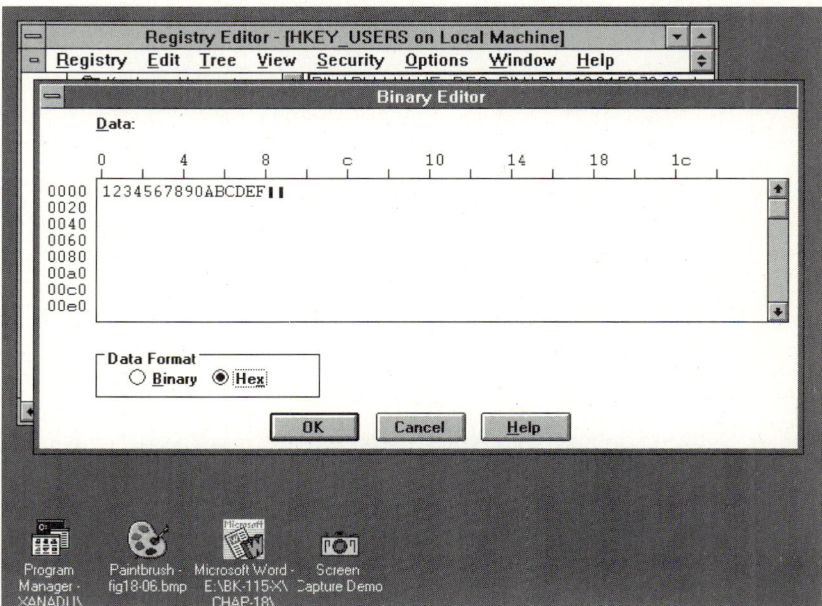

Figure 18.7
The Binary Editor dialog box

3. Select the preferred format—Binary or Hex—in the Data Format box.
4. Edit the data value as desired.
5. Select OK—the edited value appears in Registry Editor.

Help Files ▼ Value entries in the Registry quite commonly appear as binary data and are identified as REG_BINARY. For such values, Binary Editor is required for revisions. Values may, however, be edited in binary or hexadecimal formats as desired. Of course, Binary Editor can be used to edit any value entry, irrespective of the entry format.

▸ Invoking DWORD Editor

To invoke DWORD Editor:

1. Select the value entry to edit.
2. Double-click on the REG_DWORD value entry.
   - Or select the DWORD option from the Edit menu. The DWORD Editor dialog box shown in Figure 18.8 appears.
3. Select the preferred format—Binary, Decimal, or Hex—in the Radix box.
4. Edit the data value as desired.
5. Select OK—the edited value appears in Registry Editor.

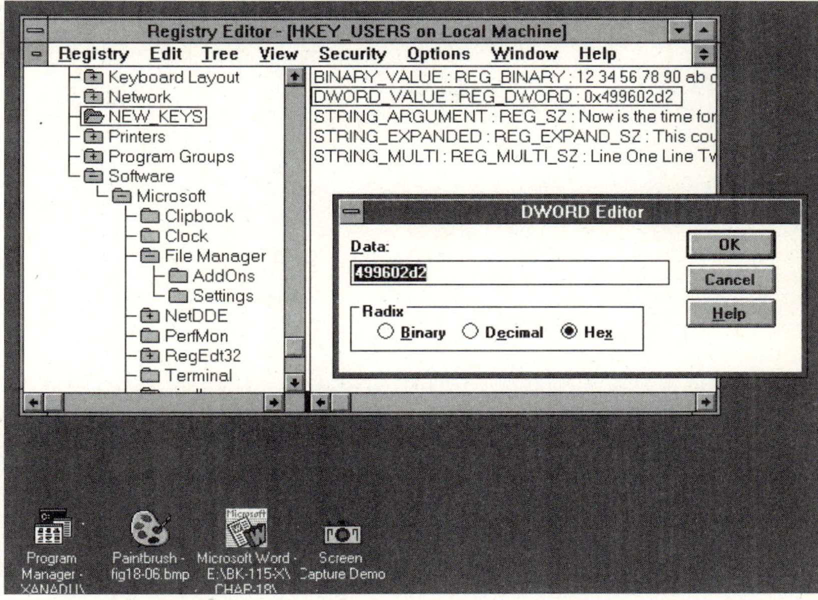

Figure 18.8
The DWORD Editor dialog box

Help Files ▼ DWORD, or Double WORD, refers to data represented by a number that is 4 bytes in size. DWORD data may, however, be edited as binary, decimal, or word values, according to your preferences.

Maintaining Registry Data Security

▶ Assigning Registry Key Permissions

To assign Registry key permissions:

1. Select the key to assign permission for.

2. Select the Permissions option from the Security menu. The Registry Key Permissions dialog box shown in Figure 18.9 appears.

   - The prompt "Registry Key" identifies the name of the selected key.
   - The prompt "Owner" identifies the name of the user or user group owning the Registry key.
   - The Name box lists the users and user groups permitted access to the Registry key plus the level of access granted to each.

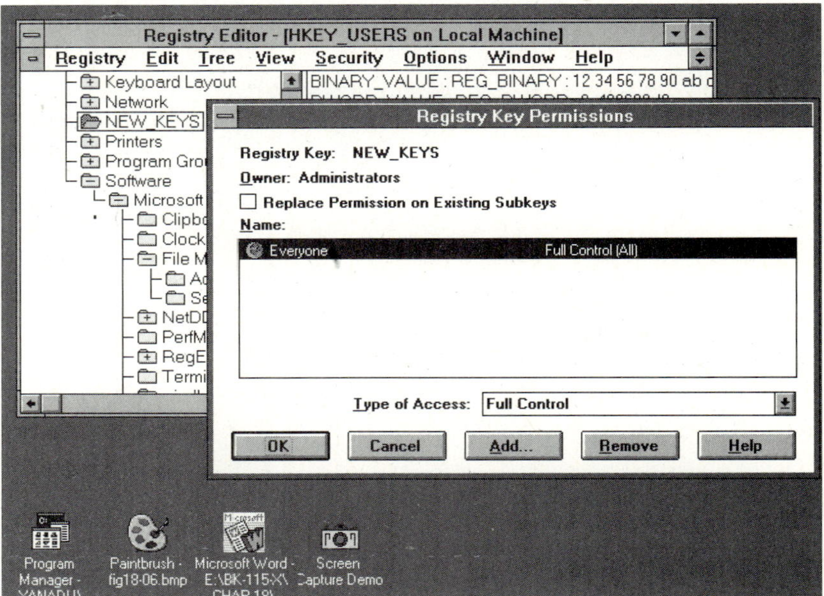

Figure 18.9
The Registry Key Permissions dialog box

3. Select the Replace Permission On Existing Subkeys check box to override permissions previously set on subkeys of the selected key.

4. Select the access type to assign from the Types Of Access pull-down list.

   - Read access permits users to read the key's contents, but does not permit changes to be made.
   - Full Control access permits users to access, edit, or assume ownership of the key.

- Special access permits designated users to access and to edit the key's Registry data.

5. Select OK to return to Registry Editor.

To add users or user groups to the Permissions list:

1. Select the Add button in the Registry Key Permissions dialog box. The Add Users And Groups dialog box shown in Figure 18.10 appears.

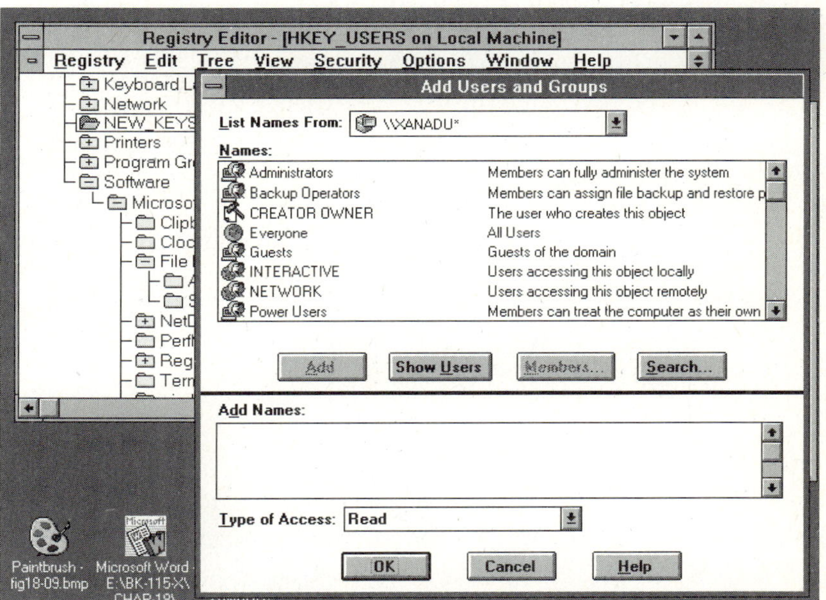

Figure 18.10
The Add Users And Groups dialog box

2. Select the workstation or domain where the user or user group has an account from the List Names From list box.
3. Select the appropriate user group from the Names list box.
   - Or select the Show Users button for a list of users who have accounts on the selected workstation or domain.
   - Or select the Members button to see the names of users in a selected user group.
4. Select the Add button. The users or user groups selected appear in the Add Names box.

5. Select the level of access to grant from the Type Of Access list box.
6. Select OK to return to the Registry Key Permissions dialog box.
7. Select OK to set the new permissions.
8. If the Replace Permissions check box is selected, a dialog box appears requesting confirmation.
9. Select OK.

To remove a user or user group from the permissions list:

1. Select the name of the user or user group to remove from the permissions list.
2. Select the Remove button. The selected user or user group is removed from the Name list.

Help Files ▼ The owner of a Registry key can set access permissions for other users, including permission for other users to assume ownership of the Registry key. At the same time, names can be added or removed from the list of users or user groups who have authorized access.

▶ Searching the Permissions List

To locate users or user groups to assign permissions:

- Select the Show Users option to see the names of all users who have accounts on the workstation.
- Select the Members option to identify members of a selected user group.
- Select the Search option to locate either a user account or a user group.

To invoke the Show Users option:

1. Select a Registry Editor key.

2. Select Permission from the Security menu. The Registry Key Permissions dialog box appears—see Figure 18.9.
3. Select the Add button. The Add Users And Groups dialog box appears—see Figure 18.10.
4. Select the workstation or domain from the List Names From list box to identify user accounts. The Names list box shows the names of user groups in the selected workstation or domain.
5. Select the Show Users button. The Names list box shows the names of user accounts on the workstation.

To identify members of a user group:

1. Select the Add button from the Registry Key Permissions dialog box. The Add Users And Groups dialog box appears—see Figure 18.10.
2. Select a user group name from the Names list box.
3. Select the Members button. The Local Group Membership dialog box shown in Figure 18.11 appears.

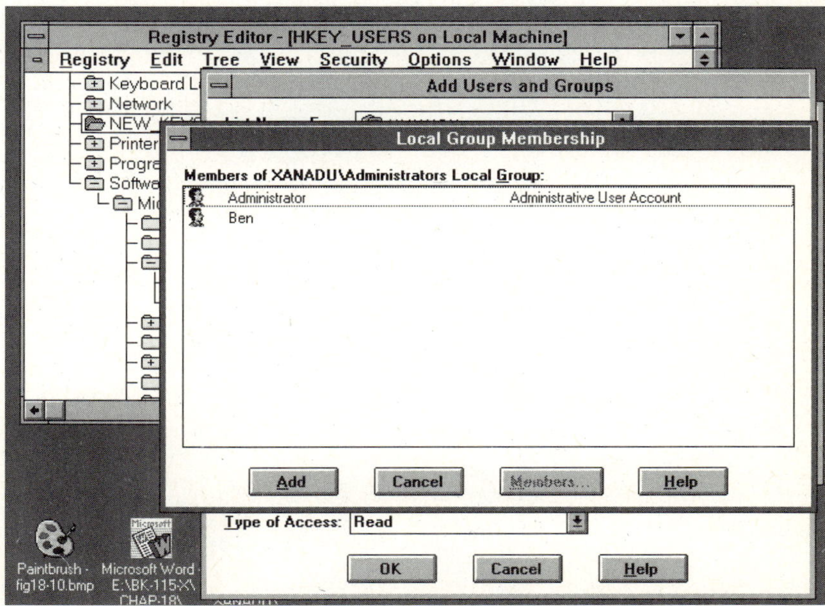

Figure 18.11
The Local Group Membership dialog box

4. If only user accounts appear in the Local Group Membership dialog box, select OK.
5. To identify members of a global group appearing in the Local Group Membership, select the group, and then select OK.
6. When the Global Group Memberships dialog box appears, select the user account to locate, and then select OK.
7. On return to the Add Users And Groups dialog box, the selected group or user appears in the Add Names dialog box.
8. Select the level of access to grant from the Type Of Access list box.
9. Select OK to return to the Registry Key Permissions dialog box.
10. Select OK to return to Registry Editor.

To search the permissions list:

1. Select the Add button from the Registry Key Permissions dialog box. The Add Users And Groups dialog box appears—see Figure 18.10.
2. Select the Search button. The Find Account dialog box shown in Figure 18.12 appears.

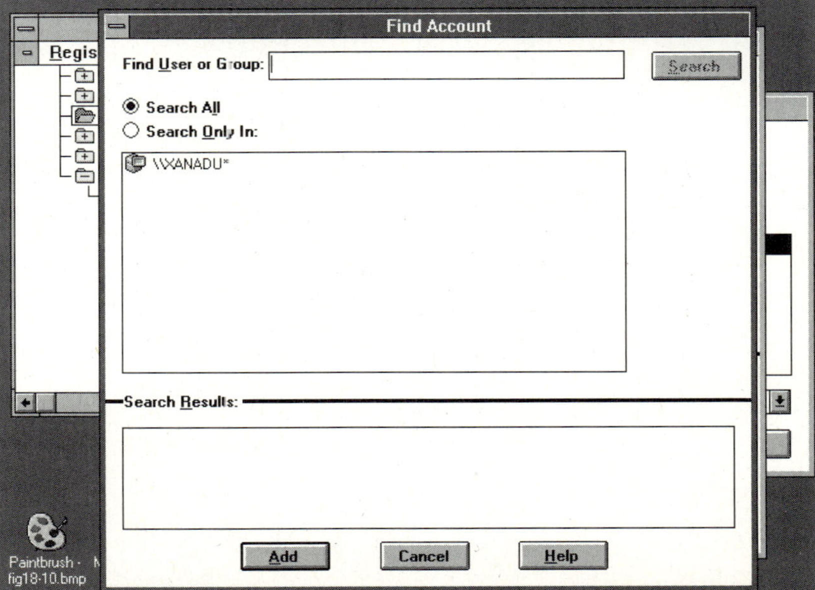

Figure 18.12
The Find Account dialog box

3. Enter the name of a user account or user group in the Find User Or Group edit box.
4. Select Search All to search all computers and domains listed.
5. Select (highlight) specific computers or domains from the listed computers to limit the search. The Search Only In option is automatically selected.
6. Select Search. The Search Results box lists all user accounts found.
7. Select Add to return to the Add Users And Groups dialog box with the located name listing in the Names list box.
8. Select the level of access to grant from the Type Of Access list box.
9. Select OK to return to the Registry Key Permissions dialog box.
10. Select OK to return to Registry Editor.

▸ Auditing Registry Key Activity

To audit activity on a Registry key:

Registry keys can only be audited by members of the Administrators group.

1. Select the Registry key to audit.
2. Select Auditing from the Security menu. The Registry Key Auditing dialog box shown in Figure 18.13 appears.
   - The prompt "Registry Key" identifies the name of the selected key.
   - The Name box lists the users and user groups being audited.
3. Select the Audit Permissions On Existing Subkeys check box to audit activity on all subkeys of the key being audited. If clear, only the primary key activity is audited.
4. Select the name of a group or user from the Name list box. The Events To Audit box is enabled and shows which events the selected group or user is already being audited for.
5. Select or clear activities in the Events To Audit box.
   - Select Success to audit successful activities on the selected Registry key.

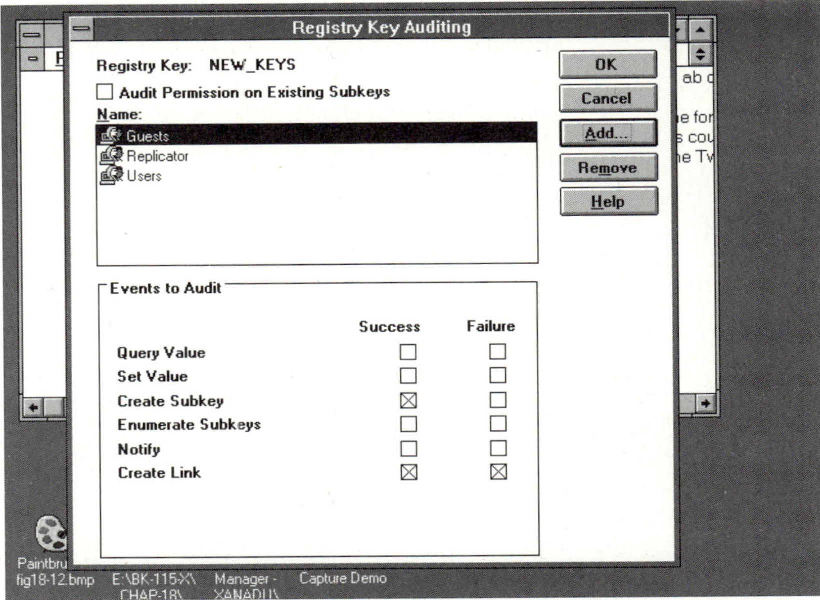

Figure 18.13
The Registry Key Auditing dialog box

- Select Failure to audit failed activities on the selected Registry key.

6. Repeat steps 4 and 5 as needed.
7. Select OK. Registry Editor audits the activities and users or groups selected.

To add users to the Audit list:

1. Select the Add button from the Registry Key Auditing dialog box. The Add Users And Groups dialog box—Figure 18.10—appears, displaying the user groups in the List Names From list box on the currently selected computer or domain.
2. To view user groups on a different workstation or domain, select the computer or domain from the List Names From list box, and then select OK. The user groups from the selected domain are now displayed.
3. Select a user or user group from the Names list.

4. Select Add. The names of the users or user groups to add to the audit list appear in the Add Names box at the bottom of the Add Users And Groups dialog box.
5. Select OK to return to the Audit dialog box.
6. Select the Events To Audit for each of the new groups.
7. Select OK. The users, user groups, and events added are now included in the Audit list.

To remove a user or user group from the Audit lists:

1. Select the user name to remove from the audit list in the Registry Key Auditing dialog box.
2. Select the Remove button—the selected user name or group is removed from the Audit list.

Help Files ▼ The Auditing option in Registry Editor tracks changes made to Registry data, identifying the users making the changes. Both successful and unsuccessful actions can be audited.

▶ Searching the Audit List

To locate users or user groups to add to the audit list:

- Select the Show Users option to see the names of all users who have accounts on the workstation.
- Select the Members option to identify members of a selected user group.
- Select the Search option to locate either a user account or a user group.

To use the Show Users option:

1. Select a Registry key from the tree pane in a Registry Editor window.

2. Select Auditing from the Security menu. The Registry Key Auditing dialog box—Figure 18.13—appears.
3. Select the Add button. The Add Users And Groups dialog box appears—see Figure 18.10.
4. Select the workstation or domain from the List Names From list box to identify user accounts. The Names list box shows the names of user groups in the selected workstation or domain.
5. Select the Show Users button. The Names list box shows the names of user accounts on the workstation.

To identify the members of a user group:

1. Select the Add button from the Registry Key Auditing dialog box. The Add Users And Groups dialog box appears.
2. Proceed in the same fashion used to identify members of a user group under "Searching the Permissions List," preceding.
3. On return to the Registry Key Auditing dialog box, select the Events To Audit options.
4. Select OK to return to Registry Editor.

To search the audit list:

1. Select the Add button from the Registry Key Auditing dialog box. The Add Users And Groups dialog box appears.
2. Proceed in the same fashion as "Searching the Permissions List," preceding.
3. On return to the Registry Key Auditing dialog box, select the Events To Audit options.
4. Select OK to return to Registry Editor.

▸ Yielding Control of a Registry Key

To yield control of a Registry key:

1. Select the Registry key.

2. Select the Permissions option in the Security menu. The Registry Key Permissions dialog box—Figure 18.9—appears.
3. Select the name of the user who will be granted full control from the Name list box.
4. Select Full Control from the Type Of Access list box.
5. Select OK.

Help Files ▼ The owner of a Registry key can grant full control to another user who can, subsequently, assume ownership of the key.

▶ Assuming Ownership of a Registry Key

Full control of a Registry key must have been granted by the previous owner before ownership can be assumed by a new owner.

To assume ownership of a Registry key:

1. Select the Registry key.
2. Select the Owner option from the Security menu. The Owner dialog box shown in Figure 18.14 appears, displaying the name of the key and the name of the present owner.
3. Select the Take Ownership button. Ownership of the selected key is granted to the current user.

Help Files ▼ Ownership of a Registry key can be assumed by any user who is logged on as an Administrator without that user having been granted permission. However, this event is audited, and the key cannot be given back to the original owner.

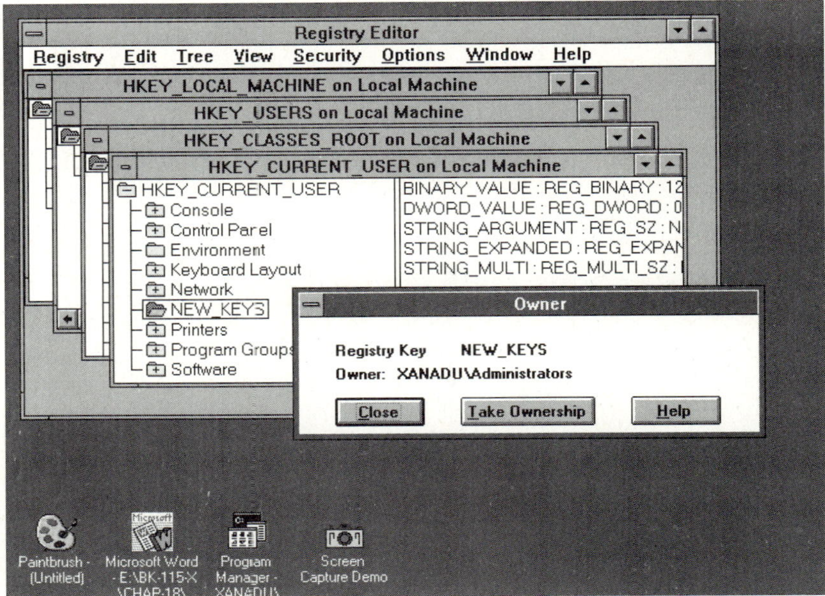

Figure 18.14
The Owner dialog box

▶ Viewing Registry Data in the Read Only Mode

To view data in the Read Only mode:

- Select the Read Only option from the Options menu. A check mark appears next to the Read Only option indicating the option is active.

Help Files ▼ The Read Only option protects the Registry data against accidental alteration. Any changes made will not be saved.

▸ Confirming Deletions

To select the Confirm On Delete option:

- Select Confirm On Delete from the Options menu. A check mark appears next to the Read On Delete option indicating the option is active.

Help Files ▼ The Confirm On Delete option protects the Registry data against accidental deletion. When enabled, Registry Editor will request confirmation before deleting a Registry key or value entry.

Changing the Appearance of Registry Editor

▸ Selecting a Font

To select a font:

1. Select the Font option from the Options menu. The Fonts dialog box appears.
2. Select a font from the Font list box.
3. Select a point size from the Size list box.
4. Select a style from the Styles list.
5. Select OK.

Help Files ▼ The Sample box displays the results of the font, size, and style selections. The font selection affects all Registry windows.

▶ Switching Views in Registry Editor

To view only the Registry key tree:

- Select the Tree Only option from the View menu.

To view only the value entries:

- Select the Data Only option from the View menu.

To view both tree and data:

- Select the Tree And Data option (default view) from the View menu.

▶ Expanding and Collapsing the Registry Tree

To expand one level of a Registry key:

1. Select a Registry key.
2. Select the Expand One Level option from the Tree menu.
   - Or press Enter.

To expand a branch of a Registry tree:

1. Select a Registry key.
2. Select the Expand Branch option from the Tree menu.
   - Or press the asterisk (*) key.
   - Or double-click on the branch icon.

To expand all of the levels of a Registry tree:

1. Select a Registry key.

2. Select the Expand All option from the Tree menu.
   - Or press Shift+@.

To collapse a branch of a Registry key:

1. Select an expanded Registry key.
2. Select the Collapse Branch option in the Tree menu.
   - Or press Enter.
   - Or press the minus (–) key.
   - Or double-click on the branch icon.

▶ Arranging Registry Windows and Icons

To cascade the Registry windows:

- Select Cascade from the View menu.

To tile the Registry windows:

- Select Tile from the View menu.

To arrange Registry window icons:

- Select the Arrange option from the View menu.

▶ Splitting Registry Windows

To split a Registry window by using the keyboard:

1. Select the split option from the View menu—a vertical bar appears in the window.
2. Select arrow keys to move the bar position.
3. Press Enter to set the bar position or Esc to cancel the command.

To split a Registry window by using the mouse:

1. Click on the vertical bar.
2. Drag the bar to the desired position and release.

Printers and Printer Options

▶ Printing Registry Data

To print a subtree:

1. Select a key in a Registry window tree pane.
2. Select Print Subtree from the Registry menu to print all data contained in the selected subtree.

Help Files ▼ When a key is printed from Registry Editor, output includes the key, the key's descendent keys, and all value entries belonging to all descendent keys.

▶ Print Setup

To set up for printing:

1. Select Printer Setup from the Registry menu. The Printer Setup dialog box appears.
2. In the Printer Setup dialog box, select the printer to use.
3. In the Form box, select the form in which to print.
4. In the Orientation box, select the page orientation.
   - Select Portrait for a vertical orientation, printing text from top to bottom.
   - Select Landscape for a horizontal orientation, printing text from side to side.
5. Select OK.

THE RESCUE PAGES: Registry Editor

Help! Windows NT seems to be totally messed up. I think I might have changed something in Registry Editor.

Well, it's definitely possible...and can, definitely, be serious...very serious. But, without knowing exactly what was changed, it's impossible to suggest a specific fix.

However, there is a general fix that, hopefully, will put you back in operation again, although it won't recover everything. You will need the Windows NT installation disk—the 3.5-inch install disk that boots the system—and the Emergency Repair Disk.

To recover the system, boot the installation disk, but instead of installing Windows NT, select the Repair option and follow directions. This should get Windows NT back into operation even if it doesn't restore everything absolutely.

Now that the system is back in operation, perform another restoration from your backup tapes. This should complete the recovery process, but in the future, be very careful before making any changes in the Registry information.

The best rule of thumb is: If you don't know what you're changing ...and why...DON'T.

CHAPTER

19

HELP! Schedule+

The Schedule+ facility is supplied as part of Windows NT's built-in networking. The Schedule+ utility replaces and extends the Calendar utility from Windows 3.1. The Schedule+ utility can be used on-line (networked) or off-line (standalone), providing facilities to maintain an appointment calendar, schedule tasks, and track project-related meetings and jobs.

Topics discussed in this chapter include

- Working with Schedule+
- Managing the Schedule+ environment
- Other scheduling programs
- Maintaining appointment schedules
- Keeping track of appointments
- Task scheduling
- Keeping track of tasks
- Communication with other users
- Accessing another user's appointment book
- Access privileges

Working with Schedule+

▶ Signing in to Schedule+

To work off-line with Schedule+ already running:

1. Select Work Off-line from the File menu.
2. Enter your mail name and password in the Password dialog box.
3. Select OK.

If Schedule+ is not running:

1. Disconnect from the Microsoft Mail server.
2. Start Schedule+.

If a prompt appears to create a local schedule file:

1. Select OK.
2. Enter the location of an existing local schedule file.

To work on-line with Schedule+:

You must be connected to your mail server to use Schedule+ on-line.

1. Select Work On-line from the File menu.
2. Enter your mail name and password in the Password dialog box.
3. Select OK.

Help Files ▼ Schedule+ can be started off-line automatically through the General Options selection from the Options menu. Also, if the Microsoft Mail facility is not available, Schedule+ will come up off-line.

Changing Passwords

To change a password:

1. Select Change Password from the Options menu.
2. Enter the current password in the Password box. The entry does not appear as it is typed.
3. Select OK.
4. Enter the new password in the Password box.
5. Select OK.
6. Enter the new password in the Password box a second time as confirmation. If this entry does not match the first, you will be prompted to type the password again until a match is entered.
7. Select OK.

HELP! *To abort password changes at any time, select the Cancel button.*

Help Files If you are using Microsoft Mail, your Schedule+ password will be the same as the Mail password.

Quitting Schedule+

To quit Schedule+, leaving the Reminders and Mail programs active:

- Select Exit from the File menu.

To quit the Schedule+, Reminders, and Mail programs:

- Select Exit and Sign Out from the File menu. When Schedule+, Schedule+ Reminders, or the Mail program is started again, an account name and password will be required.

Managing the Schedule+ Environment

▶ Customizing Schedule+ Settings

The following Schedule+ options can be customized:

The Control Panel can be used to customize date and time formats used in schedule displays.

- Reminders type and timing
- Whether week numbers are displayed on the calendar
- What day the week begins on
- The beginning and end of a normal workday
- Starting Schedule+ on-line or off-line
- Schedule accounts for resources such as conference rooms, equipment, and so on
- Colors for the Appointment Book and Planner
- Font sizes for Appointment Book entries

To customize Schedule+ display settings:

1. Select Display from the Options menu. The Display dialog box shown in Figure 19.1 appears.
2. Select settings and changes from the Display dialog box.
3. Select OK.

To customize general Schedule+ options:

1. Select General Options from the Options menu. The General Options dialog box shown in Figure 19.2 appears.
2. Select or change settings as desired.
3. Select OK.

▶ Displaying or Hiding the Status Bar

To display or conceal the status bar:

- Select Status Bar from the Options menu.

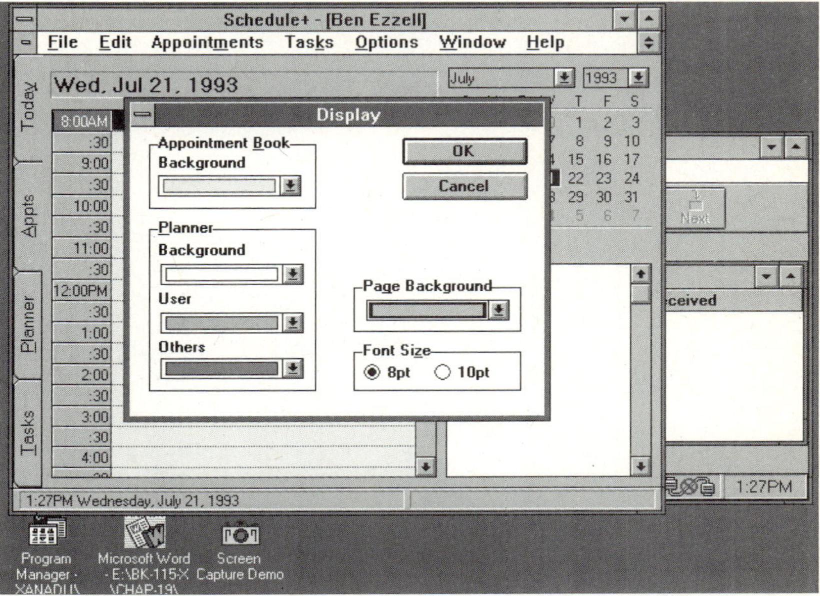

Figure 19.1
The Display dialog box

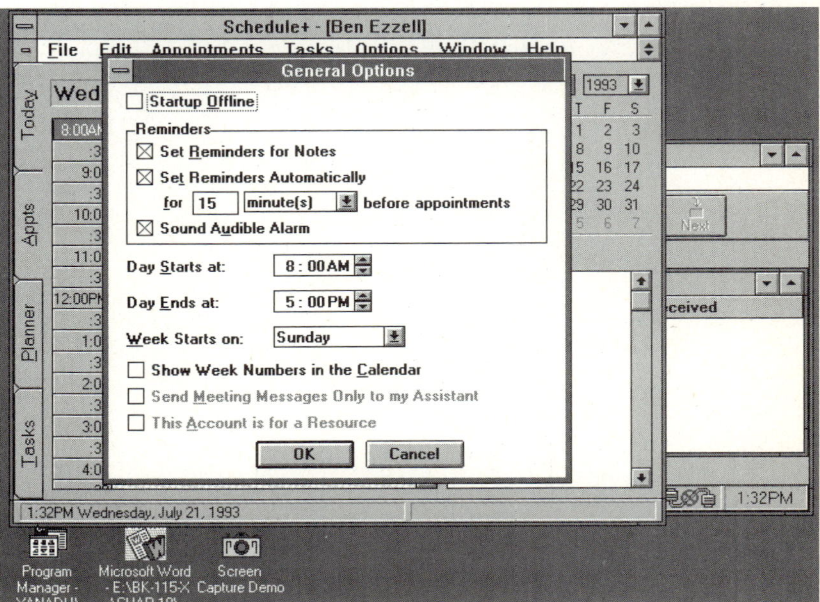

Figure 19.2
The General Options dialog box

▶ Archiving a Schedule

To save schedule information as an archive:

1. Select Create Archive from the File menu. The Create Archive dialog box shown in Figure 19.3 appears.

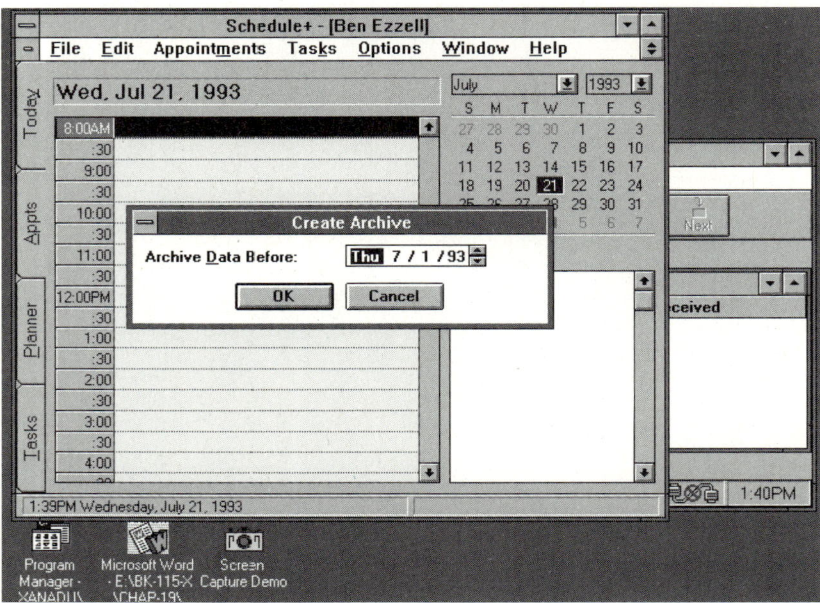

Figure 19.3
The Create Archive dialog box

2. Select a date in the Archive Data Before edit box. All entries preceding this data will be archived.
   - Enter a date directly.
   - Or use the up and down arrow buttons to change the date displayed.
3. Select OK.
4. If the archive drive, directory, or file identified in the file selection dialog box is not correct, select a new drive, directory, or file name.
5. Select OK.

Help Files ▼ The default archive file is named using the first eight characters of the schedule owner's mailbox name and the extension .ARC. If the file name already exists, the archived data is appended to the existing archive file.

▶ Viewing an Archived Schedule

To view an archived schedule:

1. Select Open Archive from the File menu.
2. Select the archive to open from the Open Archive file selection dialog box.
3. The archived schedule appears in the Schedule+ window, where it can be viewed, edited, or altered in the same fashion as a normal schedule. Changes are saved to the archive file.
4. Close the Appointment Book window to exit from the archived schedule.

▶ Moving a Local Schedule File

To relocate a local schedule file:

1. Select Move Local File from the File menu. A file selection dialog box appears.
2. Select a drive from the Drives list box.
3. Select a directory from the Directories list box.
4. Select OK.

Other Scheduling Programs

▶ Importing Information from Another Schedule Manager

If the import process is canceled before completion, appointments that have already been added to the Appointment Book are not removed.

To import information from another schedule manager:

1. Select Import Appointments from the File menu. A file selection dialog box appears.
2. Select a drive, path, and schedule file to import into Schedule+.
3. Select OK. The Import Format dialog box—Figure 19.4—appears.

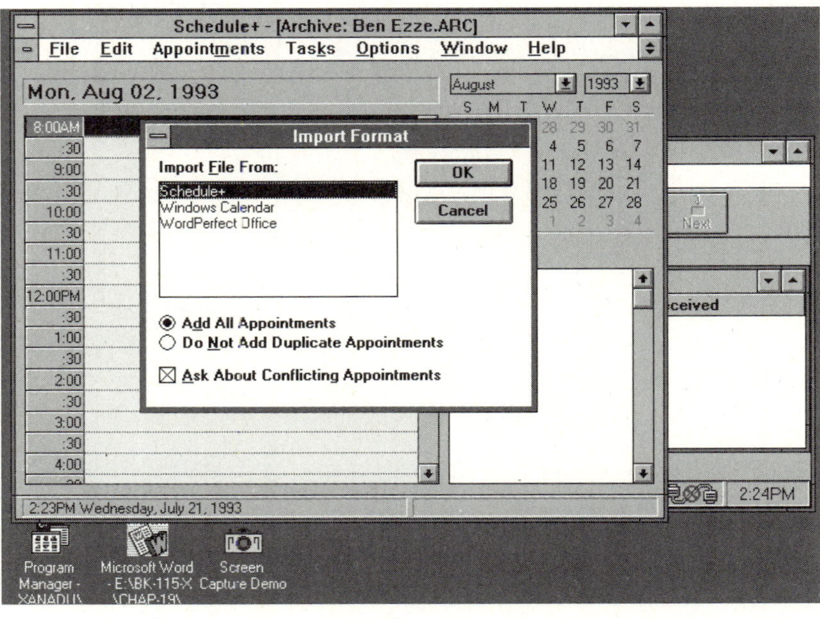

Figure 19.4
The Import Format dialog box

4. Select the schedule program type from the Import File From list box.
   - Select the Add All Appointments option to copy all appointments, including duplicate and conflicting appointments.
   - Select the Do Not Add Duplicate Appointments option to copy all appointments except duplicates.

- Select the Ask About Conflicting Appointments option to have Schedule+ prompt before copying conflicting appointments.

5. Select OK to import appointments.

Help Files ▼ Schedule+ attempts to recognize the format of the imported file. However, if no file format is recognized, a file format must be selected. Also, access privileges are required to create or modify the schedule that information is being copied to.

▶ Exporting Schedule Information

To export schedule information to another program:

1. Select Export Appointments from the File menu. The Export Appointments dialog box—Figure 19.5—appears.
2. Select an export format from the File Format list box.
3. Select All to copy the entire schedule.
   - Or select the Schedule Range option and enter first and last dates to copy appointments between.
4. Select the Include Daily Notes check box to copy daily notes.
5. Select OK. A file selection dialog box appears.
6. Select the drive, directory, file name, and an export file format from the Export Appointments file selection dialog box.
7. Select OK.

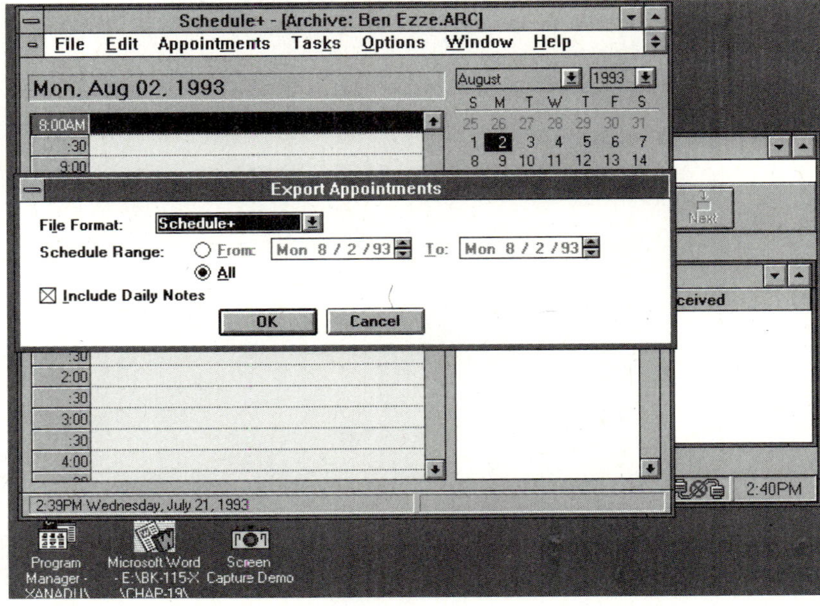

Figure 19.5
The Export Appointments dialog box

Maintaining Appointment Schedules

▶ Scheduling an Appointment

To schedule an appointment:

To enter an appointment quickly using the default settings, simply double-click on the time slot and type the description or highlight the time slot(s), press Enter, and type a description.

1. Select a time slot in the Appointment Book. The Appointment Book appears in Figure 19.6.
2. Select New Appointment from the Appointments menu. The Appointment dialog box—Figure 19.7—appears.
3. Enter a brief description of the appointment in the Description box.
4. Select the Set Reminder For check box and specify the advance interval to set a reminder for the appointment.
5. Select the Tentative check box to schedule this appointment as tentative.
6. Select the Private check box to make this appointment private.
7. Select OK.

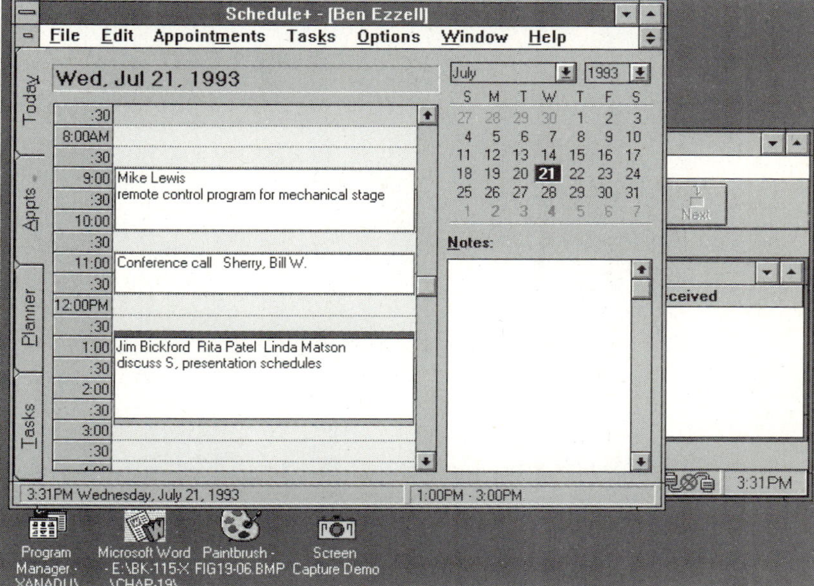

Figure 19.6
The Schedule+ Appointment Book screen

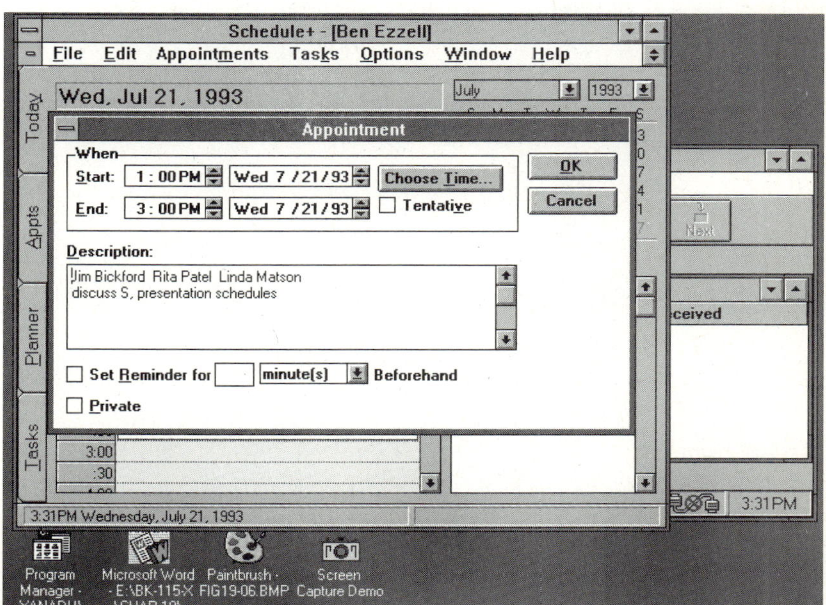

Figure 19.7
The Appointment dialog box

To duplicate an appointment:

1. Select the appointment to duplicate from the Appointment Book.
2. Select the Copy Appt command from the Edit menu.
3. Select the day in the Appointment Book to copy the appointment to.
4. Select the time slot to copy the appointment to.
5. Select the Paste command from the Edit menu.
6. Repeat steps 3 through 5 to copy the same appointment to additional time slots.

▶ Changing or Deleting an Appointment

To change an appointment description:

- Select the appointment.
- Delete the text in the time slot.
- Enter a new description.

To change an appointment time:

- Select the appointment.
- Click on the broad bar at the top of the appointment slot.
- Drag the appointment to a new time.

To change an appointment's duration:

- Select the appointment.
- Click on the bottom of the appointment slot.
- Drag the handle up or down to a new time.

Alternatively, an appointment can be changed as follows:

1. Select the appointment from the Appointment Book.
2. Select Edit Appt from the Edit menu.

3. Make changes to the start and end times, description, reminder alert and time, status and so on.

4. Select OK to save the changes.

To delete an appointment:

1. Select the appointment to delete.

2. Select Delete Appt from the Edit menu.

   - Or press Ctrl+D.

▶ Scheduling Recurring Appointments

To create a new, recurring appointment:

1. Select the time slot for the recurring appointment.

2. Select New Recurring Appt from the Appointments menu. The Recurring Appointment dialog box—Figure 19.8—appears.

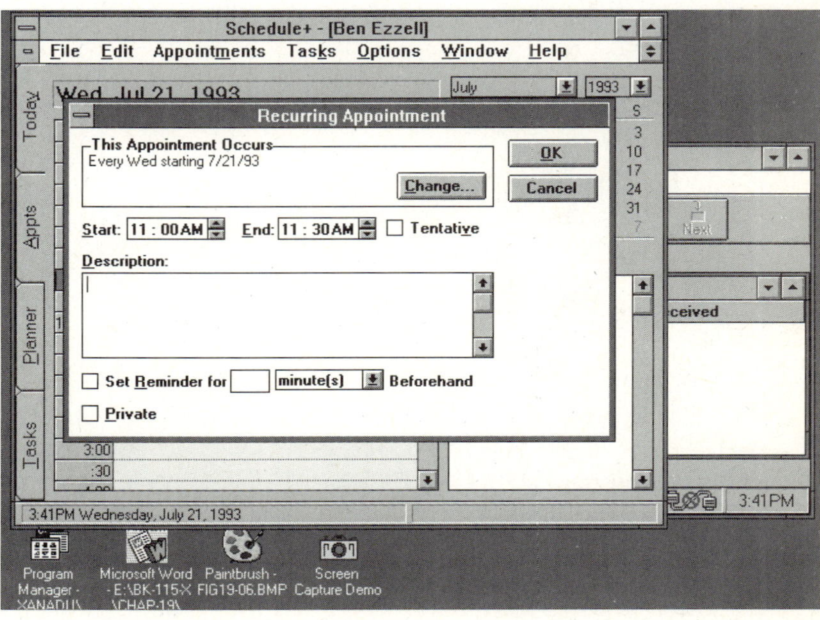

Figure 19.8
The Recurring Appointment dialog box

3. Select the Change button in the This Appointment Occurs box to revise the recurrence pattern and start date for the appointment. See "Changing Intervals for Recurring Appointments," following.
4. To change the start or end time for the appointment, select the hour or minutes from the Start or End edit boxes.
   - Use the up and down arrows to change the time.
   - Or type a new time in the edit box.
5. Enter a brief description of the appointment in the Description box.
6. Select the Set Reminder For check box and specify the advance interval to set a reminder for the appointment.
7. Select the Tentative check box to schedule this appointment as tentative.
8. Select the Private check box to make this appointment private.
9. Select OK.

To identify an existing appointment as a recurring appointment:

1. Select an existing appointment from the Appointment Book.
2. Select New Recurring Appt from the Appointments menu. The Recurring Appointment dialog box—Figure 19.8—appears.
3. Select the Change button in the This Appointment Occurs box to revise the recurrence pattern and start date for the appointment. See "Changing Intervals for Recurring Appointments," following.
4. Select OK.

Changing Intervals for Recurring Appointments

To change a recurring appointment's interval:

1. Select the Change button from the Recurring Appointment dialog box. The Change Recurrence dialog box appears—see Figure 19.9.

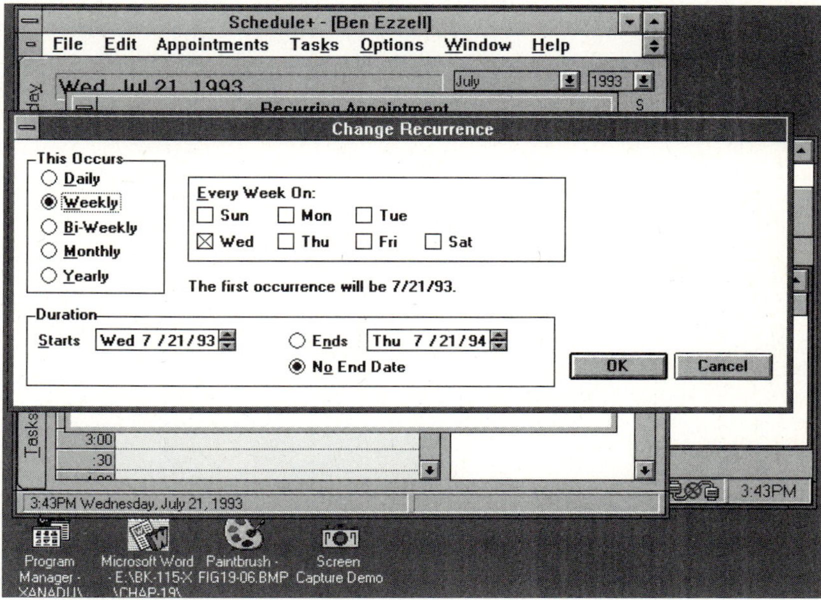

Figure 19.9
The Change Recurrence dialog box

2. Select the interval from the This Occurs box by selecting Daily, Weekly, Bi-Weekly, Monthly, or Yearly.

- For Daily recurrence, select Every day or Every weekday.
- For Weekly or Bi-Weekly recurrence, select the day of the week.
- For Monthly recurrence, select a day of the month or a week and weekday.
- For Yearly recurrence, select a day and month or select a week, day of week, and month.

3. To change the start or end date for a recurring appointment, select the hour or minutes from the Starts or Ends edit box.

- Use the up and down arrows to change time.
- Or type a new time in the edit box.
- Or select the No End Date option.

4. Select OK.

Changing or Deleting Recurring Appointments

To view a list of all recurring appointments:

- Select Edit Recurring Appts from the Appointments menu.

To change a single instance of a recurring appointment:

Changing a single recurring appointment is the same as changing a regular appointment. Other instances of the appointment are unaffected.

1. Double-click on the appointment entry.
2. Make changes in the Appointment dialog box.
3. Select OK.

To change all occurrences of a recurring appointment:

1. Select Edit Recurring Appts from the Appointments menu. The Edit Recurring Appointments dialog box—Figure 19.10—appears.

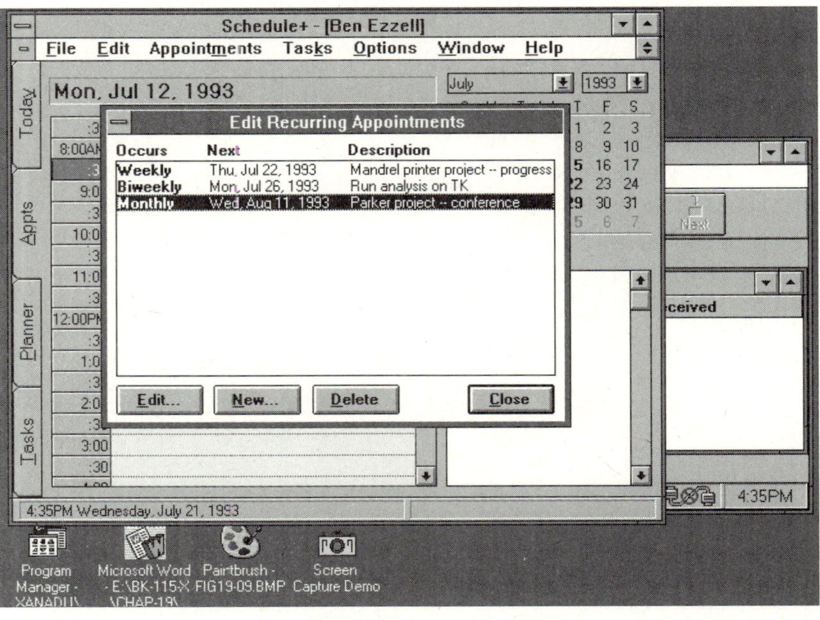

Figure 19.10
The Edit Recurring Appointments dialog box

2. Select the appointment to change from the list of recurring appointments.

3. Select the Edit button or double-click on the appointment entry.
4. In the Recurring Appointment dialog box—Figure 19.8—make any changes desired.

Deleting a single recurring appointment is the same as deleting a regular appointment.

To delete a single occurrence of a recurring appointment:

1. Select the appointment to delete from the Appointment Book.
2. Select Delete Appt from the Edit menu.

To delete all occurrences of a recurring appointment:

1. Select Edit Recurring Appt from the Appointments menu. The Edit Recurring Appointments dialog box—Figure 19.10—appears.
2. Select the appointment to delete from the list of recurring appointments.
3. Select the Delete button.
4. Select Close.

Arranging a Meeting

Some options discussed here—such as the Change button, names of attendees, and auto-scheduling—are available only on a network with the Microsoft Mail facility operating.

To arrange a meeting from the Planner:

1. Select the Planner by clicking on the Planner tab at the left side of the Schedule+ window. The Planner appears in Figure 19.11.
2. Select the Change button to change the names in the Attendees list box.
3. Enter any accompanying message in the message area.
4. Select a time slot when all attendees are available.
   - Or select the Auto-Pick button to allow Schedule+ to select a time when everyone is free.
5. Select the Request Meeting button.
6. In the Subject box, type a brief description of the meeting. The Subject entry appears in the Appointment Book after the meeting is confirmed.

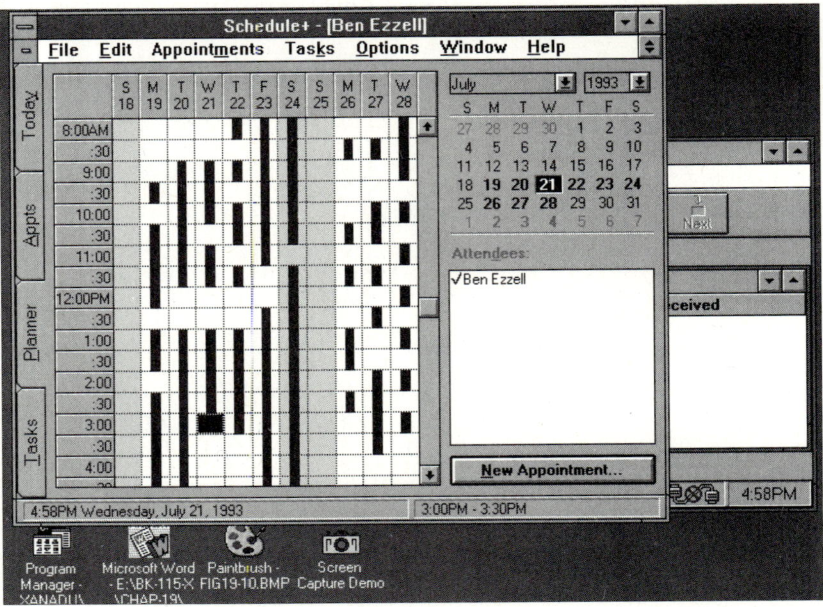

Figure 19.11
The Schedule+ Planner dialog box

7. Clear the Ask For Responses check box if responses are not required.
8. Select the Send button.

To set up a meeting from the Appointment Book:

1. Select the Appointment Book by clicking on the Appts tab at the left side of the Schedule+ window. The Appointment Book appears as shown in Figure 19.6.
2. Select a time slot for the meeting. The time can be changed later if a scheduling conflict occurs.
3. Select New Appointment from the Appointments menu.
4. Select the Choose Time button.
5. Select the Change button in the Attendees box.
6. Select the attendees' names from the address list.
7. Select OK.

8. Move the appointment to a time slot when all attendees are available.
   - Or select the Auto-Pick button to allow Schedule+ to select a time when everyone is free.
9. Enter a description of the meeting in the Description box.
10. Select the Invite button.
11. In the Subject box, type a brief description of the meeting. The Subject entry appears in the Appointment Book after the meeting is confirmed.
12. Clear the Ask For Responses check box if responses are not required.
13. Enter any accompanying message in the message area.
14. Select the Send button.

▸ Scheduling Resources

To schedule a room or resource while scheduling a meeting:

- Add the resource to the list of Attendees invited.

To schedule a room or resource without attendees:

1. Select the Planner.
2. Select the Change button in the Attendees box.
3. Select the name for the resource from the address list.
4. Select OK.
5. Select a time slot when the resource is available.
   - Select any time slot in the grid for the length of time the resource is needed.
   - Select Auto-Pick from the Appointments menu to find a time slot when the resource is available for the required time.
6. Select the Request Meeting button.
7. Optionally, enter a brief description in the Subject box.

8. Enter an optional message to include with the meeting request.
9. Select the Send button.

Canceling or Rescheduling Meetings

To reschedule a meeting:

1. Select the Appointment Book.
2. Select the meeting from the list of appointments.
3. Click and drag the meeting to a new time slot.
4. Select Yes at the Notification query to allow Schedule+ to notify other attendees of the change.
5. Enter an optional note in the message area.
6. Select Send. Attendees receive new meeting requests for the new time slot, which they may accept, tentatively accept, or decline.

To cancel a meeting:

1. Select the Appointment Book.
2. Select the meeting from the list of appointments.
3. Select Delete Appt from the Edit menu.
4. Select Yes at the Notification query to allow Schedule+ to notify other attendees of the change.
5. Enter an optional note in the message area.
6. Select Send. Attendees receive notification of the cancellation.

Setting Appointment Reminders

To set a reminder for a new appointment:

1. Select a time slot from the Appointment Book.

2. Double-click on the selected time slot.

    - Or select New Appointment from the Appointments menu.

3. Enter a description and settings.
4. Select the Set Reminder check box.
5. Enter a reminder interval in the edit box.
6. Select interval units as minutes (default), hours, days, weeks, or months.
7. Select OK.

To set a reminder for an existing appointment:

1. Select an appointment from the Appointment Book.
2. Double-click on the selected appointment.

    - Or select Edit Appt from the Edit menu.

3. Follow steps 4 through 7, preceding.

Alternatively, to set a reminder for an existing appointment by using the default interval:

1. Select an appointment from the Appointment Book.
2. Select the Set Reminder option from the Appointments menu.

To set a reminder for all occurrences of a recurring appointment:

1. Select Edit Recurring Appts from the Appointments menu. The Edit Recurring Appointments dialog box—Figure 19.10—appears.
2. Select the appointment to change from the list of recurring appointments.
3. Select Edit from the option buttons or double-click on the appointment entry.
4. In the Recurring Appointment dialog box—Figure 19.8—select the Set Reminder For check box.
5. Enter a reminder interval in the edit box.

6. Select interval units as minutes (default), hours, days, weeks, or months.
7. Select OK.
8. Select Close.

To set a reminder automatically for each new appointment:

1. Select General Options from the Options menu.
2. Select the Set Reminders Automatically check box in the Reminders box.
3. Enter a reminder interval in the edit box.
4. Select interval units as minutes (default), hours, days, weeks, or months.
5. Select OK. New appointments now set reminders using the default time selected.

To turn all reminders on or off:

- Select Turn On Reminders or Turn Off Reminders from the File menu. Reminders remain on or off until the selection is reversed again or until Schedule+, Microsoft Mail, or Windows NT is started again.

Keeping Track of Appointments

▶ Adding Daily Notes to the Appointment Book

To add a daily note to the Appointment Book:

1. Click in the Notes window.
   - Or enter Alt+N. The text cursor appears in the Notes window.
2. Add text to the note entry.

To set a reminder for daily notes:

1. Select General Options from the Options menu.
2. Select the Set Reminders For Notes check box in the Reminders box.

3. Select OK.

To delete a daily note:

1. Select (highlight) the text to delete in the Notes box.
2. Select the Del key.

▸ Changing the Dates in the Appointment Book or Planner

To change dates in the Appointment Book or Planner:

1. Click the day to view in the calendar.
2. Click on the month or year arrows to change the month or year.
3. If week numbers are displayed, the Go To Week option from the Edit menu displays a dialog box where the number of the week can be selected.
4. Select OK.

To display today's page:

- Click the Today tab at the left of the Schedule+ window.

▸ Locating Text in the Appointment Book

To locate a text string in the Appointment Book:

1. Select Find from the Edit menu. The Find dialog box—Figure 19.12—appears.
2. Enter a character string in the Search For edit box.
3. Select a search method.
4. Select Start Search.

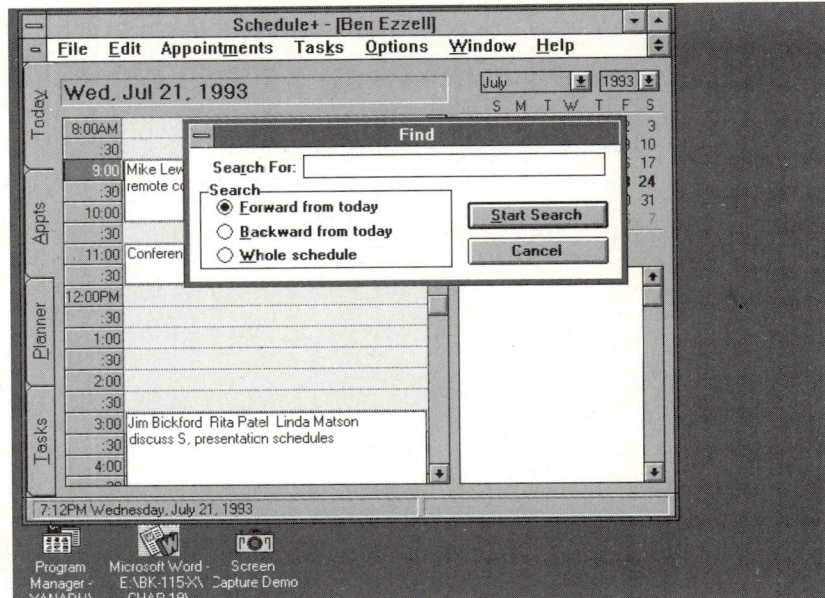

Figure 19.12
The Find dialog box

Help Files ▼ The time required for the search depends on the quantity of information in the Appointment Book. As the search proceeds, a progress bar shows the percentage completed. When the requested string is located, the Appointment Book is displayed with the matching string highlighted.

▶ Printing Appointments, Daily Notes, and Tasks

To print appointments, daily notes, or tasks:

1. Select Print from the File menu. The Print dialog box—Figure 19.13—appears.
2. Select the starting date in the Schedule Range box.

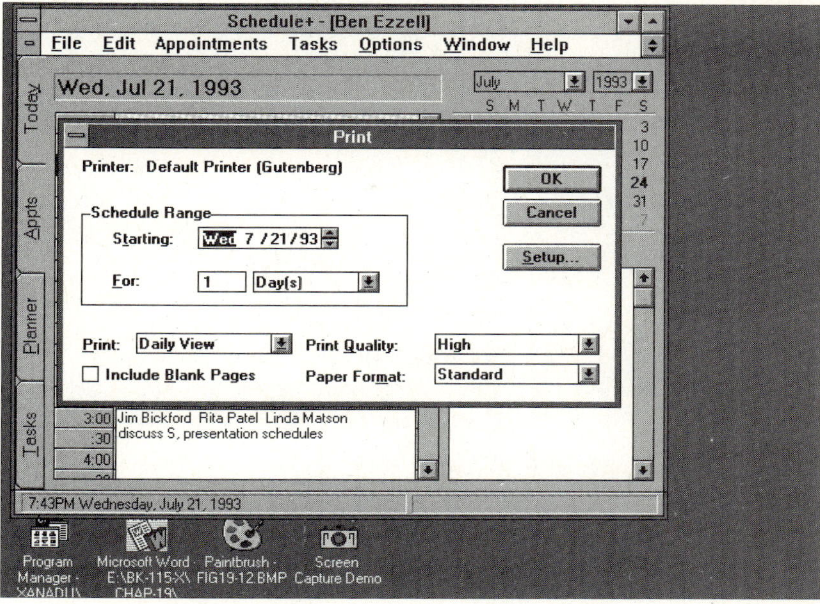

Figure 19.13
The Print dialog box

3. Select the days to print in the Schedule Range box.

- Enter a number in the For edit box.
- Select Days, Weeks, or Months from the interval list.

4. Select a print format from the Print box as:

- *Daily View* prints appointments and daily notes with each day's schedule on a separate page.
- *Weekly View* prints appointments and daily notes with each week's calendar on a separate page.
- *Monthly View* prints appointments and daily notes with each month's calendar on a separate page.
- *Text View* prints appointments and daily notes as a list using a best-fit arrangement, breaking pages as required.
- *Tasks* prints a list of all tasks. No range selection is required.

5. Select print quality in the Print Quality box.

6. Select printout size in the Paper Format box. Format sizes are
   - Standard—approximately 6.5 by 9.5 inches
   - Junior—approximately 4.5 by 7.5 inches
   - Pocket—approximately 3 by 6 inches
7. Select the Setup button to customize margins for a different printout size. The Printer Setup dialog box also permits selecting landscape (versus portrait) page layout and changing printers.
8. Select OK to print.

▶ Tracking Appointments by Associated Projects

To track appointments according to their associated projects:

1. Enter the project name as the first part of the description for the appointment.
2. Export the schedule to a file using text (.TXT) format.
3. Open the exported file in a spreadsheet or database program.
4. Sort the imported material by project name.

Task Scheduling

▶ Adding Projects to a Task List

To add a project to the Task list:

1. Select the Task list by clicking on the Tasks tab at the left of the Schedule+ window.
2. Select the New Project option from the Tasks menu. The Project dialog box—Figure 19.14—appears.
3. Enter a project name in the Name edit box.

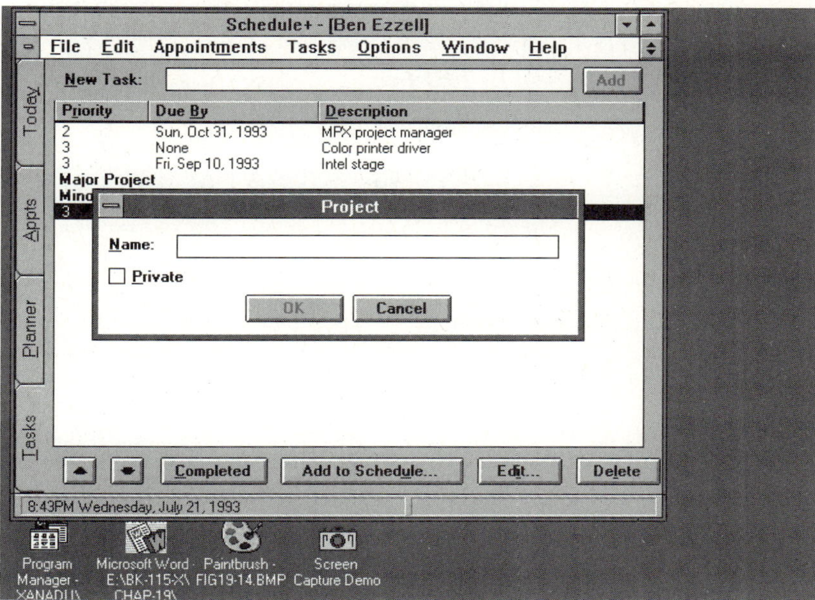

Figure 19.14
The Project dialog box

4. Select the Private check box to make the project private.
5. Select OK. The Project name now appears in the Task list.

HELP! *If the project name doesn't appear, select View By Project from the Tasks menu.*

▶ Adding a Task

To add a new task:

1. Select the Tasks list by clicking on the Task tab at the left of the Schedule+ window.
2. Click on the project to add the task to.
3. Select a New Task from the Tasks menu.
4. Enter a description of the task in the New Task edit box.
5. Click on the Add button. The Task dialog box—Figure 19.15—appears.

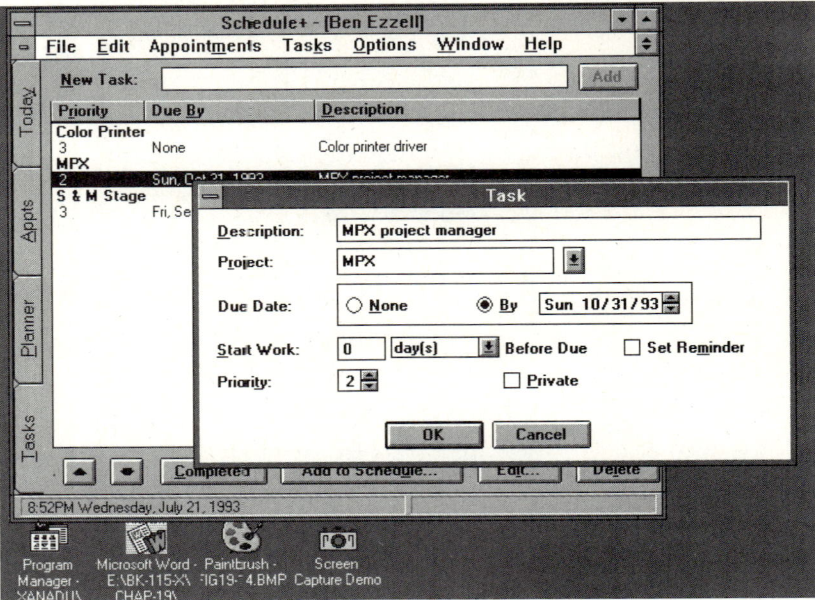

Figure 19.15
The Task dialog box

6. Select the By option and use the arrow buttons to select a due data for the task.

   ■ Or select None to assign no due date.

7. Enter an interval in the Start Work boxes for the task to become active. This sets a time interval prior to the due date when the task becomes active.

   ■ Use the arrow buttons to select Days, Weeks, or Months.

8. Select the Set Reminder check box to set a reminder for the task.

A due date is required before a reminder can be set.

9. Use the arrow buttons to select a task priority in the Priority box.

   ■ Or enter a new priority level.

10. Select the Private check box to designate the task as private.

11. Select OK.

Or:

1. Select New Task from the Tasks menu. The Task dialog box appears as preceding.
2. Enter a description of the task in the Description box.
3. Select a project name to associate the task with from the Project box or select "None" if the task is not associated with a project.
4. Conclude by following steps 5 through 11, preceding.

▸ Moving or Copying a Task

To move a task to another project:

1. Select the Task list by clicking on the Tasks tab at the left of the Schedule+ window.
2. Click on a task and drag it to another project.

To copy a task to another project:

1. Select the Task list by clicking on the Tasks tab at the left of the Schedule+ window.
2. Select a task from the displayed list.
3. Press and hold the Ctrl key while dragging the task to another project.

▸ Changing Task Priority Levels

To change a task's priority level:

1. Select the Tasks list by clicking on the Tasks tab at the left of the Schedule+ window.
2. Select a task from the displayed list.
3. Click the up or down arrow buttons at the bottom of the Task list.

▶ Changing or Deleting a Task or Project

To change a task:

1. Double-click on the task to change.
   - Or select the task and press Enter. The Task dialog box shown in Figure 19.15 appears.
2. Make any changes desired.
3. Select OK.

To delete a task:

1. Select the task to delete in the Task list.
2. Select the Delete button.

To change a project:

1. Double-click on the project to change.
   - Or select the project and press Enter.
2. Enter a new name in the Name box.
3. Select OK.

To delete a project:

1. Select the project to delete from the Task list.
2. Select the Delete button. A message dialog box appears cautioning that all tasks associated with the project will also be deleted.
3. Select the OK button.

The fastest way to remove a number of tasks from a project is to create one task that is not associated with a project, use the mouse to drag each of the other tasks to the unassociated task, and then delete the unassociated task.

To delete a project without deleting its tasks:

1. Double-click on a task.
   - Or select a task and press Enter.
2. In the Task dialog box, change the Project associated with the task to "None."
3. Repeat steps 1 and 2 for all remaining tasks.

4. Delete the project as shown in the preceding section.

▶ Creating a Recurring Task

A recurring task is a convenient way to schedule jobs—such as weekly status reports—which regularly require attention.

To create a recurring task:

1. Select New Recurring Task from the Tasks menu. The Recurring Task dialog box—Figure 19.16—appears.

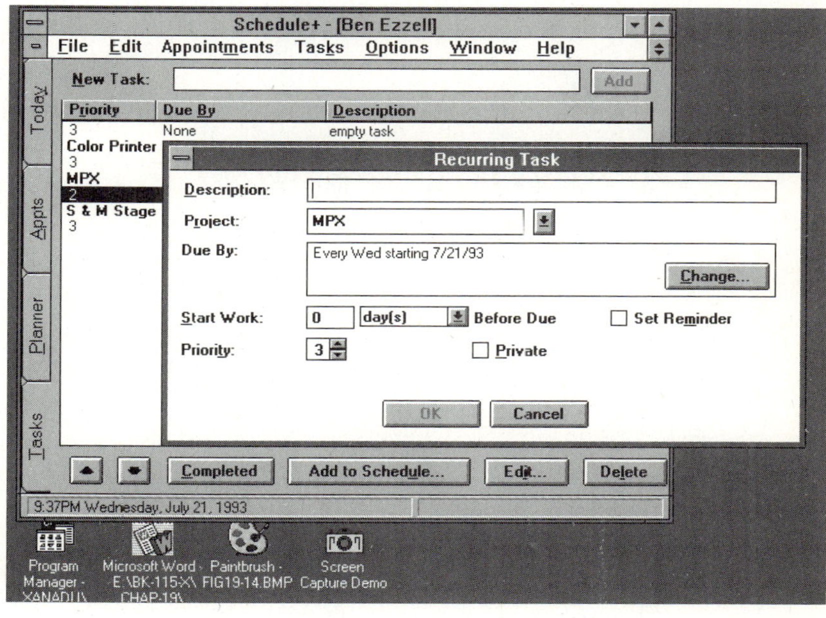

Figure 19.16
The Recurring Task dialog box

2. Enter a task description in the Description box.

3. Select a project to associate the task with or select <None> if the task should not be associated with a project.

4. Select the Change button to change the default due date. The Change Recurrence dialog box shown in Figure 19.9 appears.

5. Refer to "Changing Intervals for Recurring Appointments," preceding, for directions on setting due dates and recurrence intervals.

6. Enter an interval in the Start Work boxes for the task to become active. This sets a time interval prior to the due date when the task becomes active.
   - Use the arrow buttons to select Days, Weeks, or Months.
7. Select the Set Reminder check box to set a reminder for the task.
8. Use the arrow buttons to select a task priority in the Priority box.
   - Or enter a new priority level.
9. Select the Private check box to designate the task as private.
10. Select OK.

A due date is required before a reminder can be set.

▸ Changing or Deleting Recurring Tasks

To display a list of recurring tasks:

- Select Edit Recurring Tasks from the Tasks menu.

To change a single occurrence of a recurring task:

1. Double-click on the task to change. The Task dialog box—Figure 19.15—appears.
2. Make the desired changes in the Task dialog box.
3. Select OK. The changed occurrence appears on the Task list separate from the recurring task.

To change all occurrences of a recurring task:

1. Select Edit Recurring Tasks from the Tasks menu.
2. Double-click on the task to be changed.
   - Or select the task and press Enter. The Recurring Task dialog box shown in Figure 19.16 appears.
3. Make the changes desired in the Recurring Task dialog box.
4. Select the Change button to change the day(s) the task occurs. The Change Recurrence dialog box shown in Figure 19.9 appears.

5. Refer to "Changing Intervals for Recurring Appointments," preceding, for directions on setting due dates and recurrence intervals.

6. Select Close.

Deleting a single occurrence of a recurrent task is done in the same fashion as deleting a regular task.

To delete a single occurrence of a recurring task:

1. Select the task to delete from the Task list.
2. Select the Delete button.

To delete all occurrences of a recurring task:

1. Select Recurring Tasks from the Tasks menu.
2. Select the task to delete from the list of recurring tasks.
3. Select the Delete button.
4. Select Close.

▸ Changing a Task's Priority

To change a task's priority:

1. Select the task from the Task list.
2. Click on the up or down arrow button at the bottom of the Task list until the entry in the Priority column shows the desired priority.

▸ Setting Reminders for Tasks

The selected task must have a specific due date before a reminder can be set.

To set a task reminder:

1. Double-click on a task in the Task list.
   - Or select the task and press Enter. The Task dialog box shown in Figure 19.15 appears.
2. Enter an interval in the Start Work boxes for the task to become active. This sets a time interval prior to the due date when the task becomes active.
   - Use the arrow buttons to select Days, Weeks, or Months.

3. Select the Set Reminder check box to set a reminder for the task. The reminder will occur when the task becomes active.

4. Select OK.

Keeping Track of Tasks

▶ Sorting and Displaying Projects and Tasks

In any view, past-due tasks are displayed in red. Caution: If you are using a red background—as some people do—past-due tasks will not be visible.

To view tasks by project:

- Select View By Project from the Tasks menu. A check mark appears by the option.

To view tasks as a list not sorted by project:

- Select View By Project from the Tasks menu. The check mark by the option is cleared.

To sort tasks by priority:

- Select the Priority button at the top of the Task list.
- Select Sort By Priority from the Tasks menu.

To sort tasks by due date:

- Select the Due By button at the top of the Task list.
- Select Sort By Due Date from the Tasks menu.

To sort tasks by description:

- Select the Description button at the top of the Tasks list.
- Select Sort By Description from the Tasks menu.

The Show Active Tasks and Show All Tasks options alternate on the menu. Only one will be visible at any time.

To view only active tasks:

- Select Show Active Tasks from the Tasks menu.

To view all tasks:

- Select Show All Tasks from the Tasks menu.

Help Files ▼ Tasks can be sorted by priority, due date, or description and can be viewed by project or without project group identifiers. Tasks are sorted in ascending order, by default, from highest priority to lowest. To invert the sort order, press the Ctrl key while selecting the Sort Field option.

▶ Noting Completed Tasks

To note a completed task in the Appointment Book:

1. Select the task to be noted as completed.
2. Select the Completed button. The text description appears in the Notes section of the Appointment Book, and the task is removed from the Task list.

▶ Adding Tasks to the Appointment Book

To add a task to the Appointment Book:

1. Select the task from the Task list.
2. Select the Add To Schedule button. The Choose Time dialog box—Figure 19.17—appears.
3. Select a date and time slot for the task.
4. Select OK. The task is added to the Appointment Book, but is not removed from the Task list.

▶ Printing Tasks

To print a Task list:

1. Display either all tasks or active tasks.

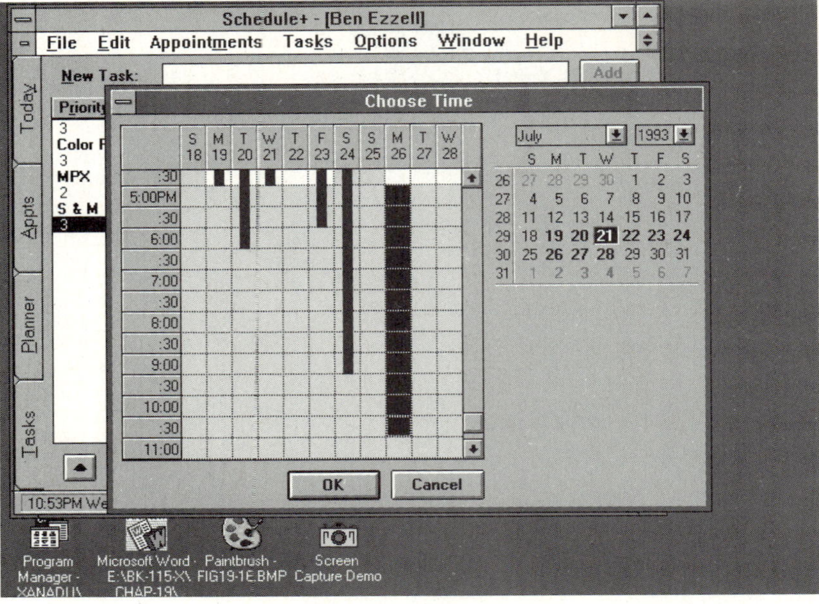

Figure 19.17
The Choose Time dialog box

2. Display tasks by project or as a flat list.
3. Sort tasks by priority, due date, or description.
4. Select Print from the File menu. Refer to "Printing Appointments, Daily Notes, and Tasks," preceding, for further options.

Communication with Other Users

Responses to meeting requests, cancellations, and other schedule-related mail appear in the Messages window and can be read without leaving Schedule+.

▶ Reading Messages

To read a message:

1. Select Messages from the Window menu.
2. Double-click on the message or response to be read.
   - Or select a message and select the Read button.

▶ Responding to a Meeting Request

To respond to a meeting request:

1. Select Messages from the Window menu.
2. Double-click on the meeting request you wish to reply to.
   - Or select the meeting request and select the Read button.
3. Select View Schedule to check your schedule.
4. Enter a message in the Message area to add to your response.

   Select Accept, Tentative, or Decline to send a response.
   - An Accept response automatically books the meeting in your Appointment Book.
   - A Tentative response books the meeting as tentative.

HELP! *If a message remains in your Messages window after you have sent an initial response (that is, the response hasn't been delivered), another reply can be sent with a different response.*

Accessing Another User's Appointment Book

▶ Viewing Another User's Appointment Book or Task List

To view another user's Appointment Book, the user must be running Schedule+, be operating on-line, and have access privileges.

To view another user's Appointment Book or Task list:

1. Select the Open Other's Appt Book option from the File menu.
2. Select the name of the user in the address list whose Appointment Book or Task list you want to view.
3. Select OK.

▸ Modifying Appointments or Tasks for Another User

To modify an appointment or task in another user's Appointment Book:

The procedures for adding, changing, or deleting appointments or tasks on another user's schedule are the same as for modifying your own. The appropriate access privileges, however, are required.

1. Select Open Other's Appt Book from the File menu.
2. Select the user's name from the address list to access his or her Appointment Book.
3. Select OK. If you have the requisite access privileges, the user's Appointment Book appears in your Schedule+ workspace.
4. Modify appointments or tasks in the user's Appointment Book as desired.
5. Select OK.

Access Privileges

▸ Viewing Users' Access Privileges for Your Schedule

To view users' access privileges for your schedule:

1. Select Set Access Privileges from the Options menu. The default access privileges for all users are displayed in the Users box as well as those of any users who have been granted specific (non-default) access privileges.
2. Select OK.

▸ Setting or Changing Users' Access Privileges

To set or change a user's access:

1. Select Set Access Privileges from the Options menu.
2. Select the name from the Users list box.

3. Select the privilege to assign in the Privileges box:
   - None
   - View Free/Busy Times
   - Read Appointments & Tasks
   - Create Appointments & Tasks
   - Modify Appointments & Tasks
   - Assistant
4. Select OK.

▶ Adding a User's Name to the Users List Box

To add a user's name to the Users list box:

1. Select the Add button. The Add Users dialog box appears.
2. Select the user's name in the address list.
3. Select the Add button from the Add Users dialog box.
4. Select OK to return.
5. Select the user's name from the Users box.

▶ Granting Access to an Assistant

To designate another user as your assistant:

1. Select Set Access Privileges from the Options menu.
2. Select the user's name from the Users box.
3. Select the Assistant option from the Privileges list box.
4. Choose the OK button.

To change assistants:

1. Select Set Access Privileges from the Options menu.
2. Select your present assistant from the Users box.

3. Set new access privileges.
   - Or select the Remove button, leaving the user with only the default access privileges.
4. Select a new user from the Users list box.
5. Select the Assistant option from the Privileges list box.
6. Choose the OK button.

To send a meeting message to your assistant without receiving a copy yourself:

1. Select General Options from the Options menu.
2. Select Send Meeting Messages Only To My Assistant.
3. Select OK.

Help Files ▼ Another user can be designated as your assistant to receive schedule-related messages and maintain your schedule, excepting, of course, appointments and tasks designated as private. Only one assistant can be designated at a time.

▶ Acting as an Assistant

To open the owner's Appointment Book:

Your assistant does not require your password for access to your schedule!

1. Select Open Other's Appt Book from the File menu.
2. Select the name of the user whose Appointment Book you want to open.
3. Select the Add button.
4. Select OK to proceed.
5. Handle tasks in the owner's Appointment Book exactly as if it were your own.

Help Files ▼ As an assistant, you receive all responses to meeting requests sent on the owner's behalf. Responses are logged in the owner's schedule automatically. To act as an assistant, you do not require the owner's password but must have Assistant access privileges.

▶ Managing Resources as a Resource's Assistant

To book appointments on behalf of resources:

- On receipt of a meeting request sent to the resource, respond as for any meeting request by confirming the resource's availability and responding to the message.

The Rescue Pages: Schedule+

This is the real world—how can I schedule overlapping appointments?

Quite easily. Simply enter each appointment for whatever time interval is appropriate. Schedule+ will handle overlaps by showing the two (or more) appointments side by side during the overlapping interval.

Schedule+ keeps sending me reminders that I don't want. Do I have to turn off the reminder for every single appointment? Can't I just get rid of them?

You have a couple of choices.

First, you can set the default conditions for appointments to not include reminders. Second, all present reminders can be turned off by selecting the Turn Off Reminders option from the File menu. Note, however, that this setting is temporary and is reset whenever Schedule+ is loaded again.

I know I have an appointment with someone, but is there any quick way of finding out when?

Use the Find option from the Edit menu to search for a name, a subject, a keyword, and so on. For details, refer to "Locating Text in the Appointment Book," preceding.

CHAPTER

20

HELP! Mail

The built-in Windows NT Mail facility is used in a network to handle message traffic between users, exchange documents, arrange schedules for meetings, and allocate shared resource scheduling.

Topics discussed in this chapter include

- Getting started with Mail
- Preparing messages
- Use of the Address Book
- Working with received messages
- Including files and objects in messages
- Folders
- Customized mail
- Management of a message file

Getting Started with Mail

▶ Logging on to Mail for the First Time

The first time you log on to Mail after installing Windows NT, a Welcome To Mail dialog box—Figure 20.1—appears, asking if you want to connect to an existing postoffice or create a new postoffice.

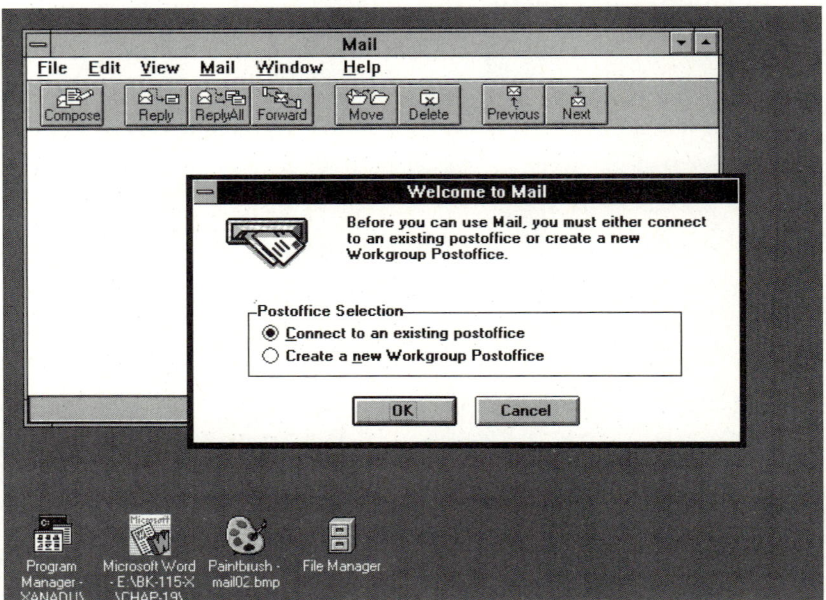

Figure 20.1
The Welcome To Mail dialog box

If you are logged on to a Windows NT Advanced Server or other network:

1. Consult your network administrator for the name and location of your postoffice.
2. Select the Connect To An Existing Postoffice option. A Connect To Postoffice dialog box appears requesting the network path where the postoffice is located.
3. Enter the complete network path in the form

   `\\COMPUTERNAME\DIRECTORY`
4. Select OK.

To install a network postoffice:

1. Select the Create A New Workgroup Postoffice option. A prompt dialog box will appear cautioning that:
   - Only one workgroup postoffice should exist within a group. If a postoffice already exists, a connection should be made to that postoffice.
   - The user creating a new postoffice becomes responsible for managing the postoffice.
2. If you have always wanted an appointment as postmaster, select Yes to proceed. The Create Workgroup Postoffice dialog box—Figure 20.2—appears.

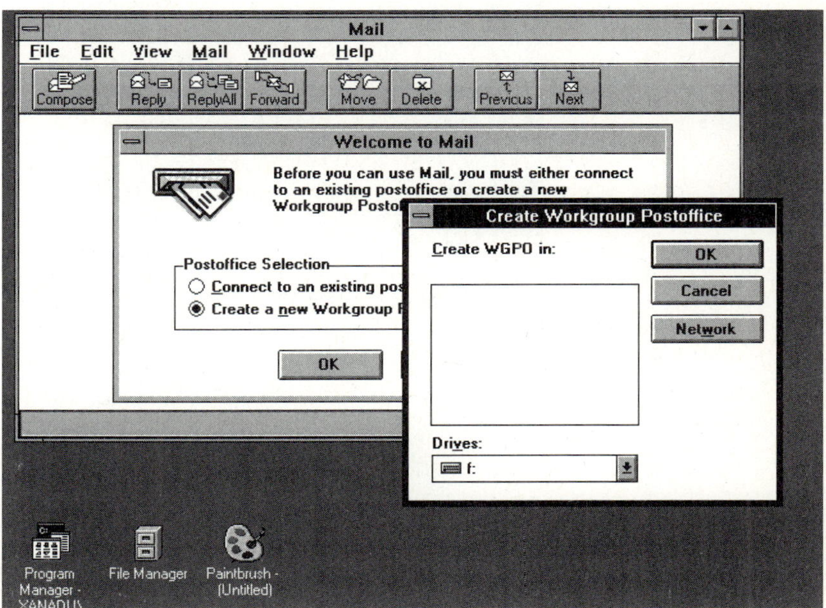

Figure 20.2
The Create Workgroup Postoffice dialog box

3. Select OK to create the WGPO postoffice subdirectory in the default location which will be \USERS\DEFAULT\WGPO on your Windows NT drive.
   - Or, enter a directory path name.

- And, optionally, select a different drive.
- Then select OK to proceed.

4. The Enter Your Administrator Account Details dialog box—Figure 20.3—appears.

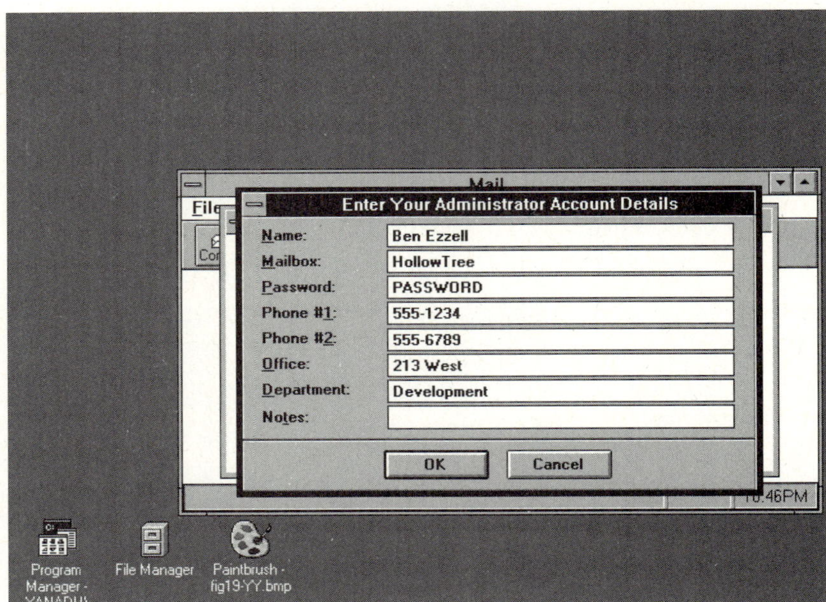

Figure 20.3
The Enter Your Administrator Account Details dialog box

5. Enter your name, a name for your mailbox account, and an optional password. The remaining phone number, office, department, and notes fields are information allowing users to reach you directly in case of difficulty. Remember, you're the postmaster responsible for this postoffice.

6. Select OK.

Help Files ▼ The directory where the postoffice was created must be available to other users on the network. Use File Manager to assign this directory as shared, and please, assign full access permission to the shared directory. Optionally, a password may also be assigned.

▶ Signing In to or Out of Mail

To sign in to Mail:

1. Select the Mail icon from the Main group. The Mail Sign In dialog box—Figure 20.4—appears.

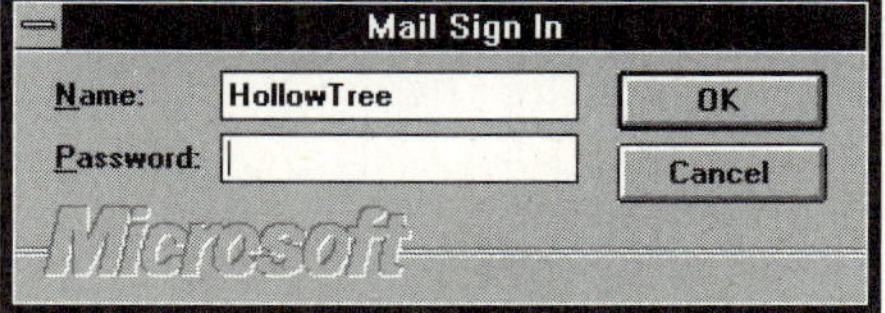

Figure 20.4
The Mail Sign In dialog box

2. Enter your mailbox name and password in the Mail Sign In dialog box. (For security, the password entry does not appear on screen as typed.)

To sign in to Mail automatically:

1. Select the Mail icon in the Main group.
2. Select Properties from the Program Manager File menu. The Program Item Properties dialog box shown in Figure 20.5 appears.
3. On the Command Line, following the entry MSMAIL32.EXE, enter a space followed by your mailbox name. If the mailbox name includes blank spaces—as, for example, "JANE JOHNS" or "Hollow Tree"—enclose the name in quotation marks.

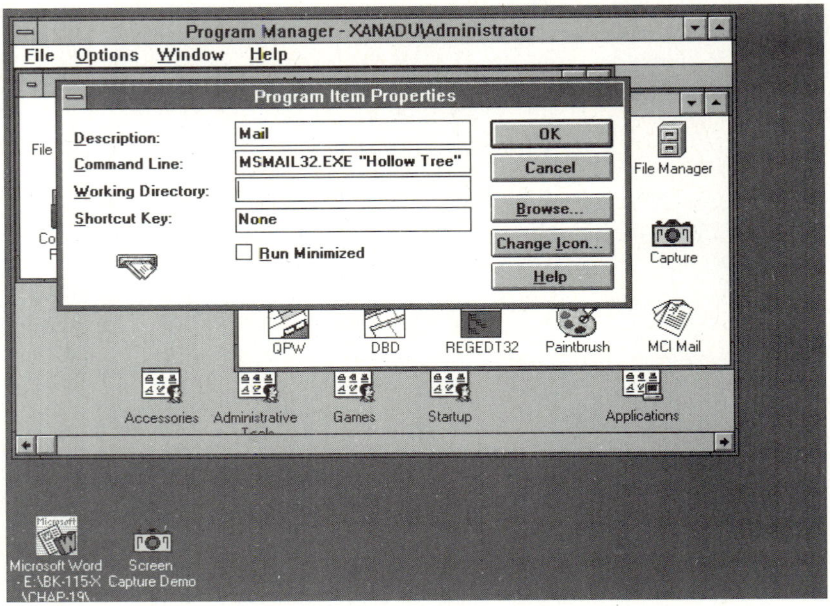

Figure 20.5
The Program Item Properties dialog box

4. For automatic log-on to the mailbox, add a space following the mailbox name, and then enter your password.

To exit Mail without signing out:

- Select Exit from the File menu. If another application using the mail facilities—such as Schedule+—is running, Mail is closed but the associated application remains open. If no associated applications are running, you are signed out of Mail.

To sign out of Mail:

- Select the Exit And Sign Out option from the File menu. If another application using the mail facilities—such as Schedule+—is running, this application will also be closed.

▶ Changing Passwords

To change your Mail password:

1. Select Change Password from the Mail menu.

2. Enter your current password and press Tab. For security reasons, the password entry is not echoed to the screen.

3. Enter your new password and press Tab. Password entries are case-sensitive.

4. Repeat the new password for verification. If the second password entry matches the first, the OK button changes from grayed-out to available.

5. Select OK. The new password is now registered and must be used when next logging on to Mail.

▸ Sending Messages

To send a message:

1. Click on the Compose button.

■ Or select Compose Note from the Mail menu. The Send Note dialog box—Figure 20.6—appears inside the Mail dialog box.

For faster entry, type the first few characters of the user name, then press Alt+K, and Mail will supply the rest of the name.

2. Enter the recipient's user name in the To box, separating multiple names with semicolons.

3. To send courtesy (carbon) copies of a message, enter the recipient's name(s) in the Cc box.

4. Enter the subject in the Subject box. The subject appears in the message list in the recipient's Inbox.

5. Enter the message in the message window (bottom).

6. Select the Send button. If the Save Sent Messages option was selected from the Options command, a copy of the message is placed in the Sent Mail folder.

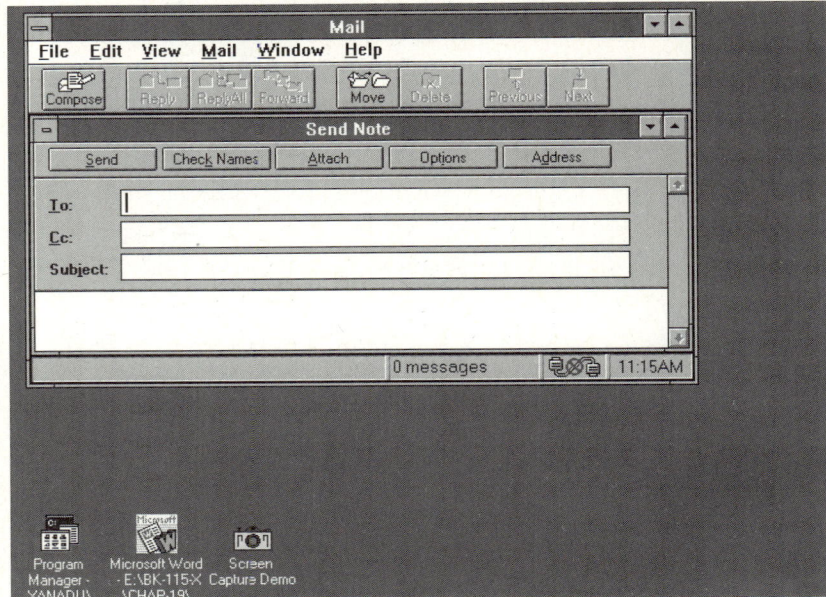

Figure 20.6
The Send Note dialog box

▶ Reading Messages

To read a message:

Double-click on a message header for quick selection and display.

1. Open the Inbox folder and, if necessary, expand the folder to display the message to read.
2. Select the message to read from the message list.
3. Select Open from the File menu.
    - Or press Enter.
4. Use the PgDn key or scroll bar, as necessary, to read the entire message.
5. Use the Previous or Next buttons or select Previous or Next from the View menu to read other messages in the list.

6. Press Esc or Ctrl+F4 to close a message window.

Deleting or Retrieving Messages

To delete a message being read:

- Click on the Delete button.

- Or select Delete from the File menu.

To delete a message from the message list:

- Drag the message to the Deleted Mail folder. The next message in the list—in chronological order—is opened.

To retrieve a deleted message:

1. Select the Deleted Mail folder.
2. Select the message(s) to retrieve.
3. Drag the message(s) to the Inbox folder.
    - Or select Move from the File menu and select a folder from the list offered.

Forwarding Messages

For fast forwarding, drag the message from the list to the Outbox. A Send Note form containing the original text will appear. Address the note in the usual fashion.

To forward a message:

1. Click on the Forward button.

    - Or select Forward from the Mail menu.
2. Specify the recipient(s) in the To box.
3. Move to the message window to add comments.
4. Select the Send button.

Preparing Messages

▶ Copying, Moving, or Deleting Information In a Message

To copy, move, or delete information:

1. Display the message.
2. Select (highlight) the information to copy, move, or delete:
   - Press Ctrl+C to copy information to the Clipboard.
   - Press Ctrl+X to move information to the Clipboard, deleting the information from the message.
   - Press Del to delete the selected information from the message.

To paste text into a message:

1. Move the text cursor (insertion point) to the location in the message where the information should be pasted.
2. Select Paste from the Edit menu.
   - Or press Ctrl+V.

▶ Copying Information between Messages

To copy information from another message:

1. Display the message to copy from.
2. Select the information to copy.
3. Select Copy from the Edit menu.
4. Press Esc to close the source message.
5. Select the destination message from the message list.
   - Or click on the Compose button to create a new message.

6. Move the text cursor (insertion point) to the location in the message where the information should be pasted.

7. Select Paste from the Edit menu.

   - Or press Ctrl+V.

Setting Message Options

To set message options:

1. Select the Options button in the Send Note window. The Options dialog box—Figure 20.7—appears.

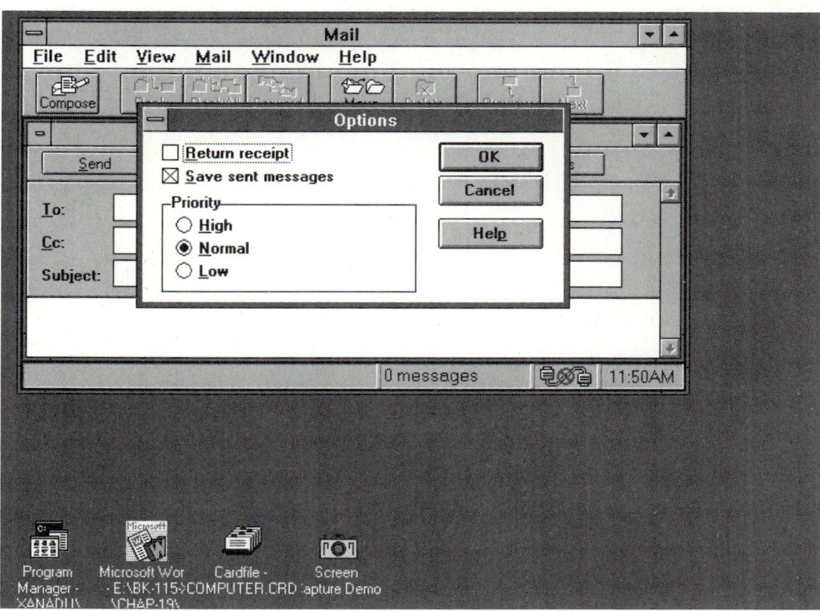

Figure 20.7
The Options dialog box

2. Select the options desired.

   - Select the Return Receipt check box to receive a return receipt message when the recipient reads the sent message.
   - Select the Save Sent Messages check box to save a copy of the message in the Sent Mail folder.

- Select a priority—High, Normal (default), or Low—for the message in the recipient's message list.

3. Select OK.

Saving an Unsent Message

To save an unsent message:

1. Double-click on the Send Note window's System menu box (upper left).
   - Or press Ctrl+F4. A query appears asking if changes to the message should be saved.
2. Select Yes to close the window, saving the message in the Inbox. The message can be later revised and then sent. Unsent messages are indicated by the Open Message icon.

Replying to a Message

To reply to a message:

1. Select a message from the message list or reply to the open message.
2. Select the Reply button.

- Or select Reply from the Mail menu to address the response message to the sender only.

Or:

- Select the Reply All button.

- Or select Reply To All from the Mail menu to address the response to everyone in the To and Cc boxes.

3. Enter a reply in the message window. The contents of the original message are already included in the message body. The response can be added to the original or the original contents can be deleted.

4. Click on the Send button.

▸ Creating and Employing Message Templates

For your convenience, create a template folder to store template messages.

To create a message template:

1. Select the Compose button.

■ Or select Compose Note from the Mail menu.

2. Address the template message to the recipients who will be receiving it regularly.

3. Enter subject and template information.

4. Double-click on the Send Note window's System menu box (upper left).

■ Or press Ctrl+F4. A query appears asking if changes to the message should be saved.

5. Select Yes to close the window, saving the template message in the Inbox. The template can be later revised and then sent. Unsent messages are indicated by the Open Message icon.

To select a template message:

1. Select a template message from the Mail folder.

2. Select Forward from the Mail menu.

■ Or click and drag the template message to the Outbox icon.

To send the template message:

1. Edit the message as desired.

2. Change the recipients list if necessary.
3. Select the Send button.

The Address Book

▶ Using Mail's Address List

To add recipients from the address list:

1. Select the Compose button.

   - Or select Compose Note from the Mail menu.
2. Select the Address button to display the Address Book listing users in your postoffice.
3. Press any key to scroll the address list to the first name beginning with the selected character.
   - To scroll to another letter, press Backspace and enter the new letter.
   - To search for a name, select the Search button or press Ctrl+F.

To add names from the address list to the To box:

1. Select the name in the address list.
2. Select the To button.
   - Or double-click on a name in the address list.
   - Or drag the name from the address list to the To box.
   - Or move to the To box and enter the name(s) directly. Multiple names should be separated by semicolons.

To add names from the address list to the Cc box:

1. Select the name in the address list.
2. Select the Cc button.

- Or drag the name from the address list to the Cc box.
- Or move to the Cc box and enter the name(s) directly. Multiple names should be separated by semicolons (;).

To remove a name from the To or Cc boxes:

- Select the name and press the Backspace or Del key.

To add addressees from a Personal Address Book:

1. Select the Personal Address Book in the Address Book.
   - Or press Ctrl+P. A Personal Address Book shows users selected from the address list together with personal groups created by the user.
2. Select recipients as preceding.

▶ Verifying User Names

To verify a user name:

1. Type all or part of the recipient's name in the To or Cc box.
2. Select the Check Names button.
   - Or select the Send button if the message is ready to send.

Help Files ▼ If a partial name has been entered and only one match is found, Mail fills in the rest of the name. If multiple matches are found, Mail presents a list of names to choose from. Verified user names appear underlined in the To or Cc boxes and cannot be modified.

Requesting Details on a User

Details can also be requested by double-clicking on any name in the Address Book or on names in the To or Cc boxes in the message form.

To ask for details about a user:

1. Select the Address Book from the Mail menu.
2. Select a user name.
3. Select the Details button. Mail displays details about the user.

Updating a Personal Address Book

To add a name to a Personal Address Book:

1. Select Address Book from the Mail menu.
2. Select a name from the address list.
3. Select the Add Names button.
   - Or press Ctrl+A.
4. Press Esc to close the Personal Address Book.

To remove a name from a Personal Address Book:

1. Select Address Book from the Mail menu.
2. Select the Personal Address Book button.
   - Or press Ctrl+P.
3. Select the name to remove.
4. Select the Remove button.

Creating or Modifying a Personal Address Group

To create a personal address group:

1. Select Personal Groups from the Mail menu.
2. Select the New button.
3. Enter a name for the group in the New Group Name edit box.

4. Select the Create button. The Address Book is displayed.
5. Select names from the address list to add to the address group.
6. Select the Add button.
   - Or press Alt+A.
7. Select OK.

To add or remove a name from a personal address group:

1. Select Personal Groups from the Mail menu.
2. Select the group name to modify from the Groups list.
3. Select the Edit button. The Address Book appears with the group members listed in the bottom window.
4. To add a group member, select a name from the address list and select the Add button.
5. To remove a name, select the name from the list and press Del or Backspace.
6. Select OK.
7. Select Done in the Personal Groups dialog box.

Working with Received Messages

▶ Printing a Message

To print a message:

1. Select Print from the File menu. A Windows Print dialog box appears.
2. Clear the Print Multiple Messages On Page check box to print each message on a separate page.
3. Select OK to continue.

Help Files ▼ Embedded objects are printed directly, while attached files must be printed by the application that originally created them.

▶ Saving Messages as Text Files

To save a message as a text file:

1. Select Save As from the File menu. The Save As dialog box appears with the first eight characters of the message's subject entered as the file name, followed by the extension .TXT.
2. Enter a new file name or extension, or change the drive or directory.
3. Select OK. If the specified file already exists, the existing file may be replaced, or the new file may be appended to the existing file.

▶ Locating a Message

If a message is deleted from the Message Finder, it is also deleted from the folder where it was located. The Message Finder window can be minimized and left on the Mail workspace for later reuse. To restart a search, expand the Message Finder and select Start. Also, multiple Message Finder windows may be kept for different searches.

To search for a message:

1. Select the Message Finder option from the File menu. The Message Finder dialog box—Figure 20.8—appears.
2. Fill in the various search fields with information to identify a message.
3. Select the Where To Look button and select the folder(s) to search from the displayed list.
4. Select Start to initiate the search.

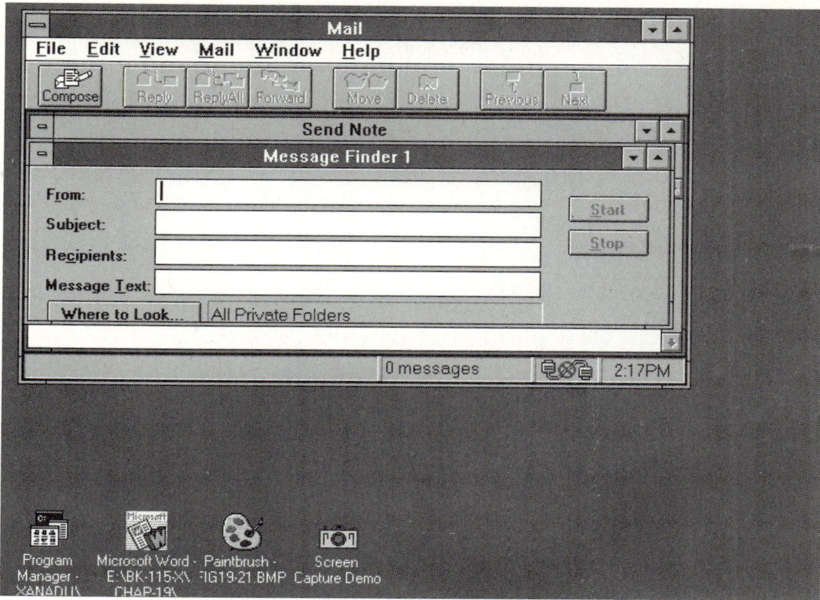

Figure 20.8
The Message Finder dialog box

Help Files ▼ Mail searches the specified folder(s), listing each message matching the search criteria as it is found. When the desired message is listed, the search can be interrupted by clicking the Stop button.

Messages can be read and processed in the Message Finder window just as in any other folder.

Moving Messages between Folders

To copy or move an open message:

1. Select the Move button.

■ Or select Move from the File menu.

2. In the Move To or Copy To box, select the folder to move the message to.
3. To create a new folder, select the New button and enter a name for the folder.
4. Select OK to proceed.

To copy or move a selected message:

- Drag the message from the message list to the folder in the folders list.

Including Files and Objects in Messages

▶ Copying Information from a File

To copy information from a file to a message:

Information can also be copied from DOS applications—executing in the DOS shell—by using the Copy options from the System menu.

1. Open the application and file containing the information to copy.
2. Select and copy the information to the Clipboard.
3. Return to the message being composed.
   - Or open a new Send Note form.
4. Select the point at which to insert the material in the message body.
5. Select Paste from the Edit menu.

To copy an entire text file into a message:

1. Select Insert From File from the Edit menu.
2. Select the text file to import from the file finder dialog box.
3. Select OK. The contents of the text file are copied to the message.

▶ Attaching a File to a Message

To attach a file:

1. Select the Compose button.

   ■ Or select Compose from the Mail menu.

2. Select the point in the body of the message where the file icon should appear. If no location is specified, the icon is inserted at the beginning of the message.
3. Select the Attach button. A file finder dialog box appears.
4. Use the file finder dialog box to select a drive, directory, and file name. The file's icon appears in the body of the message.
5. Repeat steps 3 and 4 to attach additional files.
6. Select Close.

A file icon can also be dragged from File Manager to Mail's Outbox. A Send Note form appears with the file icon in the message body.

To attach a file from File Manager:

1. Select the Compose button.

   ■ Or select Compose from the Mail menu.

2. Open the File Manager window.
3. Select a file from File Manager to attach to the message.
4. Drag the file icon from File Manager to the point in the message where it should appear.

▶ Embedding an Object in a Message

To embed an object in a message:

1. Open the document with the information to include in the message.
2. Copy the information from the application to the Clipboard.

3. Switch back to Mail.
4. Select the Compose button.

- Or select Compose from the Mail menu.

5. Select Paste Special from the Edit menu.
6. Select the Object format from the Data Type list.
7. Select the Paste button.

To create and embed a new object within Mail:

1. Move the text cursor (insertion point) to the location in the Send Note form where the object should be inserted.
2. Select Insert Object from the Edit menu. The Insert Object dialog box lists the Windows-based applications that can create objects.
3. Select an application from the list.
4. Select OK to proceed. The selected application's window opens on top of Mail.
5. Create the object within the application.
6. Select Update from the application's File menu.
   - Or close the application. The new object is inserted in the message.

▶ Opening and Saving an Attachment

To open an attached file from a message:

- Double-click on the file icon in the message body.

To save one or more attached files in the current directory:

1. Select Save Attachment from the File menu.
2. Select the file from the Attachments list.

3. Select the Save button.

   - Or select the Save All button to save multiple attached files.

To save a selected file using a different file name:

- Enter the new file name in the File Name edit box.

To save the file in a different directory:

- Select the drive and directory where the file should be written.

▶ Working with Embedded Objects

To modify an object:

1. Double-click on the object in the message body.

   - Or select the object and select the Object command from the Edit menu. The application that created the object opens with the object loaded, ready for editing.

2. Edit the object.

3. Select Update from the application's File menu.

   - Or close the application. The object in the Mail message is updated to reflect the changes.

To activate an object:

1. Select the object from the message body.

2. Select Object from the Edit menu. The menu displays all commands available for working with the object.

3. Select the appropriate menu command to activate the object.

Folders

Creating Folders or Subfolders

To create a folder:

If a folder was already selected in the folder list when New Folder is selected, the new folder is automatically a subfolder of the selected folder.

1. Select the Folders list.
2. Select New Folder from the File menu.
3. Enter a name for the folder in the Name edit box. A folder name can consist of any combination of characters and spaces.
4. Select Private or Shared as the folder type.
5. Select Options to assign access permissions to a shared folder, and then select permissions in the Other Users Can list box.
6. Select OK. The new folder is included in the Folders list in alphabetical order.

To rename a folder:

1. Select the folder to rename from the folder list.
2. Select Folder Properties from the File menu.
3. Enter the new folder name.
4. Select OK.

To create a subfolder:

1. Select the Options button from the New Folder dialog box.
2. Enter a name for the subfolder in the Name edit box.
3. Select the Subfolder Of option button under Level.
4. Select a folder.
5. Select OK.

To move a folder within a folder:

- In the Folders list, drag one folder to another folder for storage.

A subfolder can also be promoted to a top-level folder by holding the Home key while dragging the subfolder anywhere in the folder list.

To make a subfolder a top-level folder:

1. Select Folder Properties from the File menu.
2. Select the folder to move from the Level list box.
3. Select the Top Level Folder option.
4. Select OK.

Expanding and Collapsing Folders

To expand a folder:

- Click on the plus sign next to the folder to show subfolders.

To collapse a folder:

- Click on the minus sign next to the folder to hide subfolders.

To expand or collapse all folders:

- Press the Ctrl and Plus keys to show all folders.
- Press the Ctrl and Minus keys to collapse all folders.

Deleting a Folder

To delete a folder:

1. Select a folder from the folder list to delete.
2. Click on the Delete button.

- Or select Delete from the File menu. Any messages in a deleted folder or subfolder are moved to the Deleted Mail folder.

Customized Mail

▸ Setting Mail Options

To set Mail options:

- Select Options from the Mail menu. The Options dialog box—Figure 20.9—appears.

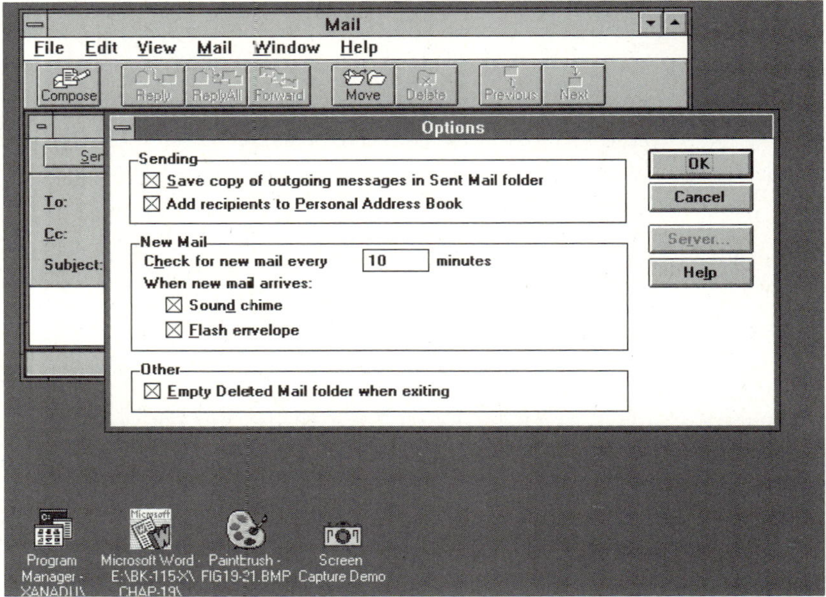

Figure 20.9
The (Mail) Options dialog box

For outgoing messages:

- Select the Save Copy Of Outgoing Messages In Sent Mail Folder check box to keep a copy of all messages sent in the Sent Mail folder.

For incoming messages:

- Enter a number—in minutes—for how often Mail should check the Inbox for new messages. (The default is 10 minutes.)
- Select the Sound Chime check box for an audio prompt when a message is received.

- Select the Flash Envelope check box to have the mouse pointer change briefly to an envelope icon when a message is received.

To empty the Deleted Mail folder when exiting from Mail:

- Select the Empty Deleted Mail Folder When Exiting check box.

Operating Off-line

To work off-line:

1. Start Mail. If the computer is not connected to your postoffice, a message asks if you wish to work off-line (off the network).
2. Select OK. A dialog box appears requesting your password.
3. Enter your password.
4. Select OK.
5. If the message file cannot be found, a request appears asking for the path where the file is located.

Help Files ▼ Messages can be composed off-line and sent using the Send button. Sent messages are moved to the Outbox and are sent automatically when Mail connects to the postoffice.

Message File Management

Backing Up and Restoring the Message File

To back up the message file:

1. Select Backup from the Mail menu.

2. Select a directory in the File Name box where the backup will be written.

3. Select OK.

If Mail is started but cannot locate the message file, a dialog box appears requesting selection of a message file.

To restore a backed-up message file:

1. Locate the backup file. A prompt appears asking if the backup file should be converted to a message file.

2. Select OK. The backup file becomes the new message file.

Help Files ▼ If the backup file isn't converted to the message file, the messages in the file can be read, deleted, or moved to folders, but no new messages can be sent or received.

▶ Exporting Mail Folders

To export one or more Mail folders:

1. Select Export Folder from the File menu. A file finder dialog box appears.

2. Select the message file (.MMF file) to export messages to.

   - Or, to create a new message file, enter a name for the new file in the File Name edit box.

3. Select OK. An Export Folders dialog box—Figure 20.10—appears with a list of message folders.

4. If the message file selected is password protected, enter a password for the message file.

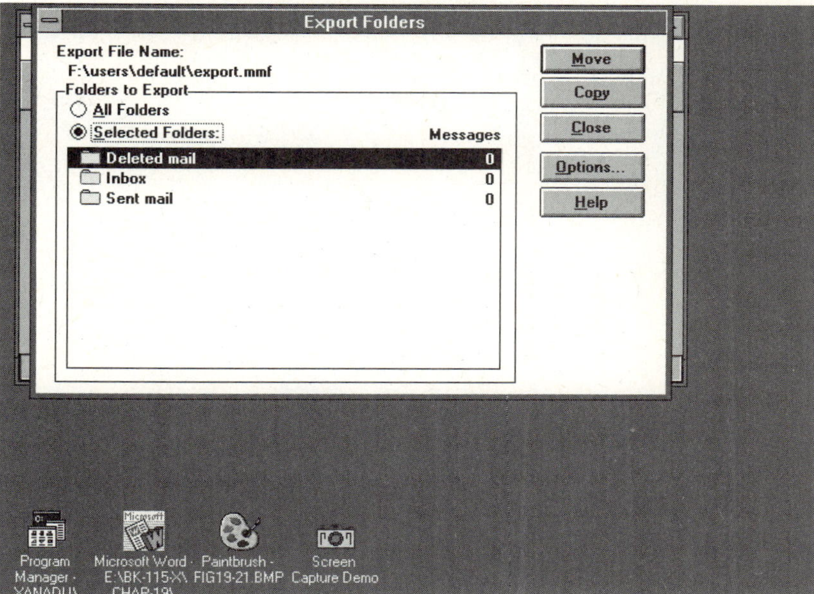

Figure 20.10
The Export Folders dialog box

5. Select the All Folders option to export all messages in the message file.
   - Or select the Selected Folders option to export only selected folders, and then select the folders to export. Subfolders are exported with their folders.
6. Select the Options button to export messages within a date range. The Options dialog box—Figure 20.11—appears, permitting export of all messages in the folders selected or of only messages received or of modified during a specific period.
   - Select the From check box and enter a date to export all messages received after that date.
   - Select the To check box and enter a date to export all messages received before that date.
   - Select both From and To to export messages received between the two dates.

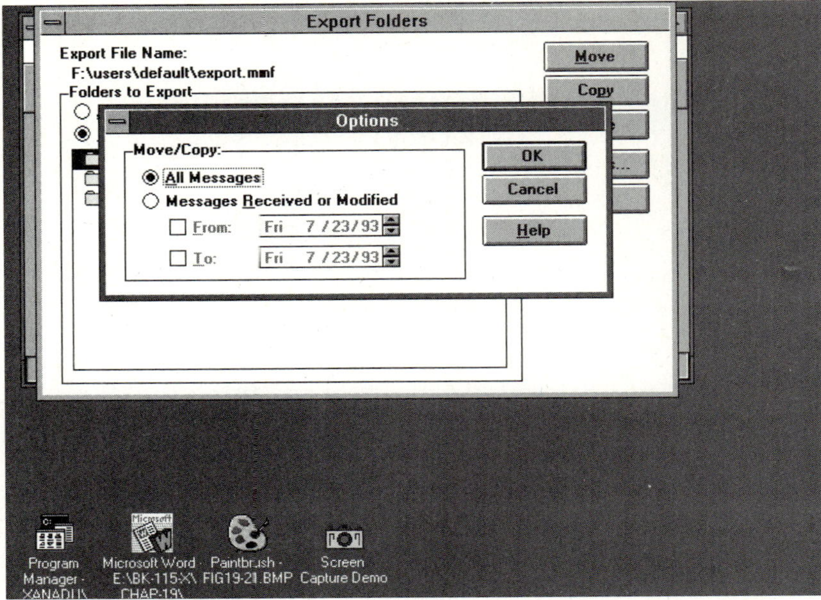

Figure 20.11
The (Export Folders) Options dialog box

7. Select the Copy button to copy the selected folders to the export message file.

   - Or select the Move button to move the selected folders to the export message file. If a conflict occurs between folder names in the export and primary message files, a prompt appears requesting a resolution of the conflicting folder names.

8. Select the Close button.

▶ Importing Mail Folders

To import one or more Mail folders:

1. Select the Import Folder option from the File menu. A file finder dialog box appears.

2. Select the message file (.MMF file) to import messages from.

3. Select OK to proceed. The Import Folders dialog box—similar to Figure 20.10—appears.

4. If the message file selected is password protected, enter a password for the message file.

5. Select the All Folders option to import all messages into the primary message file.

   - Or select the Selected Folders option to import only specific folders, and then select the folders to import. Subfolders belonging to selected folders are also imported.

6. Select the Options button to import messages within a date range. The Options dialog box—Figure 20.11—appears, permitting import of all messages in the folders selected or only messages received or modified during a specific period.

   - Select the From check box and enter a date to import all messages received after that date.
   - Select the To check box and enter a date to import all messages received before that date.
   - Select both From and To to import messages received between the two dates.

7. Select the Copy button to copy the selected folders from the import message file.

   - Or select the Move button to move the selected folders from the import message file. If a conflict occurs between folder names in the import and primary message files, a prompt appears requesting a resolution of the conflicting folder names.

8. Select the Close button.

The Rescue Pages: Mail

My mailbox is trashed but I can't get rid of it to create a new one!

First, if you can access the mailbox at all—or if any other users can access it—any messages, personal folders, saved mail, and so on, should be saved by writing them to another location.

Second, you should try to restore the mailbox directory(ies) from your tape backup. Specifically, the relevant directories should be \USER\DEFAULT\WGPO plus all subdirectories of this directory.

Third, refer to the MSMAIL32.INI file in your \WINNT directory. The first part of the file should look something like this:

```
[Microsoft Mail]
WG=1
LocalMMF=1
NoServerOptions=1
DemosEnabled=0
NetBios=1
ServerPath=F:\USERS\DEFAULT\WGPO
ServerPassword=PASSWORD
Login=HollowTree
OfflineMessages=F:\WINNT\MSMAIL.MMF
MAPIHELP=F:\WINNT\SYSTEM32\MSMAIL32.HLP
Window=22 21 636 408 1 1 1 0
```

The three most important elements here are the location of your mailbox, your server password, and your login mailbox—perhaps not the world's greatest security, but simpler than steaming open envelopes.

The file MS-MAIL.MMF contains all unsent mail. Do not delete.

Fourth, if all else fails and matters really are a total muck-up, go to File Manager and, in the \WINNT directory, delete the file MSMAIL32.INI. Then delete the directory \USER\DEFAULT\WGPO. **Caution:** This will delete the entire mailbox...lock, stock, and barrel...and its contents.

Last, call the Mail utility and re-create your postoffice.

I created a local mailbox but I want to connect to a network mailbox instead.

This is relatively simple—the first and essential step is to delete (or rename) the MSMAIL32.INI file in your \WINNT directory.

You may also, now or later, delete the directory \USER\DEFAULT\WGPO and its subdirectories, but this step is not immediately urgent.

After deleting the MSMAIL32.INI file, call the Mail utility and connect to the network postoffice as detailed, preceding, "Logging on to Mail for the First Time."

I can't log on to the mailbox with my password. What's happened?

There are three good possibilities: First, remember that your password is case-sensitive (is the Caps Lock key pressed down by accident?).

Second, are you sure you're using the right password? If this is a new postoffice and you assigned a blank password, the Mail facility reset your passwork to "password" (right, very imaginative).

Third, are you sure you're using the right password? If you've forgotten your password...well, perhaps a hypnotist or a memory course would help.

CHAPTER

21

HELP! Network Operations

Windows NT is specifically designed for network operations with all network facilities built-in rather than being add-ons after the fact. Thus, networking capabilities and features are found in every level of the Windows NT system even though, in many cases, these are transparent to the user. At some level, however, it is still necessary for an Administrator to establish user accounts, set accounting policies, and assign permissions and access rights.

Thus, topics covered in this chapter include

- Network settings
- Managing user accounts
- Managing local groups
- Managing user account policies
- Using the Chat utility
- Customizing Chat
- Using the 3270 Emulator to connect to an IBM 3270 mainframe
- Working with the active session

Network Settings

▶ Changing Network Settings

To change network settings:

- Double-click on the Network utility from the Control Panel. The Network Settings dialog box—Figure 21.1—appears.

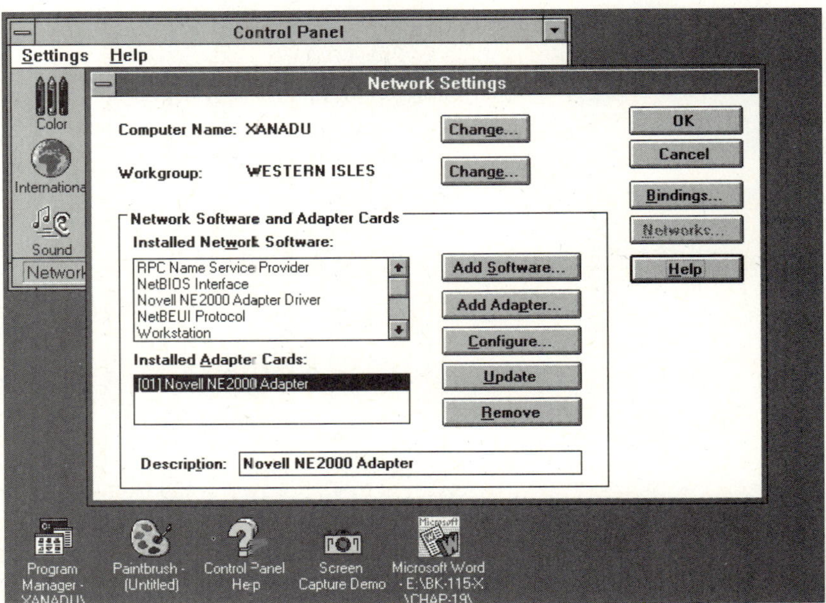

Figure 21.1
The Network Settings dialog box

▶ Naming a Computer

To change a computer's network name:

1. Select the Computer Name Change button from the Network Settings dialog box.
2. Enter a new name—up to 15 characters—in the Computer Name edit box. Windows NT forces the Computer Name entry to be uppercase characters only.

Help Files ▼ The name assigned to the computer must not duplicate a user name or any other computer name. Also, the name cannot include any embedded spaces.

> **HELP!** *If the computer is a member of a Windows NT Advanced Server domain and the name is changed to a computer name that lacks a domain account, it will not be possible to log on to the domain or to access any domain user accounts until the new name is granted a domain account from the Server.*

▶ Joining a Workgroup

To join a computer to a workgroup:

1. Select the Workgroup Change button from the Network Settings dialog box. The Domain/Workgroup Settings dialog box appears as shown in Figure 21.2.
2. Select the Workgroup option.
3. Enter a workgroup name in the Workgroup edit box. The workgroup name must be different from the computer name.
4. Select OK.

▶ Joining a Domain

If you are not sure about the correct domain name or other elements of the Domain edit box, select the Workgroup option instead.

To join a computer to a domain:

1. Select the Workgroup Change button from the Network Settings dialog box. The Domain/Workgroup Settings dialog box appears as shown in Figure 21.2.
2. Select the Domain option.

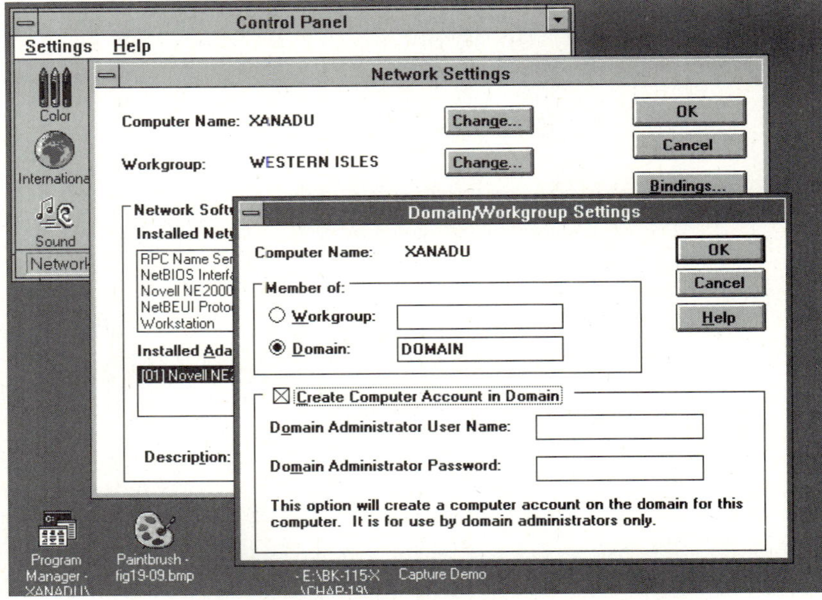

Figure 21.2
The Domain/Workgroup Settings dialog box

3. Enter a name for the domain to join in the Domain edit box. Consult the network administrator to obtain a correct domain name.
4. Select OK.

To create an account for a computer in the domain:

Only domain administrators can create a computer account in the domain.

1. Select the Create Computer Account In Domain check box.
2. Enter your user name in the Domain Administrator User Name edit box.
3. Enter your password in the Domain Administrator Password edit box.
4. Select OK.

Help Files ▼ If an account does not yet exist for the specified computer name in the selected domain, the Create Computer Account In Domain option creates an account automatically.

▸ Selecting and Installing Network Adapters

To install a network adapter:

1. Select the Add Adapter button from the Network Settings dialog box. The Add Network Adapter dialog box—Figure 21.3—appears.

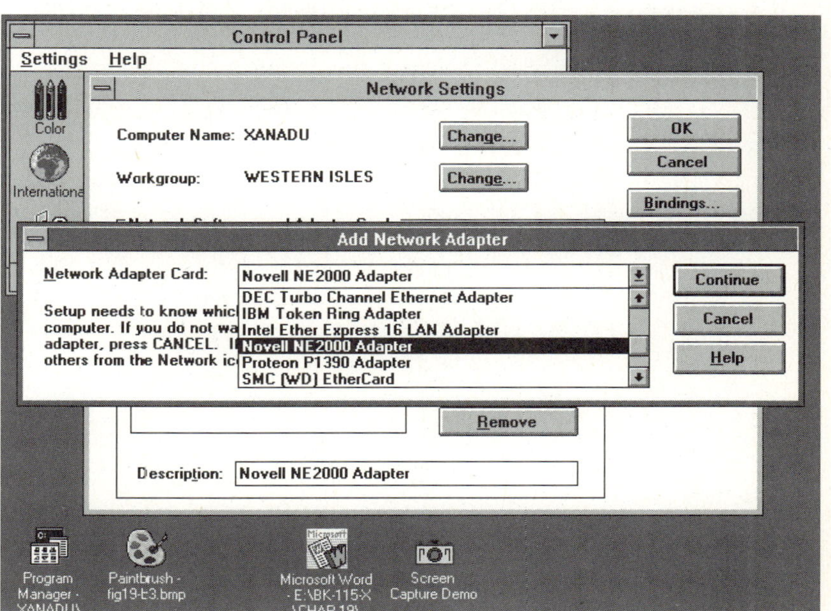

Figure 21.3
The Add Network Adapter dialog box

2. Click on the arrow at the right of the Network Adapter Card list box to call the pull-down list.
3. Select an adapter from the list.

4. Select <Other> to install an adapter that is not on the current list (in which case, a manufacturer's disk will be required).
5. Select Continue to proceed.
6. A Setup dialog box for the selected network card will appear. Enter the requested information in the Setup dialog box to complete installation of the network card.

Help Files ▼ A network adapter card must be installed before the computer can communicate over the network. In addition, a network device driver is required to coordinate adapter functions.

After new network adapters/drivers are installed, the computer must be restarted before the changes can take effect. When the Network Settings dialog box closes, a message will appear reminding you of the need to log off and then log on again.

HELP! *DOS and Windows 3.1 (16-bit) device drivers cannot be used under Windows NT. Network operations under Windows NT can only be supported using 32-bit drivers supplied by Microsoft or supplied by the manufacturer specifically for Windows NT.*

▸ Installing Network Software

To install supporting network software (not adapter drivers):

1. Select the Add Software button from the Network Settings dialog box. The Add Network Software dialog box—Figure 21.4—appears.
2. Select the software to install from the Network Software list box.
3. Select <Other> if the software to install is on a vendor-supplied disk.
4. Select Continue.

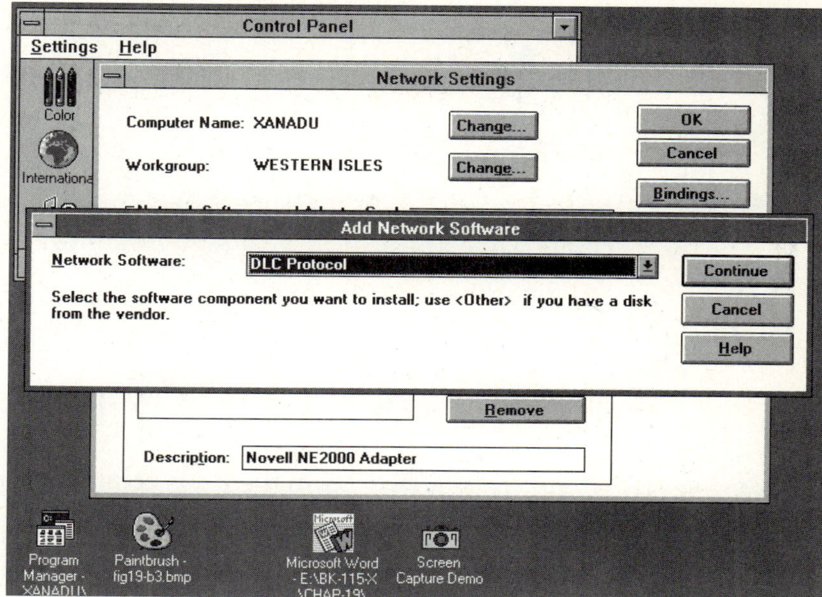

Figure 21.4
The Add Network Software dialog box

Help Files ▼ Once supporting network drivers are installed, the computer must be restarted before the changes can take effect. When the Network Settings dialog box closes, a message will appear reminding you of the need to log off and then log on again. A full power-down reset may be required to initialize some network cards.

▶ Configuring or Updating the Network

To configure or update the network:

- Select the Configure button from the Network Settings dialog box.

Help Files ▼ The Setup dialog box that appears in response to the Configure button is contingent on the installed hardware/software drivers. Options presented may include

- *IRQ Level* which sets the interrupt level used by the adapter card.
- *I/O Port Address* which sets the I/O port base address as a hexadecimal string.

Use the Help button for specific instructions concerning the dialog box and adapter card.

▶ Setting Network Bindings

The Bindings button in the Network Settings dialog box calls the Network Bindings dialog box. The network bindings should only be changed by an experienced network administrator who is thoroughly familiar with the requirements of the network software.

▶ Deleting User Profiles from Setup

To delete a user profile:

1. Select Options from the Windows NT Setup dialog box.
2. Select Delete User Profiles. The Delete User Profiles dialog box appears, listing user profiles that have been copied to the local system.
3. Select the user profile to delete.
4. Click on the Delete button to remove the selected profile.
5. Repeat steps 3 and 4 until all unwanted profiles are deleted.
6. Select Continue.

Help Files ▼ If the current user does not have permission to delete user profiles, Setup displays a message to this effect and the profile(s) are not deleted.

When the computer is a part of a Windows NT Advanced Server network and a user from another computer logs on to the network from the local computer, the user's profile is copied to the local computer. Unwanted or outdated profiles can be deleted by members of the Administrators local group or the Domain Admins global group. The original user's profile remains in the user's configuration registry on his or her remote system.

Handling User Accounts with User Manager

▶ Creating New User Accounts

To create a new user account:

1. Select New User from the User menu. The New User dialog box shown in Figure 21.5 appears.
2. Enter a user name—up to 20 characters—in the Username edit box.
   - A user name must be unique—that is, it cannot duplicate another user name or group name on the workstation.
   - A user name can contain any upper- or lowercase characters except: /\[ ] " : ; | = , + * ? < or >
3. Enter the user's complete name in the Full Name edit box.
4. Describe the user or the user account in the Description box.
5. Enter a password—up to 14 characters—in both the Password and Confirm Password boxes. (Passwords are always case-sensitive.)
6. Set or clear the check boxes for the password and account disabled options.

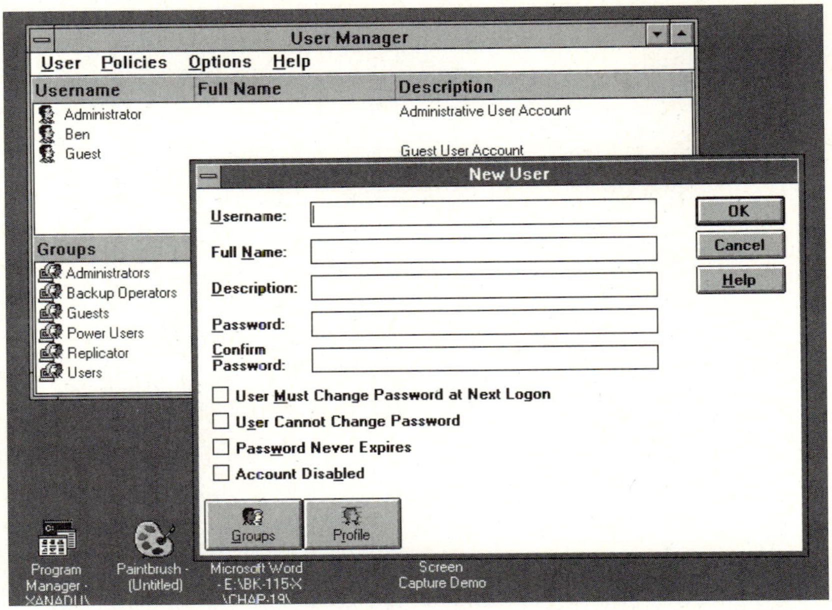

Figure 21.5
The New User dialog box

7. To administer Groups or Profile properties, select the appropriate button at the bottom of the New User dialog box.

8. Select OK.

▶ Copying a User Account

To copy a user account:

1. Select a user account from the User Manager window.

2. Select Copy from the User menu. The Copy Of *User Name* dialog box appears, identical to the New User dialog box in Figure 21.5. The Username, Full Name, and Password boxes are cleared, while the remainder of the entries are duplicated.

3. Enter a new user name—up to 20 characters—in the Username edit box.

4. Enter a new password in both the Password and Confirm Password edit boxes.

5. Update any other account characteristics as necessary.
6. Select OK.

Help Files ▼ Instead of creating a new user account from scratch, copying an existing account offers advantages, as all group memberships belonging to the original account are duplicated in the new account. You might also create one or more dummy accounts for use as templates when creating new accounts.

▶ Managing Properties for a Single User Account

To modify a single user account:

1. Double-click on a user account in the User Manager window.

   ■ Or select a user account and select Properties from the User menu.

2. The User Properties dialog box appears, identical to the New User dialog box in Figure 21.5 except that the Username cannot be edited.
3. Enter new text to change the Full Name or Description fields.
4. To change the password, enter a new password—up to 14 characters—in both the Password and Confirm Password edit boxes. For security, the existing password is represented—in both instances—by a row of asterisks with a length different from the actual password length.
5. Update any other account characteristics as necessary.
6. Select OK.

▶ Managing Properties for Multiple User Accounts

To make identical modifications to two or more user accounts:

1. Select two or more user accounts from the User Manager window.
2. Select Properties from the User menu. The User Properties dialog box appears but does not display Username, Full Name, or Password fields.
3. Enter a new description for all selected user accounts. If the selected accounts already have identical descriptions, the description text appears in the edit box. If they are different, the box appears blank.
4. Change settings for the password and account disabled options by selecting or clearing the check boxes for each. If all of the selected accounts have the same settings, the current settings will be shown as checked or cleared. If one or more accounts have different settings, the check box appears as a gray solid.
5. To administer Groups or Profile properties, select the appropriate button at the bottom of the User Properties dialog box.
6. Select OK.

Help Files ▼ Modifying multiple user accounts allows the same changes to be made to all. Of course, for multiple files, the user and individual names and passwords cannot be changed.

▶ Managing Group Memberships for Single or Multiple User Accounts

To manage group memberships for a single user account:

1. Select the user account from the User Manager window.

2. Select Properties from the User menu.
3. Select the Groups button from the User Properties dialog box. The Group Memberships dialog box shown in Figure 21.6 appears.

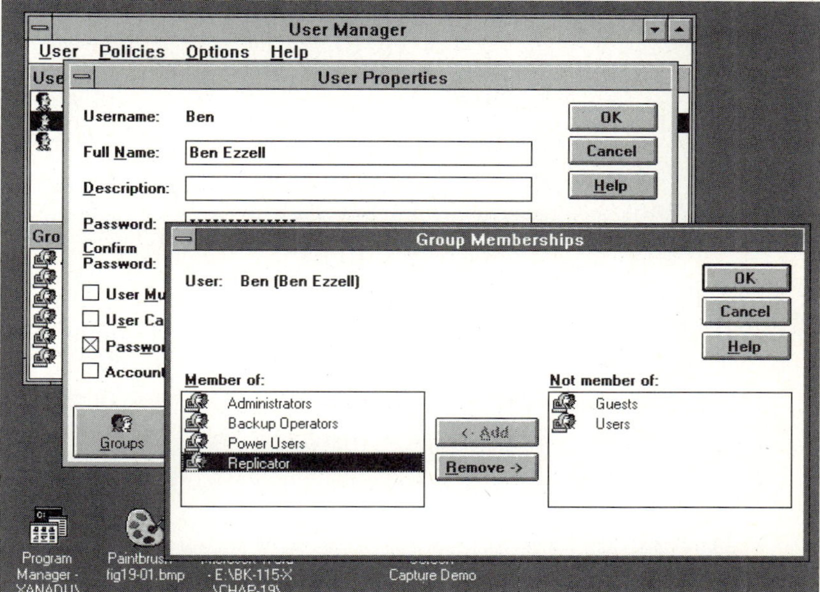

Figure 21.6
The Group Memberships dialog box

To manage common group memberships for two or more user accounts:

1. Select two or more user accounts in the User Manager window.
2. Select Properties from the User menu.
3. Select the Groups button from the User Properties dialog box. The Group Memberships dialog box shown in Figure 21.6 appears.

To add a single user account or multiple user accounts to one or more groups:

1. Select one or more groups in the Not Member Of list box.
2. Select the Add button.

- Or drag one of the selected group icons into the Member Of list box.

To remove a single user account or multiple user accounts from one or more groups:

1. Select one or more groups from the Member Of list box.
2. Select the Remove button.
   - Or drag one of the selected group icons into the Not Member Of list box.

To conclude:

- Select the OK button.

Help Files ▼ The Group Memberships dialog box is used to manage the memberships for selected user accounts in groups on the workstation.

▶ Managing Profiles for Single or Multiple User Accounts

To configure a user environment profile:

1. Select the Profile button from the New User, Copy Of, or User Properties dialog boxes. The User Environment Profile dialog box shown in Figure 21.7 appears.
2. Enter an optional file name for a log on script in the Logon Script Name box.

To identify a local directory as the home directory:

1. Select the Local Path radio button.
2. Enter a local directory, including a drive letter and a complete local path as, for example, D:\USER\BEN_E.

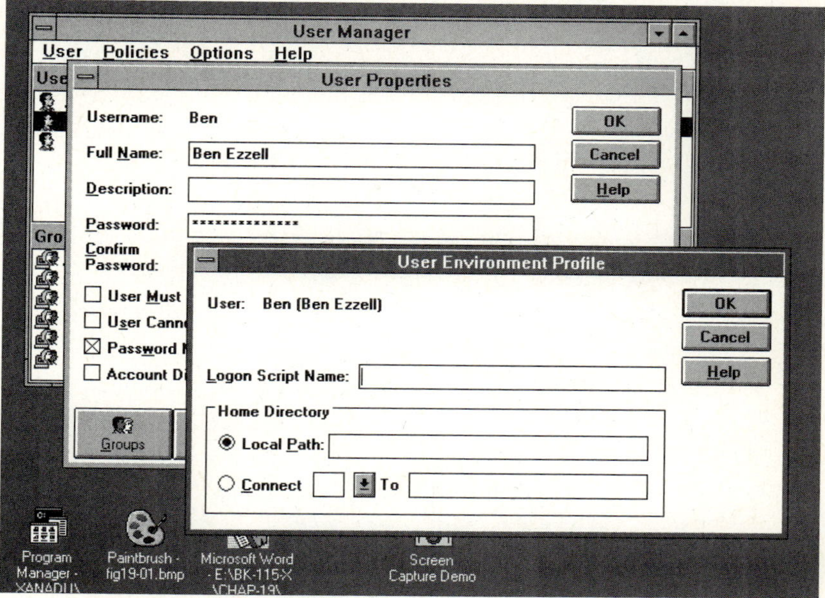

Figure 21.7
The User Environment Profile dialog box

To identify a network directory as the home directory:

1. Select the Connect radio button.
2. Enter a drive letter specification, for example, drive K.
3. Enter a network path, for example, \\TIRNANOG\USERS\BEN_E.

Help Files ▼ All entries in the User Environment Profile dialog box are optional but can be used to identify a log-on script or a home directory for user accounts. Also, the environmental variable %USERNAME% can be substituted for the final subdirectory in either path specification.

▶ Disabling User Accounts

To disable or enable one or more user accounts:

1. Select one or more user accounts from the User Manager window. (The Administrator account cannot be disabled.)
2. Select Properties from the User menu.
3. Select or clear the Account Disabled check box to prevent or permit log ons to the selected user account(s).
4. Select OK.

Help Files ▼ A disabled user account cannot be logged on but can be restored, if necessary, at a later time.

▶ Deleting User Accounts

To delete one or more user accounts:

1. Select one or more user accounts from the User Manager window. (The Administrator account cannot be deleted.)
2. Select Delete from the User menu.
3. Select OK from the confirmation message.
4. Select Yes from the Delete message.
   - Or, select Yes To All for multiple deletions.

Help Files ▼ A deleted user account cannot be recovered. Because every user account is identified internally by a unique SID (security identifier), re-creating a deleted account will not restore access to resources, rights, or permissions that were granted to the old user account. Initially disabling a user account rather than deleting the account is recommended. Deletions can be made later from the disabled accounts with less risk than initially closing the account by deletion.

▶ Renaming User Accounts

To rename a user account:

1. Select a single user account from the User Manager window.
2. Select Rename from the User menu. The Rename dialog box appears.
3. Enter a new user name—up to 20 characters—in the Change To edit box.
   - A user name must be unique—that is, it cannot duplicate another user name or group name on the workstation.
   - A user name can contain any upper- or lowercase characters except: /\[ ] " : ; | = , + * ? < or >
4. Select OK.

Managing Local Groups

▸ Creating a Local Group

To create a new local group:

1. Select one or more user accounts from User Manager as initial members of the new group.
   - Or select any group to ensure that no user accounts are initially selected.
2. Select New Local Group from the User menu. Any user accounts selected previously will be initial users of the new group. The New Local Group dialog box shown in Figure 21.8 appears.

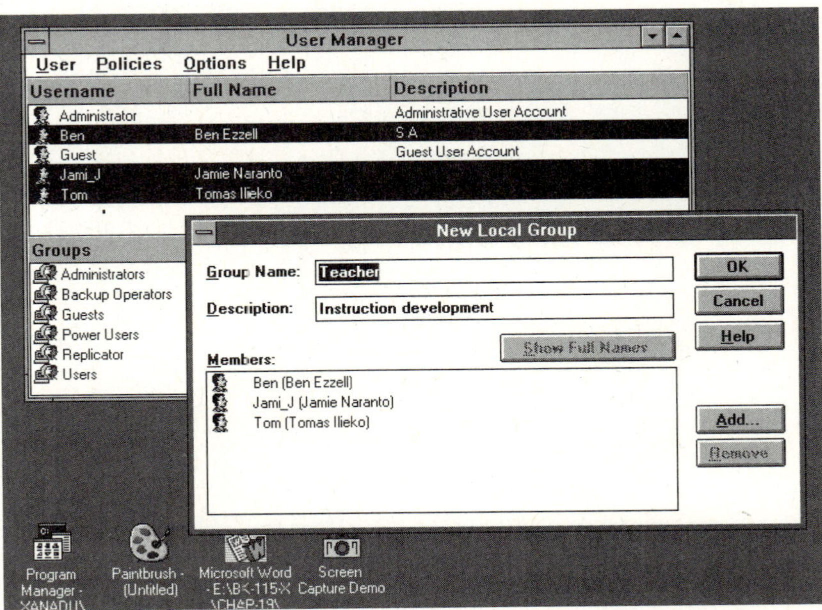

Figure 21.8
The New Local Group dialog box

3. Select the Show Full Names button to display the full names of the listed user accounts. (**Caution**: Show Full Names may be a lengthy process when the local group contains numerous users from other domains.)

4. Enter a name for the new group—up to 20 characters—in the Group Name box.
   - A user name must be unique—that is, it cannot duplicate another user name or group name on the workstation.
   - A user name can contain any upper- or lowercase characters except: /\[ ] " : ; | = , + * ? < or >
5. Enter a description for the new group in the Description edit box.
6. Select OK.

▸ Adding or Deleting Members for a Local Group

To add members to a local group:

1. Select the local group from User Manager's Groups list.
   - Select (highlight) the local group and select Properties from the User menu.
   - Or double-click on the local group. The Local Group Properties dialog box appears, identical to the New Local Group dialog box shown in Figure 21.8, with the exception that the Group Name cannot be edited.
2. Select the Add button from the Local Group Properties dialog box (or the New Local Group dialog box).
3. Select the Add button to add members to the local group. The Add Users And Groups dialog box appears as shown in Figure 21.9.
4. Select user accounts from the Add Users And Groups dialog box.
   - User accounts can be added from the local workstation.
   - If the workstation is a member of a domain, user accounts and global groups can be selected from that domain and from trusted domains.
5. Select OK.

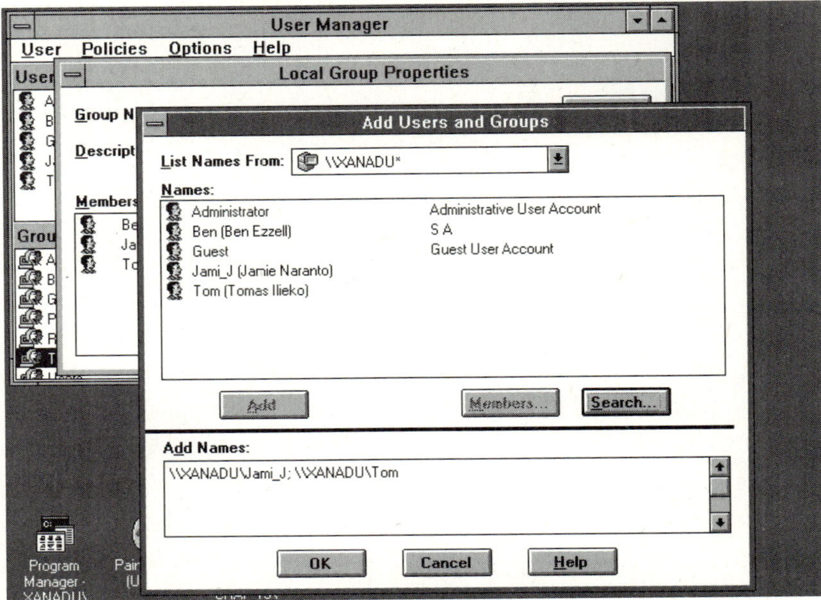

Figure 21.9
The Add Users And Groups dialog box

To remove members from a local group:

1. Select one or more members from the Members box.
2. Select the Remove button.
3. Select OK.

▸ Copying a Local Group

To copy an existing local group:

1. Select a local group from the User Manager window.
2. Select Copy from the User menu.
3. Select the Show Full Names button to display the full names of the listed user accounts. (**Caution**: Show Full Names may be a lengthy process when the local group contains numerous users from other domains.)

4. Enter a group name—up to 20 characters—in the Group Name edit box.

   - A user name must be unique—that is, it cannot duplicate another user name or group name on the workstation.

   - A user name can contain any upper- or lowercase characters except: /\[ ] " : ; | = , + * ? < or >

5. Enter a new description in the Description edit box if desired.

6. To add additional members or to remove existing members, see "Adding and Deleting Members for a Local Group," preceding.

7. Select OK.

Help Files ▼ Copying an existing group creates a new group which, initially, contains the same members as the original group. Any rights or permissions granted to the original group, however, are not assigned to the new group.

▶ Managing Local Group Properties

To modify properties for a local group:

1. Select the local group from the Groups list in User Manager and select Properties from the User menu.

   - Or double-click on the local group name. The Local Group Properties dialog box appears (refer to the New Local Group dialog box in Figure 21.8).

2. Select the Show Full Names button to display the full names of the listed user accounts. (**Caution**: Show Full Names may be a lengthy process when the local group contains numerous users from other domains.)

3. Enter a new description in the Description edit box.
4. To add additional members or to remove existing members, see "Adding and Deleting Members for a Local Group," preceding.
5. Select OK.

▶ Deleting a Local Group

To delete a local group:

1. Select a local group from the Groups list in User Manager.
2. Select Delete from the User menu.
3. Select OK from the confirmation message.
4. Select Yes from the delete message.

Help Files ▼ Once a group is deleted, it cannot be recovered. Each group is identified, internally, by a unique SID (security identifier) which authorizes access to resources, rights, and permissions. When a group is deleted, the SID is lost. When a deleted group is re-created, a new SID is generated, but the original rights and permissions are not recovered. Instead, all permissions, rights, and accesses must be reassigned under the auspices of the new SID.

Deleting a local group removes only the group but does not delete any user accounts or global groups that were members of the deleted local group. Also, built-in groups cannot be deleted.

Managing User Account Policies

▶ Managing Password Policies

To manage account passwords:

1. Select Account from the User Manager's Policy menu. The Account Policy dialog box shown in Figure 21.10 appears.

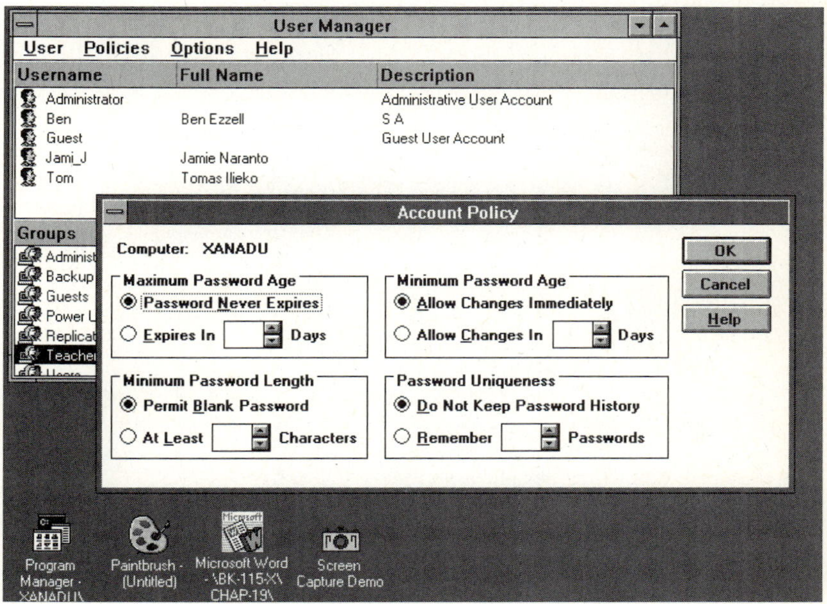

Figure 21.10
The Account Policy dialog box

2. Maximum Password Age can be set to an interval between 1 and 999 days.

   ■ Or select Password Never Expires.

3. Minimum Password Age can be set to an interval between 1 and 999 days.

   ■ Or select Allow Changes Immediately.

The Allow Changes Immediately and Remember n *Passwords options should not be used together.*

4. Enter a size from 1 to 14 characters for Minimum Password Length.

   ■ Or select Permit Blank Password.

5. Select Do Not Keep Password History if immediate password changes are allowed.

   - Or enter a history of 1 to 8 passwords.

6. Select OK.

Managing User Rights

To manage a user rights policy:

1. Select User Rights from the Policies menu. The User Rights Policy dialog box shown in Figure 21.11 appears.

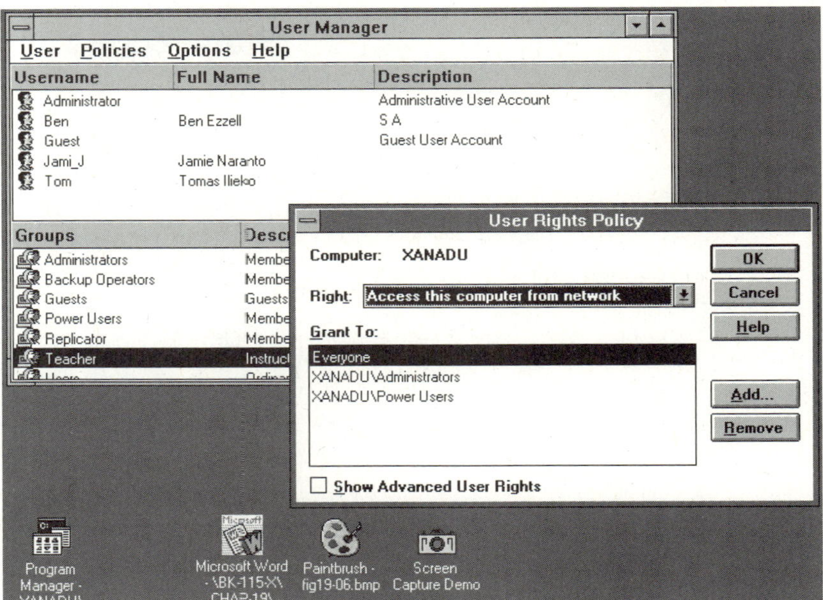

Figure 21.11
The User Rights Policy dialog box

2. Select a right from the pull-down Right list box. The Grant To list box lists the groups and user accounts granted the selected right.

3. Add or delete users from the Grant To list box.

Advanced rights are used principally by programmers creating Windows NT applications.

To administer advanced user rights:

- Select the Show Advanced User Rights check box. The pull-down Right list box now lists the advanced user rights as well.

To add additional groups or user accounts to the Grant To list:

1. Select the Add button—the Add Users And Groups dialog box appears as shown in Figure 21.9.
2. Refer to "Adding or Deleting Members for a Local Group," preceding.
3. Select OK.

To remove a group or user account from the Grant To list:

1. Select a name in the Grant To list box.
2. Select the Remove button.
3. Select OK.

Help Files ▼ Granting a right authorizes a user to perform specific actions. In general, the simplest way to provide rights to a user (instead of managing the rights directly) is to add the user's account to one of the built-in groups that possesses the required rights.

▶ Managing Audit Policies

To disable auditing:

1. Select Audit from the Policy menu. The Audit Policy dialog box shown in Figure 21.12 appears.
2. Select Do Not Audit to disable all auditing.

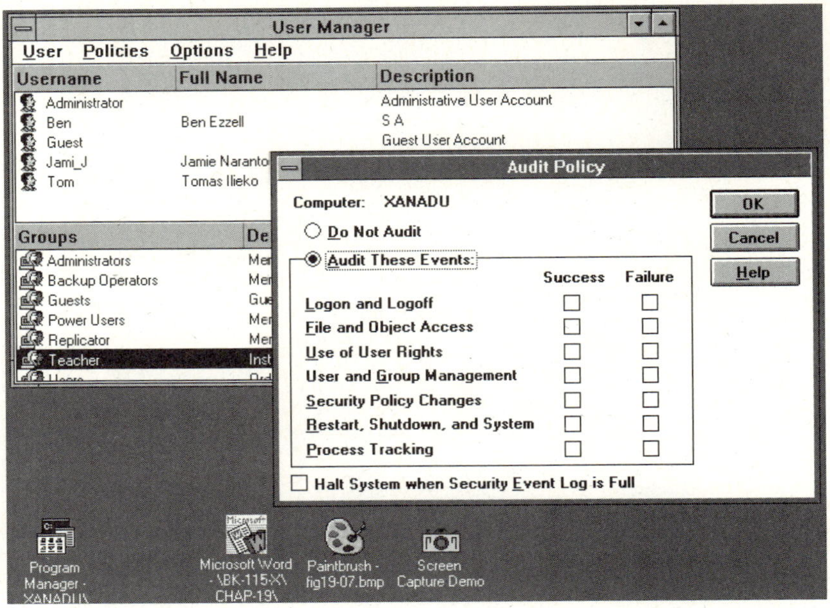

Figure 21.12
The Audit Policy dialog box

To enable auditing:

1. Select Audit from the Policies menu.
2. Select Audit These Events to enable auditing.
3. Select specific events to audit by selecting or clearing the Success and Failure check boxes for each.
4. For a totally secure environment, select the Halt System When Security Event Log Is Full check box. **Caution:** All applications halt when the security log is filled if this option is selected. Data loss is possible!

HELP! *If the system is halted because the security log is filled, log on as an administrator and clear the security log after saving the contents to a reference file.*

Help Files ▼ The Audit Policy defines which security events will be recorded in the security log. Because the size of the security log is limited, attempting to record everything that happens is wasteful and will result in the log being filled quite rapidly. The maximum size for the security log is set and the security log is viewed by using Event Viewer.

The Halt System When Security Event Log Is Full option should be selected only when a maximum security environment is required. If this option is selected, when the security log becomes filled, all applications and services halt immediately until an administrator clears the security log and enables further event logging.

The Chat Utility

▶ Placing a Call

To place a call:

1. Click on the Dial button from the tool bar.
   - Or select Dial from the Conversation menu.
2. Enter the name of the computer to call in the Computer edit box.
   - Or select the computer from the list of computers.
3. Select OK to make the connection.

Help Files ▼ Chat calls the specified computer and waits for a response. A message in the status bar provides notification when the called computer answers.

▶ Conversing via the Chat Utility

To converse with another user:

1. Call the remote computer and wait for a response.
2. Enter the message text to send in the top window.
3. Received text appears in the bottom window.
4. Press F6 or use the mouse to switch between windows.
5. Hang up when the conversation is finished.

Help Files ▼ Chat can be used to call another computer (person) in a workgroup to carry on an electronic conversation.

▶ Answering a Call

To answer a call when the Chat window is open:

- Click on the Answer button from the tool bar.

Or:

- Select Answer from the Conversation menu.

To answer a call when Chat is an icon:

- Double-click on the Chat icon.

Or:

- Select the icon and press Enter.

Help Files ▼ After answering the call, a message can be typed in the upper window and then transmitted to the remote terminal.

If Chat is already running when a call is received, an audio warning is sounded and a message appears on the status bar. If Chat is not open, Chat is executed but is initially minimized. The Chat icon, however, is amusingly animated when an incoming call rings.

▸ Hanging Up

To hang up:

- Click the Hang Up button from the tool bar.
- Or select Hang Up from the Conversation menu.
- Or exit Chat (a Hang Up instruction is issued automatically).

Help Files ▼ Once the connection is broken, messages cannot be entered in the Chat window. If the remote connection hangs up first, a message appears in the status bar.

Customizing Chat

▶ Changing Background Colors

To change a window background color:

1. Select Background Color from the Options menu.
2. Select the color to use under Basic Colors. (The color selected will be mapped to the nearest supported solid color.)
3. Select OK.

Help Files ▼ By default, the window showing the conversation from the remote terminal uses the remote background color and font.

▶ Changing Fonts

To change fonts:

1. Select Font from the Options menu.
2. Select a font from the Font list.
   - Or enter the font name in the Font edit box.
3. Select a font style from the Font Style list box.
4. Select a font size from the Size box.
5. Select strike-out or underline from the Effects buttons, if desired.
6. Select text color from the Color list.
7. Select OK to return to Chat.

Help Files ▼ Font, size, and color can be selected and will be reflected in the Chat utility at the other end of the conversation. One caution may be in order, however. Selecting a font that is not available to the person you are conversing with may make a real mess of the conversation.

▸ Changing Window Preferences

To change window preferences:

1. Select Preferences from the Options menu.
2. Select a layout under Window Style.
3. Select a font preference under Partner's Message.
4. Select OK.

Help Files ▼ Two conversation windows can be displayed side by side instead of above and below.

HELP! *When the remote terminal has selected a font that is not supported locally, selecting Use Own Font can remedy this difficulty.*

▸ Displaying and Hiding the Tool Bar and Status Bar

To display or hide the tool bar:

- Select Toolbar from the Options menu.

To display or hide the status bar:

- Select Status Bar from the Options menu.

Help Files ▼ The Chat tool bar, directly below the menu bar, offers mouse-accessible buttons for the Call, Answer, and Hang Up functions. The status bar at the bottom displays information about commands, connections, or actions. Both can be shown or hidden as preferred.

▶ Turning Sound On and Off

To turn sound on or off:

- Select Sound from the Options menu. A check mark appears when the sound is on.

Help Files ▼ Sound is used as notification of incoming calls, but can be turned off if desired. Also, if a sound card is installed, the Control Panel Sound utility can assign different .WAV sound files to the Chat Incoming Ring and Chat Outgoing Ring sound events.

Using the 3270 Emulator to Connect to an IBM 3270 Mainframe

Opening a Configuration

The DCL Protocol driver must be installed from the Control Panel before the 3270 Emulator can be used to connect to an IBM 3270 mainframe.

To load a terminal configuration:

1. Select Open from the File menu. The Open dialog box appears, listing configuration files with the extension .CFG.
2. Select a configuration file from the list.
3. Select OK to load the configuration.

Help Files The configuration file must be opened before connecting to the host application.

Defining Basic Session Settings

The DLC Protocol driver must be installed from the Control Panel before the 3270 Emulator can be used or configured. Use the Network utility from the Control Panel and select Add Software to install the DLC Protocol handler.

To define basic session settings:

1. Select Settings from the Session menu. The 3270 Settings dialog box shown in Figure 21.13 appears.
2. Enter the 12-digit hexadecimal address of the host computer in the Host Network Address box. The address used may be for a 3174, 37X5, 9370, AS/400, or similar pass-through device. Consult the host administrator for appropriate values.
3. Select the first Local Node ID edit box.
4. Enter the 8-digit hexadecimal local node ID for the local system with the three-digit block number in the first box and the five-digit node number in the second. Consult the host administrator for appropriate values.

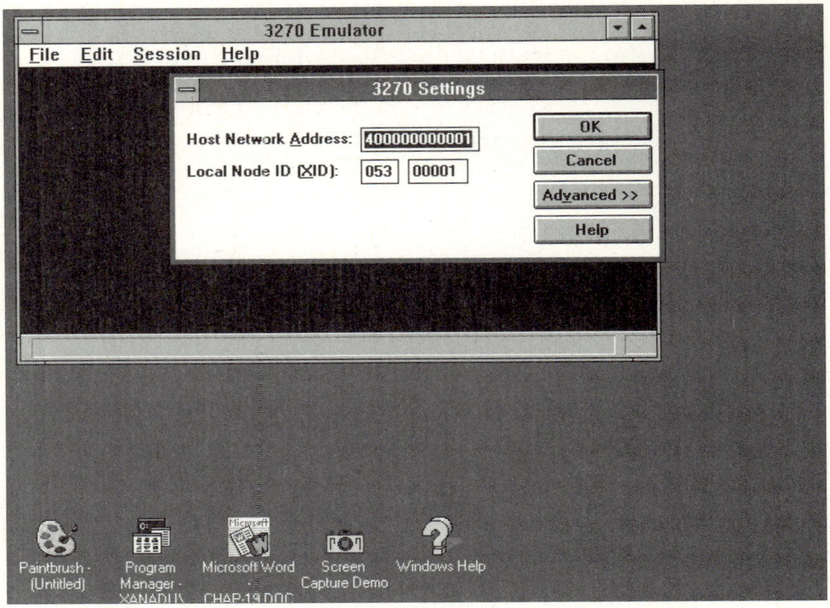

Figure 21.13
The 3270 Settings dialog box

5. Select OK.

▸ Defining Advanced Session Settings

To configure advanced session settings:

1. Select Settings from the Session menu. The 3270 Settings dialog box shown in Figure 21.13 appears.
2. Select the Advanced button. The 3270 Settings dialog box expands to show the advanced options as shown in Figure 21.14.
3. Define the local configuration, as follows:
   - *Host Code Page* selects the appropriate EBCDIC code-page translation tables from the Host Code Page list. The default is English-US.
   - *Local Adapter Name* selects the Local Adapter Name by selecting the correct adapter board.

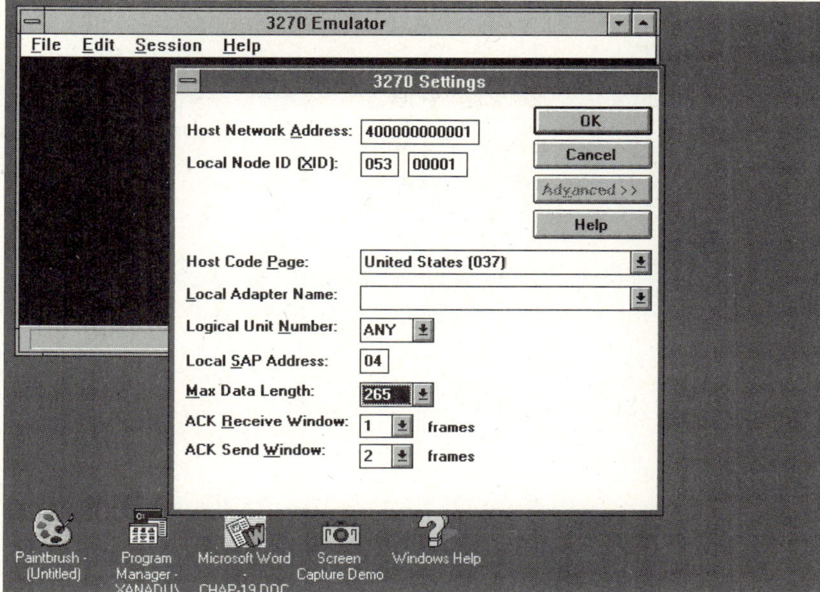

Figure 21.14
The 3270 Advanced Settings dialog box

- *Logical Unit Number* selects the two-digit hexadecimal LU number defining the physical unit (PU) on the host. Contact the host administrator for the appropriate value or select ANY.
- *Local SAP Address* enters the local system access point (SAP) address defined in the host or pass-through device. The SAP address is a two-digit hexadecimal number and must be evenly divisible by four. Contact the host administrator for the appropriate value.
- *Max Data Length* enters the maximum data transfer size that the physical unit (PU) can receive in one segment or path information unit (PIU). Size must include the transmission header (TH) and request / response header (RH). The size specified must match either the MAXDATA value configured on the host or the I Frame Size configured on the 3174. Contact the host administrator for the appropriate value.
- *ACK Receive Window* sets the maximum number of link-level frames received before transmitting an acknowledgment (ACK). The customary setting is 1 but may be changed for maximum

performance. Contact the host administrator for the appropriate setting.

- *ACK Send Window* sets the maximum number of link-level frames transmitted before waiting for an acknowledgment (ACK). The customary value is 2 but may be changed for maximum performance. Contact the host administrator for the appropriate setting.

Help Files ▼ The advanced settings cannot be changed during a session with the host, although these can be reviewed. To make changes, you must first disconnect from the host mainframe.

▶ Saving a Configuration

To save a terminal configuration:

1. Select Save As from the File menu. The Save As dialog box shown in Figure 21.15 appears.
2. In the File Name box, type a name for the configuration.
3. Select OK to save the configuration.

To create a new configuration:

- Select New from the File menu—all configuration settings revert to default values.

▶ Connecting to the Host Application

To connect to the host application:

- Select Connect from the Session menu. The 3270 host terminal appears.

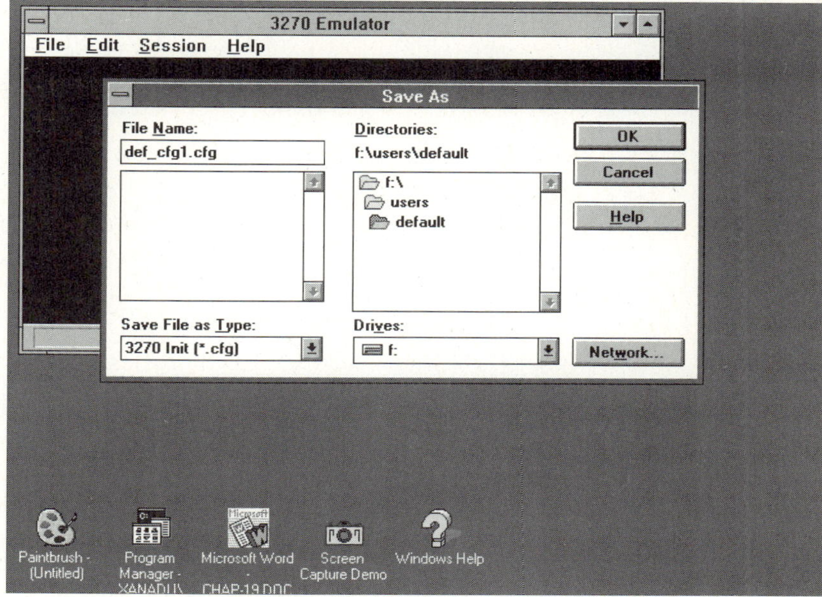

Figure 21.15
The Save As dialog box

To disconnect from the host application:

- Select Disconnect from the Session menu. The host terminal disappears.

Help Files ▼ The 3270 Emulator provides access to an IBM host application from a Windows NT system, establishing a single logical unit (LU) connection to any of the following host application environments:

- Virtual Machine/Conversation Monitor System (VM/CMS)
- Time Sharing Options (TSO)
- Customer Information Control System (CICS)

Working with the Active Session

▸ Copying and Pasting the Active Screen

To edit the active screen:

1. Select the portion of the screen to edit.
   - Or select the Select All option from the Edit menu.
2. From the Edit menu, choose Copy—the selection is copied to the Clipboard.
3. Position the cursor at the location to insert the Clipboard contents.
4. Select Paste from the Edit menu.

Help Files ▼ The 3270 Emulator permits copying all or a portion of the screen to the Clipboard and pasting the Clipboard contents to a different location in the same screen or to another screen.

▸ Printing the Emulator Screen

To print the screen:

1. Select Print from the File menu. The Print dialog box appears.
2. Select OK to print the contents of the active screen using the default printer and settings.

The term enhanced *refers to the non-numeric pad control keys found on enhanced keyboards. The term* num-pad *refers to the numeric keypad keys.*

To change printer options:

1. Select Printer Setup from the File menu or from the Print dialog box. The Print Setup dialog box appears.
2. Select a new printer from the Specific Printer list.
3. Change other printer options as desired.

4. Select OK.

Emulating 3270 Keys on the Enhanced 101 Keyboard

The IBM 3270 keyboard can be emulated from a PC Enhanced (101-key) keyboard by using the special key assignments shown in Table 21.1.

Table 21.1
IBM 3270/Enhanced 101 Keyboard Map

3270 Keyboard	Enhanced 101 Keyboard
Dup	Alt+(*enhanced*) Ins
Field Mark	Shift+(*enhanced*) Home
Erase to End of Field	Shift+(*enhanced*) Del
Erase Input	Alt+(*enhanced*) End
Reset	Shift+(*left*) Ctrl
Reset	(*left*) Ctrl
Home	Home (*num pad* or *enhanced*)
Tab	Tab
BackTab	Shift+Tab
Newline	Enter (*main keyboard*)
Newline	Shift+Enter (*main keyboard*)
Fast Cursor Left	*Not supported*
Fast Cursor Right	*Not supported*
Cursor Up	Up Arrow (*num pad* or *enhanced*)
Cursor Down	Down Arrow (*num pad* or *enhanced*)
Cursor Left	Left Arrow (*num pad* or *enhanced*)
Cursor Right	Right Arrow (*num pad* or *enhanced*)
Alternate Cursor	Alt+F11
Insert	Ins (*num pad* or *enhanced*)
Delete	Del (*num pad* or *enhanced*)
Attention	Esc

Table 21.1
IBM 3270/Enhanced 101 Keyboard Map (Continued)

3270 Keyboard	Enhanced 101 Keyboard
System Request	Alt+Ctrl+S
Clear	Pause
Enter	Enter (*num pad*)
Enter	Shift+(*num pad*) Enter
Enter	Shift+(*right*) Ctrl
PA1	Alt+(*enhanced*) Insert
PA2	Alt+(*enhanced*) Home
PA3	Shift+(*enhanced*) PgUp
PrintScrn	Alt+P
CurSel	Alt+F3
PF1	F1
PF2	F2
PF3	F3
PF4	F4
PF5	F5
PF6	F6
PF7	F7
PF8	F8
PF9	F9
PF10	F10
PF11	F11
PF12	F12
PF13	Shift+F1
PF14	Shift+F2
PF15	Shift+F3
PF16	Shift+F4
PF17	Shift+F5

Table 21.1
IBM 3270/Enhanced 101 Keyboard Map (Continued)

3270 Keyboard	Enhanced 101 Keyboard
PF18	Shift+F6
PF19	Shift+F7
PF20	Shift+F8
PF21	Shift+F9
PF22	Shift+F10
PF23	Shift+F11
PF24	Shift+F12

THE RESCUE PAGES: Network Operations

I'm trying to log on to a Windows NT Advanced Server network, but the system doesn't seem to recognize me. I've entered a domain name and everything, but nothing works.

You might be better off at the moment to select the Workgroup option. To log on to a Domain, you need the domain name (check with the domain administrator) and you must have a domain account granted to the local computer's name which is granted by the domain administrator. Of course, if you happen to be the domain administrator, you can use the Create Computer Account In Domain option to create an account.

I can't find a driver on NT's list matching my network card, but when I select <Other> and try to use the drivers supplied by the manufacturer, this doesn't work either.

Basically, you have two choices. First, you can get a network card that is supported by a Windows NT driver, or second, you can contact the card manufacturer of your present card and ask for a 32-bit Windows NT driver. What you can't do is install a 16-bit network driver—even if it does work just fine under DOS and Windows 3.1. Sorry, but 16-bit drivers just aren't compatible.

I deleted a user profile by accident. How do I get it back?

Not to worry—the original user's profile still exists in the user's configuration registry on his or her system. The profile can be restored (transferred) when the user logs on again. User accounts, of course, are a slightly different matter.

Okay, I deleted a user account by accident. How do I get the account back?

In this case, you should worry...because you can't. All you can do is re-create the account and reassign all accesses to resources, rights, permissions, and so on. Sorry, but that's the way it works when you delete an account.

Next time, however, instead of deleting a user account, why not begin by disabling the account? A disabled account prevents the user from logging on, but unlike a deleted account, can be reenabled later if necessary. And, of course, a disabled account can be later deleted when you're sure it really won't be wanted again.

What about a local group? Can I disable a group account instead of deleting it?

No, group accounts can only be deleted, and built-in groups (groups defined by Windows NT) can't be deleted at all. Still, deleting a group account isn't exactly a disaster, although re-creating a group account may involve reassigning access rights to resources and replacing permissions granted to the original account.

Of course, deleting a group account has no effect on the accounts of users who belonged to the group.

APPENDIX

HELP! Troubleshooting and Disaster Recovery

When you install Windows NT, you are instructed to create an Emergency Repair Disk. Many other operating systems have included similar instructions for creating "undo" disks or other "backup" disks during installation, and quite humanly, users have discovered these utility disks gathering dust and have appropriately erased them as worthless.

The Windows NT Emergency Repair Disk, however, is in an entirely different category, and the single biggest favor that you can do for yourself is to keep the Emergency Repair Disk in a safe but convenient location...just in case.

I repeat:

Do not wipe, erase or lose the Emergency Repair Disk!

If—emphasis, *if*—Windows NT fails because an operator error changes the configuration, erases a critical file, or alters system parameters—which can and does happen even (or, perhaps, especially) to experienced programmers—or for any other reason, the Emergency Repair Disk can be used to restore the Windows NT system. This is not by itself an absolute cure, but it is an important and critical first step.

Disaster Recovery

▸ The Configuration Recovery Menu Option

If Windows NT fails to start because of changes made to the system configuration—if an error is made in changing the video driver, for example—the Configuration Recovery menu offers an opportunity to recover from these changes without having to reinstall Windows NT.

If you are using the FlexBoot utility to load a choice of operating systems, select Windows NT from the FlexBoot options. The initial text screen will read

```
OS Loader Ver3.1
Press spacebar now to invoke last known good menu
```

Press the spacebar immediately. If you are not using FlexBoot and are booting only Windows NT, press the spacebar as soon as the words "OS Loader" appear.

In response, the Configuration Recovery menu appears as a text—not graphic—screen display:

```
Configuration Recovery menu (Last Known Good)

This menu allows you to switch to a previous system configuration, which may
overcome system startup problems.

If the system starts correctly now, choose Use Current Startup Configuration. No
changes will occur. If the system does not start correctly, choose Use Last
Known Good Configuration.

IMPORTANT: System configuration changes made since the last successful startup
will be discarded

Use Current Startup Configuration

Use Last Known Good Configuration

Restart computer

Use the up and down arrow keys to make your selection
Press enter when you have made your selection
```

By default, the Use Current Startup Configuration option will be highlighted. If, however, you are having problems booting Windows NT because of configuration changes, use the arrow keys to highlight the Use Last Known Good Configuration option and press Enter to continue booting. This option selects the system configuration which was last successfully used—in effect, the configuration in use before the system was last modified. The saved configuration replaces the more recent configuration, undoing recent changes to the system.

If the Last Known Good Configuration option does not work, refer to "Restoring the Windows NT System," below.

Restoring the Windows NT System

To restore a damaged Windows NT system:

The Emergency Repair Disk is not intended for use on a new hard drive or a computer other than the system where it was originally created. This is a repair disk, not an installation disk.

1. Reboot the system by using the Windows NT installation disk. After the installation utility checks the system hardware, a screen appears offering a choice of actions which include

```
To attempt repairs on a damaged Windows NT system, press R.
```

2. To attempt repairs, press R.
3. At the prompt, insert the Emergency Repair Disk. After repairs are completed, Windows NT should be bootable again.
4. To complete repairs, continue restoring the system from your tape backup.
5. Return the Emergency Repair Disk to a safe storage location in case it is needed again.

Reinstalling Windows NT

If the Emergency Repair Disk fails—or if you erased the Emergency Repair Disk, discarded it, or can't find it—your remaining choice for disaster recovery is to reinstall Windows NT. Following are a few suggestions to minimize your losses.

First, Windows NT can be reinstalled "on top" of your old installation. While this will not re-create your lost program groups, shared network directories and other custom changes, this will minimize the elements that have to be re-created.

Second, store the new Emergency Repair Disk in a safe but convenient location.

Third, after reinstalling Windows NT, restore the system from your tape backup. This may involve overwriting some new files with older backup files to re-create your system configuration.

Fourth, re-create any lost program groups and drive assignments, reassign shared directories, and so on.

Restoration from Backup Tapes

Most of us lack the time and patience to create complete backups with ideal frequency, so we tend to create complete tape backups at long intervals and create differential backups (backups containing only changed files) more regularly.

When restoring from tape, this often means that we begin with our most recent full backup and then restore from a series of partial backups. When doing so, it may be useful to run a test after each set is restored to ensure that the problem has not been restored as well. In the event that the problem is also restored, then you have certainly narrowed the problem down and should have a good lead on where and how the problem occurred.

System Troubleshooting

Since Windows NT is quite new, system troubleshooting remains a relatively hazy area simply because time and experience have not yet taught us what problems to expect or where to look for solutions. In general, however, problems seem to be relatively few and correctable principally through an exercise of common sense and careful observation.

The system event logs will be among your most important troubleshooting tools. These may, however, require a bit of practice to understand because of the wealth of information that they can be generate.

For example, installing a network card and a sound card that both use the same interrupt will generate a truly generous list of error events. To troubleshoot a problem, the trick is to look at the first error in the

string and then decide where the real problem is. And, as a general rule, the solution will be simple...once the actual problem is identified.

When common sense fails and the problem really is a software or hardware failure, try to have as much information as possible at hand before calling for help. Items that you will probably be asked for may include the event log, the Registry contents, and your system configuration. Thus, before calling for assistance, have Windows NT booted and ready...unless, of course, the problem is that Windows NT won't boot at all.

APPENDIX

B

HELP! Installing Windows NT

Installing Windows NT is a bit different than installing a conventional application, because Windows NT is not an application but an operating system. It is also unlike upgrading to a new version of DOS, because Windows NT is a 32-bit operating system instead of a 16-bit revision of an existing OS, so it is incompatible with your existing operating system.

For both of these reasons, installing Windows NT first requires a boot Windows NT loader disk. To install Windows NT, begin by placing the boot loader disk in drive A, then reboot the system either by pressing the reset button on the front of the computer, or by powering down and then powering up again. The traditional warm reboot (Ctrl+Alt+Del) may also be used.

On reboot, the boot loader disk loads an installation stub—the Windows NT Setup program—and begins by performing a system hardware test to determine what equipment is available on the system.

Hardware Requirements

There are five initial hardware requirements to run Windows NT:

- You must have a computer with either an 80386 or 80486 or Pentium CPU, or a MIPS ARC/R4x00 CPU. Your 80286 CPU system will not support Windows NT.
- You will require a single high-density floppy disk for your A drive—either a 1.2MB 5.25-inch or 1.4MB 3.5-inch disk. This disk does not need to be formatted but should be labeled "Emergency Repair Disk" and set aside until requested. (See Appendix A for notes on using the Emergency Repair Disk.)
- A minimum of 8 megabytes of RAM is required (12 megabytes are suggested and 16 or more are helpful).
- You will need about 70 megabytes of space on your hard drive for a complete installation. This space does not necessarily have to be on your C (boot) drive. Unlike DOS—which must be installed on the C drive—your Windows NT operating system can be installed on any system drive desired and, using the FlexBoot utility, can be installed to allow you to boot either DOS or Windows NT.
- You should have a mouse (or other pointing device). This is not an absolute requirement, but operating Windows NT without a mouse is awkward at best.

A Choice of Installations

Windows NT is distributed in two forms: as a 3.5-inch boot loader disk with a CD-ROM to load the bulk of the operating system, or as a set of 3.5- or 5.25-inch disks for those who do not have a CD player or whose CD controller is not compatible with Windows NT.

Installation Using CD-ROM

To install Windows NT using a CD-ROM, both a 1.2MB 5.25-inch and a 1.4MB 3.5-inch disk are supplied—each labeled "Setup Disk for CD-ROM Installation"—together with a single compact disc in a shrinkwrapped envelope. To install Windows NT from the CD, remove the CD from the envelope and place it in your CD-ROM drive. Next, place either the 5.25-inch or 3.5-inch Setup disk in your A drive, then boot or reboot (reset or power up) the computer.

The Setup program will begin by checking your hardware for the presence of a SCSI controller. If no SCSI controller is identified—meaning that your controller is not recognized or supported by Windows NT—reboot and use the floppy-disk installation procedure.

Installation Using Floppy Disks

To install Windows NT using floppy disks, you must have a 3.5-inch drive, although this does not necessarily have to be your boot drive. Begin by selecting the appropriate Setup disk—either the 5.25- or 3.5-inch disk—and placing it in your A drive, then boot or reboot (reset or power up) the computer.

As with the CD-ROM installation, the Setup program will begin by checking your hardware for the presence of a SCSI controller. If your hard drive is a SCSI drive but the controller is not recognized, refer to the Hardware Compatibility List for the names and model numbers of compatible SCSI controller cards.

If your hard drive is a conventional IDE drive, the absence of a SCSI controller is irrelevant and installation will proceed without comment.

The Setup Program

After checking for SCSI drives, the Windows NT Setup program performs a series of system checks, including

- Identifying the correct hardware settings for the computer.
- Confirming drive partitions and selection.
- Confirming the computer file system.

- Confirming the installation drive and directory.
- Copying all essential files.

Installation Options

To begin installation, place the Windows NT boot disk in your boot drive and reboot your computer. After an initial system check, you will be presented with several options:

- To learn more about Windows NT Setup before continuing, press F1.
- To Setup Windows NT now, press Enter.
- To attempt repairs on a damaged Windows NT system, press R. (Refer to Appendix A for notes on Disaster Recovery.)
- To quit Setup without installing Windows NT, press F3.

Regardless of your installation sources—CD-ROM or floppy disks—when you continue with the installation, your next choice will be between express and custom installation. The latter is strongly recommended—particularly if you are installing Windows NT for the first time.

Custom Installation

If you select custom installation, you will be prompted for a series of system characteristics, including

- Display (video card) type
- Mouse
- Printer type and port address (LPT1, and so on)
- Keyboard and keyboard layout (standard, enhanced, and so on) and language (English, French, and so on)
- If you have a network card, the network adapter type, IRQ setting, base port address and other network settings
- If you are joining a Windows NT Advanced Server domain, the computer name and the domain name assigned by network administrator

Express Setup

Express Setup relies on the Setup utility to make decisions about the system hardware, automatically configuring Windows NT for your system. Any initial settings can be changed later—if desired—after Windows NT is installed. Express Setup is recommended.

Selecting the Installation Directory

If Windows NT identifies Windows 3.1 as already installed, the Setup program will recommend installation in the same path. However, if you intend to use both Windows 3.1 and Windows NT or if there is insufficient space on the drive where Windows 3.1 is installed, you may select a new drive and/or directory in which to install Windows NT by doing the following:

- Press N to select an alternate drive/directory.
- If there is insufficient space to install Windows NT, press F3 to exit. Then reboot DOS and delete unneeded files to make space for Windows NT.

A Choice of File Systems

After you have selected a drive and directory for installation, Setup will display the selected drive, showing the drive ID, the current file system, the total size of the drive (or partition), and the amount of free space.

```
Drive:  Type (Used for)              Size    Free
------- ---------------------------- ------- -------
D:      FAT (MS-DOS, Windows, OS/2)  115 MB  104 MB
```

Following the drive/capacity report, you will be offered a choice of four file systems:

- Convert to NTFS (preserves existing files)
- Reformat to NTFS (destroys existing files)
- Reformat to FAT (destroys existing files)
- Keep existing file system intact (no changes)

The FAT acronym stands for File Allocation Table, and is used by DOS, Windows 3.1, Windows NT ,and OS/2 systems.

The last option is recommended and should be highlighted. Before converting any drive to the NTFS file system, you should be aware of the NTFS system characteristics, particularly the fact that an NTFS drive is not visible or accessible from DOS or Windows 3.1. On the other hand, an NTFS drive offers a number of advantages that a FAT file system does not.

After you select a file system, the default directory for installation is identified as *winnt* but may be changed if desired.

If you are installing from either 3.5- or 5.25-inch floppy disks, you will then be prompted to insert disks one at a time in the customary and tedious fashion. Alternatively, if you are installing from CD, you have the freedom to take a break while files are transferred to the hard drive.

If you are using floppy disks, after the ninth disk has been inserted you will be prompted to remove the floppy disk from the boot drive and to reboot by pressing the Ctrl+Alt+Del combination to load Windows NT. (Yes, there are still another 13 floppies to be loaded.)

After Windows NT reboots, the initial screen will prompt you to press Ctrl+Alt+Del again to log on to Windows NT, after which you will be asked for registration information—specifically, your name and (optionally) a company name.

Next, you'll be prompted for a computer name, with a maximum of 15 characters. This is the name by which the computer will be called for network operations.

You will then be asked to make a language selection. A pull-down list offers a wide variety of choices ranging from English (American) to Turkish.

The printer type selection is also presented as a pull-down list asking for a model (printer type) and port (normally LPT1). The supported printer list is quite extensive but is arranged alphabetically. If you have more than one local printer, multiple selections are permitted. This selection should, however, be used only for local printers—network printers have their drivers installed on the system where they are located and do not require local installation. If you prefer, printer selection can be left for later—refer to the Control Panel for printer installation.

The network card selection also offers a pull-down list with a variety of choices. Network card selection can be deferred for later installation—refer to the Control Panel for network drivers. When the network card is installed, the base address and IRQ number will be requested.

After these settings have been made, the Setup utility will continue loading files. If you are loading from the floppy disks, you will be prompted to insert disk 9 (again) and then continue through disk 22.

Once all the files have been loaded, the Setup utility will install applications and create program groups—beginning with the Accessories, Administrative Tools, Game, Main, and Startup groups—before configuring the registry and system information.

▶ Account Settings

After the principal program groups have been established, you will be asked to provide information for the Administrator Account setup. For the Administrator account, the user name is fixed as *Administrator,* but you will be asked to enter and confirm a password. You may have the option of leaving the password blank, although this is very poor security for any shared system.

The next step is to set up a personal account. You will be asked for a name (yours or someone else's), a password, and confirmation.

After the administrative and personal account information is entered, the Setup utility will continue setting up non-Windows NT applications in a common Applications group.

▶ Setting the Date and Time

Next, the Setup utility will ask you to select Date/Time information, which will require setting the date and the local time and selecting a time zone from a pull-down list. Also, if you want automatic daylight saving time to be selected, check the Daylight Savings check box.

▶ The Emergency Repair Disk

Last, the Setup utility will prompt you to insert the Emergency Repair disk in your boot drive. This disk must be high density, but does not need to be formatted. Setup will format the disk automatically before copying the emergency repair information to the ERD. Do NOT discard or erase the Emergency Repair disk. Refer to Appendix A for further information.

Once the Emergency Repair disk is completed, remove the disk and select the reboot button to continue.

Booting Using the FlexBoot Utility

The FlexBoot utility is installed automatically on all PCs with an existing DOS system. On boot, the Flexboot screen will appear as shown:

```
OS Loader V3.1

Please select the operating system to start:

    Windows NT Version 3.1
    MS-DOS

Use ↓ and ↑ to move the highlight to your choice.
Press Enter to choose.

Seconds until highlighted choice will be started automatically:  17
```

The Windows NT selection is highlighted by default, but the up and down arrow keys can be used to change the selection. Press Enter to boot immediately or wait for the countdown (which is set by default for 30 seconds) to boot the highlighted selection.

Both the default selection and the default time delay can be changed either by editing the BOOT.INI file (on your C drive) or by using the System utility from the Control Panel.

In any case, you now are ready to boot Windows NT and are free from the archaic limitations of a 16-bit operating system.

But, don't forget, when you boot Windows NT, you will be requested to press Ctrl+Alt+Del before logging on—this is not an error, but helps prevent a Trojan horse virus from intercepting your password.

INDEX

A

B

D

E

I

J

K

L

M

N

Q

R

S

T

U

V

W

X

Z